The Historic Defences of Plymouth

Andrew Pye & Freddy Woodward

Exeter Archaeology
Fortress Study Group South West

Sponsored by
English Heritage
Devon County Council
Cornwall County Council
Caradon District Council
Fortress Study Group South West

July 1996

Cover Photograph : The Hoe, Drakes Island and Mount Edgcumbe, from the Citadel, c. 1850 (Reproduced courtesy of Plymouth City Museum and Art Gallery)

Inside Front Cover Photograph : Staddon Fort and glacis (Photograph: F.M. Griffith, Devon County Council. Frame DAP/US5. Copyright Devon County Council)

Inside Back Cover : Maker Heights in 1808 (PRO: MR 1209)

for

Eileen,

Eleanor & Katherine

List of Contents

List of Illustrations

FOREWORD

The three principal English historic dockyards of the Royal Navy were Portsmouth, Plymouth and Chatham. Henry VII was responsible for Portsmouth, Chatham developed under Elizabeth, and Plymouth Dock, coming somewhat later on the scene, was begun in the 1690s. Each of them had their particular peaks of activity up to and including the Second World War. They were at all times crucial for the maintenance of the fleets that were Britain's first line of defence and which for long enjoyed world-wide naval power. They were also important industrial complexes, employing huge numbers of people, and often technically innovative. Their protection from attack was vital. Each was progressively fortified with measures to guard against bombardment from the sea and against an enemy force attempting a landward attack. As the great periods of national crisis - the Spanish Armada of 1588, the invasion threat of Napoleon Buonaparte in 1803-5, or from Hitler's Germany in 1940 - stimulated emergency measures along the coasts, so the fear of recurring danger from possible invasions and coastal raids was present intermittently throughout the centuries. As the range and destructive power of guns advanced, so the defences moved outwards to counter the physical threat to the dockyards and the towns which served them. This led to the creation of successive rings of fortifications of ever greater complexity around all three naval bases. Such defences may be seen as an extension of earlier medieval town walls and castles.

Portsmouth, together with the anchorage of Spithead, has the most extensive spread of fortification stretching from the Needles in the west to Langstone Harbour in the east, and including the Isle of Wight and the Solent sea-forts. At Plymouth the defences were more compact, gradually expanding beyond to Drake's Island, then to the Breakwater and on to the very entrance to Plymouth Sound. They also included the Antony Position and Whitsand Bay on the Cornish side of the Tamar. As at Portsmouth, Plymouth's landward approaches were eventually protected by a line of detached forts along the high ground north-east of the Dockyard in the 1860s.

The main period of fortress building at all three naval bases came in the 19th century, particularly following the Royal Commission on the Defences of the United Kingdom Report of 1860, but at each there is a substantial sequence of surviving defence works going back to the 15th century in one direction and continuing to the end of the 19th century and through to two World Wars in another. It is at Portsmouth and Plymouth in particular where a remarkable collection of fortifications of many dates and forms has developed from which the evolution of British military engineering can be understood.

The defences of Portsmouth have been well studied in recent years. Most of the surviving forts and batteries there have been statutorily protected but also it is where a representative sample is displayed and available to the public. The same level of appreciation and evaluation of Plymouth's forts did not occur until the appearance of F.W. Woodward's *Plymouth's Defences* in 1990. This provided a general overview but it is the absence of a detailed inventory which accounts for a general unawareness of what survives at Plymouth and its historical significance at both national and local levels. It became clear to English Heritage and local planning authorities that there was insufficient objective data to set in hand a rational conservation policy.

The Plymouth Defences Survey project was set up in 1991, largely as a result of concern at the accelerating deterioration of many of the defence sites and the increasing pressure of development affecting them. The overall objectives were twofold: to provide the information for the respective planning authorities and English Heritage to carry out their roles more effectively and to promote the appreciation of the fortifications in a more positive light. The survey carried out by Exeter Archaeology began with the Devonshire side during 1991 and 1992, the first draft gazetteer being completed in 1993. Fieldwork in Cornwall followed in 1994 and that draft gazetteer was completed in the summer of 1995. The survey was commissioned by English Heritage, in association with Cornwall County Council (Cornwall Archaeological Unit), Devon County Council and Caradon District Council, and has been undertaken by Exeter Archaeology in conjunction with the South-West branch of the Fortress Study Group and the Cornwall Archaeological Unit.

The gazetteers have established the extent of survival and provided an inventory of some 216 individual defence works. The purpose of the survey was to identify all known defence sites in and around Plymouth, to catalogue their present use and condition, and to make broad proposals regarding their future management and use. This has not only involved background research to locate the sites and summarise their history and function but also site visits to define as far as possible the extent of surviving surface and below-ground remains, to assess their present condition and to indicate the extent and nature of any statutory or other protection they currently enjoy. The survey has broken new ground in that it spans such a wide range, and includes the great variety of 20th-century structures from anti-aircraft batteries to pillboxes which remain from the response to Britain's last great invasion crisis in 1940.

The Plymouth defences are of particular value in demonstrating the whole range of British coastal defences from the 16th century to 1945. From the ramparts of the Royal Citadel or from Western King, the whole historic development of Plymouth's seaward defences can be seen progressing from the cliffs of the Hoe and out beyond Drake's Island and the Breakwater to the limits of the Sound. The restoration of Crownhill Fort, inland, gives the visitor another dimension. With imagination, other surviving fortifications can contribute distinctive value in the future development and promotion of Plymouth and its environs. Individual sites can be managed in a positive way if allowance is made for proper consultation, conservation and recording, and a suitable degree of public access. What is now needed is a strategy to bring greater public awareness to the overall significance of what remains of an exceptional group of defence works built in response to past dangers and to guide future policy and practice for their protection and conservation.

Andrew Saunders
Chairman, Fortress Study Group, and former Chief Inspector of Ancient Monuments, English Heritage

INTRODUCTION

The city of Plymouth and its surrounding countryside on both sides of the Tamar is home to a massive range of fortifications spanning 500 years. These include examples of almost every type of fortification built in this country during this time, and are of considerable national importance, reflecting the status of Plymouth as one of the country's principal naval bases. Indeed, they rival only those of Portsmouth in their sheer number, range and extent of survival. However, whilst at Portsmouth many of the fortifications are protected, used in ways which retain and enhance their character, and are actively promoted as an integral part of the city's heritage, Plymouth has to date lagged behind. It was in response to this that the Plymouth Defences Survey was set up in 1991 by English Heritage, Devon and Cornwall County Councils, Caradon District Council, and Fortress Study Group South West (FSGSW). This publication presents the results of this survey, which has been undertaken over the last five years by the authors and their colleagues in Exeter Archaeology and FSGSW.

The scope of the survey reflects its primary purpose, namely to provide an inventory of the historical defensive works of Plymouth and to promote the appreciation of them as a positive resource and as a major part of Plymouth's history.

The survey is wide ranging, encompassing some 216 sites of all periods and types from the late medieval blockhouses of Devil's Point and Mount Edgcumbe through to the later Royal Citadel and Victorian forts, and to the searchlights, pillboxes and anti-aircraft batteries of the present century. However, it is not intended to be a full, comprehensive history or permanent record of every site; rather it is a snapshot of our current state of knowledge, compiled from historical information gathered over a number of years, and from site visits. Nor does it cover the many other military sites and buildings surviving in and around Plymouth, such as barracks, reservoirs and dockyard facilities, except where these fall within the circuit of individual fortifications or have been adapted for defensive purposes. These are as much part of Plymouth's military role and heritage as the fortifications, and should be assessed in the same way and for similar reasons; a task made all the more urgent by the continuing release of MoD property for other uses. Neither does the survey constitute the final word on the subject: new fortification sites emerged during the survey, and have continued to emerge since. Yet more will almost certainly come to light, particularly of the periods of the First and Second World Wars and of the recently ended Cold War, through the current Defence of Britain Survey (Note 1).

Only a brief, incomplete review of the fortifications of the medieval and 16th century period and of the Civil War has been attempted here, as undertaking the in-depth research required to identify and locate most of these fell outside the remit of this survey. Detailed studies of the early defences have already been published elsewhere (2), and the number of sites and the understanding of their history and role will undoubtedly increase as new research is published and new discoveries made (3). Likewise there remains much scope for more accurately locating the sites of the Civil War on the ground, from the exact line of the inner town defences to the positions of the outer redoubts and more temporary fortifications. Although much of the groundwork has already been done (4), more specific historical and archaeological work is now needed to achieve this and to assess the extent of any remains there may be (5). For later periods also, although much information has already been gathered and published, both on the general background and on particular sites (6; Chapter 1 below), there is further information to be gained from the archives of the Public Record Office and elsewhere, and from the detailed study and recording of individual sites.

The layout of the book is as follows. Chapter 1 is an account of the historical background to the defences, describing their development in the context of the topography of Plymouth, and of political, military and technological developments. Chapter 2 looks to the future, setting out a national view from English Heritage on how a conservation strategy for the fortifications should develop. Chapter 3 is a gazetteer of some 216 individual sites. This is principally arranged on a geographical basis, although the general order of presentation is intended to reflect the historical shift of the defences (the 'ring of fire') outwards from the centre of Plymouth and the Dockyard as the range of artillery increased. For most sites there is a plan illustrating the character and layout of the site, and the extent of its present survival; a list of abbreviations used is provided in Appendix 1, with a glossary of terms in Appendix 2. For ease of reference an alphabetical index is also provided, and each entry has a list of specific sources; general sources are listed in Appendix 3.

In conclusion, this book is intended both as an introduction to Plymouth's defences and to the potential they contain, and as a source of information about individual sites. However, it is important to recognise that each individual site was intended as an integral component of the defences of the time. The less physically imposing and attractive fortifications of the last 100 years or so, such as concrete pillboxes, searchlights, and gun emplacements, are therefore as important to Plymouth's history and its continuing appreciation as the more spectacular and well known sites such as the Citadel, Crownhill Fort or Drake's Island. The retention of a few of the more attractive sites is meaningless if the rest of the system of which they formed part is allowed to eventually disappear without trace.

The challenge now is to follow Portsmouth in actively conserving and encouraging the sympathetic use of what remains of the defences which have served Plymouth so well in the past, for though often threatened Plymouth has not been attacked by sea or land in the last 500 years. They can then be used to promote the city, and serve as a reminder to future generations of Plymouth's central role in the country's military history. Plymouth's defences are undeniably of national importance, and it is the authors' and sponsors' hope that the publication of this book and the accompanying exhibition will enable this to be more widely appreciated and will assist in the effort to retain this central part of Plymouth's heritage well into the next millennium.

Andrew Pye & Freddy Woodward, July 1996.

Notes

1. Brown, I et al. 1995 *20th Century Defences in Britain.* CBA

2. Barber, J 1979 'New Light on Old Plymouth' *Proceedings of the Plymouth Athenaeum,* **IV**, 55-66

   Brayshay, M 1987a 'Tudor Artillery Towers and their role in the Defence of Plymouth in 1588' *The Devon Historian* **35**, 3-14

   Brayshay, M 1987b 'Plymouth's Coastal Defences in the Year of the Spanish Armada' *Report and Transactions of the Devonshire Association,* **119**, 166-196

3. Pye, A.R., Rance, C., Stead, P.M., & Watts, M.A 1994 *Archaeological Assessment and Evaluation of the Elizabethan Fort, Royal Citadel, Plymouth* Exeter Archaeology Report No. **94.81**

4. Stoyle, M 1993 *A List of Civil War fortifications at Plymouth* Exeter Archaeology Report No. **93.82**

   Worth, R.N 1875/76 'The Siege of Plymouth' *Report and Transactions of the Plymouth Institution,* **5**, 250-300

5. Henderson, C.G 1995 'Excavations at Plymouth Whitefriars, 1989-94', in Ray, K (ed) *Archaeological Investigations and Research in Plymouth, Volume 1: 1992-93* Plymouth Archaeology Occasional Publication No. **1**., 47-58

6. Cobb, P & Moore, D 1990 *Crownhill Fort, Plymouth.* Palmerston Forts Society

   Pye, A.R 1992 'An archaeological survey of Mount Pleasant Redoubt, Plymouth' *Proceedings of the Devon Archaeological Society* **50**, 137-161

   Woodward, F.W 1987 *Citadel*

   Woodward, F.W 1990 *Plymouth's Defences*

ACKNOWLEDGEMENTS

Many people, too numerous to name individually, have assisted over the last five years in the work leading to this book and its publication. The main sponsors, English Heritage and Devon and Cornwall County Councils, have been of considerable assistance and support throughout; in particular, Nick Johnson (Cornwall County Archaeologist), Frances Griffith (Principal Archaeologist, Devon County Council) and were instrumental, with FWW, in setting the project up with English Heritage, and Rob Iles of English Heritage has seen the project through to its conclusion and contributed Chapter 2. Caradon District Council have also given financial assistance. The project has benefitted considerably from the pioneering work undertaken over the last decades by Andrew Saunders, who has kindly provided the foreword to this book. Considerable support has also been provided by Chris Henderson (Director of Exeter Archaeology), and by several members of FSGSW, notably Tom Hitchins, Keith Rawlings and John Symons, who have kindly provided much information they have gathered over the years and assisted in arranging access. Helpful discussion and assistance has also been provided by the late James Barber, Adam Sharpe, Richard Linzey, Ian Hogg, Bill Horner, Steve Hartgroves, Keith Ray, Tony Bayfield, Cynthia Gaskell-Brown and her colleagues at Mount Edgcumbe, and the staffs of Plymouth City Museum, the Plymouth Local Studies and Proprietary Libraries, the Westcountry Studies Library, the Devon and West Devon Record Offices, the former Property Services Agency of the DoE, and the British Library, Public Record Office, National Maritime Museum, Royal Artillery Institution, Royal Commission on Historic Monuments and English Heritage. The survey would not have been possible without the assistance of the MoD and Armed Services, the Mount Edgcumbe Estate, the Mount Edgcumbe Country Park, Landmark Trust and other landowners and tenants, who kindly facilitated access to their properties.

The recent aerial photographs have been taken by Frances Griffith, Steve Hartgroves and Adam Sharpe, with financial assistance from Devon and Cornwall County Councils and the Royal Commission on Historic Monuments. The fine set of figures are the work of Tom Dixon, Sarah Noble, Tony Ives and Sarnia Blackmore, and the text has been produced by Pam Wakeham and AP (all of Exeter Archaeology); desk-top publishing has been undertaken by Mike Tippett and Kevin Kerslake of Cornwall County Council Planning Department. The following also kindly gave permission for illustrations to be used: the Imperial War Museum, MoD, British Library, Public Record Office, RCHME, Plymouth Proprietary Library, Plymouth City Museum and Art Gallery, Landmark Trust, R.C.F Serpell, the late W.G.M Jones, Austin C Carpenter, Ian V Hogg, and Tom Hitchins. Various sections of the text were read and commented upon by Andrew Saunders, Austin C Carpenter, Nick Johnson and Frances Griffith, who also assisted in proof reading. Ian Hogg and Andrew Saunders also kindly provided material on the defences from their own researches, and the glossary in Appendix 2. Last, but not least, we would like to thank our families for their patience and tolerance throughout!

1. HISTORICAL BACKGROUND

Plymouth, or Sutton as it was then called, was no more than a fishing village at the time of the Norman Conquest. But it grew as a result of trade first with the King's possessions in France and later with the New World so that its increasing prosperity made it a target for sea raiders. A castle, a fort and a great citadel were successively built to protect its harbour and the anchorage in the Cattewater.

When in 1690 a royal dockyard was begun in the Hamoaze estuary to the west new batteries were needed to cover the channel to it. In the mid-eighteenth century Dock Lines were begun and later an arc of redoubts was built from Mount Pleasant round to Maker Heights to cover the dockyard. By the end of the Napoleonic Wars the dockyard was one of the largest industrial complexes in the country, so that the threat of invasion in the nineteenth century called for not only improved coast defences but later a ring of land forts covering both the town of Plymouth and the dockyard.

Two world wars saw the coast defences modernised to give protection from long-range bombardment and in World War II priority was soon given to air defence. It is not surprising that there are still the remains of well over 100 principal sites which record the long development of Plymouth's defences.

Natural features affecting the defences

(Fig. 1)

Geography played a large part in Plymouth's development. Until the mid-eighteenth century communication even with Exeter was by narrow and notoriously muddy tracks. The growing town was almost cut off from the rest of the country except by sea. Being the principal port in the west it traded progressively with France, the Mediterranean and the New World. Later, with Dock as the naval base in the west, it was the port of refuge and repair for ships damaged by storm or enemy action, and for prizes. In the seventeenth century it played its part in cutting off the Dutch trade through the Channel with their colonies, and until the early nineteenth century was the base for the blockade of Brest and the French bases in

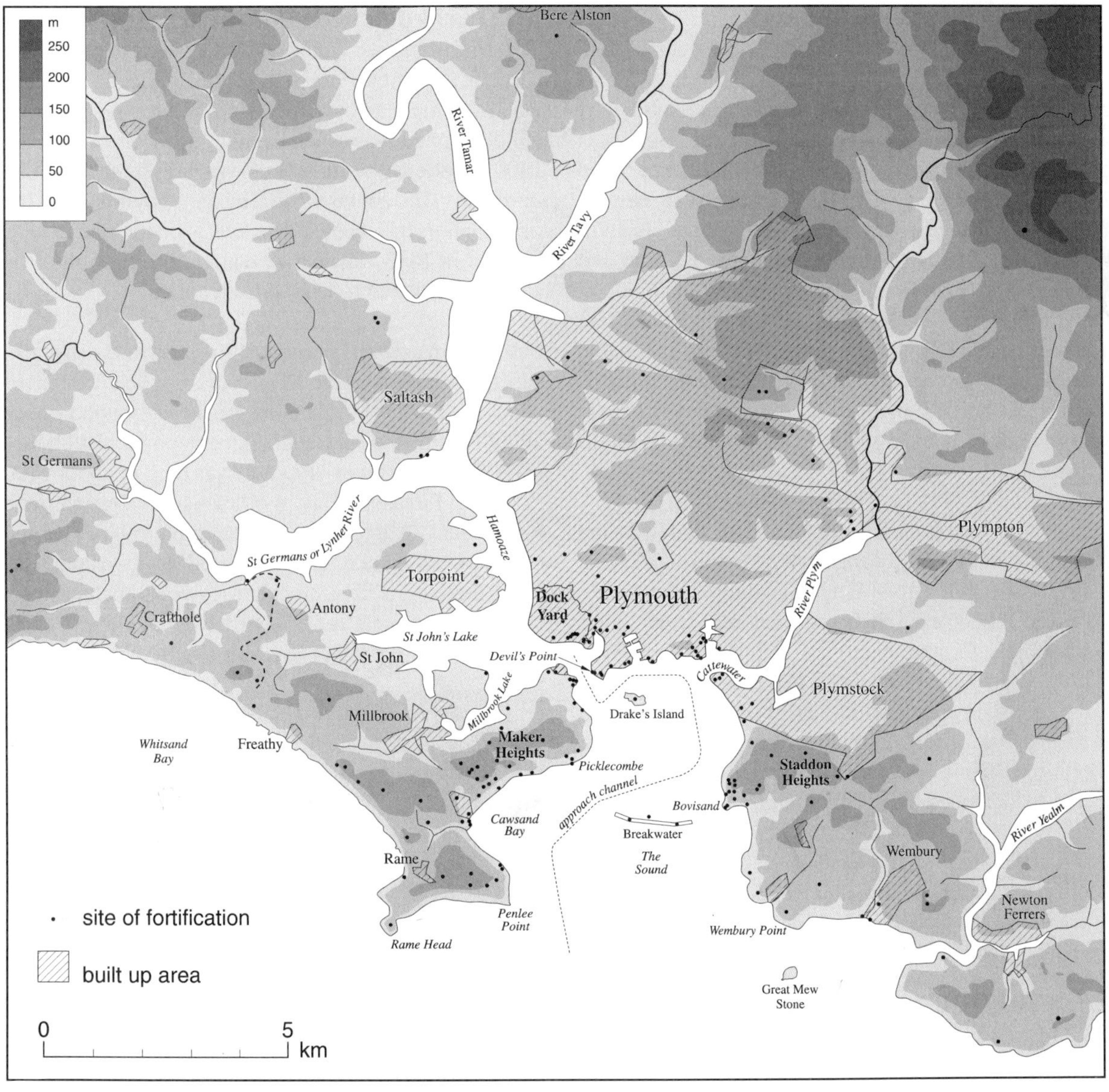

Fig. 1 The topography of Plymouth and the surrounding area

the Bay of Biscay. Its growing importance to the Royal Navy made it a prime target for attack from both the sea and the land.

The detailed layout of the defences of Plymouth was influenced by the unusual topography. The waters of Plymouth Sound are dominated from the east and west by Staddon Heights and Maker Heights and are fed from the north by the two estuaries of the Plym and the Tamar. The latter embraces the smaller estuary of the Lynher, or St Germans, River flowing from the west. The mouth of the Plym estuary, known as the Cattewater, provided a sheltered anchorage in earlier years, until larger ships and the need for a more secure anchorage turned attention to the deep water of the Hamoaze where the dockyard was built.

Ships anchored in the Sound were exposed to winds from SE to SW until the Breakwater was completed in 1844. From then on it offered safe anchorage to a modern fleet but one that was exposed to bombardment from the sea. The coast defences were moved out to cover first the channels to the east and west of the Breakwater at close range and then, as the range of guns rapidly increased 100 years ago, out to Renney to the east and Penlee to the west.

Before the Breakwater was built the dockyard at Devonport was relatively close to the open sea by comparison with, say, that at Rochefort, built about the same time and sited 15km up a narrow river. But it was protected by its twisting and easily defended deep water approach (Fig. 1). The channel runs east of Drake's Island (earlier called St Nicholas Island), turning west through 90° between Drake's Island and the Hoe and then north through more than 90° at Devil's Point before winding west past Mount Wise and north again into the Hamoaze. As soon as reliable cannon were developed Drake's Island was fortified and it remained the pivot of the sea defences for 300 years, reinforced by a series of batteries on Western King.

A potential threat to the growing dockyard was the possibility of bombardment from Maker Heights, less than 2000m away, following a landing to the south. Cawsand Bay offers a sheltered anchorage with a good landing beach, and even the exposed beaches at Whitsand Bay could be used in favourable weather. From Cawsand guns could be dragged the 3000m onto the Heights in a few hours and from there could in a short time fire the dockyard. In time of war the Heights had to be defended even from a raid.

Staddon Heights to the east are far away from the dockyard but they do threaten the old town as well as overlooking the Sound and the Royal Citadel. When the ring of land forts was planned in the 1860s a strong position was built on the Heights both to secure them against a small landing at Newton Ferrers and to hold out against a large force advancing from the east following large-scale landings at Torbay, later using Dartmouth as a base.

To the west, land forts were pushed well beyond Maker to a line running south from the village of Antony to the sea, so that following a landing at Looe or Fowey the enemy could be kept out of view of the dockyard. A longer and more difficult approach lay north of the Lynher estuary. Defences west of Saltash to cover this approach would have to be pushed out to the high points at Burrell and Elmgate to prevent the dockyard coming under observation.

Plymouth itself is a city of many hills and has a series of ridges running roughly east to west at North Hill, Hartley, Manadon and Crownhill. In the seventeenth-century Civil War the town's defences were on North Hill and the besieging Royalists were based on Hartley. In the 1860s the land forts of the North Eastern Defences were originally to have run through Hartley, but were pushed out to the line Ernesettle - Crownhill - Laira to reduce the cost of the land required and to take advantage of the steep valleys either side of Crownhill.

In World War II enemy bombers used the estuaries to guide them onto the dockyard and the heaviest anti-aircraft batteries were sited in prolongation of these and other lines of approach.

The early defences *(Plan A; Fig. 2)*

The first defence against an attack by ships on the harbour at Sutton Pool was in the fourteenth century when a chain across the entrance was raised by a windlass in a tower when the alarm was given. Before 1400 a castle with four towers was built by the town on Lambhay Hill above the Barbican. By this time the first cannon had been made and a major raid on the harbour in 1403 was met by cannon fire from the Hoe so the French had to land at Cattedown.

Later, guns were mounted in bulwarks (usually earthworks) on the Hoe whenever there was a threat of attack. To prevent a landing on the only good beach along the north of the Sound an octagonal blockhouse (The Artillery Tower - *Plate 1*) was built in about 1490 to cover Firestone Bay. Following his breach with Rome Henry VIII was at odds with both the Pope and the King of France, and he feared an invasion. By 1540 there were five blockhouses covering the north shore of the Sound from Fisher's Nose to Devil's Point *(Fig. 2)* and a further one was built below Mount

Plate 1: Artillery Tower, Firestone Bay c. 1490 (Exeter Archaeology)

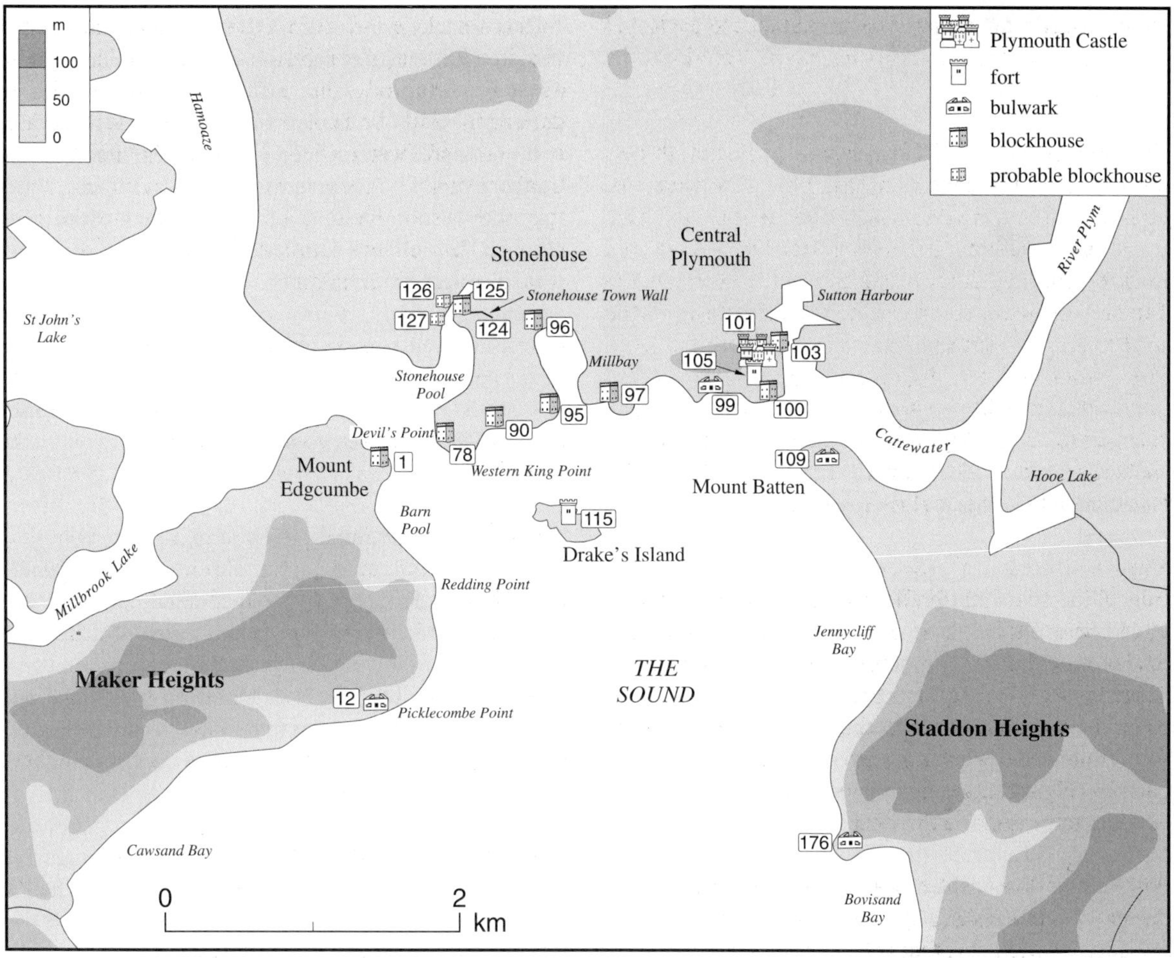

Plan A: Medieval and 16th century defences

Schedule *1 Mount Edgcumbe blockhouse; 12 Picklecombe bulwark; 78 Devil's Point blockhouse; 90 Firestone Bay Artillery Tower; 95 Millbay West blockhouse; 96 Millbay North blockhouse; 97 Millbay East blockhouse; 99 Bulwarks on the Hoe; 100 Fishers Nose blockhouse; 101 Plymouth Castle; 103 Barbican blockhouse and chain; 105 Plymouth Fort (Drake's Fort); 109 Mount Batten bulwark; 115 Drake's Island fort; 124 Stonehouse Town Wall; 125 Stonehouse blockhouse; 126 Stonehouse Pool blockhouse, north; 127 Stonehouse Pool blockhouse, south; 176 Staddon Point bulwark*

Fig. 2: 1540 Panorama (BL: Cott. MS Aug. I i 35-36)

Plate 2: Bedstock cannon in Dartmouth Castle (Austin C. Carpenter)

Edgcumbe shortly after. There was also a wall with a blockhouse on the shore at its western end protecting Stonehouse, and probably two others across Stonehouse Pool on the opposite shore. All these blockhouses which had been built with local money were intended to mount two or three of the early cannon (Plate 2). As cannon became more powerful and reliable, fire from Drake's Island could help to cover the entrance to the Cattewater and a fort was built on top of the island in 1549 on the instructions of the Privy Council.

When in 1586 the threat of invasion by the Spanish first developed, a plan was drawn showing the proposed positions of guns, supported by companies of militia, around the Sound. These covered the possible landing beaches from Bovisand to Cawsand and included Drake's Island. After the Armada of 1588 further attacks were still likely and work began on a fort on the east end of the Hoe in 1592 (Plymouth Fort, *Fig. 3*). Cannon were now powerful enough to demolish castles with their high but thin walls. Thick earth ramparts were needed to absorb cannon shot and on these could be mounted the defenders' guns. From this the bastion system of defence was developed *(Plate 3)*. From each four-sided projecting bastion fire was directed from the two outer faces against the advancing enemy. Guns in the two inner flanks covered the curtain on either side and the face of the next bastion. This system was incorporated in Plymouth Fort. Guns were also mounted in open batteries in the Lower Fort to cover the entrance to the Cattewater.

The Civil War and after *(Fig. 4; Plan B)*

When the Civil War broke out in 1642 Plymouth declared for Parliament and occupied the Fort and Drake's Island. In response to the threat of a Royalist attack in the following year new defences were begun. A line of redoubts was built based on North Hill and the town itself was surrounded by a stone-revetted rampart and ditch *(Fig. 4)*. Isolated redoubts were built to cover possible landing places such as Prince Rock and Western King, and the entrance to the Cattewater was covered from Stamford Hill. At one stage the defences at Stamford were overrun and shipping had to take refuge in Millbay. As a result, soon after the war was over a gun tower was built at Mount Batten and named after the commander of the Parliamentary navy in Plymouth during the war. It was needed at the time because of the threat of attack by the Dutch.

Charles II was aware of the importance of Plymouth - he had nominally commanded the besieging army in

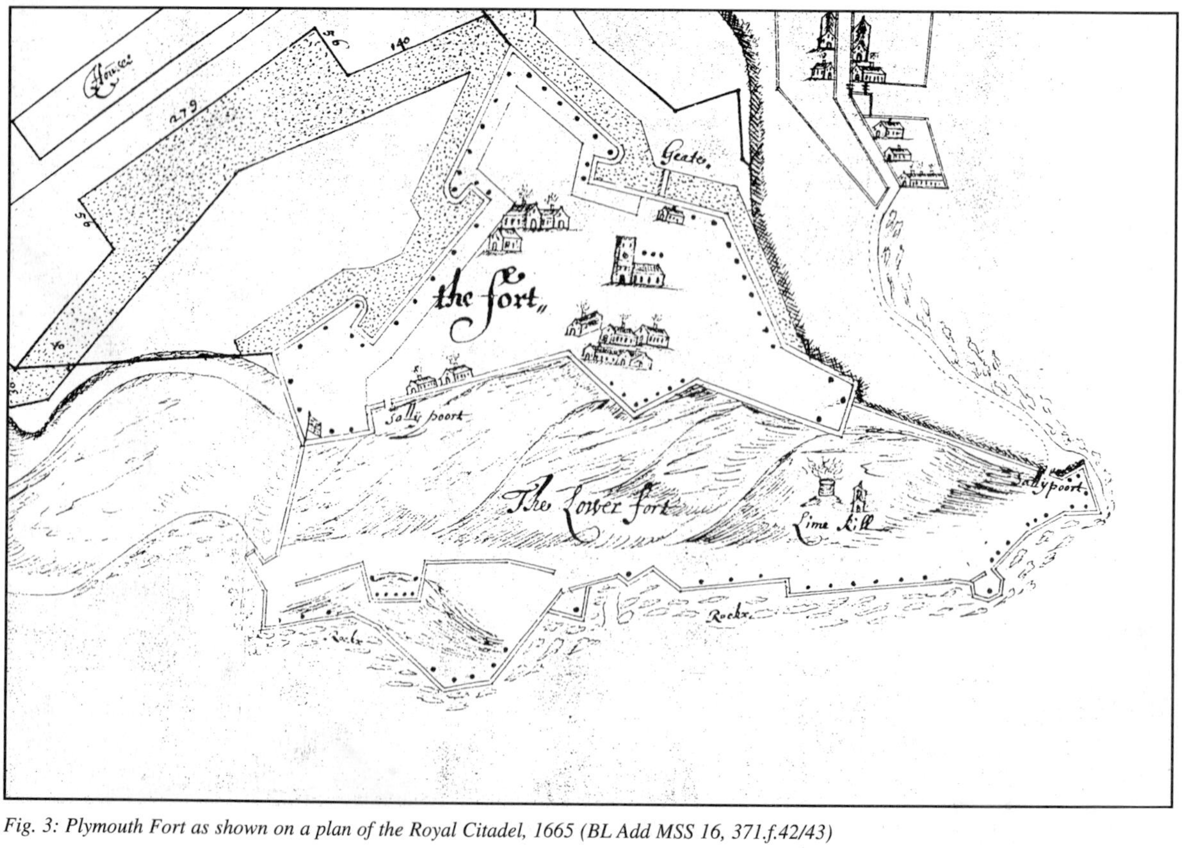

Fig. 3: Plymouth Fort as shown on a plan of the Royal Citadel, 1665 (BL Add MSS 16, 371.f.42/43)

Plate 3: Bastion system of fortification at the Royal Citadel (FWW)

1645-6 - and he planned to build a royal dockyard there (originally at Hooe Lake). In 1665 work began on the Royal Citadel, one of the most important seventeenth-century fortifications in the country. When completed *(Fig. 5)* it dominated not only the Hoe and the town, but also the channel across to Drake's Island and, from an enlarged Lower Fort, the entrance to the Cattewater. Batteries were also built at this time at Queen Anne's Battery and at Mount Batten (Plan B). In 1667 Dutch, and again in 1690 French, squadrons approached but declined to face the guns of the Citadel.

War with France *(Plans B-D)*

The conflict with France which began in 1690 was the first of a series of wars which continued until the end of the Napoleonic Wars in 1815. During this time eight invasions of varying sizes were launched from France though none landed in England in any strength thanks to the Royal Navy; another half dozen were planned. After the building of the Royal Dockyard on the Hamoaze began in 1690, new batteries were planned to cover the passage between Drake's Island and the Hoe and round Devil's Point to Mount Wise. In 1700 batteries were proposed at Drake's Island and Devil's

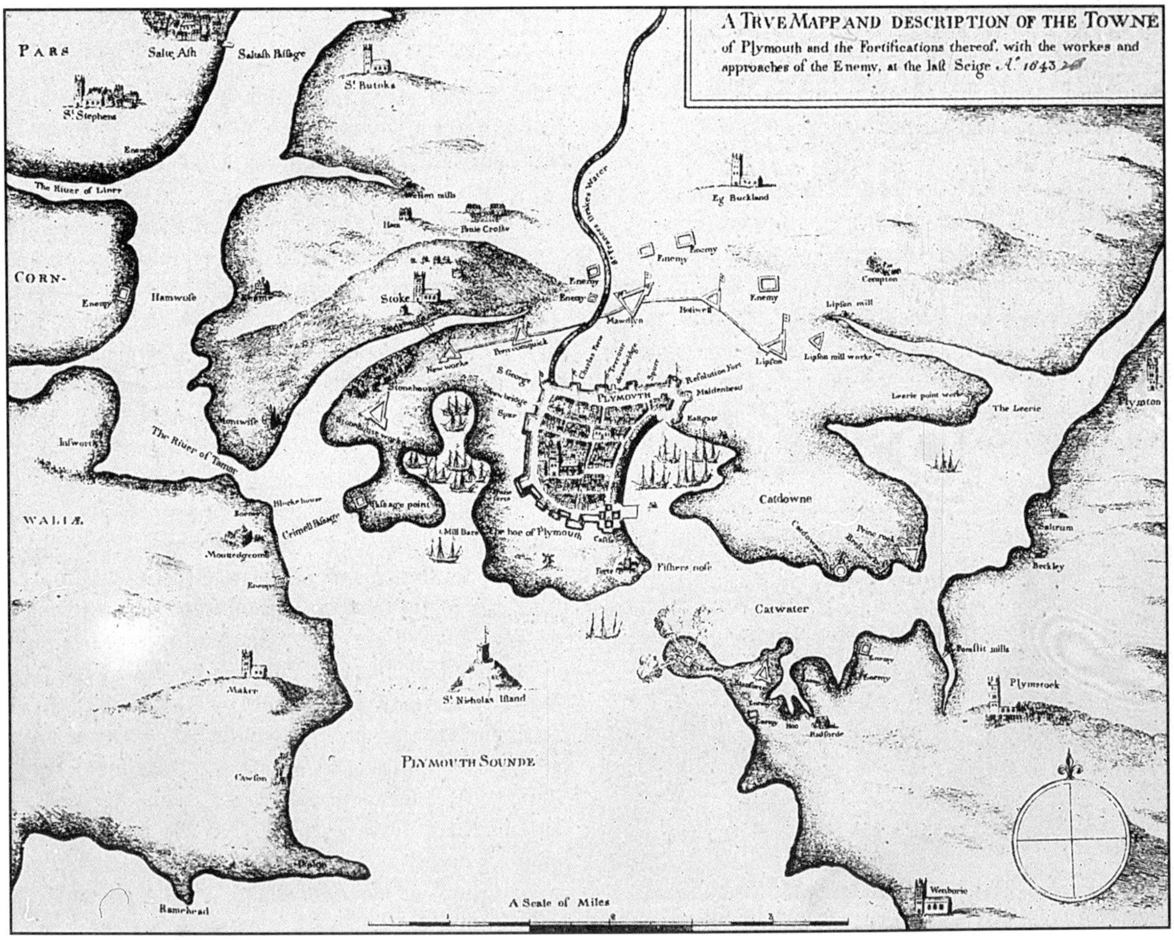

Fig. 4: Siege Map of Plymouth 1644, by W. Hollar (Plymouth Proprietary Library)

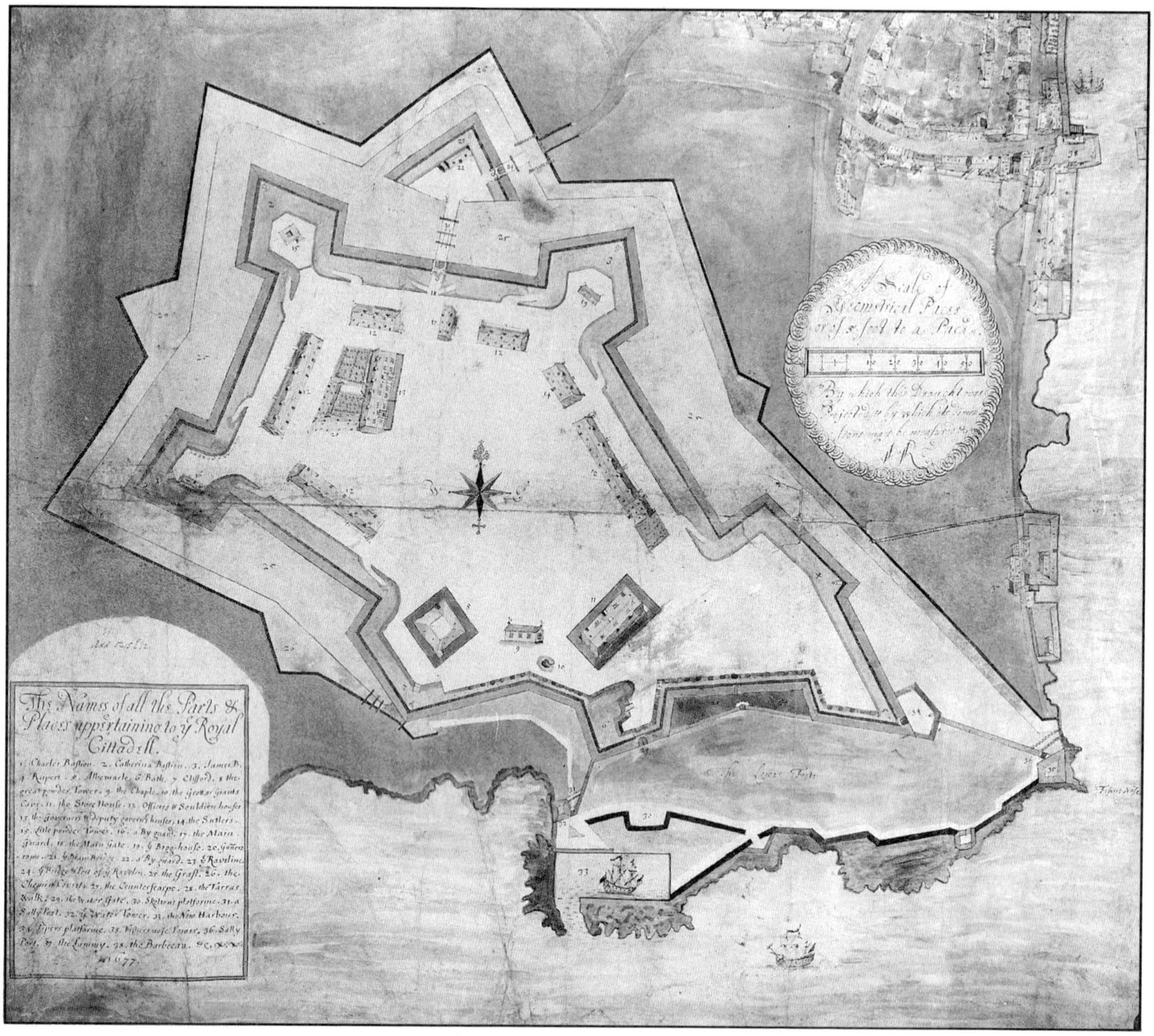

Fig. 5: Plan of Royal Citadel by J.R., 1677 (BL: Add 5415.E.2)

Point and for the first time a permanent battery was to be built at Cawsand to cover the bay *(Plan B)*.

In anticipation of the outbreak of the Seven Years War, in 1753 the Citadel's fortifications were extended, larger cannon mounted *(Plate 4)* and three new batteries built in the Lower Fort facing west to cover the passage along the front of the Hoe. The war started in 1756 and in the following year work began to surround the Dockyard, the town of Dock and the barracks being built around it with a rampart and ditch (Dock Lines, *Fig. 6*). During the war batteries were built or old ones strengthened at Devil's Point, Redding Point, Wilderness Point (Mount Edgcumbe) and Cawsand (Amherst Battery) *(Plan C)*.

Plate 4: 32-pdr cannon on garrison standing carriage at Royal Citadel (Exeter Archaeology)

In 1779 during the American War of Independence the threat of a combined Franco-Spanish invasion resulted in a crash building programme of earthwork redoubts (*Plan D*). To cover Dock Lines, which were at that time not strong enough to resist a determined attack, redoubts were proposed at high points within and in front of the Lines. Only those at Mount Pleasant *(Plate 5)*, Mount Wise, Western King and Stonehouse *(Fig. 7)* appear to have been completed. A line of redoubts was built to block the approach to Maker Heights from Cawsand, where three new batteries were built covering the beach and bay. The crossing at Cremyll was secured by Obelisk Redoubt and the associated musketry lines. Shortly after, the first battery was built on Staddon Heights near Withy Hedge, facing onto the Sound. A proposal by the Duke of Richmond, Master General of the Ordnance, to build a large bastioned fort on Maker Heights and another at Merafield (now Maryfield), near Antony House, was defeated in Parliament in 1786 but by 1790 the two flanking redoubts (Nos 4 and 5) on Maker had been strengthened and stone-revetted.

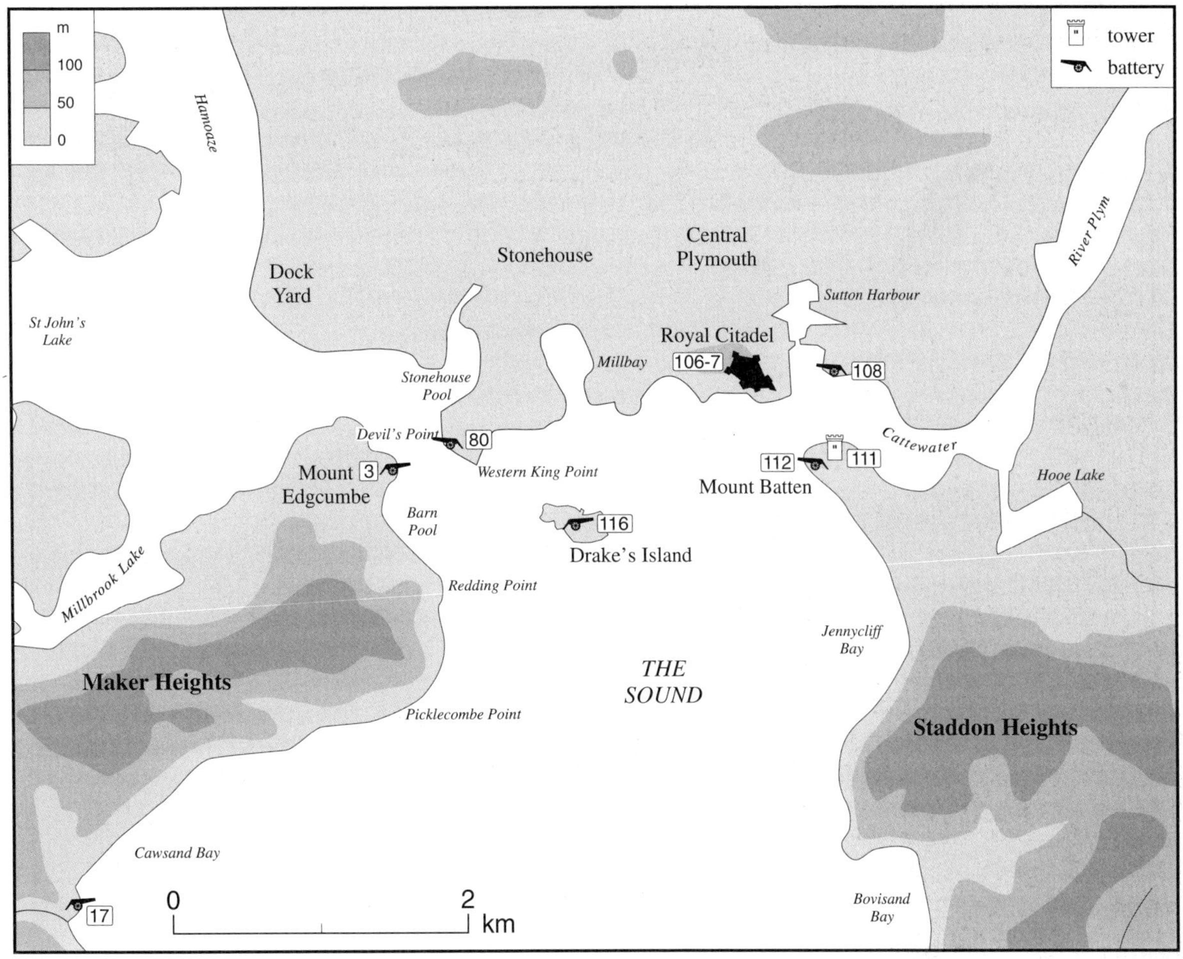

Plan B: After the Civil War: the Restoration and early defences of the Dockyard, 1645 - 1755
Schedule *3 Mount Edgcumbe Battery; 17 Cawsand Battery A; 80 Devil's Point Battery A; 106/7 The Royal Citadel and Lower Fort; 108 Queen Anne's Battery; 111 Mount Batten tower; 112 Mount Batten Battery; 116 Drake's Island batteries*

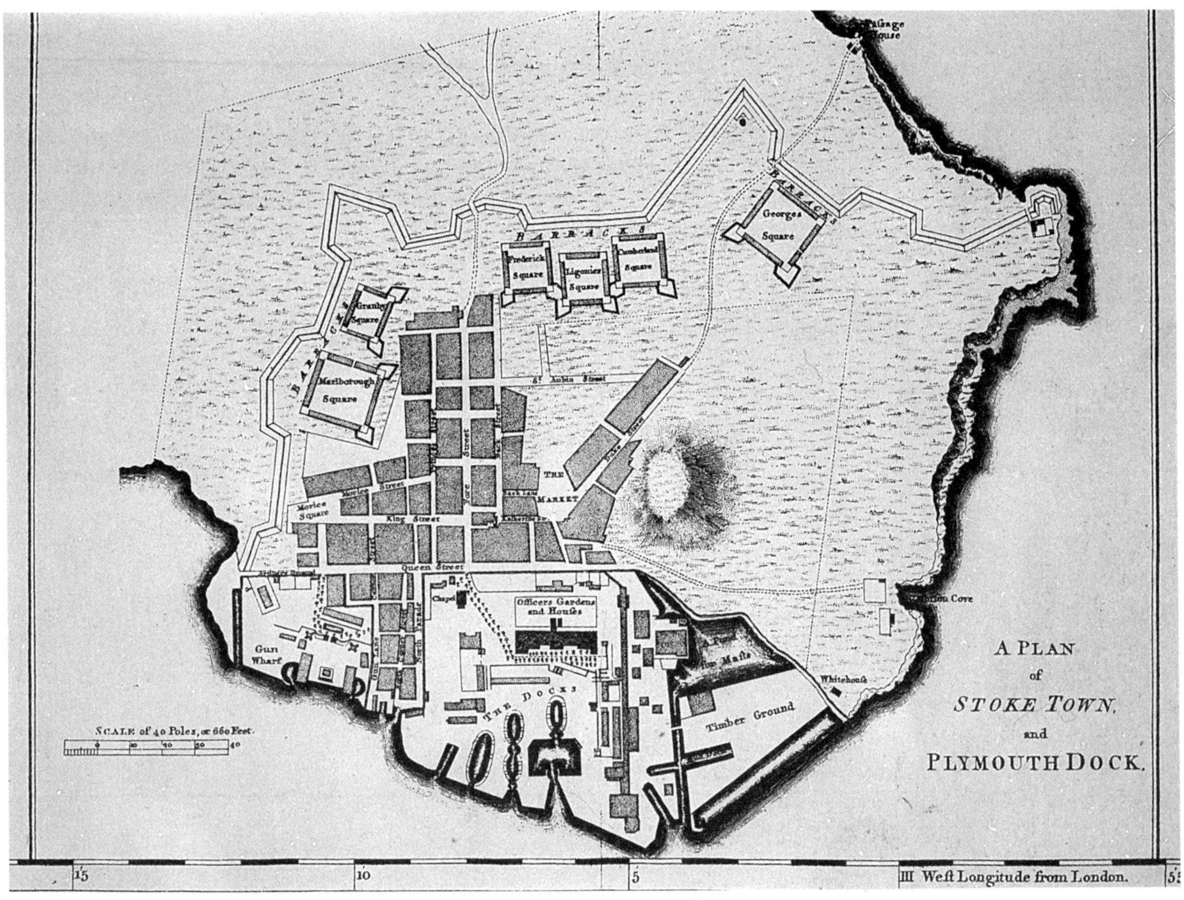

Fig. 6: Plan of Dock Lines by Benjamin Donn, 1765

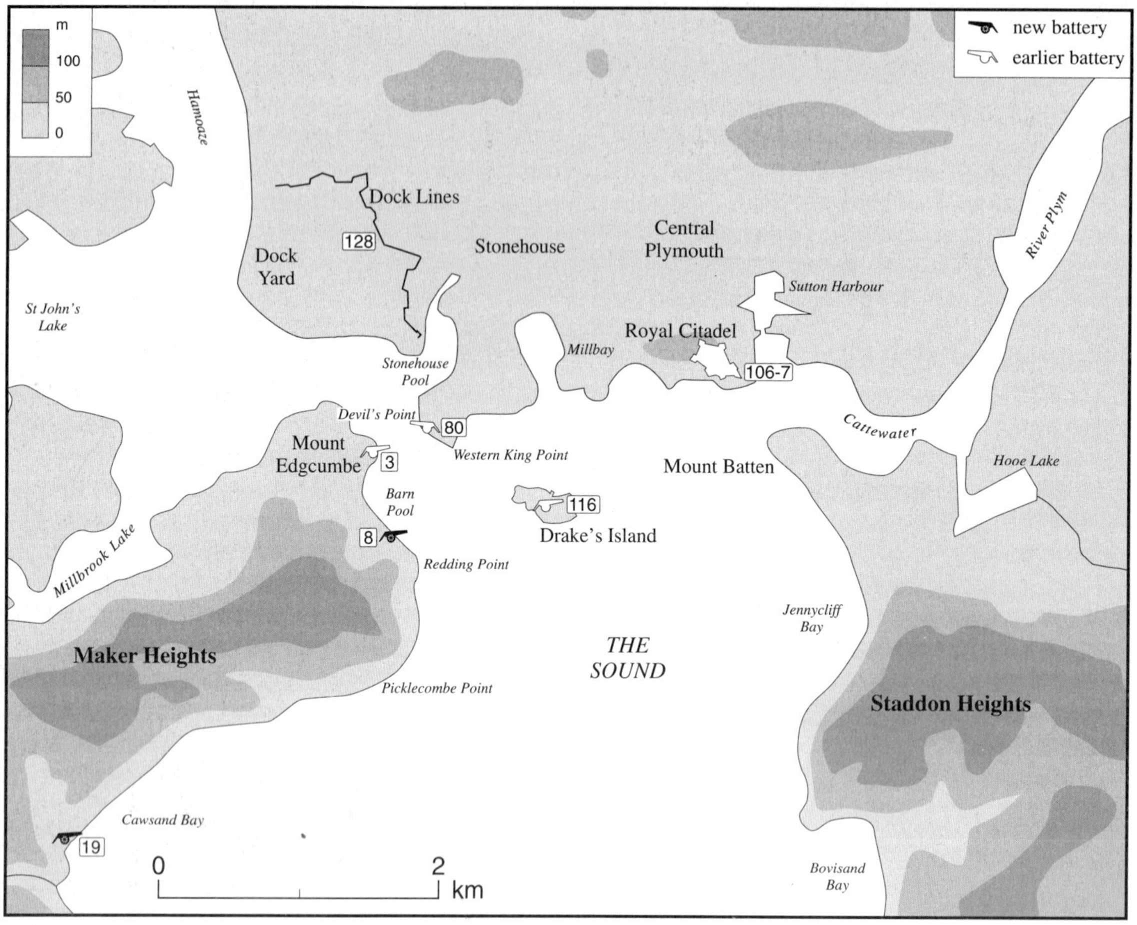

Plan C: Mid 18th century defences: the Dock Lines
Schedule *128 DockLines;* ***New batteries*** *8 Redding Point Battery; 19 Amherst Battery* ***Earlier fortifications, still armed*** *3 Mount Edgcumbe Battery; 80 Devil's Point Battery A; 106/7 The Royal Citadel and Lower Fort; 116 Drake's Island batteries*

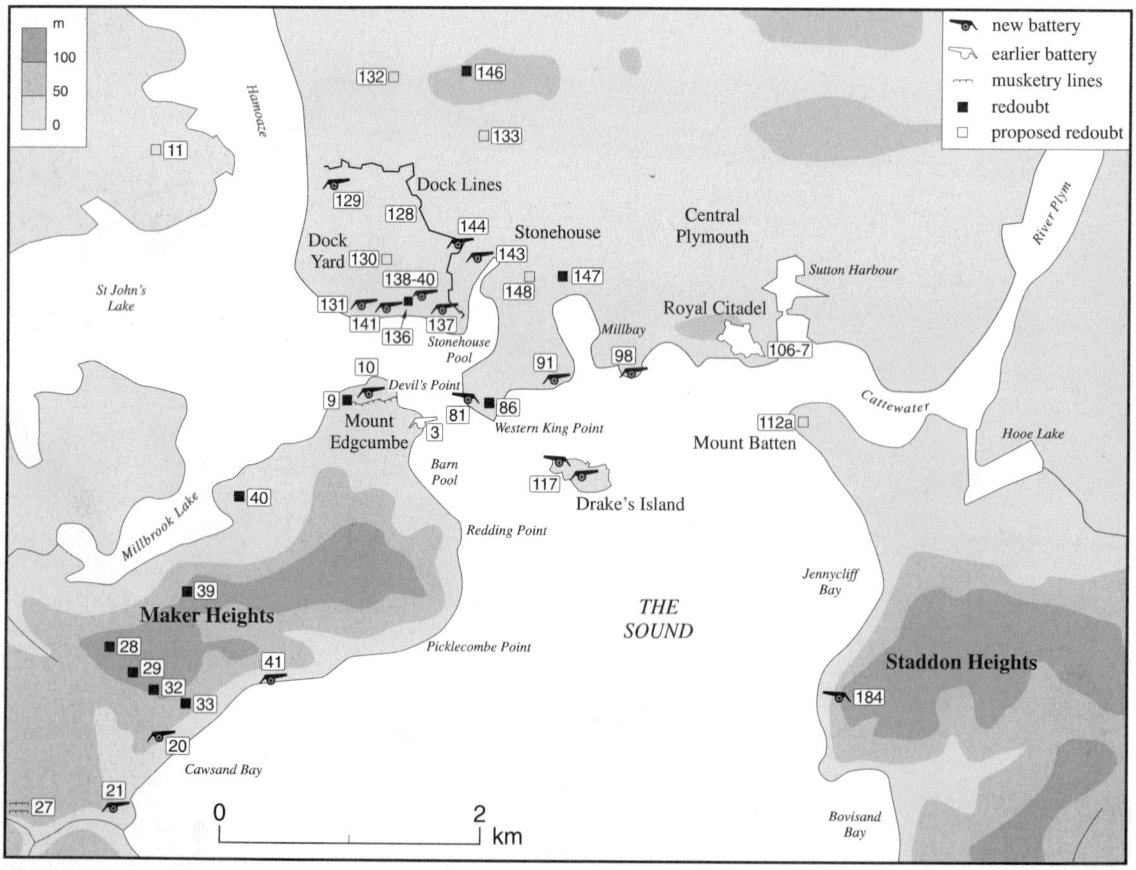

Plan D: The late 18th and early 19th century: wars with France and Spain
Schedule *128 The Dock Lines; 106/7 The Royal Citadel and Lower Fort; 27 Wringford Farm picket post and roadblock* ***New batteries*** *10 Retreat Battery and musketry lines; 20 Minadew Brake Battery; 21 Cawsand Battery B; 41 Sandway Battery; 81 Passage Point Battery; 91 Eastern King Battery; 98 West Hoe Battery; 117 Drake's Island batteries; 129 Cavalier Battery; 131 Bunker's Hill Battery; 137 Lower Mount Wise Battery (No. 1); 138-141 Mount Wise Batteries Nos 2 - 5; 143 Bluff Battery; 144 George's Bastion battery; 184 Staddon Battery;* ***Earlier battery, still armed*** *3 Mount Edgcumbe Battery;* ***Redoubts*** *9 Obelisk (Cremyll) Redoubt; 28 Maker Redoubt No. 1; 29 Maker Redoubt No. 2; 32 Maker Redoubt No. 3; 33 Maker Redoubt No. 4; 39 Maker Redoubt No. 5; 40 Empacombe Redoubt (Maker Redoubt No. 6); 86 Western King Redoubt; 136 Mount Wise Redoubt; 146 Mount Pleasant Redoubt; 147 Stonehouse Redoubt A;* ***Proposed redoubts*** *11 Torpoint; 112a Mount Batten; 130 Windmill Hill; 132 Keyham; 133 Stoke; 148 Stonehouse Redoubt B*

Plate 5: Mount Pleasant Redoubt (Photograph: F. M Griffith, Devon County Council. Frame DAP/UU12, taken 10 Jan 1992. © Devon CC)

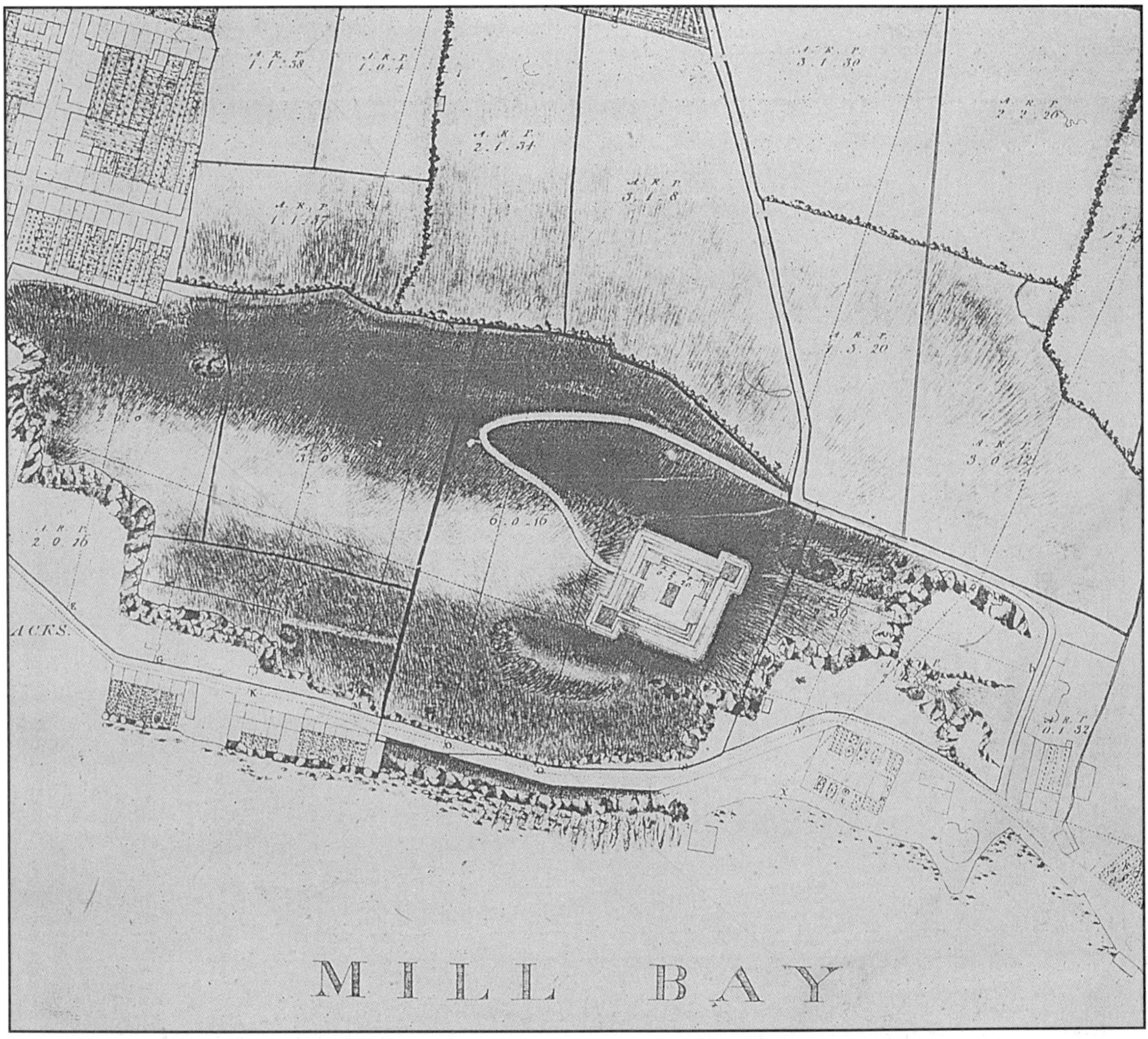

Fig. 7: Stonehouse Redoubt, 1808 (PRO: MR 1202)

Plate 6: 24-pdr on garrison traversing carriage (FWW)

The coast of the West Country was not seriously threatened with invasion during the Napoleonic Wars. The coast batteries at Plymouth were in most cases re-armed with larger guns, often on traversing carriages *(Plate 6)*, shot furnaces for red-hot shot were built and mortars added to the armament of the Citadel. A further redoubt with tower flanks - similar to the one at Stonehouse - was built at Empacombe to the NW of Maker Heights and a barracks and hospital for the garrison were built behind the line of redoubts on the Heights. A start was made in 1810 to strengthen Dock Lines but work was abandoned in 1816 when only two-thirds of the improved ditch and rampart was complete *(Plan D)*.

The fear of invasion in the mid-nineteenth century *(Plans E and F)*

During 30 years of peace after 1815 Britain's defences were neglected, until renewed alarm at French intentions resulted in a survey in 1844 of the coast defences which now had to face the threat of steam-driven wooden men-of-war. As a result by 1849 three new fortified limestone batteries had been completed at Plymouth (Plan E). Two of the batteries, at Staddon Point (Bovisand) and Picklecombe, covered the channels into the Sound on either side of the newly-completed breakwater. The third at Eastern King (known as Prince of Wales Redoubt) covered the channel past Drake's Island and dominated the high ground above Firestone Bay. In the following years the existing coast batteries began to be equipped with the latest cannon: 68-pdrs and 8-in and 10-in shell guns (firing explosive cannon balls). In 1853 work began on the remodelling of Dock Lines and a musketry keep was built on George Bastion in 1855-6 *(Plan E; Fig. 8)*.

Rapid developments began in 1858 which, over the next fifteen years, culminated in the building at Plymouth of new types of coast batteries, a ring of land forts and the arming of both with guns of entirely new design. The impetus for this was increasing alarm about the intentions of the French Emperor, Napoleon III. In that year he opened a large new basin at the heavily-defended naval dockyard at Cherbourg and the French navy, using their experience in the Crimean

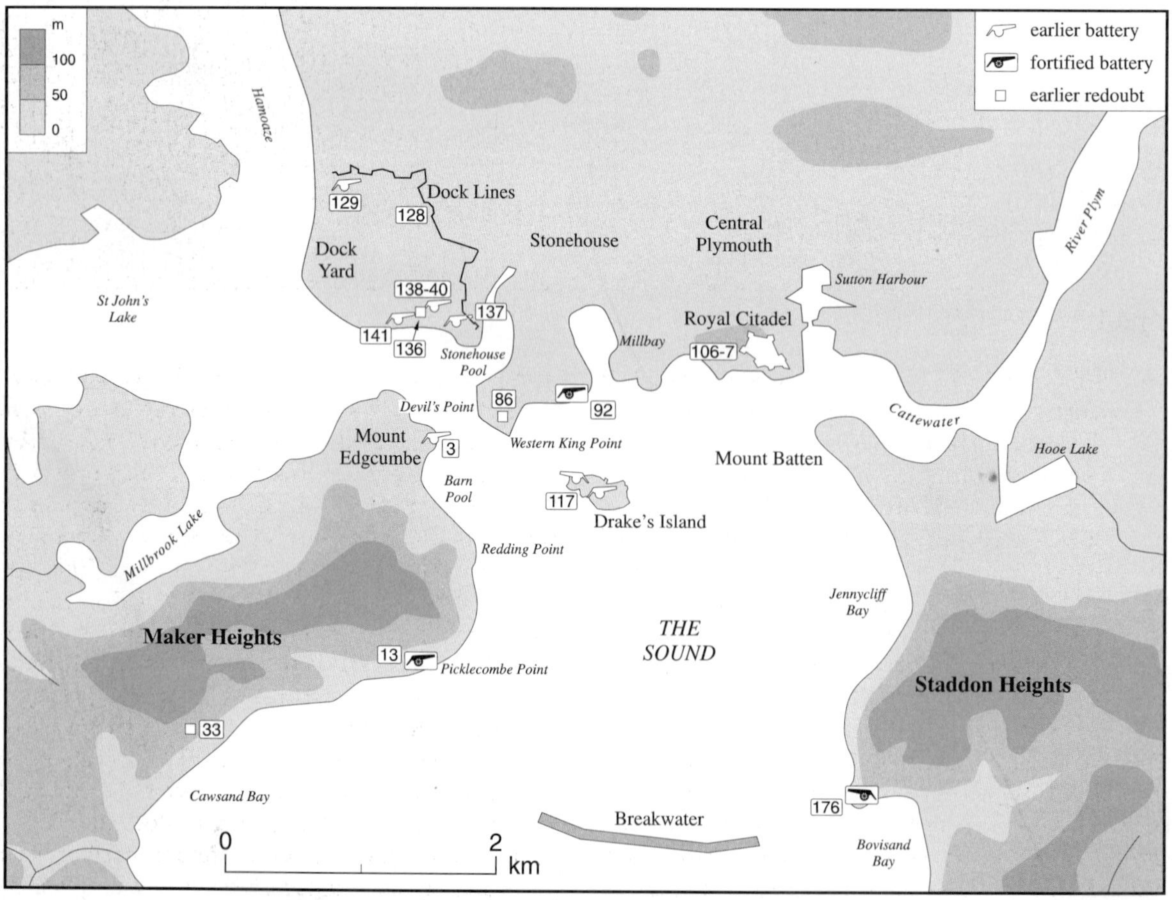

Plan E: The defences in the 1840s

Schedule *128 The Devonport Lines (Dock Lines); 106/7 The Royal Citadel and Lower Fort;* ***New fortified batteries*** *13 Picklecombe; 92 Prince of Wales Redoubt (Eastern King); 176 Staddon Point Battery A;* ***Earlier batteries, still armed*** *3 Mount Edgcumbe Battery; 117 Drake's Island batteries; 129 Cavalier Battery; 137-141 Mount Wise Batteries Nos 1 - 5;* ***Earlier redoubts, still armed*** *33 Maker Redoubt No. 4; 86 Western King Redoubt; 136 Mount Wise Redoubt*

Fig. 8: 1872 Panorama from Illustrated London News

War, laid down the first iron-clad wooden frigate. Our government was aware that an iron-clad warship was proof against the fire of the existing coastal batteries and that with the Army dispersed around the growing Empire the reserve of troops available to resist an invasion was very small. Popular alarm increased until in May 1859 the government was persuaded to permit the formation of volunteer units for home defence and in August the prime minister, Lord Palmerston, announced the formation of a Royal Commission "to consider the defences of the United Kingdom".

The recommendations of the Royal Commission were greatly influenced by the developments taking place at the time in gunnery, and their influence in turn on the design of coast batteries and land fortifications. Muzzle-loading smooth-bore cannon, similar in principle to those used in Henry VIII's time, were still in use though they had become larger and more powerful. Apart from the development of explosive cannon balls with primitive time-fuses, their main characteristic was still horizontal fire at short ranges. In 1859 Sir William Armstrong was appointed Superintendent of the Royal Gun Factory, Woolwich, to produce his revolutionary design of gun. This was rifled and breech-loading (RBL). It fired a pointed shell to nearly three times the range of a cannon, a shell which had much greater penetration and carried up to ten times the amount of explosive. At the longer ranges of which the Armstrong gun was capable the trajectory was no longer nearly horizontal and the vulnerable parts of fortifications needed in future to be protected from plunging fire with at least a six-foot covering of earth. Coast guns would in future need greater protection against pointed shells than that given by granite-faced embrasures.

The Royal Commission's report, 1860

(Plan F)

The Royal Commission's recommendations for Plymouth, after pruning by the Cabinet, resulted in the completion by 1872 of six new coast batteries, together with Breakwater Fort (finished about 1880), and a ring of eighteen land forts and batteries based on three principal forts at Staddon, Crownhill *(Fig. 9)* and Tregantle. The land forts were linked by a system of military roads protected from the likely direction of attack by banks, with a firing-step on the rear slope where appropriate. The defences were also strengthened in several cases by extended ditches and scarps across the front of groups of forts and batteries.

Plate 7: Bovisand Battery and (above) Staddon Point Battery in the 1890s (R.C.F. Serpell)

During the building of the casemated coast batteries it was decided to replace the original design of granite embrasures with wrought-iron shields up to three feet thick made of sandwiches of wrought-iron plates with shock-absorbent material between them *(Plate 7)*. The land fortifications were polygonal in design, the shape and number of sides depending on the ground on which they stood and which they were required to cover. Each face was covered by the fire of guns and rifles from galleries projecting into a deep ditch, called *caponiers*.

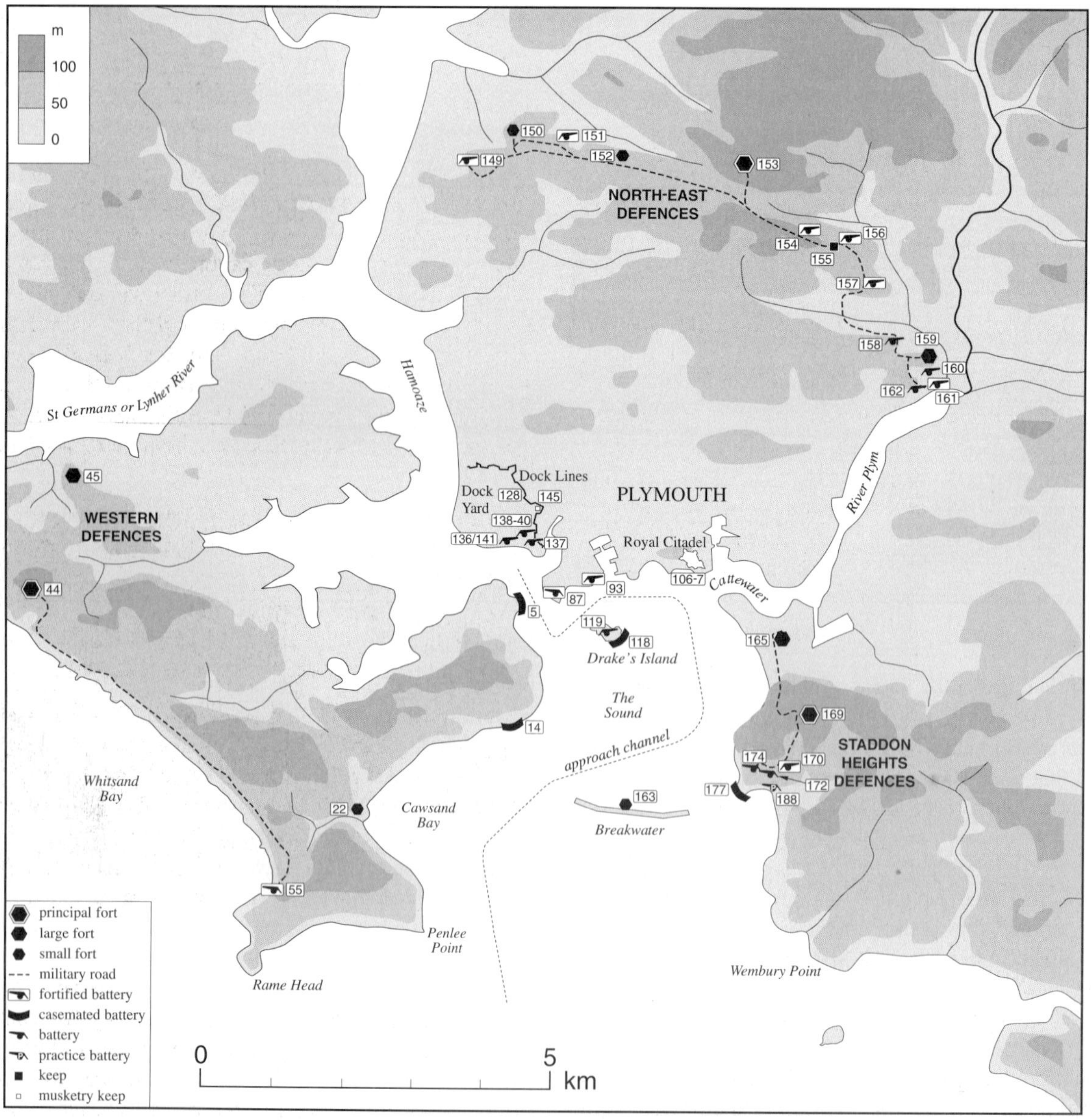

Plan F: The re-building of the Dock Lines, and the Victorian forts and batteries, 1853-1880

Schedule *106/7 The Royal Citadel and Lower Fort; 128 The Devonport Lines (Dock Lines); 145 George's Bastion - musketry keep; 155 Eggbuckland Keep* ***Principal forts*** *44 Tregantle; 153 Crownhill; 169 Staddo;* ***Large forts*** *45 Scraesdon; 159 Efford; 165 Stamford* ***Small forts*** *22 Cawsand; 150 Agaton; 152 Woodland; 163 Breakwater Fort* ***Fortified batteries*** *55 Polhawn; 87 Western King Battery A; 93 Eastern King Battery B; 149 Ernesettle; 151 Knowle; 154 Bowden; 156 Forder Battery; 157 Austin; 161 Laira; 170 Brownhill;* ***Casemated batteries****; 5 Garden Battery; 14 Fort Picklecombe; 118 Drake's Island; 177 Fort Bovisand* ***Batteries and emplacements*** *119 Drake's Island, upper RML battery; 136 Mount Wise Redoubt; 137-141 Mount Wise Batteries Nos 1 - 5; 158 Deer Park Emplacement; 160 Efford Emplacement; 162 Laira Emplacement; 172 Twelve Acre Brake Battery; 174 Watch House Brake Battery; 188 Bovisand Practice Battery*

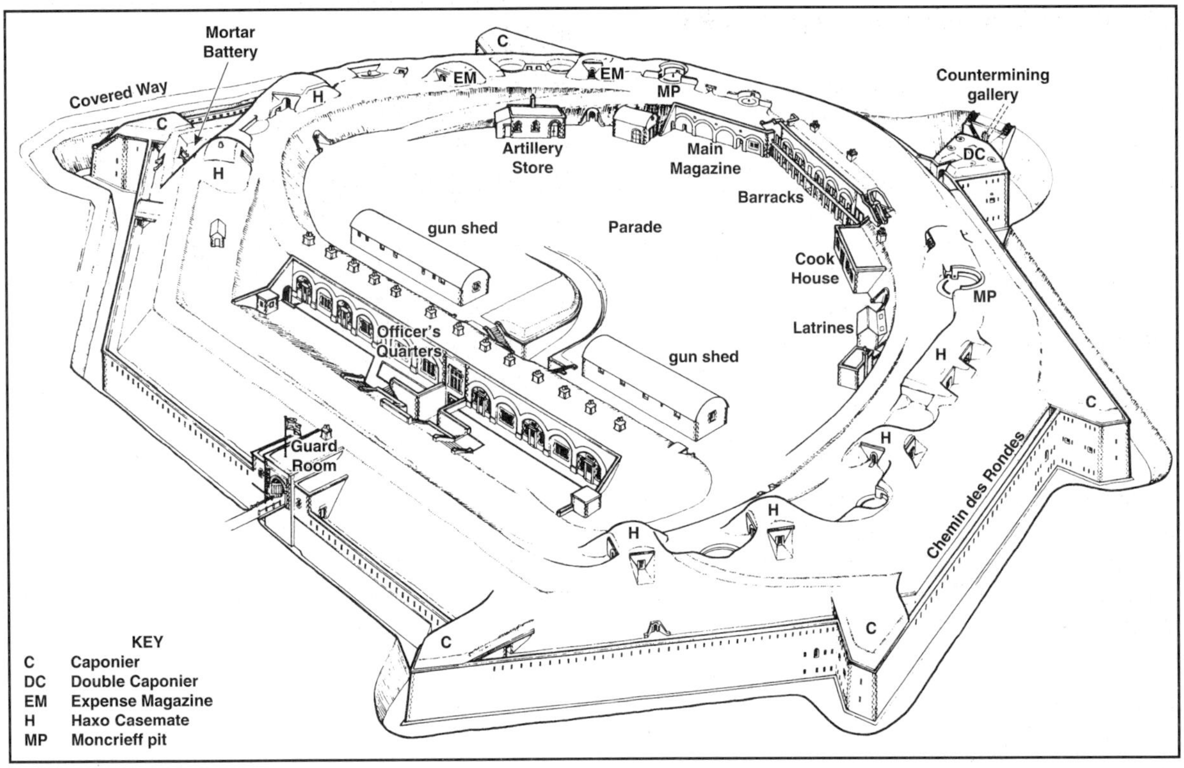

Fig. 9: Plan projection of Crownhill Fort (based on an original provided by the Landmark Trust)

In front of the ditch was a parapet which concealed the ditch from the enemy *(see Fig. 9)*. In front of the parapet sloped a cleared *glacis* covered by the guns on the ramparts behind the ditch. Beyond the *glacis* was an extensive 'clearance area' *(see Fig. 99)* which could be cleared of obstructions such as buildings and trees when invasion threatened. Guns mounted on the front rampart of the fort fired over an open parapet; those on the flanks of the fort were vulnerable to fire from the side so were in casemates on top of the ramparts, earthed over (bombproofed) and known as Haxo casemates. Magazines and casemates used as barracks were also bombproofed. A practice battery was established at Bovisand where the militia and volunteer artillerymen who were to man the forts and batteries in war could fire the various types of guns out to sea.

Armstrong's breech-loading gun was later rejected by the navy in favour of a new generation of guns developed in the 1860s. These returned to the principle of muzzle-loading but the projectile was made with studs which fitted into deep rifling in the bore and so they were able to fire pointed shell. The main advantage of these rifled muzzle-loading (RML) guns was their ease of manufacture. Consequently in a few years guns of much larger calibre were being built, although their range (up to 5000 yards) was only about half that of the Armstrong guns and they were less accurate. By 1873 the coast batteries had all been armed with 9-in *(Plate 8)* and 10-in RMLs, 12-in RMLs were being mounted on Drake's Island *(Plate 9)* and by 1880 12.5-in RMLs were being emplaced in Breakwater Fort.

Plate 8: 9-in RML in open emplacement with iron shield at New Tavern Fort, Gravesend (FWW)

Plate 9: 12-in RML on reproduction mounting on Drake's Island (FWW)

The completion of the land defences was slow. The ramparts of the last batteries were finished by 1872 but by then the smooth-bore guns for which they had been intended were obsolete. Their armament was low in priority - after the navy and the coast batteries - and when emplacements were finally built on the ramparts they were designed for the obsolescent Armstrong guns *(Plate 10)* and for 64-pdr RMLs *(Plate 11)* as they became available. The larger forts were armed first and were also given one or two emplacements for the

Plate 10: 7-in RBL in a Haxo casemate at Fort Nelson, Portsmouth (FWW)

Plate 11: 64-pdr RML (blocked up) in 360 degree centre pivot emplacement at Fort Nelson, Portsmouth (FWW)

Moncrieff pattern 7-in BL disappearing guns *(Fig. 10)*. A revised scale of armament was produced in 1885 and largely implemented by 1893. The result was a smaller number of more powerful guns than originally proposed and also a much reduced scale of armament for the smaller forts and batteries.

Following the overwhelming defeat of Napoleon III in the Franco-Prussian War in the year 1870, the immediate threat of invasion was finally removed. This accounts for much of the subsequent delay in completing the armament and for the later charge that the fortifications were unnecessary and therefore 'follies'. In fact their building was in response to a threat which had been perceived by the government for some years and became the cause of widespread popular alarm by 1859. Historically, this chain of forts and batteries, especially those in the North Eastern defences between Laira and Ernesettle, remain a fine and in some respects unique example of a developing system of fortification, each designed for its particular site and having the strength given by granite and limestone. The progress in design over some ten years can be seen by comparing Tregantle, the earliest, with Crownhill, the last, both in general layout and in the design, for example, of the double caponiers.

The modernisation of the coast defences

(Plan G)

The collapse of France in 1870 only removed the threat to our dockyards for a short time. Increasing industrialisation in western Europe was followed by the modernisation of the Italian and German navies as well as the French. In the 1870s the larger RMLs being mounted in the coast batteries were in response to the increasing size of naval guns. At the same time great efforts were made to improve the effectiveness of their fire against the armoured, steam-driven warships of the day by improved methods of rangefinding and fire control. This resulted in the development of accurate optical depression rangefinders (DRFs) and position finders (PFs), which were eventually able to pass the range and bearing of the projected future position of the target to the electric dials on the guns. Observation

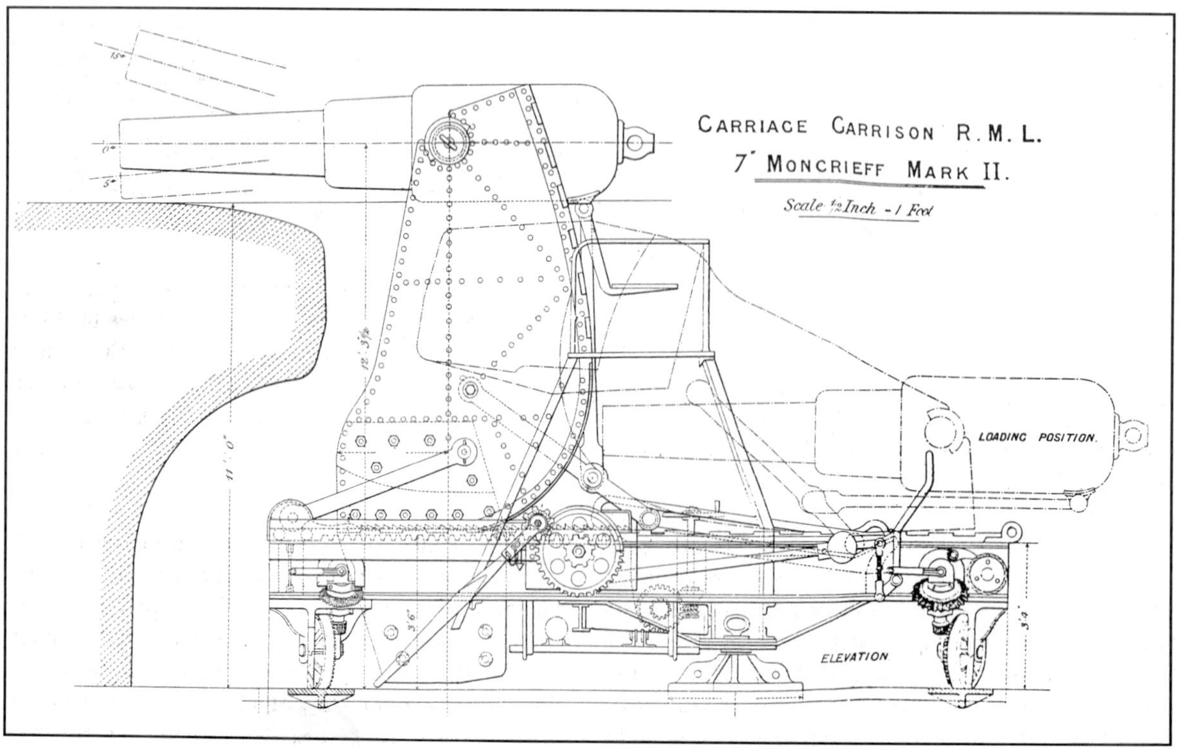

Fig. 10: Moncrieff Mark II disappearing carriage, (the gun shown is a 7-in RML. By 1885 7-in RBLs had been mounted at Crownhill, Scraesdon & Stamford on these carriages) (Austin C. Carpenter)

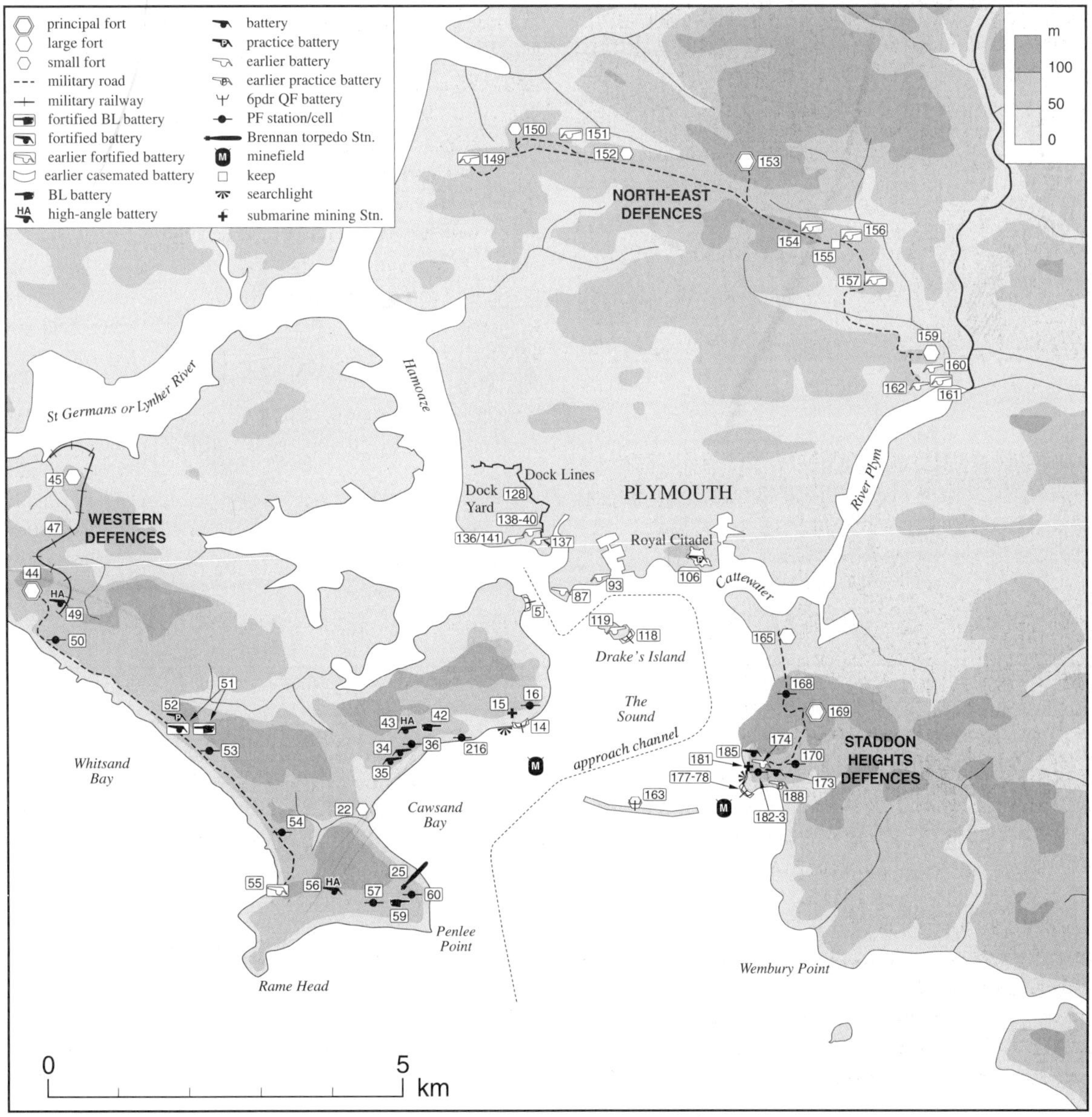

Plan G New coast batteries, and rearmament with RML and RBL guns, 1880-1898

Schedule *25 Pier Cellars Brennan torpedo station; 47 Wacker-Tregantle military railway; 106 The Royal Citadel - Queen's Battery (practice); 128 The Devonport Lines (Dock Lines); 155 Eggbuckland Keep (still armed)* **New batteries** *49 Tregantle Down Battery (high-angle), 9" RML; 51 Whitsand Bay Battery, 12.5" RML & 6" BL (disappearing); 52 Whitsand Bay Practice Battery, 64pdr RML; 56 Rame Church Battery (high-angle), 9" RML; 59 Penlee Battery, 6" & 13.5" BL (disappearing); 34 Grenville Battery, 12.5" RML; 35 Maker Battery, 12.5" RML; 42 Raleigh Battery, 10" BL; 43 Hawkins Battery (high-angle), 9" RML; 83 Royal Naval Reserve Battery, Western King; 173 Frobisher Battery, 12.5" RML; 185 Staddon Heights Battery, 12.5" RML* **6pdr QF batteries** *5 Garden Battery; 14 Fort Picklecombe; 118 Drake's Island; 178 Fort Bovisand Battery B; 163 Breakwater Fort;* **Earlier batteries, still armed/re-armed**; *5 Garden Battery; 14 Fort Picklecombe; 55 Polhawn Battery; 87 Western King Battery A; 93 Eastern King Battery B; 118 Drake's Island casemated battery; 119 Drake's Island upper battery; 136 Mount Wise Redoubt; 137-141 Mount Wise Batteries Nos 1 - 5; 149 Ernesettle Battery; 151 Knowle Battery; 154 Bowden Battery; 156 Forder Battery; 157 Austin Fort; 160 Efford Emplacement; 161 Laira Battery; 162 Laira Emplacement; 174 Watch House Brake Battery; 177 Fort Bovisand; 188 Bovisand Practice Battery* **Earlier forts, still armed/re-armed** *22 Cawsand; 44 Tregantle; 45 Scraesdon; 150 Agaton; 152 Woodland; 153 Crownhill; 159 Efford; 163 Breakwater Fort; 165 Stamford; 169 Staddon* **Position finding (PF) stations/cells** *16 Redding Point PF station; 36 Maker PF station; 50 Crowstone Field PF station; 53 Trenninow PF station; 54 Knatterbury PF station; 57 Middle Barton PF station; 60 Folly Tower PF station; 168 Jennycliff PF cell; 170 Brownhill PF cells; 182 Watch House Brake PF station; 183 Staddon Heights PF cells; 216 Hooe Lake Point PF cell* **Submarine mine observing stations** *15 Picklecombe; 181 Bovisand*

posts sited above the batteries and clear of their smoke passed orders to the guns by telephone to indicate targets and to control their fire.

Towards the end of the century, apart from the heavier armour on battleships and the greater size and range of their guns, new forms of attack developed. Blockships were being used at night to block the narrower parts of channels and, as steam and later diesel engines gave small craft much higher speeds, small torpedo boats were used to attack ships at anchor and in harbour. To keep blockships and other raiders from entering the Sound, minefields were laid at both ends of the Breakwater, controlled from observation posts above Bovisand and Picklecombe. At night they were illuminated by the first searchlights, known simply as 'electric lights'. Fast-moving torpedo boats were countered by a new development: small (3-pdr and 6-pdr) quick-firing (QF) guns able to fire up to 25-30 rounds per minute, assisted by searchlights which illuminated the sea area in front of the battery at night. The first QF guns were sited at Breakwater Fort, Picklecombe, Bovisand, Drake's Island and Garden Battery.

The most unusual defensive weapon developed at this time was the Brennan torpedo, and one that was kept remarkably secret. Years of development by its designer had produced an underwater wire-guided torpedo capable of considerable accuracy in the hands of a trained operator. Only eight stations were built for them, one of which was at Pier Cellars. The Brennan torpedo was operational from about 1890 to 1905 when it was withdrawn from service.

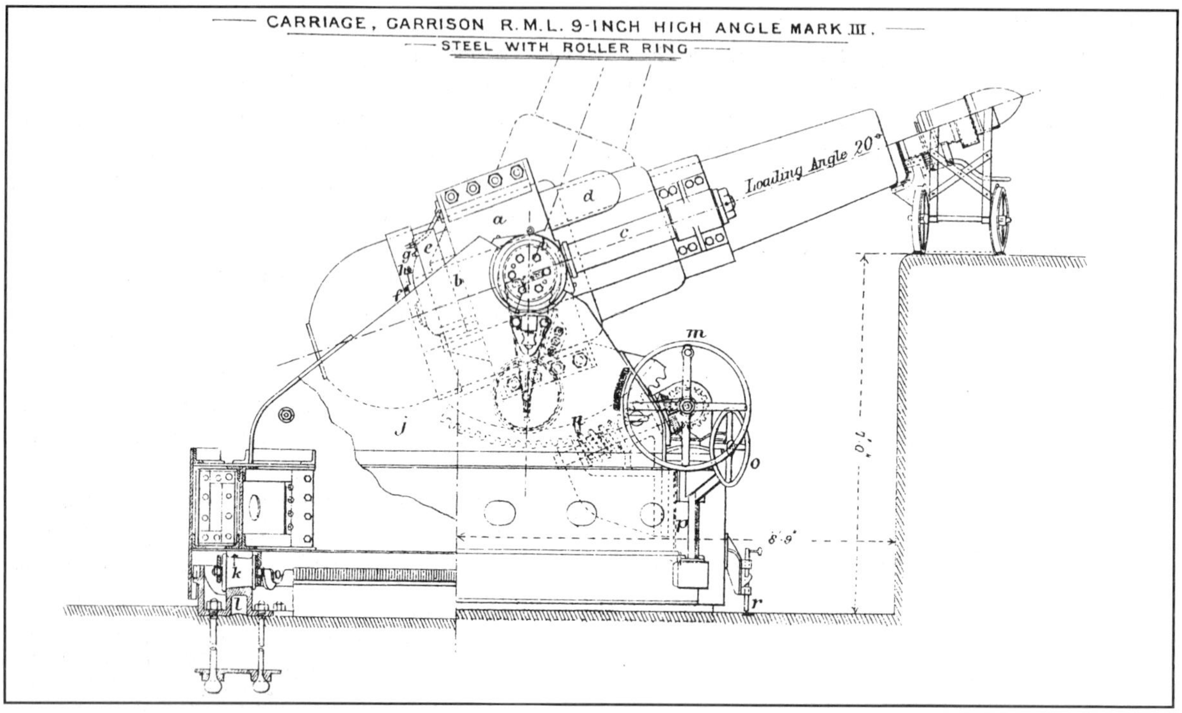

Fig 11: 9-in RML High Angle Mark III gun, from the official handbook

These developments were the background to a review of the coast defences in 1887, as a result of which a large building programme began in 1890 *(Plan G)*. A start was made before 1887 when two 12.5-in RML guns were mounted in No. 4 Redoubt at Maker overlooking Cawsand Bay. These guns were moved in 1890 to a new position known as Maker Battery and further 12.5-in RML batteries were built at Frobisher, Staddon and Whitsand Bay at this time. The latest guns being fitted to battleships at this time were capable of lying off Whitsand Bay and bombarding the dockyard from there. In order to attack their thinner deck armour three batteries of high-angle 9-in RML guns *(Fig. 11)* were built at Hawkins, Rame Church and Tregantle Down in 1893 and a battery of two 10-in BL guns was completed about the same time at Raleigh.

The most remarkable addition to the coast defences was the emplacement of a 13.5-in 68-ton BL disappearing gun *(Fig. 12)* at Penlee in 1894. It took

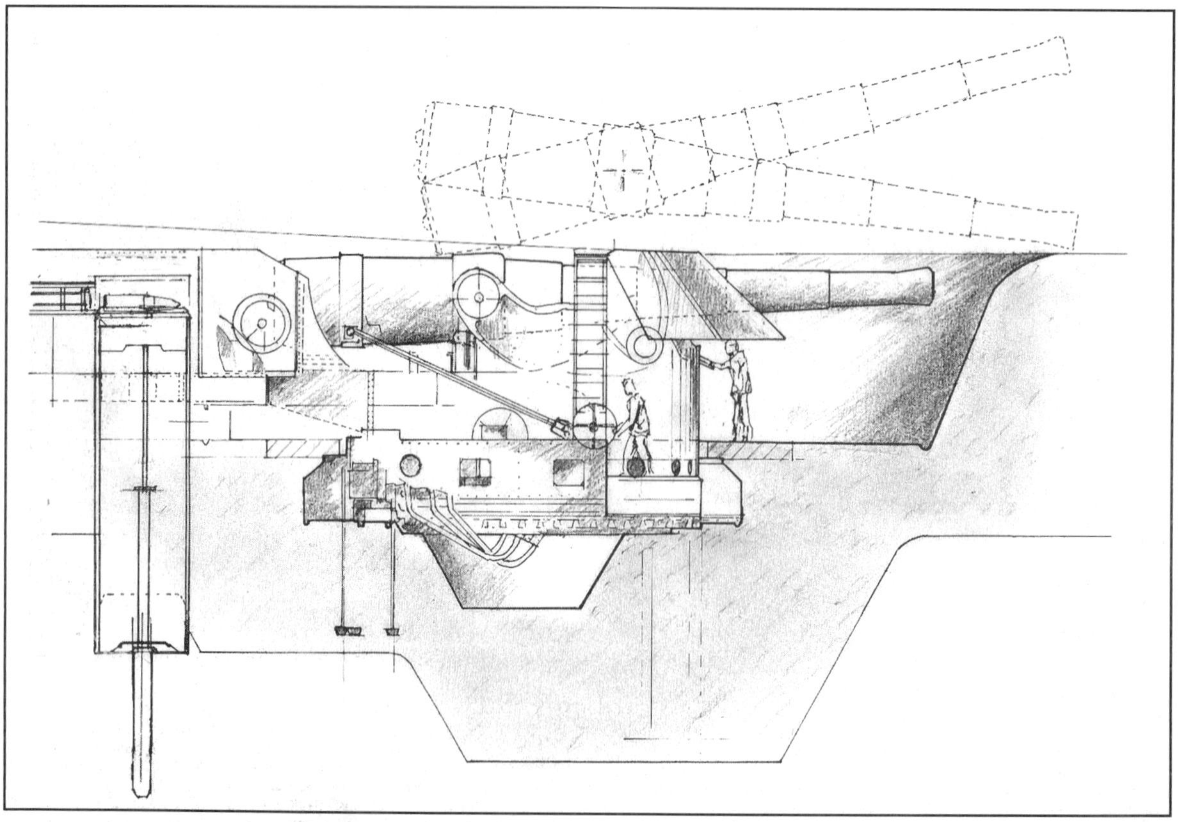

Fig. 12: An artist's impression of the complete mounting for the 13.5-in BL disappearing gun at Penlee Battery, 1894, based on the official handbook (Ian V. Hogg)

200 men and 80 horses two weeks to drag it up the hill from specially-built landing steps at Penlee Point where it was landed from a pair of barges. But its massive mounting proved unreliable in practice firing and it remained the only one emplaced in the country until dismantled after 1908.

To assist the programme of rearmament at this time a military railway was completed in 1893 from a jetty at Wacker Quay on the Lynher River up to Scraesdon Fort and on to Tregantle Down Battery. A new design of battery surrounded by a ditch with caponiers at the salients was built at Whitsand Bay in 1893 to mount three 12.5-in RMLs and two 6-in BL guns on improved hydro-pneumatic disappearing carriages. Consideration began to be given to the local defence of the larger batteries about this time and unclimbable fences and infantry strongpoints were also introduced.

To provide ranges and bearings to targets for all these new batteries, groups of PF stations were built along the high ground overlooking Whitsand Bay and on either side of the Sound. A practice battery for the coast gunners in the garrison was built in front of Whitsand Bay Battery in 1895. RML, and later BL and QF, guns were mounted there.

The development of modern coast defences *(Plan H)*

Within 15 years another step in the development of guns had made most of the 1890s rearmament obsolete. Wrought-iron RMLs were succeeded by steel and wire-wound guns, gunpowder by cordite. The result was the production of long, slim tapered gun barrels such as we know today, which fired shells at much higher muzzle velocities, and therefore to longer ranges, and with greater accuracy. Mountings no longer recoiled up

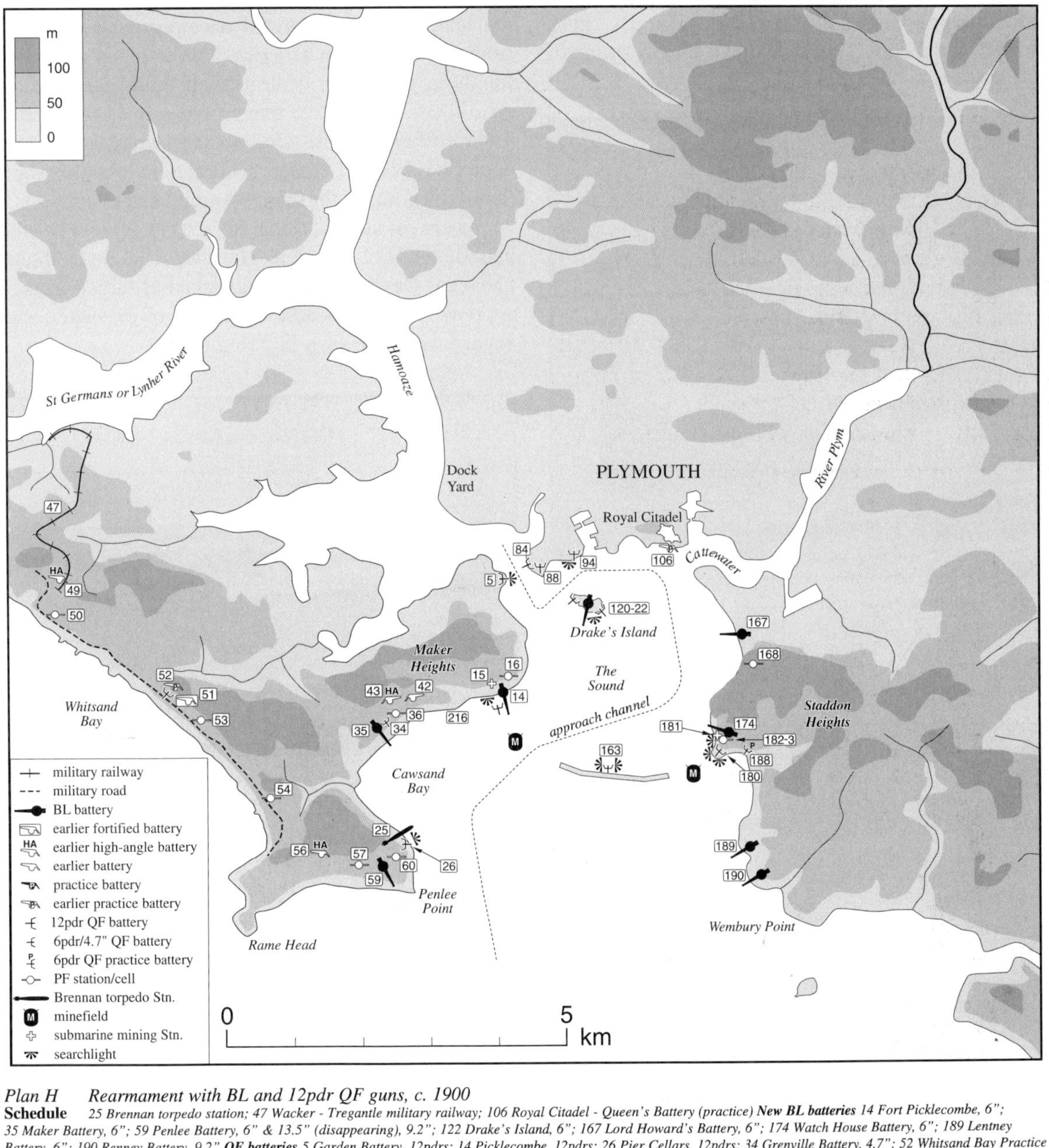

Plan H Rearmament with BL and 12pdr QF guns, c. 1900

Schedule *25 Brennan torpedo station; 47 Wacker - Tregantle military railway; 106 Royal Citadel - Queen's Battery (practice)* ***New BL batteries*** *14 Fort Picklecombe, 6"; 35 Maker Battery, 6"; 59 Penlee Battery, 6" & 13.5" (disappearing), 9.2"; 122 Drake's Island, 6"; 167 Lord Howard's Battery, 6"; 174 Watch House Battery, 6"; 189 Lentney Battery, 6"; 190 Renney Battery, 9.2"* ***QF batteries*** *5 Garden Battery, 12pdrs; 14 Picklecombe, 12pdrs; 26 Pier Cellars, 12pdrs; 34 Grenville Battery, 4.7"; 52 Whitsand Bay Practice Battery, 3pdrs, then 12pdrs; 84 Devil's Point Battery B, 12pdrs; 88 Western King Battery B, 12pdrs; 94 Eastern King Battery C, 12pdrs; 120 Drake's Island, Western QF Battery, 12pdrs; 121 Drake's Island, Eastern QF Battery, 12pdrs; 163 Breakwater Fort, 6pdrs; 180 Staddon Point Battery B, 12pdrs; 188 Bovisand Practice Battery, 6pdrs* ***Earlier batteries, still armed*** *42 Raleigh Battery, 10" BL; 43 Hawkins Battery (high-angle), 9" RML; 49 Tregantle Down Battery (high-angle), 9" RML; 51 Whitsand Bay Battery, 12.5" RML; 52 Whitsand Bay Practice Battery, 64pdr RML & 6" BL; 56 Rame Church Battery (high-angle), 9" RML* ***Position finding (PF) stations/cells*** *16 Redding Point PF station; 36 Maker PF station; 50 Crowstone Field PF station; 53 Trenninow PF station; 54 Knatterbury PF station; 57 Middle Barton PF station; 60 Folly Tower PF station; 168 Jennycliff PF cell; 182 Watch House Brake PF station; 183 Staddon Heights PF cells* ***Submarine mine observing stations*** *15 Picklecombe; 181 Bovisand*

Plate 12: 6-in BL gun at Lentney practice battery (Ian V. Hogg)

slides; recoil was absorbed by a hydraulic system and the gun was returned immediately to the firing position pneumatically. These developments, combined with a quick and effective system of breech-loading, resulted in much higher rates of fire from mountings which were soon developed to allow 360° traverse and relatively high angles of elevation. The BL guns mounted in the early 1900s were still the backbone of coast artillery in World War II.

Plate 13: Coast artillery searchlight
(Imperial War Museum, H 39430)

Plate 14: Coast artillery searchlight emplacements and Battery Observation Post on crest at Penlee Point (S. Johnson)

Developments in Germany were the impetus behind the reorganisation and modernisation of the coast defences which took place between 1900 and 1905 *(Plan H)*. Admiral Tirpitz became Minister of Marine in 1897 and in the following year a Naval Law was passed which established a major programme of naval construction including 12 new battleships. The building programme was doubled by the Naval Law of 1900; a direct challenge to British naval supremacy had emerged.

Forerunners of the new generation of guns which were introduced after 1900 were the 10-in 29-ton breech-loading (BL) guns which had been mounted at Raleigh Battery in 1893. By then an improved breech system had been developed. This was used in the 6-in BL guns *(Plate 12)* which were emplaced between 1900 and 1905 in batteries at Lentney, Watch House, Lord Howard's, Drake's Island, Picklecombe and Maker, replacing all the RMLs and disappearing guns, apart from the high-angle batteries. The eventual mounting for these guns on a central pivot with 360° traverse gave them an effective range of nearly 16,000 yards. Their role was Close Defence for which they were equipped with a very accurate automatic sight (autosight). For night firing, searchlights *(Plates 13 & 14)* were mounted close to sea level, below the batteries where possible. Further out, searchlights known as Observation Lights picked up targets as they approached, and passed them to one of the batteries to engage with their own Fighting Lights.

Plate 15: 9.2 in BL gun firing at Renney Battery (T.K. Hitchins)

At Renney and Penlee, batteries of three 9.2-in BL guns *(Plate 15)* were built in the same period. Until 1908 Penlee, with one 13.5-in BL, two 9.2-in BL and two 6-in BL on hydro-pneumatic disappearing mountings, was the most powerful battery in the defences. After 1908 only three 9.2-in BL were approved. They were sited in the Counter Bombardment role and as far from the dockyard as practicable to keep battleships out of range of it. Their maximum range was originally 24,000 yards but this was later improved at Renney.

The first 6-pdr QF guns were already by 1900 being replaced by 12-pdr QFs *(Plate 16)*, with batteries at Staddon Point, Drake's Island, Eastern and Western King *(Fig. 13)*, Devil's Point, Garden Battery,

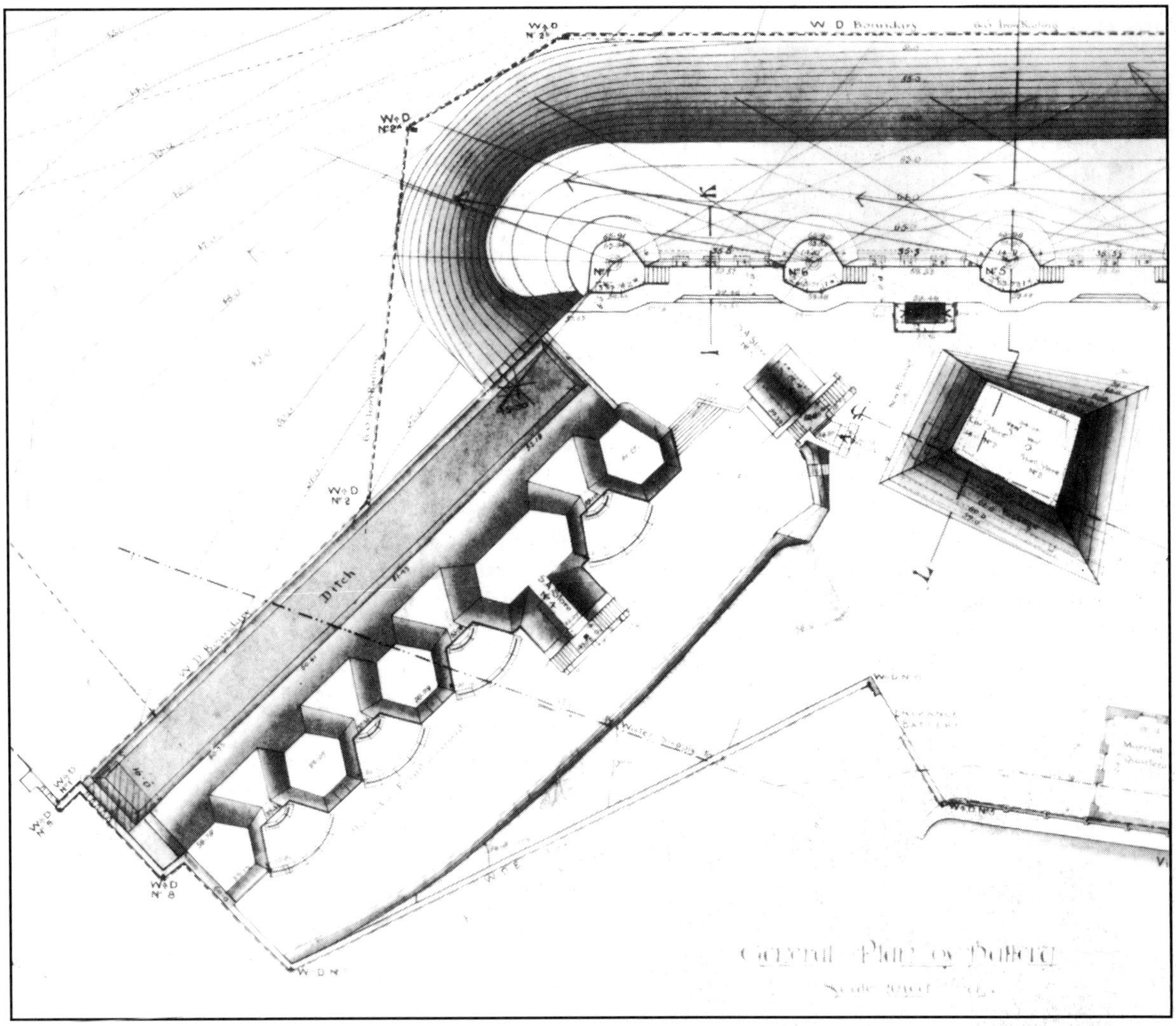

Fig. 13: Plan of part of 12-pdr QF battery at Western King superimposed on 64-pdr RML emplacements of 1862 (PRO: WO 78/5047)

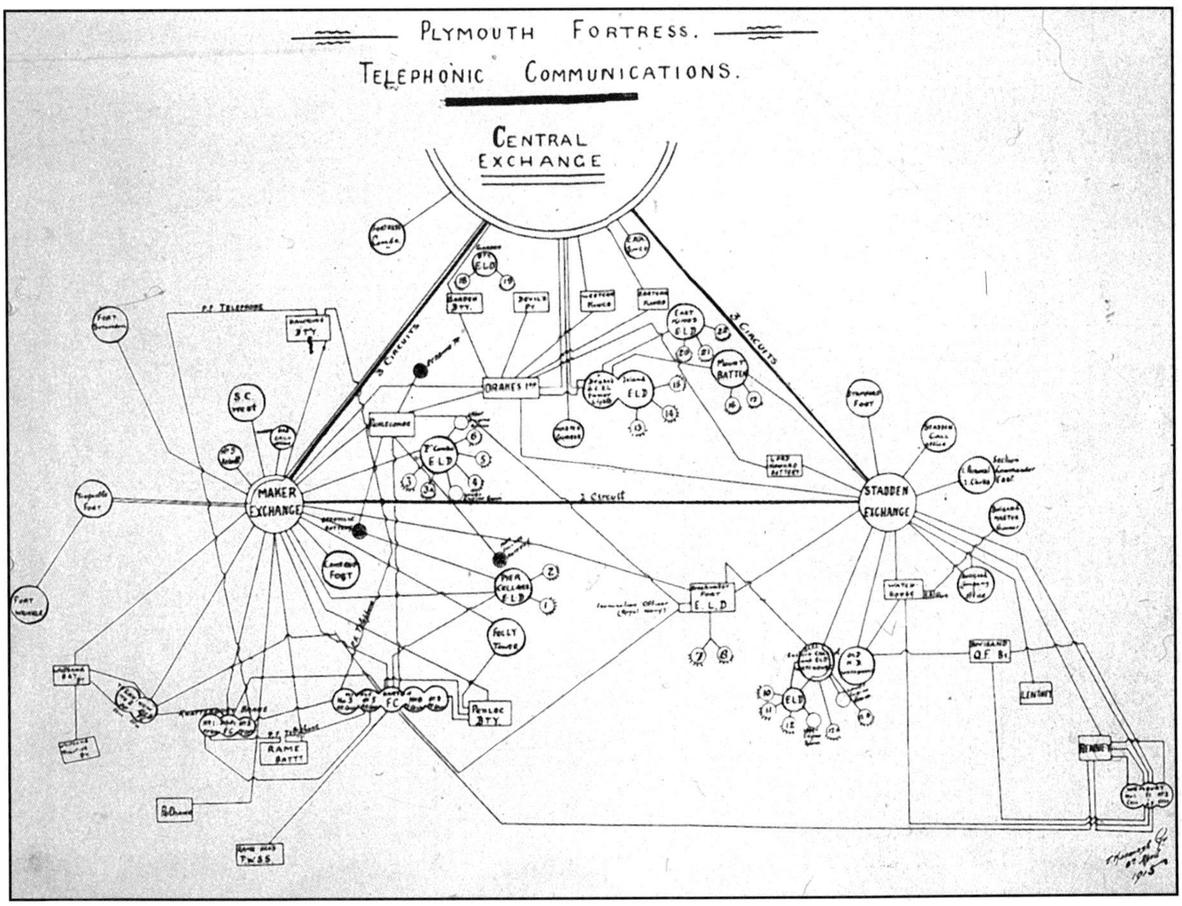

Fig. 14: Plymouth fortress telephone communication layout in 1915 (PRO: WO 192/122)

Plate 16: 12-pdr QF gun at Staddon Point Battery in 1939 (the late W.G.M. Jones)

Picklecombe and Pier Cellars. Some 3-in and 4.7-in QF guns were mounted (or at least proposed) for Picklecombe, Grenville and Polhawn to cover possible landing beaches. All the 12-pdr batteries had two or more wide-angle searchlight emplacements to provide at night an illuminated water area covering their fields of fire.

The 6-in and 9.2-in batteries had DRFs to give them ranges to targets relatively close in and were linked to groups of PF stations along the cliffs. These passed the ranges and bearings of targets further out to the guns by telephone and later by electric dials. Batteries were grouped, according to their proximity and their role, into Fire Commands. At Plymouth there were three Fire Commands, one each commanding the defences to the east and west of the Sound and one based on Drake's Island. The Fire Commander exercised tactical control over his sea area and was in turn under the Fortress Commander, Plymouth. The latter had his own Fortress Plotting System, based on observation posts (OPs) further up the coast to east and west, to give early warning of approaching targets. All positions down to individual searchlights were linked by telephone *(Fig. 14)*. This was the organisation of the coast defences by 1914 when, in the words of the official historian, "coast artillery in the British Army had never been more ready for war".

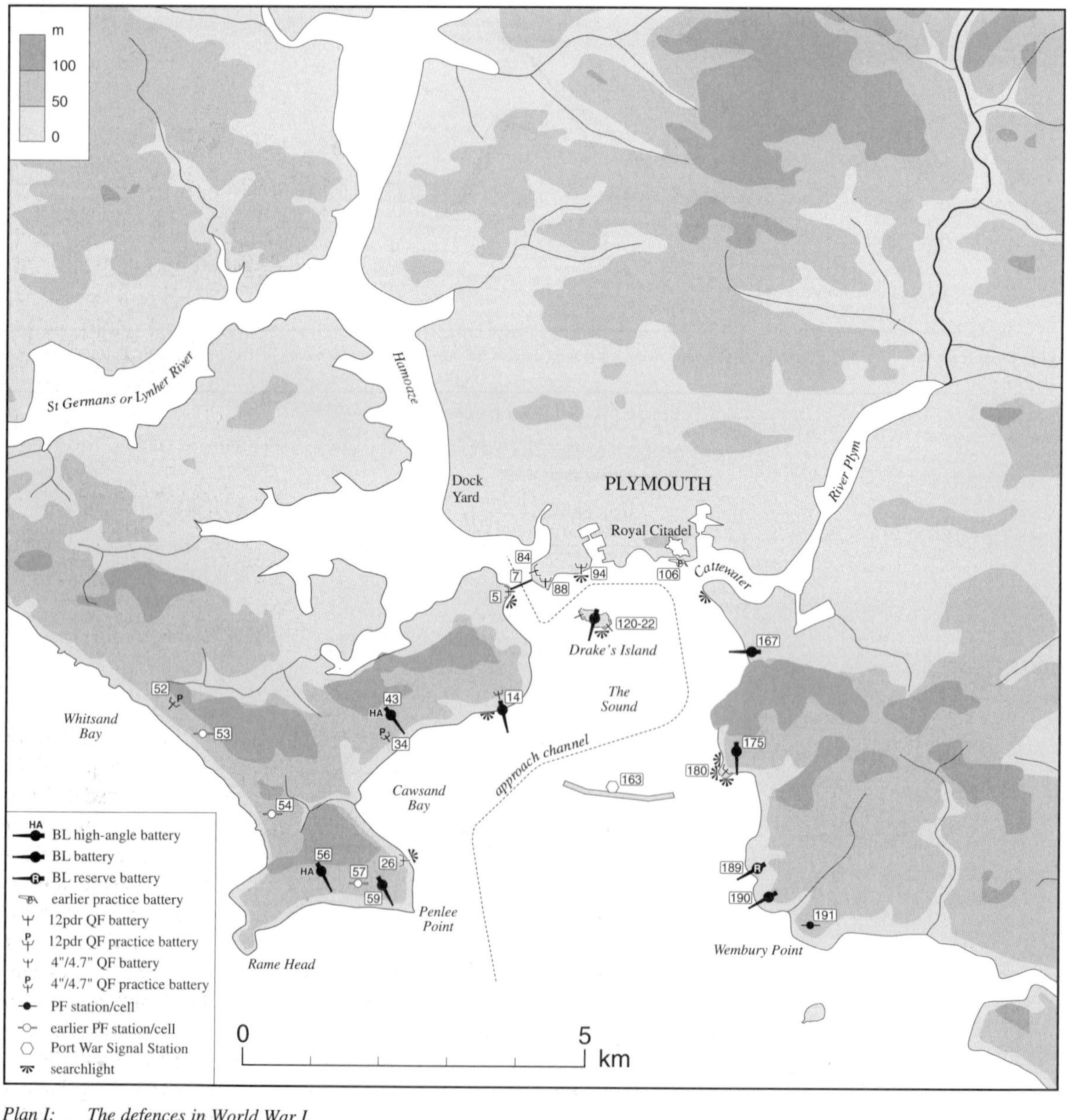

Plan I: The defences in World War I

Schedule *7 Boom; 106 Royal Citadel - Queen's Battery (practice); 163 Breakwater Fort - Port War Signal Station* ***BL batteries*** *14 Picklecombe, 6"; 43 Hawkins Battery, 9.2" (high-angle); 56 Rame Church Battery, 9.2" (high-angle); 59 Penlee Battery, 9.2"; 122 Drake's Island, 6"; 167 Lord Howard's Battery, 6"; 175 Watch House Battery, 6"; 189 Lentney Battery, 6" (in reserve); 190 Renney Battery, 9.2"* ***QF batteries*** *5 Garden Battery, 12pdrs; 14 Picklecombe, 4"; 26 Pier Cellars Battery, 12pdrs; 34 Grenville Battery, 4.7" (practice?); 52 Whitsand Bay Practice Battery, 12pdrs; 84 Devil's Point Battery B, 12pdrs; 88 Western King Battery B, 12pdrs; 94 Eastern King Battery C, 12pdrs; 120 Drake's Island, Western QF Battery; 12pdrs; 121 Drake's Island, Eastern QF Battery; 12pdrs; 180 Staddon Point Battery B, 12pdrs* ***Position finding (PF) stations*** *53 Trenninow PF station; 54 Knatterbury PF station; 57 Middle Barton PF station; 191 Wembury PF station*

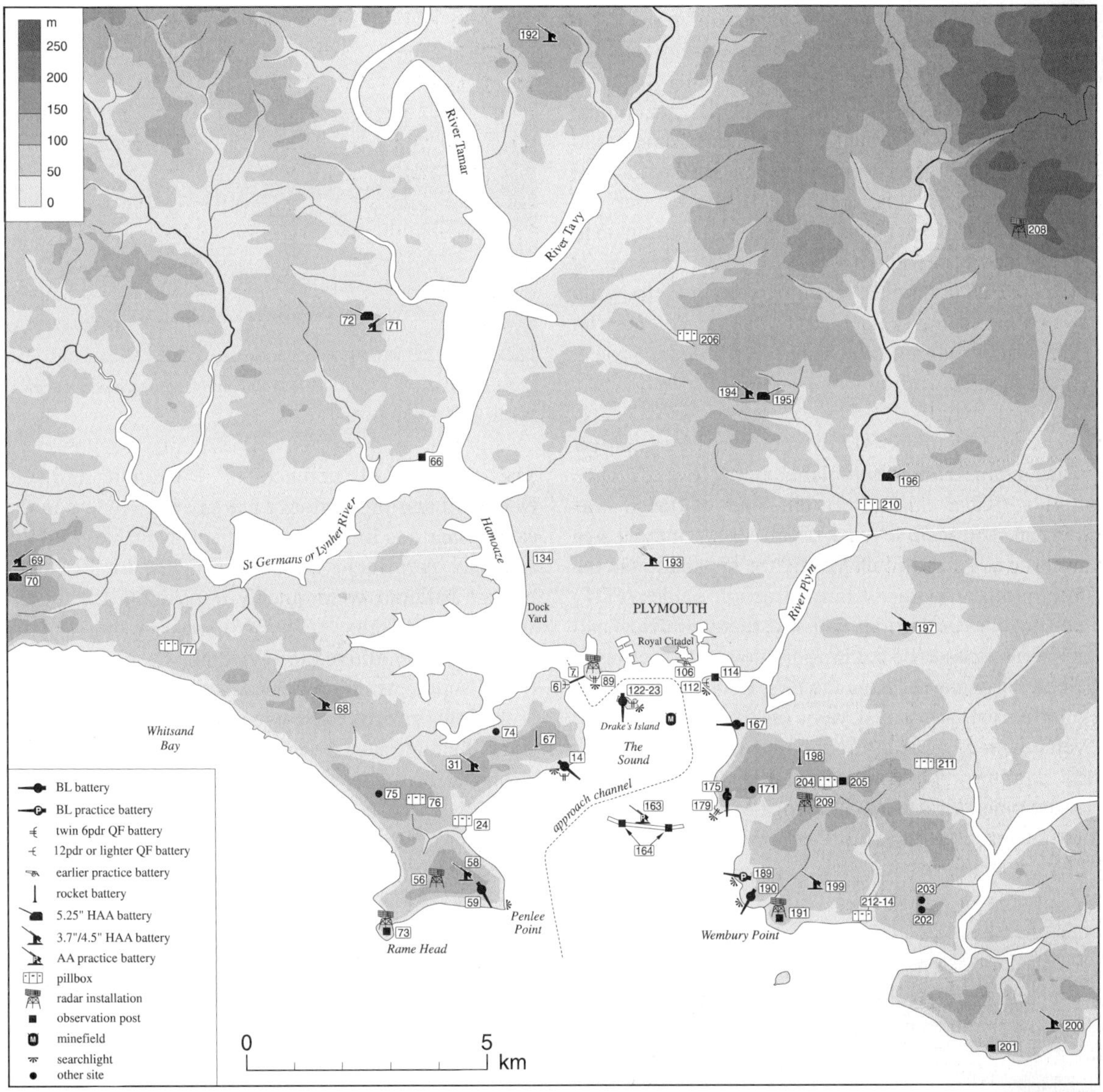

Plan J: *The defences in World War II*

Schedule *7 Boom; 106 Royal Citadel - Queen's Battery (practice); 163 Breakwater Fort - Port War Signal Station & anti-aircraft training battery* **BL coastal batteries** *14 Picklecombe, 6"; 59 Penlee Battery, 9.2"; 122 Drake's Island, 6"; 167 Lord Howard's Battery, 6"; 175 Watch House Battery, 6"; 189 Lentney Battery, 6" (practice/reserve); 190 Renney Battery, 9.2"* ***QF batteries*** *6 Earl's Battery (boom defence), calibre not known; 14 Picklecombe, twin 6pdr; 89 Western King Battery C, twin 6pdr; 113 Mount Batten Battery B, 12pdr; 123 Drake's Island, twin 6pdr; 179 Fort Bovisand Battery C, twin 6pdr* **Heavy anti-aircraft batteries** *31 Maker, 3.7"/4.5"; 58 Penlee, 3.7"/4.5"; 68 St John's Down, 3.7"/4.5"; 69 St Winoll's Battery A, 3.7"/4.5"; 70 St Winoll's Battery B, 5.25"; 71 Carkeel Battery A, 3.7"/4.5"; 72 Carkeel Battery B, 5.25"; 192 Bere Alston, 3.7"/4.5"; 193 Central Park, 4.5"; 194 Seaton Barracks Battery A, 3.7"/4.5"; 195 Seaton Barracks Battery B, 5.25"; 196 Woodford, Plympton, 5.25"?; 197 Colesdown Hill, Plymstock, 3.7"/4.5"; 199 Down Thomas, 3.7"/4.5"; 200 Netton, 3.7"/4.5"* **Rocket ('Z') batteries** *67 Mount Edgcumbe; 134 Devonport dockyard; 198 Hooe Hill* **Radar installations** *56 Rame Church Battery; 73 Rame Head; 89 Western King; 191 Wembury; 208 Wotter; 209 Staddiscombe* **Fortress observation posts** *73 Rame Head; 191 Wembury; 201 Netton* **Other observation posts** *66 Wearde Quay; 114 Mount Batten; 164 Breakwater; 205 Staddiscombe* **Pillboxes** *24 Kingsand; 76 Wiggle Farm; 77 Crafthole; 204 Staddiscombe; 206 Looseleigh Lane, Crownhill; 210 Longbridge, Marsh Mills; 211 Higher Spriddlestone Farm; 212 Wembury beach (east); 213 Wembury beach (west); 214 Wembury* **Miscellaneous** *74 Maker torpedo boat station; 75 Trenninow; 171 Brownhill; 202 Wembury bombing decoy site; 203 Wembury - building*

World War I *(Plan I)*

Few additions were made to the coast defences during World War I apart from the rearmament of Hawkins Battery and Rame Church Battery with 9.2-in BL H/A guns, completed by the end of 1914. Hawkins was largely rebuilt using the latest techniques in concrete for the walls and caponiers. Local defences round all the batteries were strengthened. The 1860s land forts and batteries were by now only used from time to time as barracks and stores, apart from Crownhill which was a depot for coast artillery and Tregantle with its rifle ranges. After the end of the war the last of the obsolete guns in the land forts were withdrawn. Peacetime retrenchment resulted in the dismantling of some of the guns in the coast batteries no longer considered essential, though they were duly remounted in most cases in 1940. The battery at Renney was equipped with 30° mountings which increased the range to over 30,000 yards.

World War II *(Plan J)*

By the summer of 1940 the defences of Plymouth were facing threats out of all proportion to the preceding ones. To the need for coast defences was added defence against low-level and high-level air attack and, when France had fallen, against airborne assault and full-scale invasion. Local defences of vulnerable points, and road blocks, were established. Pillboxes were built to cover the beaches at Wembury, Bovisand, Kingsand and Cawsand. The 1860s forts were used for a variety of purposes, not only as barracks. Crownhill was a strongpoint in the local defence plan and foxholes can be found on the ramparts of most forts and batteries in the North Eastern defences. Agaton was the principal supply depot for Devon and Cornwall, Staddon was the barracks for a coast artillery training regiment and the rifle ranges at Tregantle were an important training area.

The framework of the coast defences was in place but required filling out. The 6-in BL guns were remounted at Lentney and Lord Howard's and other batteries made up to strength in guns. Local defence of the batteries became important. Renney and Penlee (and Hawkins) had already been given pillboxes and unclimbable fences before World War I, but the vulnerability of these isolated batteries to a commando raid was obvious. Renney eventually had three spigot mortars for local defence and a party of infantry from the main garrison was detailed to man the defences on 'stand to'. Two 40mm LAA guns were added to protect the guns against strafing.

There were only minor improvements in the equipment of the counter bombardment and close defence batteries (9.2-in and 6-in) but one of these was important. The accuracy and effectiveness of the 9.2-in batteries was greatly improved by the installation in the battery plotting rooms of Fire Direction Tables (FDT) which enabled the various ballistic, meteorological and other corrections to be fed in continuously to the ranges and bearings received from the PFs. Range-finding was revolutionised as the war went on by the progressive development of coast artillery radars of two types - for early warning and for fire control. Eventually there was a fire commander's radar (CA No. 2 Mk I) at Wembury Point, for example, and a fire control radar (CA No. 1 Mk IV) at Renney Battery for the battery commander's use.

Plate 17: Typical wartime 6-pdr Twin gun position (Imperial War Museum, HU 39429)

In 1942-3 the 6-pdr twin QF gun *(Plate 17)* was introduced as the anti-motor torpedo boat (AMTB) equipment in place of the 12-pdr QFs. These were removed apart from two guns from Drake's Island which were emplaced at Mount Batten. The 6-pdr twin had a rate of fire of 72rpm or more and an improved system of sighting and control of fire. The opportunity was taken to simplify the layout and control of the AMTB guns and pairs of guns were emplaced at Bovisand, Drake's Island, Western King and Picklecombe with additional searchlights to improve the illuminated areas in front of them.

Plate 18: 40-mm LAA gun in position on the coast (Imperial War Museum, H 39438)

The anti-aircraft defence of Plymouth and the Dockyard was high priority but its effectiveness in the early years was limited by the guns available. Mobile, and later permanent (Staddon Heights, for example) barrage balloons were quickly in position. Light anti-aircraft (LAA) guns *(Plate 18)* were in short supply and the battery allotted to Plymouth was not complete. It was supplemented by obsolescent 3-in 20-cwt guns of doubtful effectiveness which were allotted singly to points liable to attack such as Bovisand Battery. Low-level defence was supplemented by 'Z' or rocket batteries, each of 64 individual 2-in (and later 3-in) rocket projectors known as 2UPs (2-in unstabilised projectiles, *Plate 19*). These were sited at Hooe Hill, the Dockyard and Mount Edgcumbe.

Plate 19: Multiple rocket projectors firing (Imperial War Museum, H 32335)

Plate 20: Typical 3.7-in HAA troop command post (Imperial War Museum, H 1265)

Plate 21: 3.7-in HAA troop gun position at Down Thomas (Photograph: F. M. Griffith, Devon County Council. Frame DAP/YW7. Copyright: Devon County Council)

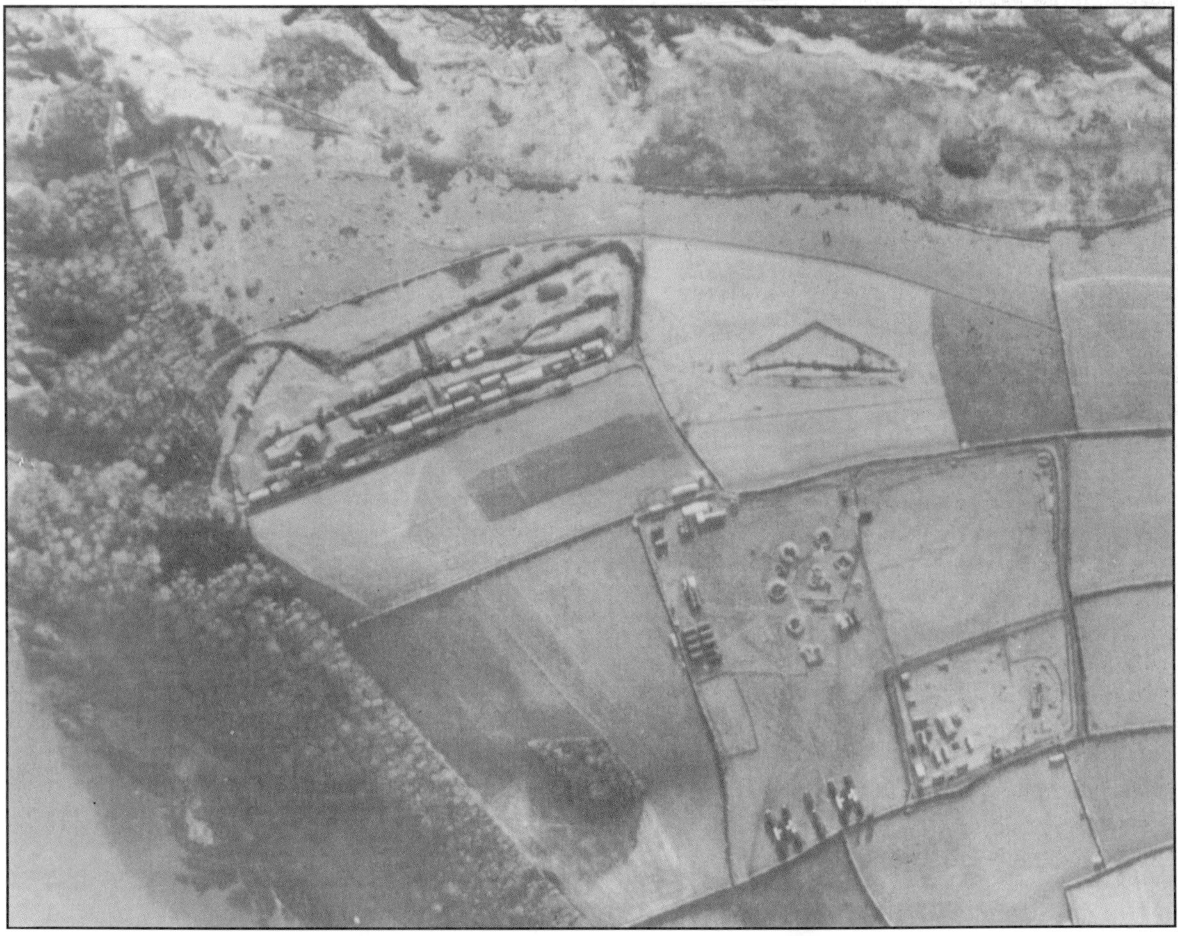

Plate 22: Aerial photograph of Penlee Battery, Middle Barton PF Station and Penlee HAA Battery in 1946 (Crown Copyright/MoD)

Defence against high-level bombing was provided by heavy anti-aircraft (HAA) guns which in the early years were 3.7-in *(Plate 20)*. At the time of the 1941 blitz a HAA regiment was deployed around Plymouth in a ring from Down Thomas, through Crownhill to Maker Heights. The first and last of these positions can still be seen *(Plates 21 & 40)*. There were then 6 troop positions, each of four guns, and a searchlight battery. The defences were supplemented by the use of Bombing Decoys (at Wembury for example) to persuade the bombers to attack open country. As more guns became available several positions were increased to 6 guns (e.g. Maker and Down Thomas, *Plate 21*) and additional positions were built further out to give depth to the defences - at Netton and Penlee *(Plate 22)* for example - as well as one in Central Park (to bolster civilian morale?). More searchlights became available and they were deployed as far out as the edge of Dartmoor. With the introduction of the 4.5-in HAA gun with its greater range, positions as far out as St Winnols were practicable, covering the approach to the dockyard by planes using the Lynher estuary as a guide. Towards the end of the war the latest gun, the 5.25-in HAA *(Plate 23)*, was emplaced at Crownhill, St Winnols and probably at Carkeel, near Saltash, and Woodford near Plympton.

Plate 23: Typical 5.25-in Twin HAA troop command post & gun position (Imperial War Museum, H 32361)

After the end of the war the defences were 'stood down', but although the local defences were abandoned the HAA positions were maintained and for several years were improved (St Winnols, for example). Crownhill Fort contained a Gun Operations Room associated with the HAA brigade headquarters at Seaton Barracks nearby. The layout of the coast defences was confirmed as similar to that before the war, and the guns were once more put on a care and maintenance basis.

As a result of the appreciation in the 1950s that an attack on a target of the size and importance of the dockyard would be by atomic bombs delivered by rockets, AA Command was eventually disbanded and in 1956 coast artillery was declared obsolete. Any guns on fixed mountings, which included all coast artillery, were cut up for salvage, the optical and fire control instruments were sent for scrap and the radars removed. Subsequently many of the HAA gun positions were built over, several of the 1860s forts were sold, and later damaged, and some of the coast batteries were filled in.

However, some of the modern coast and HAA batteries remain more or less intact. With the nineteenth-century forts and the remains of the redoubts and earlier coast batteries they form links in the historical chain which is the story of Plymouth's defences, stretching back for more than 500 years to the Castle Quadrate and the blockhouses below the Hoe.

2. A CONSERVATION STRATEGY FOR PLYMOUTH AREA HISTORIC FORTIFICATIONS

It is now recognised that Plymouth Sound is one of the best locations in Britain to see the evolution of coastal defences. However this recognition has come relatively recently. In the introduction to his pioneering work 'Plymouth's Defences' (1990) Freddy Woodward contrasted the lack of effort in the Plymouth area with Portsmouth, Chatham and Dover. He went on to point out the need for a co- ordinated conservation policy embracing all the local authorities, English Heritage and other interested bodies.

The publication of the recent survey of the defences around Plymouth Sound provides an the ideal time to initiate such a policy. The survey was commissioned by English Heritage, in association with Cornwall and Devon County Councils along with a number of groups like Fortress Study Group South West. The purpose of the survey was to provide baseline data for all the historic defence sites in the area for planning and management purposes.

There were a number of issues about present day management that this survey was not able to tackle in the time available and so a very limited project, appraising the management and current use of defence sites, was undertaken by Sheila Weston. This helped clarify a number of difficult ownership issues. It also provided the opportunity to discuss with a sample of the main owners and occupiers their own thoughts on the use and management of some of the more extensive sites.

The survey and the management appraisal have shown that a large proportion of the historic fortifications do survive to some degree but many of the more important ones are in poor condition or have inappropriate uses and have been damaged. In addition military considerations meant they were originally built on some of the most prominent locations but in recent decades they have become clothed in a mantle of vegetation so they are now frequently overlooked and often local pcople are not aware of them.

A conservation strategy is required to bring to public attention the overall significance of what remains of an exceptional group of sites, and to guide policy and practice for their preservation wherever that is possible. The key role must lie with the six local planning authorities concerned, but the understanding and commitment of owners will be an important ingredient of success. It is important to recognise that this is not just a question of funding. There is a range of possibilities for enhancing and interpreting this important collection of sites over the short and long term, the success of which will depend on a consistent strategy and planning. The critical issue in many cases may be the use which can be found and sustained for a site compatible with its character. Approached in the right way, and recognising the need for flexibility, the defence heritage offers an opportunity as well as a challenge to the City and the surrounding area.

The outline of this strategy has now been adopted or endorsed by the relevant Committees for the Councils of Plymouth, Caradon, South Hams, Cornwall and Devon and Plymouth Development Corporation. It is pleasing to report that those same Councils (with the exception of South Hams) and Plymouth Development Corporation have co-operated in the financing and the provision of material for the exhibition. What follows is an abridged version of the strategy.

THE STRATEGY

The main objectives of the strategy are:

a) actively to conserve the more important and better preserved examples of these fortifications;

b) to protect at an appropriate level all other fortifications still in reasonable condition through the planning process;

c) to increase public awareness of the historic fortifications and, where appropriate, encourage public access on a regular or occasional basis.

While that is fairly easy to state, it will be impossible to achieve real progress if the associated problems and recent land use history are not taken fully into account. Many of the problems are long-standing and result partly from limited or inappropriate uses and abandonment. Another difficult issue is the conservation of concrete defences of the last 100 years; they have no architectural pretension and are frequently removed as eyesores or dismissed as semi-derelict. Bearing in mind those difficulties it is essential that any conservation strategy embraces the following principles:

- it must be explicitly long term (15-20 years) if it is to counter effectively existing inappropriate land usages and management regimes;
- it is a co-operative exercise on the part not only of the six local authorities but also all other agencies and groups involved as well as those owners that are interested;
- more consideration should be given to the historical and technological significance of fortifications.

Many of the larger fortifications are now situated throughout the suburbs of Plymouth and rural parts of Caradon and South Hams. Therefore it is important to recognise the needs of people in those areas in developing the strategy and to specifically explore the potential of some of the forts for community uses. From these principles follow eight action points.

1. Exhibition about Plymouth's Historic Defences

There is at the moment relatively little public regard for the fortifications in the area. An exhibition has therefore been set up, telling the story of the development of the fortifications and their future. It is in a form that allows it to be transported to several venues in Plymouth as well as the surrounding rural area. There has been a formal launching ceremony to mark its opening. The exhibition will act as a focus for other public events like special public open days and guided tours for those forts not normally open to the public. A similar exercise could be laid on for local schools.

2. Publication of the Plymouth Defences Survey and National Guidance Notes on their Repair and Maintenance

The Plymouth Defences Survey is the first historical survey of its kind to have been undertaken. The guidance notes, which provide basic advice on the approach to repairs and maintenance, are specifically for later fortifications (1880-1945) and will also have application for defence sites throughout England.

3. Interpretation and Access

Only a small number of sites will ever be suitable for visits on a regular basis in the manner done so successfully by the Landmark Trust at Crownhill Fort. However, there is great scope for laying out trails along the military roads linking the forts and this type of work has been started in the area by Groundwork Plymouth. There is a good case for a working party to develop a co-ordinated approach to interpretation and access where that is possible; this could include the Groundwork Trust, the Landmark Trust (Crownhill Fort), English Heritage Historic Properties Group (Citadel and Mount Batten Tower), local authorities, local members of the Fortress Study Group and interested owners.

4. Evaluation and Selection of Fortifications for Statutory Protection

English Heritage intends that any further proposals for statutory protection of known defence sites should be considered within a comprehensive framework embracing both scheduling and listing as appropriate. Scheduling is principally for buried remains and other structures where minimal use or only limited change would be envisaged (e.g underground structures, ramparts and ditches) and listing for the those structures (casemates and other buildings) where there is potential for adaptive reuse, particularly for buildings now inhabited as scheduling is specifically excluded for them. A joint policy would allow for complementary designations rather than the present confusing overlap.

The joint programme for scheduling and listing will be developed on a staged basis with the first part taking place in 1996. Initially only fortifications dating from 1660 will be considered as most surviving earlier forts already have some form of statutory protection. It will be necessary for this policy to be rigorous and based on a complete database for the whole of England to evaluate what is nationally important prior to establishing exactly which of the designations is appropriate. It is intended that this work should tie in closely with existing initiatives like the identification of 20th century defences and thematic studies carried out for barracks and airfields.

For 19th and 20th century fortifications it will be necessary to be much more selective as to what is regarded as of sufficient importance for listing or scheduling as so much does survive. This means that fairly large numbers of those fortifications will not receive any form of national designation but may still be important in regional or local terms. The latter is almost certain to be the case for many of the Commission fortifications of the 1860's around Plymouth. For that reason other more locally based designations like conservation areas should be seriously considered. Indeed there are many features, such as the *glacis* (cleared ground around a fort) and military roadways linking forts, which could not otherwise be protected. Conservation area status is also a useful mechanism for enhancement schemes such as the restoration of partially damaged or missing features.

5. Development Plan Policies and Supplementary Guidance

As noted above there will inevitably be quite a large number of fortifications and defences which cannot be given any statutory protection, especially for works of the last 150 years. They may well nonetheless merit positive protection through the planning system. In addition the setting of these features are best protected through planning controls. Recent planning legislation and DoE guidance notes have stressed the primacy of approved development plan policies prepared by local planning authorities when considering proposals for development. The policy (EV12) recently adopted in the Plymouth Local Plan provides a starting point for others to follow and then to develop in subsequent revisions. In particular it should be possible to go further and encourage positive management and enhancement schemes for individual sites and areas.

The extensive survey of the Plymouth defences can help guide policies in local authority planning documents and indeed their consideration of what might be made conservation areas. Other guidance specifically prepared for the management of these fortifications (such as the items described below) should be referred to in the text accompanying development plan policies as it will then be given greater weight in the planning system generally. Particular issues that supplementary planning guidance should address are the actual setting of these fortifications and access as statutory protection cannot itself deal with these wider issues. These matters should also be integrated with other land use policies and opportunities such as the 'Green Corridors' proposed in the Plymouth Local Plan.

6. Conservation Management Proposals

Many of these fortifications are large and complex sites. The uses to which they are put need careful planning to ensure, on the one hand, that they make use of all significant structures so that some parts are not under-used and become derelict, and on the other hand, that certain uses do not become so intensive that they lead to unacceptable changes and even damage. This is a difficult balance as too little use can lead to almost as many problems as too intensive and inappropriate uses. Another important issue for the small number of forts with a large amount of original fittings is how those items are curated during the transition period when their use changes or they are temporarily without a use.

General guidelines could be given for different types of forts and batteries as to what uses might be encouraged and the likely overall capacity to be exploited for any new development. There are also occasions when it might be possible to draw up more detailed guidance for individual fortifications such as for:

scheduled ancient monuments -
when a site is scheduled for the first time or its designation is confirmed the documentation for each site includes a management statement. A similar statement may be useful when listing these structures and should certainly be done if a complementary scheduling is done for the same site.

conservation area proposal -
it is now generally accepted that it is no longer sufficient for local authorities just to designate conservation areas. The actual designation must also include statements on the need for the designation and a character appraisal. The latter could be expanded to include suggestions about how the area could be used and managed as well as the more usual proposals for enhancement.

development briefs -
these are occasionally produced by local authorities to provide guidance for the redevelopment of difficult or sensitive areas for owners and prospective developers and are particularly desirable in the case of large and complex sites where change of use is unavoidable. They will describe the constraints of the site and outline what might be acceptable in terms of new development. Again such a document could include guidance on how the historic features can be protected and enhanced.

It may also be worth commissioning similar management proposals for important or difficult sites where none of the above channels is available. The production of such documents also provides a useful opportunity to discuss management issues with owners and occupiers, to raise awareness of the fortifications and to help develop conservation proposals as a precursor to what is described in section 8 below.

7. Research and Archaeological Recording

The recent survey of Plymouth defences has provided an excellent record of all the currently known examples of defence sites in the area. However, the survey is not very detailed and there will be occasions when further recording is necessary where individual defences are subject to proposals for conservation or development. In addition the survey has highlighted several potential areas of research which hopefully can be pursued in the future.

8. Sources of Funding and Programme of Work

In the coming year the local authorities, English Heritage and other interested parties will explore sources of funding for conservation and management of these fortifications. This can then develop into a programme of work possibly on a partnership basis. It might also be worth considering strategies for particular groupings of fortifications such as the Commission forts or defences along the waterfront.

3. GAZETTEER OF SITES

3.1 Introduction

The gazetteer includes 216 sites; each is individually numbered and depicted on one of three overall maps (1 to 3), and each appears (with the same number) on at least one of the period plans illustrated in Chapter 1. Each site has a text entry, and many are illustrated by character plans and some by historic maps, where these are available; a selection of photographs is also included. The abbreviations used in the plans and text are set out in Appendix 1, and the technical terms are explained in the Glossary (Appendix 2). As sites of different periods occur on the same character plan, the overall arrangement of the gazetteer is geographical, with other Civil War and WWII sites appearing in separate sections at the end. General sources are listed in full in Appendix 3, and sources specific to the site are listed at the end of the relevant entry.

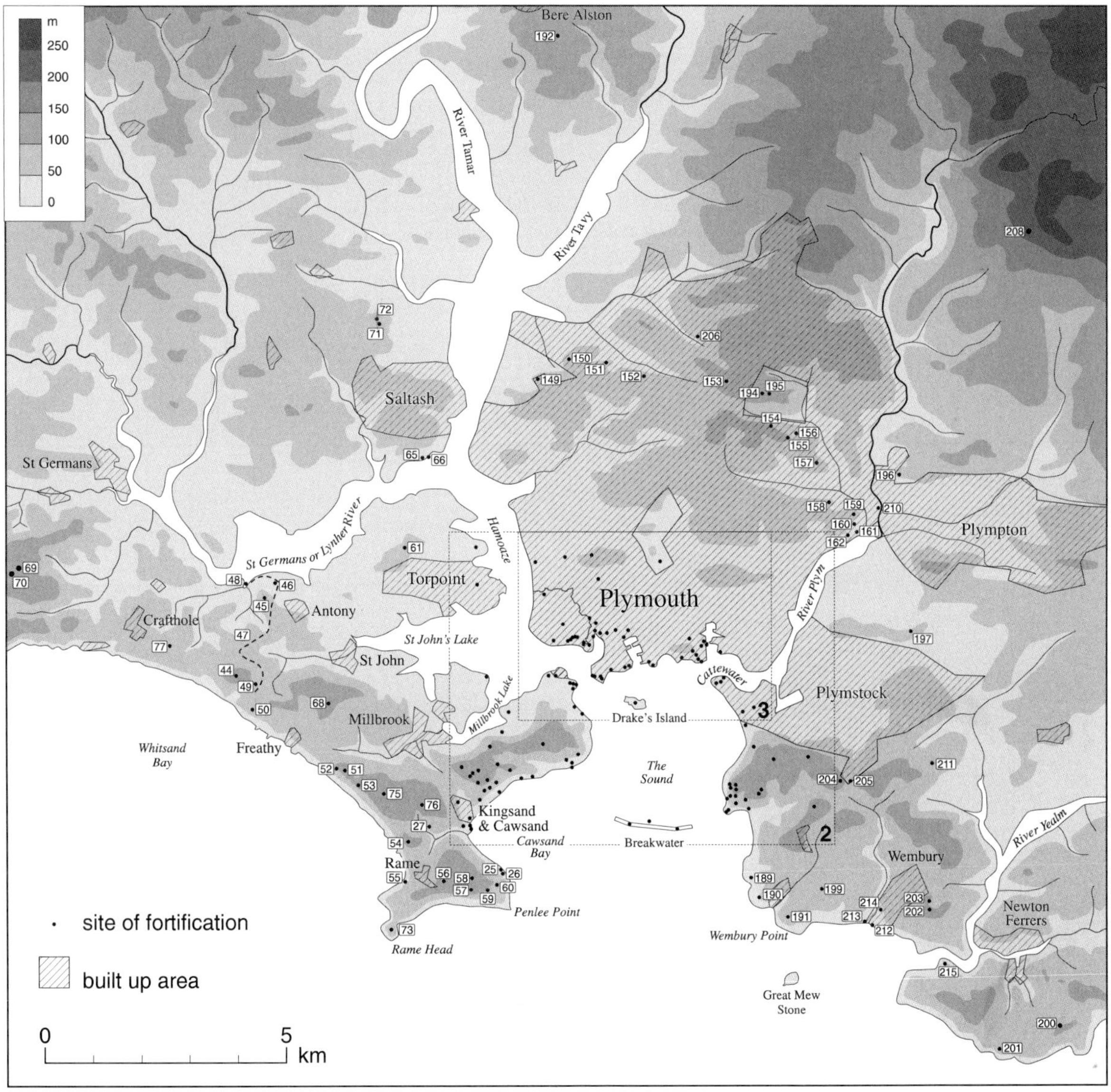

Gazetteer Map 1

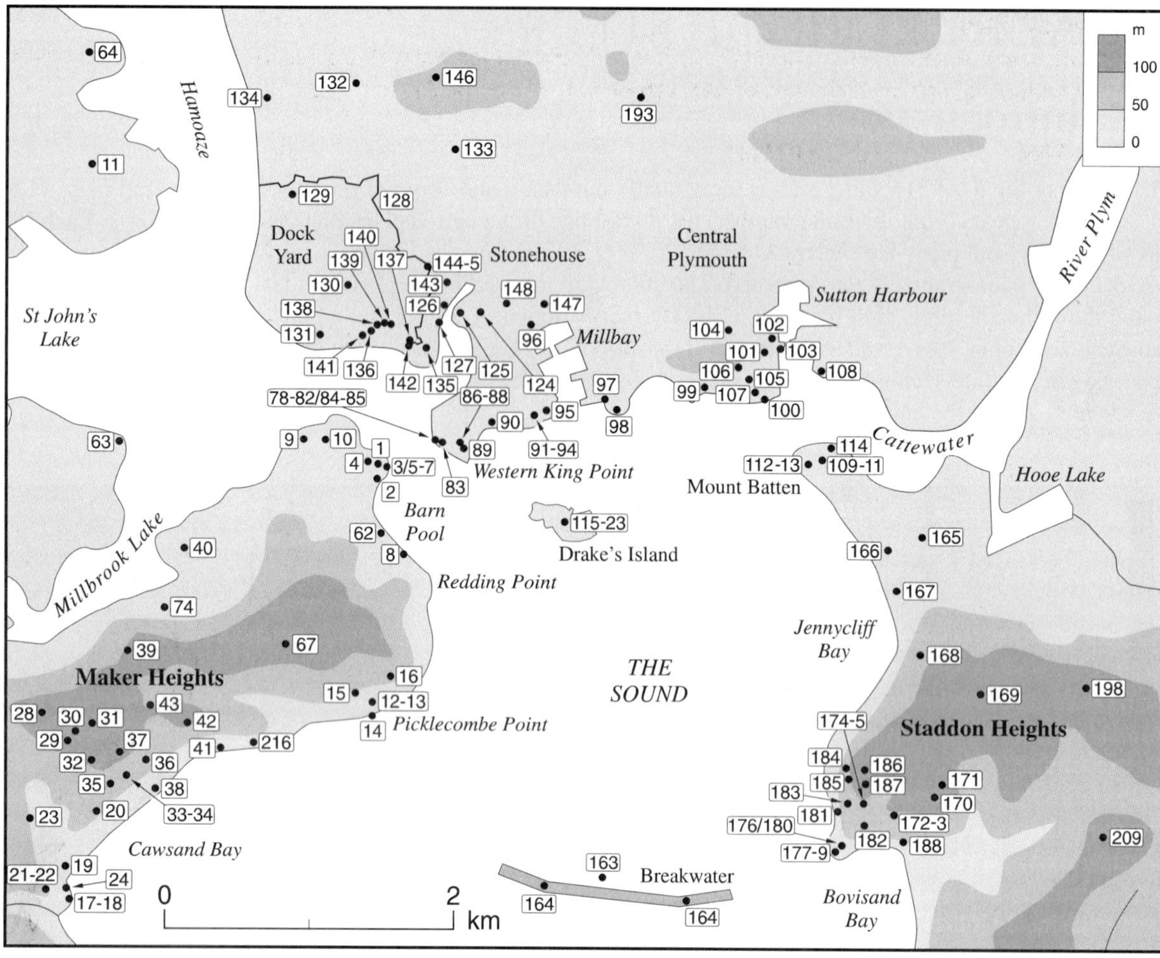

Gazetteer Map 2

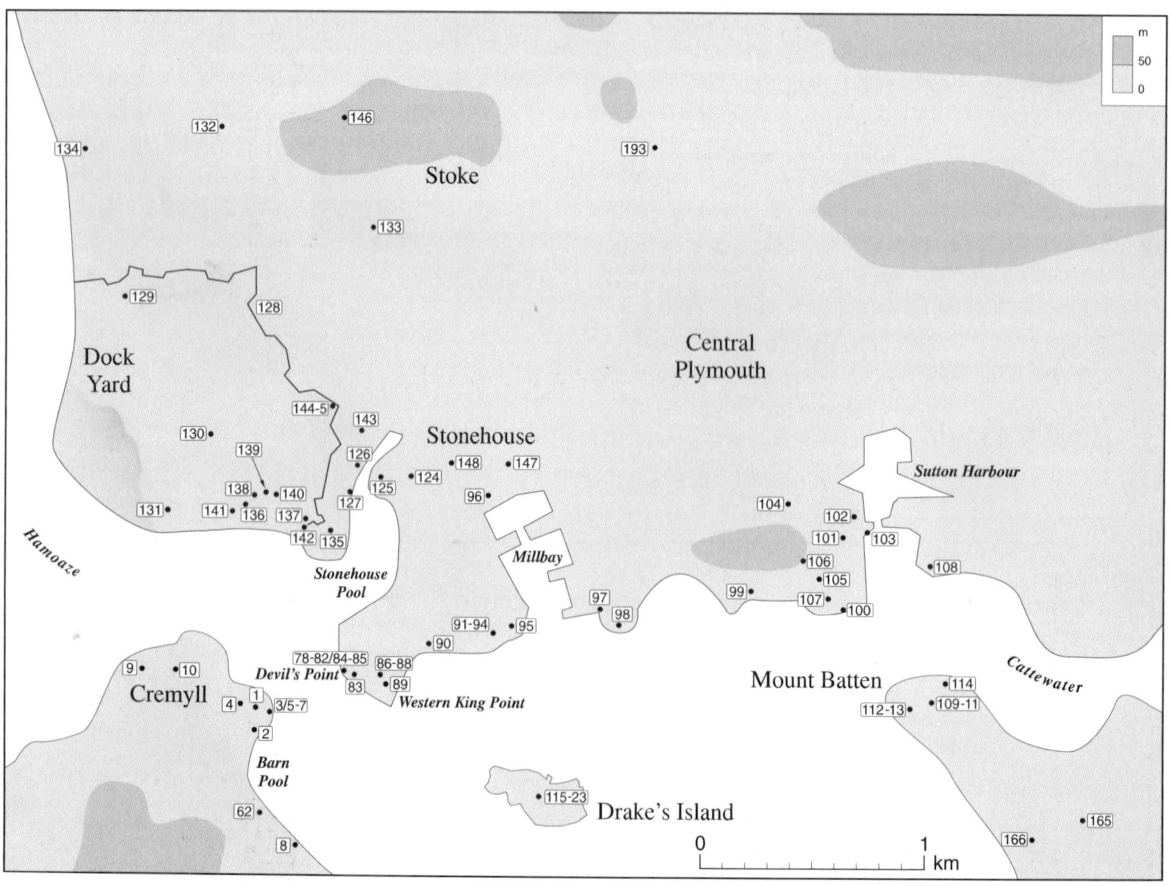

Gazetteer Map 3

Schedule of sites

Each site depicted on the gazetteer maps (1 -3) is listed below, together with the section no. of the gazetteer in which it appears. An alphabetical index of sites can be found after the Appendices.

No.	Map	Defensive Work	Section
1	3	Mount Edgcumbe Blockhouse	3.2.1
2	3	Bowling Green Battery	3.2.1
3	3	Mount Edgcumbe Battery	3.2.1
4	3	Mount Edgcumbe Powder House	3.2.1
5	3	Garden Battery	3.2.1
6	3	Earl's Battery	3.2.1
7	3	World War II Boom	3.2.1
8	3	Redding Point Battery	3.2.1
9	3	Obelisk/Cremyll Redoubt	3.2.1
10	3	Musketry Lines/Retreat Battery	3.2.1
11	2	Torpoint Redoubt (proposed)	3.2.1
12	2	Picklecombe Bulwark	3.2.1
13	2	Picklecombe Battery	3.2.1
14	2	Picklecombe Fort	3.2.1
15	2	Picklecombe Submarine Mine Station	3.2.1
16	2	Redding Point PF Station	3.2.1
17	2	Cawsand Battery A	3.2.3
18	2	Pemberknowse Fort	3.2.3
19	2	Amherst Battery	3.2.3
20	2	Minadew Brake Battery	3.2.3
21	2	Cawsand Battery B	3.2.3
22	2	Cawsand Fort	3.2.3
23	2	Bakers Battery	3.2.3
24	2	Kingsand WWII Pillbox	3.2.3
25	1	Pier Cellars Brennan Torpedo Station	3.2.3
26	1	Pier Cellars QF Battery	3.2.3
27	1	Wringford Farm Picket Post & Roadblock	3.2.3
28	2	Maker Redoubt No. 1	3.2.2
29	2	Maker Redoubt No. 2	3.2.2
30	2	Maker Barracks	3.2.2
31	2	Maker HAA Battery	3.2.2
32	2	Maker Redoubt No. 3	3.2.2
33	2	Maker Redoubt No. 4	3.2.2
34	2	Grenville Battery	3.2.2
35	2	Maker Battery	3.2.2
36	2	Maker PF Station	3.2.2
37	2	Maker Hospital & Reservoir	3.2.2
38	2	Sandway Fort	3.2.2
39	2	Maker Redoubt No. 5	3.2.2
40	2	Empacombe Redoubt (Maker Redoubt No. 6)	3.2.2
41	2	Sandway Battery	3.2.2
42	2	Raleigh Battery	3.2.2
43	2	Hawkins Battery	3.2.2
44	1	Tregantle Fort	3.2.4
45	1	Scraesdon Fort	3.2.4
46	1	Scraesdon Foxholes	3.2.4
47	1	Wacker - Tregantle Down military railway	3.2.4
48	1	Wacker Quay	3.2.4
49	1	Tregantle Down Battery	3.2.4
50	1	Crowstone Field PF Station	3.2.5
51	1	Whitsand Bay Battery	3.2.5
52	1	Whitsand Bay Practice Battery	3.2.5
53	1	Trenninow PF Station	3.2.5
54	1	Knatterbury PF Station	3.2.5
55	1	Polhawn Battery	3.2.5
56	1	Rame Church Battery	3.2.6
57	1	Middle Barton PF Station	3.2.6

No.	Map	Defensive Work	Section
58	1	Penlee HAA Battery	3.2.6
59	1	Penlee Battery	3.2.6
60	1	Folly Tower PF Station	3.2.6
61	1	Beggars Fort	3.2.7
62	3	Barn Pool Civil War Battery	3.2.7
63	2	Inswork Point Battery	3.2.7
64	2	Thanckes Civil War Redoubt	3.2.7
65	1	Wearde Quay Battery	3.2.7
66	1	Wearde Quay WWII Observation Post	3.2.7
67	2	Mount Edgcumbe Rocket Battery	3.2.8
68	1	St Johns Down HAA Battery	3.2.8
69	1	St Winolls HAA Battery A	3.2.8
70	1	St Winolls HAA Battery B	3.2.8
71	1	Carkeel HAA Battery A	3.2.8
72	1	Carkeel HAA Battery B	3.2.8
73	1	Rame Head Radar Installation	3.2.8
74	2	Maker Torpedo Boat Station	3.2.8
75	1	Trenninow WWII Depot	3.2.8
76	1	Wiggle Farm Pillbox	3.2.8
77	1	Crafthole Pillbox	3.2.8
78	3	Devil's Point Blockhouse	3.3.1
79	3	Devil's Point Civil War Redoubt	3.3.1
80	3	Devil's Point Battery A	3.3.1
81	3	Passage Point Battery	3.3.1
82	3	Three Gun Battery	3.3.1
83	3	Royal Naval Reserve Battery	3.3.1
84	3	Devil's Point Battery B	3.3.1
85	3	Devil's Point Boom Mooring Rings	3.3.1
86	3	Western King Redoubt	3.3.1
87	3	Western King Battery A	3.3.1
88	3	Western King Battery B	3.3.1
89	3	Western King Battery C	3.3.1
90	3	Firestone Bay Artillery Tower	3.3.1
91	3	Eastern King Battery A	3.3.1
92	3	Eastern King (Prince of Wales) Redoubt	3.3.1
93	3	Eastern King Battery B	3.3.1
94	3	Eastern King Battery C	3.3.1
95	3	Millbay (West) Blockhouse	3.3.1
96	3	Millbay (North) Blockhouse	3.3.1
97	3	Millbay (East) Blockhouse	3.3.1
98	3	West Hoe Battery	3.3.1
99	3	Bulwarks on Hoe	3.3.1
100	3	'Fisher's Nose Blockhouse'	3.3.1
101	3	Plymouth Castle	3.3.1
102	3	Barbican Gate	3.3.1
103	3	Barbican blockhouse & chain	3.3.1
104	3	Hoe Gate	3.3.1
105	3	Plymouth (Drake's) Fort	3.3.1
106	3	Royal Citadel	3.3.1
107	3	Lower Fort	3.3.1
108	3	Queen Anne's Battery	3.3.1
109	3	Mount Batten Bulwark	3.3.1
110	3	Mount Batten Civil War fortifications	3.3.1
111	3	Mount Batten Tower	3.3.1
112	3	Mount Batten Battery A	3.3.1
112a	3	Mount Batten Redoubt (proposed)	3.3.1
113	3	Mount Batten Battery B	3.3.1
114	3	Mount Batten WWII Observation Post	3.3.1
115	3	Drake's Island Fort & 16th century defences	3.3.1
116	3	Drake's Island - early 18th century defences	3.3.1

No.	Map	Defensive Work	Section
117	3	Drake's Island - late 18th century defences	3.3.1
118	3	Drake's Island - casemated battery	3.3.1
119	3	Drake's Island - main & lower batteries	3.3.1
120	3	Drake's Island - Western QF Battery	3.3.1
121	3	Drake's Island - Eastern QF Battery	3.3.1
122	3	Drake's Island - 6-inch BL Battery	3.3.1
123	3	Drake's Island - WWII QF Battery	3.3.1
124	3	Stonehouse Town Wall	3.3.2
125	3	Stonehouse blockhouse	3.3.2
126	3	Stonehouse Pool blockhouse (North)	3.3.2
127	3	Stonehouse Pool blockhouse (South)	3.3.2
128	3	Dock (Devonport) Lines	3.3.2
129	3	Cavalier Battery	3.3.2
130	3	Windmill Hill Redoubt (proposed)	3.3.2
131	3	Bunker's Hill Battery	3.3.2
132	3	Keyham Redoubt (proposed)	3.3.2
133	3	Stoke Redoubt (proposed)	3.3.2
134	3	Devonport Rocket Battery	3.3.2
135	3	Old Gun Wharf Battery	3.3.2
136	3	Mount Wise Redoubt	3.3.2
137	3	Lower Mount Wise Battery	3.3.2
138	3	Mount Wise Battery No. 2	3.3.2
139	3	Mount Wise Battery No. 3	3.3.2
140	3	Mount Wise Battery No. 4	3.3.2
141	3	Mount Wise Battery No. 5	3.3.2
142	3	Richmond Walk fortified gates	3.3.2
143	3	Bluff Battery	3.3.2
144	3	George's Bastion battery	3.3.2
145	3	George's Bastion musketry keep	3.3.2
146	3	Mount Pleasant Redoubt	3.3.2
147	3	Stonehouse Redoubt A	3.3.2
148	3	Stonehouse Redoubt B (proposed)	3.3.2
149	1	Ernesettle Battery	3.3.3
150	1	Agaton Fort	3.3.3
151	1	Knowle Battery	3.3.3
152	1	Woodland Fort	3.3.3
153	1	Crownhill Fort	3.3.3
154	1	Bowden Battery	3.3.3
155	1	Eggbuckland Keep	3.3.3
156	1	Forder Battery	3.3.3
157	1	Austin Fort	3.3.3
158	1	Deer Park Emplacement	3.3.3
159	1	Efford Fort	3.3.3
160	1	Efford Emplacement	3.3.3
161	1	Laira Battery	3.3.3
162	1	Laira Emplacement	3.3.3
163	2	Breakwater Fort	3.3.4
164	2	Breakwater WWII Observation Posts	3.3.4
165	2	Stamford Fort	3.3.4
166	2	Stamford Hill Civil War fortifications	3.3.4
167	2	Lord Howard's Battery	3.3.4
168	2	Jennycliff PF cell	3.3.4
169	2	Staddon Fort	3.3.4
170	2	Brownhill Battery	3.3.4
171	2	Brownhill WWII Radar Installation	3.3.4
172	2	Twelve Acre Brake Battery	3.3.4
173	2	Frobisher Battery	3.3.4
174	2	Watch House Brake Battery	3.3.4
175	2	Watch House Battery	3.3.4
176	2	Staddon Point Battery A	3.3.4

No.	Map	Defensive Work	Section
177	2	Fort Bovisand Battery A	3.3.4
178	2	Fort Bovisand Battery B	3.3.4
179	2	Fort Bovisand Battery C	3.3.4
180	2	Staddon Point Battery B	3.3.4
181	2	Bovisand Submarine Mine Station	3.3.4
182	2	Watch House Brake PF Station	3.3.4
183	2	Staddon Heights PF cells	3.3.4
184	2	Staddon Battery	3.3.4
185	2	Staddon Heights Battery	3.3.4
186	2	Target Butts	3.3.4
187	2	WWII Barrage Balloon	3.3.4
188	2	Bovisand Practice Battery	3.3.4
189	1	Lentney Battery	3.3.4
190	1	Renney Battery	3.3.4
191	1	Wembury PF Station	3.3.4
192	1	Bere Alston HAA Battery	3.3.5
193	3	Central Park HAA Battery	3.3.5
194	1	Seaton Barracks HAA Battery A	3.3.5
195	1	Seaton Barracks HAA Battery B	3.3.5
196	1	Woodford HAA Battery	3.3.5
197	1	Colesdown Hill HAA Battery	3.3.5
198	2	Hooe Hill Rocket Battery	3.3.5
199	1	Down Thomas HAA Battery	3.3.5
200	1	Netton HAA Battery	3.3.5
201	1	Netton Observation Post	3.3.5
202	1	Wembury Bombing Decoy	3.3.5
203	1	Wembury WWII building	3.3.5
204	1	Staddiscombe Pillbox A	3.3.5
205	1	Staddiscombe Pillbox B	3.3.5
206	1	Looseleigh Lane Pillbox	3.3.5
207		Yennadon Down WWII site	3.3.5
208	1	Wotter Radar Installation	3.3.5
209	2	Staddiscombe Radar Installation	3.3.5
210	1	Long Bridge Pillbox	3.3.5
211	1	Higher Spriddlestone Pillbox	3.3.5
212	1	Wembury Beach Pillbox (East)	3.3.5
213	1	Wembury Beach Pillbox (West)	3.3.5
214	1	Wembury Pillbox	3.3.5
215	1	Worsewell Battery	3.3.4
216	2	Hooe Lake Point PF cell	3.2.1

3.2. Cornwall Gazetteer

3.2.1. The Inner Defences

MOUNT EDGCUMBE BLOCKHOUSE

PAR = MAKER, NGR = SX 45625318, PRN = 6228, MAP 3 No. 1

This is located immediately to the rear of the later Garden Battery. It does not appear on the c. 1540 panorama of Plymouth, unlike the other blockhouses at Devil's Point and Firestone Bay for example. It is thought to have been built shortly after, either in 1540 or perhaps in 1545 by the Edgcumbe family, although Shepherd dates it to 1586. It is shown on Grenvyle's map of 1586-88 and is referred to in Carew's survey of 1602. It was held by the Royalists during the Civil War and was captured in a Parliamentarian raid of 1644 when they carried off several guns. It was supplemented and perhaps replaced by a battery (Mount Edgcumbe or Bowling Green Battery) built by Killigrew in 1690. It is not known, however, for how long the blockhouse itself remained armed. On an 1820 print a pavilion is shown built against its eastern wall with Mount Edgcumbe Battery in the background.

Plate 24 Mount Edgcumbe Blockhouse (Exeter Archaeology)

The blockhouse is square and built of local rubble stone with granite details around the doorway, gun embrasures and loop-holes. It contains two loop-holes at first-floor level, one in the W wall and one just below the crenellations in the N wall. There are two gun embrasures in the S and E walls; there is no apparent indication however of a third embrasure noted in the List description as being in the N wall. Instead there is an inserted doorway. Each wall is crenellated, although it is possible that the crenellations may be later additions, as slate levelling present in the walling immediately below does not appear elsewhere in the structure. The original doorway is sited in the W wall and is protected by a loop-hole to one side of the door and by a *machicolation* or portcullis slot above which extends down from roof level. The present roof probably dates to the late 19th/early 20th century and consists of concrete supported on decaying RSJs. The present stairway is probably contemporary; earlier brickwork however around the bottom of it indicates that there was an earlier staircase(s) in this position, which would have provided access to the loop-holes in

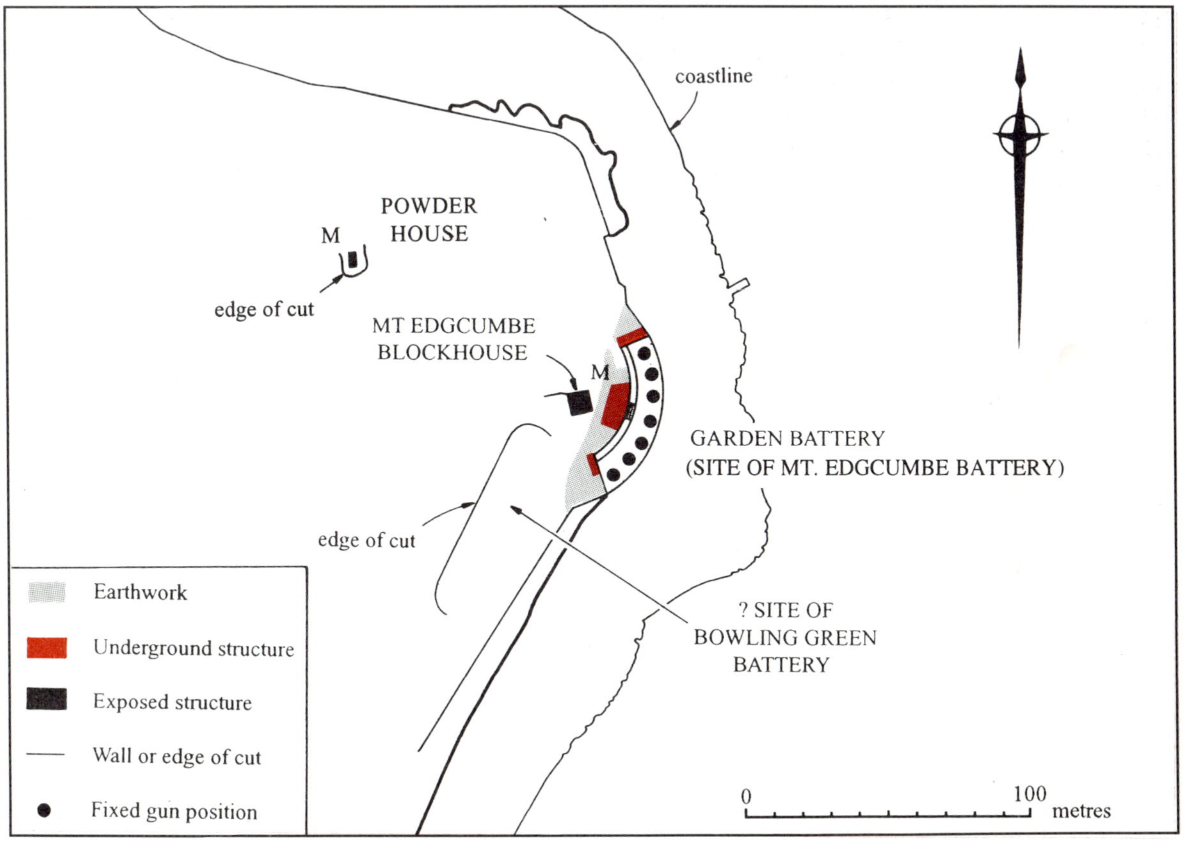

Fig 15: Mount Edgcumbe Blockhouse, Battery & Garden Battery

the W and N walls. The interior is further divided by an E - W stone wall, and the interior and surrounds of the embrasures have been rendered; they contain sockets for later window frames/mullions. On the outside of the E wall there are infilled scars where the structure of the pavilion was keyed in; putlog- and/or vent-holes are visible elsewhere. A later rubble stone wall adjoins the N.W corner.

Present condition

The condition of the masonry is relatively good although the roof level/ceiling requires monitoring and has been closed off, presumably because it is deemed unsafe. The masonry of the crenellations also requires monitoring and intermittent repair.

Sources

General

1, 2, 3; B, K, L, M, Q.

Specific

1602	Carew's survey of Cornwall
1820	Print (copy). MECP
n.d.	Notes entitled 'The Blockhouse & Battery'. MECP
1919	Pearse Chope, R *Early Tours in Devon & Cornwall*

BOWLING GREEN BATTERY

PAR = MAKER, NGR = SX 45555315, PRN = 6230, MAP 3 No. 2

This has been thought to be the site of a battery mentioned as existing in 1599 by Carew in his survey of 1602, and possibly also of the battery constructed by Vice-Admiral Killigrew in 1690. Alternatively, it is possible that this battery was sited immediately to the N on the site of the Mount Edgcumbe Battery; this was refurbished in 1747 and lay on the site of the later Garden Battery.

The proposed site of the Bowling Green Battery consists of a level grassy area bounded by a large hedge to the rear and fronted by a masonry revetment/sea wall. There is no visible evidence of any gun positions or associated structures such as magazines. The sea wall consists of a series of mortared masonry piers infilled with dry-stone and mortared local rubble walling and topped by a decorative course of shillet; it has been raised in height. There is no evidence of a battery parapet or of any gun embrasures.

Present condition

There are no visible remains of a battery. The site is grassland and is traversed by a public path. The sea wall is in reasonable condition overall although some sections are eroding.

Sources

General

Q.

Specific

1602	Carew's survey of Cornwall
1890	Worth, R.N *History of Plymouth*
1922	Historical MSS Commission report. Vol **12**, 334 (for 1690 ref. re Admiral Killigrew)
n.d.	Notes entitled 'The Blockhouse & Battery'. MECP
1919	Pearse Chope, R *Early Tours in Devon & Cornwall*

MOUNT EDGCUMBE BATTERY

PAR = MAKER, NGR = SX 45605320, PRN = 38552, MAP 3 No. 3

This consisted of a private 21-gun saluting battery located on the site of the later Garden Battery. It was refurbished or rebuilt in 1747 by George, first Earl of Edgcumbe. It may represent the site of the guns mentioned by Carew in 1602 and/or the battery which was established in 1690 by Vice-Admiral Killigrew on or near the site of the bowling green. This is described in 1701 as having 20 guns and in 1717 by Col. Lilly as being ruinous. Alternatively this battery may have been sited slightly to the S on the site of the present bowling green (see under Bowling Green Battery). However, the 1747 reference to the battery being restored as opposed to being built, suggests that it was already in existence. It is shown on an 1820 print as consisting of guns on an open gun platform pointing over a low parapet and is named on the 1856 1st edition OS 6-inch map.

No remains of the battery are visible, except for an associated powder magazine (Mount Edgcumbe Powder House); it was presumably completely demolished on the construction of Garden Battery. It was replaced by Earl's Battery, which was armed with 21 French guns which had been mounted on the original battery in c. 1800.

Present condition

Demolished; no remains visible.

Sources

General

Q.

Specific

1602	Carew's survey of Cornwall
1856	O.S. Ist edition 6-inch map sheet no. 123. WDRO
1890	Worth, R.N *History of Plymouth*
1922	Historical MSS Commission report. Vol **12**, 334 (for 1690 ref. re Admiral Killigrew)
n.d.	Notes entitled 'The Blockhouse & Battery'. MECP
1919	Pearse Chope, R *Early Tours in Devon & Cornwall*

MOUNT EDGCUMBE POWDER HOUSE

PAR = MAKER , NGR = SX 45505322, PRN = 38552.1, MAP 3 No. 4

This is sited within the Park, c. 120m to the N.W of the site of Mount Edgcumbe Battery, with which it was probably associated. It is sited within a rock-cut terrace designed to provide protection against an explosion, channelling the main force of any explosion upwards rather than sideways. Its style of construction is consistent with an 18th century date, and it may be contemporary with the documented reconstruction of Mount Edgcumbe Battery in 1747. It is a single-storey rubble stone building, with granite details and an internal brick barrel vaulted roof. There are vents in each side wall, closed off on the outside with pierced slates. The interior was not viewed.

Present condition

Very good; it has recently been refurbished.

Sources

Specific

1995 Gaskell-Brown, C. pers comm.

GARDEN BATTERY

PAR = MAKER, NGR = SX45605320, PRN = 37091, MAP 3 No. 5

This is a granite casemated battery dating to 1862-3 and located on the western side of the mouth of the Hamoaze, on the site of an earlier saluting battery (Mount Edgcumbe Battery). It lies within Mount Edgcumbe Country Park, adjoining the French gardens and immediately N of the Bowling Green. It was recommended by the Royal Commission in 1860 as part of the inner sea defences; it was intended to defend both the main channel to the N of Drake's Island and the shallower channel to the S and to be armed with ten guns (with no barrack accommodation). The contract for construction was awarded in January 1862 and the battery was completed in April 1863, excluding the iron shields which were added after 1869 when alterations were proposed to the magazines. It was built to the original plan which was for seven guns in casemates with magazines to the rear. The original armament was seven 68-pdr SB cannon on wooden traversing carriages. It had been armed by 1882 and in

Plate 25: Garden Battery from Devil's Point (Exeter Archaeology)

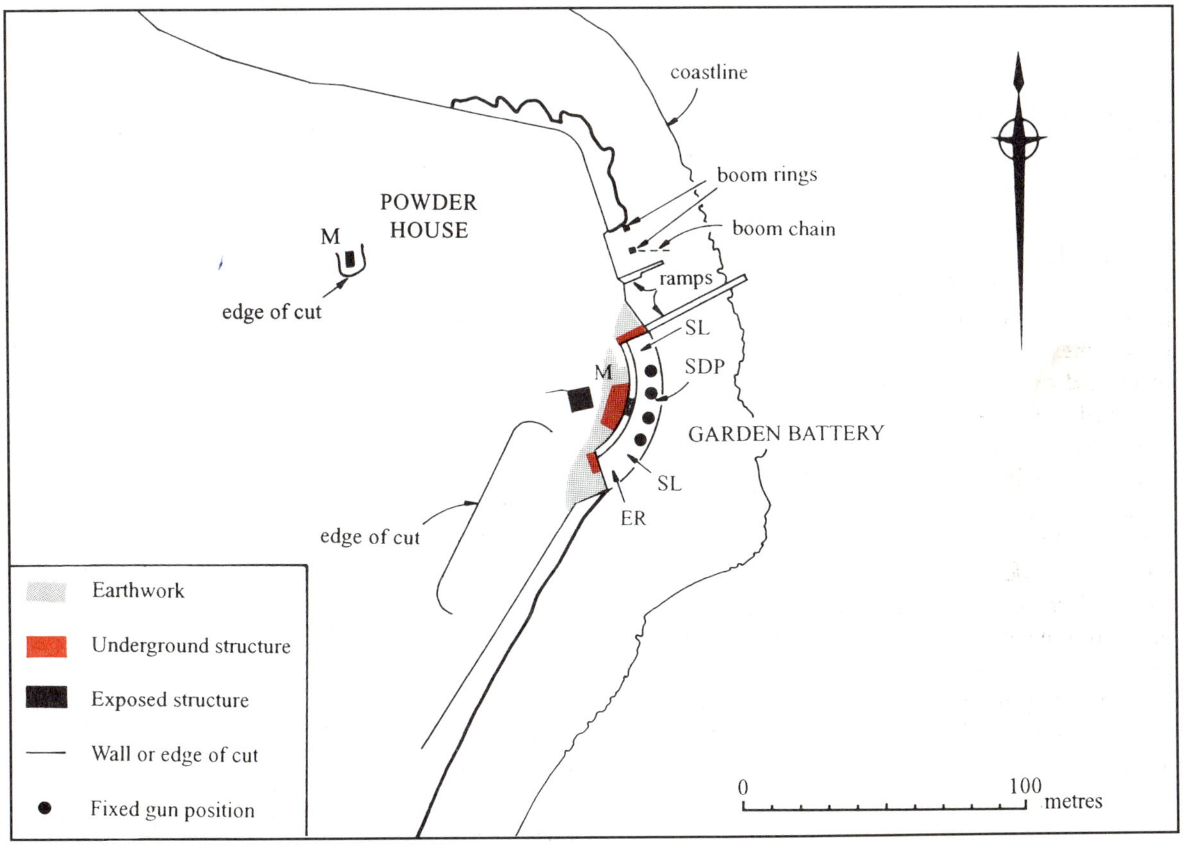

Fig 16: Garden Battery re-armed with QF guns, c.1900

Plate 26: Garden Battery casemates (Exeter Archaeology)

1885 seven 9-inch RML guns were approved as an updated armament, of which six appear to have been mounted. In 1893 four 64-pdr RMLs were approved and at the same time three 6-pdr QF guns were dismounted in Ordnance care; when and where the latter were mounted (if at all) is not known. In 1895 these were replaced by four 12-pdr QF guns, reduced to two in 1905. By 1910 these were accompanied by two searchlights placed in two of the former gun casemates. The guns and lights were removed in 1927 and the MoD gave up the battery in 1946.

The battery is sited on the rocky foreshore, with high tide reaching up to the base of the outer wall. It projects out slightly from the shore line and is built on a curving frontage (containing the casemates) with at each end short straight lengths of wall ending in square piers. It is single-storey, and on its roof there is an ornamental saluting battery (Earl's Battery), replacing the earlier Mount Edgcumbe Battery. In plan it consists of seven gun casemates with a further five magazine chambers to the rear. The main entrance is from the seaward side at the N end and is at the top of a later concrete landing ramp; the doorway is topped with wrought-ironwork containing the letters 'VR' flanked by 18 and 62; there is another datestone ('1862 VR') in the outer wall underneath casemate No. 4. The battery is faced with large ashlar granite blocks; the internal structure consists of local rubble stone with brick vaults overlain by an asphalt roof. Of the five magazine chambers, two lie within the rear of the gun casemates and three lie beyond the casemates; these consist of separate brick-vaulted chambers protected by a mound of earth. A small passage, possibly a storeroom, at the S end mirrors the entrance passage at the N. The present entrance lies at the rear of casemate No. 1 and has been inserted, possibly when the QF guns were installed. The gun casemates (numbered from N to S) all survive complete. No. 1 retains its original paving, racer rail and tackle-loops for a 68-pdr SB or 9-inch RML gun. Elsewhere the floor is largely cement, although impressions of the racer rails can be discerned. Concrete platforms supporting mounting-plates for 12-pdr QF guns have, together with ammunition lockers, been built later within casemate Nos 2 - 5. The platforms in Nos 4 and 5 are different to those of Nos 2 and 3, and it is in Nos 4 and 5 that two 12-pdr QF guns are shown on later additions to a plan of 1880. These additions also include searchlight emplacements in Nos 1 and 6, an engine-room in No. 7 and an electric light direction post in No. 3. Casemate Nos 2 - 5 retain their original iron shields, the remainder having been removed and replaced with shuttered concrete, presumably when the searchlights were installed. Concrete plinths for engines and generators and also partition walls were originally inserted within the rear of the gun casemates and within some of the magazine chambers also, but have been removed since the 1970s. The magazines have been much altered since their original construction, presumably reflecting the changes in design recommended in 1869 and possibly modifications contemporary with the installation of the QF guns. The chamber within the rear of No. 2 may be of later construction.

Present condition

Overall in very good condition although it suffers from damp; when visited there was standing water up to an inch deep within Casemate No. 1. Some internal fixtures such as tackle-loops in the ceiling and rings at each end of some of the rear racer rails still survive. However little remains of any ironwork associated with the mantlets except for some hook positions.

Sources

General

12, 13, 15, 17, 19, 21 - 24; K, Q.

Specific

1880 Plan, with later additions. PRO: WO78/5056

EARL'S BATTERY

PAR = MAKER, NGR = SX 45645318, PRN = 6229, MAP 3 No. 6

This is located on the roof of Garden Battery which was completed in 1863; Earl's Battery was present by 1871. It succeeded Mount Edgcumbe Battery, which was demolished on the construction of Garden Battery. It was armed with the 21 French guns from Mount Edgcumbe Battery. Only three of these now remain; the others were apparently disposed of during WWII, perhaps for scrap to help the war effort. During WWII it appears to have been the site of two light ?QF guns covering the anti-submarine boom/net extending across to Devil's Point.

It is an open battery with a low parapet wall at the front with a 2m-wide gently sloping granite gun platform immediately behind. Access is via a flight of steps from the rear and also originally via subsidiary entrances through the N and S flanks. The flanks and the rear are bounded by stone balustrades. The rear balustrade is on the line of the rear wall of the vaulted gun casemates of Garden Battery below. At the S end of the battery platform there is a small domed pagoda of unknown function; there may have been an equivalent at the other end.

Plate 27 Earl's Battery, cannon and later ammunition lockers (Exeter Archaeology)

Two later gun positions have been cut into the top of the parapet wall at the N end of the battery, served by two pairs of inserted store recesses. Some of the mounting-bolts still survive, together with a bracket; this may have held a davit to bring up ammunition from the magazines below via the main seaward entrance to Garden Battery. These two gun positions may be the sites of two light QF guns defending this end of the WWII or possible earlier WWI boom (see boom mooring-rings below).

Present condition

Good. Very well maintained. The N and S entrances are blocked off with a mixture of timber and shrubs.

Sources

General

K, Q.

Specific

n.d. Notes entitled 'The Blockhouse & Battery'. MECP

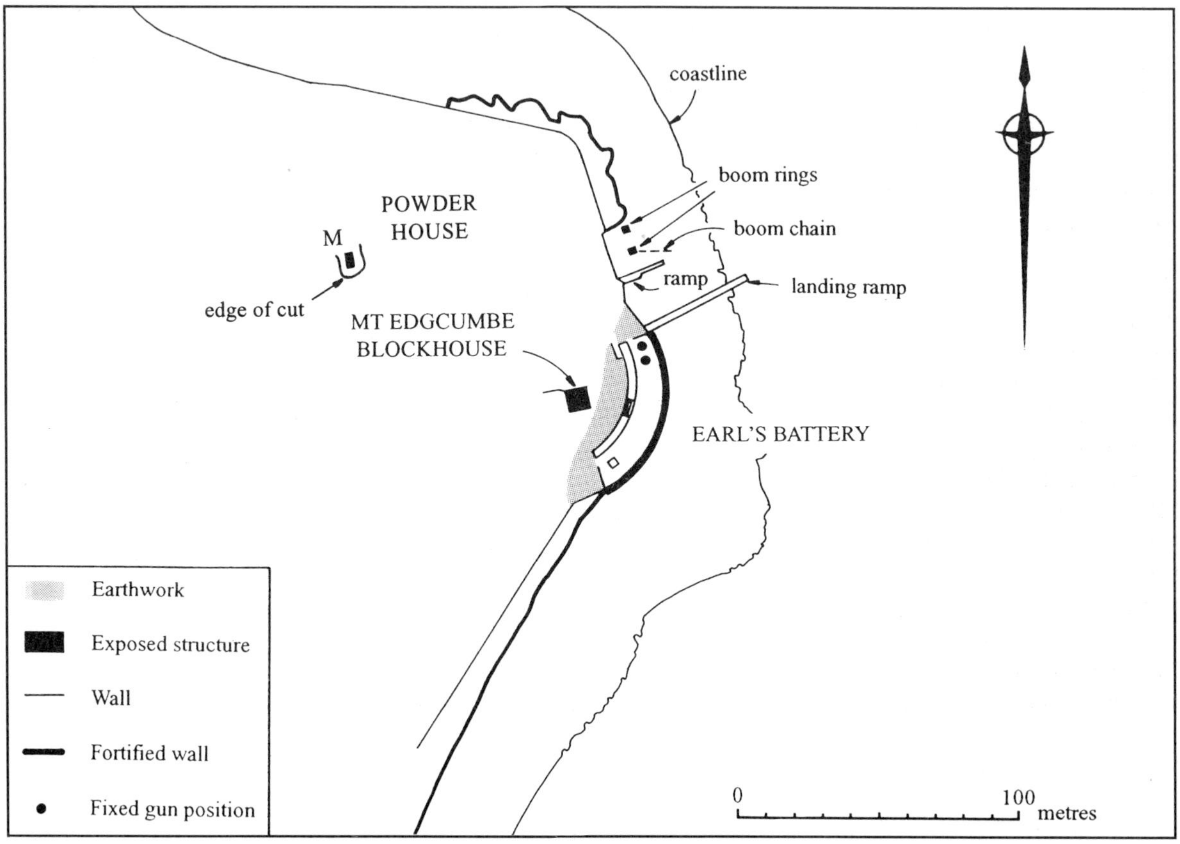

Fig. 17: Earl's Battery & QF guns protecting the boom

BOOM MOORING-RINGS

PAR = MAKER, NGR = SX 45635323, PRN = 38550, MAP 3 No. 7

Consists of two large iron rings, the southern of which has a chain attached. They are located on the seaward side of a later concrete platform sited between high and low water mark. The rings, together with a concrete ramp immediately to the S, may originally have belonged to an anti-submarine net and/or boom (although they may not be contemporary). They may date to WWI and/or WWII. The other end is located on the foreshore immediately to the S of Devil's Point Blockhouse, where there are four similar mooring-rings set into the rock. A boom was placed across the entrance to the Hamoaze from May 1941 to November 1943 and it is likely that a similar protection was also extended across the Hamoaze in WWI when submarines were beginning to be a threat. It would also have given some protection against light vessels such as motor torpedo-boats. The boom appears to have been protected by two light QF gun positions sited at the N end of Earl's Battery, immediately S of the concrete ramp. It may have been lit by a searchlight, possibly sited within the N casemate of Garden Battery.

Present condition

Fair, although the ironwork is decaying and the ramp is being undermined by wave action.

REDDING POINT BATTERY

PAR = MAKER, NGR = SX 45785265, PRN = 6236, MAP 3 No. 8

This is shown on charts of 1768, 1782 and 1786, sited immediately to the N of the modern Raveness Point (named on these charts as Redding Point). However, it is not referred to by Dixon in his report of 1780 and is not depicted on Cowl's plan of 1780 or on Gardner's of 1784, suggesting that the 1782 and 1786 plans may be based on out-of-date information (probably based on an original survey of 1770). It has previously been thought to have been located near the modern Redding Point which lies just N.E of Picklecombe Point. It covered the anchorage of Barn Pool and to some extent the shallow channel to the S of Drake's Island. On the 1786 chart it is marked as being armed with 24 cannon. It was probably constructed during the Seven Years' War in the late 1750s when other fortifications works were in progress, notably the Dock Lines and alterations to the Citadel.

The most likely location of the battery is immediately to the E of Milton Temple within the Country Park, where there is a level terraced area revetted on its N and E sides by masonry walling. It lies just above high tide level, at the S end of Barn Pool, and is in the logical position for a battery covering the anchorage. It is thus the most likely site of the battery unless others have been eroded into the sea.

Present condition

It is a grassy area traversed by the main coastal path. The walling on the E side is in bad condition and is slumping into the sea; it was very difficult to view. The N wall is partly covered by vegetation, and towards the W revets the pathway; it may contain later fabric.

Sources

General

5, 6, 8; M, Q.

Specific

1768	Plan of the town, ports and the Citadel of Plymouth by ?M. de Beville (Stuart No. 135)
1782	A Chart of Plymouth Sound, Cattwater & Hamoaze. PLSL
1786	Chart of Plymouth Sound & Catwater. Surveyed in 1786, printed for Robt Sayer (possibly based on a 1770 survey). Copy in PLSL

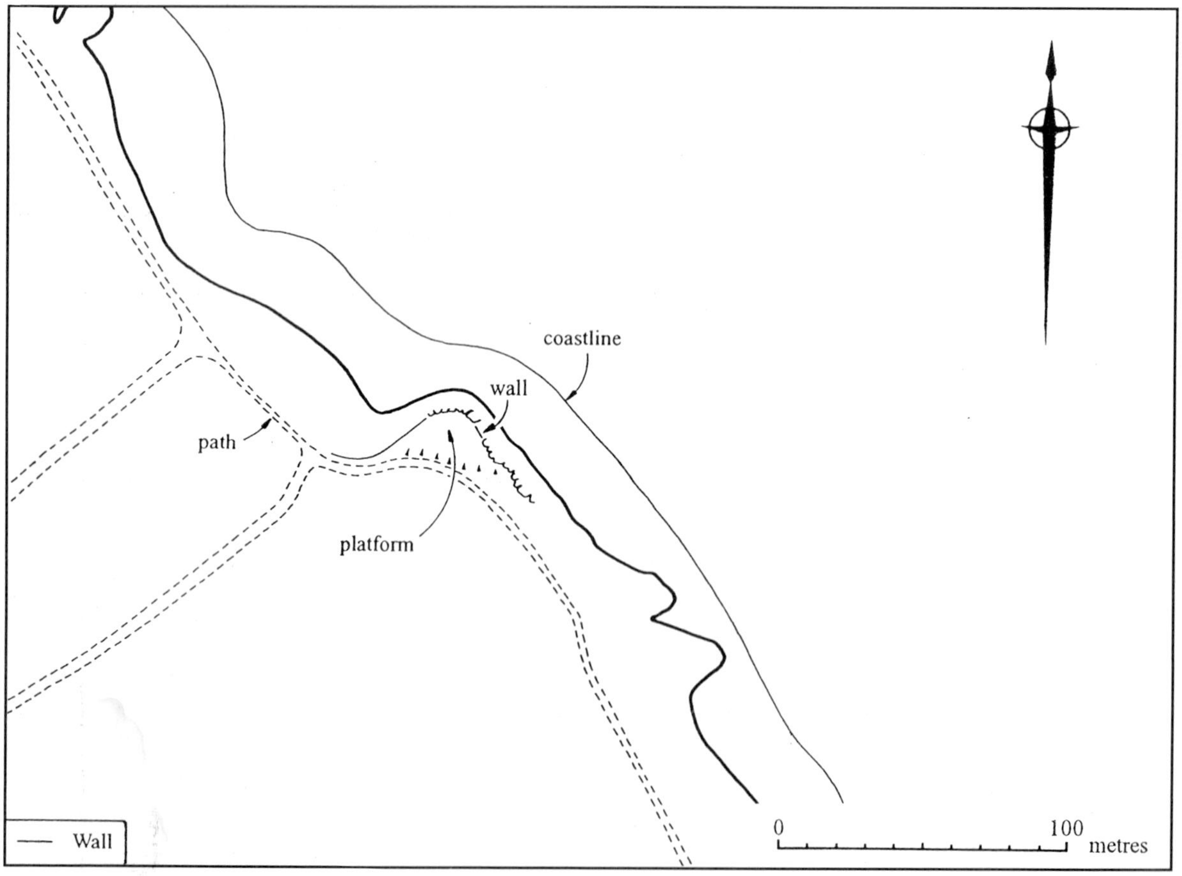

Fig. 18: Redding Point Battery

OBELISK REDOUBT

PAR = MAKER, NGR = SX 45065340, PRN = 37241, MAP 3 No. 9

This is located at the W extremity of a small ridge of limestone, the E end of which forms Cremyll Point. As a defensive work it operated in conjunction with the musketry lines and Retreat Battery along the ridge to the E. The redoubt was begun on 19 August 1779, just after the Franco-Spanish fleet anchored in Cawsand Bay. It is one of a series of fortifications built or proposed by Lt. Col. Matthew Dixon in response to the threat posed by the enemy fleet. In his report of 10 January 1780 he described it as being intended for 500 men and to be covered at the rear by Mount Wise Redoubt. Its intended role, along with the musketry lines and gabion battery to the E (which were armed with six 12-pdr field guns, and, along with the redoubt, were protected by a ditch with fraising and fronted by a strong thorn barrier), was to protect the retreat of forces from Maker Heights, should the positions there be forced by the enemy, and also to inhibit the enemy from bombarding the Dockyard. On Cowl's map of 1780 it is marked as being armed with eight 18-pdr guns. In a further report (possibly by Dixon) dating to after March 1780 it is described as being for 200 men. It is depicted as existing on Gardner's map of 1784, together with the musketry lines to the E. It is also apparently depicted on maps of 1857 (not located) and 1783, and is also called Cremyll Redoubt.

The Redoubt is sited on a prominent knoll in one corner of a pasture field. The obelisk still survives. The knoll has a fairly level top and drops away steeply and with a regular slope to the S and E. This probably represents the outline of the redoubt. The N limit is formed by a rock face, below which runs the footpath. This, and some of the E slope, is heavily overgrown. The W slope has been partly removed by a cut made to accommodate an oil storage tank; however no masonry or other remains are visible in the side of it. The site of the entrance shown (on the E side) on Gardner's 1784 plan is obscured by undergrowth. Although the immediate slopes to the S and E appear to be landscaped, presumably during the construction of the redoubt, there appears to be no extensive *glacis* beyond this, just an open hillside and valley bottom which could presumably be effectively covered. There are no surface remains of the redoubt and the junction of the musketry lines with it is not clear, although they may have occupied the top of a small ridge running E from the S.E corner of the redoubt.

Present condition

The top and S and E flanks survive complete and are presently under pasture. Below-ground remains are likely to survive. Part of the W side has been truncated just below the summit, whereas the N limit was probably always defined by the present rock face.

Sources

General

4 - 8; Q.

Specific

1783 Plan of Retreat Battery. CRO

1857 Plan of Cremyll Redoubt (PLSL - however not located there, nor at PCM or WDRO)

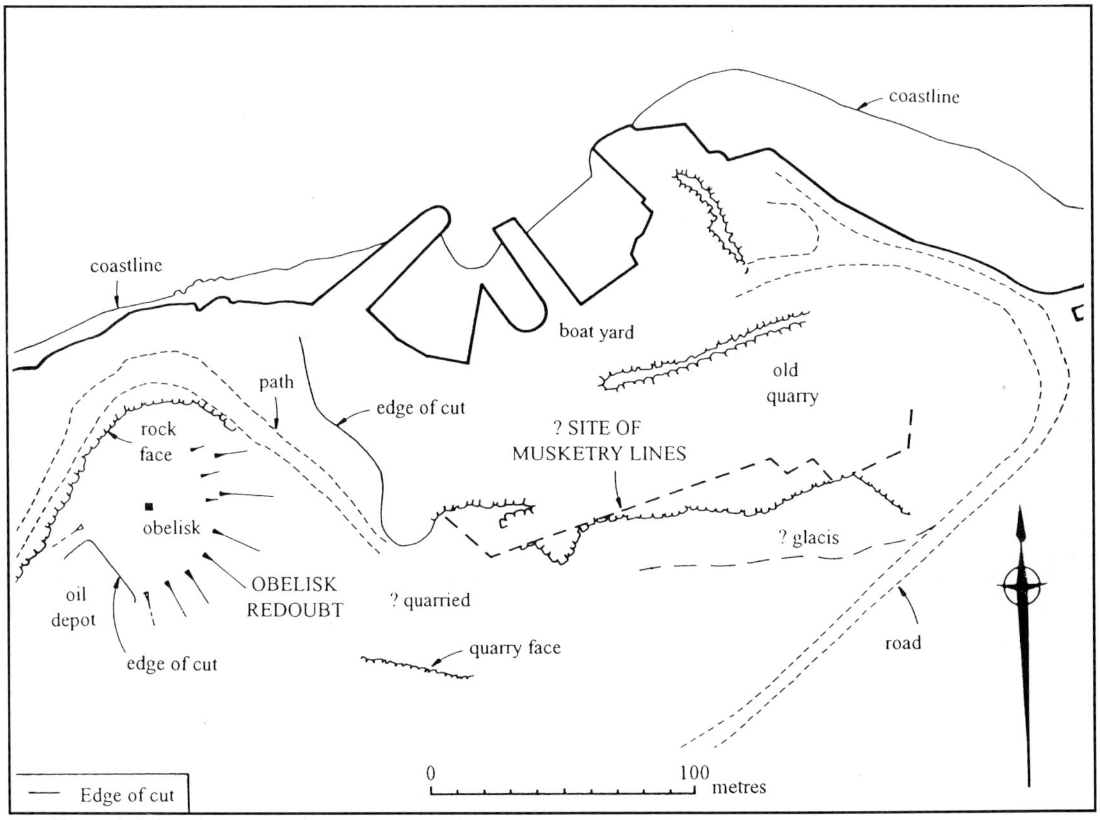

Fig. 19: Obelisk Redoubt & Musketry Lines

MUSKETRY LINES / RETREAT BATTERY

PAR = MAKER, NGR = SX 45075233 - 45335243, PRN = 6238, MAP 3 No. 10

This was constructed at the same time as Obelisk Redoubt and was intended to cover the retreat of troops from Maker Heights and also to hold up the enemy and inhibit them from effectively bombarding the Dockyard. Construction was probably begun at a similar time to the Redoubt after August 1779 and probably completed in the first half of 1780; it is not however described in Dixon's January 1780 report. Remarks written later in 1780 describe it as a gabion battery for six 12-pdrs, the field pieces sited above Passage House (at Cremyll Point) and linked (to the redoubt) by a breastwork of about 200 feet in length. Mount Wise Redoubt covered its rear. On additions probably dating to about 1779 on a 1777 chart by Mackenzie the armament of this battery is given as five 6-pdr guns. It is apparently depicted on a map of 1783 and is on the map of 1784 by Gardner. 'Retreat Battery' is not named as such in any of the available historical sources and is therefore probably a modern name.

The lines and gabion battery occupied a low E/W ridge extending from Cremyll Point in the E to Obelisk Redoubt in the W. However, much of the ridge to the N, probably including its summit, has been quarried away up to the line of the present pathway along the rear of the gardens of the properties fronting the main road. Quarrying has also occurred at the top end of the present car park. Part of the S facing slope of the ridge still survives as the back gardens of these properties but does not contain any visible remains of musketry lines. Indeed it is unlikely that they would be located on this slope as the area immediately behind and above them would have been exposed to fire from an enemy below, thus rendering any reinforcement of the Lines hazardous; it is more likely that the Lines ran along the top of the ridge. There are no identifiable remains along the present quarry face, which at its E end turns S and follows the W property boundary of 'Karenza'. Thus the wall forming the N limit of 'Karenza', previously thought to be part of the Lines, lies on the quarry floor below the level of the top of the ridge; it is of rubble stone masonry and contains no military features, and its location on the quarry floor suggests that it is not associated with the musketry lines. Thus it is probable that the musketry lines and the gabion battery have largely been quarried away, except to the W where they adjoined Obelisk Redoubt.

Present condition
Largely quarried away, except for possibly at the W end where there is a small limestone ridge adjoining Obelisk Redoubt.

Sources
General
4 - 8; Q.
Specific

1783	Plan of Retreat Battery. CRO
1857	Plan of Cremyll Redoubt (PLSL - however not located there, nor at PCM or WDRO)

PROPOSED REDOUBT AT TORPOINT

PAR = ANTONY, NGR = approx SX?43605520, PRN = 38548, MAP 2 No. 11

Torpoint is the site of a redoubt proposed by Dixon in his report of January 1780; it is marked 'O' on his plan and was intended to provide 'a further security of the Navy and Ordnance Arsenals as (it) would oblige the enemy to break ground in order to make a regular attack against them before they could come sufficiently near to bombard the Arsenals'. It is shown as sited on the hill immediately to the W of Torpoint; the top of which is now occupied by housing. There is no evidence that it was ever built or started; it does not appear on any other contemporary or later plans.

Source
General
5.

PICKLECOMBE BULWARK

PAR = MAKER, NGR = SX 45605150?, PRN = 6235.1, MAP 2 No. 12

The slight promontory occupied by the later Fort Picklecombe is a possible site for the bulwark and gun battery (of three guns) proposed on Sir Richard Grenvyle's map of 1586-88; another equally possible site is Hooe Lake Point (NGR = SX 44905140) along the coast to the W. On Grenvyle's map three guns are shown firing W, S.W & S across the Sound and Cawsand Bay, and are enclosed to landward by a fence or rampart labelled 'the new bulworke.' This is a secondary addition to the map; the original lettering reads 'three peices of ordinance to be new placed to defend the landinge in Cawsan baye to master the roade'. However there is no known evidence that these proposals were put into effect, and there are no known surface remains or reported observations of defences of this date.

Sources
General
2; M, Q

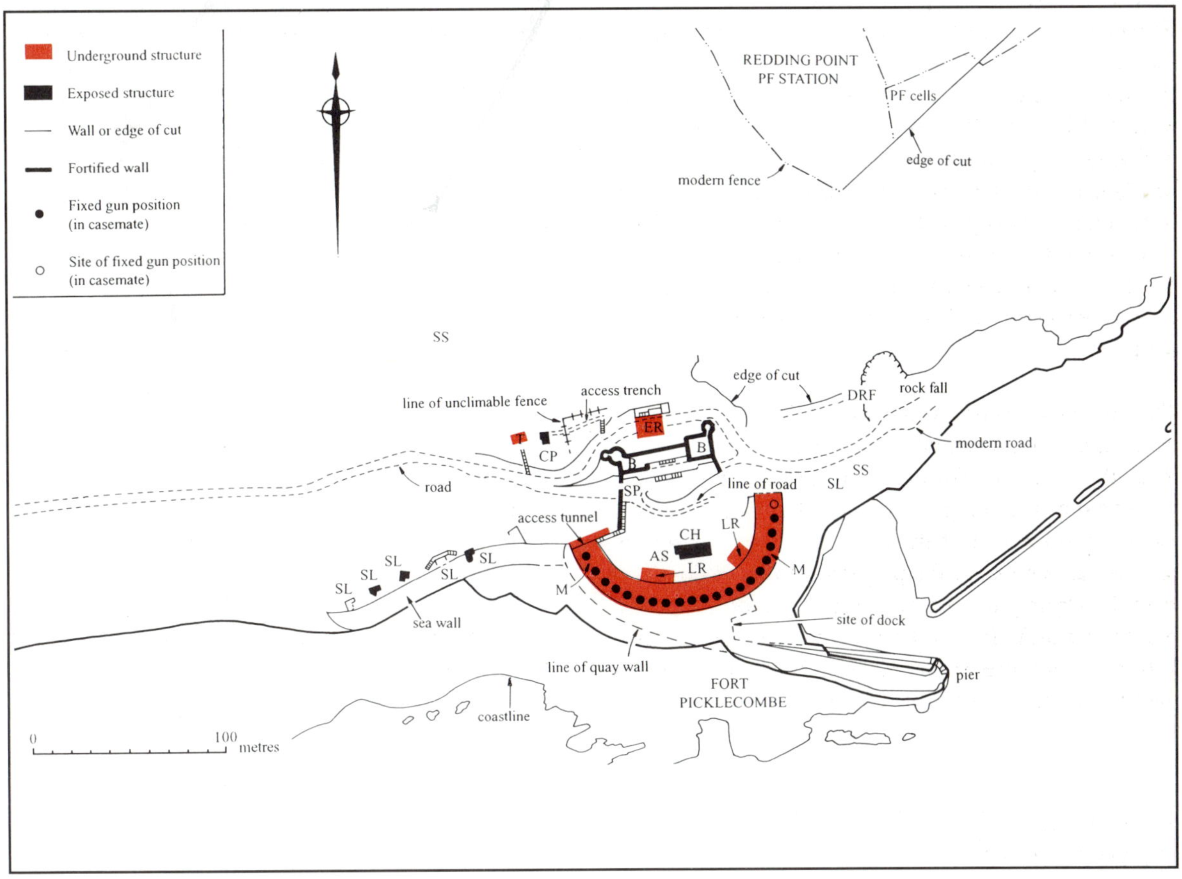

Fig. 20: Fort Picklecombe & Battery

PICKLECOMBE BATTERY

PAR = MAKER, NGR = SX 45545161, PRN = 6235.2, MAP 2 No. 13

This was a limestone battery and barracks located on the slope immediately above the later Fort Picklecombe. Its construction was recommended on 23 October 1844 by the Committee considering the Harbour Defences of Plymouth to close off the gap around the W end of the newly completed breakwater; another similar battery (Staddon Point Battery) was to close off the E gap. Construction had begun by December 1845, when it is described as having two towers and soldiers' quarters surrounded by a ditch, with an intended armament of three 56-pdr guns and six 32-pdr guns on traversing carriages, with a shot furnace. A datestone over the entrance gate indicates that it was completed (at a cost of £9001 12s 5d) in 1848, and by 1851 the guns were mounted and the magazines filled. It was superseded by Fort Picklecombe, which was begun in 1861-2, but the barracks continued in use as officers' quarters and hospital facilities until the release of the fort by the MoD in 1956. The W tower is thought to have been used as an R.O.C Post in the last war.

Only the barracks belonging to the battery and remnants of the surrounding ditch survive; the gun platform was sited on a terrace to the S of the barracks and may have been at least partly removed when Picklecombe Fort was constructed. The guns appear to have fired through an embrasured wall (shown on a print of *c.*1850 below and to the S of an arched entrance through the W flanking wall). The barracks

Plate 28: Fort Picklecombe & Battery (Photograph: S. Hartgroves. Frame: ABP/F35/68. Copyright: Cornwall Archaeological Unit)

Plate 29: Picklecombe Battery (Exeter Archaeology)

are an ornate two-storey structure with dressed limestone facework, apparently built in the style of Warwick Castle to please the landowner, the Earl of Mount Edgcumbe. Three-storey towers (one polygonal and the other round, with a stair turret attached) are sited at the N.E and N.W corners, and the barracks were originally entered via an arched doorway (and presumably a drawbridge) through the N wall. At the front there is an arched verandah, with stairs giving access to a first-floor balcony; the gun platforms were sited below the verandah. Local defence was provided by the ditch, which has been largely infilled and remodelled to accommodate the later submarine establishment and the present road, loopholes in the gorge (rear) wall of the barracks and in the flanks of the towers, and crenellated parapets on the flanks and along the gorge of the building. Loopholed walls also protected the flanks between the barrack building and the gun platform; the W wall is shown on the c.1850 print as containing an arched entrance similar to that existing today and three loopholes to the S of it. However structural evidence indicates that it was rebuilt to contain more loopholes and a remodelled monumental entrance (with the original 1848 datestone retained) to form an impressive entrance and contiguous flanking defence with the new Fort Picklecombe in the 1860s. The E loopholed wall (with an entrance inserted after 1896) may however represent original 1840s work. A masonry sentry box (probably dating to the 1860s) with loopholes is sited immediately inside the W entrance. The interior of the barracks was not accessible, but the external windows and doors contain some original (or at least 1860s) joinery and detail, and more is likely to survive inside.

Other surviving details include some of the original ornate railings at the front of the verandah and on the stairs to the first-floor balcony, and an iron plaque set into the verandah floor reading 'Seychelles Asphalt' and 'Claridges'.

Present condition

At present the barracks lie empty and derelict. Refurbishment/conversion work has been started but has ceased for some time; there are piles of timbers visible inside and a heap of spoil on the outside. The condition of the stonework is generally very good, although the rendering is peeling off and the iron girders supporting the York stone first floor balcony are rusting and rotting. The condition of the interior could not be assessed, but the need for renewal of timber floors in the towers for example is clear from architects' drawings of 1991.

Sources

General

10, 11, 12, 19; K, Q.

Specific

1845	Description of proposed works PRO: WO 44/522
*c.*1850	Print, depicting the 'New Fort: Mount Edgcumbe' PLSL: P623.1 PIC
*c.*1850	Print or drawing of the Breakwater, showing the battery in the background. MECP (Picklecombe file, not sourced)
1851	Letter or report. PRO: WO 55/807
1853	Letter or report. PRO: WO 44/523
*c.*1875	Postcard, showing old battery above new one. Copies held by MECP (Picklecombe file, not sourced) & in D. Quarmby Collection (FSG)
1880	Block plan PRO: WO 78/5050(2)
1899	General plan PRO: WO 78/5050(1)
n.d (1890s)	Photographs of barracks & fort PLSL: P623.1
1907	Plan of alterations PRO: WO 78/5048
1940s	Fort Record Book PRO: WO 192/297
1983	Plan drawn by P.J. Cobb of UK Fortification Club (possibly based partly on 1907 plan). Copy held by CAU.

FORT PICKLECOMBE

PAR = MAKER, NGR = SX 45555153, PRN = 6235.3, MAP 2 No. 14

This is a two-tier granite casemated battery dating to the 1860s, located on the shore below the earlier 1848 battery; it is one of only two such multi-tier casemated batteries to be built in the country (the other being at Garrison Point, Sheerness). The construction of a heavy battery in this position to more effectively close off the western entrance around the Breakwater was proposed by Jervois in February 1858. It was to mount sixty guns in three tiers (two casemated) with accommodation for 300 men, and was to operate in conjunction with another proposed battery on the Breakwater opposite. After the Royal Commission of 1860 recommended a casemated battery of forty guns garrisoned by 200 men, the initial design (by Maj. Porter) of November 1860 was for a casemated battery mounting forty-two 68 & 110-pdr guns in two tiers with a further sixteen guns on an open platform above, and with a detached magazine to the rear; the guns were to be protected by iron shields. Remodelling in 1864 involved the removal of the roof tier and the re-location of the magazine to the basement; forty-two 12 and 18-ton RML guns were to be mounted in two tiers protected by iron shields. By 1867 the structure had been completed (except for the shields) by Hubbard & Co. at an estimated cost of £79845, and by November 1872 (when test firing was carried out) the shields were in position and the fort was apparently armed with thirty-two 10-inch 18-ton, 9-inch 12-ton and 7-inch 7-ton RML guns, six of which were fired. By 1880 the fort was fully armed with heavy 10-inch guns on the upper tier and lighter 9-inch guns below, and the 7-inch guns on the flanks; two look out stations were constructed on the roof. In 1885 the armament was reduced to eighteen 10-inch, fourteen 9-inch and four 7-inch RMLs, and remained at this level until shortly after 1893. By 1898 the number of RMLs had been further reduced, and two 6-pdr QF guns had been emplaced to cover the minefield. In 1899 six 12-pdr QF gun positions are shown on the roof; these guns were mounted by 1903 and were probably dismounted shortly after 1908, together with the remaining RMLs. These were replaced by two 6-inch BL guns proposed in 1907, together with two 4-inch QF guns (presumably in the old 12-pdr emplacements). The 6-inch BL guns formed the Examination Battery during World War I. The 4-inch QF guns were removed between 1927 and 1931, with the armament at the beginning of World War II apparently consisting of the two BL guns and some 12-pdr QF guns; these were replaced in 1941 with two twin 6-pdr QF guns. During World War II the 6-inch BL guns again formed the Examination Battery; all the remaining guns were dismounted in or by 1956.

Plate 30: Fort Picklecombe before conversion, 1973

Other installations were also constructed around the fort to provide direction and lighting for the guns. By 1896 a Depression Range Finder (DRF) had been built on the slope to the E of the fort, together with a Battery Commander's station (also perhaps containing a DRF) to the E; a submarine mining PF station and the Redding Point PF station had also been built (see separate entries). Between 1896 and 1899 three Electric Light (EL, i.e. searchlight) emplacements were built on the shore to the E, presumably serving the 12-

pdr QF battery on the roof and lighting the minefield; these are shown on maps of 1903 and 1915. This minefield and its associated PF station presumably became redundant in 1905, when submarine mining of harbour entrances was ended on the orders of Admiral Lord Fisher, the First Sea Lord. In 1910 four ELs are recorded, perhaps including at least one sited on the coast to the W, and five were present by 1920; at least two of these presumably represented fighting lights for the BL guns, with the remainder illuminating the area for the QF guns. Four lights were present in 1936, and additional ones were probably constructed to accompany the new twin 6-pdr QF guns installed in 1941 (as happened at Bovisand).

The main fort structure consists of a series of 42 granite-faced casemates built in two tiers on a curving frontage and sited on the rocky foreshore just above high tide level; all survive complete, except for the easternmost pair (where the main entrance gate has been cut through) and the iron shields (all now removed) and most of the internal fittings. The fort was accompanied on its seaward side by a quay, landing slip and pier, part of which still remains. Access from the quay into the interior of the fort was via a passage at the W end; this contains several tackle loops, and presumably represents the route by which some guns were brought into the fort. Each gun and the gun directly above was protected by a single iron shield, and each pair of neighbouring casemates was supplied from the magazines in the basement via a cartridge lift at the front and a shell lift to the rear. All the casemates have now been converted into flats and are generally inaccessible; most internal detail such as mantlet bars and pulley and tackle loops appears to have been removed. The basement level is of very similar plan to Fort Bovisand, with alternating cartridge and shell stores and access passages to the rear and around the front. The rear passage contained a lamp passage in its upper part, served from two sets of lamp rooms. Circular shell lifts occur at intervals off the rear passage, and two pairs of shell and cartridge stores have subsequently been adapted as magazines for the BL guns on the roof and have had shell lifts inserted. The roof of the front passage contains cartridge lifts at intervals, together with serving hatches (some of which retain their original wooden lining) into the cartridge stores. To the rear of the casemates at ground level the masonry shell of the cook house (used as an artillery store in 1899) survives; the coal house and the access road up the slope behind have however been removed and incorporated into the landscaping scheme. Local defence was provided by loopholed walls on the flanks linking the fort with the earlier 1848 barracks behind; the W wall survives, the E wall has been largely demolished.

Five concrete and brick searchlight emplacements are sited on the coast to the W of the fort. Three are of pre World War II design, with a broad semi-circular curving opening at the front protected by a sliding iron shutter, whilst the fourth is probably of World War II

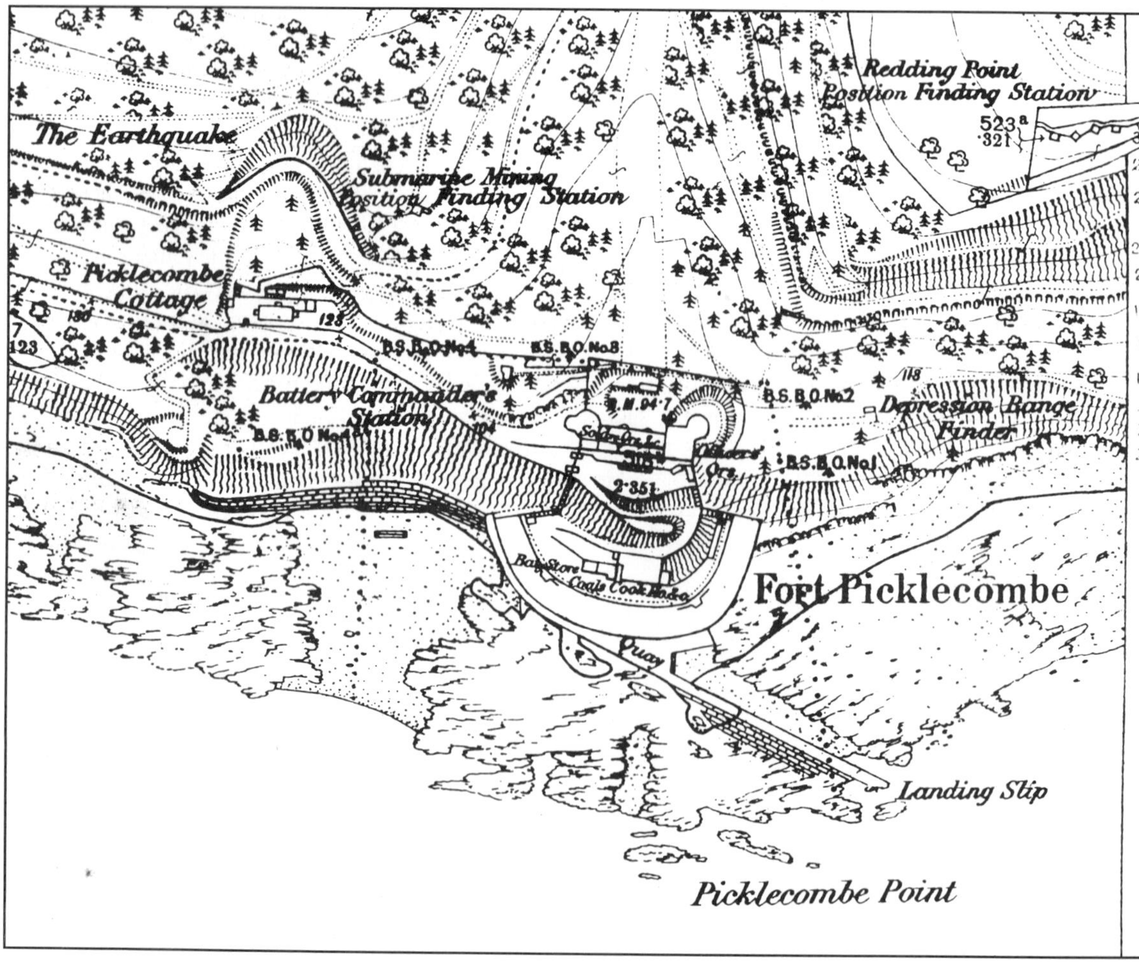

Fig. 21: Fort Picklecombe in 1896 (PRO: WO 78/2314)

Plate 31: Fort Picklecombe after conversion (Exeter Archaeology)

Plate 32: Searchlight emplacement at Picklecombe (Exeter Archaeology)

date, and has a single vertical slit at the front; the fifth has been demolished. The three early emplacements probably acted at some point as fighting lights for the 6-inch BL guns; the other(s) probably illuminated the area for the QF guns. Three emplacements were also sited on the shore to the E, but have been demolished and replaced by garages.

The battery commander's post lies on the hillslope (at NGR = SX 45475162) to the N.W of the fort, and consists of a single-storey concrete and brick building; this is terraced into the slope and has a curved viewing window (originally protected by an iron shutter) at the front. Access is via a stone revetted trench from the east, where sections of unclimbable fence also survive (of a style dating to c. 1900). No visible remains survive of the DRF position on the hillside (at approx NGR = SX 45645164) to the N.E of the fort, except a terraced accessway.

Present condition

Overall the shell of the fort structure appears to be in good condition, although the construction of new flats on the roof has removed all trace of the later BL and QF gun positions and the conversion of the casemates has removed almost all internal detail except for some remnants in the magazines. The easternmost casemate has been removed by the insertion of an arched entranceway, and the E flanking wall and access road up to the 1848 battery have been demolished and incorporated into terraced gardens. At the front the original quay has been removed by the construction of an underground car park around the front of the fort, and the searchlights to the E have been demolished and replaced by garages. One of the searchlights to the W has been completely demolished and another largely demolished; the remainder, together with the battery commander's post, appear at present to be in reasonable condition although they are liable to be deemed unsafe for health and safety reasons and demolished.

Sources

General

11 - 15, 17, 19 - 24; F, G, K, Q.

Specific

?1872	Description of test firing at Picklecombe. MECP (on the back of a print sold in the shop, 1984)
*c.*1875	Postcard, showing the fort with shields in place. MECP & D. Quarmby collection (FSG)
1880-1	Plans PRO: WO 78/5050 (2, 3)
1892	Letters or report PRO: WO 196/29
1898	?armament table or report PRO: CAB 7/6
1899	General plan. PRO: WO 78/5050(1)
?1890s	Photographs of fort from west. PLHL: P623.1
1901	Drawings re installation of ELs (Electric Lights) PRO: WO 78/5040
1905	?armament table or report PRO: CAB 16/1
1906	Defence scheme map PRO: WO 33/400
1907	Plans of ?BL gun emplacements PRO: WO 78/4146
1907	Plans of alterations PRO: WO 78/5048
1907	Plans of magazines PRO: WO 78/4064
1927	?armament table or report PRO: CAB 36/16
1931	?armament table or report PRO: CAB 16/105
1941	?armament proposal, table or report PRO: WO 199/523
1943	?armament table or report PRO: WO 199/954
1940s	Fort Picklecombe Fort Record Book PRO: WO 192/297
n.d	Section drawing through casemates and shields. Copy held by FWW.
1983	Plan drawn by P.J. Cobb of UK Fortifications Club. Copy held by CAU.
n.d	Gerrard, J. *Book of Plymouth*. Late 19th cent. photo, p.85.

PICKLECOMBE SUBMARINE MINING ESTABLISHMENT AND P.F. STATION

PAR = MAKER, NGR = SX 45535163 & 45425167 (PF Station), PRN = 6235.4, MAP 2 No. 15

By 1896 a submarine mining establishment (shown on a plan of 1899) had been built underground and to the rear of the 1848 barracks, together with a Position Finding (PF) station on the hillslope to the N.W. Both are probably contemporary with the equivalent establishment and observation station built within and above Fort Bovisand in 1896, and controlled and observed minefields laid across the two entrances into the Sound at each end of the breakwater; these minefields are shown on a plan of 1903. They presumably became redundant in 1905, when submarine mining of harbour entrances ceased on the order of Admiral Lord Fisher, the First Sea Lord.

The submarine mining establishment consists of three underground brick vaulted masonry chambers built within the ditch of the 1848 battery. The counterscarp wall of the ditch forms the N wall of the stairwell, off which the chambers open to the S. Most were inaccessible; one is labelled as an engine room and another had a central serving hatch. The position finding station has been demolished, and no identifiable remains are visible above-ground.

Present condition

Submarine mining establishment

Structurally in reasonable condition although the interiors of the vaults were not seen; some internal detail may therefore survive.

P.F. Station

This has been thoroughly demolished and its site covered by a heap of spoil. Below ground remains however may survive, especially if the roof has been pushed in and the side walls left intact.

Sources

General

19, 23.

Specific

1899 Plan of barracks and fort, including Mining Establishment. PRO: WO 78/5050(2)

REDDING POINT POSITION FINDING STATION

PAR = MAKER, NGR = SX 45675178, PRN = 37095, MAP 2 No. 16

This is located on the brow of the coastal ridge c. 200m to the N.E of Fort Picklecombe, and was built in the early 1890s, presumably to serve the heavy RML guns still emplaced in Fort Picklecombe and Breakwater Fort, and possibly the new Raleigh Battery (built in 1890-93). Three cells had been built by 1894, increasing to five by 1896. These were still in operation in 1903, but by 1915 had become redundant.

The cells are shown in 1896 as facing S and S.W. They were connected by a sunken accessway to the rear, access to which was via a flight of steps at the E end. The cells and the accessway have been demolished and infilled; the latter is visible towards its E end as a nettle-filled hollow, and slight mounds covered with brambles probably represent the sites of the cells. An overgrown terrace immediately to the S probably represents earlier landscaping associated with the drive lower down the slope.

Present condition

Demolished and levelled; site partly occupied by a pine plantation which has been felled. The cells would have been built within a terrace, which has been infilled; it is therefore probable that remains of the walls of the cells survive below ground.

Sources

General

18, 19, 23, 24.

HOOE LAKE POINT PF CELL

PAR = MAKER, NGR = SX 44675142, PRN = 38549, MAP 2 No. 216

A single PF cell is marked on the map of 1896, sited on the coastal slope some 300m to the W of Hooe Lake Point. It is not marked on a map of 1903, which depicts the PF stations extant at the time. It was presumably intended to serve the guns of Fort Picklecombe and/or Raleigh Battery, or was perhaps associated with the submarine minefield, and had become redundant by 1903.

No identifiable surface remains of the PF cell are visible; the most likely location would seem to be a small quarry or rock cut terrace cut into the slope some 10m or so above the coastal footpath.

Present condition

The terrace contains a tree and dense vegetation. Below ground remains of the demolished PF cell may still survive.

Sources

General

19.

3.2.2. Maker Heights

MAKER REDOUBT No.1

PAR = MAKER, NGR = SX 43255155, PRN = 6113.01, MAP 2 No. 28

This is located on Maker Heights immediately to the north of Kingsand overlooking a watershed and a valley aligned NW/SE. It is the northernmost of a line of four redoubts constructed during the War of American Independence. A temporary redoubt was probably built on the site in *c.* 1779 by the Royal Cornwall Militia; a more permanent redoubt was designed by Dixon and the Duke of Richmond, begun in July 1782 and largely completed by November 1782 (Evans 1990). It, and Nos 2-4, were originally intended to form detached bastions of a large fort on the high ground behind, which was not built. By 1784 it was armed with eight guns (18-pdr and 32-pdr SB cannon), and on a map of 1788 is labelled as No. 1 (Royal Cornwall) Redoubt. It is shown on maps of 1808 & 1811 as having earthen ramparts on its northern, western and southern flanks with a ditch enclosing the gorge; a building is shown immediately to the south-east, together with (in 1811) a possible guardhouse in the interior of the redoubt opposite the entrance, and 10 gun embrasures: five on the front face, two on the south flank and three on the north flank. Both buildings had been demolished by 1896 when the redoubt is marked as dismantled. It was apparently disarmed at the end of the Napoleonic Wars in 1815, although A. Saunders quotes a reference to the armament of the northern redoubt dated 1820 in which three 18-pdrs were mounted on the front face, one 18-pdr on the right flank, and two 18-pdrs and four 32-pdrs on the left flank (this does not however match the no. of embrasures).

The redoubt consists of a three-sided work with a ditch closing off the rear. The ramparts and interior is largely overgrown, as is the ditch on the western and southern flanks. The ramparts as shown on the 1950s O.S map have been largely levelled, probably on the construction of an underground 1950s R.O.C. Monitoring Post in its centre (surrounded by a fence). This replaced the earlier (*c.* 1951) Orlit type B post, the

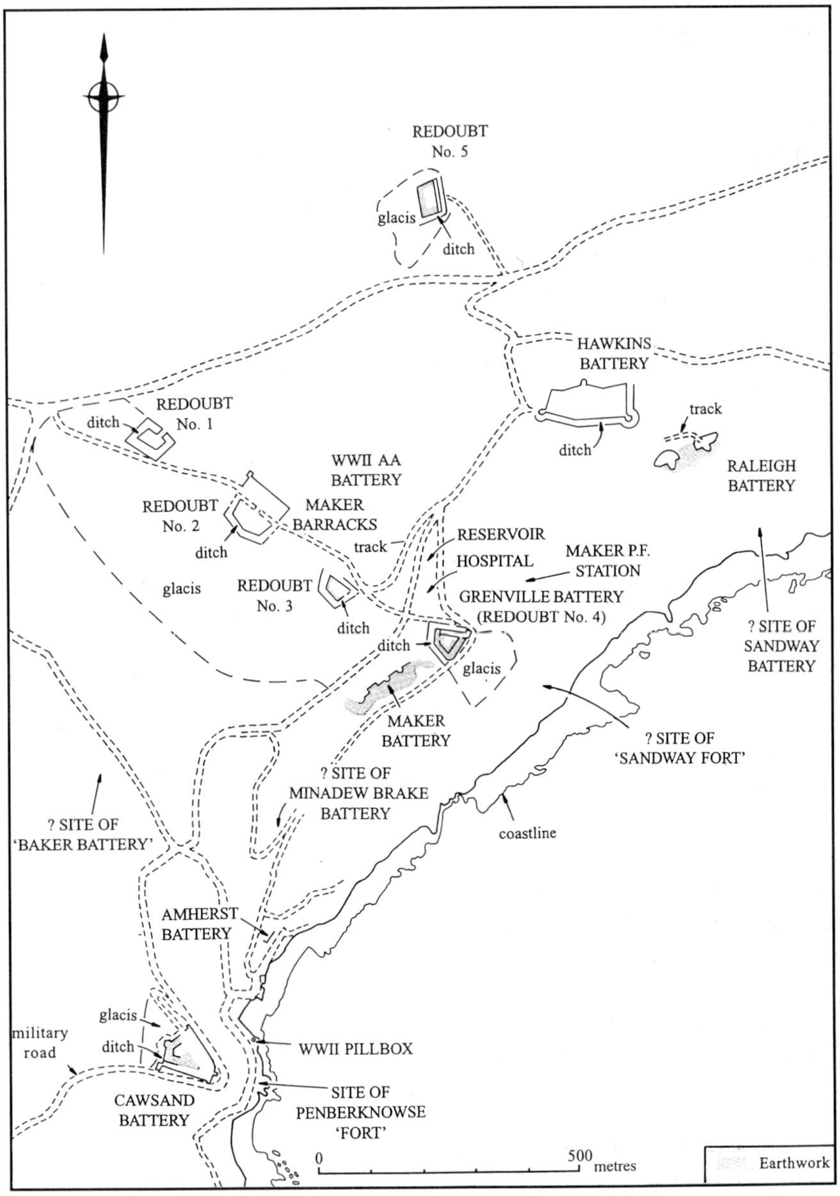

Fig. 22: Maker Heights & Cawsand Bay

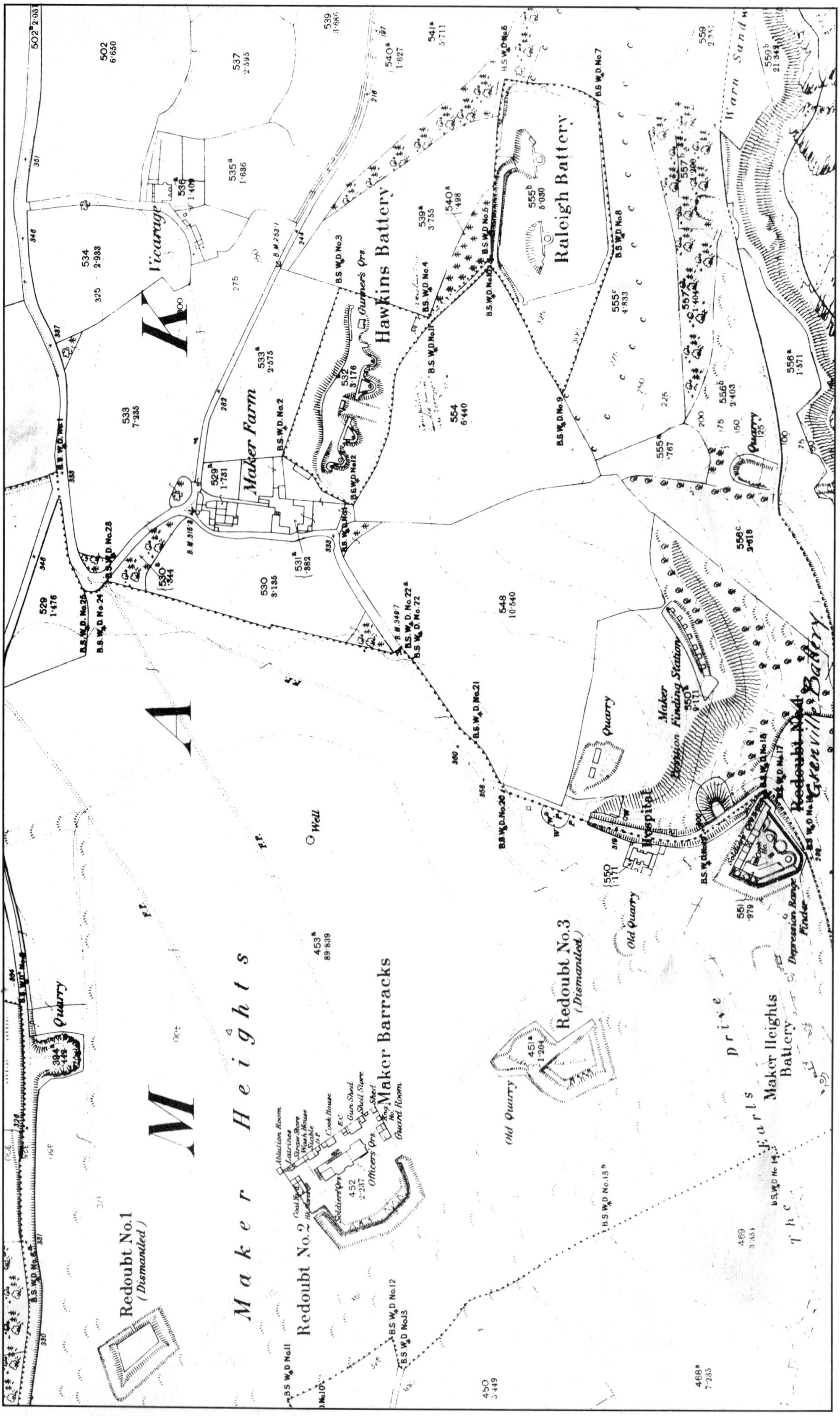

Fig. 23: *Maker Heights in 1896 (PRO: WO 78/2314)*

Plate 33: Maker Redoubts (Photograph: S. Hartgroves. Frame: ABP/F4/50. Copyright: Cornwall Archaeological Unit)

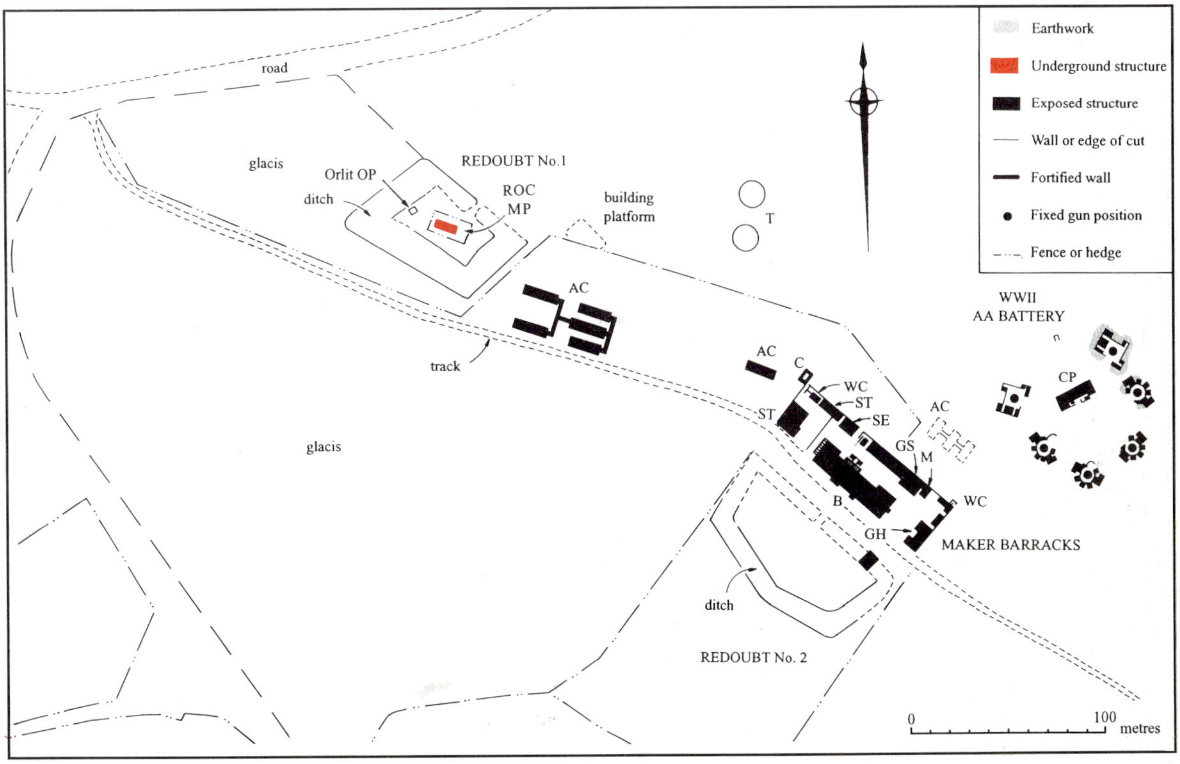

Fig. 24: Maker Redoubts Nos 1 & 2, the Barracks & the WWII HAA Battery

concrete platform of which survives immediately to the north. The redoubt is entered via an entrance causeway over the ditch in the centre of the gorge to the rear. The *glacis* is visible to the front and to the north where it is largely overgrown. Outside to the south-east the site of the building shown in 1784 & 1811 is visible as a platform, with some walls being visible in outline.

Present condition

Interior grassland and occupied by the ROC Post and

Plate 34: Redoubt No. 1, rubbish infilling the ditch (Exeter Archaeology)

earlier Orlit platform; the ditches and rampart are largely overgrown and inaccessible. Gorge ditch partly infilled with modern dump material.

Sources

General

8, 11, 12, 15, 19; C, D, E, K, L, M, O, Q, R.

Specific

1779-82	Sketch of encampments on Maker Heights. BL: Add Mss 15533 (Stuart No. 168)
1782	Plans for redoubts PRO: MPH 377
1782	Proposed fort on Maker Hgts PRO: MPH 382
1783	Projected works on Maker Hgts PRO: MR 1391
1783	Proposed fort on Maker Hgts PRO: MPHH 551
Oct 1783	Letter to Lord Townsend, Master General of Ordnance PRO: WO 30/54
1784	Projected works on Maker Hgts PRO: MR 916
1784	Maker Hgts PRO: MR 1387
1785	Maker Hgts PRO: MPH 341
1785	Main fort section and plan PRO: MPHH 131
1785	Proposed fort PRO: MPHH 537
1785	Plan for fort PRO: MPHH 536
1788	Plan of Maker Heights and surrounds by R. Sturt. PRO: MR 1434
1789	Plan of fort and redoubt PRO: MPH 717
1789	Plan of proposed defences PRO: MPH 719
1789	Plan of defences and ground they cover PRO: MPHH 535
1808	Proposed redoubt on Maker Hgts PRO: MR 1211
1808	Plan of Maker Hgts PRO: MR 1209
1809	Proposed defences on Maker Hgts PRO: MR 1392
1810	Section of proposed redoubt PRO: MPH 733
1811	Plan of Maker Heights Redoubts PRO: MPH 233/6
1820	Reference to armament PRO: WO 44/578
1844	Maker Tithe Map

MAKER REDOUBT No. 2

PAR = MAKER, NGR = SX 43475136, PRN = 6113.02, MAP 2 No. 29

This forms the centre right of the line of four redoubts constructed on Maker Heights during the War of American Independence. It was probably begun as a temporary redoubt in *c*. 1779 by the Somerset Militia; it was subsequently designed in a more permanent form by Dixon and the Duke of Richmond, begun in July 1782 and largely completed by November 1782 (Evans 1990). All four were originally intended to form detached bastions of a large fort on the high ground behind, which was not built. No. 2 is depicted on Gardner's map of 1784 together with a small building outside the gorge to the rear, and is labelled in 1788 as No. 2 (Somerset) Redoubt, when it was armed with seven 18-pdr guns. In 1788, 1808 and 1811 it is shown as being enclosed by a ditch to the rear and to be five-sided; in 1811 ten gun embrasures are shown, six on the two front faces and two on each of the flanks; it was entered via a central causeway across the gorge

Plate 35: Maker Barracks & Redoubt No. 2 (Photograph: S. Hartgroves. Frame: ABP/F35/79. Copyright: Cornwall Archaeological Unit)

ditch. Opposite the entrance in the interior there is a small building, possibly a guardhouse. By this time the barracks had been built to the rear, and by 1808 sections at least of the ditch scarps had been revetted in stone. Apparently it was disarmed in 1815, and by 1896 the ditch to the rear had been infilled. During WWII several Nissen huts and buildings were built within the redoubt but were demolished (except one) in the 1970s. It is probable that the ramparts present on the front face and on the flanks were also largely removed at this time as the embrasures shown on the 1950s O.S map are no longer particularly visible.

The outline of the redoubt is clear with the ditches on the western and southern flanks still open to a considerable depth although heavily overgrown. Very small sections of the scarp revetment wall are visible towards the south. The line of the gorge ditch is visible as a slight hollow to either side of the central causeway. Its southern end lies under a modern building. The rampart has been completely levelled, and at the time of the site visit no clear traces of gun embrasures were visible. There is a marked *glacis* slope to the west.

Present condition

Ditches to the west and south are heavily overgrown. The ditch to the north has been largely infilled with relatively recent dumping, as has the eastern end of the southern ditch. The interior is now rough grassland.

Sources

As for Redoubt No. 1

MAKER BARRACKS

PAR = MAKER, NGR = SX 43475136, PRN = 6113.07, MAP 2 No. 30

The main barrack block, together with the guardhouse, magazine and other ancillary buildings, were built within a walled enclosure immediately to the east of Redoubt No. 3 between 1804 and 1808, to provide permanent accommodation for the garrison of the redoubts. They are depicted on maps of 1808, 1811, 1844, and 1896, and some of the buildings are described in a document of 1882. In 1808 and 1811 the barrack, guardhouse and magazine are shown, together with buildings on the sites of the engine house, toilets,

Plate 36: Maker Barracks (Exeter Archaeology)

ablution block/wash house, womens wash house, straw store, latrines and barrack stores (as labelled on a map of 1896). In 1858 Jervois recommended the provision of a barrack for 1000 men and a battery of field artillery to the rear of the redoubts, to act as a reserve to defend the Anthony Line and Cawsand Bay, & the Royal Commission of 1860 also recommended a barrack for 300 men and the repair and strengthening of the existing redoubts; in neither case was the existing barrack mentioned or the recommendations apparently fully carried out. Additions and alterations which did occur comprised the construction of the officers' stable block and the provision of a musketry *caponier* (later used as an ablution room) at the N. corner of the enclosure in 1848, the reconstruction of the first floor of the barracks in 1858-59, the probable construction of the gun shed and the barrack stores in

Plate 37: Maker Barracks, boot scraper (Exeter Archaeology)

the 1860s/70s, the mens' latrines in 1879, the womens' wash house and straw store in the early 1880s, and the replacement of the earlier cook house by an ablution block in the early 1900s, when another building (now demolished) was built outside the enclosure to the east. Later additions and modifications were also made, probably during WWII when further accommodation blocks were built within the interior of Redoubt No. 2 and between Nos 1 & 2, together with an anti-aircraft battery and associated structures to the east. Latterly it has been used as a school camp, but now lies empty; many of the WWII accommodation buildings were demolished in the 1970s.

Plate 38: Maker Barracks, magazine & gun shed (Exeter Archaeology)

Most of the buildings and the enclosure wall survive complete, although some have been substantially modified. The main barrack is a two-storey building of rubble stone with brick and granite details and a slated hipped roof; it has projecting wings and a cellar under its N.W end; the S wing contained separate officers' quarters. It is entered via loopholed porches at the front and S.E end, a flight of granite steps to the rear, and doors at the N.W end, and retains some detail such as iron boot scrapers, fireplace surrounds, panelling, wooden window joinery (occasionally) and internal shutters, bannisters, 1860s wooden pegs and Victorian/Edwardian iron kitchen ranges/stoves; most of the internal detail survives within the officers' quarters. The guard house is a single storey rubble stone building with a hipped slated roof and two wings, the southern of which is a later brick addition. It contains a cell block at the S end, which retains its original door, 1860s wooden pegs, and a series of graffitti; wooden panelling survives elsewhere. Other buildings of particular interest include:

(i) a small magazine, built of rubble stone with limestone ashlar details with a brick barrel-vaulted roof and internal brick cavity walling, and containing 1860s wooden pegs;

(ii) a gun shed of 4 bays, built of limestone with an open front (later bricked in), possibly for the battery of field artillery recommended in 1858. It retains its original (iron) roof and to the rear is a contemporary extension containing shelf racking; this is probably the shell store marked in 1896;

(iii) the officers' stable, a two-storey red sandstone building with a pitched Delabole slate roof and an 1848 datestone over the doorway; it contains wooden stalls on the ground floor with a hayloft over;

(iv) the wash house, a single-storey red sandstone and limestone building, with a pitched (originally slated) roof; probably 1840s or earlier in date;

(v) the straw store, a single-storey stone building with a central double-doorway (later narrowed and flanked by two inserted windows) and a hipped roof;

(vi) the latrines, which retain their original slate divides;

(vii) the roofless caponier, with an 1848 datestone over its entrance; and

Plate 39: Maker Barracks, latrines (Exeter Archaeology)

(viii) the barrack stores, consisting of a two-storey sandstone building with a pitched roof (now collapsed) and a lean-to and former coal store behind; the former retains some original joinery whilst the latter contains several vertical measuring posts. The enclosure wall displays evidence of several breaks of build, particularly in the sections adjoining the *caponier*, and elsewhere is topped with a decorative course of pitched stone.

Present condition

The whole complex is at present empty; most of the buildings are in reasonable condition, except the latrines and *caponier*, which lie derelict, and the barrack stores, which are of especial concern; its roof has collapsed into the first floor, which has itself largely collapsed as a result, and the structure and the remaining joinery is rapidly deteriorating. The main barrack block has recently been repaired, although some of the beams are still supported on Acrow props.

Sources

General

11, 12, 15, 19; C, K, L, Q.

Specific

1808	Plan of Maker Heights PRO: MR 1209
1811	Plan of Maker Heights redoubts PRO: MPH 233/6
1844	Maker Tithe Map
1882	Plan of Maker Barracks. PRO: WO 78/2975
1886	Plan of Maker Barracks and Devonport. PRO: WO 78/3655

MAKER WWII ANTI-AIRCRAFT BATTERY

PAR = MAKER, NGR = SX 43625147, PRN = 37104, MAP 2 No. 31

This is located on the top of Maker Heights, some 80m N.E of Maker Barracks, and was sited to defend against aircraft using Plymouth Sound as a line of approach. In 1940 it seems to have been armed with four 3.7-inch HAA guns, with the later addition of two more of unknown calibre, but otherwise its history is not documented.

The site lies in a pasture field adjoining the earlier barracks, which were probably used as accommodation for the battery. It consists of a ring of six gun emplacements facing from the N.E around to the N.W, arranged around a partly sunken command post at the centre. There are no visible remains of a central magazine, subsidiary shelters, radar platform or gun store for example, although there is a possible site of a

Plate 40: Maker HAA Battery (Photograph: S. Hartgroves. Frame: ABP/F35/80. Copyright: Cornwall Archaeological Unit)

demolished building built sunk into the ground c. 20m to the N of the command post. The command post is terraced slightly into the hillside and is the same in plan as that at St Winolls Battery A, with a large plotting room to the rear flanked by wing rooms and with various instrument platforms at the front, facing S.S.E towards the sea. No internal fixtures and fittings survive. The six gun positions are of two different types, reflecting the arrangement at Down Thomas. The four positions facing E, S & W are 13 sided in plan, and are of exactly the same design as the emplacements at Bere Alston. They are built of concrete blockwork, with earth mounded over and against the outside for extra protection; a blast wall across the entrance offered the gun crews some additional protection from strafing. Around the sides are a series of ammunition lockers, with a separate shelter on each flank. Where visible the mounting bolts are oval in layout, with a cable duct leading to the centre from a control box next to the entrance (probably at the terminus of cables originating at the control post). A flaking illegible ?regimental or unit crest survives just inside one of the emplacements; no other fixtures survive. The two emplacements facing N.E & N.W are rectangular in plan, and from their position appear to be later additions to the armament. The mounting bolts are different and are arranged in a circle, and may either have held different guns or the same guns on a different type of mounting. Ammunition lockers are arranged around the sides, but there are no separate shelters.

Access to the battery appears to have been via a slightly embanked trackway from the S, and possibly via a footpath to a ramp cut through the N.E wall of the barrack enclosure at this time. Three hut bases located to the S.W just outside the barracks are probably also associated with this battery.

Present condition

The site is at present partly overgrown and used to pasture and shelter stock. Most of the gun positions and the command post are very well preserved, although some concrete block walls have been partly demolished and are beginning to crumble.

Sources

General

25; R.

Plate 41: Maker HAA Battery command post (Exeter Archaeology)

Plate 42: Maker HAA Battery, 3.7" emplacement (Exeter Archaeology)

MAKER REDOUBT No.3

PAR = MAKER, NGR = SX 43645123, PRN = 6113.03, MAP 2 No. 32

This forms the centre left of the line of four redoubts constructed on Maker Heights during the War of American Independance. It was probably started as a temporary redoubt in *c*. 1779 by the 50th Regiment of Foot; subsequently a more permanent redoubt was designed by Dixon and the Duke of Richmond, begun in July 1782 and largely completed by November 1782 (Evans 1990). All four were originally intended to form detached bastions of a large fort on the high ground behind, which was not built. No. 3 is depicted on Gardner's map of 1784 together with a small building outside the gorge to the rear, and is labelled in 1788 as No. 3 (50th Regiment) Redoubt, and was armed with 10 guns. In 1784, 1788, and 1811 it is shown as being enclosed by a ditch to the rear and to be four sided; in 1811 ten gun embrasures are shown, two on the N flank, and four each in the front face and S flank. By 1811 part of the gorge ditch had been removed by quarrying, probably to provide stone for the remodelling of Redoubt Nos 4 & 5 between 1787 and 1791; the entrance is via a bridge over the gorge. It was apparently disarmed in 1815, and marked as dismantled in 1896, when the small building outside had been demolished. During ?WWII Nissen huts were built within the gorge ditch, together with a small building at the E. end of the S. rampart.

The redoubt is very well preserved, although part of the S rampart has been removed and partly dumped into the ditch. It consists of a four sided ditched work, with an overgrown rampart surviving on the N, W, and part of the S faces; one possible embrasure is visible in the W face. The gorge ditch has a drystone masonry scarp, which has been removed at the south when the ditch was widened and partly infilled, presumably to create access to the quarry; traces of a stone scarp also survive elsewhere. The interior is open, and contains a soldier's grave slab dating to the 1890s (now obscured by vegetation); the site of the building to the east is heavily overgrown and inaccessible; its N.W end may have been quarried away after 1811. Two concrete Nissen hut bases lie within the gorge ditch; there is no trace of the bridge. Outside the redoubt the extensive *glacis* slope is visible to the south and west.

Present condition

The ramparts and the bottoms of the W & S ditches are overgrown; the S end of the gorge ditch and the E. end of the S ditch have been partly infilled, and most of the S rampart demolished (since the 1950s). The *glacis* forms part of a pasture field; the redoubt is not used at all.

Sources

As for Redoubt No.1.

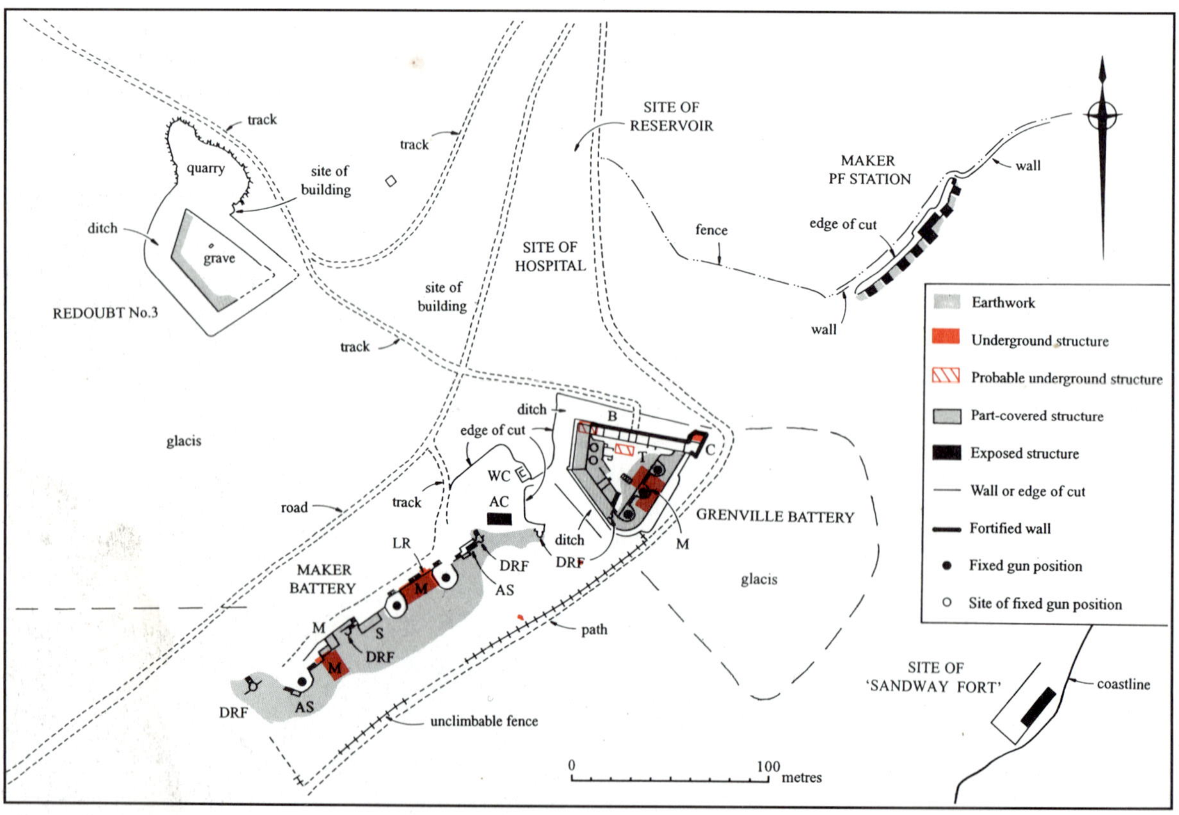

Fig. 25: Maker Redoubts Nos 3 & 4, Grenville & Maker Batteries & the PF Station

MAKER REDOUBT No. 4

PAR = MAKER, NGR = SX 43855113, PRN = 6113.04, MAP 2 No. 33

This forms the southernmost of the line of four redoubts constructed on Maker Heights during the War of American Independance. It was probably started as a temporary redoubt in *c*. 1779 by the North Gloucester Militia; it was designed in a more permanent form by Dixon and the Duke of Richmond, begun in July 1782 and largely completed by November 1782 (Evans 1990). All four were originally intended to form detached bastions of a large fort on the high ground behind which was not built. On the defeat of this scheme Redoubt Nos 4 & 5 were strengthened between July 1787 and summer 1791 by the addition of stone revetments, loopholed stone barrack blocks along the gorge, bomb proof magazines and gun platforms; a musketry *caponier* protected the southern sea facing flank of No. 4, with the later addition (in Dec. 1787) of another to protect the gorge. The stone was obtained from a quarry adjoining the road (at SX 43765123, see Evans 1990), and possibly from the quarry to the rear of Redoubt No. 3. In 1788 it was labelled as No. 4 (North Gloucester) Redoubt, and in 1808 & 1811 is shown as having eight gun embrasures, one on the short southern flank, four on the S.W flank, and three on the west flank; none are shown on the S.E sea-facing flank. In 1790 it was armed with 8 guns, probably 32-pdrs, and was disarmed in 1815. By 1849 however three 10-inch, three 68-pdr and four 32-pdr guns had been approved. In 1887 it was remodelled and in 1899 was renamed Grenville Battery. During and shortly after WWII the barrack blocks in Nos 4 & 5 were apparently occupied by Plymouth families displaced by the Blitz.

Plate 44: Barracks in Redoubt No. 4 (Exeter Archaeology)

The redoubt lies about 325 feet above sea level, at the summit of a steep slope down to the sea. Much of the 1791 structure remains despite the later remodelling, which is largely restricted to the southern sea-facing flank. It is defended by a stone-revetted ditch on the land-facing flanks and the gorge, and by two musketry *caponiers* at its S.E corner; one of two levels enfilading the gorge, and the other the southern flank. The gorge is further defended by a long brick vaulted building containing musketry loops slanted so as to cover the main entrance. This is single storey, was originally slated, and was subdivided to provide heated barrack accommodation; some detail survives, such as the iron frames of shutters on the inside of the musketry loops, and one of the main double gates; the surviving joinery is of unknown date. In the interior there is a gun platform behind a rampart on the N.W & S.W faces, with a store room (later used as an Artillery Store) under. Later buildings adjoin the rear of the platform

Plate 43: Maker Battery & Redoubt No. 4 (Photograph: S. Hartgroves. Frame: ABP/F35/50. Copyright: Cornwall Archaeological Unit)

and the barrack block. On the outside the *glacis* slope to the west has been largely removed by the construction of Maker Battery; the steep slope down to the sea does appear to have been landscaped and was presumably covered by musketry fire from the S flank and *caponier*.

Present condition

The redoubt is derelict, and the ramparts and ditches on the landward side are heavily overgrown. The S.end of the gorge ditch has been partly infilled, and a causeway has been built across the site of the bridge to provide access. The interior is used as a boat store, together with the barrack block; the magazines and artillery store remain empty. Since WWII the slates have been removed from the roof of the barrack, and in places holes have developed in the brick vaulting; it is only a matter of time before substantial sections collapse.

Sources

General

As for Redoubt No. 1

Specific

1786 Proposed alterations to North Gloucester Redoubt PRO: MPHH 549

1790 N. Gloucester Redoubt PRO: MPH 731

1849 Maps showing armament. Royal Citadel Officers Mess.

Rest as for Redoubt No. 1

GRENVILLE BATTERY

PAR = MAKER, NGR = SX 43855113, PRN = 6113.04, MAP 2 No. 34

A sea-facing battery built within the earlier Maker No. 4 Redoubt. It was proposed in 1885 for two 38-ton 12.5-inch RML guns and was completed in 1887. Also proposed was a moveable armament of 4 ?40-pdr RBL guns; a shed for moveable armament was present at Maker Battery to the south of Grenville by 1901. A plan of 1896 shows the two gun emplacements, together with a cook house adjoining the rear of the earlier N.W. gun platform. In either 1890 (Fort Record Book) or 1892 (Naval and Military Magazine) the guns were removed to the recently constructed Maker Battery, and in 1899 Grenville was remodelled to accommodate three 4.7-inch QF guns, which were mounted in 1901. These were flanked by two 'lookout' posts, and remained in place until at least 1927; they were used as a practice battery in 1908. Grenville was abandoned by the MoD in 1948.

Plate 45: Grenville Battery, 4.7-in QF emplacements (Exeter Archaeology)

The earlier RML and subsequent QF emplacements were constructed on the S. flank of the earlier redoubt, which was extended and revetted in concrete to accommodate the guns and the underlying magazines. The three QF positions survive complete, although most of the guard rails and the doors of the store recesses have been removed and the mounting bolts are not visible. Ammunition was brought up from the magazines below via a shaft and davit; a similar arrangement may have served the RML guns. One observation post is visible on the right flank, the other was not identified. The magazines have been adapted, presumably in 1899-1901, with a flat ceiling replacing the earlier jack vaulting of the RML magazines. Remains of the brick cook house abut the rear of the earlier gun platform.

Present condition

Derelict. The magazines are empty, but are structurally sound; a recent attempt has been made by trespassers to remove the davit. The cook house is a ruin. The ramparts are overgrown, and the outer concrete revetment wall is cracked at its W. end.

Sources

General

17, 19, 21, 24; F, K, L, O, Q.

Specific

1892 ?Naval and Military Magazine.

1896 Plan of battery. PRO: MR 1412

1901 Plan of modification for 4.7-inch guns. PRO: WO 78/5051

1901 Arcs of fire PRO: WO 78/4149

n.d ?Armament refs PRO: CAB 16/1 & 36/16

MAKER BATTERY

PAR = MAKER, NGR = SX 43735105, PRN = 6121, MAP 2 No. 35

This was built in 1886-87 to cover Cawsand Bay and the western approaches to the Sound, as part of the modernisation of the coastal defences recommended by the Stanhope Report of 1887. With the two heavy RML guns mounted at Grenville immediately to the E, and other batteries in Cornwall at Hawkins, Raleigh, Penlee, Rame Church, Whitsand Bay and Tregantle Down, it was intended to defend the dockyard against battleships standing off and bombarding it by providing plunging fire down onto their decks. It is therefore sited at about 300 feet above sea level, and on the seaward side is deliberately masked from view by earthworks landscaped into the natural contours.

Plate 46: Maker Battery, 12.5-in RML emplacement (Exeter Archaeology)

The detailed history of the armament and buildings of the battery is closely linked with that of Grenville Battery, from which at times it is difficult to distinguish; in some sources both batteries are collectively referred to as Maker Battery until the re-naming of No. 4 Redoubt as Grenville Battery in *c.* 1899. The initial armament of the present Maker Battery was one 38-ton 12.5-inch RML gun, accompanying the two installed at Grenville. In 1890 the latter were moved to new emplacements to the W, possibly represented by the two western emplacements of Maker Battery shown on the 1896 map (these are the only ones shown with aprons and form a pair), and in 1892 Maker Battery is recorded as mounting three 38-ton RML guns. In 1894 the battery is recorded as having been completed as a two-gun battery, with the subsequent addition of another emplacement and magazine; the re-emplacement of the original two guns is not mentioned. In the early 1900s the northern two RML emplacements were replaced by two 6-inch Mark VII BL gun emplacements; these guns were mounted by 1903. They were still present in 1908, but appear to have been removed by WWI as they are not shown on maps of 1911 and 1915. Other buildings referred to include two stores and a shed for moveable armament; the latter is not shown on the 1896 map and probably, together with the toilet block, dates to the construction of the BL Battery in 1901-3. One Depression Range Finder (DRF) is marked to the east of the battery in 1896, with three others being added later; two of these flank the BL gun positions and probably date to the early 1900s; the other lies beyond the western limit of the battery and probably dates to the late 1890s before the RMLs were replaced. No known military use was made of the site during the two World Wars. The site was released by the MoD in 1956.

The battery is sited along the top of a ridge extending westwards from Grenville Battery. The two 6-inch BL gun positions and the westernmost RML position survive complete, together with accompanying earth-covered bomb-proof magazines, shelters and stores, and the four DRF positions. The battery was surrounded by an unclimbable fence, large sections of which still survive along the coastal path; this probably dates to the 1890s, as it encompasses the surviving RML position. This retains its circular racer rails and a central pivot (which is an upturned SB gun), with an underground ?artillery store to the W and an underground cartridge store and hoist to the E, with a shell store above. The two concrete 6-inch BL positions retain their aprons, sawn-off mounting bolts, and some of the fighting-light brackets and the iron shutters of the cartridge lifts, but the guard rails, davit, and most of the shutters of the store recesses have been removed. The eastern position is constructed on the site of the eastern RML position, whilst the western position is sited to the W of the central RML position, which is occupied by an earth-covered shelter. An underground magazine is sited between the two BL guns, and consists of a central shifting lobby flanked by shell and cartridge stores, with a lamp-room off the entrance stairwell. At each end there is a serving hatch and separate cartridge and shell lifts. Few internal

Plate 47: Maker Battery, unclimbable fence (Exeter Archaeology)

fittings survive except for the shell lifts; these appear largely intact except for their winding handles and chains. To the E of the gun positions there is a bomb-proof brick-built artillery store with armoured door and barred windows with armoured shutters; it is contemporary with the RML battery. A later rectangular brick building with double doors (possibly the shed for moveable armament) occupies a terrace to the E, together with a brick toilet block. All four DRF positions survive complete, and consist of a central instument pillar flanked by recesses within the retaining walls; the two central positions are approached via steps and the earlier eastern one via a sunken way from the rear of the battery; the western one is inaccessible.

Present condition

Largely derelict. The shelter and magazines of the BL guns and the ?shed for moveable armament are used as fishermens' stores and workshops; the magazines however are not maintained and are heavily cluttered, and have recently suffered fire damage. The RML magazine is derelict and empty and is used for dumping rubbish; the hoist mechanism may survive largely complete under a heap of rubble; the only other contemporary example known to survive in the Plymouth area is at Staddon Heights Battery. The artillery store and the toilet block lie empty, and the latter together with the western DRF position is heavily overgrown. The structure of the battery is largely intact, although gradually deteriorating through lack of maintenance and damp. However, the section of retaining wall to the W of the western BL position is leaning outwards and is in danger of collapse, and dumping is occurring to the rear of this area. The area surrounding the emplacements and buildings is scrub and heath land.

Sources

General

17, 18, 19, 21, 23, 24; C, K, Q.

Specific

1892	?Armament tables. PRO: WO 196/29
1893	?Armament tables. PRO: CAB 7/6
1899	Plan. PRO: WO 78/4259
1900	Plan. PRO: WO 78/2610
1902	Plan of arcs of fire. PRO: WO 78/4148
1905	?Armament tables. PRO: CAB 16/1

MAKER POSITION-FINDER STATION

PAR = MAKER, NGR = SX 44005125, PRN = 6113.11, MAP 2 No. 36

This is located on the brow of a steep slope down to the sea, some 200m to the N.E of Grenville Battery on the other side of a coombe. It consists of seven PF cells built in the late 1880s, presumably to direct the guns emplaced at the new Maker Battery and perhaps Raleigh and Cawsand Batteries also. They were built by 1894, and were still in use in 1903. By 1915 however they had become redundant, as they are not shown on a plan of the fortress telecommunications network of that date.

The PF cells are built along the front of a terrace cut into the hillside, spoil from which has been embanked between and in front of the lower part of the cells below their windows to mask them from the enemy's view and protect them from incoming fire. Access is shown on the 1896 map in the form of a footpath from the W, but there is a surviving flight of steps at the E end, and a possible trackway below the cells at this end leading away downhill to the E. Six of the cells survive in the form depicted in 1896, and consist of simple square buildings with brick walls and concrete roofs sloping down from rear to front. The roofs are supported at the sides on iron RSJs, and at the front overhang a rectangular window which affords views to the front and sides; each cell is entered from the rear, and none retain instrument pillars. One cell has however been extended to the rear and has had an extra room added, necessitating some further terracing; this occurred after 1896 and probably after 1903, and may represent the conversion of one of the PF cells into a Fire Commander's cell.

Present condition

The cells are derelict, and heavily overgrown, although accessible with effort. In several the front part of the roofs have collapsed or are in the process of collapsing due to the corrugated iron on the underside of the concrete having rusted and fallen off and the RSJs to each side rusting and rotting away. The converted cell however is in a reasonable state of preservation. The whole area is heavily overgrown.

Sources

General

18, 19, 23, 24.

MAKER HOSPITAL

PAR = MAKER, NGR = SX 43825123, PRN = 6113.9, MAP 2 No. 37

This is sited to the rear of No. 4 Redoubt, overlooking a steep coombe leading down to the sea. It was present by 1808, and was probably built with the barracks in 1804. It is depicted on maps of 1808, 1811, 1844, 1896, and ?1914, and probably became disused shortly afterwards.

The hospital building is shown as having two wings projecting eastwards from each end, with an extension to the rear, and enclosed by a wall. By 1896 a smaller enclosure had been added to the south. The remains of the hospital are sited within an impenetrable area of thorn scrub, although some wall foundations are visible at its S.E corner adjoining the track; no standing buildings or walls are visible.

Present condition

The buildings and enclosure wall have been demolished down to just above their foundations; the site lies undisturbed within an area of scrub and undergrowth.

Sources

General

19; C, K.

Specific

1808	Plan of Maker Heights PRO: MR 1209
1811	Plan of Maker Heights PRO: MPH 233/6
1844	Maker Tithe Map
1914	O.S 1:2500 Sheet LV6

MAKER HEIGHTS RESERVOIR

PAR = MAKER, NGR = SX 43835130, PRN = 6113.10, MAP 2 No. 37

This is sited *c.*30 metres north of the hospital, and was built between 1896 and ?1914, possibly to serve the new batteries of Grenville and Maker. It has been infilled (or is a covered chamber), and was surrounded by Norton iron fencing, some stanchions of which are still visible; its site is visible as a terrace. It was built on the site of a shed marked on maps of 1808 and 1811 (which had been demolished by 1896), and contained a pump house, the site of which is not visible. Some 10-20 metres to the north (at SX 43835134) is an earlier small stone shed with a brick barrel-vaulted roof; although 1860s or earlier in character and marked on the 1896 map, it contains a later concrete slab roof and may have been associated with the reservoir; its original function is not known, it may have been an earlier pump or well house, or possibly a sentry post (although rather isolated).

Present condition

Reservoir overgrown, S part more so, and waterlogged in very wet weather. The earlier building to the north is partly ruinous, with one side wall largely demolished.

Sources

General

19

Specific

1808	Plan of Maker Heights PRO: MR 1209
1811	Plan of Maker Heights PRO: MPH 233/6
1950s	O.S. 1:2500 map

'SANDWAY FORT'

PAR = MAKER, NGR = SX 44035103, PRN = 6129, MAP 2 No. 38

A fort or battery has been thought to have been sited on the coastal slope just above the Sandway fish cellars, and directly below Maker Redoubt No. 4 (Grenville Battery). Sheppard (1975) dates it to 1865, whilst Woodward (1990) thought it may have been built in *c.*1804 to cover the southern flank of the Maker Heights position. However, there is no direct evidence for a fort in this location, and it would seem to be an unlikely site for the following reasons:

(i) it is overlooked, and presumably exposed to fire from, Maker Redoubt No. 4 (of earlier date) on the hill above;

(ii) there is no evidence of a ditch, rampart, or fortified walling on any of the historic or O.S maps or on the ground; the only physical remains consist of the stone walls of the fish cellars on the foreshore below, stone field walls with later brick piers flanking the track down to the cellars, and three brick buildings housing concrete machinery plinths in the undergrowth above (these, together with an enclosure, are shown on maps after 1914 and probably date to the last war; their exact functions are not clear);

(iii) there is no reference to such a fortification in the Royal Commission recommendations of 1860 or in the subsequent reports of 1867 & 1869, which otherwise detail all the fortifications planned and built at this time (with the exception of naval reserve batteries adjoining the dockyard); and

(iv) there may be some confusion with a battery depicted by Dixon and Cowl in 1780 at or near 'Warn Sandway', some 500m to the N.W (see under entry for Sandway Battery).

Present condition

An area of coastal slope, with rough grazing and scrub adjoining the sea cliff. The brick buildings survive largely complete although heavily overgrown. One has been used as temporary accommodation by tramps.

Sources
General
5, 6, 12, 14, 15; L, O, Q.

MAKER REDOUBT No. 5

PAR = MAKER, NGR = SX 43815196, PRN = 6113.05, MAP 2 No. 39

This protects the northern flank of the line of four redoubts (Nos 1-4) constructed on Maker Heights during the War of American Independence. It was probably begun as a temporary redoubt in *c.* 1779 by the 2nd Devon Militia; subsequently it was designed in a more permanent form by Dixon and the Duke of Richmond in 1781-82. Construction began in July 1782, and was mostly complete by February 1783, when bad weather stopped work (Evans 1990). All five redoubts were originally intended to form detached bastions of a large fort on the high ground to the south of No. 5 which was not built. On the defeat of this scheme No. 5 was strengthened between July 1787 and summer 1791 by the addition of stone revetments, a loopholed stone barrack/storeroom/guardroom along the gorge, and gun platforms. The stone may have been obtained from a small quarry *c.* 100m to the south (at SX 43765182), or from other quarries to the rear of No. 3 and adjoining Earl's Drive (at SX 43765123). In 1788 it was labelled as No. 5 or 2nd Devon Redoubt, and in 1808 and 1811 is shown as having nine gun embrasures, two on the north flank, three on the south, and four on the west face, with a small building outside the gorge to the rear; its armament (if any) is not known. It was apparently ruinous by 1866, and in WWII the barrack block was occupied by Plymouth families displaced by the Blitz.

The redoubt lies at the top of a steep wooded slope down to Millbrook Lake to the north, and covers the north flank of Redoubt No. 1 and the road from Millbrook to Cremyll. All the 1791 structure remains intact, apart from the drawbridge (now gone) and the building outside the gorge (demolished by 1896). The steeply battered scarp and ditch counterscarp are revetted with coursed dressed stone, and the scarp is topped with a limestone/granite cordon, with an earthwork rampart above protecting gun platforms behind. The stone barrack block along the gorge is similar in form to No. 4, and contains musketry loops aligned so as to protect the entrance; this was via a bridge (the stone piers are still present) over the gorge. The interior is no longer accessible except by rope, and was not viewed; any bomb-proof magazines were presumably sited under the gun platforms (*terreplein*). Outside the redoubt is surrounded by a rock-cut ditch to the south and east, and a terrace to the north and west; a well-preserved landscaped *glacis* slope lies to

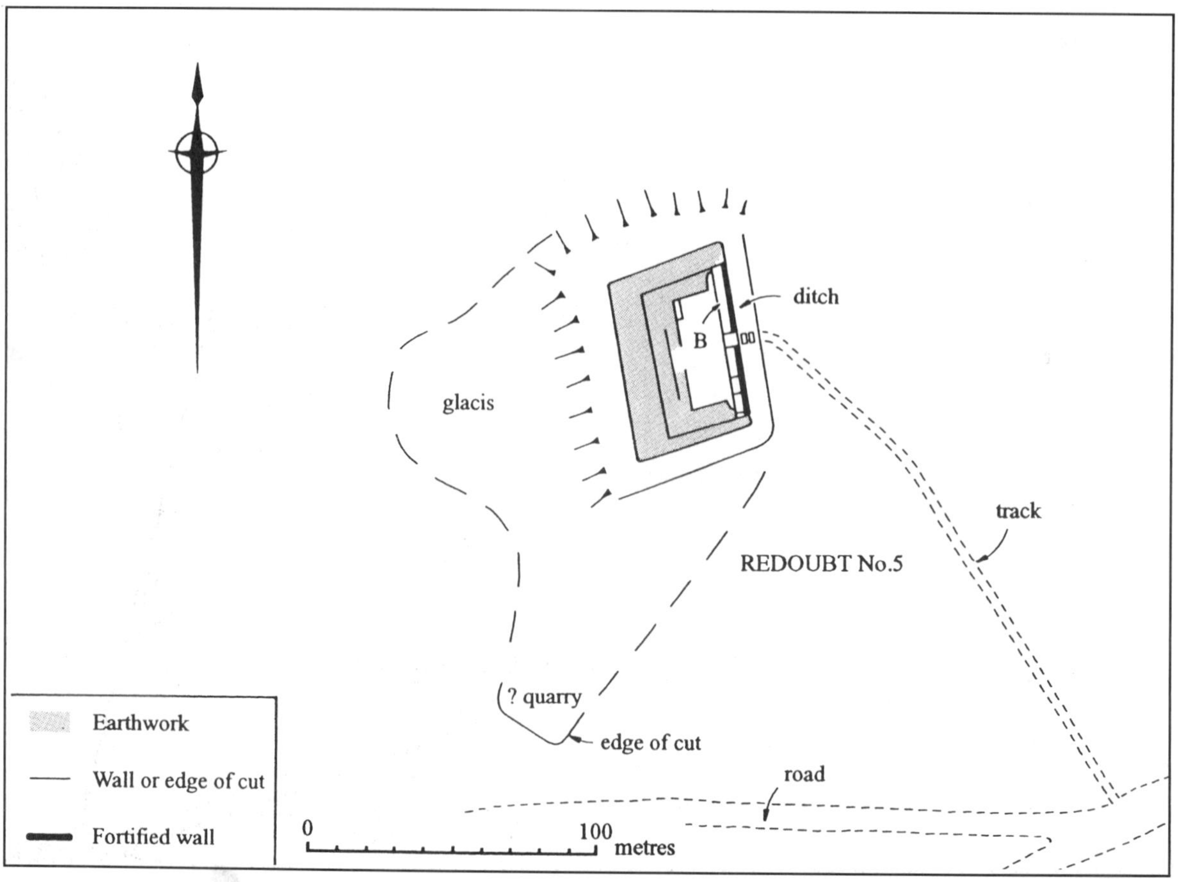

Fig. 26: Maker Redoubt No. 5

the west and around to the south-west, whilst to the north the ground slopes away very steeply and does not appear to be landscaped. The site of the small building survives as a small terrace, and access to the redoubt is via the original embanked metalled trackway from the road to the south.

Present condition

The redoubt is derelict, empty and largely inaccessible, and the ramparts and probably much of the interior are heavily overgrown. Sections of the stone facing of the scarp are loose and some of the facing stones have been lost, although overall the scarp and counterscarp walls are in reasonable condition, as is the exterior of the barrack block. The field is used for pasturing cattle;

Plate 48: Maker Redoubt No. 5 (Photograph: A. Sharpe. Frame: ACS 3034. Copyright: Cornwall Archaeological Unit)

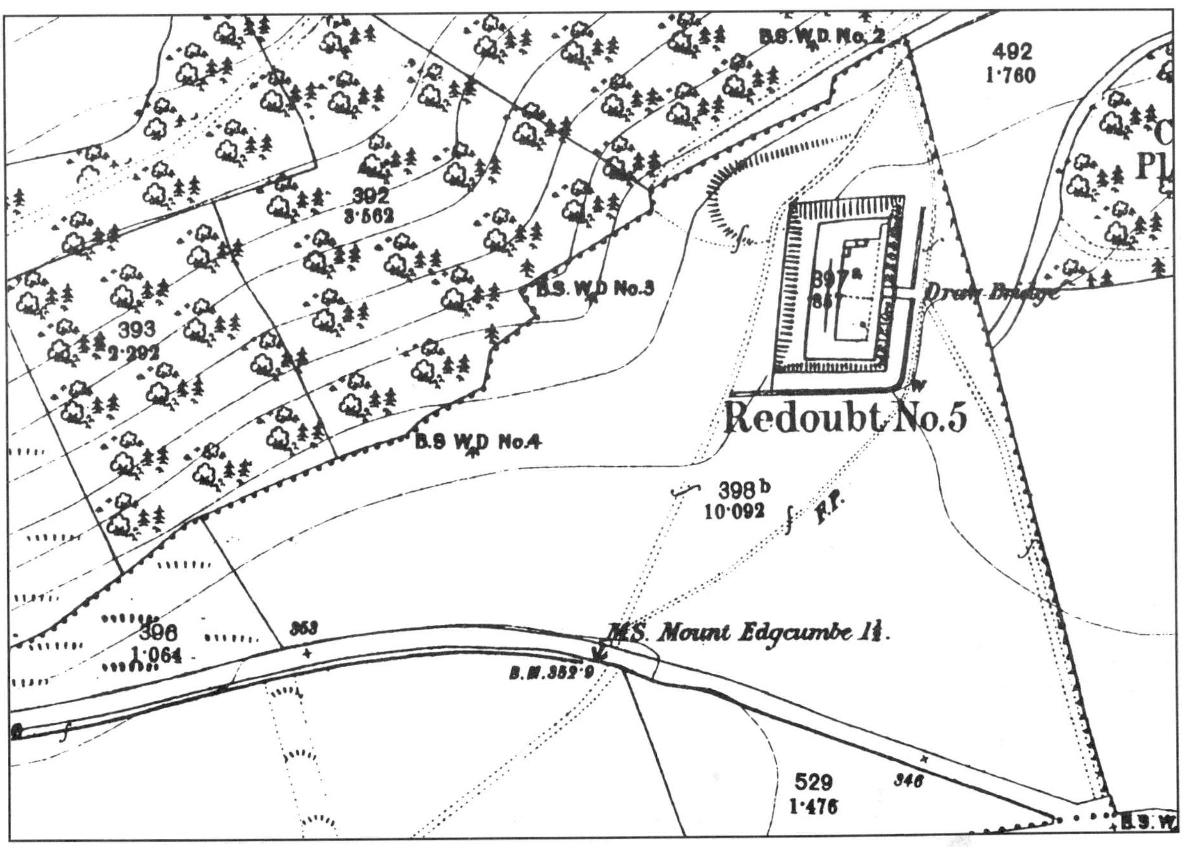

Fig. 27: Maker Redoubt No. 5 in 1896 (PRO: WO 78/2314)

Plate 49: Maker Redoubt No. 5 & glacis (Exeter Archaeology)

these shelter in the gorge ditch, and feed is left here and in the area to the east immediately above. This area, including the site of the small building, is being churned up by cattle and by the storage and movement of heavy logs, and the access track is used by farm vehicles.

Sources
As for Redoubt No. 1.

EMPACOMBE REDOUBT (MAKER REDOUBT NO. 6)

PAR = MAKER, NGR = SX 44255264, PRN = 6113.06, MAP 2 No. 40

This is sited some 1 - 1.5km to the N.E of the other five Maker redoubts, just below the brow of a low hill and overlooking Millbrook Lake. It faces WSW and was intended to command the northern flank of the Maker Heights position to the N of Redoubt No. 5 and Millbrook Lake, and possibly to cover the King's Brewhouse at Southdown. It was proposed in 1808 during the Napoleonic War and completed by 1811, when a plan was produced to accompany Lieutenant General Mercer's inspectional report on the fortifications. It is shown as square in plan and surrounded by a ditch, with projecting *caponiers* at its S.E & N.W corners containing the magazine and store room, a gun platform along its W side and infantry firing steps along the other three sides, a guardhouse in the centre, and the main entrance and bridge in the centre of its E side. It was probably disarmed by 1815 (if indeed guns were mounted in the first place), and was apparently partly ruinous by 1866, when it housed some forty artillerymen and officers.

The redoubt is square in shape and surrounded by a stone-revetted ditch at least *c.* 4m deep. It has a stone-revetted gun platform on the W side, fronted in part with the remnants of an earthen parapet and containing faint impressions of possible individual gun platforms. Remains of the infantry firing steps may survive to the S of the entrance; elsewhere the profile seems to have been removed by gardening activity. The single-storey ?brick-built guardhouse remains intact and has a

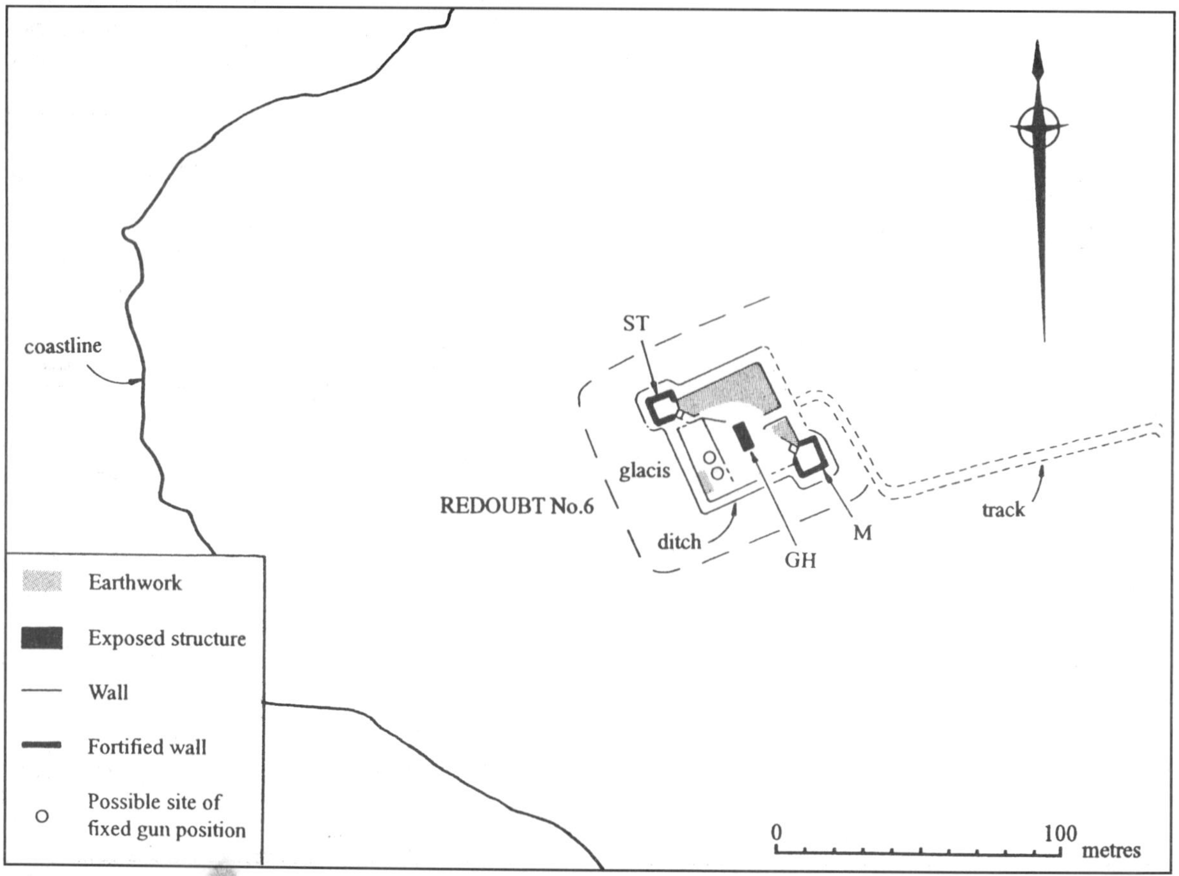

Fig. 28: Empacombe Redoubt

Plate 50: Empacombe Redoubt, musketry caponier (Exeter Archaeology)

pitched slated roof. Both *caponiers* contain a single level of horizontal sandstone musketry loops covering the area beyond the ditch as well as along it; these have either been blocked up, rendered over, or converted into larger windows. The S.E *caponier* has a parapet at roof level, whilst the other has been subsequently heightened and a second floor added. No original internal detail is visible in any of the structures, which are all well-decorated and occupied. The immediate area surrounding the redoubt on the N, W and S sides forms a levelled *glacis* (in effect the levelled upcast from the ditch); there is no clear evidence of landscaping within the fields beyond, although presumably this area was kept free of obstructions.

Present condition

Overall the structure is in good condition; more recent additions and alterations have been made to the buildings and some sections of the ditch have been infilled or are heavily overgrown.

Sources

General

C, L, O, Q.

Specific

1808	Plan of proposed redoubt. PRO: MR1211
1810	Sections through proposed redoubt. PRO: MPH 733
1811	Plan accompanying Mercer's inspectional report. PRO: MPH 233(5)
1817	Gilbert, C.S. *Historical survey of Cornwall* **2**, 382
1824	Hitchens, F. & Drew, S. *History of Cornwall* **2**, 445

SANDWAY BATTERY

PAR = MAKER, NGR = SX 44465135, PRN = 38554, MAP 2 No. 41

A battery of four 18-pdr guns is shown in this approximate location on both Dixon's map of 1780 (as battery F) and Cowl's map of the same date (as battery Q). In Dixon's report of January 1780 it is listed as one of the batteries completed in 1779 and as 'furnished with four 18 pdrs and intended to flank shore between Kinsand and Reading Point'; a further document dating to *c.* 1780 gives its height above sea level as 106 feet. It is not shown on any later plans such as those drawn up by Gardner in 1784 or Sturt in 1788, and therefore appears to have become redundant at the end of the American War of Independance in 1783.

The most likely site for the battery is a relatively level area of land which projects out from the coastline and lies at a height of 100-120 feet above sea level. It lies on the seaward side of the coastal track, and is covered by impenetrable scrub. Alternatively, it may have been sited slightly to the S, where it appears to be depicted by Cowl; however this lies at 150 feet, and is a steep

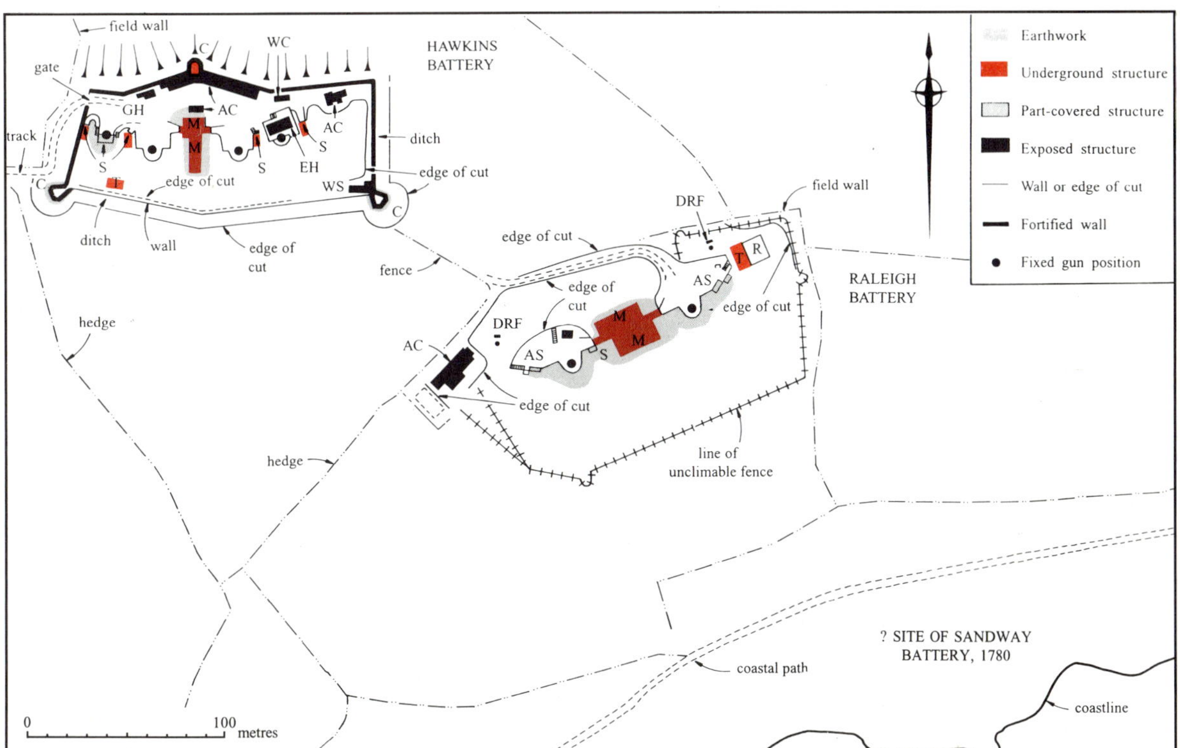

Fig. 29: Raleigh, Hawkins & Sandway Batteries

slope, containing terracing belonging to a disused quarry. The first site appears most likely, given its height above sea level and its suitability for commanding the bay.

Present condition
The site is completely overgrown with scrub, covering any surface remains or indications there may be.

Sources
General
4 - 7, 8.

RALEIGH BATTERY

PAR = MAKER, NGR = SX 44355147, PRN = 6126, MAP 2 No. 42

This is located on the crest of the ridge to the E of Maker Farm and Hawkins Battery, and faces S over Cawsand Bay and the approaches to the Sound. It was intended to fulfill a counter-bombardment role, and was deliberately landscaped into the natural contours so as not to be easily visible to enemy ships below. Following a recommendation in 1885 for the emplacement of a 17-inch BL gun to the E of Maker Farm, the present battery was named in 1890 and completed by 1893 (by Messrs Lapthorn & Goad of Plymouth), when an armament of two 10-inch 29-ton breech-loading (BL) guns was approved. These were mounted *en barbette* by January 1894, and remained in place until 1908, when they were placed in reserve. The guns had been dismounted by 1910, and the battery was abandoned by the MoD in 1946.

The battery and its associated buildings survives intact. It consists of two concrete gun emplacements, access to which is via a sunken trackway to the rear and flights of steps to each side. The gun emplacements are terraced into the slope, and consist of a curved concrete apron and parapet wall containing shell recesses and tackle loops, with store recesses, fighting lights and recesses for control and telephone panels flanking the emplacements to the rear. A central pivot and racer rail survive in the E emplacement, and a ring of tie bolts in the other. Each emplacement is accompanied by an earth covered artillery store with barred windows and an arched recess, and a shelter or lamp room adjoins the W emplacement. The main magazine lies under an earthen traverse between the emplacements, to which ammunition was brought via a sloping concrete ramp. A pair of cartridge stores separated by a shifting lobby

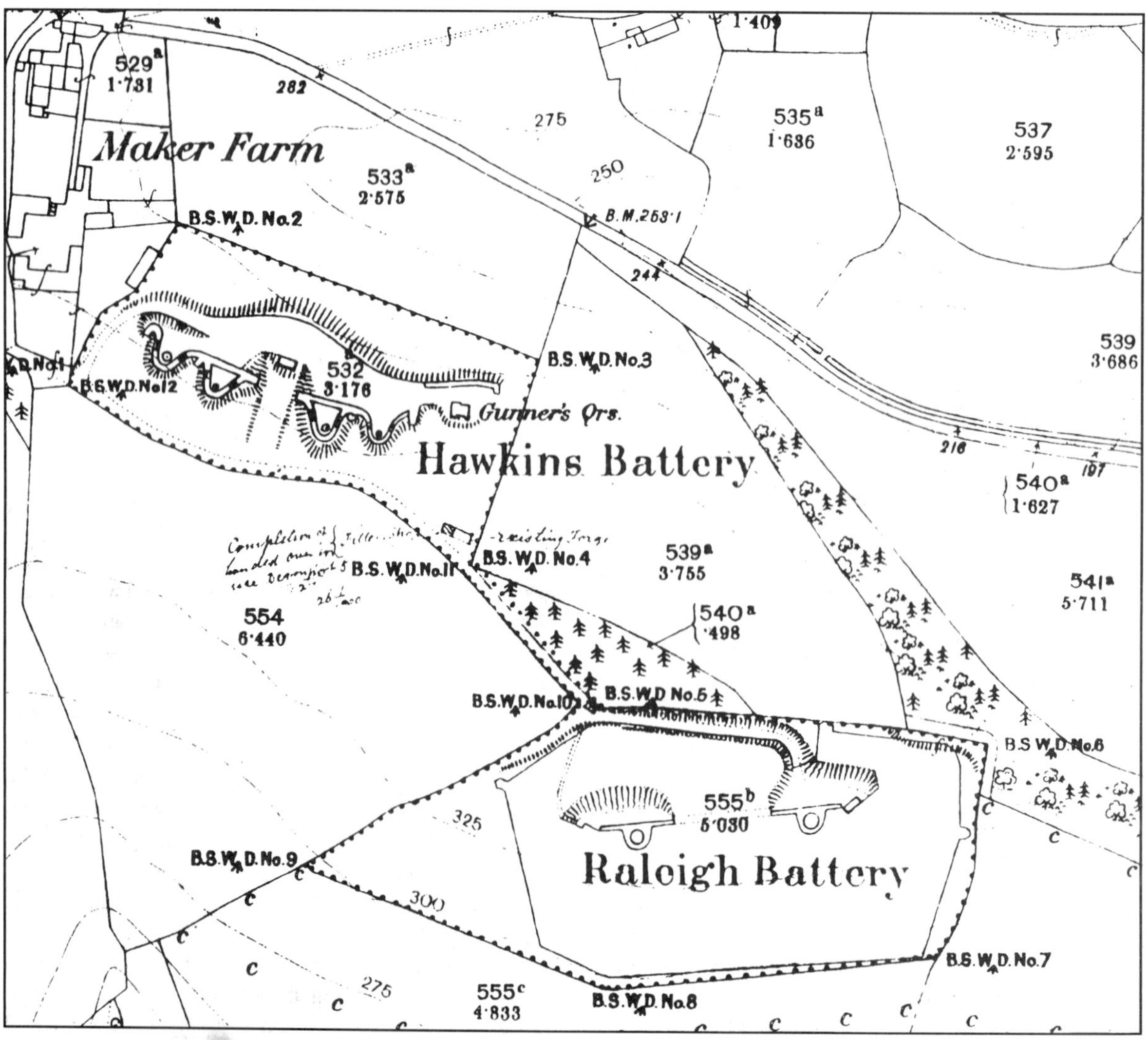

Fig. 30: Raleigh & Hawkins Batteries in 1896 (PRO: WO 78/2314)

open off the central access passage to the S, with a pair of filled shell stores opposite. Structures added after 1896 include a shelter or artillery store to the rear of the W emplacement, two DRF positions flanking the emplacements to the rear, and a brick built accommodation block with verandah and an accompanying ablution block in a terrace to the W. Other structures include a probable toilet and a reservoir and cistern or tank adjoining the E emplacement. In 1896 local defence was provided by an unclimbable iron fence, which included three projecting *caponier* type features; subsequently the fence was extended to the W to include the accommodation block. No lengths of fence remain upright, although sawn off stumps are visible at intervals.

A considerable number of the original fixtures and fittings remain in situ, including the pivots and racer rails, tie-bolts, tackle loops and fighting light brackets of the gun emplacements, the original iron gates, lamp window shutters, shelf brackets and joinery (with room labels) in the main magazine (together with some

Plate 51: Raleigh Battery, 10-in BL emplacement (Exeter Archaeology)

Plate 52: Raleigh Battery, DRF emplacement (Exeter Archaeology)

ammunition boxes), and iron fireplaces and joinery in the accommodation block.

Present condition

Overall the battery is in very good condition considering that is has lain open and derelict since its abandonment in 1946. The gun emplacements are largely clear (and occupied by bee hives), although the terraces to the rear are overgrown, as is the E DRF position. No structural stress is apparent. Much internal detail survives in the magazines, which are open and filled with general rubbish as well as loose ammunition boxes for example; the accommodation block has been largely gutted and the interior filled with mud, although one fireplace remains. The DRF positions survive complete.

Sources

General

13, 17, 18, 19, 21, 23, 24; K, Q.

Specific

1892	Report, letters or proposals. PRO: WO 196/29
1893-1901	Plan and additions. PRO: WO 78/4248
1898	?Armament table. PRO: CAB 7/6
1905	?Armament table. PRO: CAB 16/1
1913	Survey maps. PRO: WO 78/4329

HAWKINS BATTERY

PAR = MAKER, NGR = SX 44105160, PRN = 6125, MAP 2 No. 43

This is located immediately below the crest of a ridge to the E of Maker Farm, and was sited so as not to be visible from the sea; its purpose was to provide plunging fire down on to the decks of enemy ships, so deterring them from bombarding the dockyard. The guns were served by the Position Finding Stations at Middle Barton and Knatterbury. The battery was first proposed in 1885, with an intended armament of six high-angle 12-ton 9-inch RML howitzers; it was completed in 1892-93 (by Messrs Pothick Bros of Plymouth) for four guns, which were mounted in December 1893. These were present (although not operational between 1906-08) until 1913-14, when the battery was rebuilt to accommodate the two high-angle Mk VI 9.2-inch BL guns approved in 1910. These were mounted in November 1914 and were still present in 1927; however they were dismounted by WWII and the battery was released by the MoD in 1946.

The battery occupies a rectangular plot of land immediately to the E of Maker Farm; the gun emplacements have been terraced into the slope, with the spoil forming a terrace to the rear. Two general phases of (wholly concrete) construction are evident, belonging to the original battery of 1892-93 and the rebuilding and alterations of 1913-14. The original plan of the battery is clearly illustrated on the 1896 map. The four 9-inch RML positions are still evident, although much modified, together with remnants of the ramps for bringing shells up on to the concrete parapet to be loaded into the muzzles of the guns and the four expense magazines or stores in the earthen traverses between each gun pit. Other original structures include the main magazine, a shelter to the rear of it, the Gunners' Quarters (a single-storey brick-built house), and the forge adjoining the original track to Raleigh Battery. The main magazine is sited in a central traverse between the two pairs of guns, and consists of a cartridge and a shell store, and a lamp room. There is no remaining evidence of any original local defence arrangements for the battery; this may have consisted of an unclimbable fence along the War Dept. boundary, which would have subsequently been removed in 1913-14.

Plate 53: Hawkins Battery, 9.2-in H/A BL emplacement (Exeter Archaeology)

The 1913-14 alterations included the complete re-building of the two central gun positions to take the two high-angle 9.2-inch BL guns, entailing the removal of the earlier ramps and trolleyways, the construction of a larger circular gun pit (the outlines of both of which are evident), and a new concrete parapet containing store recesses at the sides. Other new structures included a guardroom and a series of accommodation blocks (including a wash room and separate toilet block) along the rear of the emplacements, and a generator house and shelter constructed within the redundant RML emplacements. The gunners' quarters was also extended at this time, and a new ammunition store added to the main magazine, in which electric lighting replaced the lamps. The defence of the battery was also considerably strengthened by the construction of a concrete loopholed wall along the rear and flanks, and a dry moat along the front and flanks. Firing-steps and raised walkways were provided for the (armoured) loopholes, whilst a parapet wall (with a walkway behind) ran along the scarp of the front ditch. Further protection was provided by concrete loopholed *caponiers* at each front corner and in the centre of the rear (gorge) wall.

Plate 54: Hawkins Battery, loopholed wall (Exeter Archaeology)

Present condition

The structure of the battery remains almost wholly complete, except for some minor alterations and extensions relating to the present use of the site as holiday accommodation. However, the structures of the S.W & S.E *caponiers* are beginning to crack and deteriorate, and the armoured loophole plates in the main wall are rusting, expanding and causing the concrete to crack and fall away; a similar problem is probably being caused by rusting RSJs within the walls and supporting the flat concrete roofs of the buildings. The moat is also heavily overgrown and partly waterlogged, and there has been some dumping into it at the W end. Overall much of the original joinery survives, including door and window frames, the louvred vent of the generator house, and sliding wooden vent covers and room labels within the main magazine; other surviving details of particular interest include hammock hooks within the 1914 accommodation blocks, armoured loophole shutters within all three *caponiers*, and the remaining tie-bolts for the eastern RML gun mounting.

Sources

General

17, 18, 19, 21, 23; K, Q.

Specific

1885-92	Recommendations and proposals. PRO WO: 196/19
1905	Plan. PRO: WO 78/5068
1905	?Armament table. PRO: CAB 16/1
1913	Plan. PRO: WO 78/4329
1927	?Armament table. PRO: CAB 36/16

3.2.3. Kingsand and Cawsand

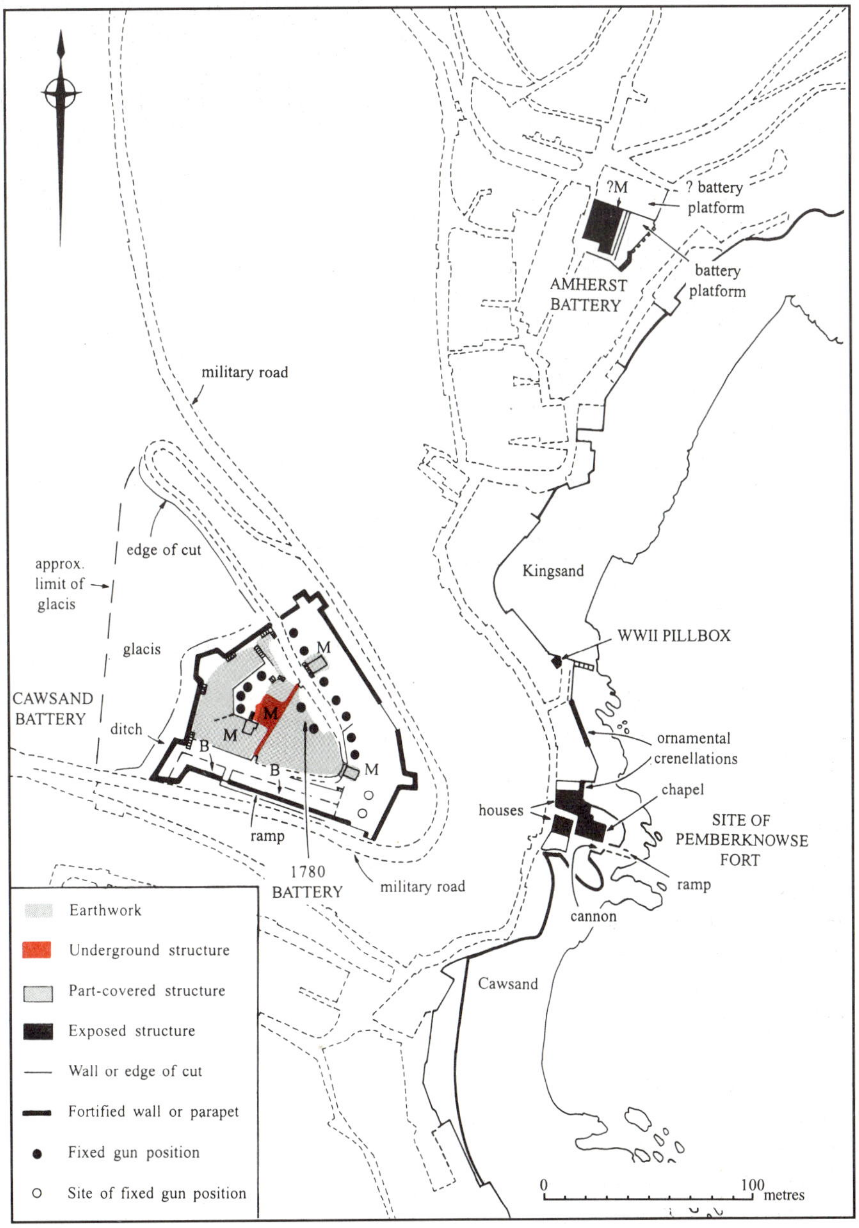

Fig. 31: Fortifications in Kingsand & Cawsand

CAWSAND BATTERY 'A'

PAR = RAME, NGR = SX 43355034 or 43495031, PRN = 6156.1, MAP 2 No. 17

A battery, maintained by the Edgcumbe family and armed with two demi-culverins and two sakers, is recorded at Cawsand in 1616 & 1625, and may be the battery of four guns apparently present in 1690 and recorded by Colonel Christian Lilly in 1716. Earlier a proposed garrison of 300 men for the bay is shown on Grenvyle's map of 1586-88, but no batteries or bulwarks are depicted. A Royalist 'fort' or battery of three guns is also recorded in Cawsand during the Civil War. No fortifications however are depicted in charts of the mid or later 18th century, except for Amherst Battery in Kingsand in 1770 and the later Cawsand Battery B built in 1779 (see separate entries). The earlier battery or batteries have been thought to lie up on the spur separating Kingsand from Cawsand, on the site of the later battery and fort; an alternative site is represented by the prominent rocky promontory of Pemberknowse Fort (see separate entry), which would have offered a seemingly ideal position for the guns of the time (which were of limited range and accuracy) to command the beaches to either side.

There are no visible surface remains of the earlier batteries, although the area of the War Memorial has been thought to represent the earthworks of an earlier fortification. A half-exposed cannon is sited at Pemberknowse Point.

Present condition
No visible remains are identifiable. Earlier remains on the site of Pemberknowse Fort and on the sites of the later battery and fort above may have been removed to some extent by the construction of the chapel and the later fortfications (which may also have covered up and thus protected any earlier remains).

Plate 55: Cawsand, before development of the fort

Sources
General
2, 3; K, L, Q.
Specific
1616 unspecified reference. PRO: SP 14/87
1625 unspecified reference. PRO: SP 16/6/12
1716 Survey by Col. Lilly. BL: Kings MS 45 f.34.
1875/76 Worth, R.N 'The Siege of Plymouth' *Rep. & Trans of the Plymouth Institution*, **5**, 279

PEMBERKNOWSE FORT

PAR = RAME, NGR = SX 43485031, PRN = 6141, MAP 2 No. 18

This is sited on a rocky promontory dividing Kingsand from Cawsand and overlooking both beaches, particularly Cawsand beach. It is thought to have been the site of a temporary battery or fort built in 1779 during the invasion scare (when a Franco-Spanish fleet anchored in Cawsand Bay) to strengthen the beach defences, which was subsequently demolished in 1792 just prior to the construction of the present Congregational Chapel in 1793. However, it is not mentioned in Dixon's report of 1780 or depicted in his map of that date, nor mentioned or depicted in other contemporary sources which otherwise include all the fortifications built at this time. However its prominent position and its siting close to sea level and adjoining the beaches indicate that it may have been the sites of the blockhouse (labelled as 'not made') shown on the panorama of *c.*1540, the battery mentioned in the early 17th and 18th centuries and the Royalist 'fort' or battery of three guns mentioned in accounts of the Civil War Siege of Plymouth (see under separate entry for Cawsand Battery 'A'); an alternative site for the latter batteries is represented by the hill to the west (the site of the Cawsand Battery 'B' (1779) and the present Cawsand Fort (1863)), although this may have lain too far away from the beaches for the guns of the time (which were of limited range and accuracy) to command them effectively. At various periods it may also have linked in with other defences along the sea front.

The site is presently occupied by a Congregational Chapel, dated, according to the board listing times of services, to 1793. This is built on an outcrop and/or platform which is retained on the seaward side with a stone wall, the lower part of which consists of high quality masonry with a rougher, later build above. It does not contain any evidence of loopholes or crenellations however. To the south there is a courtyard area bounded on its seaward side with a rendered stone wall; this contains a rough hole at floor level which has been thought to represent a loophole; alternatively it may represent a drain, allowing sea water to return from whence it came during times of storm. Adjoining the small slipway is a half-buried cannon (thought to be a ship's cannon); this may either have been brought ashore from a ship and/or have formed part of the armament of one of the batteries. To the north of the chapel there is a length of east-facing crenellated wall, which may either represent fortification or a later decorative feature. Another length of crenellated wall overlooks South Rock to the north (at SX 4348506); this however forms part of a late heightening of the sea wall and as such probably represents a late 19th-century decorative feature. Therefore there appears to be no clear visible evidence of a fortification at Pemberknowse, although given its location and prominence it is a natural location for the early 17th and 18th-century fortifications.

Present condition

The sea wall and the crenellated wall immediately to the north are both in good condition, as is the wall of the courtyard to the south. The gun is half-buried and corroding, and has recently had concrete laid against and slightly over one side of it (perhaps infilling an attempt to dig it up). The courtyard to the south of the chapel is presently open space, whilst lean-tos abut the sea wall to the east and north of the chapel.

Sources

General

1, 3, 5, 6, 7; C, L, Q.

Specific

1875/76 Worth, R.N. 'The Siege of Plymouth' *Rep. & Trans. of the Plymouth Institution*, **5**, 279.

AMHERST BATTERY

PAR = MAKER, NGR = SX 43505058, PRN = 6136, MAP 2 No. 19

This is sited within Kingsand, overlooking Cawsand Bay, and is first depicted on a chart surveyed in 1770 as Amherst Battery, mounting twelve 18-pdr guns. It may have been constructed during the Seven Years War in the late 1750s, when the Dock Lines were begun, and was named after an Admiral Amherst, who was in command in Plymouth sometime in the second half of the 18th century. Although it appears on later 18th century charts (Nos 146 & 148 in Stuart, which claim to have been surveyed in 1786 and 1797 respectively but which were probably largely based on the 1770 survey as they depict none of the fortifications built in 1779-80), it does not appear on maps of 1780 by Dixon and Cowl, nor on Mackenzie's 1779 survey, which otherwise show all the fortifications built or in use at that time. A battery of eight 18-pdrs was indeed built at that time (see under Minadew Brake Battery), but is depicted to the N.E of Kingsand and is described as lying at a height of 176 feet (Amherst Battery lies at about 50 feet). Therefore, as it is not referred to by Dixon, it appears that Amherst Battery had become redundant by the invasion scare of 1779.

The probable site of the battery was identified by P. Sheppard and one of the landowners, G.R Daniel, in 1973. It lies on a terrace *c.* 50 feet above the sea, which is now occupied by the Grey House (now split into two) and its garden. There is also a slightly higher terrace immediately to the N (now the garden of Minadew Brake Cottage), which may also have formed part of the battery as there is not enough room in the Grey House garden to mount and work twelve cannon. The Grey House terrace is fronted by a 20 feet high and 85 feet long buttressed rubble stone wall; a demi-bastion containing small embrasures or loops projects out from its S end. At its N end the upper part of it has been rebuilt, although the lower part of the build abuts an earlier wall running N.E - S.W, which appears to be continuous with the E/W wall retaining the garden terrace of Minadew Brake Cottage to the N. This therefore appears to be the earliest wall on the site, suggesting that the N terrace is earlier than the Grey House terrace (although its present N/S front retaining wall has been built after the early E/W dividing wall) and/or that the present front wall of the Grey House terrace is a later extension. Also the loops at the S end appear too small and closely spaced to represent cannon embrasures, and either represent loops for infantry to fire along the front of the battery or a later decorative garden feature. To the rear the basement of the Grey House lies slightly below the garden and is thought to be the site of the powder magazine; it is fronted by an unusual raised stone pathway, which may have protected the magazine from incoming fire. The front wall of the basement is slightly thicker than those above, indicating perhaps that it incorporates the remains of an earlier building, but there is no identifiable internal evidence of this and there is no difference in build visible within the S gable end. Therefore it is probable that this represents the site of the battery (which may well also have included the terrace to the N), although it is not clear how much of the visible fabric is contemporary with the battery.

Present condition

The site consists of very well maintained private gardens and houses, and the retaining walls display no obvious signs of stress, although parts have been repaired in the past.

Sources

General

4, 5, 6, 7; K, L, M, Q.

Specific

1770 Chart of Plymouth Sound. PLHL. (Stuart No. 141)

1783 Map. CRO: Carew Pole Ms No.F1/10

1785 Map. CRO: Carew Pole Ms No.F1/10

1786 Chart of Sound. NMM: 419/111 PB D8407 (Stuart No. 146)

1797 Chart of Sound. BL: Maps 151 f.1(3) (Stuart No. 148)

1973 Sheppard, P 'The Amherst gun battery, Kingsand' *Cornwall Archaeology* **XII** 75-76.

MINADEW BRAKE BATTERY

PAR = MAKER, NGR = SX 43555079, PRN = 38539, MAP 2 No. 20

A battery is shown by both Dixon and Cowl (Batteries E and R respectively) on the seaward side of the road down into Kingsand from Maker Church, outside the built-up area of the village to the N.E., and is also shown in this position on a chart by Mackenzie completed in 1779. It is described by Dixon as having been completed by 17th August 1779, when it was armed with eight 18-pdr guns (the armament also given by Cowl & Mackenzie). It was one of three batteries (totalling sixteen 18-pdrs) in and around Kingsand and Cawsand at the time (along with Cawsand Battery B and Sandway Battery; see separate entries), and was intended by Dixon to command the beaches of Kingsand and Cawsand and to annoy any enemy attempt to land within Penlee Point. In a contemporary document it is given as lying at a height of 176 feet. Based on this evidence and the siting on the 1780 maps the most likely site for the battery would seem to be at or near the junction of the path forming a continuation of Devonport Hill in Kingsand with the 'New Road' running around the 55-60m contours above, where there is presently an overgrown garden terrace. This battery has previously been identified with the earlier Amherst Battery in Kingsand, but this is unlikely for the following reasons:

(i) Amherst Battery only lies at a height of *c*.50 feet, and the heights given for other batteries in the same document are accurate;

(ii) the three contemporary maps clearly depict the battery as lying outside Kingsand, whilst Amherst Battery clearly lies within it; and

(iii) it appears from Dixon's report that the battery was newly built in 1779, whilst Amherst Battery is shown on an earlier chart of c.1770.

The battery appears to have become redundant at the end of the American War of Independence as it is not shown on either Gardner's maps of 1784-86 or on Sturt's of 1788.

There are no identifiable remains of the battery currently visible, except for the garden terrace itself; the walls retaining this terrace and the pathways above and below are generally heavily overgrown.

Present condition

A heavily overgrown, apparently redundant garden terrace.

Sources

General

4, 5, 6, 7, 8; M

Specific

1788 Map by R. Sturt. PRO: MR 1434

CAWSAND BATTERY 'B'

PAR = RAME, NGR = SX 43355036, PRN = 6156.2, MAP 2 No. 21

This was sited on the spur separating Cawsand from Kingsand which is now occupied by the later Cawsand Fort. It is depicted on maps of 1779, 1780 & 1784, and described by Dixon in his report as having been completed by 17th August 1779, when it had stores and ammunition and was armed by seamen. It was intended with Minadew Brake Battery to command the beaches and annoy enemy attempts to land within Penlee Point, and was armed with four 18-pounders. In a contemporary document it is described as a '4 Gun Battery in Boulward' and as lying at a height of 127 feet; although this and the other two batteries in Cawsand Bay are described by Maurice Jones as redoubts there is no indication in contemporary sources that it was converted into a redoubt, and the eight gun battery referred to in the documents represents Minadew Brake Battery. Cawsand is the only battery of the three to be depicted on the 1784 map, suggesting that it continued in use during the Napoleonic Wars, probably becoming redundant in *c*.1815.

Plate 56: Gun platforms (foreground) of Cawsand Battery B (Exeter Archaeology)

The only visible remains consist of two granite gun platforms sited within the later fort. These face due east out over the bay, and are located on a raised grassy platform above and immediately to the rear of the later gun positions below. They are partly covered with turf, and do not appear to be contemporary with the gun positions below, which belong to the sea face of the later fort. No more than nine guns are recorded on this face; these are represented by the seven emplacements depicted below on the 1896 map and two others at a higher level at the S.E corner of the fort.

Present condition

The two gun platforms remain complete, although partly covered; they may have been exposed during clearance and landscaping undertaken as part of the current development. Any parapet and rampart at the front of the platforms has been levelled. Other remains of gun platforms and magazine foundations for example may survive below-ground, although parts may have been removed by the construction of the later gun positions and underground magazine of the later fort.

Sources

General

4, 5, 6, 7, 8; J, K, L, Q.

Specific

1779 Armament table dating to 17th August, by Lieut. Col. Dixon. WDRO: Ph 355 13-24 (MFC).

CAWSAND FORT

PAR = RAME, NGR = SX 43355035, PRN = 6156.4, MAP 2 No. 22

This is sited on the spur separating Cawsand and Kingsand, overlooking the villages and the bay, but overlooked itself by higher ground immediately to the west. It was built on the site of the 1779 battery, on the recommendations of a memo by Maj. Jervois dating to 1858, and is therefore of similar date to Tregantle and Scraesdon forts and with them slightly predates the recommendations of the 1860 Royal Commission. Its construction was recommended in 1858 to defend against ships entering the bay and to enfilade the shore; it was to act as a keep to *c*.10 guns placed along its front, with accommodation for 100 men under its *terreplein*. In the preamble to the 1860 report it is described as being under construction, although in 1869 the date of commencement is given as 1861. It was completed in 1863 at a cost of £16171, and in 1867 was described as an earthwork for 10 guns, enclosed by a defensible wall and barrack. In the minutes of evidence in the 1869 report it was stated as having thirteen 68-pdr, 8- and 7-inch RBL guns, nine on the sea front and four on the land front, although in the summary fourteen are listed on the land front (a probable typing error, given the minutes of evidence and the physical lack of room). It was noted that it was overlooked and exposed to attack from the rear, because the proposed work on Knatterbury Hill and the strengthening of the Maker redoubts had not been undertaken, and the remodelling of the battery to take heavier guns was recommended. In 1885 it was armed with nine 64-pdr RML guns and four 8-inch SB guns, and in 1893 with just the nine 64-pdrs. These had been removed by 1903, although the fort continued in occupation during WWI; it was released by the MoD in 1926. Subsequently it remained derelict until its recent redevelopment.

The fort remains largely complete, although the barrack block has been converted and adapted into modern housing and new houses and garages have been built on top of the ramparts along the sea faces. The road around the fort ('New Road') originated as a military road built at the same time in the early 1860s.

Plate 57: Cawsand Fort after development (Photograph: S. Hartgroves. Frame: ABP/F35/93. Copyright: Cornwall Archaeological Unit)

Plate 58: Cawsand Fort, later emplacement (Exeter Archaeology)

Access to the fort was (and is) via a trackway from the N, which originally entered over a drawbridge, and via a ramp and gateway through the barrack block from the S. It is enclosed by a loopholed wall, which is flanked by a pair of musketry *caponiers* at the N corner, a further two along the sea face, and another at the S corner; further protection on the land face is provided by a loopholed bastion and demi-bastion and dry moat. At the N.E corner of the curtain wall there is a War Dept. boundary stone and benchmark dated 1867, which has previously been interpreted as the date of completion of the fort; this however conflicts with the completion date of 1863 given in the parliamentary report. Within the fort seven gun positions, mostly retaining their racer rails and in two cases having central pivots comprising re-used cannon and a different type of carriage, are still visible on the sea face, flanking an earth-covered expense magazine. Another two guns were sited on the roof of the officers' quarters at the S corner, but have been removed or overlain by new houses; they were served by an expense magazine under the archway connecting the other seven gun positions with the rear of the barracks. In the centre of the battery there is a large earthen traverse on two levels, the upper of which forms a cavalier overlooking the land face and contains four granite gun platforms. These are served from an expense magazine, which is connected to the main magazine below via a lift; there is also a spiral staircase between this upper gun platform and the magazine. The main magazine is sited under the central traverse, off a passage; it consists of a shell store and a cartridge store entered via a shifting lobby and surrounded by a lamp passage, off which are the lift and staircase to the upper gun platform above. Several fixtures and fittings still remain, including most of the racer rails and pivots for the gun carriages, original door frames and timber battening (for wooden lining) within the cartridge store, part of the original mechanism for the lift and the guard 'cage' at its top; further features may survive within the barracks but these were not viewed as they are now private homes. The sockets for the drawbridge chain and mechanism are also visible in the W side of the N gate (now demolished). Two further granite gun platforms are visible facing E on the grass platform to the rear of the sea-facing gun positions; these probably belong to the earlier 1779 battery on the site (see under Cawsand Battery 'B'). Outside the fort to the W is a small levelled area of ground (now much obscured by dumping) which represents a *glacis*.

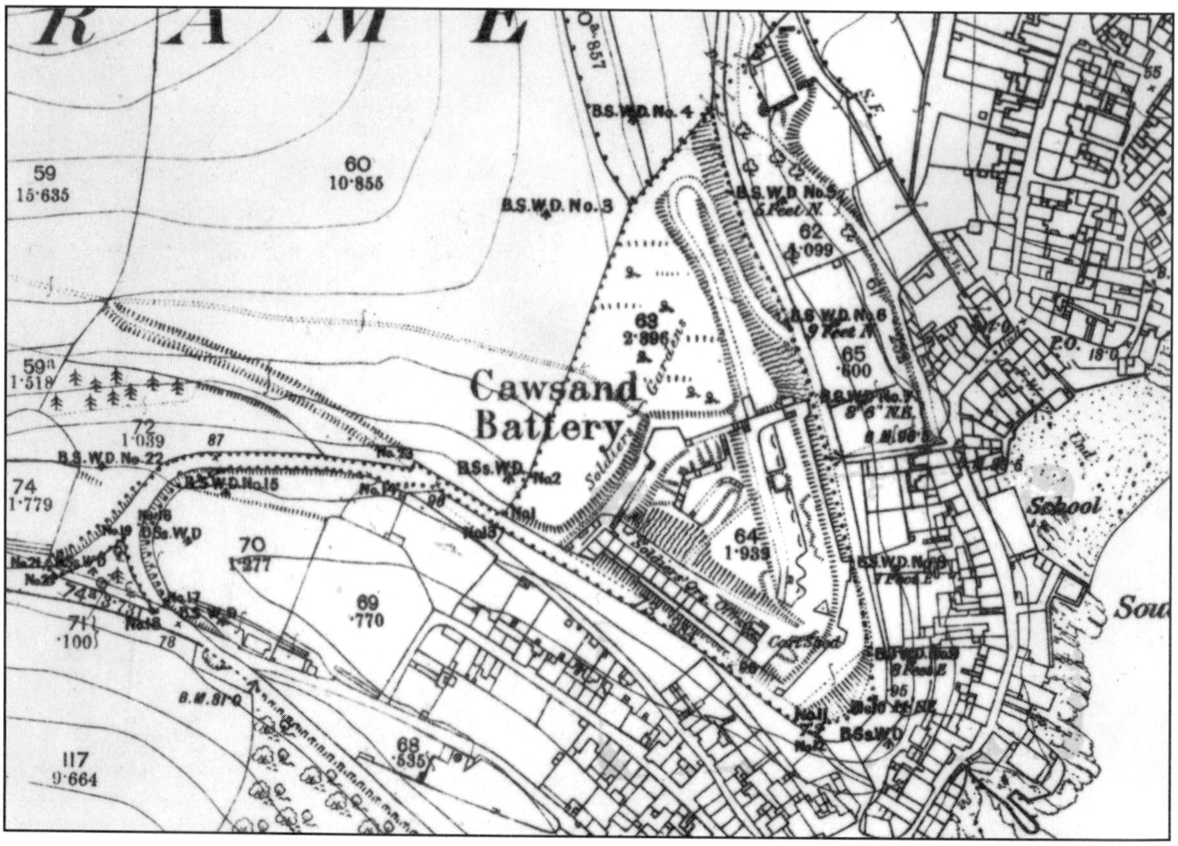

Fig. 32: Cawsand Fort in 1896 (PRO: WO 78/2314)

Present condition.
Overall the fort is structurally sound and in good condition, although large parts have been altered and in part removed. This has involved the following:

(i) the conversion, heightening and extension to the rear of the original barrack blocks, so that relatively little of the original facework is visible except at the front and towards the E end at the rear;

(ii) the construction of new housing along the E sea face, which has entailed the removal of the rampart in front of the seven extant gun positions, the removal of the material around most of the racer rails, leaving them high and dry and destroying their context, and the removal or covering (without trace) of the two gun positions and the protective earthwork traverses on the roof of the officers' quarters at the S corner;

(iii) the construction of new garages to the rear of the gun positions, which may have removed evidence of the earlier 1779 battery (or earlier fortifications);

(iv) the conversion of the extant gun positions into garden features; and

(v) the construction of new garages outside the entrance, entailing the removal of part of the ditch, and the dumping of material over the *glacis* to the west and into the ditch adjoining the bastion; further infilling has occurred to the S, within the garden of the neighbouring house ('Green Hedges').

However, landscaping and clearance work associated with the development have resulted in the exposure of the upper gun positions, stairways, and the earlier 1779 gun platforms. The main magazine and expense magazines are in reasonable condition.

Sources
General
11, 12, 14, 15, 17, 23, 24; K, L, Q.
Specific
1900 Plan. PRO: WO 78/4428.
1924 Reference. PRO: CAB 36/17.

'BAKERS BATTERY'

PAR = MAKER, NGR = SX 432 509, PRN = 37086, MAP 2 No. 23

This has been identified as the site of a barracks built for 1000 troops in 1864. However, no original source is cited and only fields are depicted in this location on the 1914 O.S. map. It is not mentioned in the 1860 Royal Commission or in subsequent reports dating to 1867 and 1869.

A post-war housing estate now occupies this site; there is no visible evidence of any structures which may have belonged to barracks or any other military buildings.

Present condition
No surface remains; currently a housing estate.

Sources
General
12, 14, 15; Q

KINGSAND WWII PILLBOX

PAR = MAKER, NGR = SX 43465038, PRN = 38540, MAP 2 No. 24

This is located in a back garden adjoining the landing steps at South Rock, at the S end of Kingsand beach. It commands the steps as well as the beach, and there presumably would have been an equivalent pillbox guarding Cawsand beach also. It is constructed of shuttered concrete and is roughly hexagonal in shape, with a doorway in the side facing Garrett Street to the S.W. This is flanked by two armoured loopoles, and there is a pair of loopholes in each of the broader sea-facing sides; the remainder have one loophole each. The interior was not viewed.

Present condition
It is very well preserved, and currently used as a garden shed; it is painted pink.

WRINGFORD DOWN PICKET POST AND ROAD BLOCK

PAR = RAME, NGR = SX 42555038-42615041;42615033-42685033;42715023, PRN = 6160, MAP 2 No. 27

This is located in a valley immediately to the W of Cawsand, and would have been on the route inland of an enemy landing at the S end of Whitsand Bay, as it would enable him to skirt around to the rear of the fortifications at Cawsand. It consists of a possible road block across Forder Hill, some 500m to the north of the hamlet of Forder, and two lengths of loopholed field walls further up the slope on the W side of the road; no field walls survive to the E of the road however. It is thought to date to the invasion scare of August 1779, when a Franco-Spanish fleet anchored in Cawsand Bay, or to the subsequent Napoleonic Wars.

The 'road block' consists of two mortared rubble stone walls projecting out *c*. 0.50m and 4m from the drystone field walls flanking the lane. In 1974 there were two stone piers which contained sockets for a timber bar to be slotted in between, but these have both now gone. The masonry walls appear to postdate the flanking field walls, although the relationships were difficult to establish due to vegetation cover.

The southern of the two loopholed field walls appears to have loops each 80m or so; it is a relatively low rubble stone wall, and there appears no other practical reason (e.g animal access or drainage) for the holes other than as loopholes for musketry, although they seem too widely spaced to provide complete cover (though others may have been removed by wall repairs for example).

To the N the ground slopes up to another loopholed wall which forms the S boundary of the Wringford farm buildings; several loopholes were visible at the E end and appeared to be more closely spaced. Their extent westwards and their condition was not assessed due to access being denied; much of the W section has apparently been removed by a house extension. For the same reason it was not possible to view the adjoining field walls to the W to ascertain whether they also formed part of the defences.

Present condition

The remaining road block walls survive in reasonable condition although heavily overgrown, and truncated by the removal of the piers. The E sections of the two loopholed walls appeared to be in reasonable condition, although it was not possible to view the W sections.

Sources

General

L, Q.

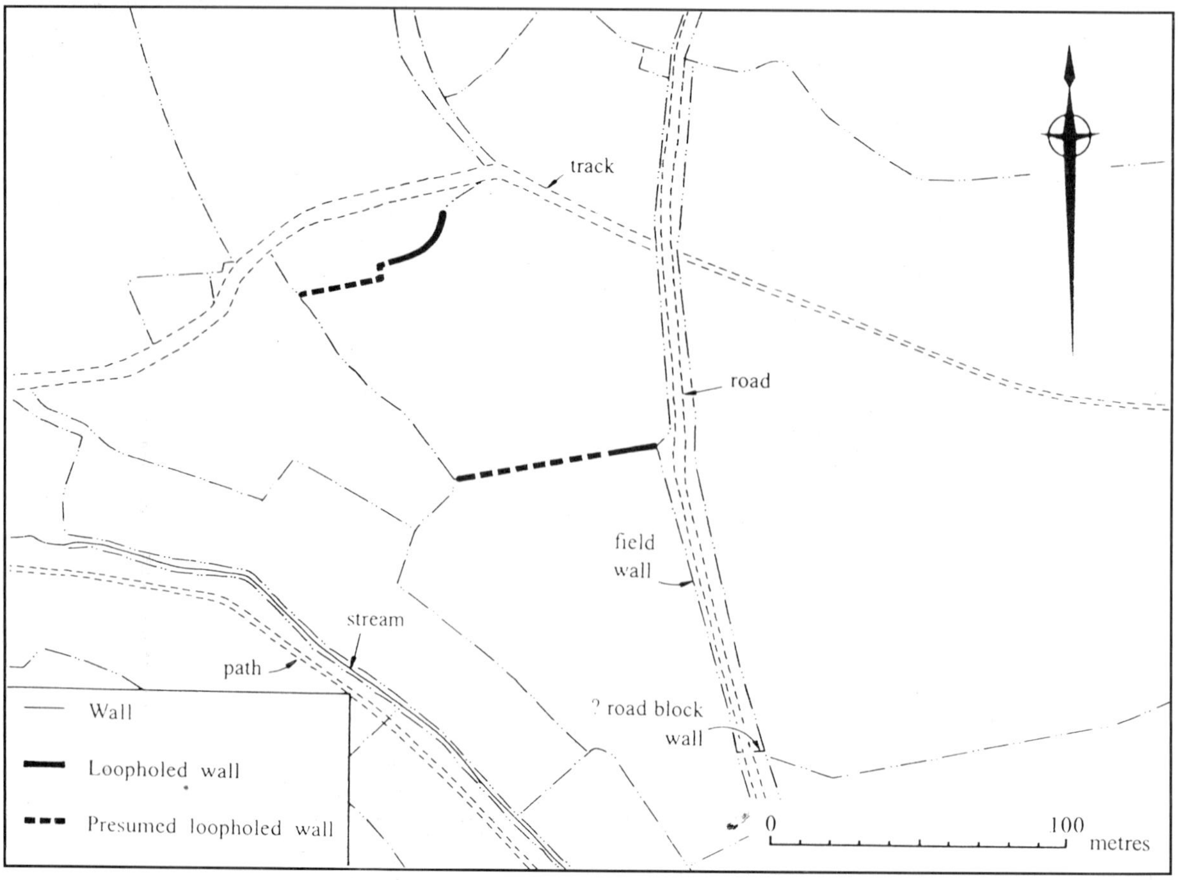

Fig. 32a: Wringford Picket Post

PIER CELLARS BRENNAN TORPEDO STATION

PAR = RAME, NGR = SX 43574951, PRN = 6019, MAP 1 No. 25

This is located on the S side of Cawsand Bay, immediately to the N.E of Penlee Battery and at the rear of an earlier harbour. It was armed with the Brennan torpedo, a wire-guided land-based anti-ship weapon, and was intended to guard the W entrance to the Sound around the Breakwater. The torpedo was first invented by Louis Brennan in 1876 and subsequently further developed with the Royal Engineers in the 1880s; it was adopted by the British Government in January 1887. The station at Pier Cellars was one of eight completed in Britain and abroad, and was almost certainly built in 1888-89 by Messrs Hill & Co.; it was probably complete by 1890 and was certainly complete by 1894. Alterations undertaken after 1896 included the addition of a searchlight (Brennan Light) adjoining the harbour mouth and the 175 foot long iron landing pier, and the construction of a battery of 12-pdr QF guns and accompanying searchlights in 1898 (see separate entry); the QF guns, together with a Maxim machine-gun at the end of the pier, had been approved (but not mounted) by 1895. The station still remained operational in 1903, but was closed in September 1906; the searchlight adjoining the pier appears to have remained in use during WWI. During WWII the station was used as a HDA Station (HDA - Harbour Defence Asdic (i.e. sonar)), together with the northern of the two QF gun searchlights. It remains in the occupancy of the MoD (Navy).

Plate 59: Pier Cellars Brennan Torpedo Station (Exeter Archaeology)

The bulk of the torpedo station is built within a terrace cut into the hillside at the rear of an earlier stone-built harbour. The station is constructed of shuttered concrete and brickwork, and is earth-covered to protect it from incoming fire and obscure its exact position from an enemy. Its layout is shown on a contemporary plan (which probably dates to the late 1890s), which also includes sections and elevations of the buildings and details as to materials and dimensions; it may therefore have been partly based on the original design plans (although it does include the Brennan Light which was built later). The launching slipway is sited immediately to the E of the harbour, and shares the entrance into the station with the tramway bringing torpedoes from the landing pier. Adjoining the

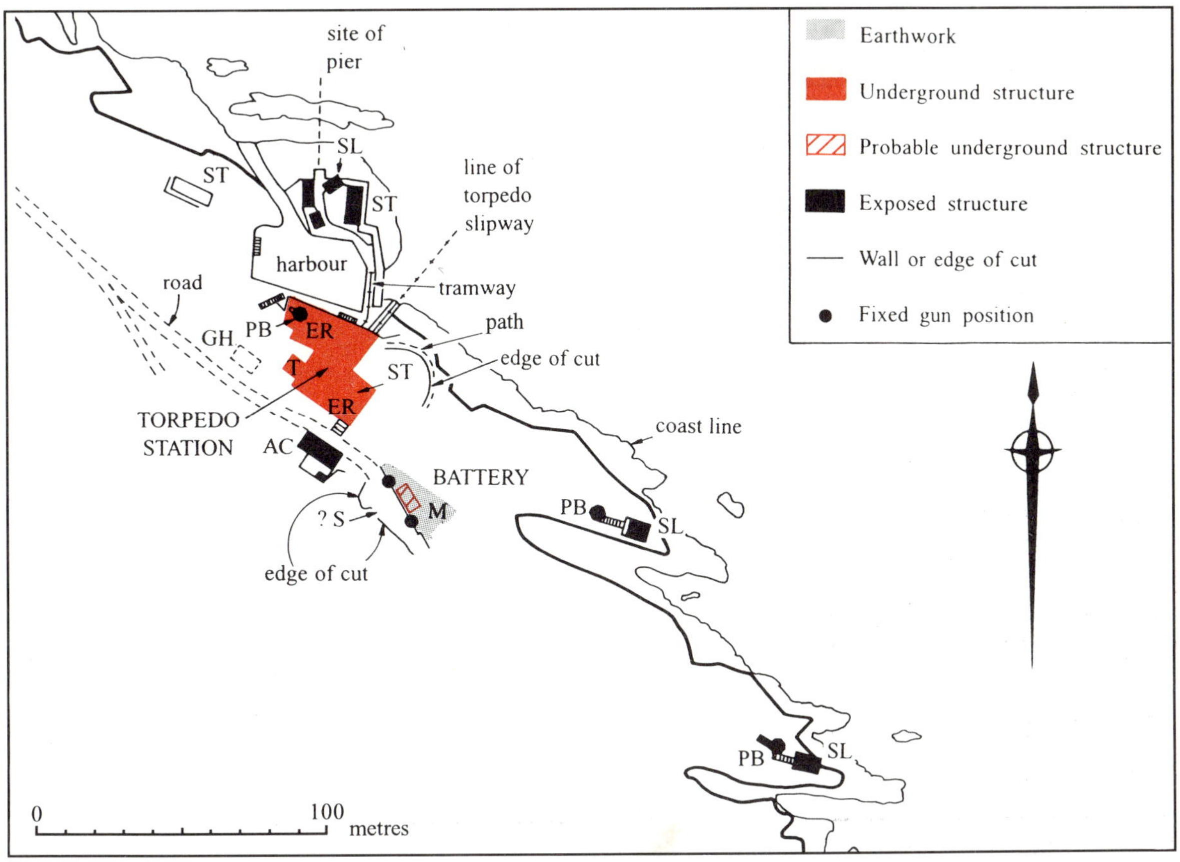

Fig. 33: Pier Cellars

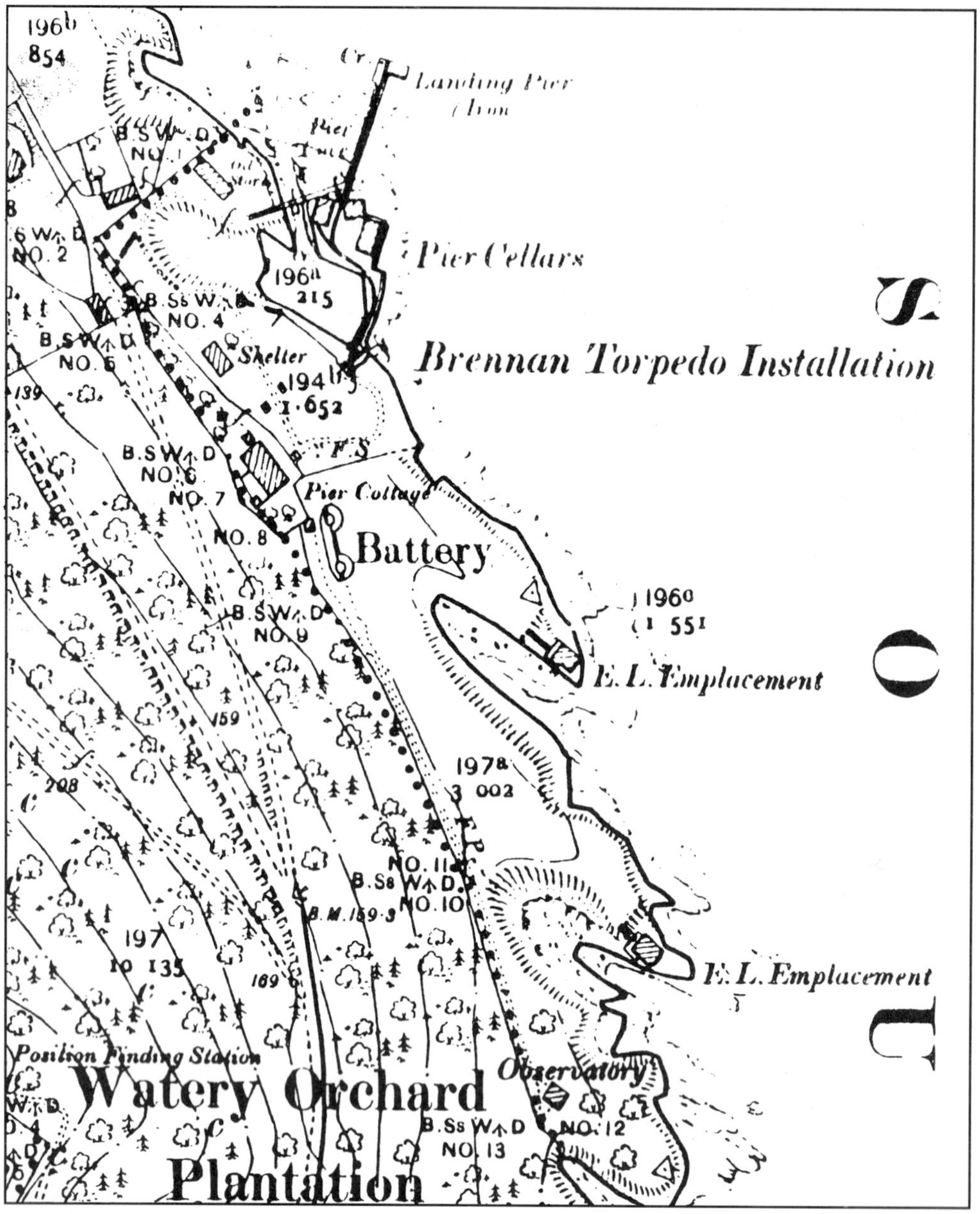

Fig. 34: Pier Cellars in 1911 (PRO: WO 78/2314)

tramway to the W are a range of rooms fronting onto the harbour which housed the accumulator, dynamo, oil-fired engine and expense oil store (the reserve oil store still exists and is sited to the west of the harbour entrance). Flanking the rear of the slipway are the wire-winding store and torpedo store, with engine and boiler rooms and adjoining coal store and ventilation shaft/emergency exit behind; all these are now blocked off except the torpedo store. Several important features are still visible within the station, including the launching rail in the slipway, a horizontal wooden beam attached to the partition along its W side which supported the racked girder for the universal pulley (via which the torpedo was guided), the girder in the ceiling of the torpedo store for the overhead traveller (with which the torpedoes were manoeuvred into position), the brick bedding for the pair of boilers, and the concrete plinths for the main steam winding-engine and the oil-fired engine, together with iron supports presumably relating to the dynamo. Outside there are the remains of the tramway from the landing pier, with some rails still in situ. At the harbour mouth only the stub of the landing pier remains. It is flanked by a rectangular brick building to the E (which, as rails entered it, may have originally been a temporary torpedo store) and by the Brennan searchlight to the W. This was built after 1896 and lies over earlier tramway rails; it faces E, and has a later octagonal observation post on the roof. Other buildings include a store and a later 'galley' (built by 1943).

On the slope above the station is Pier Cottage, a two-storey house with yard and coal house to the rear which appears to pre-date the station and to which has been added a large chimney serving the flues from the engine boilers below. This may have accommodated the observation post directing the course of the torpedo, as it is the only building to lie on the line of the launching slipway, but there is no indication of the location of the O.P. on the plans in this building or elsewhere. Other remains include the concrete slab foundation of the shelter (later guard house) adjoining the road, and a two-storey octagonal concrete pillbox, observation post and/or mine observation or control station sited directly above the accumulator room; this is very similar in character to those which accompany

Plate 60: Pier Cellars, launching slipway (Exeter Archaeology)

the two QF gun searchlights (which probably date to *c.*1900) but is not marked on any plan or map.

Present condition

The main part of the station is little used, except for the oil-fired engine room (a boat store), expense oil store, and torpedo store (five-a-side football); the rooms to the rear are empty, blocked off and derelict, and partly occupied by piles of rubble; rubbish has been thrown down the ventilation shaft. At the harbour mouth the Brennan light has been blocked up and is used as accommodation, the temporary torpedo store is a dining room, served by the adjoining galley; the former store is an ablution block. Pier Cottage is used as the guardhouse and as accommodation; the harbour and the surrounding area are used for adventure training.

Sources

General

17, 18, 19, 23, 24; Q.

Specific

1888 Drawings of launching way for torpedoes. PRO: WO 78/4468

late 1890s? Plan of station and elevations. J. Symons, FSGSW.

late 1890s? Sheet of sections belonging to above. PSA: 035141B

1943 Site plan of HDA Station. PSA: 035145B

1943 Site plan and plan of searchlight (range buildings). PSA: 035143B

1992 Richards, D 'A Brennan Torpedo Station at Hong Kong' *The Redan*, **26**, 25-32.

1993 Beanse, A 'Brennan Torpedo: Winding Engine and Steering Gear' *The Redan* (forthcoming).

PIER CELLARS QF GUN BATTERY

PAR = RAME, NGR = SX 43594946, PRN = 37090, MAP 1 No. 26

This is sited adjoining the Brennan Torpedo Station, and was built in 1898 (after approval in 1895) to protect the station and also covered (with Grenville Battery) the examination anchorage in Cawsand Bay and perhaps the minefields around the W end of the Breakwater. It was armed with two 12-pdr QF guns which were dismounted by 1908 (probably when the torpedo station was closed in 1906); these were re-mounted during WWI and removed between 1920 and 1936. The battery was accompanied by two searchlights (protected by adjoining pillboxes and located at SX 43674946 & 43734937), which had been built by 1910, and also probably utilised the Brennan searchlight at the harbour mouth. In 1943 contemporary drawings show that the N searchlight was intended to be a 'D/G Range', with the searchlight cell forming the instrument room and the pillbox the signal office, with a T.E.O. Office also being built; there is no physical evidence of this conversion however.

Both the gun positions survive complete with mounting-plates, store recesses, parapets and aprons. The magazine (now infilled) is sited underground between the gun positions, and to the rear of the N position was a small brick shed (now demolished). Both searchlights and their accompanying pillboxes survive complete, although only the N one was accessible. The searchlight cell is brick-built and concrete-roofed, and contains a fireplace and a square window opening; this faces due E and retains one half of its protective armoured shutter. At the top of the stair there is an octagonal concrete pillbox which has horizontal firing-slits protected by armoured shutters.

Present condition

The gun positions are in reasonable structural condition although part of the earthwork fronting them has been terraced away and the guard rails, store recess doors and davits have been removed and at least the stairwell of the magazine infilled. The N searchlight and pillbox survive complete with remnants of iron shuttering, whilst the S pair also appear to be complete; it was not possible to ascertain the survival of internal fittings however.

Sources

General

17, 19, 21, 23, 24; K, Q.

Specific

1898 Armament table? PRO: CAB 7/6

*c.*1900 Plan. PSA: 035141B

1905 Armament table? PRO: CAB 16/1

1907 Plan of battery magazines. PRO: WO 78/4063

1927 Armament table? PRO: CAB 36/16

1943 Site plan. PSA: 035145B

1943 Plan of proposed range buildings. PSA: 035143B

n.d. Plan of Electric Light Emplacement. PRO: WO 78/4063

n.d. Plan. Held by K. Rawlings, FSGSW.

3.2.4. Western Defences

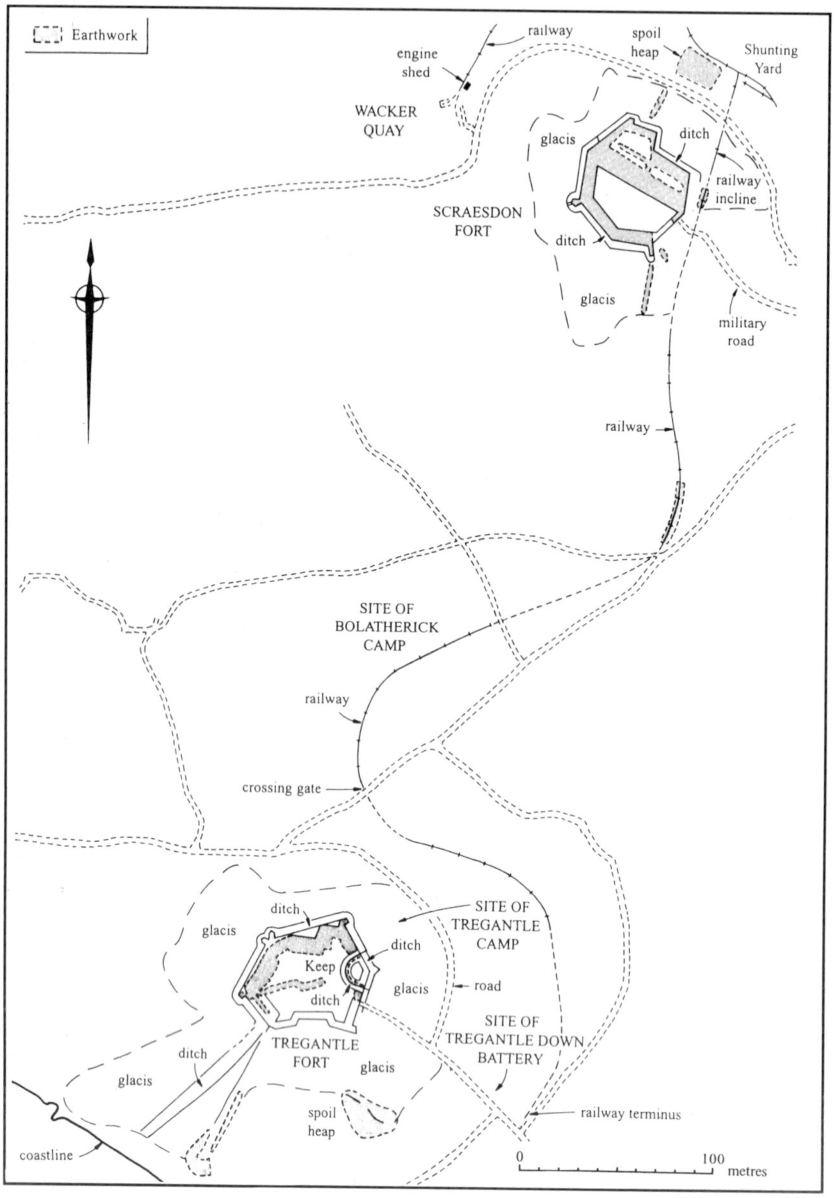

Fig. 35: The Western Defences

TREGANTLE FORT

PAR = ANTONY, NGR = SX 38625332, PRN = 6354, MAP 1 No. 44

This forms the principal fort of the western defences of Plymouth (the Antony Position), the construction of which was originally recommended by Jervois in February 1858. With Scraesdon Fort and another proposed fortification in between (not built) it was intended to command the western approach to Plymouth between the St Germans river and the coast and prevent the bombardment of the Dockyard. Jervois originally recommended an armament of *c.* 60 guns, the provision of a parapet and ditch on the seaward side to provide a flanking defence, and the construction of 'towers' at the gorge. It was to contain bombproof barracks for 450 of the total of 1000 men proposed for the garrisoning of the Antony Position. In March 1858 it was placed at the top of the list of relative importance and construction began in December. In 1860 the Royal Commission reported it as being already under construction and recommended the addition of permanent lines (not built) to link it with Scraesdon Fort; the fort was completed in March 1865. The 1869 report listed the intended armament as 87 guns and the remodelling of the magazines and other additions were mentioned. It recommended the placement of additional guns on the seaward flank to keep ships at a distance and prevent them from bombarding the fort; this arose out of comments made by General Todleben during a visit in 1864. In 1869 the total cost was estimated at £189,999. In 1875 it had not yet been armed; the recommended armament was 22 7-inch RBLs, 13 64-pdr RMLs, five 8-inch rifled howitzers and 24 SB flank guns. In 1885 it was armed with six 64-pdr RMLs, seven 7-inch RBLs and 10 32-pdr SB BL guns, and there were 26 other guns lying within the fort. In 1893 three 64-pdr RMLs and three 7-inch RBLs were mounted on the N face, one 64-pdr RML and one 7-inch RBL on the N.W face, one 7-inch RBL on the salient and six 64-pdr RMLs on the S.W face, together with six other 64-pdrs on the upper tier of the Keep. Although 10 32-pdr SB guns were recommended for the *caponiers* none were apparently

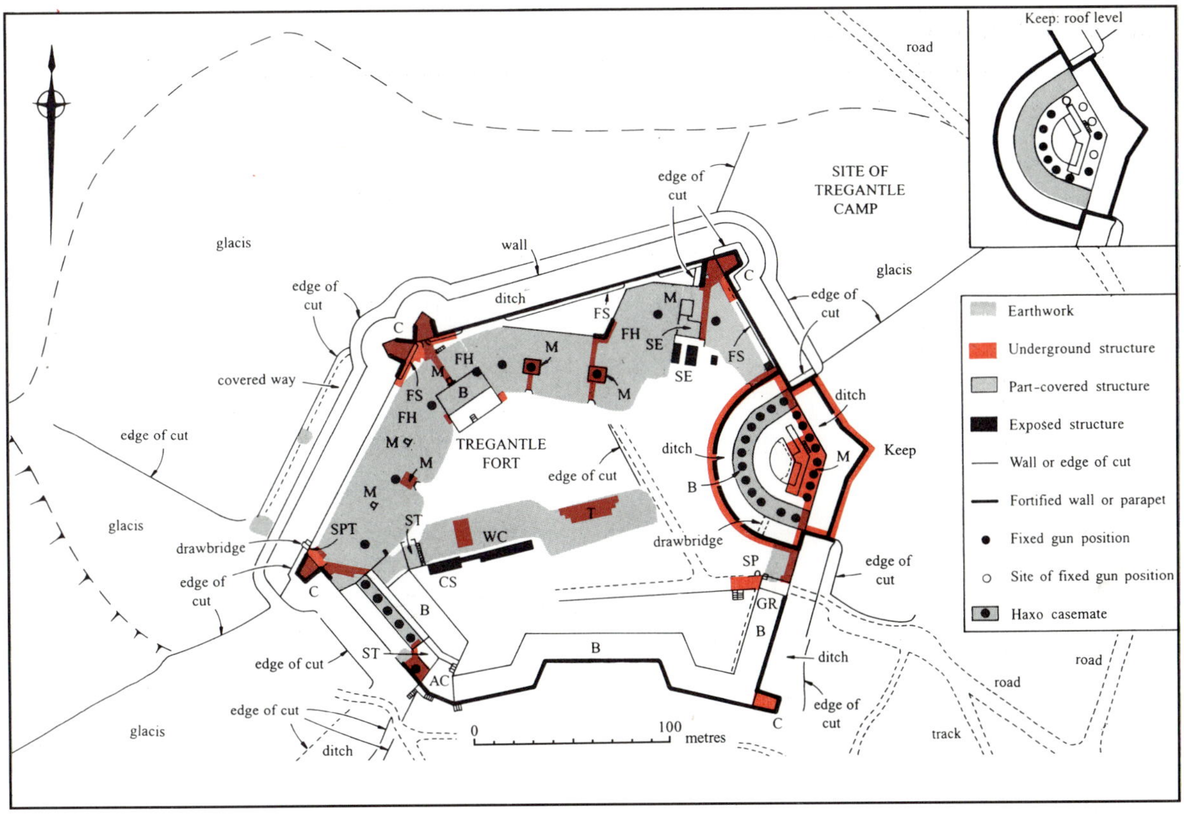

Fig. 36: Tregantle Fort

mounted. There were also three 64-pdr RMLs in the upper parade for drill purposes. The fort was probably disarmed towards the end of the century and since then has been used as barrack accommodation for the firing ranges to the S and S.W; at least one range had been built by 1896.

The fort is sited on a hill about 360ft above sea level immediately adjoining the coast and astride the main road through to Maker Heights from the W. It commands a wide area to the W and N and Scraesdon Fort is visible. It is a hexagonal work containing a keep at the apex of the gorge and barrack casemates along the S and E flanks and in the keep. It is surrounded on

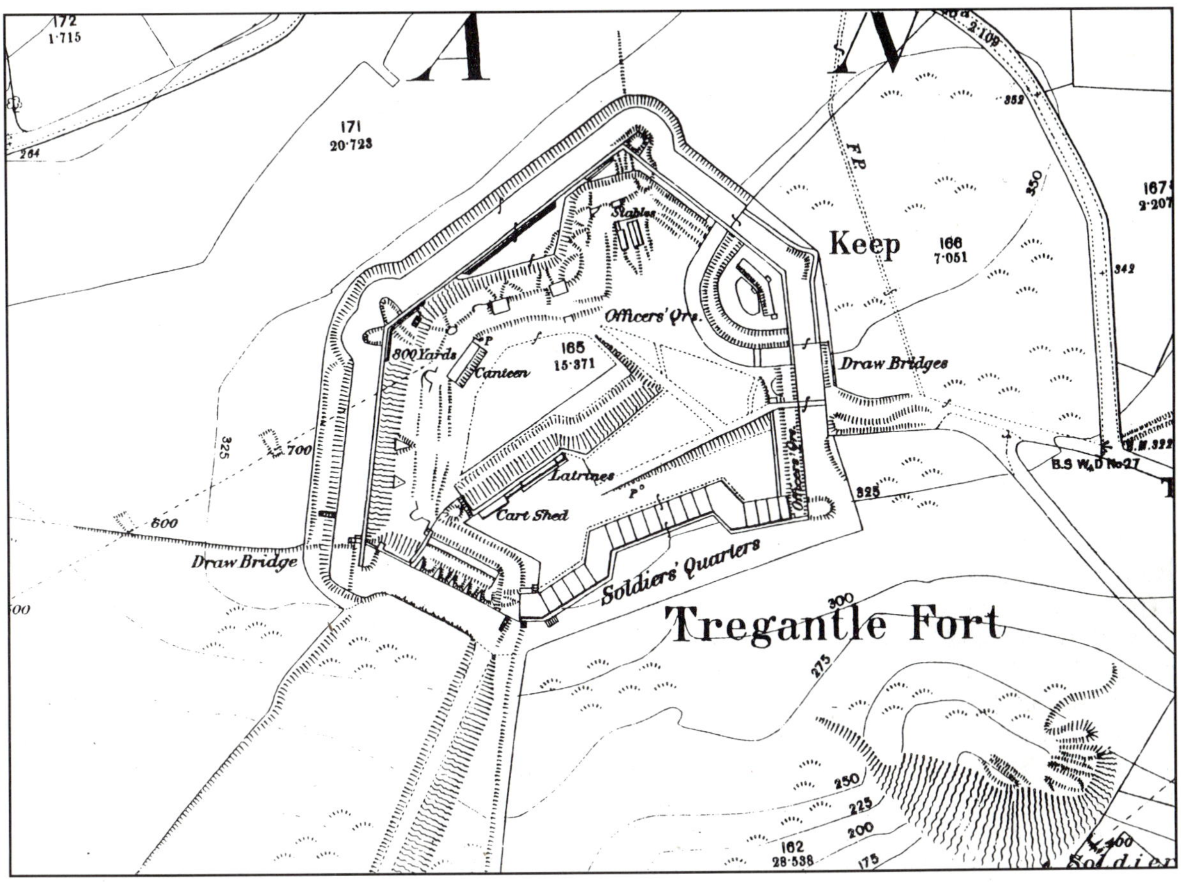

Fig. 37: Tregantle Fort in 1896 (PRO: WO 78/2314)

Plate 61: Tregantle Fort (Photograph: S. Hartgroves. Frame: ABP/F24/1. Copyright: Cornwall Archaeological Unit)

all sides except for the S by a *c*. 20ft deep dry rock-cut ditch which is defended by bombproof *caponiers* (1 double and 3 single) and musketry galleries (mostly defended by drop ditches). Beyond the ditch is an extensive *glacis*, defended on the N.W flank by a covered way containing traverses. Spoil from the construction of the fort is dumped to the S & S.W., in the area of the former soldiers' gardens. A deep ditch (recommended by Jervois in 1858) runs from the S.W salient down to the sea, with an embankment and roadway running at an angle behind; this diverges from the ditch towards the S.

Plate 62: Tregantle Fort, N.W salient & double caponier (Exeter Archaeology)

The Keep is semi-circular in plan and is protected by ditches to the E and W; both are flanked by counterscarp galleries. At each end of the ditch on the outside are musketry galleries; these face the N and S.E *caponiers*, which fire in the opposite direction. The main entrance to the fort is from the E and was originally entered via a drawbridge, and there is also a small sallyport with drawbridge adjoining the S.W *caponier* and another at the S salient, opening onto the roadway down to the sea. The W, N.W and N flanks were further protected by a partial *chemin des rondes* and firing-step, itself protected by flanking galleries. Access to the *chemin des rondes* is via a passage into the double *caponier* (via a small drawbridge), and from another adjoining the keep ditch. On the N flank the effective length of the face was increased by constructing the rampart in an indented, zig-zag form (a *crémaillère*), thus allowing more guns to be mounted.

The armament was concentrated on the N, N.W and S.W flanks and in the Keep. Three of the original stone gun embrasures survive on the N & N.W flanks, two of which have been modified to take guns of later pattern. In addition there are two single Haxo casemates served by expense magazines underneath (although there are no ammunition lifts), which presumably mounted 7-inch RBL guns. There are two Moncrieff emplacements, again probably originally for 7-inch

Plate 63: Tregantle Fort, double caponier (Exeter Archaeology)

Plate 65: Tregantle Fort, 1880s emplacement for a 64-pdr RML (Exeter Archaeology)

RBL guns, one at the W salient and one at the N.W salient (overlooking the double *caponier*); both have been adapted to take different guns. There are two other concrete gun emplacements of the 1880s, probably for 64-pdr RML guns. Other original features include an expense magazine on the N flank and masonry store-recesses on the N.W rampart and on the roof of the Keep. There are a further five Haxo gun casemates on the S.W flank facing down a landscaped *glacis* towards the sea. These were probably built after 1869 on the recommendations of the report and of General Todleben in 1864. At the southern end there is a further gun casemate at a lower level covering the ditch. The S flank was defended by gun embrasures and musketry loops in each of the barrack casemates. The roof of the barracks was defended by a parapet wall similar to that at Crownhill. The barracks along the gorge side however were, together with the *caponiers*, originally earth-covered and bombproof. The Keep has a series of bomb-proof gun casemates facing out across the fort, each of which is flanked by musketry-loops, and a set on the same level facing out across the ditch to the E. At roof level there are further emplacements firing over earthen ramparts into the interior of the fort and through embrasures in the parapet wall out to the E. The Keep has a central courtyard and is entered via a drawbridge from the S and up a stair from the galleries below. It contains the main magazine of the fort.

Within the fort is a central traverse dividing the upper and lower parades and protecting the rear of the barracks; it contains one room (now filled in) and some water tanks. There is a further set of three barrack

Plate 64: Tregantle Fort, 1860s emplacement (Exeter Archaeology)

casemates behind the central *caponier* and there is also accommodation in the *caponiers*. Other surface buildings consist of a stable-block to the N and stores and barrack casemates to the rear of the Haxo casemates on the S.W flank, together with a cart-shed and washrooms/urinals on the lower parade and a defended guardroom adjoining the main entrance at first-floor level. The access road was originally protected by an embankment to the S (now removed).

Later remains include two viewing or firing platforms for target ranges above the double *caponier* and at the W salient, another short range in the N ditch, and a series of foxholes, probably WWII in date, along the N and N.W ramparts. Others probably existed elsewhere but have been filled in. Some more modern buildings have been built within the lower parade adjoining the access road and water tanks installed on the roof of the Keep. Other 20th-century buildings have recently been removed from the upper parade and from the gorge ditch of the fort outside the S.E *caponier*.

Outside the fort there was originally a camp which dates to the early 20th century and has now been demolished. A few hut-bases and walls are still visible and, although their construction has disturbed the surface of the original *glacis*, the extent of the latter can still be discerned.

Present use/condition

The fort is still in MoD ownership and is used as barrack accommodation for units utilising the target ranges and training areas. Ranges occupy the *glacis* to the S.W of the fort. Most of the expense magazines and the small barrack block in the N.W flank of the fort, together with the stable-blocks, are empty. The Keep is unused but it has recently been cleared out and is awaiting repairs to the roof. The S barrack blocks are still in use and those to the rear of the Haxo casemates have just been refurbished. None of the *caponiers* are used in any way and have suffered due to damp, intermittent fires and general neglect. The ditch on the N side has recently been cleared of trees and vegetation, as has the rampart, affording a very clear view of the defences on this side. Some of the newly exposed parts of the structure however, such as the firing-step along the *chemin des rondes* and parts of the counterscarp wall and possibly scarp wall of the ditch,

Plate 66: Tregantle Fort, casemate in keep (Exeter Archaeology)

now need consolidation. The remainder of the fort is in relatively good condition although what appears to be serious subsidence is visible within the lower gun casemate to the S of the Haxo battery on the S.W flank. MoD are monitoring the cracked wall.

Sources
General
11 - 15, 17 - 19; K, O, Q.
Specific

1857-62	Plans of Plymouth and Devonport defences. PRO: MPH 629
1895	Plan of Scraesdon, Tregantle and railway. PRO: WO 78/3479
1913	Plan of fort. PRO: WO 78/3698
1915	Plan PRO: WO 78/3689
1915	First floor plan. PSA: 023268B
1920	Plan of Scraesdon and Tregantle Forts (landowners) (held by K. Rawlings, FSGSW)
1936	Plan of Keep and main magazine. PSA: 023279B
1942	Basement plan of fort. PSA: 023269B
1952	Plans of N.W *Caponier*. PSA: 023281B
1955	First-floor plan of fort, and camp. PSA: 023283X

SCRAESDON FORT

PAR = ANTONY, NGR = SX39305490, PRN = 6361, MAP 1 No. 45

This represents (with Tregantle) one of the two forts of the Western Defences of Plymouth (the Antony Position), the construction of which was originally recommended by Jervois in a memo of February 1858. With Tregantle and another proposed fortification sited in between (not built) it was intended to deny the Maker peninsula, and the opportunity to bombard the Dockyard, to an enemy approaching from the west, and to cover both the new turnpike road from St Germans to Devonport and the Lynher River. Jervois originally recommended an armament of 35 guns, the provision of a permanent line of defence between the fort and the river, the construction of a tower at the gorge, and the provision of bombproof barracks for 300 men. Construction (by George Roach and Co. to a design by Captain Crossman) probably began in late 1858, at the same time as Tregantle, and was largely complete by July 1868. The original design (submitted in 1859 and signed by Queen Victoria) included a keep within the upper parade and barrack accommodation around its perimeter; the keep, and much of the latter, were subsequently omitted in the early 1860s. The 1860 Royal Commission recommended in addition the construction of a permanent ditch and rampart between Scraesdon and Tregantle, and of the intermediate works recommended by Jervois; none of these were in the event built. The 1869 report stated that the fort was largely complete and listed the intended armament as 57 guns, of which 27 were to be on the rampart; each expense magazine was to serve 4 - 5 guns, and three

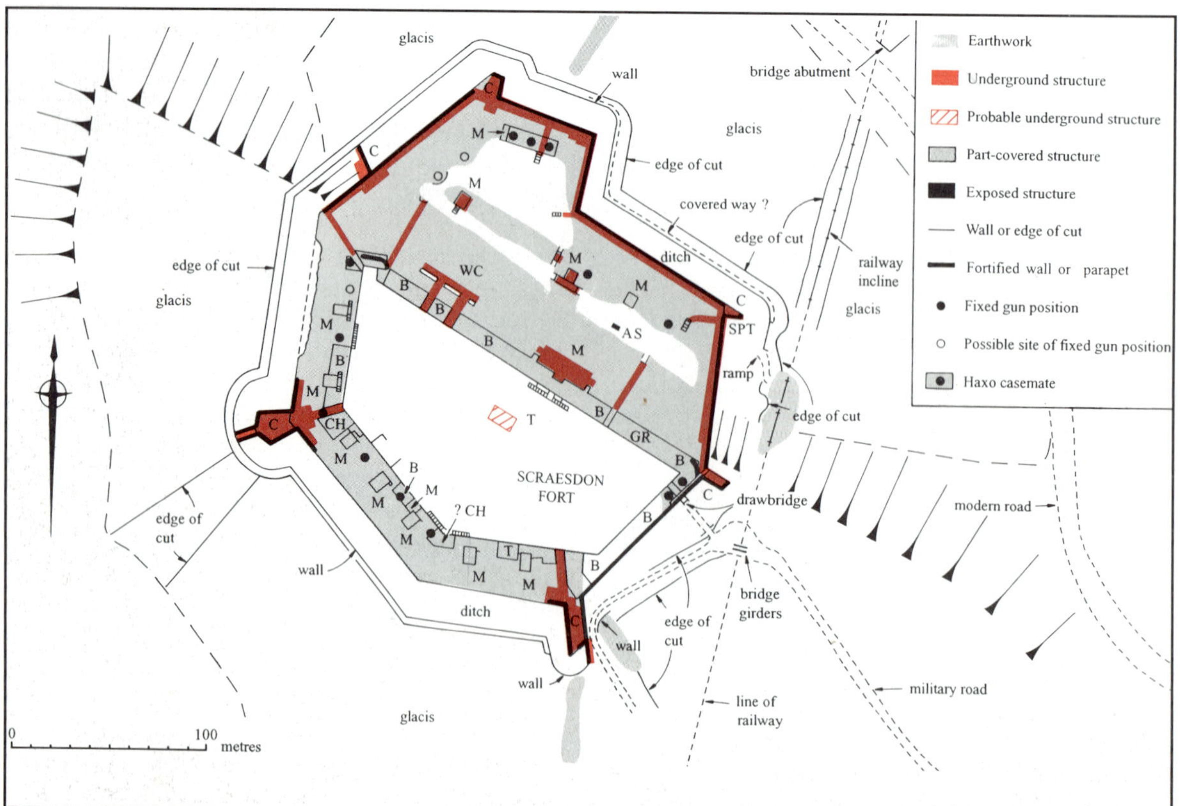

Fig. 38: Scraesdon Fort

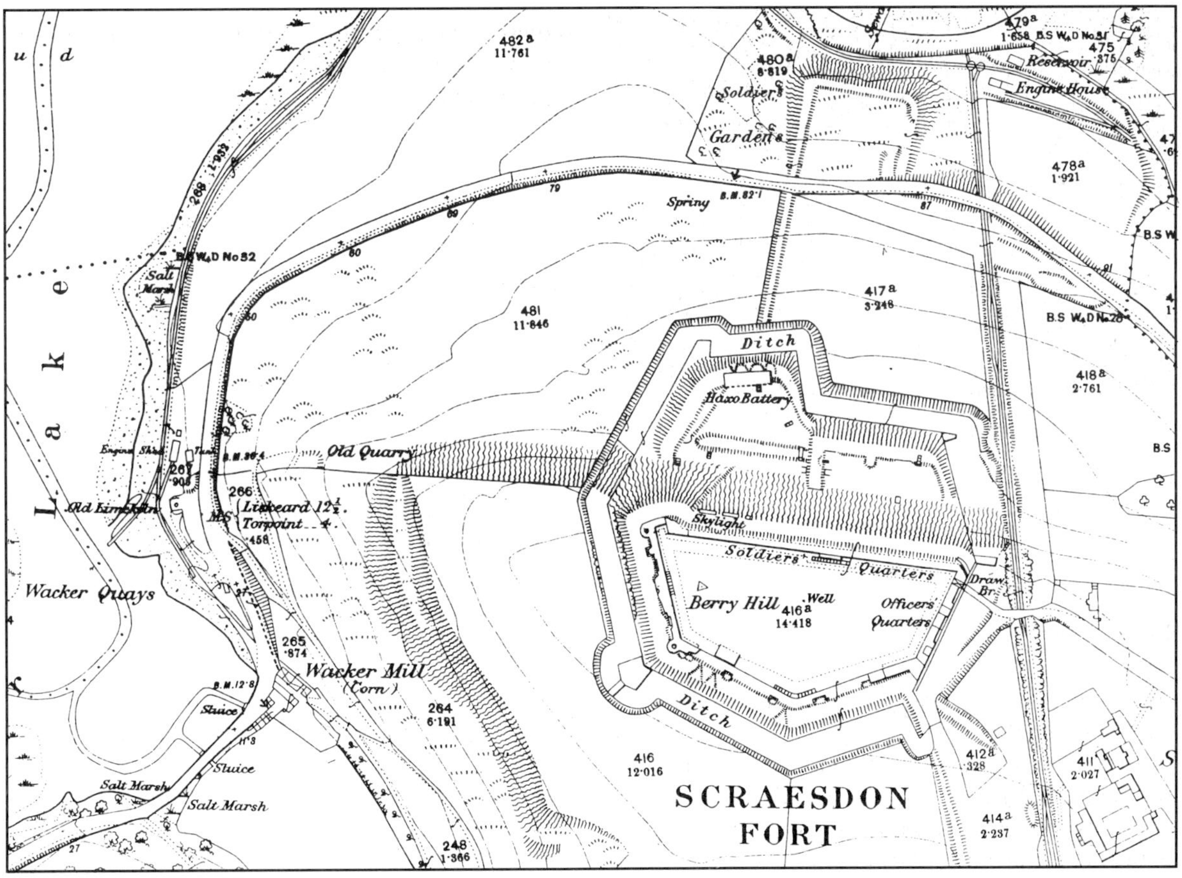

Fig. 39: Scraesdon Fort in 1896 (PRO: WO 78/2314)

had been built by 1868. The central traverse held the main magazine, and was intended to protect the upper parade from fire from across the river to the N; the report also advocated the provision of a traverse (containing further barracks) within the upper parade to protect the magazine from fire from the S, and the remodelling of the magazine itself; the completion of the gun embrasures and positions was only advocated in the event of a specific threat. The three Haxos on the lower parade are also mentioned, and are depicted on a plan of 1870. The fort apparently remained unarmed at least until 1875, when an armament of twenty-five 7-

Plate 67: Scraesdon Fort (Photograph: S. Hartgroves. Frame: ABP/F35/162. Copyright: Cornwall Archaeological Unit)

inch RBL guns, six 8-inch howitzers and ten SB flank guns was recommended. By 1885 two 7-inch RBL guns had been mounted at the N and N.W salients of the upper parade, and three in the Haxo battery; in addition the mounting of several other guns had been either approved or proposed, and several guns were lying in the fort. By 1893 the mounted armament had increased by the addition of one 64-pdr RML gun on the N.W face and three 7-inch RBLs on the west (i.e. S.W) face of the upper parade, two 5-inch BL guns on the middle parade (the E part of the lower parade), and two 32-pdr SBBL guns in the lower tier of the double *caponier*. The fort was probably disarmed towards the end of the century, and is currently used by the Armed Services for dry training.

Plate 68: Scraesdon Fort, upper parade (Exeter Archaeology)

The fort is sited on a hill overlooking the Lynher River and Wacker Lake, and commands a wide area to the W and S. It is built on two levels, with the upper level (upper parade) lying at 254 feet a.s.l. and the lower level (lower and middle parades) at 173 feet. It is a polygonal work surrounded by a 30 feet deep rock cut ditch on all sides except the gorge, which is fronted by a shallower ditch and faces S.E. The main entrance gate is sited within the gorge and is approached via an iron girder bridge with a drawbridge (which still survives) adjoining the gate itself. The ditch and gorge are defended by six (1 double and 5 single) *caponiers* (mostly fronted by drop ditches) and by musketry galleries, and by a loopholed escarp gallery along the scarp wall of the lower parade. In addition the gorge could be defended by guns mounted in the barrack casemates along this side, which each contain a gun embrasure flanked by musketry loops; further protection to the gate was provided by two gun positions sited immediately above it. The fort is surrounded by an extensive *glacis* (except on the gorge side), within which several distinct landscaped planes can be discerned; the area to the rear (S.E) of the fort is protected by a continuation of the natural escarpment running NW-SE through the fort and by an embankment running southwards from the S *caponier*. The area between the fort and the river is protected by an earthen embankment (the slight earthen breastwork referred to by the Royal Commission), access to the rear of which appears to have been via a covered way leading around the outside of the ditch from a sallyport adjoining the E. *caponier*; access to the covered way from the bottom of the ditch was via a ramp. At its N

Plate 69: Scraesdon Fort, S.E Caponier (Exeter Archaeology)

end the embankment is continuous with, and extends around, the edge of a large dump of spoil (presumably from the excavation of the ditch), which is also the site of an extensive system of later infantry trenches and foxholes (see separate entry). This, and the fort, are skirted by the military railway built from Wacker Quay to Tregantle Down in the early 1890s (see separate entry); the railway incline clips the fort ditch, and the girders of the bridge carrying the access road to the fort over the railway cutting (now infilled) outside the fort gate remain visible.

Within the fort, the guns which were eventually mounted were concentrated on the W and S.W faces of the upper parade, and on the N faces of the lower and middle parades. Two well-preserved emplacements (complete with pivot, racer (or tracking) rails and tackle loops) for 7-inch RBL guns on Moncrieff (disappearing) mountings lie at the N and W salients of the upper parade, together with concrete emplacements for the 64-pdr RML gun and the three 7-inch RBL guns (mounted *en barbette*) listed in 1893. On the lower parade the three Haxo gun casemates remain complete with racer rails, tackle-loops and adjoining expense magazines, and the concrete emplacements for the two 5-inch BL guns listed in 1893 remain visible on the N

Plate 70: Scraesdon Fort, Moncrieff emplacement (Exeter Archaeology)

Plate 71: Scraesdon Fort, Haxo casemates (Exeter Archaeology)

face of the middle parade, separated by a contemporary expense magazine, and with a later surface ?shelter building to the rear. Earlier empty gun platforms are visible to the W of the Haxo battery, together with expense magazines sited under the traverse to the rear and within the traverse separating the lower and middle parades, and a total of seven on the ramparts of the upper parade. Should an enemy have gained the lower parade, additional protection for the upper parade was afforded by an earthen rampart and firing step along the top of the central traverse, strengthened by a stone parapet wall and firing step at each end. There may also, as in other forts elsewhere, be the remains of later infantry trenches within the top of the ramparts, but these are heavily obscured by vegetation.

Plate 72: Scraesdon Fort, main magazine (Exeter Archaeology)

The main magazine, toilets, soldiers' quarters and a guardroom/cell are sited in vaulted casemates under the central traverse, with access from the upper parade; two flights of steps connect the upper and lower/middle parades, with further access being provided via the escarp gallery. The officers' quarters were sited in casemates along the gorge and along part of the S.W face; the remaining faces of the parade held casemates used for stables, a cookhouse, expense magazines, stores, and additional soldiers' quarters. There is also the remains of a freestanding building, which was built between 1870 and 1896 and was used as a dining room in 1907. The main gate is flanked on the north by a guardroom containing the remains of the drawbridge mechanism. Although largely derelict and open to the elements, important fixtures and fittings do survive, including ornate and plain guard rails around the rampart walk, and around stairwells and the stairs within the escarp and musketry galleries and *caponiers*, shelving/racking and fireplaces in some of the barrack casemates, wooden flooring and some joinery in these and in the main magazine in particular, original slate divisions within the urinals, and the pivots, racer rails and tackle-loops belonging to several of the guns, most particularly the Moncrieff mountings.

Present use/condition

The fort is still in MoD ownership, and is used intermittently for dry assault training. It is generally therefore empty, with the rooms open to the elements. The upper parade is clear, and recent Nissen huts within it have been demolished, together with much of the 'dining room'. The casemates and *caponiers* are all open (except the double *caponier*), and as a result relatively few internal fixtures and fittings survive unscathed; several of the suspended wooden floors have been replaced with concrete and the fireplaces have mostly been blocked up. Many of the ornate iron railings have been removed, and several sections lie loose in the escarp gallery, together with probably other fittings such as iron shutters from the *caponier* embrasures. Most of the gun positions however survive in very good condition, except the concrete of one of the Moncrieff pits, which is badly cracked. Overall the masonry structure of the fort is in good condition, although the ramparts, lower parade and much of the ditches are heavily overgrown. The ditch is largely free of infilling, except around the S *caponier* adjoining the farm. The *glacis* and embankments survive largely complete and uncluttered, except for disturbance caused by the construction of the railway in the 1890s.

Sources

General

11, 12, 13, 14, 15, 17, 18, 19; K, Q.

Specific

1784	Plan of Heights of West Anthony by Lieut. Col. Dixon PRO: WO 78/859
1857-62	Plans of Plymouth and Devonport defences. PRO: MPH 629
1859	Plan. PRO: WO 78/482
1859	Plan and sections. PRO: MR 1271. (WO 78/483)
1870	Plans and sections of the fort. PSA: 023262-5B
1895	Plan of Scraesdon, Tregantle, and railway. PRO: WO 78/3479
1907	Plan. PSA: 023260B (also copy held by K. Rawlings, FSGSW)
1920	Plan of Scraesdon and Tregantle Forts (landowners) (held by K. Rawlings, FSGSW)
1931	Plan. PSA: 023261B (also copy held by K. Rawlings, FSGSW)

SCRAESDON FOXHOLES

PAR = ANTONY, NGR = SX 39425515, PRN = 6361.1, MAP 1 No. 46

These are a series of interlinked infantry trenches and positions located on the spoil heap to the N.E of Scraesdon Fort, overlooking the St. Germans or Lynher River. There are a series of positions truncating the slight rampart along the W and N sides of the heap, with communication trenches extending to the rear. They probably date to WWI or WWII, but display no evidence of corrugated iron and stake revetment, as found elsewhere on the ramparts of the forts to the N of Plymouth; they may therefore have been dug for training, or have been earlier in date. Another set of apparent foxholes show up as cropmarks on recent aerial photographs; these are sited on the fort *glacis* to the S.

Present condition

The area is currently heavily overgrown and wooded, as are some of the trenches. Apart from this, the system appears to survive intact.

Sources
General
19.

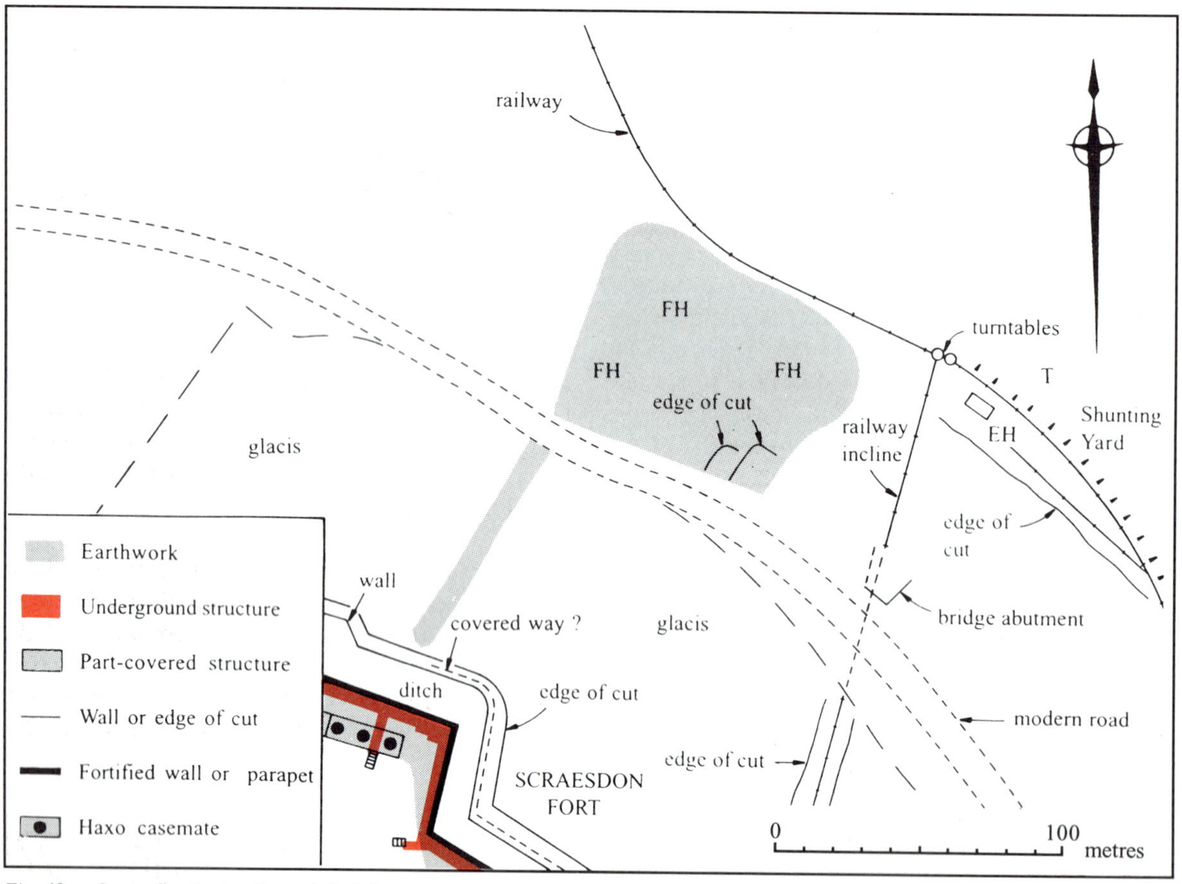

Fig. 40: Scraesdon Fort, railway & foxholes

WACKER - TREGANTLE RAILWAY

PAR = ANTONY, NGR = SX 38935509 - 39125305, PRN = 6360, MAP 1 Nos 47 & 48

This extended from Wacker Quay (No. 48) on the St Germans or Lynher River to Tregantle Down Battery (No. 49) on Whitsand Bay, and was built between June 1886 and 1893 to supply Tregantle and Scraesdon Forts and the new batteries being built along Whitsand Bay and between Rame Head and Penlee Point. It was originally intended to construct it as far as Penlee but in the event was only built as far as Tregantle Down. Its course, extent and associated structures are clearly depicted on the map of 1896, with Engine Sheds at Wacker Quay (SX 38955503), at the shunting yard at the foot of the incline near Scraesdon Fort (SX 39525515), and at the end of a passing loop at the top near Scraesdon Farm (SX 39385463). Most of the line was single track, except for the incline and passing loops near Wacker Quay and Scraesdon Farm. At the foot of the incline was a shunting yard and a pair of turntables. Much of the rolling stock and at least some of the prefabricated structures had originally been shipped out to the Sudan in 1885, but were not in the event used and were brought back. By 1905 the railway had shut down.

Much of the line of the railway is still visible, with especially well-preserved sections extending from Wacker Quay around to the shunting yard, up the incline to Scraesdon Fort (although the cutting at the top has been infilled), from Scraesdon Farm to the main road, within and to the S.W of Bolatherick Camp, and above Lower Tregantle; the site of the terminus at Tregantle Down also survives. At Wacker the prefab. engine shed still survives, together with a water tank nearby; the other two engine sheds have been demolished however. Other surviving features consist of a crossing gate in a hedge on the main road at SX 38755370, a bridge abutment where the main road crosses the incline, the girders of a bridge crossing the infilled cutting at the gate of Scraesdon Fort, an ?inspection pit above Lower Tregantle at approx SX 39015355, and one of the 'kissing gates' which was originally sited where a footpath crossed the railway near Lower Tregantle; this gate has since been resited at the top of this path on the main Crafthole-Millbrook road (at SX 38865350).

Present condition

Most of the course of the railway and the shunting yard is overgrown, although passable on foot. Most of the incline remains open, though some dumping is occurring at the top end. The cutting to the S has been infilled, and its S end is occupied by a slurry pit; a slurry pit also lies on the site of the demolished engine shed to the S. To the S of Scraesdon Farm the railway is used as a farm track. The section upslope from Lower Tregantle is overgrown; elsewhere the railway has either been ploughed out or lies in pasture fields. An important survival is the engine shed at Wacker Quay, which survives virtually complete, although vulnerable to vandalism.

Sources

General

18, 19; Q.

Specific

1886	'An important military railway'. Western Morning News, 6th Sept. 1886.
1895	Plan of Scraesdon, Tregantle, and railway. PRO: WO 78/3479
1987	Payton, P. 'Tregantle and Scraesdon - their Forts and Railway'
n.d.	Sambourne, R.C. 'Story of a Cornish Military Railway'

TREGANTLE DOWN BATTERY

PAR = ANTONY, NGR = SX 39005315, PRN = 6355, MAP 1 No. 49

This is sited at the head of a coombe some 200m to the S.E of Tregantle Fort and was first proposed in 1885 with an armament of six 10-inch BL howitzers to cover Whitsand Bay and (with Rame Church and Hawkins Batteries) to prevent ships from standing off and bombarding the Dockyard. It was also sited at the terminus of the military railway from Wacker Quay. It was constructed by Messrs Debnam and Sons between *c.*1890 and 1892, when it was completed; by 1893 it was armed with four 12-ton 9-inch RML howitzers on high-angle mountings. In 1895 another two 9-inch guns were recommended but were not mounted. A plan of 1905 shows two pairs of gun positions, separated by two pairs of cartridge and shell stores, a shelter, and an artillery store. By 1908 the guns appear to have been dismounted as the battery is not shown on the Defence Scheme maps or on the Plymouth Fortress telephone network of 1915. The battery was apparently abandoned in 1922.

The site of the battery was infilled in the 1970s to form the present car park. However the outlines of at least two of the gun pits are visible at surface as slight hollows containing differential fills. The sunken access way at the N end is still evident, as is the terminus area of the railway immediately to the S of and beyond the car park.

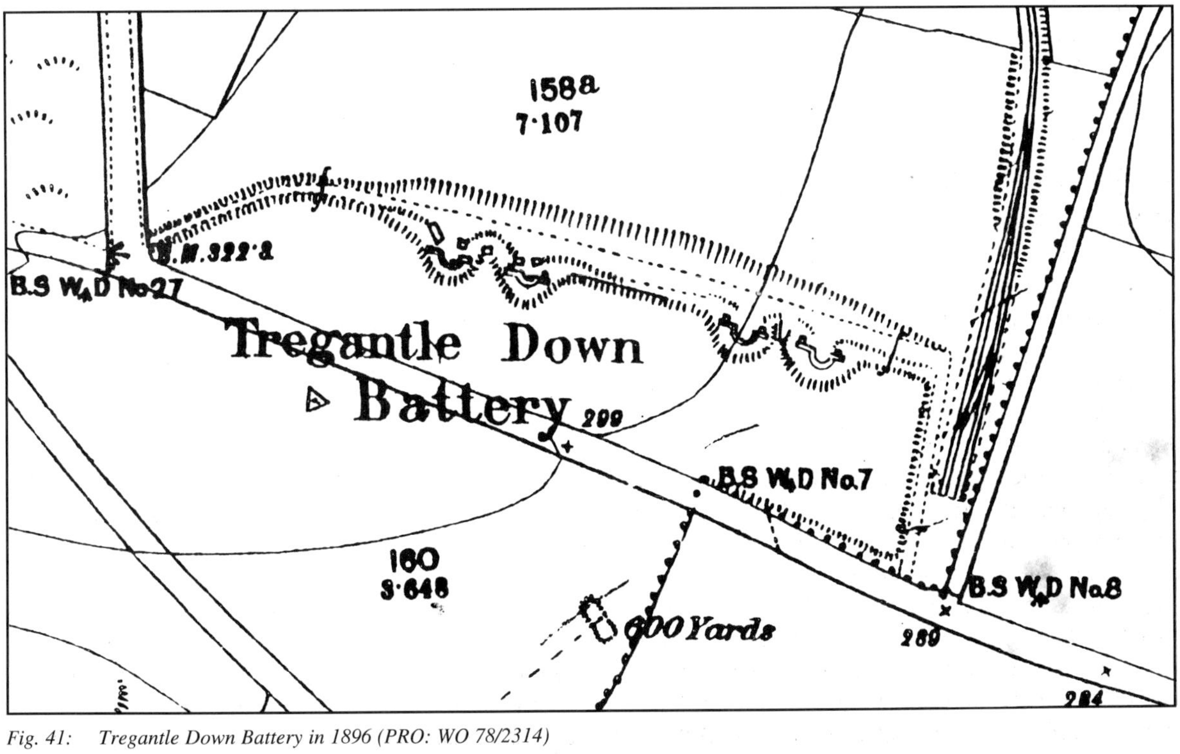

Fig. 41: Tregantle Down Battery in 1896 (PRO: WO 78/2314)

Present condition

The battery has been infilled to the level of the tops of the gun pits. Therefore the mountings and other fittings, together with the underground structures (which may still remain as voids), probably still survive largely complete as archaeological remains. It is currently a car park.

Sources

General

17, 18, 19, 21, 24; F, K, Q.

Specific

1892	? Report. PRO: WO 196/29
1898	?Armament table. PRO: CAB 7/6
1905	Plan, showing the four 9-inch RML emplacements. PRO: MR 1068

3.2.5. Whitsand Bay

CROWSTONE FIELD POSITION FINDING STATION

PAR = ANTONY, NGR = SX 38975263, PRN = 37101, MAP 1 No. 50

This is sited on the brow of the coastal slope, some 0.5km to the S of Tregantle Down Battery, whose guns it presumably served. Two cells were built by 1894, but had become redundant by 1915, as it does not feature on the Fortress telephone network of that date. The current O.S. map shows two cells with a sunken accessway to the rear, surrounded by an ?unclimbable fence and a larger area of War Dept. land.

The two cells are sited on the brow of the coastal slope just above a quarry, and enjoy wide views S.W across Whitsand Bay. Both have been demolished to the level of their viewing windows, with the interior being infilled and the side walls surviving below ground. The concrete sill of the W cell is visible, whilst the E cell is visible as a hollow. The accessway to the rear is visible as a linear hollow, and the boundary stone remains in situ to the N; there is no trace of the surrounding fence or of the other stones.

Present condition

The cells have been demolished and infilled, although substantial remains of the side walls probably survive below ground. The area is rough grazing, with occasional low scrub.

Sources
General
18, 19, 24.

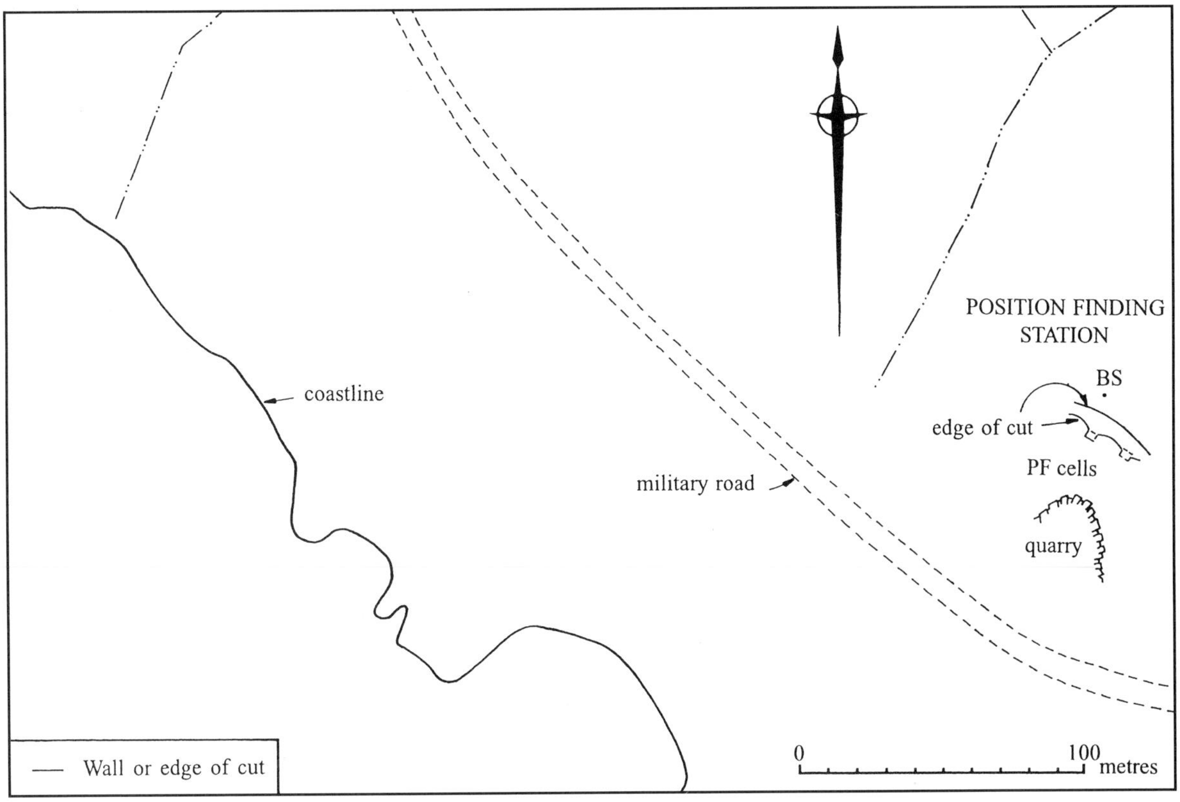

Fig. 42: Crowstone Field PF Station

WHITSAND BAY BATTERY

PAR = ST. JOHN, NGR = SX 40855150, PRN = 6106, MAP 1 No. 51

This is sited on a hill overlooking the bay, *c.* 0.5km to the S of Stone Farm, and was first proposed in 1885 as a battery of three 12.5-inch RML guns intended to defend against long-range bombardment of the Dockyard. Construction began after summer 1888 and was probably complete by 1890; by 1893 the three RMLs had been mounted, together with two 6-inch BL guns on hydraulic disappearing (Elswick) mountings. The battery was built by W.T Jinkin of Plymouth and in 1894 was surrounded by a 20 feet deep trench revetted on the inside with a vertical wall 1 to 8 feet thick and protected by three octagonal concrete *caponiers*; it contained casemated barracks and also caretaker's quarters, and the drawbridge was yet to be completed or the *caponiers* armed. In 1897 or shortly afterwards the 6-inch guns were removed, followed by the RML guns in 1912; there was also an abortive proposal in 1906 to mount two 9.2-inch guns in two of the central emplacements. In the early 1900s there were also three Depression Range Finders (DRFs) within the battery, and a command post on each flank. The battery was not apparently armed during WWI or WWII, and was released by the MoD in 1951.

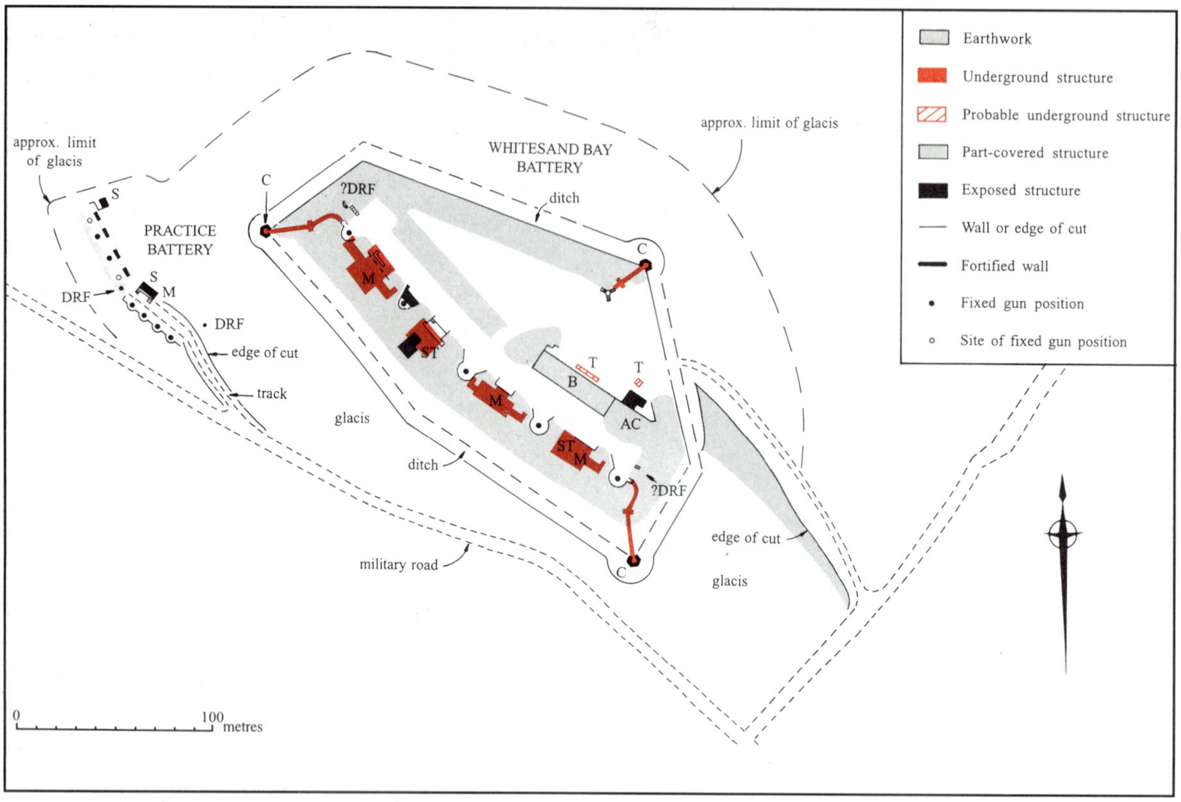

Fig. 43: *Whitsand Bay Batteries*

It was not possible to view the site during the survey, and therefore the following description and comments on condition are based on the study of aerial photographs taken in 1989, and on historical and current maps. The battery is protected by a rock cut ditch, covered by three musketry *caponiers*; additional protection on the land facing sides was provided by an earthen firing platform to the rear of the rampart, and the surrounding area within War Dept. ownership was kept clear to form a *glacis*. However, due to the subsequent construction of the practice battery to the S.W and the recent terracing of the N and N.W flanks to provide additional caravan spaces, the extent to which this *glacis* was deliberately landscaped and levelled is not clear. Access to the battery is via a road from the E; this is sited within a cutting, and is further protected on its seaward side by an embankment formed from the spoil. In the interior of the battery,

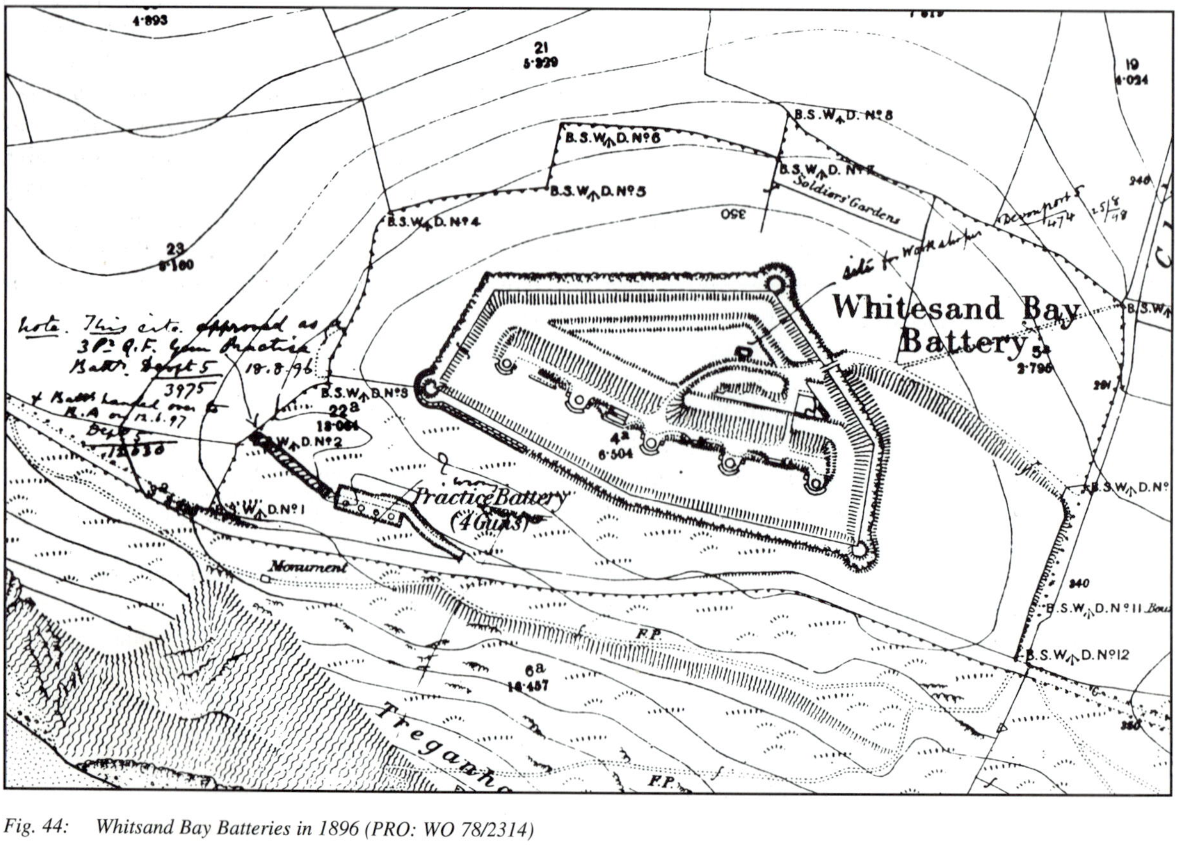

Fig. 44: *Whitsand Bay Batteries in 1896 (PRO: WO 78/2314)*

Plate 73: Whitsand Bay Battery (Photograph: S. Hartgroves. Frame: ABP/F24/3. Copyright: Cornwall Archaeological Unit)

five gun pits (the three 64-pdr RML guns to the E and the two 6-inch guns to the W) are sited along the rear of the sea-facing rampart; underground magazines and Artillery Stores are sited in between, and on each flank there was/is a flight of steps, presumably leading up to Depression Range Finder (DRF) positions. An earthen traverse protects the rear of the gun positions and magazines, and towards its E end contains barrack accommodation. This, together with the nearby caretaker's quarters, were protected by another earthen traverse sited along the S side of the (?sunken) accessway to the guns. Subsequently other surface buildings were added, including two structures on the sea-facing rampart.

Present condition

This can only at present be determined from study of the 1989 aerial photographs and from reports by FSGSW. The *glacis* to the S and S.E remains intact, together with the Practice Battery and the access road and embankment; the *glacis* slope to the N.W and N has however been largely destroyed by terracing for caravans. Large sections of the ditch have been partially infilled and in part widened to accommodate caravans; this is particularly noticeable on the seaward side, where the scarp wall appears to have been demolished and the rampart behind partly removed - it is this material which has presumably been used to infill the ditch. The *caponiers* at the S.W and N.E corners are visible in outline, although it is not clear whether they survive complete (with the ditch being infilled around them) or have been partly demolished; the S.E *caponier* is not visible on the photographs. In the interior the rampart has been removed from either side of the entrance, which has been widened, and modern buildings constructed; the caretakers' quarters, and presumably the barracks, have been retained however. Elsewhere other sections of rampart and traverse have been removed to accommodate caravans, most noticeably to the rear of the gun positions. All five of these remain in outline, although partly occupied by later buildings and caravans; it has been reported that the pivot (a re-used cannon) and racer rail have recently been removed from one of these. The condition of the underground magazines and other structures is not known; from the air the areas they occupy appear undisturbed, and therefore they may remain largely intact. Overall, although there has been collateral damage, much of the basic structure of the battery still appears to remain.

Sources

General

17, 18, 19, 21, 23; K, Q.

Specific

1896	Plan of battery. PRO: WO 78/5052
1898	Armament table? PRO: CAB 7/6
*c.*1900s	Whitesand Bay Battery Fort Record Book. PRO: WO 192/121
1906	Plan showing proposed 9.2-inch gun positions. PRO: MR 1068

WHITSAND BAY PRACTICE BATTERY

PAR = ST. JOHN, NGR = SX 40675151, PRN = 6106.1, MAP 1 No. 52

This is sited on the upper part of the coastal slope immediately to the W of Whitsand Bay Battery. It consists of two sets of four gun mountings for QF and heavier guns. The E set was originally for four 64-pdr RML guns and was built between February 1895 and 1896; subsequently two of the mountings appear to have been adapted, possibly for 6-inch guns on Vavassour mountings. The W set was built from August 1896 and handed over to the Royal Artillery in June 1897, and initially mounted 3-pdr QF guns; these were replaced by 12-pdr QF guns in 1903, although the original approved site for these apparently lay to the E of the RML positions. The RMLs may have been dismounted in 1903, followed by the QFs in *c.*1919 or in the 1950s (Hogg).

Both sets of the four open gun positions survive intact, although the QF positions to the W are not depicted on the current O.S. map. Access to the battery was via a sunken trackway from the military road below. The E set of four gun positions consist of two types of mounting placed alternately, fronted by a low concrete parapet wall. To the rear is a combined brick-built shelter/magazine, sited at a lower level, and there are the pillars of a DRF position high up on each flank. To the W, at a slightly higher level, are the partly covered remains of four QF positions, each of which has a freestanding store recess to the rear, and overgrown concrete parapets at the front. The mounting plates of the two central positions are visible, the flanking positions are completely overgrown and overlain with soil. It is accompanied by a sunken shelter building at the W end.

Plate 74: Whitsand Bay Practice Battery (Exeter Archaeology)

Present condition

The battery is sited within rough grassland and low scrub, and is largely complete. The racer rails and pivots of the RML positions remain intact, as do the mounting plates of at least two of the QF positions. The buildings and DRF positions are also generally in good condition, although overgrown; small parts of the internal brick walls of the magazine have also been demolished, although the labels remain legible.

Sources

General

19; F, K, Q.

Specific

*c.*1900 Whitesand Bay Battery Fort Record Book. PRO: WO 192/121

TRENNINOW POSITION FINDING STATION

PAR = ST. JOHN, NGR = SX 41155114, PRN = 37102, MAP 1 No. 53

This is sited on the brow of the coastal slope, adjoining the military road and some 400m to the S.E of Whitsand Bay Battery. It was built in the early 1890s, presumably to serve the guns in the battery, and five cells were present by 1894 and are shown (enclosed by an ?unclimbable fence) in 1896. These were reduced to three between 1903 and *c.* 1905, and in 1915 two cells are shown, one of which is labelled as the old Fire Commander's cell. These may have been used with the practice battery prior to its disbandment in 1919, since the main battery seems to have been disarmed in 1912.

A total of six cells are present on the site. Three occupy a terrace cut into the slope just above the road, whilst another three are sited on the brow of the hill above; these have a sunken accessway to the rear. Earth has been mounded up between and in front of each set of cells, so that only their viewing windows are visible from the seaward side; this was to mask them from view and to provide some protection from incoming fire. Five of the cells were present in 1896 and are of the same standard design and construction (shuttered concrete with internal brick lining; concrete roofs reinforced with steel girders and lined with corrugated iron). Most retain a set of three instrument pillars. The remaining cell is a larger 'L'-shaped building, and has been added after 1896; it almost certainly represents the old Fire Commander's cell of 1915. It consists of two rooms and is built of shuttered concrete throughout, and retains three instrument pillars.

Present condition

Four of the cells are heavily overgrown, together with the terrace and accessway to their rear; one however, together with the Fire Commander's cell, is largely clear. Overall the site survives largely complete (except for the loss of some brick walling, some damage to pillars, and loss of perishable internal detail) with the F.C. cell being a particularly important and complete survival. However, several of the concrete

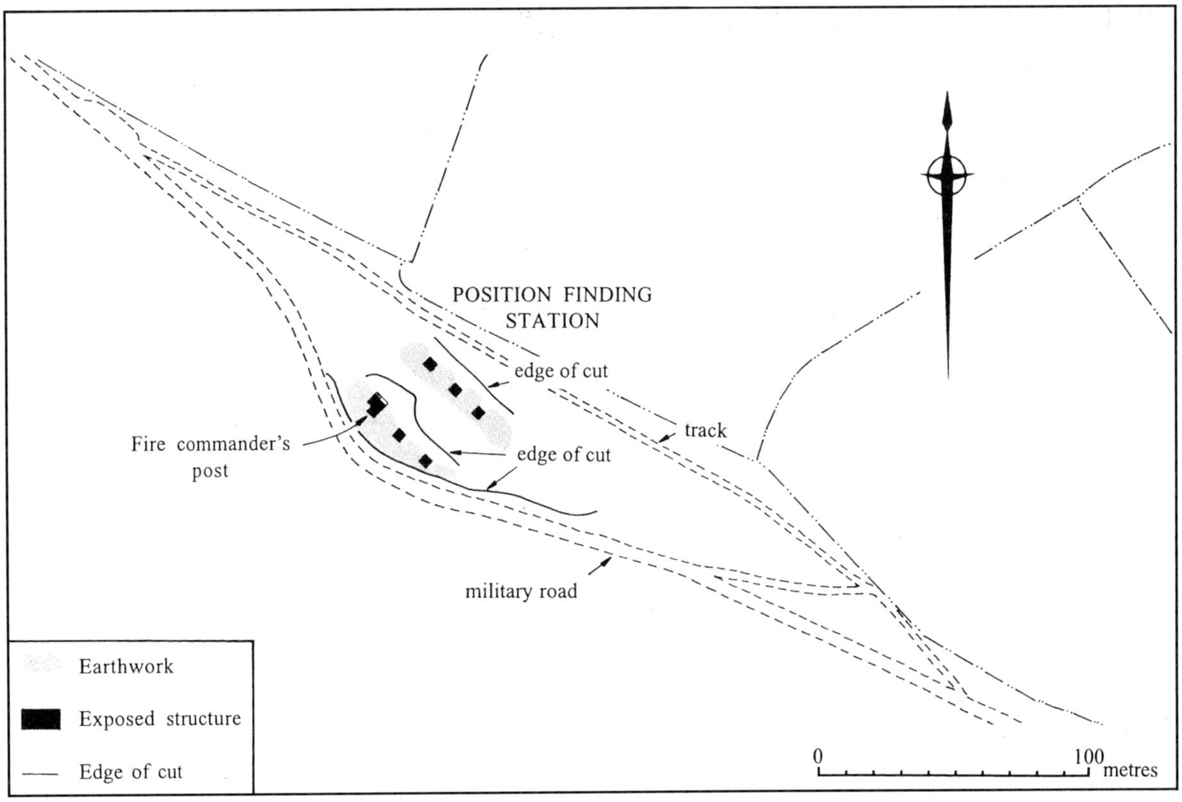

Fig. 45: Trenninow PF Station

roofs of the earlier cells are cracking and have lost their corrugated iron lining, and are probably technically unsafe; lumps of concrete are also flaking off in places.

Sources
General
18, 19, 23, 24.
Specific
*c.*1905 Whitesand Bay Battery Fort Record Book. PRO: WO 192/121

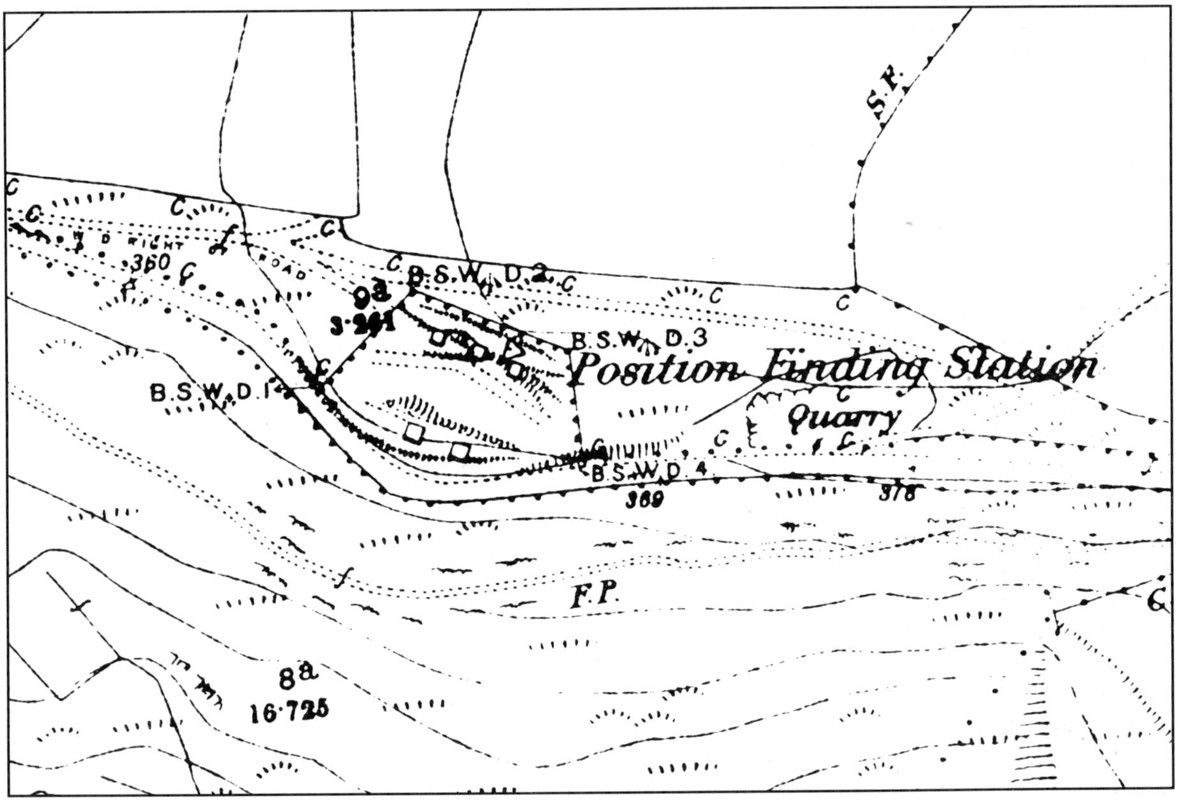

Fig. 46: Trenninow PF Station in 1896 (PRO: WO 78/2314)

Plate 75: Trenninow PF Station (Photograph: S. Hartgroves. Frame: ABP/F35/128. Copyright: Cornwall Archaeological Unit)

KNATTERBURY POSITION FINDING STATION

PAR = RAME, NGR = SX 42125006, PRN = 37093, MAP 1 No. 54

This is sited on Knatterbury Hill, overlooking Whitsand Bay, and has previously been thought to have been the site of an unfinished Palmerstonian fort. The construction on this hill of a small work (mounting 5 guns and with barrack accommodation for 100 men) was recommended in 1860 to protect Polhawn and Cawsand Batteries against assault, but in the event it appears that the funds intended for its construction

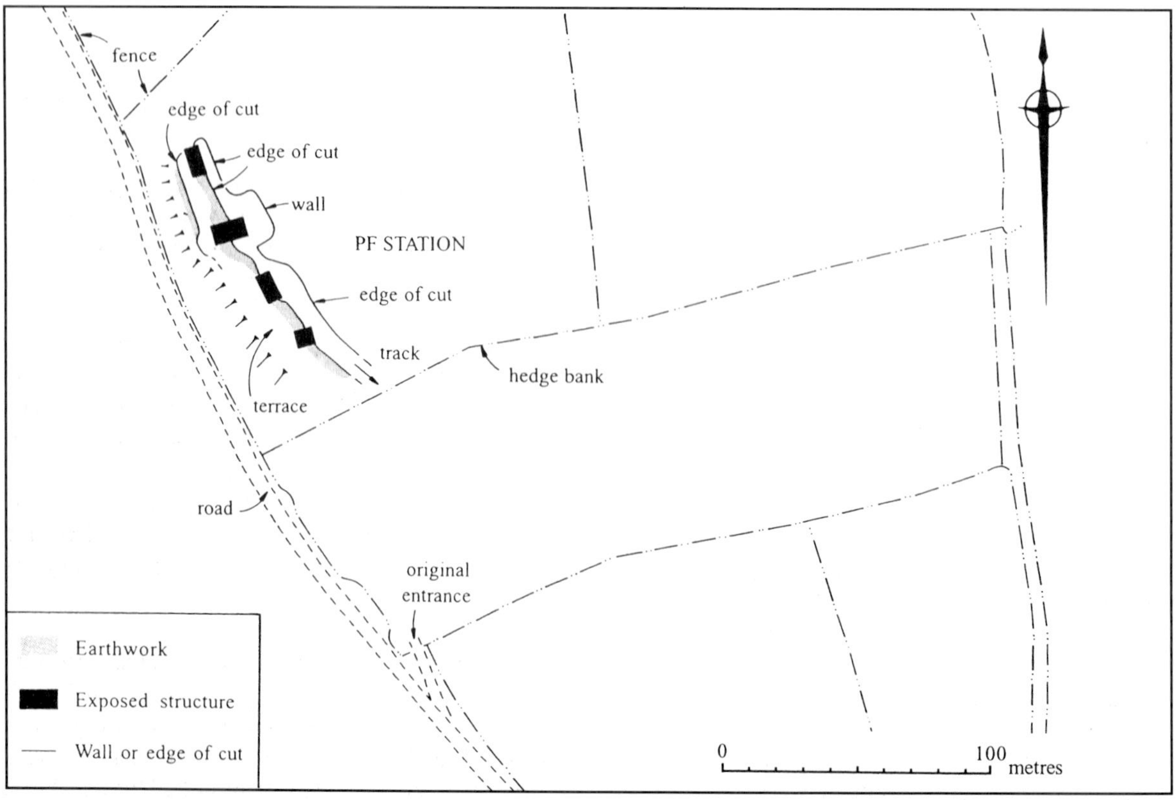

Fig. 47: Knatterbury PF Station

Plate 76: Knatterbury PF Station (Exeter Archaeology)

Plate 77: Knatterbury PF Station, instrument pillars (Exeter Archaeology)

were spent on the military road linking Tregantle with Polhawn and Cawsand, although the report of 1869 does still comment that the construction of such a work would be necessary to complete the defences. No mention is made however in subsequent correspondence that a start was ever made.

The PF station was constructed in the early 1890s to serve Hawkins and Rame Church Batteries and consisted of four cells. By 1915 this had been reduced to two cells, with the addition of a Deputy Fire Commander's cell. It became redundant with the disarming of the batteries shortly after WWI.

Four brick-walled concrete-roofed cells survive within a terrace cut into the hillside; they have been built in a very similar fashion to the other PF stations at Maker and Trenninow for example, and are separated and protected by a stone-revetted earthen bank. A sunken trackway provided access from the S.E., originally leading to a gateway in the adjoining field giving onto the military road. All four cells survive complete, two of them each containing three instrument posts and three of them having evidence for trig points or instrument settings on their roofs; all four have later been extended, either to the rear or to the side. As far as the scrub cover allows, all the visible earthworks, walling and structures on the site are consistent with the terracing, embanking and revetment accompanying the construction of the PF station and do not appear to belong to any earlier unfinished works; in addition, no clear evidence of banks on the other sides was noted, and the drop in level at the rear of the site where it borders the ploughed field is probably due to the level being reduced by ploughing.

Present condition

The station and access track is heavily overgrown with scrub and brambles, and survives complete, although some of the concrete roofs have lost their internal corrugated-iron lining and are probably technically unsafe.

Sources

General

12, 13, 15, 18, 23, 24.

POLHAWN BATTERY

PAR = RAME, NGR = SX 42074922, PRN = 6006, MAP 1 No. 55

Polhawn Battery is located halfway up the sea-cliffs at the S end of Whitsand Bay. In the invasion scare of the late 1850s the Bay was identified as a possible landing place to the rear of the proposed forts at Tregantle and Scraesdon, and to defend against this it was initially proposed to construct four artillery towers along the Bay between Tregantle and Rame Head, each to be armed with twenty guns and garrisoned with fifty men. These were not built, and in 1860 the Royal Commission recommended the construction of a ten gun battery (Polhawn) at the S end of the bay, where a landing was thought to be most likely; this was to be protected on the landward side by a small work on Knatterbury Hill (not in the event built). The battery was constructed between 1861 and 1863 at a cost of £8850, and was armed with seven 68-pdr RML guns; it was defended by a loopholed gorge on its landward side and was linked to Tregantle and Cawsand Forts with a military road (the present coastal road), along which reinforcements could be brought. In the Parliamentary Inquiry of 1869 the battery was thought to be insufficient as it was not supported on the landward side, was armed with out-of-date guns of limited range, and its western flank was exposed to fire from the sea; the construction of a small battery of heavy guns was recommended to support it, a role eventually fulfilled by Whitsand Bay Battery. The armament of 68-pdrs remained in place until 1898, and shortly after it was recommended that the armament be modernised by the installation of two 4.7-inch QF guns on the roof; there is no evidence that these were emplaced however. During or shortly before WWI the battery was apparently used as accommodation, and the magazine as a cell; the battery was released by the War Dept. in 1928.

The battery is a two-storey rubble limestone structure with dressed granite and limestone details, and brick vaulting in the interior. It consists of two wings, with loopholed single storey *caponiers* to the rear and to the W; the main entrance is via a refurbished drawbridge at roof level. The exterior is protected by a rock-cut dry

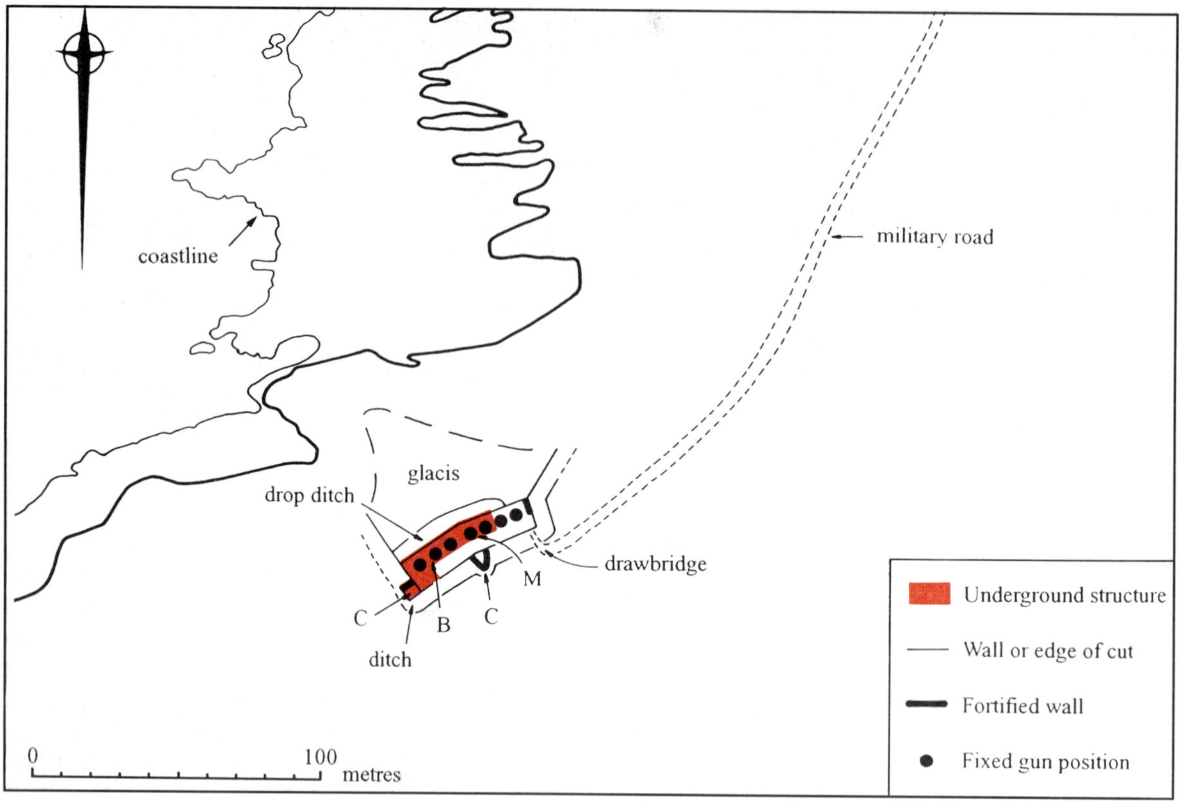

Fig. 48: Polhawn Battery

ditches along the rear and W flanks, both of which are protected by musketry *caponiers*. A further length of wet ditch extends eastwards from the E flank, and is protected by musketry loops and a *machicolation* (murder hole) in the E wall of the battery. At the front the basement level is protected by a drop ditch, and a levelled area may form a *glacis* in front of the guns (although it may be in part due to garden landscaping). Further protection was afforded by limestone firing-steps (now replaced by a flower bed) and parapets at roof level. Access to the battery is via a branch of the military road.

Access to the seven vaulted gun casemates on the first floor level is via spiral granite staircases at each end of the roof; further stairways provide separate access to the magazines and barrack casemates below, which are sited under the central and western gun casemates. The

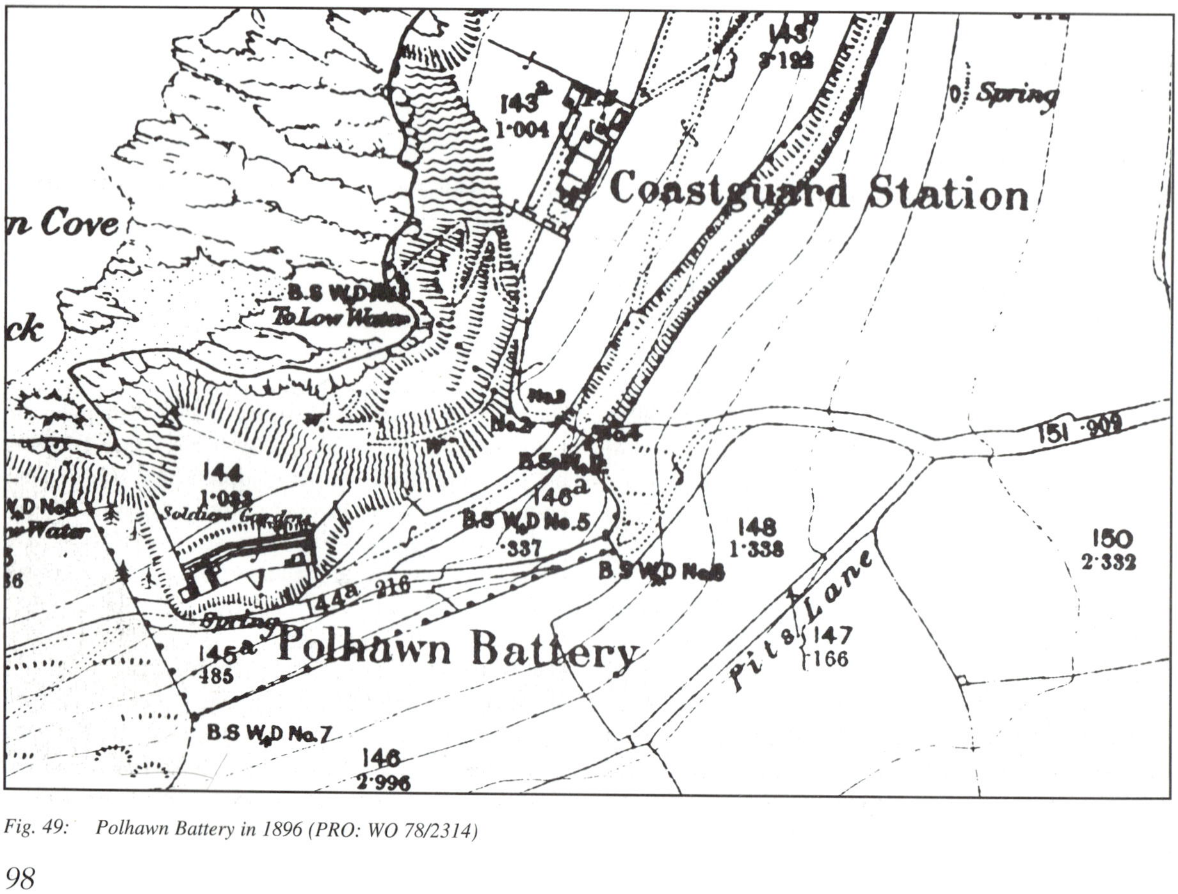

Fig. 49: Polhawn Battery in 1896 (PRO: WO 78/2314)

Plate 78: Polhawn Battery (A. Sharpe. Frame: ACS/3111. Copyright: Cornwall Archaeological Unit)

gun casemates retain the inner racer rails of the gun carriages (the outer ones have been removed and picked out in brick), expense ammunition lockers and recesses for tackle loops, and fireplaces to the rear; no mantlet bars or other fittings survive around the embrasures. They were lit by windows to the rear, some of which still retain their original armoured folding shutters. At basement level there are three barrack casemates, each of which had a fireplace and are lit by shuttered windows opening to the front, and the magazine. This consists of a cartridge store and shell store, and a lamp room or shifting lobby to the W. A separate lamp passage lit the two stores. The shell-store, lamp room/shifting lobby and access passage all retain their original suspended wooden floors. Other fixtures and fittings which survive include the wooden door (complete with brass fittings) of the cartridge store and later ?WWI graffiti on the walls inside, the shutters of a store recess and vent at casemate level, iron guardrails to the stairs, armoured window shutters, and much of the drawbridge mechanism.

Present condition

The building is currently used as a self-catering hotel and is well maintained. The drawbridge has recently been refurbished and is now in working order. The ditch to the E is waterlogged and heavily overgrown, whilst the counterscarp of the flanking wall to the W has been removed and the hillside terraced relatively recently; the ditch to the rear has been partially infilled to the S of the *caponier* and contains garden terracing. The *glacis* area to the front has been landscaped and is used as a garden.

Sources

General

11, 12, 14, 15, 17, 19; K, Q.

Specific

n.d. Plan showing proposed 4.7-inch QF guns. PRO: WO 78/4055

Plate 79: Polhawn Battery, gun casemates & drop ditch (Exeter Archaeology)

Plate 80: Polhawn Battery, gun casemate (Exeter Archaeology)

3.2.6. Rame Head to Penlee Point

RAME CHURCH BATTERY

PAR = RAME, NGR = SX 42924924, PRN = 6009, MAP 1 No. 56

This is sited immediately behind the brow of the coastal ridge just to the E of Rame, and was intended to cover the approaches to the Sound. A battery of six 10-inch BL howitzers was first proposed on or near this site in 1885, together with another of two 10-inch and two 6-inch BL guns near Rame Head (not built). A battery of four 9-inch BL guns on high-angle mountings was constructed on the present site by Messrs Reed, Blight & Co. of Plymouth in the early 1890s and was armed by 1893; a caretaker's quarters was also constructed. Initially the battery was probably protected by an unclimbable fence with *caponiers* at the corners (see 1896 map), but by WWII this seems to have been replaced by a concrete wall on a slightly different alignment (see 1983 sketch plan), with the entrance protected by a concrete pillbox. The removal of the 9-inch guns was proposed in 1905, and their replacement by two 9.2-inch BL guns on high-angle mountings (sited on the two central 9-inch positions to each side of the magazine in the central traverse) was proposed in 1909 and approved in 1911; they were present during WWI and in 1920 but were dismounted between 1927 and 1929, when the battery was declared redundant. During WWII it is thought to have been used as a radar station, with a mast being sited between the two 9.2-inch gun positions.

No above ground remains of the battery or of the surrounding wall are visible.

Present condition

The site was demolished in the 1970s and is now rough grassland and waste covered with dumping. The area to the N (rear) of the gun positions however appears to remain at its original level. Substantial below-ground remains of the gun positions and magazines may well survive.

Sources

General

17, 18, 19, 21, 23, 24; F, K, Q.

Specific

1892	?report. PRO: WO 196/29
1898	?Armament table. PRO: CAB 7/6
1905	?Armament table. PRO: CAB 16/1
1905-08	Plans PRO: WO 78/5069
1909	Plan of 9.2-inch emplacements. PRO: WO 78/5049
1909	Plan of magazines. PRO: WO 78/4061
1913	Plan of battery, incl Hawkins Battery. PRO: WO 78/4329
1927	?Armament table. PRO: CAB 36/16
1939	Plan, incl. Cawsand & Penlee. PRO: WO 78/5037
1946	Vertical air photograph. RCHME: CPE/UK/1890 Frame 3115.
1972	Plan and schedule of existing buildings and proposed demolition and landscaping works. Cornwall County Council.
1983	Interpretative sketch plan drawn by UK Fortifications Club. Copy held by CAU.

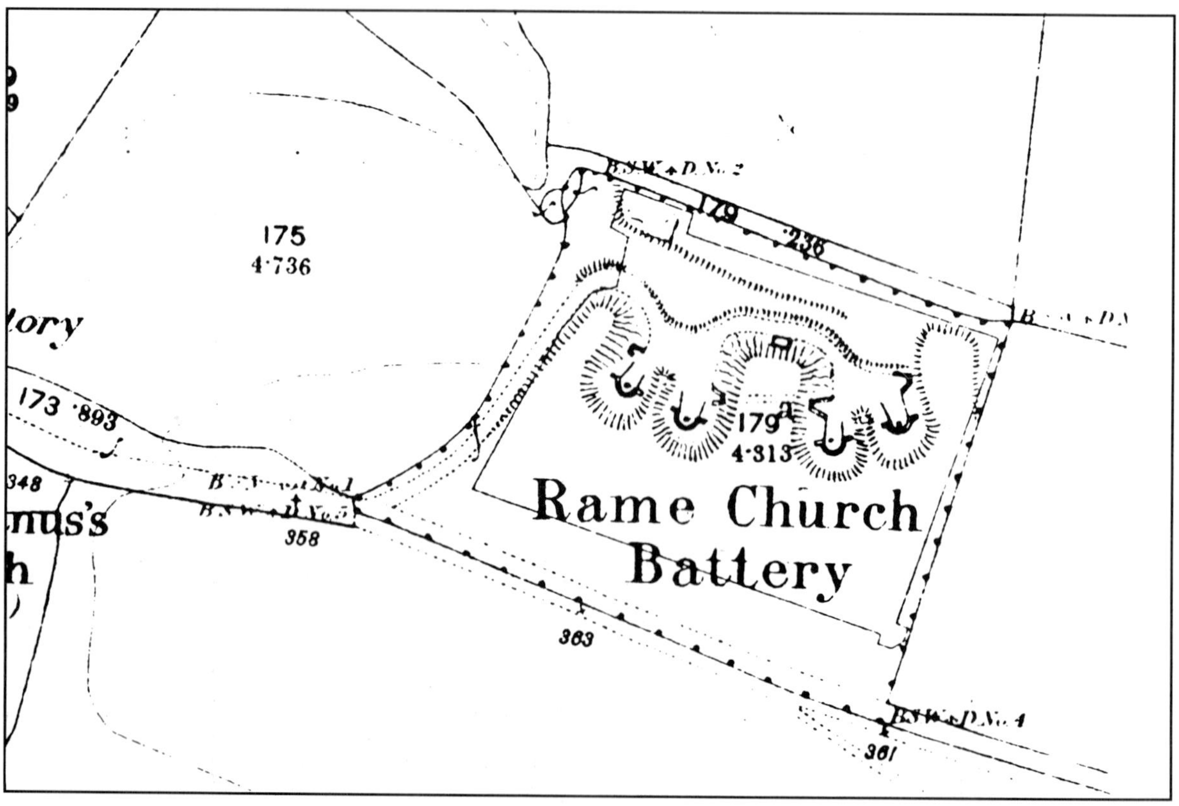

Fig. 50: Rame Church Battery in 1896 (PRO: WO 78/2314)

MIDDLE BARTON POSITION FINDING STATION

PAR = RAME, NGR = SX 43524912, PRN = 37094, MAP 1 No. 57

This is sited on the brow of the coastal slope immediately to the W of Penlee Battery, and was built at the same time as the battery in the early 1890s. Nine cells are recorded in 1894 and 1903, and are shown with a ?shelter building to the rear on a plan of 1911. In 1915 the Fire Command post was based on the site and at least four cells were in operation. The site has previously been interpreted as a WWI practice battery and WWII flank battery, although there is no known historical or physical evidence for this. An aerial photograph of 1946 appears to show it as being protected by an ?unclimable fence and ditch on its seaward side, ending in projecting '*caponier*'-type features on each flank.

The PF cells were built within a terrace cut into the hill slope, and linked by a sunken accessway to their rear. All the nine cells have been demolished down to the sills of their viewing windows, and together with the access way have been infilled with rubble (some of which may have come from the AA Battery to the N). The access way is still discernible as a hollow, and the outlines of four of the cells are visible; the line of the ?unclimbable fence/ditch is represented by the present limit of cultivation.

Present condition

The site has been largely demolished and infilled, although substantial below-ground remains of the lower two-thirds of each cell still survive, perhaps with internal detail such as instrument pillars. The immediate area of the station is rough grassland strewn with rubble and with light scrub, and is sited within an arable field.

Sources

General

18, 19, 23, 24.

Specific

1946	Vertical air photograph. RCHME: CPE/UK/1890 Frame 3115.
1972	Plans and schedules of existing buildings and propose demolition and landscaping works. Cornwall County Council.
1983	Interpretative sketch plan drawn up by UK Fortifications Club. Copy held by CAU.

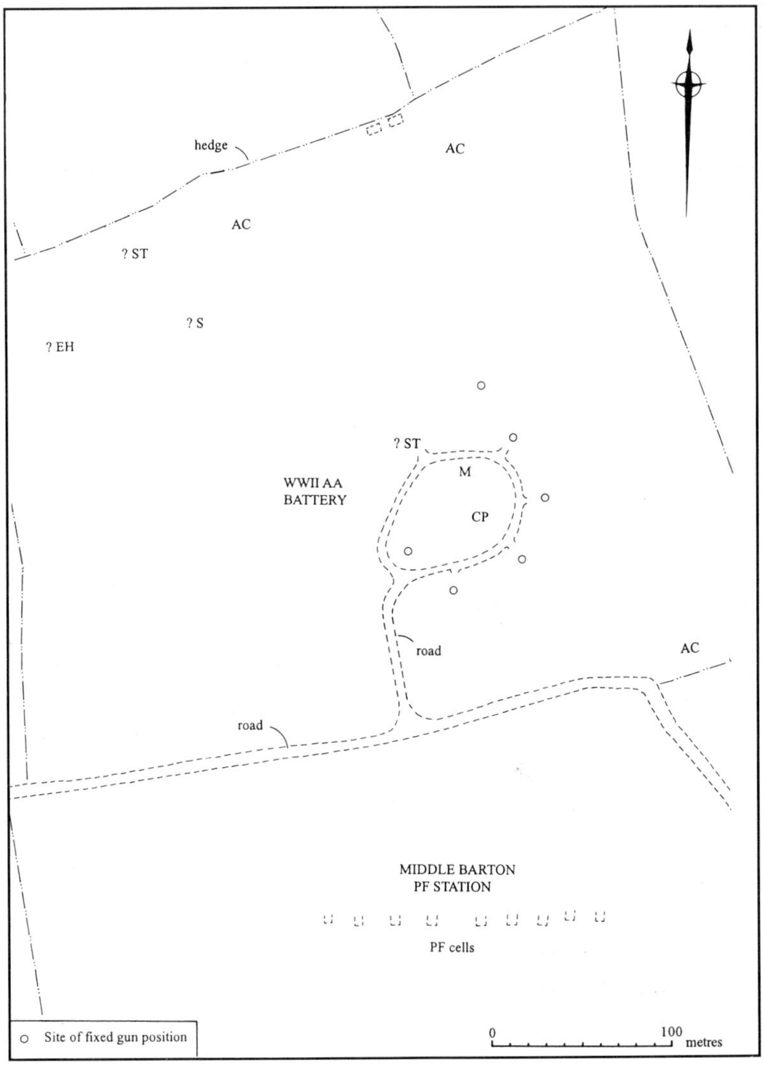

Fig. 51: Penlee HAA Battery & Middle Barton PF Station

PENLEE ANTI-AIRCRAFT BATTERY

PAR = RAME, NGR = SX 43484935, PRN = 38542, MAP 1 No. 58

This is sited on the brow of the ridge to the N.W of Penlee Battery, presumably to defend against aircraft using the Sound as an approach to Plymouth. It was probably built in 1940 and in 1941 four ?3.7-inch HAA guns are recorded on the site, manned by 203 HAA Battery. An air photograph of 1946 and a plan drawn in the 1970s prior to its demolition however show five to six gun positions, all apparently circular or polygonal and facing S, E and N.E and linked by an access road, with a sunken magazine and command post sited within the circuit of the latter, another surface building (possible gun store) off to one side, and sentry posts at the entrance. Service and accommodation buildings covered the field to the N, N.W and E of the battery, and seemed to have included rectangular stores/?magazines as well as a mast-base and other blastproof buildings. It is of exactly the same layout as the battery at Down Thomas in the South Hams, although the latter had two rectangular and four polygonal emplacements.

The whole site was levelled in the 1970s, although the access road still survives and the sites of the gun positions remain clearly discernable. The magazine and command post have been infilled. All the structures to the N have been completely removed, although the sites of two buildings are identifiable to the S.E of the battery.

Present condition

The battery has been demolished, although substantial below-ground remains of the infilled magazine and central command post are likely to survive, together with the hardstandings and bolt mountings of the individual gun positions. The sites of the buildings to the N have been largely removed and ploughed out. The site of the battery is rough grassland surrounded by arable; intermittent dumping is occurring.

Sources

General

25 (listed as Rame); R.

Specific

1946 Vertical air photograph. RCHME: CPE/UK/1890 Frame 3115.

1972 Plans and schedules of existing works and proposed demolition and landscaping works. Cornwall County Council.

1983 Interpretative sketch plan by UK Fortifications Club. Copy held by CAU.

PENLEE BATTERY

PAR = RAME, NGR = SX 43804916, PRN = 37103, MAP 1 No. 59

This is sited at the brow of the coastal slope above Penlee Point and was a battery of heavy long-range guns intended to defend against battleships standing off and bombarding the Dockyard from long range. Originally intended as a 'masked battery' for a 101 or 110-ton gun, it was first proposed in 1885 as a battery

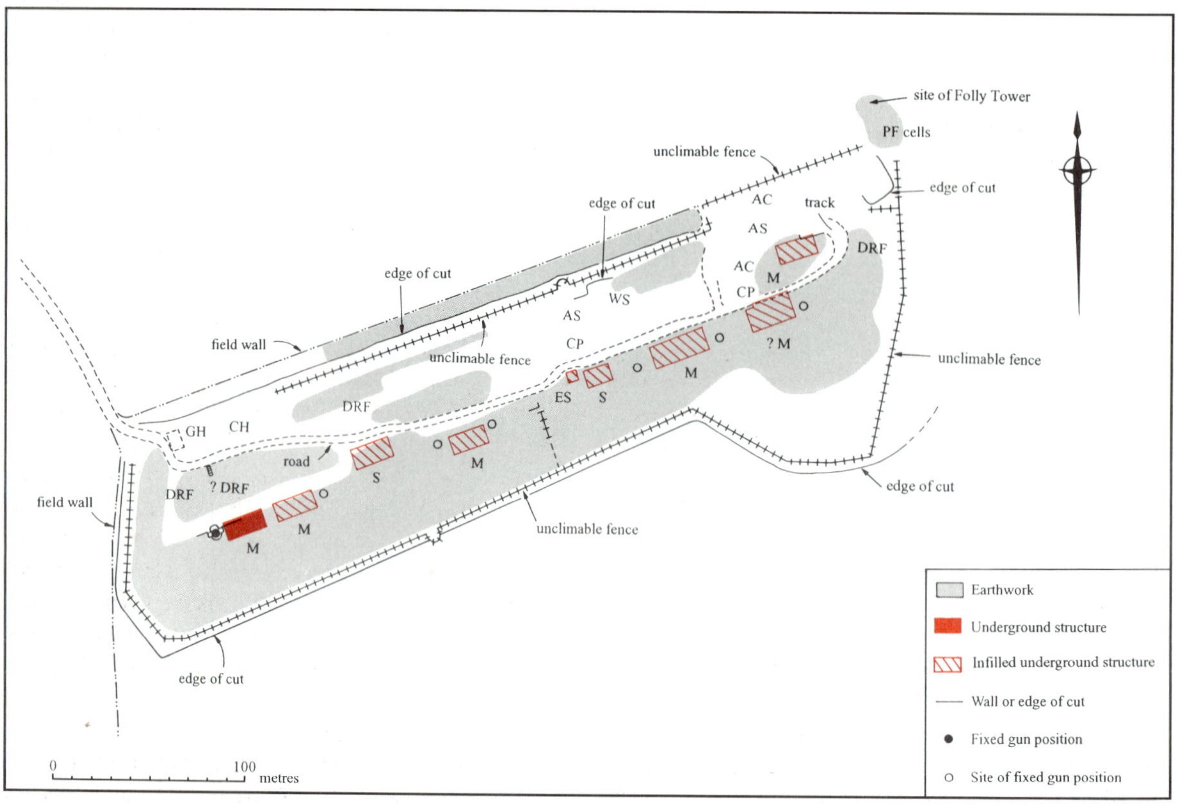

Fig. 52: Penlee Battery

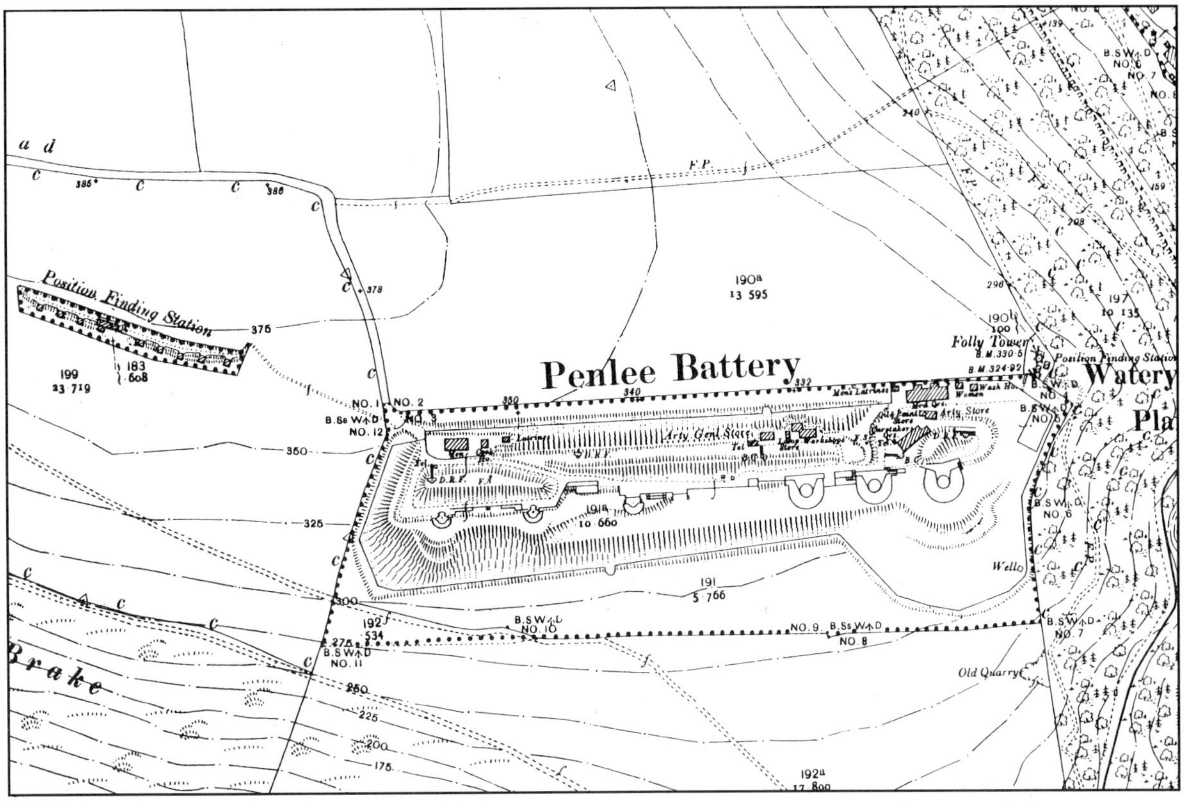

Fig. 53: Penlee Battery in 1911 (PRO: WO 78/2314)

for two 67-ton 13.5-inch BL guns and four 6-inch BL guns on Elswick disappearing mountings. Construction of one 13.5-inch and two 6-inch emplacements started in autumn 1889, and the two 6-inch guns were mounted by 1892. However, although the barrel for the 13.5-inch had been brought in 1892 to specially constructed landing steps at Penlee Point, by January 1894 it had only just been mounted and was not yet operational. It was the largest gun mounted at Plymouth at the time and was sited in a large emplacement at the eastern extreme of the battery and 'powered' by a tank filled with scrap-iron sited in an accumulator pit; it was accompanied by a large two-level underground magazine to the rear. Other buildings constructed at the time included underground storerooms and accommodation casemates, magazines to accompany the 6-inch guns at the west end of the battery, and at ground level the master gunner's (subsequently the caretaker's) quarters. The battery was protected by a trench, which by 1896 had been strengthened by the addition of an unclimbable fence. The guns were served by the neighbouring contemporary Position Finding Stations at Folly Tower and Middle Barton. In 1898 two other 6-inch emplacements were under construction to the E of the original two, and one of these guns had been mounted by 1903; the eastern emplacement is shown on a map of 1911 as being either infilled or (more likely) unfinished, and there is no record of a fourth 6-inch gun being mounted. In 1899 two 9.2-inch BL guns were also proposed, with the emplacements being sited immediately to the W of the earlier 13.5-inch emplacement; these guns were mounted by 1903, joining the 13.5-inch gun and the three 6-inch BL guns. In 1907 a third 9.2-inch gun was proposed to replace the 13.5-inch gun, and had been emplaced by 1910, by which time the 13.5-inch and 6-inch guns had been dismounted. By 1911 more surface buildings had been added, including married quarters and workshops. During WWI the armament was three 9.2-inch guns, which were reduced to two in 1920. By 1929 the third gun had been re-mounted and the battery was used for practice; by 1936 all three had been re-mounted on 35° mountings which gave them a maximum range of 35,000 yards. In 1932 they were accompanied by two searchlights (SX 44214877 & 44234875) and an observation light (SX 44264872) at Penlee Point, and a new Battery Command Post and Searchlight and Observation Light Directing Posts were sited on the hillside above (SX 44154885 & 44164885), together with an engine room (SX 44174891). During WWII all three guns were operational, and were manned by 164 Coast Battery Royal Artillery; the guns were removed in 1956 and most of the emplacements infilled and the buildings demolished in the 1970s. An aerial photograph of 1946 (*Plate 22*) also shows (at approx. SX 44104888) a further unidentified installation downslope of the battery, immediately to the N.W of the Admiralty Signal Station, and also three semi-circular features sited downslope of and adjoining the W end of the battery (at approx. SX 43704898); two of these are accompanied by buildings to their rear, and all three appear similar in shape and form to gun positions. However, there are no other historical sources for guns in this position, and it is possible that they may either represent temporary positions for training or test firing, or have an altogether different function.

All the surface buildings have been demolished down to their foundations and all the underground shelters and magazines and all bar one of the gun

Plate 81: Penlee Battery, showing 9.2-in BL emplacements (A. Sharpe. Frame: ACS/3090. Copyright: Cornwall Archaeological Unit)

emplacements have been infilled, although parts of the concrete retaining walls and aprons of the infilled emplacements are still visible. The westernmost 6-inch BL emplacement however survives intact, together with its underground magazine to the E and a Depression Range Finder position on the earthwork to its rear and the steps to another to the E. Details such as the fighting light brackets for the gun still remain, although the gun pit has been infilled and other fixtures such as guard rails and the doors of store recesses have been removed. Elsewhere most of the earthworks still survive, although substantial sections have been levelled; long sections of the unclimbable fence survive however, including projecting *caponiers*, and the earlier trench is visible along the W and S flanks. Another section of unclimbable iron fence in a shallow trench seems to divide off the 9.2-inch emplacements from the earlier 6-inch positions to the W, and probably dates to WWI. At Penlee Point the landing steps still survive, although the searchlights, Battery Command Post, Searchlight and Observation Light Directing Posts and engine room have been demolished.

Present condition

Although all surface buildings and some sections of the earthwork traverses and unclimbable fence have been demolished and the underground structures and gun emplacements mostly infilled, most of the battery in fact survives largely complete as 'below-ground remains'. It is currently a low-intensity public amenity area and nature reserve, and the S face of the rampart and the trench is heavily overgrown with scrub. The overgrown slab foundation of the BC Post at Penlee Point survives, although nothing remains of the searchlights except rubble spreads.

Sources

General

17, 18, 19, 21, 23, 24; F, K, Q.

Specific

1892	Report? PRO: WO 196/29
1896	Series of 8 plans of emplacements and magazines. PRO: WO 78/5055
1896-1905	Series of 5 plans of proposed construction of 6" and 9.2" emplacements. PRO: WO 78/4145
1898	Armament reference. PRO: CAB 7/6
1899-1932	Series of plans of proposed new 9.2" in old 13.5" emplacement, searchlights etc. PRO: WO 78/5039
1904	Plans of 9.2" positions. PRO: WO 78/4144
1905	Armament reference. PRO: CAB 16/1
1929	PRO: WO 33/1201/3
1932	Plan of searchlights (ELs). PRO: WO 78/5067
1936	Plan. PRO: WO 78/5036
1939	Plan/map. PRO: WO 78/5037
1941	PRO: WO 199/523/941
1943	PRO: WO 199/954 13/1
1946	Vertical air photograph. RCHME: CPE/UK/1890 Frame 3115
1972	Plans and schedules of existing buildings and proposed demolition and landscaping works. Cornwall County Council.
1983	Interpretative sketch plan by UK Fortifications Club. Copy held by CAU.

FOLLY TOWER POSITION FINDING STATION

PAR = RAME, NGR = SX 44054927, PRN = 38541, MAP 1 No. 60

This is sited immediately to the E of and adjoining Penlee Battery and was built to serve its guns in the early 1890s. Three cells were present in 1894 and are shown in 1896, although only two were apparently operational in 1903. No cells are shown in 1915, although it was part of the telephone network.

No above-ground remains of the cells survive, except for overgrown heaps of rubble. The adjoining Folly Tower has also been demolished.

Present condition

The buildings have been demolished, although this may only have involved breaking the roofs and infilling the interiors; substantial below-ground remains therefore may still survive. The site is largely overgrown with scrub, although partly traversed by a pathway.

Sources

General

18, 19, 23, 24.

Specific

1972 Plans and schedules of existing buildings and proposed demolition and landscaping works. Cornwall County Council.

1983 Interpretative sketch plan by UK Fortifications Club. Copy held by CAU.

3.2.7. Other early and Civil War fortifications

BEGGARS FORT

BEGGARS FORT

PAR = ANTONY, NGR = approx SX ?42105590, PRN = 6256, MAP 1 No. 61

'Beggars Forte' is depicted on a map of *c.* 1591 showing the landscape N of Plymouth; it is not apparently shown however on any other maps of the period. On the plan it is shown to the S of Antony House, and inland of an inlet which is probably Thanckes Lake. On this evidence the most likely site for such a fortification would seem to be the relatively broad, flat-topped hill to the W of Maryfield.

Present condition

Open field and woodland.

Sources

General

M, Q.

Specific

c. 1591 Map showing landscape north of Plymouth (Stuart No. 8).

CIVIL WAR 'BATTERY' ON BARN POOL

CIVIL WAR 'BATTERY' ON BARN POOL

PAR = MAKER, NGR = approx SX 45605275, PRN = 38551, MAP 3 No. 62

A cannon denoting the possible site of a battery is depicted in the centre of Barn Pool Bay on the Hollar Siege Map of 1644. It is depicted as being equidistant from Mt Edgcumbe Blockhouse and the S limit of the bay. Cannon are also shown in a similar position on Grenvyle's map of *c.* 1586-8, although these may refer to proposed gun positions around or immediately to the S of Mount Edgcumbe Blockhouse and may therefore not have been emplaced. Likewise it is not clear to what extent the cannon on the 1644 map represents the likely site of a battery as opposed to the presence for example of mobile artillery covering the bay. There are no obviously identifiable remains or site of such a battery.

Present condition

Part of Mount Edgcumbe Country Park; alternate grassland with wooded areas in between two coombes.

Sources

General

2, 3; M.

INSWORK POINT BATTERY

INSWORK POINT BATTERY

PAR = MAKER, NGR = SX 43835335 & 43755335, PRN = 6056, MAP 2 No. 63

This consists of a low earthen breastwork located on a low bluff immediately above the foreshore at the tip of Inswork Point, together with the site of a possible gun platform on the spur behind (at NGR SX 43755335). No fortification is marked at this location on the Hollar

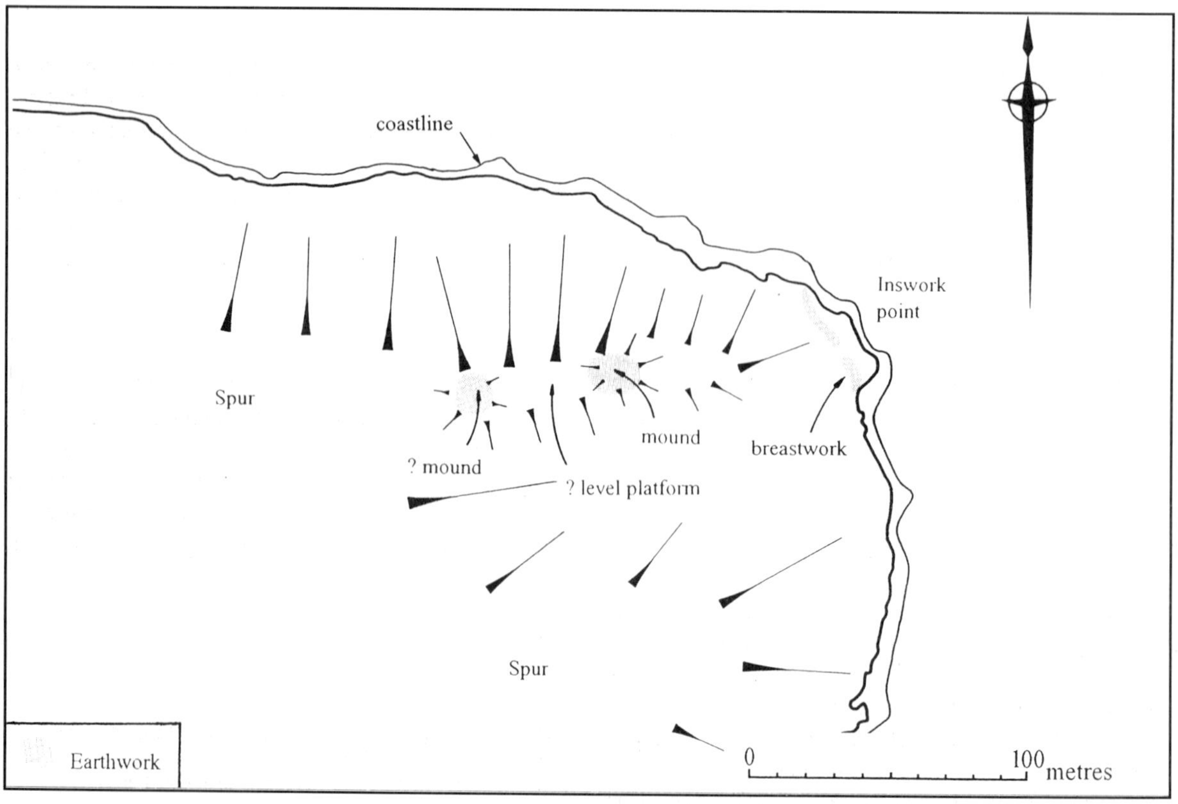

Fig. 54: Inswork Point

Siege Map of 1644, although reference to one is apparently made in a pamphlet of 1644.

The breastwork survives in two sections, separated by a gully; this may represent an accessway from the beach or a later truncation. The N end appears to stop just short of the bluff, whilst the S end has probably been eroded away by the sea. Ploughsoil has mounded up against the rear of the bank.

On the top of the spur to the W there is a slightly levelled area, which is thought to have represented a gun platform (as the height would have given them greater visibility and range), together with slight mounds at its eastern and perhaps western extremities. Alternatively the guns may have been sited behind the breastwork, closer to targets on the Hamoaze, and the mound(s) on the spur above may represent natural ground levels and/or earlier man made features. No trace of the breastwork was identified elsewhere along the bluff; to have been effective as a defence it must originally have been much more extensive.

Present condition

The bank is in good condition, although its S end has been eroded by the sea, as is some slumped bank material near its N end. Much of its length is obscured by scrub. The platform and mound(s) are within a field (currently pasture) which is periodically ploughed; they are discernable, but will presumably suffer continuing plough damage unless an appropriate management scheme is adopted.

Sources

General

3; L, Q.

Specific

1644 Martin, Col. R *Siege pamphlet.* PLSL.

THANCKES CIVIL WAR REDOUBT

PAR = ANTONY, NGR = approx SX 43505595, PRN = 6269, MAP 2 No. 64

A square Royalist fortification is marked on the Hollar Siege Map of 1644 near the W bank of the Hamoaze, approximately midway between the Lynher River and St Johns Lake, and opposite Keyham Lake on the E bank. On this evidence the most likely site for the fortification is on Yonderberry Point, immediately N of Thanckes Lake. This is presently occupied by a Royal Naval Oil Storage Depot; the site was not visited.

Present condition

Probably largely destroyed by construction of tanks and associated buildings and roads, although some below-ground remains may well still survive.

Source

General

3.

WEARDE QUAY BATTERY

PAR = SALTASH, NGR = SX 42455770, PRN = 6278, MAP 1 No. 65

An artillery fortification, sited above and slightly to the W of Wearde Quay, overlooking the mouth of the Lynher River and the Hamoaze, and between the road down to the quay and the railway to the N. It has been identified with a Royalist battery depicted on the Hollar siege map of 1644, which places it further around the coast to the E. The S bastioned wall of the battery is depicted on the tithe map of 1841, when it forms the S limit of plot No. 175, which was used as a garden and called 'Battery'. The N part was truncated on the construction of the Cornwall Railway in c. 1857, and the S wall is again depicted on the O.S. 1st edition 1:2500 map surveyed in *c.* 1859. The site was identified and surveyed in the 1950s by C.J. Squires, and his measured sketch plan and section remains the primary record of the site.

The remains consist of a battered mortared stone wall *c.* 3.50m high, which is topped by a vertical section of wall (a possible parapet) *c.* 0.5m high; the top of the wall lies flush with the ground level behind, and therefore it is not clear whether there was a parapet. The wall forms a central, pointed bastion, and decreases in height to each side, reflecting the rising slope of the ground. The site has been interpreted as representing a fortified battery platform, with symmetrical side walls flanking the central bastion, and with an apparently open rear. Alternatively, the sophistication of the wall and the effort invested in constructing it indicates that it may have formed part of a self-contained, fully defended redoubt, the rear of which would also have been defended by a similar wall and perhaps a ditch.

Present condition

Although heavily overgrown, and affected by the roots of ivy and other vegetation, the structure of the wall, where it is visible, is in very good condition. However, vegetation has recently been removed from the apex of the bastion, loosening several keystones in the process. The interior of the site is heavily overgrown and impenetrable.

Sources

General

3; Q.

Specific

1841 St Stephens-by-Saltash tithe map and apportionment

1859 1st edition 1:2500 map. Sheet 46.5

n.d. Squires, C.J. Annotated measured sketch plan.

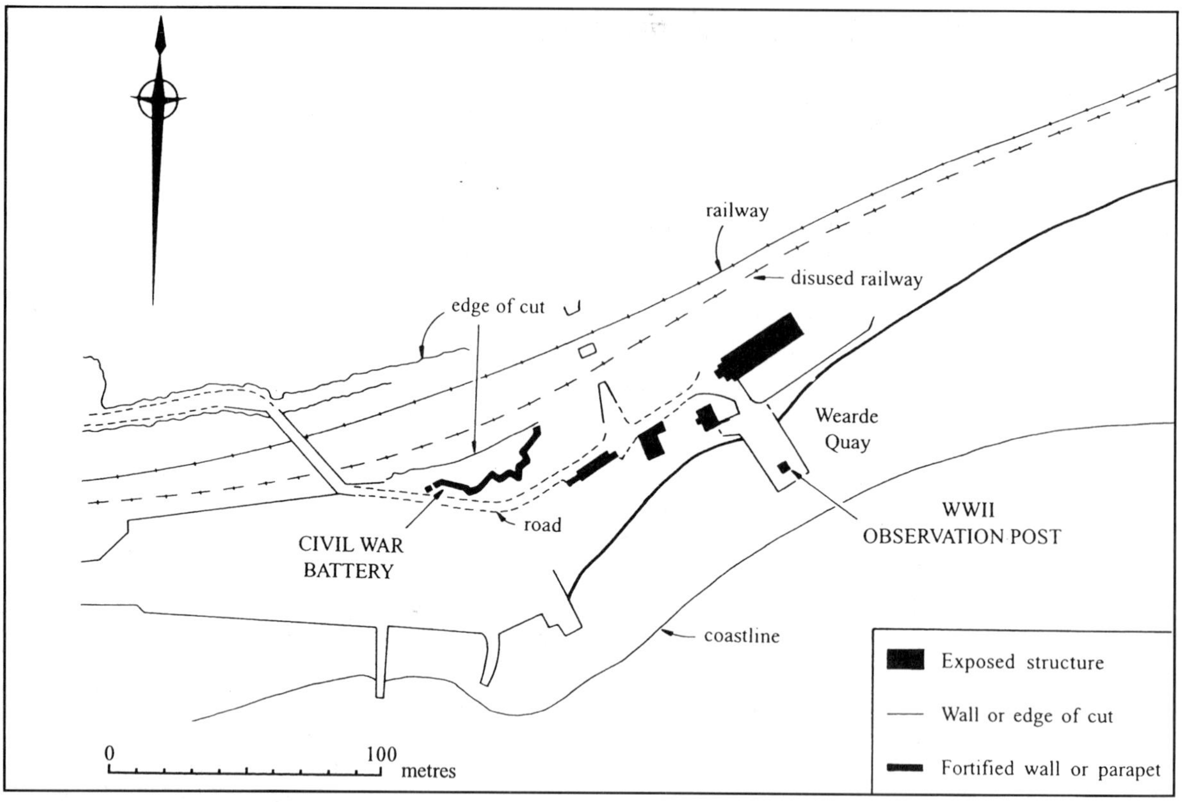

Fig. 55: Wearde Quay

WEARDE QUAY WW II OBSERVATION POST

PAR = SALTASH, NGR = SX 42565770, PRN = 38544, MAP 1 No. 66

A square shuttered concrete single-storey building located on the end of Wearde Quay, looking out over the junction of the Lynher River with the Hamoaze. Has a viewing slit at each of its front corners, and a doorway (retaining its original armoured door) to the rear. Interior not accessible at the time of visit. May represent a minewatcher's post.

Present condition
Good, the structure remains complete.

3.2.8. Other World War Two fortifications

MOUNT EDGCUMBE WWII ROCKET BATTERY

PAR = MAKER, NGR = SX 44905200, PRN = 38545, MAP 2 No. 67

A rocket ('Z') battery, with an armament of 64 ?3-inch rockets mounted on two multiple launchers, is recorded on Mount Edgcumbe in c.1941, when it was known as No. 143 Z Battery. It was located in the field *c.* 200m to the E of Maker Church, which is called Rocket Field on a map held by the Mount Edgcumbe Country Park.

Present condition

Demolished; a pasture field.

Sources

General

25; R.

Specific

n.d. Map held by MECP

ST JOHNS DOWN WWII ANTI-AIRCRAFT BATTERY

PAR = ST JOHN, NGR = SX 40605280, PRN = 37098, MAP 1 No. 68

This is sited on a hill to the rear of Whitsand Bay, and was armed with four 3.7-inch HAA guns in 1941, when it was manned by No. 202 HAA Battery. Access was via a road branching off southwards from the main Crafthole - Millbrook road, along which were sited various accommodation buildings (shown on the 1951 O.S 1:2500 map). The gun positions are not shown, but were almost certainly sited beyond the S end of this road, under and around the S end of the present factory building. An aerial photograph of 1962 shows most of the site, including four gun positions in an arc facing S, with what appears to be a command post behind. The main accommodation buildings were sited in a field immediately to the W (at SX 40355298), where several of the Nissen huts remain; further accommodation may have been provided in buildings sited in the field to the S; these have now mostly been demolished and replaced with modern farm buildings. An accompanying sewage works lies to the S.

Present condition

The site of the main battery is occupied by a more recent factory building. Below ground remains may however survive immediately to its south. To the W, the western complex of nissen huts survives complete, together with one building belonging to the eastern complex; all are used for farm storage.

Sources

General

25; R.

Specific

1951 O.S. 1:2500 map sheet SX 4051.

1962 R.A.F. vertical aerial photograph. RCHME: 58/5095. Frame F21 070.

ST WINOLLS ANTI-AIRCRAFT BATTERY A

PAR = ST GERMANS, NGR = SX 34205545, PRN = 37099, MAP 1 No. 69

This is an early WWII HAA battery which lies some 500m to the N.E of Hendra Farm, on the crest, N and E facing slopes of a hill; it was subsequently replaced by another battery (St. Winolls Battery B) sited some 200m to the S.W. In about 1942 it appears to have been armed with four 4.5-inch HAA guns. These were arranged in an arc around the central command post which still survives complete with its internal fittings, such as fuseboxes to the individual guns and overall electric fusebox. As such it is the only one of its date to survive with such complete internal detail in the Plymouth area. A later observation post/tower has been added to its S end. This and two of the gun positions on the N.E side survive within an area of scrub, bordered on the S by a hedge. The other two gun positions were probably sited on the slightly higher crest of the hill some 40m or so to the N.W of the command post. This area, together with the accommodation buildings to the north and N.E (which probably continued in use with the later battery), have all been demolished and the land reclaimed and cultivated. However, two hut-bases survive near the main gate of the WWII battery (at SX

Plate 82: St Winolls HAA Battery A, fuse boxes inside command post (Exeter Archaeology)

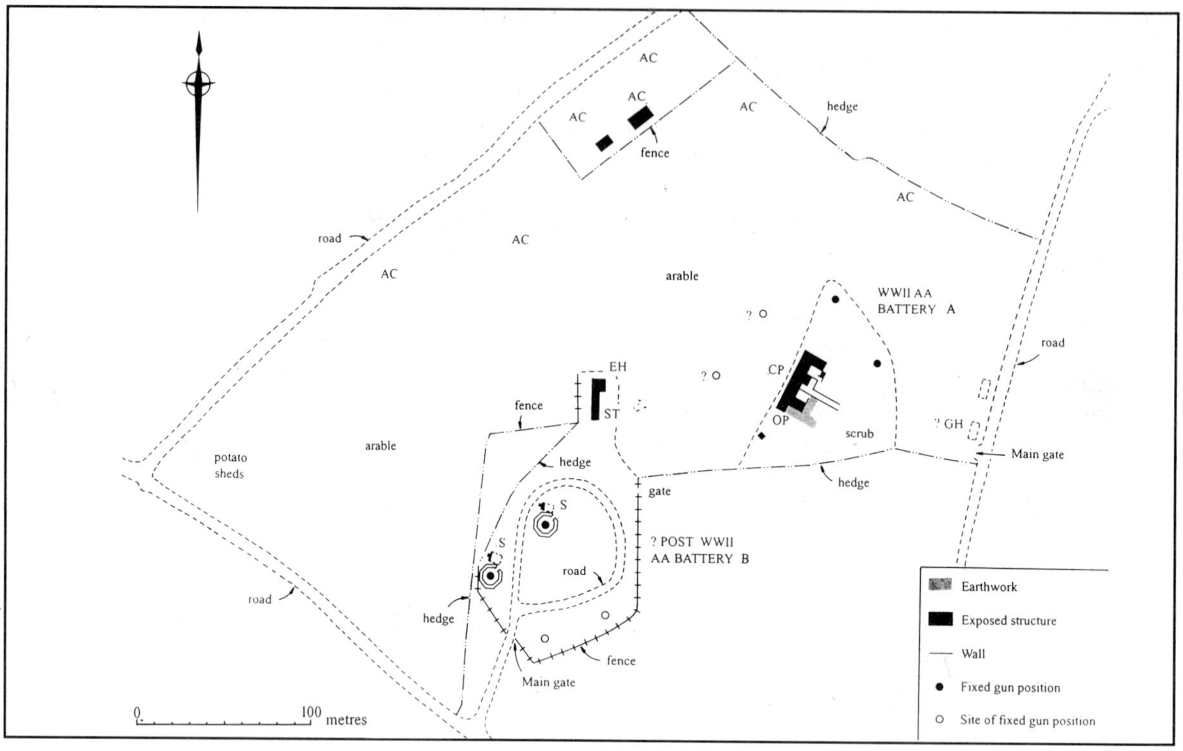

Fig. 56: St Winolls HAA Batteries

34285546), together with the remnants of accommodation buildings to the N (at SX 34105562). The guns faced N.W., N and N.E., and were orientated so as to fire on aircraft using the easily visible approach to the Dockyard provided by the St Germans River, rather than against aircraft approaching across the coastline to the S.

Present condition

Half the site survives complete and the command post in particular is in extremely good condition with rare survival of internal detail and fittings. The concrete hardstandings, together with the mounting-bolts and cable ducts, of the two gun remaining positions are visible but overgrown; the surrounding ammunition lockers and shelters have been demolished. The other two gun positions have been ploughed out. Another small building *c.* 100m to the S.W also survives and contains fuse or junction boxes.

Sources
General
25; R.

ST WINOLLS ANTI-AIRCRAFT BATTERY B

PAR = ST GERMANS, NGR = SX 34055540, PRN = 37099.01, MAP 1 No. 70

This is a HAA battery dating to late in WWII or immediately after, and was constructed for four 5.25-inch guns. It was built on the southern crest of the hill occupied by the earlier WWII battery (St. Winolls Battery A) some 200m to the N.E., and is of typical plan. Access was from the S via a concrete road branching off from the lane, and the battery was surrounded by a concrete post fence on the E and S flanks. A hedge forms the W boundary. The access road completed a full circuit, giving access to four gun positions, three of which were sited outside the circuit to the S and W, and one within it. Two examples are visible and survive complete, although partly infilled with rubbish. The others have been infilled and covered by a large mound of earth. Each consists of a 14-sided concrete walled surround containing ammunition lockers, with an infilled gun pit in the centre. In each case there is a partly-covered, flat-roofed engine room (with projecting ventilator) immediately to the N; these are built partly underground. To the N there is a service building, consisting of a probable gun store with louvred windows and double iron door at its N end and stores and accommodation and perhaps a control room in the range to the S. To the N and N.W there were accommodation buildings of a camp accompanying this battery (or the earlier one); these have been removed and the area reclaimed for arable cultivation.

Present condition

The site survives largely complete despite the infilling and covering of two of the emplacements and partial infilling of the two remaining ones. The access road is being progressively covered over with manure and rubbish. The gun store is used for low-intensity storage whilst the remainder is open and derelict; the overall structure appears sound. The land use is rough grassland and the site is used for dumping with some encroachment of scrub from the W.

Sources
General
25; R.

CARKEEL WWII ANTI-AIRCRAFT BATTERY A

PAR = SALTASH, NGR = SX 41506020, PRN = 50033, MAP 1 No. 71

CARKEEL WWII ANTI-AIRCRAFT BATTERY A

This was sited on a hill *c.* 1km to the N of Saltash, with a least three and probably four gun positions facing N and N.W, defending against aircraft using the Tamar as a route of approach to Plymouth from the N. It was armed with four 3.7-inch guns in 1940, when it was manned by No. 165 HAA Battery. An O.S. 1:2500 map of 1967 shows a central command post within a typical road loop, off which would have been sited the gun emplacements (the beginnings of branch roads to these can be seen down the W and N sides of this loop), with a sunken magazine and possible gun store to the S of the road. A probable guard house lies adjoining the entrance onto the main road to the W.

Present condition

The site now lies within a recently developed industrial estate, and it is unlikely that any remains survive; none are visible at surface.

Sources

General

R.

Specific

1967 O.S. 1:2500 map sheet SX 4160.

CARKEEL WWII ANTI-AIRCRAFT BATTERY B

PAR = SALTASH, NGR = SX 41486040, PRN = 50033.1, MAP 1 No. 72

CARKEEL WWII ANTI-AIRCRAFT BATTERY B

This is depicted on the O.S. 1:2500 map of 1967, and was sited 200m to the N of the earlier 3.7-inch battery. It is of exactly the same plan as the later battery at St Winnols (Battery B), consisting of four gun pits facing N and W, each accompanied by a rectangular engine room. Three are sited outside the looped access road, and one within; to the S, adjoining the access road, is a probable gun store and ?command post. This was probably built towards the end of the war, or shortly after, for four 5.25-inch guns. The site now lies within a partly developed industrial estate, probably under a gas depot; no surface remains are visible.

Present condition

Recently demolished. It is unlikely that any below ground remains survive as the industrial estate has been terraced into the hill; the N limit of this terrace runs along the field boundary depicted in 1967 as immediately on the N side of the battery.

Sources

General

R.

Specific

1967 O.S. 1:2500 map sheet SX4160.

RAME HEAD RADAR INSTALLATION

PAR = MAKER , NGR = SX 41834832, PRN = 38547, MAP 1 No. 73

RAME HEAD RADAR INSTALLATION

The following radar installations have been noted at Rame Head by Wing. Co. M. Dean, from his study of relevant War Office records: a Type 31/43 small cabin at Rame Chapel, and two Chain Home Low (CHL) installations and a Ground-Controlled Interception (GCI) hut/mobile installation at Rame Head. These date from WWII, and may not all be contemporary, and would not necessarily have left substantial physical remains indicating their former presence.

Physical remains consist of a concrete platform sited immediately on the S side of the medieval St Michael's Chapel; this contains two circular mounting plates and a niche containing tie bolts has been inserted into its seaward side. There is no evidence of side walls and therefore this may represent the mast or gantry base, with the equipment perhaps being housed in the chapel. To the S steps lead down towards the point and an earlier quarry terrace (another possible site for an accompanying building). Two ?hut terraces sited (at SX 41914852) on the neck of land connecting the promontory to the shore may also have been associated with a radar installation, although the presence of the headland in front would have obstructed the coverage of any equipment installed at this location. Several huts are shown at this location on an aerial photograph taken in 1946.

Another probable site(s) for one of these radar installations is at or near the Coastguard Station (SX 42054870); no specific remains dating to WWII are visible in this area, except possibly for some earlier mast stanchions.

Present condition

In reasonable condition, although any superstructures have been removed.

Sources

General

R.

Specific

1946 R.A.F. vertical aerial photograph.
RCHME: CPE/UK/1890 Frame 3116.

MAKER TORPEDO BOAT STATION

MAKER TORPEDO BOAT STATION

PAR = MAKER, NGR = SX 44105225, PRN = 6113.12, MAP 2 No. 74

This lies on the N slope of Maker Heights above Millbrook Lake, and comprises a concrete built tunnel extending at least 10m back into the hillside, and elements of a man-made harbour jutting out from the coastline *c.* 150m to the N. Both have been identified by R. Linzey who made a site visit, and presumably date to WWII. A local resident interpreted it as an unfinished motor torpedo boat station, with the tunnel representing the magazine.

Present condition
Not assessed.

TRENNINOW WWII SITE

TRENNINOW WWII SITE

PAR = MAKER, NGR = SX 41705100, PRN = 38555, MAP 1 No. 75

This is sited on a hill overlooking Whitsand Bay, and consists of four buildings connected to the coastal road by a concrete roadway. Its function is not at present known; it may have operated as a depot of some kind, as most of the buildings appear to have direct vehicle access. The site was not viewed in any detail, and there may well be other features in addition to those shown on the map.

Present condition
The field is at present arable. The condition of the individual structures has not been assessed.

WIGGLE FARM PILLBOX

WIGGLE FARM PILLBOX

PAR = RAME, NGR = SX 42405077, PRN = 38543, MAP 1 No. 76

This is sited in the corner of a field some 100m to the E of Wiggle Farm, and commands the approach up the valley from the S. It is a six-sided shuttered-concrete structure of WWII date, and has a single splayed square embrasure in each side, except the rear (N) side where two embrasures flank a central doorway. No armoured shutters or other fittings survive.

Present condition
In good structural condition with no obvious stress evident within the walls; at present empty.

Plate 83: Wiggle Farm pillbox (Exeter Archaeology)

CRAFTHOLE PILLBOX

CRAFTHOLE PILLBOX

PAR = SHEVIOCK, NGR = SX 37255390, PRN = 38546, MAP 1 No. 77

A hexagonal Type 24 pillbox sited on the crest of a hill, in the corner of a field at the junction of Trethill Lane and the main road leading E from Crafthole towards Millbrook and Torpoint. Built during WWII. Of shuttered concrete construction, with a pair of loopholes flanking the doorway, and a single loophole in each of the remaining five sides. Does not retain any traces of iron shutters, or of the internal anti-ricochet wall.

Present condition
Not very good, as the concrete is heavily fissured on the N.E side of the pillbox.

Sources
General
R.

3.3 DEVON GAZETTEER

3.3.1. Inner Defences: Western King to Mount Batten

DEVIL'S POINT BLOCKHOUSE

PAR = E. STONEHOUSE, NGR = SX45945335, PRN = SX45SE-14, MAP 3 No. 78

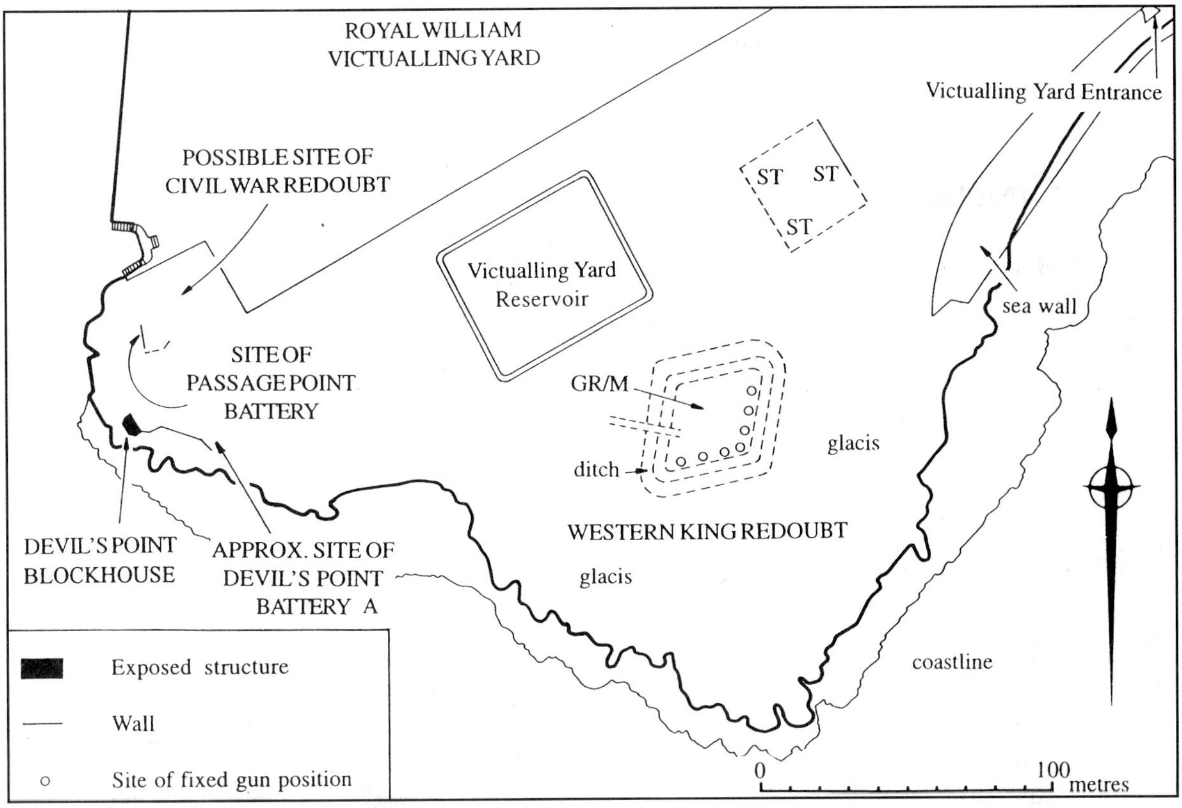

Fig. 57 Western King & Devil's Point, medieval to 18th century defences

Plate 84 Devil's Point, Western King & the Royal William Victualling Yard (Photograph: F.M. Griffith, Devon County Council. Frame DAP/UU5. Copyright Devon County Council)

DEVIL'S POINT BLOCKHOUSE

Plate 85 Devil's Point Blockhouse (Exeter Archaeology)

This is located just above the high water mark, and was probably built in the late 15th or early 16th century by the Edgcumbe family to protect their harbour and settlement at Stonehouse from raids by the French and others, in conjunction with the other blockhouses on Firestone Bay and flanking Stonehouse Pool, and the town wall. It is depicted in *c.*1540 as a square single-storey blockhouse (*Fig. 2*). It was probably used intermittently for defence in subsequent periods, and was probably the site in 1902 of a heavy machine-gun sited to cover the boom across the narrows. Subsequently the boom appears to have been covered by two light QF guns sited at the N end of Earl's Battery.

The blockhouse is a single-storey heptagonal structure built of rubble limestone, with dressed granite details around the square gun embrasures and the arched doorway. There are five embrasures, two pairs (one blocked) facing W across the narrows and a single embrasure (now blocked and only visible from the interior) facing N. It was entered through a pointed arched doorway at the rear, which is flanked by vents. The interior is vaulted, and the present floor level may be higher than the original, since it lies flush with the base of the embrasures. Sockets in the walls may indicate partitioning and later use of the structure. The roof is grass covered and contains some later brickwork; there is no visible evidence of a later gun position.

Present condition
Generally sound, although there is some loose stonework at the top. It is empty and the doorway and most of the embrasures have been blocked.

Sources
General
1
Specific

1886	Worth, R. N 'Notes on the early history of Stonehouse' *Jnl. Plymouth Institution* **9**, 338-74.
1992	Brayshay, M Lecture, 14 Oct
n.d	Western King Fort Record Book. PRO: WO 192/198

DEVIL'S POINT CIVIL WAR REDOUBT

DEVIL'S POINT CIVIL WAR REDOUBT

PAR = E. STONEHOUSE, NGR = SX45965337,
PRN = SX45SE-713/2, MAP 3 No. 79

A square Parliamentarian redoubt is shown immediately to the E of Passage (later Devil's) Point on the Hollar siege map of 1644 (*Fig. 4*). It is sited to defend the narrow passage against enemy (Royalist) shipping and to fire on enemy positions shown on the Cornish side, and to be defended against land attack.

The most likely site is the knoll immediately to the N of the blockhouse. This knoll was subsequently occupied by the later Passage Point and 3 Gun Batteries (Nos 81 & 82). No above-ground remains are visible.

Present condition
Demolished, although below-ground remains may survive.

Source
General
3

DEVIL'S POINT BATTERY A

DEVIL'S POINT BATTERY A

PAR = E. STONEHOUSE, NGR = SX45965335,
PRN = SX45SE-713/1, MAP 3 No. 80

This battery was located at or near Devil's Point and was first proposed in February 1700, when it was to have eleven guns. It was intended to protect the approach to the newly built Dockyard, construction of which had begun in the 1690s. In *c.*1716 it was armed with fifteen culverins. The battery appears to be shown on a map of 1765, which depicts an embrasured wall extending along the shoreline eastwards from the blockhouse to the site of the later Naval Reserve Battery (No. 83). By 1779 it had become redundant, as it is not referred to in any of the contemporary documents. The exact location of the battery is unknown; it may have been sited anywhere between the blockhouse and the reserve battery, or the guns may have been spread out along this stretch of coast. No surface remains are identifiable, although some of the coastal walling may contain earlier fabric.

Present condition
Demolished, although below-ground remains may be sited under the present coastal path, or perhaps partly under the earthwork belonging to the later Devil's Point Battery B. It is possible that coastal erosion since 1765 may have removed some of any remains which may survive, although this is unlikely as map evidence indicates that the general line of the coastline has remained the same since that period.

Sources
General
M, O, Q.
Specific

1700	Defence estimates for securing the various dockyards. BL: Add Mss 5439. f. 193
1714-17	Report & Survey by Col Christian Lilly. BL: Kings Mss 45
1765	Plymouth Sound. BL: Kings Top XI 78.2

PASSAGE POINT BATTERY

PAR = E. STONEHOUSE, NGR = SX45955337, PRN = SX45SE-713, MAP 3 No. 81

This is depicted on a plan drawn up in January 1780 by Lieutenant Colonel Matthew Dixon as a three sided work sited immediately to the N of the earlier blockhouse. It was probably sited on the S part of the knoll later occupied by the 3 Gun Battery (No. 82), where thicker walls are shown on a plan of the latter dating to 1830; these may represent the remnants of the battery which were subsequently incorporated into the structure of the later battery.

Passage Point Battery was thrown up hastily during the emergency of August 1779, when a Franco-Spanish invasion fleet anchored in Cawsand Bay during the American War of Independence, and by January 1780 had become a permanent work mounting two 18-pdr guns and two 8-inch howitzers (although other sources dating to 1780 or shortly after give the armament as four or six 18-pdrs). The purpose of the battery as described by Dixon was to 'take a ship when she comes round the point of Wester King, [and] to flank the ground of Mount Edgcumbe in front of the Obelisk Redoubt' (No. 9). It is clear from this and from the depiction of the battery on the accompanying map that the guns faced both S towards Western King Point and W over the top of the blockhouse and across to Mount Edgcumbe and Wilderness Point. By 1811 it had been re-modelled as the 3 Gun Battery (No. 82).

No surface remains specifically belonging to this battery have been identified to date, although it is probable that the retaining walls sited on the slope immediately to the N of the blockhouse may contain some fabric belonging to the walls depicted in 1824 and subsequently.

Present condition
Largely demolished, although some fabric may survive within later walling and below-ground remains may survive on the slope and under the S part of the later 3 Gun Battery.

Sources
General
4 - 8, 19; O, Q.
Specific

1811	Plan of Western King & Devil's Point. PRO: MPH 233
1824	Plan showing Three-Gun Battery. PRO: MPH 681
1823	?Plan. PRO: WO 78/405
1831	Plan of Three-Gun Battery. NMM: Photo A.2639
1820	?Plan. PRO: WO 44/158

THREE GUN BATTERY

PAR = E. STONEHOUSE, NGR = SX45965339, PRN = SX45SE-713/3, MAP 3 No. 82

This is located on a prominent knoll immediately to the N of the blockhouse, on the probable site of the earlier Passage Point Battery. It was probably built shortly before 1811, when it is first depicted; this and later, more detailed, plans show the gun platform as facing S.E towards Western King Point, with a guardhouse behind. It appears to have been re-modelled during the late 1850s, as the 1860 plan shows iron shutters (presumably covering gun embrasures) in the S.E. wall and a four (as opposed to three) gun battery. It is illustrated in 1872, although the guns are not evident, and probably became redundant during this period due to the construction of the Royal Naval Reserve Battery in its line of fire; this probably occurred in the 1860s, as a building is depicted on the site of the Reserve Battery in 1872 (*Fig. 8*). By 1891 it had become a drill battery. No armament is recorded in 1885 & 1893. By 1896 it is no longer labelled as a battery and a building has been constructed immediately on the downslope side of the gun platform.The site consists of a level terrace. A short section of rubble limestone wall (with granite details) survives on the line of the S wall of the battery. The wall separating the battery from the garden to the N has been demolished, together with the guardhouse and the wall fronting the gun platform.

Present condition
The remaining section of wall is in a relatively stable condition, although partly overgrown. Potential below-ground remains of the other walls and the gun platform

(which may have been surfaced with timber or granite setts) are likely to survive, as there has been no obvious ground disturbance.

Sources
General
17, 19; Q.

Specific
1811 Plan of Western King & Devil's Point. PRO: MPH 233
1823 Plan of Cremyll Passage Point in Plymouth Sound. PRO: WO 78/405
1824 Plan showing Three-Gun Battery. PRO: MPH 681
1830 Sketch of the Three Gun Battery at Devil's Point. PRO: MFQ 241(2)
1831 Plan of Three Gun Battery. NMM: Ph A2639
1860 Western King Redoubt & area. PRO: MR 1323
1872 Illustrated London News panorama.
1891 Military map. WDRO: Acc 81X/34

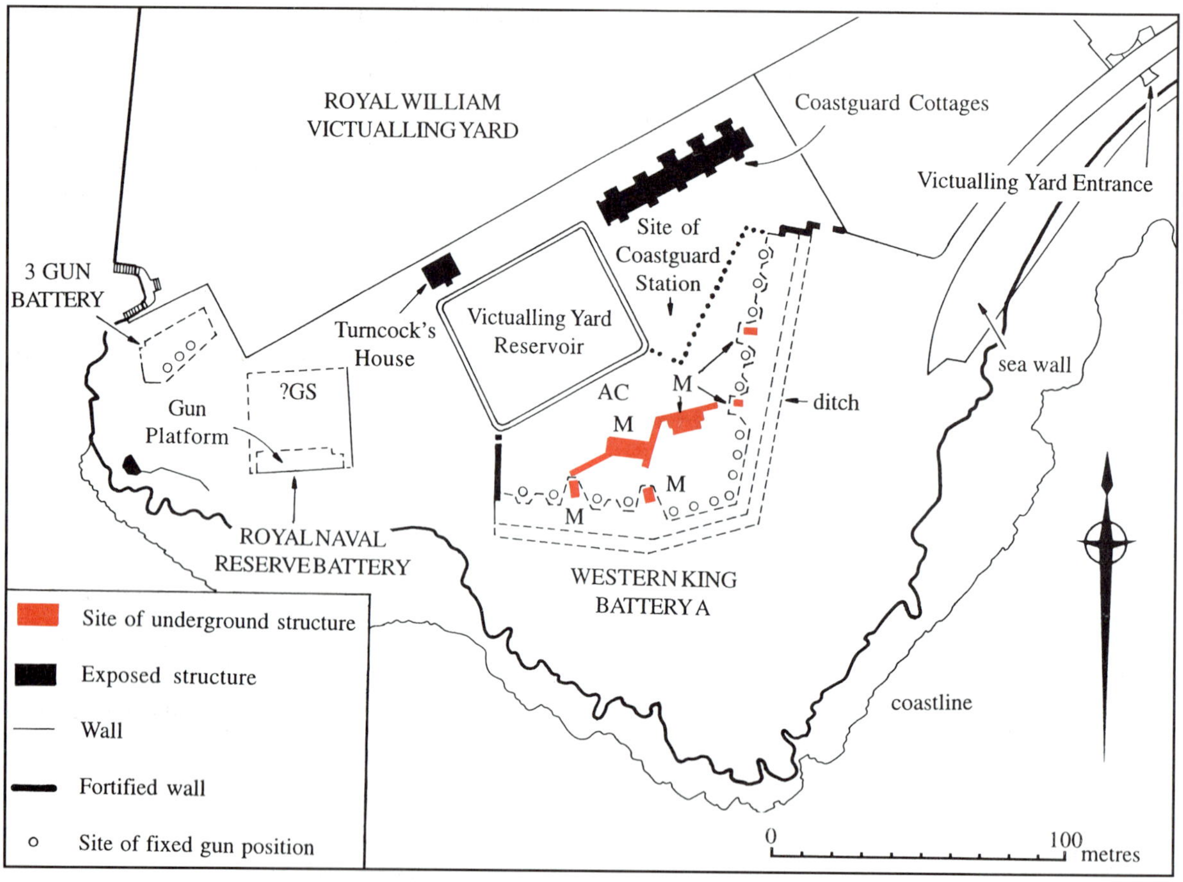

Fig. 58 Western King & Devil's Point, 19th century defences

ROYAL NAVAL RESERVE BATTERY

PAR = E. STONEHOUSE, NGR = SX46005336, PRN = SX45SE-702, MAP 3 No. 83

This was located on a terrace cut into the hillslope between Devil's Point and the reservoir, facing S over the Sound. Although not referred to in the Royal Commission report of 1860, it was probably built during the 1860s as a building is depicted in this position on the 1872 panorama (*Fig. 8*). In 1891 a rectangular gun platform or building at the front of the terrace is labelled drill batteries, and a 'drill shed' (possibly also a covered gun shed) is shown to the rear. By 1911 another small building had been constructed in the N.E corner. It is not clear when the battery was dismantled; it is still labelled as a battery in 1911.

The terrace remains, but the two buildings to the rear have been demolished and the terrace surfaced in tarmac. The terrace is revetted by a contemporary brick wall (later heightened) to the E and a later shuttered concrete wall to the N & W. The gun platform at the front is retained by a low dressed limestone wall topped with granite coping stones; perforated air bricks occur at intervals, suggesting that the platform had a suspended timber floor rather than stone setts.

Present condition
The revetment walls & the gun platform are in good condition, although some of the granite coping stones are missing. The drill shed has been demolished, though below-ground remains of this & of the platform are likely to survive.

Sources
General
12, 19.
Specific
1872 Illustrated London News panorama
n.d. Plan. PRO: WO 78/4147
1891 Military map. WDRO: Acc 81X/34
1958 Plan. PSA: 030260B

DEVIL'S POINT BATTERY B

PAR = E. STONEHOUSE, NGR = SX45965335,
PRN = SX45SE-714, MAP 3 No. 84

This is located immediately to the rear of the blockhouse & the early 18th century battery (A). It was built in 1901-2 and mounted two 12-pdr QF guns to cover the narrow entrance to the Hamoaze (and possibly a boom and/or anti-submarine net strung across it), in conjunction with other QFs mounted within the casmates of Garden Battery opposite. In 1905 two more 12-pdr emplacements were proposed on the shore below but were not built. In 1908 and 1910 it was fully armed, but by 1920 one gun had been removed; no guns were present in 1936, but in 1941 the battery buildings were taken over by those manning the boom defence.

A plan of 1901-2 shows the two gun emplacements, with a telephone room, coal store and latrines against the retaining wall to the rear. A stairwell to the rear of the guns provided access down to the shelters for officers and other ranks, and to the artillery store and lamp room at the W end and the main magazine (a cartridge and filled shell store separated by a shifting lobby) sited under and between the gun positions.

The battery occupies a small terrace, the rear of which is defined by a concrete retaining wall. The two gun positions are visible, complete with concrete aprons and one steel mounting plate; the other has either been removed or covered by concrete. The stairwell and magazines have been infilled, and the buildings to the rear demolished.

Plate 86 Devil's Point Battery B, 12-pdr QF emplacements (Exeter Archaeology)

Present condition

The gun positions and retaining wall remain in good condition. Substantial below-ground remains of the magazine, shelter and other rooms probably survive intact.

Sources

General

19, 21, 22, 24; O, Q.

Specific

1901-2	Battery for 2 12-pdr QF Guns. PRO: WO 78/5054
1905	Plymouth Devil's Point: proposed additional 2 12-pdr QF Guns. PRO: WO 78/4147
1912-30	Plymouth Defences Index Plan. PRO: WO 78/5066
1927	? Armament table. PRO: CAB 36/15
1958	Plans. PSA: 030260B, 030264B
n.d.	Western King Fort Record Book. PRO: WO 192/298

BOOM MOORING RINGS

PAR = E. STONEHOUSE, NGR = SX45945334,
PRN = SX45SE-715, MAP 3 No. 85

A boom across the narrow entrance to the Hamoaze is first referred to in *c*.1900, and was present during World War I and World War II, when the buildings belonging to the nearby QF battery were taken over by boom defence. The ends were anchored by chains fixed to the foreshore immediately to the S of the blockhouse and immediately to the N of Garden Battery (where one chain still survives). Two light QF guns or heavy machine guns were sited on Earl's Battery to fire along the boom, and, although the siting of a Maxim machine-gun on the roof of the blockhouse was proposed in 1902, there is no reference to this or other armament being emplaced. An anti-submarine net may also have been installed with the boom in the last war.

Four massive iron rings are embedded in the foreshore immediately to the S of the blockhouse, on or just below the high water mark. These anchored the other end of the chain which still survives attached to equivalent rings on the opposite shore. There are no visible remains of a gun position on the roof of the blockhouse.

Present condition

The iron rings are firmly set into the rock and largely complete, although corroded.

Source

Specific

n.d.	Western King Fort Record Book. PRO: WO 192/298

WESTERN KING REDOUBT

PAR = E. STONEHOUSE, NGR = SX46155336, PRN = SX45SE-257/1, MAP 3 No. 86

This was located on gently rising ground to the rear of Western King Point, and lies under the later Western King QF Battery (B, No. 88). It dates to the same period as Passage Point Battery, and was described by Dixon in 1780 as being completed in July 1779 and armed (with twelve 18-pdr guns) on 16 August, when the Franco-Spanish fleet anchored in Cawsand Bay. Other contemporary sources however mention ten and eight 18-pdrs; it is possible that the armament was reduced when the immediate emergency had passed. Dixon's 1780 plan of the redoubt shows twelve embrasures (with a *terreplein* behind) on the sea-facing sides, with a *banquette* on the land-facing sides; a very similar arrangement to both the contemporary redoubts of Mount Pleasant and Mount Wise. It was surrounded by a ditch and *glacis*, with access via a drawbridge from the W; a building housing a guardroom, storeroom and magazine (which may have been partly underground) is shown in the centre, together with a reservoir or cistern. In 1805 it was armed with ten 18-pdr guns, and in 1811 only eleven embrasures are shown. In 1850 it was armed with ten 8-inch and 32-pdr guns, and a map of 1856-57 shows seven embrasures on the sea-facing sides & a possible eighth in the N.E corner. In 1860 seven emplacements are shown, complete with racer rails for the gun carriages, and shortly after the armament was strengthened by the addition of nine further emplacements on the flanks in 1861-62 (Western King Battery A). At this time the buildings were demolished, the land-facing ramparts

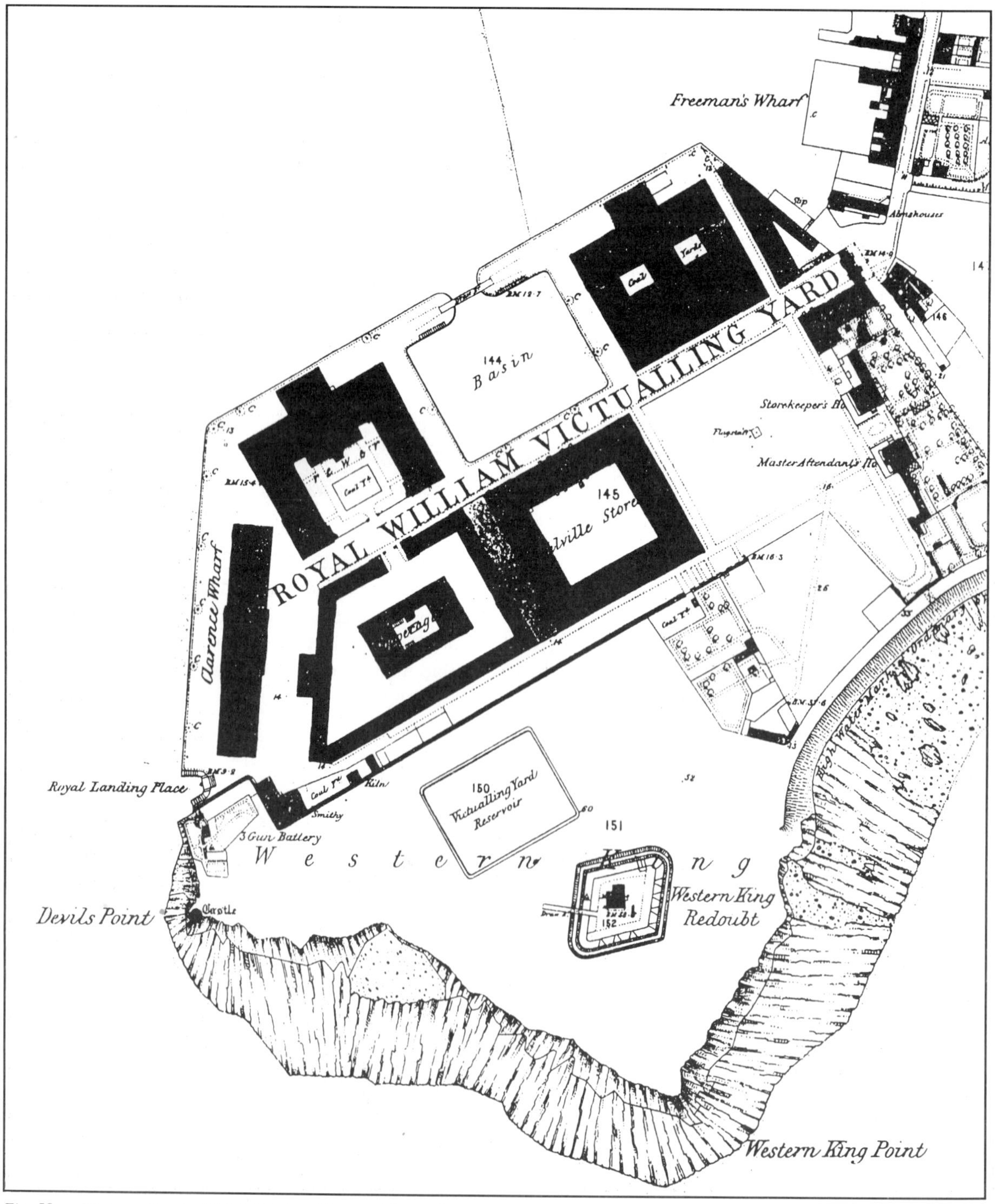

Fig. 59 Western King in 1857 (WDRO: military edition of O.S. 1:2500 map)

levelled and the ditches filled in, and bomb-proof magazines built. In 1885 three 64-pdr RMLs were mounted on the sea-faces, but had been removed by 1893. In *c*.1899 the remaining faces were overlain by the earthwork of the QF Battery (B, No. 88).

The remains of the redoubt lie buried under the QF battery and the area to the N, and part of the ditch and a brick parapet wall were revealed in 1995. One of the bomb-proof magazines built in 1861-62 and the connecting passages were built within the ditch of the earlier redoubt.

Present condition

Demolished, although substantial below-ground remains survive.

Sources

General

4 - 9, 12, 13, 15, 17, 19; O, Q.

Specific

1780	Dixon's plan of Western King Battery. PRO: MPH 373
1811	Plan of Western King & Devil's Point. PRO: MPH 233
1823	Plan of Cremyll Passage Point in Plymouth Sound. PRO: WO 78/405
1824	Plan showing Three-Gun Battery and Redoubt. PRO: MPH 681
1851	?Letters. PRO: WO 55/807
1856-7	Military edition of O.S. 1:2500. Devon sheet CXXIII.11 WDRO.
1872	*Illustrated London News* panorama
1891	Military map. WDRO: Acc 81X/34
1995	*Stonehouse Urban Development Area, Plymouth, Devon. Environmental Assessment: the Archaeological & Built Heritage.* (Appendix 3) Wessex Archaeology Ref. No. 37964

WESTERN KING BATTERY A

PAR = E. STONEHOUSE, NGR = SX46155336, PRN = SX45SE-257/2 & 3, MAP 3 No. 87

This incorporated and replaced the earlier redoubt, with additional gun positions being built on the flanks (*Fig. 8*). Its construction was proposed by the 1860 Royal Commission to strengthen the defences of the entrance to the Hamoaze, in conjunction with a similar battery flanking the earlier redoubt at Eastern King, and new casemated batteries on Drake's Island and at Garden Battery on the shore opposite. Its design was approved in November 1860, was built in 1861-62, and consisted of nine new gun emplacements, four on the W flank and five on the E, together with the seven emplacements on the sea-facing sides of the old redoubt. The guns were served by a pair of bomb-proof expense magazines on each flank, two of which were built within the truncated ends of the W & N ramparts of the old redoubt. Two bomb-proof main magazines

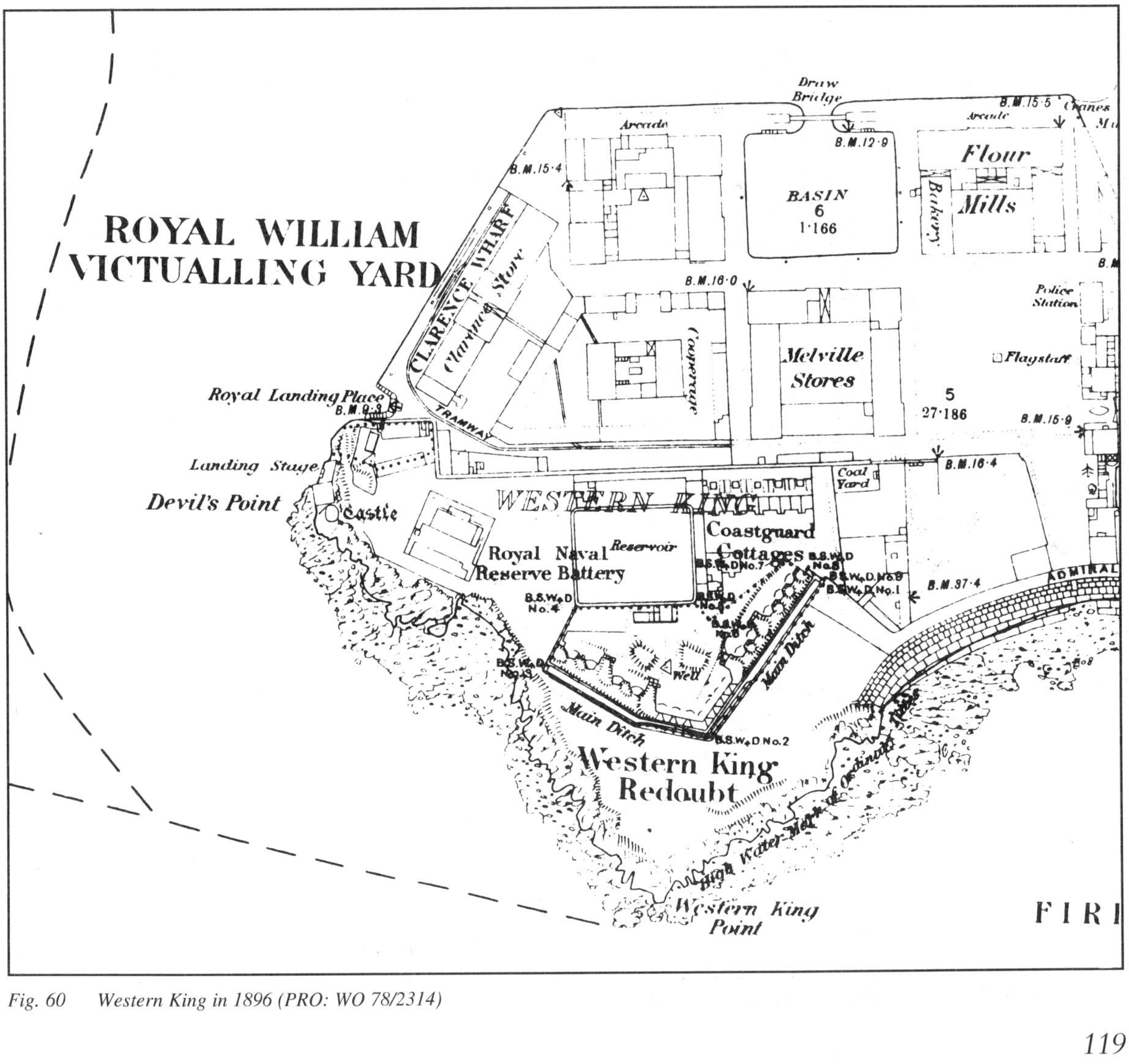

Fig. 60 Western King in 1896 (PRO: WO 78/2314)

(each containing a shell store and a cartridge store) were constructed to the rear (one largely within the infilled ditch of the former redoubt) and were linked to each flanking battery by underground passages. Accommodation for the gunners was provided by a masonry building adjoining the reservoir to the rear, and the battery was defended by a ditch along the front and by loopholed walls on each flank. To the rear the Victualling Yard reservoir was utilised as part of the defensive perimeter.

Originally an armament of fifteen guns was recommended in 1860, and sixteen emplacements were provided in 1861-62. In 1885 it was armed with twelve 64-pdr RML guns, nine of which were on the flanks and three in the redoubt, declining to nine by 1893. In 1899 it was replaced with a QF battery (B, No. 88) which was built over the W flank of the battery and the redoubt; the E flank remained open until the extension of the present car park in the 1970s.

Few above ground remains are visible due to the later QF battery being built over the top of it, the extension of the car park in the 1970s, and the demolition at the same time of the gunners' quarters and magazines and infilling of the area between the QF battery and the reservoir. However, the loopholed walls flanking the battery remain largely complete. Both are constructed of rubble limestone and topped with a decorative course of brick, and contain dressed granite loops. The wall on the W flank extends from the ditch up to the corner of the reservoir, and faced west. The wall on the E flank extends from the rear of the gun positions around the end of the ditch, includes a monumental gateway (giving access to the battery and the former Coastguard Cottages & Station) and ends at the corner of the Victualling Yard wall. It includes windows belonging to a demolished building, granite loops facing S & S.W along the ditch in front of the battery, and limestone loops facing S & flanking the gateway. The defensible perimeter constructed in 1861-62 therefore extended from this gateway and around to the S.W corner of the reservoir. Within the battery, the foundations of the gunners' quarters and substantial remains of the bomb-proof magazines were revealed in 1995. The ditch at the front has been infilled, although its rock scarp is visible in places.

Present condition
The remaining sections of loopholed wall are in good condition, although the N end of the W wall has been demolished where it adjoins the reservoir. The potential for below-ground remains of the battery surviving within and under the rampart of the later QF battery is high, and further remains of the magazines and gunners' quarters are likely to survive within the infilled area to the N. To the E the present car park slopes up to the wall at the rear of the former battery, and is not terraced into the hillside; therefore the survival of remains of the E emplacements and of the ditch fronting them is likely.

Sources
General
12 - 15, 17, 19; O, Q.
Specific

1898	General plan of battery. PRO: WO 78/5047
1942	Layout & summary history of battery (in Fort Record Book). PRO: WO 192/198
1956-8	Plans. PSA: 030264B, 030258X, 030259X

WESTERN KING BATTERY B

PAR = E. STONEHOUSE, NGR = SX46135334, PRN = SX45SE-257, MAP 3 No. 88

This was built in 1897-98 directly over the rampart and gun positions of the W flank of the 1861-62 battery, and over the front faces of the earlier redoubt. It was armed with seven 12-pdr QF guns which covered the channels to each side of Drake's Island against attack by motor torpedo boats and other light and speedy craft. It was the only 7-gun QF battery in the country, and remained fully armed to at least 1910, but by 1920 only four guns were mounted, which by 1930 had been reduced to two; by 1936 these were accompanied with one searchlight. In 1941 or shortly after they were replaced by two twin 6-pdr QF guns (C, No. 89).

A plan of 1898 (*Fig. 13*) shows the seven gun positions, together with the 1861-62 main magazines (which continued to be used) and the four expense magazines, which were used as small arms stores. Two new passages were built to connect the main magazines with the QF gun positions, and derricks brought the ammunition up to the gun platform. To the rear the 1861 gunners' quarters continued in use, and by 1911 a shelter, cook house and ablution block had been built to the E. Between 1896 & 1898 the loopholed wall on the E flank was extended N & W to the S.E corner of the reservoir to form a new boundary wall; this contained the main entrance to the battery. A fire control post was later sited at the apex of the battery.

All seven concrete emplacements survive complete, together with their steel mounting plates (one of which is engraved 'CAR GAR Q.F. PL' with 'EOC WD (and) 1897' below), and the concrete aprons, gun platforms (with ammunition lockers to the rear) and walkway. However most of the guard rails and all the derricks have been removed, and the area to the rear of the gun positions infilled up to the level of the walkway. The boundary wall is built of random stone rubble, and incorporates the earlier War Dept. granite boundary stones depicted in 1896.

Present condition
The condition of the above-ground remains is very good, although one of the mounting plates is partly covered by modern steps. To the rear, substantial below-ground remains of the magazines and of the

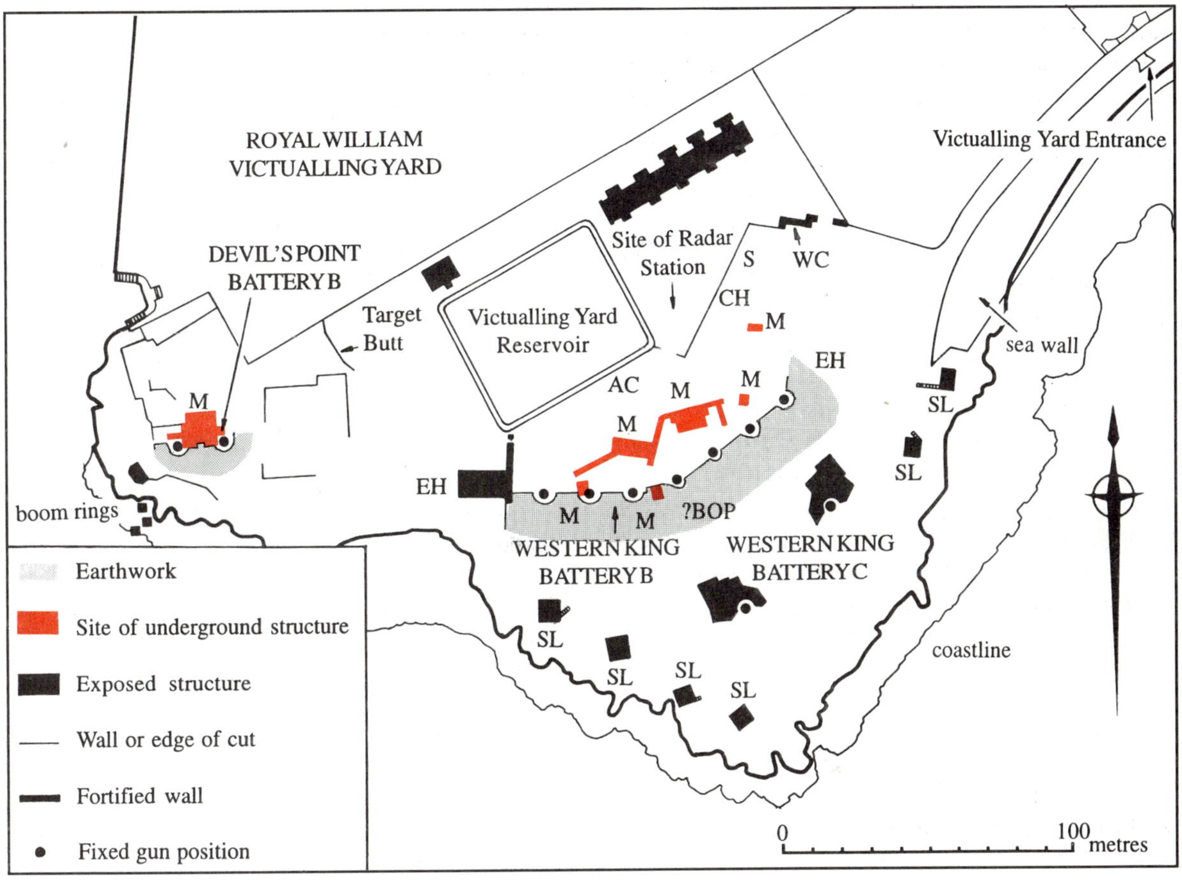

Fig. 61 *Western King & Devil's Point, defences from c.1900 to WWII*

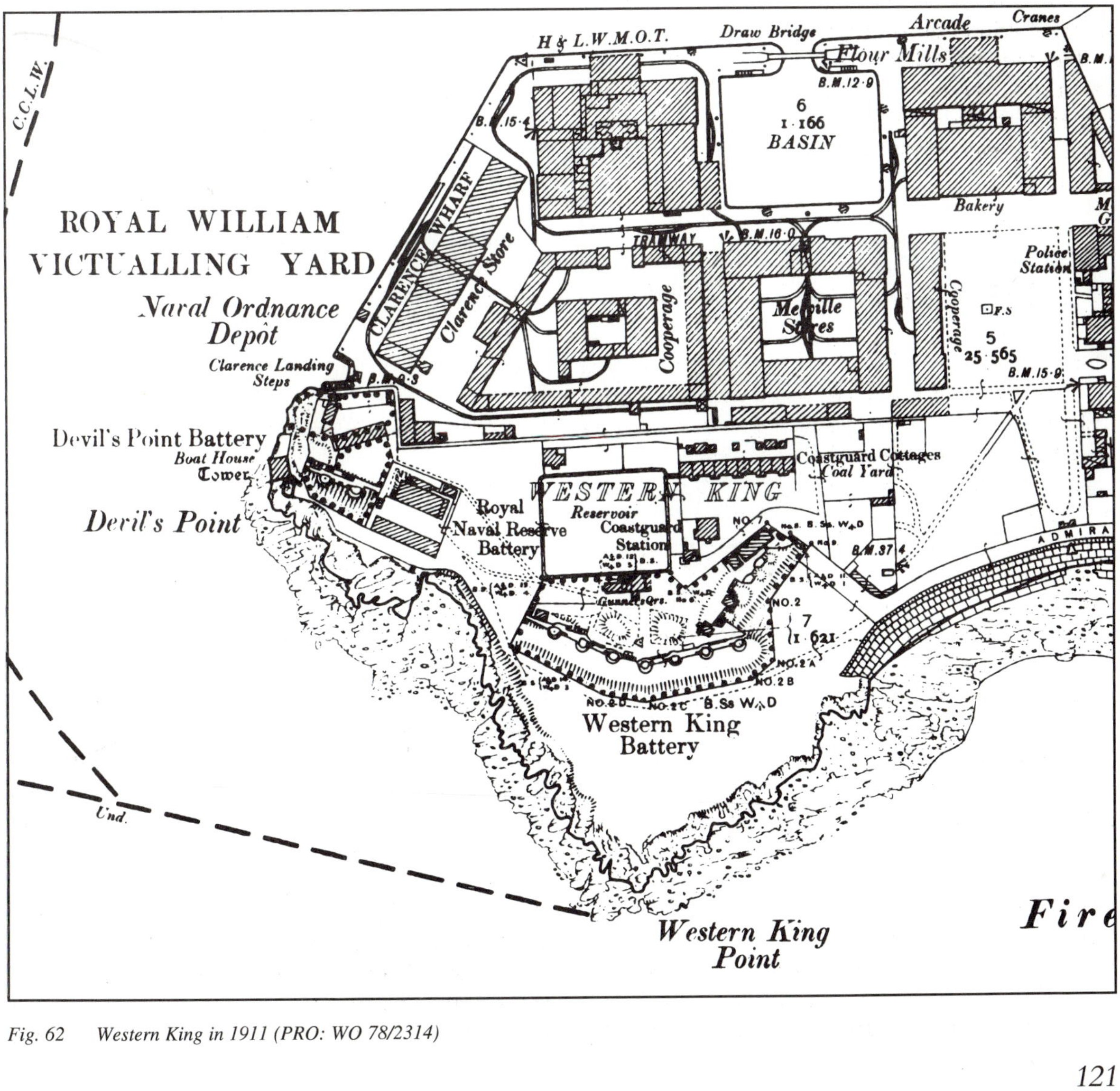

Fig. 62 *Western King in 1911 (PRO: WO 78/2314)*

connecting passages were observed in 1995. Foundations of the demolished shelter & cook house may survive under the N end of the present car park.

Sources
General
19 - 22, 24; O, Q.

Specific

1898	General plan of battery. PRO: WO 78/5047
1905	Armament table? PRO: CAB 16/1
1927	Armament table? PRO: CAB 36/16
1941	Plans? PRO: WO 192/135 & 199/523
1942	Layout & summary history of battery (in Fort Record Book). PRO: WO 192/198
1956-8	Plans. PSA: 030264B, 030258X, 030259X, 030262X.
1970	O.S. 1:2500 map sheet SX4653. WCSL

WESTERN KING BATTERY C

PAR = E. STONEHOUSE, NGR = SX46155330 & 46185334, PRN = SX45SE-258, MAP 3 No. 89

This consists of two twin 6-pdr QF gun positions located downslope from the earlier 12-pdr QF battery. The emplacements were built in 1941. The guns provided a more efficient and up-to-date defence against fast motor torpedo boats and other light fast-moving craft trying to enter the Hamoaze, and operated in conjunction with six searchlights. These incorporated or replaced one built in 1930-36, and are sited on the coast just above high water mark; they were powered by two engine houses sited on the flanks of the earlier QF battery. After 1942 a radar station was established in the former coastguard station to the N, but its role is not clear as its field of view would have been distorted by the ground in front and by Drake's Island. The guns were dismounted in 1956 on the disbandment of Coast Artillery, and the observation towers to the rear were probably demolished in the early 1960s. There were also numerous other service and accommodation structures built within the area of the old QF Battery in the 1940s; these are shown on plans of 1942 and 1958 and were demolished in the 1960s and early 1970s.

Plate 87 Twin 6-pdr QF emplacement at Western King (Exeter Archaeology)

The two gun positions, together with the adjoining concrete and brick-built storage buildings, shelters and observation towers (now demolished), were built within terraces cut into the *glacis* slope of the earlier redoubt. The guns were sited facing out to sea, and were surrounded on the other three sides by an area covered by a cantilevered roof, which now forms a public shelter. The roofs of related structures to the rear are still visible; the structures themselves have presumably been infilled. The structures within the QF battery and the former coastguard station have been demolished.

Plate 88 Searchlight emplacements at Western King (Exeter Archaeology)

All six searchlight emplacements accompanying the battery survive complete, and have been constructed within terraces cut into the coastal cliffs behind the foreshore. Four are sited on the W shore of Western King Point and face S, whilst two are sited on the E shore and face E & S.E. All are of concrete and brick construction and consist of a single concrete cell with a brick access stairwell to the rear. Each has a central vent in the roof directly above the search light below. Five have a pair of light slits each, which would originally have had protective steel shutters, whilst the westernmost cell only has a single slit; this may be the earlier searchlight built in 1930-36.

The W engine house powering the battery and searchlights survives intact, and is built within a terrace immediately to the W of the earlier loopholed wall; the E one was demolished in the 1970s. The engine house is a flat roofed single-storey concrete structure, entered via a ramp and doorway from the south. The windows and door retain their original armoured shutters, and the walls contain ventilation grilles just below eaves level. The interiors of this and of most of the

Plate 89 Searchlight engine house (Exeter Archaeology)

searchlight emplacements are not accessible and have not been viewed.

Present condition

The condition of the gun positions is reasonable, as they have been converted for use as public shelters. The gun mountings have been concreted over, and the buildings to the rear blocked off and probably infilled with rubble; their bitumen roofs however survive intact and lie flush with the current ground surface. The six searchlight cells survive complete, although only one apparently still retains its armoured shutters; all except the easternmost one have been blocked off and have had their access stairwells infilled. The western engine house also survives complete, although the survival of any internal fittings was not ascertained; foundations of the eastern engine house probably survive under the surface of the present car park. Remnants of the other demolished buildings may survive below ground.

Sources

Specific

1941	Plan? PRO: WO 192/135 & 199/523
1942	Layout of battery and notes in Fort Record Book. PRO: WO 192/198
1956	Admiralty plan. Copy held by Mr Firth of Admiralty Cottages.
1956-7	Plans. PSA 030258X, 030262X

FIRESTONE BAY ARTILLERY TOWER

PAR = E. STONEHOUSE, NGR = SX46375352, PRN = SX45SE-8, MAP 3 No. 90

This is located within Firestone Bay to deter any landings on the beach. It is probably one of a system of blockhouses built by the Edgcumbe family in the late 15th/early 16th century to defend Stonehouse from French and other raids. It is depicted on the panorama of c.1540 (*Fig. 2*) as a two-storey polygonal tower with guns on two floors and crenellated battlements above. It formed part of the 'fortress of Stonehouse', together with a bulwark and Devil's Point Blockhouse to the W and the town wall to the N. Worth thought that it was built between 1485 and 1525; Brayshay dates it to the 1490s. Graffiti apparently indicate some military occupation in 1810 but by 1857 it had become a coastguard watch-house. Between 1891 & 1896 an extension was built onto the W end and the building converted into public conveniences. The 1857 O.S. plan shows it as having five embrasures in its W, S.W, S, S.E, & E.S.E walls with a doorway and stairwell to the rear.

Two blocked granite cannon embrasures are visible (*Plate 1*) at the lowest level in its S & S.E walls with loops and possible smaller gunports on the floor above, and further loops within the crenellations above that. It is not clear without closer inspection whether the present crenellations are primary or secondary. The roof level apparently contains emplacements for pivoted hand-held artillery of the time (Dalton & Terry 1993). To the rear there is an arched doorway at first-floor level, access down to which is now via a stairwell, indicating that the ground level behind the blockhouse has been raised considerably since its construction. The building is built of rubble limestone with granite quoins and embrasures and other detail. The interior was not viewed.

Present condition

It is in good structural condition; recent conversion into a restaurant has involved some alteration.

Sources

General

1, 19; O, Q.

Specific

1857	1st edition of O.S. 1:500 map sheet No. 100. PCM
1864	1st edition O.S. 1:2500 map sheet CXX.III.11. WDRO
1886	Worth, R.N 'Notes on the early history of Stonehouse' *Jnl. of Plymouth Institution* **9**, 338-74
1891	Military map. WDRO: Acc 81X/34
1977	Plan. EH
1992	Brayshay, M Lecture, 14 October.
1993	Letter from John Dalton & David Terry, Architects, Plymouth
1995	Brayshay, M 'The Sixteenth Century Protection of Sutton Harbour and Plymouth Sound: the documentary evidence' in Ray, K (ed) *Archaeological Investigations and Research in Plymouth, Vol. 1, 1992-93* pp 83-90. Plymouth Archaeology Occasional Publication No. **2**

EASTERN KING BATTERY A

PAR = E. STONEHOUSE, NGR = SX46615358, PRN = SX45SE-21, MAP 3 No. 91

This battery was built between 17 August 1779 and 10 January 1780 on the orders of Col. Dixon to counter the threat of the Franco-Spanish fleet which anchored in Cawsand Bay in August 1779. The battery was armed with four 18-pdr guns mounted *en barbette* and was intended to fire on ships using the approach channel between Eastern King and Drake's Island. On Gardner's 1784 map it is depicted on or near the site of the later Eastern King Redoubt (built 1844-49), at the north end of a small ?quarry, probably the same as that present on the site now.

There are no identifiable surface remains of the battery; it would have been demolished when the later redoubt was built.

Present condition

Demolished, although fragmentary below-ground remains may survive.

Sources

General

4 - 8; N, O, Q.

EASTERN KING (PRINCE OF WALES) REDOUBT

PAR = E. STONEHOUSE, NGR = SX46615358, PRN = SX45SE-21, MAP 3 No. 92

This was named the Prince of Wales Redoubt and was one of three (Picklecombe Battery and Staddon Point Battery A being the others) recommended by the 1844 Inter-Service Committee on Harbour Defences. It was completed in 1849 (as recorded by a datestone over the entrance arch), and had two gun casemates with embrasures for eight guns mounted *en barbette* in open battery on the roof above; in *c.* 1850 it was armed with 8-inch and 10-inch SB guns. It was protected by loopholed walls and a dry ditch, and is the earliest fortification in the Plymouth defences to possess musketry galleries (*caponiers*) projecting out into the ditch and gun casemates. In 1861-2 further gun emplacements were added to the flanks (Eastern King Battery B), followed by four 12-pdr QF guns on the roof in c. 1900 (Battery C).

The redoubt is approximately arrow-shaped, with a range of single-storey barrack casemates flanking two gun casemates at the front and a separate two-storey keep to the rear. This contained the officers' quarters and main magazine, and was linked to the barrack range and the gun platform (*terreplein*) on the roof above by curtain walls and a walkway; there was a further small magazine at the E end of the barrack range. Much of the structure is faced with high quality, monumental limestone ashlar, with internal brick vaulting and partition walls. The ground floor of the keep contains two magazine chambers with lamp windows to the rear and heated officers' quarters above and to the front. Water was stored in granite cisterns under the courtyard. The roof of the barrack range has a stone parapet with embrasures for eight guns; these, and the area to the rear, were infilled with concrete on the construction of the QF positions in c.1900. The gun casemates below retain tackle loops and one pivot, and the impressions of racer rails for the traversing carriages. Some internal detail survives elsewhere, such as wooden ventilation louvres between the barrack casemates and fireplaces and later racking within them, and the iron shutter to the lamp window in the small magazine. The redoubt was entered through a monumental gateway (with the royal crest and 1849 datestone above) in the N.E flank, approached via a 'horned' entrance and an outer gate. The redoubt was protected by a dry ditch and by a quarry to the S, which also afforded the guns in the casemates a clear field of fire over the channel; the

Plate 90 Eastern King Redoubt, the keep (Exeter Archaeology)

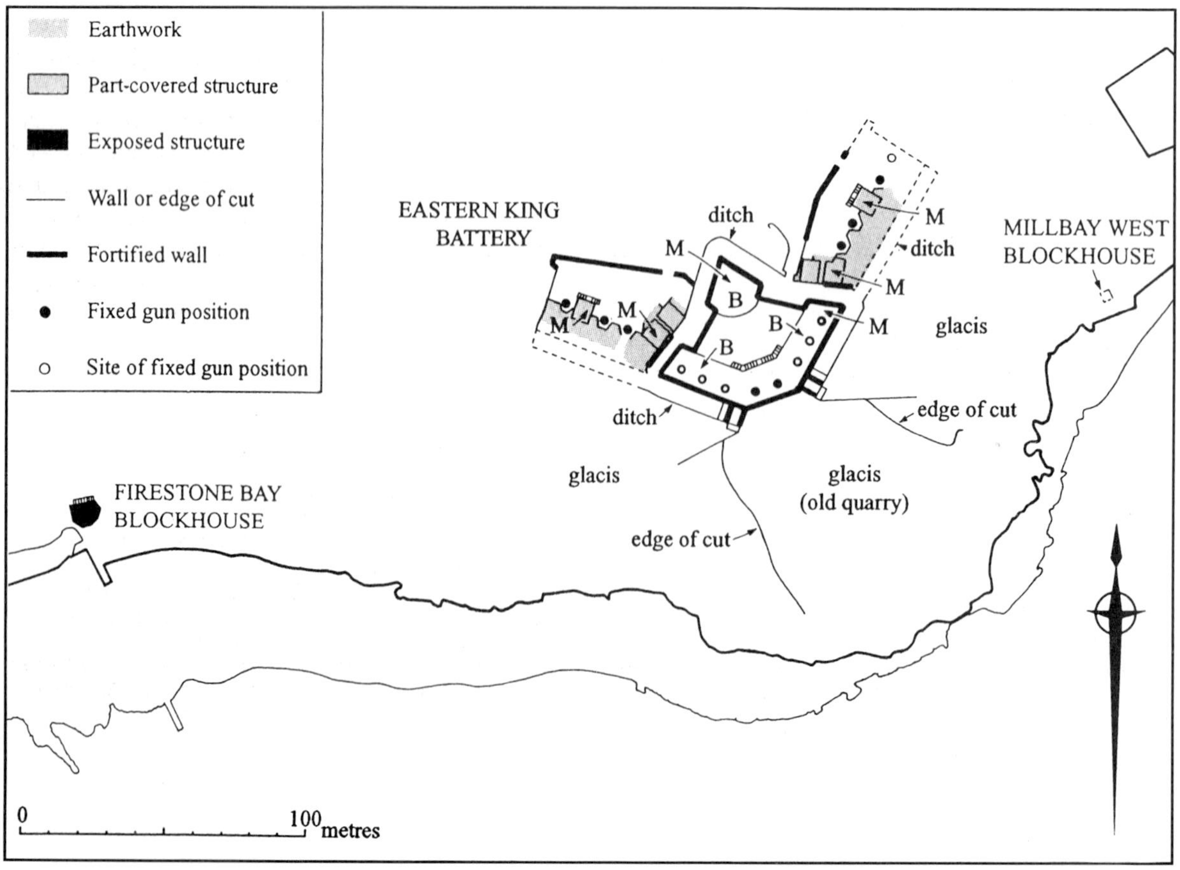

Fig. 63 Firestone Bay Artillery Tower, Eastern King & Millbay (East) Blockhouse

Plate 91 Eastern King Redoubt, ditch & caponier (Exeter Archaeology)

ditch was itself protected by two musketry *caponiers* fronted by drop ditches, musketry galleries at each end of the barrack range, and loopholes in the flanks of the keep and along the curtain walls. Further defence to the flanks and rear was provided by a parapet on the roof of the keep and by an upper level of loopholes in the curtain walls; there were also two sets of loopholes in the counterscarp wall opposite each end of the barrack range, access to which was via the main gate and a sally port. These were blocked up and the ground level in front of them raised when the additional emplacements were added in 1861-62.

Present condition

The redoubt is in very good structural condition and has recently been refurbished by the MoD, although prior to this the upper part of the N.E curtain wall above the gate had been removed. Most surviving internal features have been retained, although asphalte now covers the QF gun positions and the earlier parapet and embrasures on the roof. The dry ditch has also recently been emptied of later structures and re-pointed.

Sources
General
10; O, Q.
Specific
1850 Armament table and plan. Officers' Mess, Royal Citadel
1857 Plan of Prince of Wales Redoubt. PRO: MPHH 629(3)
1866 Plan. RCHME: PLM/536
1993 Pye, A *Refurbishment of Eastern Kings Fort, RMB Stonehouse, Plymouth. Archaeological Assessment* Exeter Archaeology Report No. **93.47**
forthcoming Pye, A. & Bishop, P *Archaeological survey of Eastern King Redoubt, Plymouth* Exeter Archaeology Report.

EASTERN KING BATTERY B

PAR = E. STONEHOUSE, NGR = SX46615358, PRN = SX45SE-21, MAP 3 No. 93

An extension (mounting 12 guns) to Eastern King Redoubt was first proposed by Jervois in 1858, and additional armament was subsequently recommended by the 1859-60 Royal Commission. The design and construction was approved in November 1860 and the gun emplacements were built in 1861-62. In 1868 powder was still brought from the magazine in the keep, and the provision of additional expense magazines were recommended. Four emplacements were built on the E flank and three on the S flank; these were originally intended for 68-pdr SB guns but by 1885 were armed with seven 64-pdr RML guns, together with a further ten 64-pdr RMLs in the casemates and on the roof of the redoubt. The latter were removed shortly afterwards, and the flanking batteries remained armed until 1895, when it was proposed to replace them with four 12-pdr QF guns. Emplacements for these were built on the roof in *c.*1900.

The flanking batteries contained a total of seven emplacements for guns mounted *en barbette*; each contained two bomb-proof expense magazines and one guardroom/magazine and were protected at the rear and flank by a loop-holed wall (with small projecting musketry galleries at the rear corners) and at the front by a ditch (now infilled). The S magazine in the E battery retains its original suspended wooden floor. A door opened from each guardroom into the ditch of the redoubt, and into the latter via the sally port and main gate. A sloping *glacis* extended to the shoreline, enabling ships standing close in to be fired on.

Present condition

The W battery survives complete, although a track has been cut through one emplacement; the buildings are used for storage and the gun positions remain visible. The flanking wall is overgrown and the ditch infilled. In the E battery one emplacement has been covered by a recently-built house; the remainder are either open or infilled; the magazines are either empty or are used for storage, whilst the ditch has been infilled. Part of the loopholed wall to the rear and the flanking wall has been demolished.

Sources
General
11 - 15, 17, 19; O, Q.
Specific
1866 Plan. RCHME: PLM/536
1898 Plan. E & W King. PRO: WO 78/5047
1899 Eastern King Redoubt. PRO: WO 78/5045
1912 O.S. plan. RCHME
1993 Pye, A *Refurbishment of Eastern Kings Fort, RMB Stonehouse, Plymouth. Archaeological Assessment* Exeter Archaeology Report No. **93.47**
forthcoming Pye, A & Bishop, P *Archaeological survey of Eastern King Redoubt, Plymouth* Exeter Archaeology Report.

EASTERN KING BATTERY C

PAR = E. STONEHOUSE, NGR = SX46615358, PRN = SX45SE-21, MAP 3 No. 94

In 1895 a battery of four 12-pdr QF guns was proposed for the site for anti-torpedo boat defence. Plans were produced in 1898-99 and the battery, together with three searchlights (Electric Lights) on the shore, was constructed shortly after. By 1908 three guns were mounted, with another being added in 1911-12, when a Searchlight Directing Post and engine room were present in the redoubt. Two guns had been removed by 1920, followed by the others by 1930; the three searchlights remained present throughout, with two still being operational in 1936 and possibly one in WWII. At least one 40mm LAA gun was apparently mounted in 1940, and an observation post built on the roof. It is still occupied by the MoD and four 3-pdr Hotchkiss guns are emplaced on the parapet and used as a saluting battery.

The four concrete QF emplacements are sited on the roof behind the 1849 parapet, and were served by a magazine in the E gun casemate below. They survive complete with ammunition lockers, and the E emplacement retains its original steel mounting-plate and the steel loading platform and guard rails to the rear. Ammunition was brought up via the cantilevered 1849 granite stairway from the magazine; this consisted of a cartridge store with serving hatch and shifting lobby, lit by two lamp-windows from a shell-store/lamp-room to the E. The embrasure of the W gun casemate was modified and the gun pivot removed to accommodate the searchlight directing post. The three searchlight emplacements are present on the shoreline, and consist of a pair sited to the W and a single one to the E; both have been modified and are used; the interiors were not viewed. Later remains include a concrete World War II observation post in one of the QF emplacements, complete with iron doors and viewing window, and the four Hotchkiss guns on the parapet.

Present condition

The four QF emplacements and the WWII observation post survive complete, although the recent application of asphalte has masked several of the features. The magazine has been demolished. The E searchlight is in good condition, although modified by the addition of a (new) flat roof and a rebuilt front wall. The W pair appears to be in good condition, although the extent to which the original structure survives is not clear.

Sources

General

17, 19 - 24; O, Q.

Specific

1898 Plan. E & W King. PRO: WO 78/5047

1899 Eastern King Redoubt. PRO: WO 78/5045

1912 O.S. plan. RCHME

1993 Pye, A *Refurbishment of Eastern Kings Fort, RMB Stonehouse, Plymouth. Archaeological Assessment* Exeter Archaeology Report No. **93.47**

forthcoming Pye, A. & Bishop, P *Archaeological survey of Eastern King Redoubt, Plymouth* Exeter Archaeology Report.

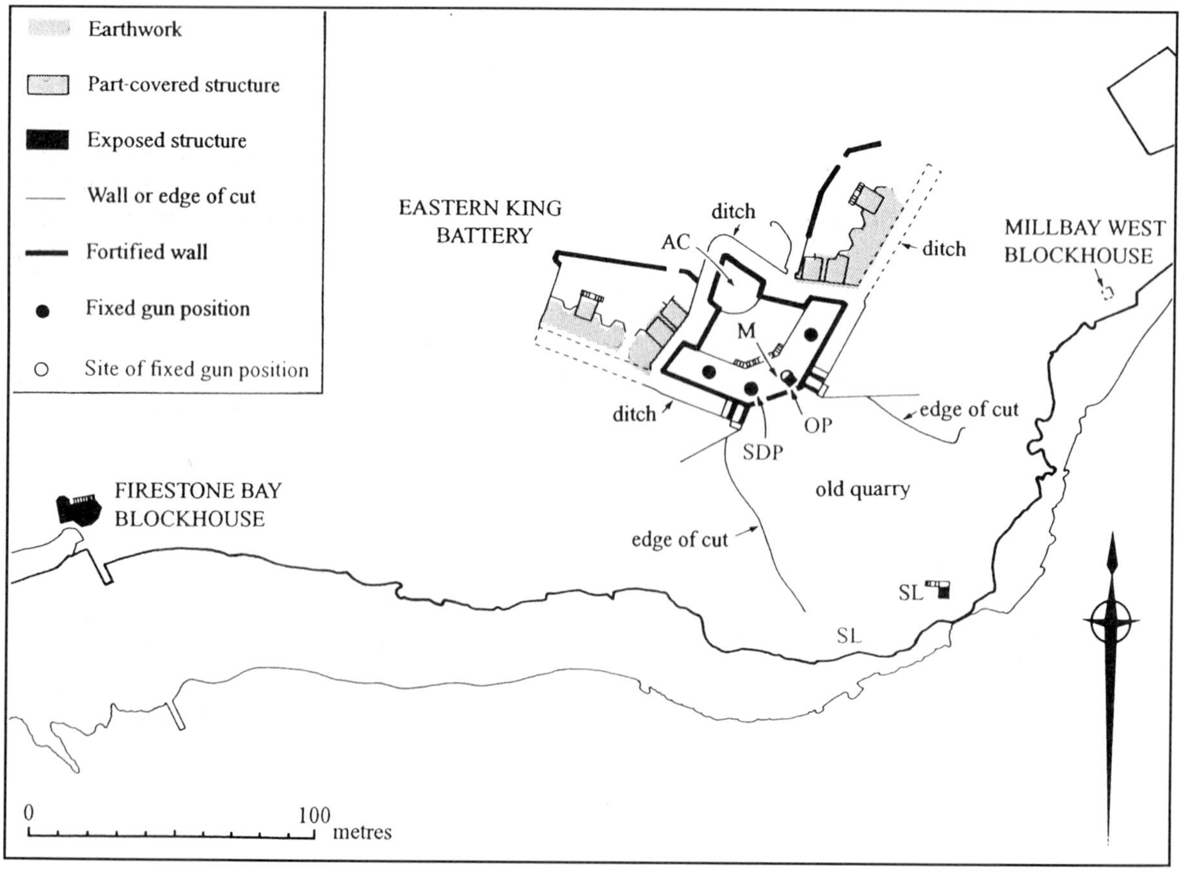

Fig. 64 Eastern King Battery C

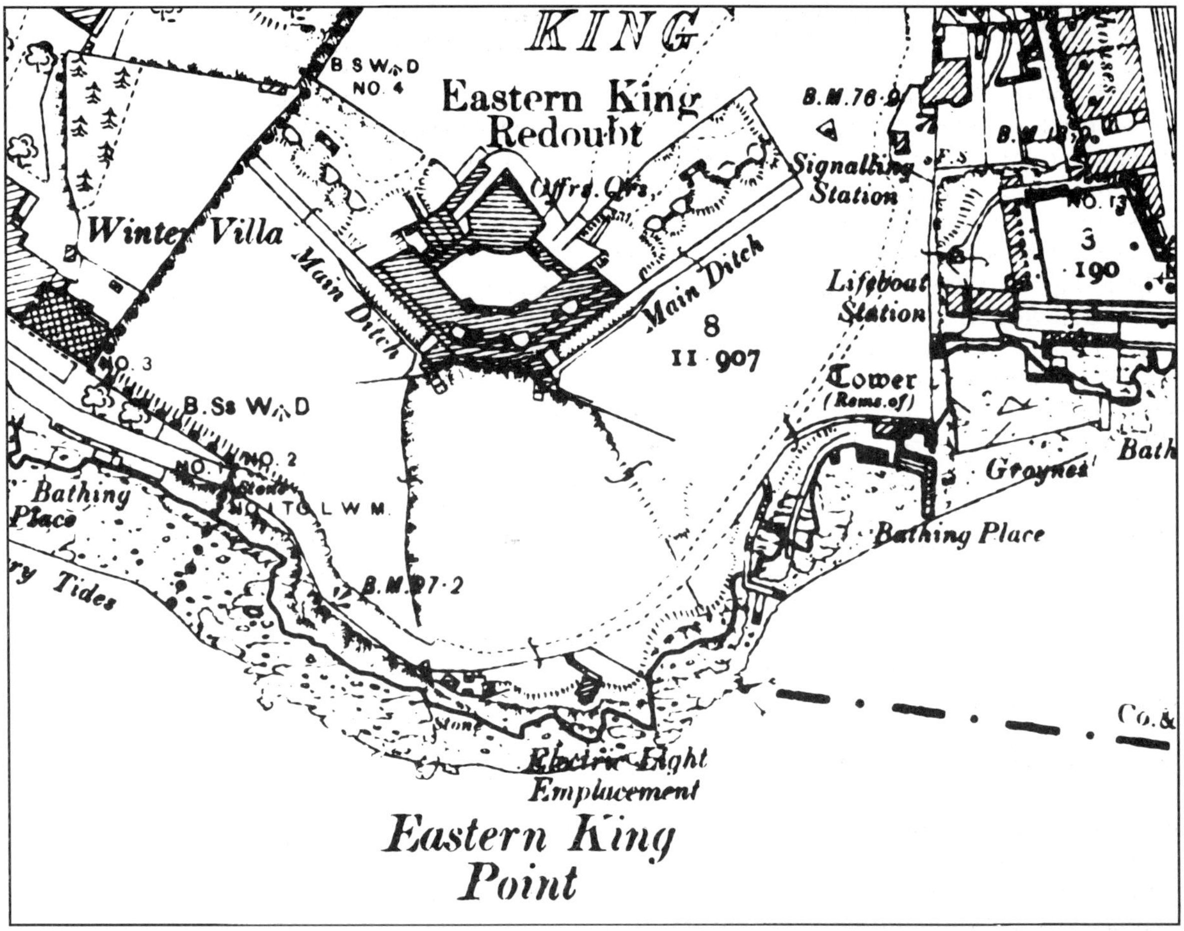

Fig. 65 Eastern King in 1911 (PRO: WO 78/2314)

MILLBAY (WEST) (or EASTERN KING) BLOCKHOUSE

PAR = E. STONEHOUSE, NGR = SX46735359, NUM = SX45SE-9, MAP 3 No. 95

This is thought to be of early 16th-century date, one of a series built along the N shore of the Sound to protect Plymouth and Stonehouse against French and other raids, and in this case perhaps to hinder a landing in Millbay. It is first depicted on the panorama of *c.*1540 (*Fig. 2*); and was partly demolished by 1868 when only the W, N & E walls are shown. The original granite doorway was apparently removed and set up outside the Drill Battery near the Long Room (at SX 46605370) in 1861. There is a detailed description of the blockhouse in Worth (1886).

It is located just above high-water mark at the S.W corner of Millbay, immediately W of the boundary wall of the docks. The E section of the N wall and the N section of the E wall survive to a height of *c.*2m and are built of undressed rubble stone, which has been heavily repointed and whitewashed. Both sections of wall have been truncated; the S end of the E wall has been partly rebuilt with the later boundary wall it supports, and a stairway has been cut through the N wall, which acts as a retaining wall for the modern bathing-place now on the site. There is no trace of the W or S walls.

Present condition

Parts of the N & E walls survive in reasonable structural condition; the other walls have been demolished.

Sources

General

1, 2, 19; M, O, Q.

Specific

1868 O.S 1st edition 1:2500 map. Sheet No. 123.11 WDRO

1886 Worth, R.N 'Notes on the Early History of Stonehouse' *Journal of the Plymouth Institution* **IX** 367.

1891 Map. WDRO: Acc 81X/34

1958 Copeland, E.W & Masson Phillips, E.N 'The Ancient Buildings of Plymouth' *Old Plymouth Society*

MILLBAY BLOCKHOUSE (NORTH)

MILLBAY BLOCKHOUSE (NORTH)

PAR = E. STONEHOUSE, NGR = ?SX46605310, PRN = SX45SE-761, MAP 3 No. 96

This is depicted on a map of 1738 and apparently on later maps dating to the 1750s, but is not shown on the panorama of *c*.1540. It is sited on the N shore of Millbay, presumably to defend against an enemy landing there, and may perhaps have been contemporary with or slightly later than those at the mouth of Millbay. There are no visible remains.

Present condition

Demolished, although below-ground remains may survive.

Source

General

M (Nos 114 & 124)

Specific

1738 Board of Ordnance plan. PRO: MPH 129

MILLBAY BLOCKHOUSE (EAST)

MILLBAY BLOCKHOUSE (EAST)

PAR = ST. ANDREW, NGR = ?SX47155367, PRN = SX45SE-585, MAP 3 No. 97

This is an artillery blockhouse probably built in the late 15th/early 16th century as part of the system of blockhouses defending the shores of the Hoe and the entrance to the Hamoaze and Stonehouse Pool to the W. It is depicted as a single-storey crenellated structure on the panorama of *c*.1540 (*Fig. 2*), and may appear on some later 18th century maps. Any remains were probably finally demolished when the present Millbay Docks were built at the end of the 1850s. Its approximate site may be occupied by the former 19th-century dock police station. The octagonal shape of this building may reflect that of the earlier blockhouse, although this must remain pure speculation as the blockhouse in *c*.1540 appears to be circular, and not polygonal.

Present condition

The original blockhouse has been demolished, although below-ground remains may survive. The dock police station has been recently refurbished and is occupied. It lies within a waterfront housing development which has replaced earlier industrial buildings.

Sources

General

1; M

WEST HOE BATTERY

WEST HOE BATTERY

PAR = ST. ANDREW, NGR = SX47245361, PRN = SX45SE-703, MAP 3 No. 98

This was erected on Col. Dixon's orders between 17 August 1779 and January 1780 at the western extremity of the Hoe adjoining the entrance to Millbay. It mounted six 18-pdr guns and was intended to take the ships in their stern as they rounded Drake's Island and sailed towards Devil's Point. It is depicted on plans of 1780 and 1784, and was probably an earthen battery with the guns being mounted *en barbette*. No remains of it are now visible; it was sited in the gardens of West Hoe Terrace.

Present condition

Site occupied by West Hoe Terrace, gardens and rebuilt public path and coastal defence wall. The battery has been demolished but below-ground remains may survive.

Sources

General

4 - 8

BULWARKS ON THE HOE

PAR = ST. ANDREW, NGR = Various, PRN = SX45SE-17/1 & SX45SE-593, MAP 3 No. 99

On the panorama of *c.*1540 (*Fig. 2*) a series of fortified walls ('bulwarks') containing gun embrasures (some occupied) and a triangular battery emplacement are depicted along the coastline between Millbay & Fisher's Nose, with two further triangular emplacements shown on the hill behind and on Firestone Bay to the W. There are various references to the construction of bulwarks (a total of five are named at various times) and other defences on the Hoe from the early 15th century (Brayshay). From the c.1540 map there appears to have been a bulwark perhaps at Tinside, and that on the hill above may have been sited near the contemporary site of St Katherine's Chapel (now within the Citadel), or near Plymouth Dome and/or Smeaton's Tower.

There are no visible remains of any of these walls or bulwarks as the area has been heavily developed and landscaped during the construction of later fortifications, and by the insertion of Madeira Road in the late 1880s and the construction of subsequent pathways and retaining walls along the coastline.

Present condition
Demolished, although below-ground remains may survive.

Sources
General
1, 2; B, M, N, O, Q.
Specific
1992 Brayshay, M Lecture, 14 Oct.
1995 Brayshay, M 'The Sixteenth Century Protection of Sutton Harbour and Plymouth Sound: the documentary evidence' in Ray, K (ed) *Archaeological Investigations and Research in Plymouth, Vol. 1, 1992-93* pp 83-90. Plymouth Archaeology Occasional Publication No. **2**

'FISHER'S NOSE BLOCKHOUSE'

PAR = ST. ANDREW, NGR = SX48275365, PRN = SX45SE-10, MAP 3 No. 100

This is a polygonal rubble limestone tower sited just west of Fisher's Nose Point, guarding the approach to Sutton Pool & the Cattewater and the shore of the Hoe. It is depicted on the panorama of *c.*1540 (*Fig. 2*) as a two-storey crenellated tower with cannon embrasures at the lower level. It may have been built in the late 15th century (Brayshay, 1992) and extensively modified in 1523; alternatively it has been suggested that it may have begun life as a powder store built in 1542 (Brayshay, 1995), partly on the basis that the 1540 panorama is of a later date, and that perhaps the earlier references refer to a blockhouse sited at Fisher's Nose itself. However, it would seem unlikely for a powder store to be sited so close to the shore where it would be exposed to damp and sea spray and also to enemy fire. The blockhouse, and another tower or platform sited at Fisher's Nose itself, was incorporated into the lower fort of Plymouth Fort in 1595, and remained as part of the Lower Fort of the Royal Citadel from the 1660s. In 1716 it was named 'Queen Elizabeth's Tower', and that at Fisher's Nose itself 'Fisher's Nose Tower'. During WWII it was apparently used as an air-raid post.

It is architecturally dissimilar to the other blockhouses at Firestone Bay and Devil's Point as it has no granite embrasures (the rear doorway is not visible). It has granite quoins at its corners, however (although these may be secondary) and two blocked archways with shillet voussoirs in its S.E & S.W faces; a further blocked doorway also with shillet voussoirs is visible in its W face. The seaward S face cannot be seen from

Plate 92 'Fisher's Nose Blockhouse' (Exeter Archaeology)

the land. The archways probably represent cannon embrasures. It also contains one (blocked) late inserted doorway in its W face, and the upper section has been subsequently rebuilt and modified. The blockhouse may be contemporary with a stretch of coastal wall running N.E., but the exact relationship with this and with the wall running westwards could not be examined.

Present condition
Good. Top occupied by public pavement and viewing platform.

Sources
General
1; O, Q.
Specific
1716 Plan by C. Lilly. BL: Kings Ms 45 f.34
1992 Brayshay, M Lecture, 14 Oct
1995 Brayshay, M 'The Sixteenth Century Protection of Sutton Harbour and Plymouth Sound: the documentary evidence' in Ray, K (ed) *Archaeological Investigations and Research in Plymouth, Vol. 1, 1992-93* pp 83-90. Plymouth Archaeology Occasional Publication No. **2**

PLYMOUTH CASTLE

PAR = ST. ANDREW, NGR = SX48275397, PRN = SX45SE-48, MAP 3 No. 101

This was built in *c.* 1380 immediately to the W of the entrance to Sutton Harbour as a defence against French and Spanish raids. Amongst other sources, it is depicted on the panorama of *c.* 1540 and on de Gomme's plan of 1665, when it was demolished to provide material for the Citadel. It is shown in 1665 as a square structure with towers at each corner; the depiction on the 1540 panorama is less clear. In neither case is a gateway depicted in its S wall; the main entrance probably lay to the N, towards the town and out of view of a potential sea-borne enemy.

In the 1530s a short stretch of crenellated wall was built from the S.W corner of the castle up the slope to the W., from the W end of Lambhay St up to the line of Castle Dyke Lane (NGR = approx. SX48255396 to SX48175398). It was demolished with the castle in 1665-7 by de Gomme, although its probable line was maintained by property boundaries up until WWII. Until recently Plymouth was thought (Worth) to have been defended by a continuous wall of medieval origin, subsequently altered and refurbished in the Elizabethan and Civil War periods. However, it has recently been argued that this stretch of wall to the W of the castle was the only length to have been built prior to the Civil War, when a continuous bastioned rampart was built around the town, although there are earlier references to ditches and other defences lying to the E & W of the town, and it is therefore possible that a medieval defensive circuit (not necessarily continuous) of some kind did exist.

The single element of the castle thought to remain is the base of a small semi-circular tower lying near the E end of the present Lambhay St. This has been interpreted in the past as one tower of a possible gateway, although others (Barber) have interpreted it as perhaps being a tower within the castle or as an 18th century folly; no gateway is depicted in the S wall of the castle in any of the historic sources. Short lengths of wall survive to E & W, although substantial repointing makes it difficult to determine whether these are of one build with the tower.

Plate 93 Plymouth Castle, tower or folly on Lambhay St. (Exeter Archaeology)

Present condition

The remains of the tower or folly have been repointed and conserved. The remainder of the castle has been demolished, together with the wall to the W. However, it is possible that some elements of the structures may survive within the foundations or walls of later buildings, and there is potential for below-ground remains to survive.

Sources

General

1; A, B, M, N, O, Q.

Specific

1665	de Gomme's first plan of the Citadel & surrounds. BL: Add Mss 16,370. f.43
1879	1st edition (surveyed in 1856-7) O.S 1:2500 map sheet CXXIII.12. WDRO
1890	Worth, R.N *History of Plymouth*
1992	Brayshay, M Lecture, Oct. 14th.
1995	Brayshay, M 'The Sixteenth Century Protection of Sutton Harbour and Plymouth Sound: the documentary evidence' in Ray, K (ed) *Archaeological Investigations and Research in Plymouth, Vol. 1, 1992-93* pp 83-90. Plymouth Archaeology Occasional Publication No. **2**
1995	Ray, K ' 'Sutton-Super-Plymouth': a Medieval Port' in Ray, K (ed) *Archaeological Investigations and Research in Plymouth, Vol. 1, 1992-93* pp 59-81. Plymouth Archaeology Occasional Publication No. **2**

BARBICAN GATE

PAR = ST. ANDREW, NGR = SX48325399, PRN = SX45SE-228, MAP 3 No. 102

This was located across the road at the S end of Southside (later the Barbican) Quay where it adjoined the West Pier at the mouth of Sutton Harbour. The date of construction is not clear, but it may be contemporary with other such gates built across the main access routes into the town elsewhere in the 16th century. It is depicted on de Gomme's plans of the 1660s and on subsequent 18th century plans; it was demolished in *c.* 1834 when Southside Quay was extended to the E.

Present condition

There are no obvious above-ground remains of the gate, although below-ground remains may survive.

Sources

General

A.

Specific

1665-72	Plans by de Gomme. BL: Add Mss 16730 f.43; 16731 D. NMM: P/45
1786	Plan of Sutton Pool by William Simpson. DCO: Maps & Charts 741
1831	Plan of Sutton Pool by Wm Rendall. DRO: DP 97
1993	Pye, A.R et al. *NRA Plymouth Barbican Tidal Defence Scheme: Historical & Archaeological Survey* Exeter Archaeology Report No. **93.57**

BARBICAN BLOCKHOUSE & CHAIN

PAR = ST. ANDREW, NGR = SX48325398, PRN = SX45SE-288, MAP 3 No. 103

On the *c.* 1540 panorama (*Fig. 2*) a fortified single-storey blockhouse with cannon and crenellations is shown on the site of the western pier with a chain extending across the mouth of the harbour to the fish-house. It appears to date from 1511, and by 1523 the chain had been installed. The blockhouse appears to have been sited on the S side of the pier, which has been much modified and extended to the E since that period. It had been demolished by 1665.

Present condition

Demolished, although below-ground remains may still survive.

Sources

General

1

Specific

1665-72	Plans by de Gomme. BL: Add Mss 16730 f.43; 16731 D. NMM: P/45
1992	Brayshay, M. Lecture, Oct. 14th
1995	Brayshay, M 'The Sixteenth Century Protection of Sutton Harbour and Plymouth Sound: the documentary evidence' in Ray, K (ed) *Archaeological Investigations and Research in Plymouth, Vol. 1, 1992-93* pp 83-90. Plymouth Archaeology Occasional Publication No. **2**

HOEGATE

PAR = ST. ANDREW, NGR = SX48015408, PRN = SX45SE-56, MAP 3 No. 104

This is depicted at the S end of Hoegate St. on most O.S maps and also on de Gomme's plans from 1665 onwards. It was probably erected in the 1590s to assist in controlling access to the town (Barber). In 1666-7 de Gomme names it 'Great How Geate', and depicts another gate ('Litle How Geate') sited at the S end of Castle Dyke Lane, at the W limit of the length of wall built westwards from the Castle in the 1530s.

Present condition

Demolished, although below-ground remains may survive.

Sources

General

A

Specific

1665-72	Plans by de Gomme. BL: Add Mss 16730 f.43; 16731 D. NMM: P/45

PLYMOUTH (DRAKE'S) FORT

PAR = ST. ANDREW, NGR = SX48155374, PRN = SX45SE-49, MAP 3 No. 105

This was first proposed in 1590 by Sir Francis Drake and the town of Plymouth in the aftermath of the Spanish Armada, and plans for a fort on the Hoe and a complete circuit of fortification around the town were compiled in 1591-92. Following the rejection of the circuit and the production of a modified fort plan by Robert Adam construction began later in 1592 and was largely complete by 1596, when the first garrison under Sir Ferdinando Gorges was installed. The fort was built at the E end of the Hoe to cover the entrance to the Cattewater and Sutton Harbour, and in 1623 mounted three brass and twelve iron cannon. It consisted (*Fig. 3*) of two bastions and a 13 foot high curtain wall facing N, fronted by a rock cut ditch 8-10m wide and 2-2.5m deep and with cannon mounted on a rampart behind. A defensible circuit (the Lower Fort) down the slope to the S included earlier blockhouse(s) and protected a series of cannon commanding the approach channel to the Cattewater and the Hamoaze. Within the main part of the fort were several buildings including the earlier chapel, the Governor's House and a probable guardhouse near the gate, which was sited in the centre of the N curtain wall.

After initially being left outside Plymouth Fort was incorporated into de Gomme's plans for the Royal Citadel from 1666 onwards, but was largely demolished in the late 1660s as the plan was finalised, although its 'lower fort' became the Lower Fort of the Citadel and was subsequently much altered and repaired, particularly in the 1750s.

The S curtain of the Citadel between Cumberland Battery and Prince Henry's Demi-Bastion generally follows the line of the S flank of the earlier fort. Some early masonry belonging to Plymouth Fort may survive at the base of the apex of Prince Henry's Demi-Bastion and in the side walls of Piper's Platform. This, and the wall to the S.E., were built on the line of the earlier flanking wall down to Fisher's Nose. Some early work probably also survives in the coastal wall to either side of the early blockhouse to the W of Fisher's Nose (referred to here as 'Fisher's Nose Blockhouse', No. 100) especially to the E of it where there is an arched doorway with shillet voussoirs of a very similar style to those in the blockhouse itself. The W bastion of the fort still survived in 1716, when a plan shows it on the site of Clifford's Bastion (now Cumberland Battery); its W face lines up with that of the later bastion and therefore it is possible that some of the masonry (perhaps only the core or footings) may be of early date. Recent trial trenching in the interior of the Citadel has also revealed the remains of the ditch and scarp wall of the earlier fort in three locations.

Present condition

Most of the early fort has been demolished or incorporated into the later Citadel. However, remnants of its structure probably survive within some of the later walls, and substantial below-ground remains of the ditch and wall have been shown to be present within the Citadel itself, together with potential remains of the chapel, governor's house and other demolished buildings within the fort.

Sources

General

M, N, O, Q.

Specific

1593	Plan by Robert Adams. PRO: SP 12/245 f.31
1596	Plan by Sir Ferdinando Gorges. PRO: MPH 262
1601-2	Plan of 'Plimouth Forte' by Genibelli. BL: Cott. Ms Aug. I i 42
1665	Plan by Bernard de Gomme. BL: Add 16,371 F.42/43
1716	Plan by C. Lilly. BL: Kings Ms 45 f.34
1994	Pye, A et al. *Archaeological Assessment and Evaluation of the Elizabethan Fort, Royal Citadel, Plymouth* Exeter Archaeology Report No. **94.81**
1995	Brayshay, M 'The Sixteenth Century Protection of Sutton Harbour and Plymouth Sound: the documentary evidence' in Ray, K (ed) *Archaeological Investigations and Research in Plymouth, Vol. 1, 1992-93* pp 83-90. Plymouth Archaeology Occasional Publication No. **2**

ROYAL CITADEL

PAR = ST. ANDREW, NGR = SX48105385, PRN = SX45SE-17, MAP 3 No. 105

This was built between 1665 and 1671 at the E end of the Hoe overlooking the mouth of Sutton Harbour and the Cattewater and was intended to protect the Cattewater anchorage and the approach to the proposed dockyard at Hooe Lake and to ensure the town's loyalty to the Crown. A full history of the Citadel, including its construction, the structures within it and its armament and changing role has been published by F.W Woodward (1987).

The Citadel replaced and incorporated Plymouth Fort and its Lower Fort and was designed by Bernard de Gomme, a Dutch military engineer. After a series of proposed plans and revisions, the final plan consisted of a continuous *enceinte* containing seven bastions, surrounded by a ditch and covered way with a *ravelin* protecting the main northern entrance and two places of arms, to E & W. The latter was replaced in the 1750s by another *ravelin*. To the S.E it included the whole area of the earlier Plymouth Fort (which was mostly demolished) and utilised the earlier Lower Fort (which was retained); a harbour was also built after the King's visit in 1671 and was present by 1672. A ditch and rampart is depicted on the E side of the Citadel on de Gomme's 1672 plan and on a French plan of 1677 leading from Rupert's Bastion down to Lambhay, enclosing a small group of buildings around a harbour there and containing a drawbridge and gate; a line representing this (at that stage proposed) ditch is also depicted on de Gomme's earlier plan of 1668. It is not depicted on any maps after 1677 (*Fig. 5*).

In 1667 the Citadel was temporarily armed against the Dutch fleet and fully armed in 1680, when the internal buildings had been completed. The original armament was 113 assorted guns in the Citadel and 40 in the Lower Fort covering the harbour approaches. Improvements in the 1720s to 1750s included the final completion of the casemates and rampart along the S curtain, the construction of traverses on the covered

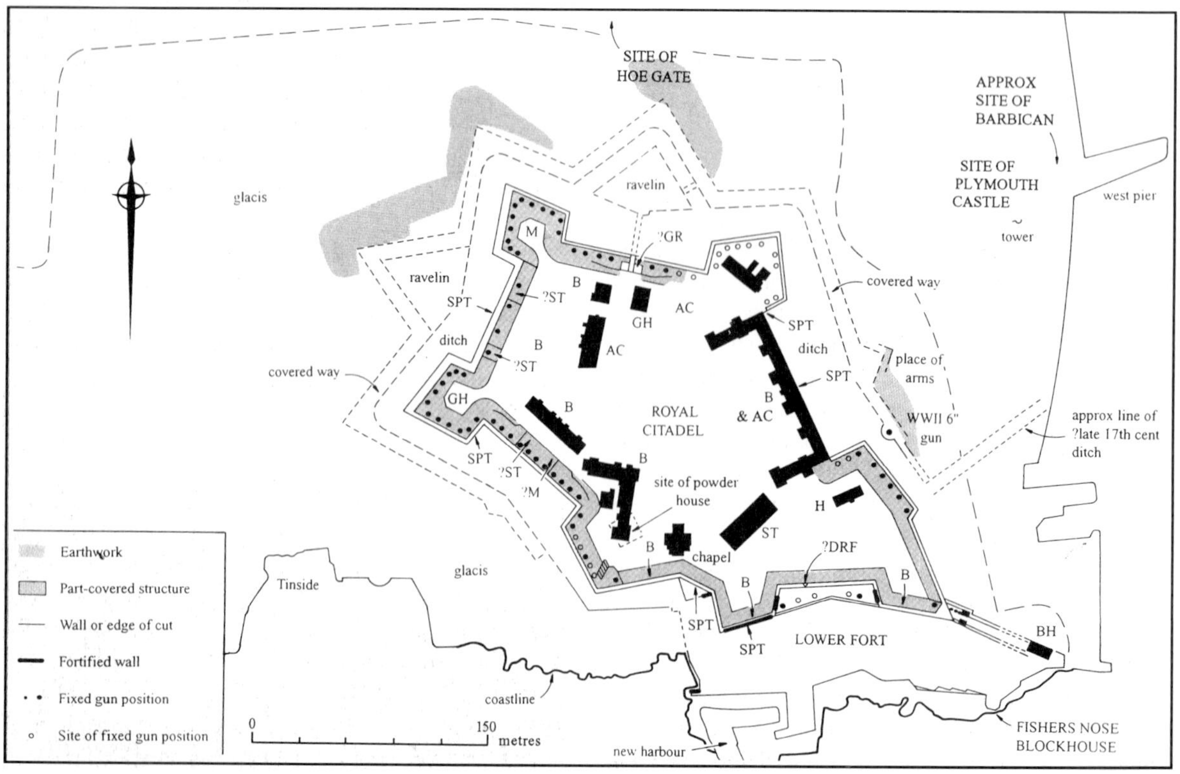

Fig. 66 Royal Citadel, Lower Fort, and earlier defences

way, the demolition of the gatehouse above the main gate, a reduction in the number of embrasures on the land-facing bastions and an increase in their number elsewhere, and finally the construction of the W *ravelin*, S.W coverport, and three new batteries (Upper and Lower Ligonier Batteries and Fredericks Battery) in the Lower Fort by General Ligonier in the 1750s. Batteries were also established at the E extremity of the Lower Fort at Fisher's Nose, and on the old octagonal 'Fisher's Nose Blockhouse' to the W. In the emergency of August 1779 89 guns were mounted at the Citadel, including 20 on the Lower Fort. Armament was modernised in 1804 and again in 1847, and in *c*.1850 there were 123 guns in place (and twenty-three 6-pdr saluting guns), including 32-pdr, 60-pdr & 8-inch SB guns in the Lower Fort, similar guns on the sea-facing bastions & curtains of the Citadel above, and a mix of lighter guns (mainly 18-pdrs) with some heavy guns and howitzers on the remaining bastions & curtains and within the two *ravelins*.

The 1860 Royal Commission considered the Citadel to be generally of limited importance, although it was recommended as a depot and barracks supporting the E end of the N.E Defences before they were moved further out to their final position; to this end the deepening of the ditch and the construction of modern casemated barracks was recommended, neither in the event carried out. By 1880 the sea front of the Citadel had been remodelled to mount medium (64-pdr) RML guns, and in 1882 its armament consisted of 28 of these guns, one 9-inch RML and 69 SB guns, with most of the RMLs being on the sea fronts. In this year the removal of the armament of the land fronts was proposed, together with the demolition of the two *ravelins* and the counterscarp of the ditch. In 1885 twenty-three 64-pdr RMLs, two 7-inch RBLs, five 8-inch SB howitzers and four 10-inch land-service mortars were present on the sea fronts (excluding the Lower Fort); the RBLs, mortars and eight of the 64-pdrs were to be retained for drill, together with an existing twenty-one gun saluting battery (18-pdr SB guns) on Queen's Battery. All the guns (seven 32-pdr and six 8-inch SB guns, and six 64-pdr RMLs) mounted in the Lower Fort were to be removed. This remained the armament for the rest of the century, although by 1895 the mortars and ten of the 18-pdrs had been removed and two 9-inch RMLs and one 6-inch BL gun added. Queen's Battery had become the main drill battery, including several of the guns in current use at the time, and continued in this role until at least WWI. During WWII or shortly before a further 6-inch BL emplacement was added on the E covered way below the Citadel, for practice in mounting and dismounting (rather than firing) the gun.

In 1888, following earlier approval in 1882, the outworks and ditches on the land front were sold to Plymouth City Council and demolished, followed by much of the Lower Fort when Madeira Road was constructed. Between 1895 and 1904 several of the old buildings within the Citadel were demolished and replaced by new accommodation blocks, including the Officers' and Sergeants' Messes. From 1902 it was garrisoned by a regiment of the Royal Garrison Artillery, who used the guns on Queen's Battery for drill. Shortly after WWII it housed the Coast Artillery Training Centre, and is now home to a commando regiment of the Royal Artillery.

Plate 94 Citadel, gun platforms on N.curtain (Exeter Archaeology)

The circuit of the Citadel survives intact (*Plate 3*) but the interior and outworks have been much altered and partially demolished. The garrison was originally accommodated in two 17th-century barrack blocks (both now demolished) and in casemates underneath the *terreplein* along the S flank between Bath Bastion and Prince Henry Demi-Bastion. The curtain between the Prince of Wales Bastion and Prince Edward Battery was lowered during the late 1890s and a new barrack block built. At the same time the rampart was removed from the rear and from within Prince of Wales Bastion. Numerous gun platforms and embrasures (including some earlier examples which have since been blocked) survive elsewhere along the walls as well as later armament, including racer rails for guns on traversing carriages on Charles Bastion and at the apexes of Bath Bastion and Prince Henry's Demi-Bastion. At the rear of the *terreplein* there are several late 17th or early to mid-18th century expense magazines, together with Napoleonic *garde-fou* walls and artillery and/or small arms stores. Emplacements for later guns (as illustrated in Woodward's 'Citadel') survive on Queen's Battery with a depression range-finder position cut into the parapet above.

Despite partial demolition and infilling in the 1880s the outlines and much of the external earthworks of the two *ravelins* clearly remain, together with the main

Plate 95 Citadel, Queen's Battery (Exeter Archaeology)

ditch (now occupied by Hoe Road and the Marine Laboratory). To the W the whole of the Hoe was originally Government property and formed the Citadel *glacis*. To the E subsequent construction of a gun park and MT park has demolished or covered most of the defences, although a length of the ditch and of the covered way still remains, together with the apex of the place of arms and the later concrete 6-inch BL emplacement.

The Citadel is entered through a main gate which has a magnificent Baroque sculpted surround; a similar, smaller gate was originally sited at the outer entrance into the *ravelin* to the N, but was moved to its present position at the W Sally Port when the *ravelin* was demolished in the 1880s. In the interior surviving early buildings include the guardhouse, the governor's house/HQ building (altered in 1902-5), the great storehouse, the aisle of the chapel, and a mid 18th-century hospital building. The casemates along the S flank, which were begun in the 1670s but only finally completed in the mid 18th-century, include some stores and guardrooms as well as living accommodation, and include embrasures and loops flanking Queen's Battery and the entrance passages to it and down to the S. Sally Port & S.W Coverport. Despite subsequent modification and conversion they retain early features such as chimneys and early fittings such as cleats for small arms, and later 19th century racking for example. The rest of the buildings either represent new accommodation built between 1895 - 1904 or date to the most recent refurbishment (1989-92).

Plate 96 Citadel, main gate (Exeter Archaeology)

Present condition

The ramparts and the curtain and bastion walls are in a very good state of preservation, together with the fine ornamented main gate and W sally port. To the N & W the remains of the *ravelins* are still visible within public parkland as is the *glacis* which now forms the Hoe. The slopes to the E however are occupied by the structures of a rebuilt MT yard, although surface remains of the covered way and place of arms survive, together with below-ground remains of the ditch counterscarp. To the S.W a marine laboratory and aquarium occupies the ditch between King Charles's Bastion and Bath Bastion, although the defences remain largely intact to the E. The interior has been refurbished. The surviving early buildings remain structurally complete and in good condition, although the extent to which any internal fixtures and fittings survive is not at present clear. Substantial below-ground remains of the earlier barrack block to the W of the HQ Block were revealed during the recent re-furbishment, together with remnants of the main magazine to the S. The refurbished casemates are in good condition and retain a range of 18th and 19th century fittings in varying states of preservation. The Lower Fort is described separately.

Sources

General

4 - 7, 9, 12, 13, 17; J, M, N, O, Q.

Specific

1665	De Gomme's first plan. BL: Add Mss 16371 F.42/43
1666-7	De Gomme's second plan. NMM: A.997 Mss 9844/2
1668	De Gomme's third plan. BL: Add Mss 16371 D
1672	De Gomme's plan & panorama. NMM: A.996 9844/1
1677	Plan by 'J.R.' BL: Add Mss 5415 E.2
c.1677	Plan (French). [Stuart No. 42]
1715	Plan by Col. C. Lilly. BL: Kings Mss 45.f.34
1716	Plan and report by Col. C. Lilly. BL: Kings Mss 45.f.33
1725	Plan. BL: Kings Top.XI 82
1725	Board of Ordnance plan. PRO: MR 902
1737	Print of Citadel. Sandford Mace
1741	Plan. PRO: MPH 728
1750-52	Plan by ?Durnford. BL: Add Mss 22875 f.20 [Stuart No. 101 (p. 57)]
1794	Plan. PRO: MPHH 61
1813	Plan. PRO: MPH 223
1879	Barrack atlas plan. PRO: WO 78/3045; copy in PCM
1900	Plan. PRO: WO 78/2976
1936	Plan. EH
1936	Plan. RCHME
1936	Plan of casemates. BPFM
1990	Halpin, C (ed) *The Work of the Central Excavation Unit 1988-89* English Heritage
1994	Bishop, P & Gibbons, P *Archaeological Survey of Casemates 201-216, Royal Citadel, Plymouth* Exeter Archaeology Report No. **94.25**
1994	Pye, A. R. et al. *Archaeological Assessment and Evaluation of the Elizabethan Fort, Royal Citadel, Plymouth* Exeter Archaeology Report No. **94.81**
1995	Bishop, P et al. *Archaeological Recording of Casemates 217-233 and construction of new Vehicle Washdown Facility at the Royal Citadel, Plymouth* Exeter Archaeology Report No. **95.28**

Various old photos & prints reproduced in Woodward's 'Citadel'.

LOWER FORT

PAR = ST. ANDREW, NGR = SX48205368, PRN = SX45SE-694, MAP 3 No. 107

This is located immediately to the S of the Citadel, and formed part of Plymouth Fort. It was incorporated into the Citadel in de Gomme's plans, and partly remodelled when the 'new harbour' was built in 1671-72, but major work was only carried out here in the mid-18th century after it had fallen into disrepair. Access was gained to the fort through the S sally port and there were gun embrasures along the S wall and on an old tower (Withen's Tower) at the W end. 'Fisher's Nose Blockhouse' was incorporated within its coastal defences. In the 1750s the Lower Fort was heavily altered and refortified by General Ligonier. Two batteries (Lower and Upper Ligonier) facing W were built at its W end, access to which was gained via a new S.W coverport, sited between Bath Bastion and Cumberland Battery. Their purpose was to fire on the sterns of ships sailing through the channel towards the dockyard, whereas the purpose of most of the earlier gun emplacements on the Lower Fort had been to defend the mouth of the Cattewater and Sutton Harbour; this reflects the change in location of the intended dockyard from the Cattewater to the Hamoaze. The southern section of the retaining wall of the lower battery is still evident, together with a projecting tower at its S end enfilading the face of the battery and a wall to the S obscuring it from the view of (and protecting it from the cannon of) ships sailing up the Sound. Fredericks Battery was built at the E end of the 'new harbour' and faced W; its site is now occupied by a Yacht Club. Other batteries were mounted on the top of the old 'Fisher's Nose Blockhouse' and on the platform at the eastern extremity of the fort at Fisher's Nose itself. Access to this end was via a covered way (still surviving) down from Piper's Platform. The 18th century armament consisted of 32 and 42-pdr cannon, but by *c.*1850 these had been augmented by 8-inch SB guns on the lower Ligonier Battery. By 1885 some 64-pdr RMLs had also been mounted, but shortly afterwards all the guns were removed and a large part of the Lower Fort demolished when Madeira Road was constructed in 1888.

The interior of the Lower Fort was much altered after 1888, and the covered way down from Piper's Platform was then truncated in 1936 by the same road. However, much of the W & S walls, together with the platform of Frederick's Battery and the platform above Fisher's Nose, still survive, together with the covered way and a later stone 'blockhouse' or guardhouse at Fisher's Nose dated 1847. This contains two entrances through its S wall and is protected by loop-holes in its S & N walls and by a parapet on the roof. The 'new harbour' built in 1671-72 is an L-shaped rock-cut inlet. The wall along its N side probably dates to the 1750s and to the construction of Ligonier's batteries.

Present condition

Most of the external walls of the fort - the covered way down from Piper's Platform and the sea walls running W and around the new harbour - still survive in reasonable structural condition, although they presumably contain alterations made when Madeira Road was constructed in 1888 and subsequently. Frederick's Battery is occupied by a yacht clubhouse, and the 'new harbour' by yachts. The flanking wall on the W and the covered way has been punctured in two places by Madeira Road, and the slopes to the N landscaped to some degree. The extent to which the 1750s batteries and the earlier gun platforms were demolished in 1888 is not clear; substantial below-ground remains may well still survive in places.

Sources

As for the Citadel and Plymouth Fort.

QUEEN ANNE'S BATTERY

PAR = CHARLES, NGR = SX48655380, PRN = SX45SE-615, MAP 3 No. 108

Also named Peake's, Spike or Gun point, this is an earthwork battery located on the E side of the entrance into Sutton Harbour; its site now lies within the S part of a yachting marina. It was originally built in 1667-68 on the recommendation of de Gomme, and was probably armed in that year and again in 1690, and permanently by 1710, initially against the Dutch. In *c.*1716 it was armed with 14 guns, and later apparently had stone-revetted embrasures. It was not manned in the emergency of 1779; it is not mentioned in Dixon's report or depicted on his map, nor on Cowl's 1780 map. It is depicted on the 1st edition 1:2500 O.S map as 'Remains of' and was demolished shortly after.

Present condition

Demolished; sited under tarmac and buildings. Below-ground remains may survive.

Sources

General

5, 6; M, O, Q.

Specific

1668	Plan by Bernard de Gomme. BL: Add Mss 16371D
1714-17	Report & Survey by Col Christian Lilly. BL: Kings Mss 45
1868	1st edition O.S. 1:2500 map (surveyed in 1855-7). PCM

MOUNT BATTEN BULWARK

PAR = PLYMSTOCK, NGR = SX48535332, PRN = SX45SE-680, MAP 3 No. 109

On Grenville's map of the fortifications of Plymouth dating to 1586-8 'a new bulwark and three new pieces to be placed' are illustrated on Mount Batten. The three cannon are facing W & S.W. There is also a record in the 1590s of a barricade on Howstert (the earlier name for Mount Batten). No surface remains of this period are identifiable.

Present condition

Demolished, although below-ground remains may survive.

Sources

General

2

Specific

1988 Gaskell-Brown, C 'The later history of Mount Batten' in Cunliffe, B *Mount Batten, Plymouth. A Prehistoric and Roman Port* Oxford University Monograph No. **26**

MOUNT BATTEN CIVIL WAR FORTIFICATIONS

PAR = PLYMSTOCK, NGR = SX4862532, PRN = SX45SE-681, MAP 3 No. 110

Mount Batten (Hoo Stert) and the heights of Fort Stamford above it to the S.E were fought over by Royalists and Parliamentarians during the siege of Plymouth from 1643 to 1645. In November 1643, or slightly before, the Parliamentarians built a linear work across the headland facing S.E to retreat into should they lose Fort Stamford on the hill above. When the latter was lost in November 1643 it was then taken by the Royalists who established a fort there which is shown on the contemporary siege map published in 1644 (*Fig. 3*). They also established, it appears, three gun batteries firing at shipping in the Cattewater and towards Drakes Island, although these cannon may represent the actions that the Royalists were undertaking rather than the exact sites of particular batteries. By June 1644 the headland had been abandoned by the Royalists, and in August a Parliamentary work was constructed upon Hoo Stert Point by 300 Parliamentary seamen, commanded by William Batten, hence the name Mount Batten.

In 1882 faint traces of Civil War earthworks were apparently observed close to the tower, and a possible slight bank is still visible beneath the vegetation around the top of the hill slope to the S.W.

Present condition

A slight bank is visible, and there is potential for below-ground remains. The E end however may have been removed by later quarrying.

Sources

General

3

Specific

1860 'Account of the siege of Plymouth by the Royal Army in 1643', accompanied with notes by Capt E.F. du Cane. *Professional Papers of the Royal Engineers* Paper **XVI**

1875-6 Worth, R.N 'The siege of Plymouth' *Reports & Transactions of Plymouth Institution* **5**

1988 Gaskell-Brown, C 'The later history of Mount Batten' in Cunliffe, B *Mount Batten, Plymouth. A Prehistoric and Roman Port* Oxford University Monograph No. **26**

1993 Stoyle, M *A List of Civil War fortifications at Plymouth* Exeter Archaeology Report No. **93.82** (City of Plymouth Archaeology Report **GD. 1293**)

1994 Gray, T & Stoyle, M 'A Cavalier Cartographer' *History Today* **44(3)**

MOUNT BATTEN TOWER

PAR = PLYMSTOCK, NGR = SX48655335, PRN = SX45SE-15, MAP 3 No. 111

Plate 97 Mount Batten Tower (Exeter Archaeology)

Previously this has been thought to date to about 1665 although it has been named after the Parliamentary naval commander in Plymouth during the siege (Captain Batten). Woodward has pointed out that therefore it is unlikely to date to after the Restoration as it would then not have been named after a Parliamentarian. It is more likely to have been built between 1645 and 1660 during the Commonwealth, perhaps in *c*.1646-52 prior to war with the Dutch. It was intended as a gun platform to co-operate with the guns on the Lower Fort opposite to protect the entrance to the Cattewater & Sutton Harbour, and also as a means of fortifying the headland, which had been taken by the Royalists during the recent siege.

The tower is shown on a chart of Plymouth Sound dated to *c*.1646 by Stuart (M). It had certainly been

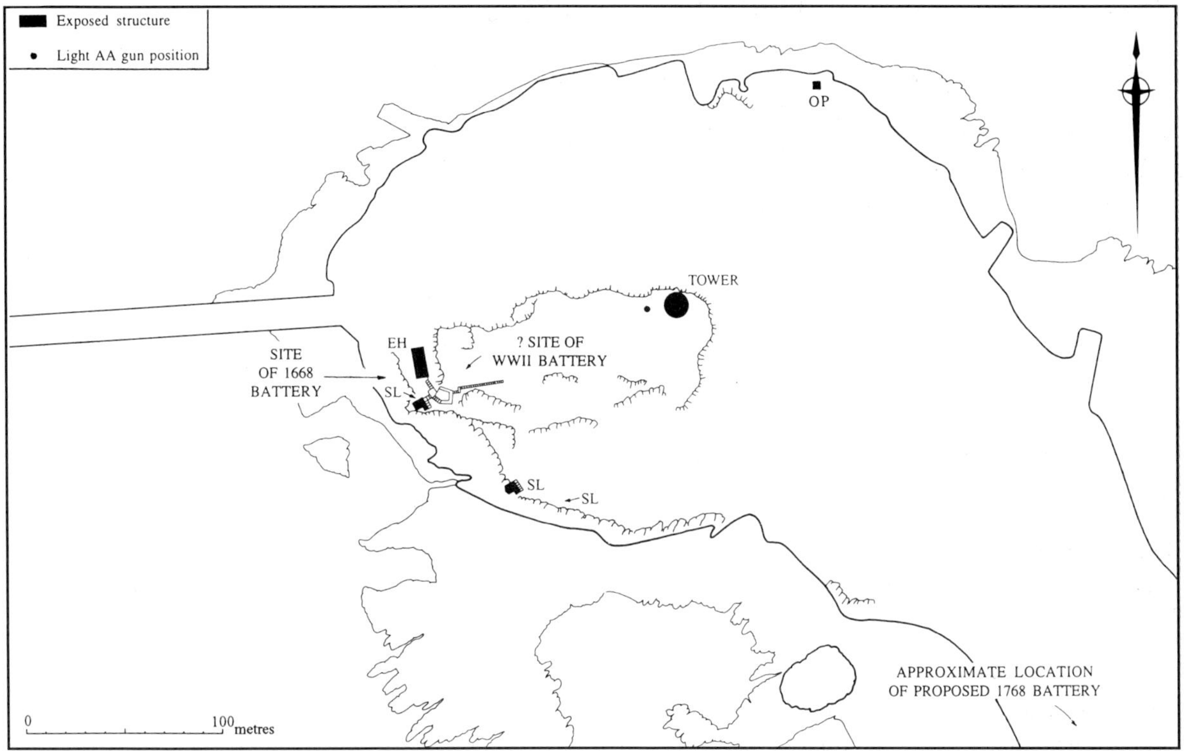

Fig. 67 Mount Batten

built by 1665, when de Gomme recommended increasing its height and building a fort around it with 2 half-bastions on the land side and a ditch and covered way. It was still armed in 1716 when Col. Lilly noted 6 guns mounted on the roof.

The masonry tower is circular & has a castellated parapet with embrasures for 10 guns. Within the tower are two floor levels with a cellar under. Access is gained at first-floor level and there is a stairway within the wall up to the second-floor & roof. There are fireplaces at first- and second-floor levels, the second-floor one being particularly ornate. The tower has a corbelled roof, and the City of Plymouth coat of arms above the main doorway.

Present condition

Very good.

Sources

General

M, N, O, P.

Specific

c.1646	Chart of Plymouth Sound. BL: Add Mss 15737 f.24v
1668	Plan of Citadel and Defences by de Gomme. BL: Add Mss 16731D
1716	Map by Col. C. Lilly of defences of Plymouth. BL: Kings Mss 45 f.34

MOUNT BATTEN BATTERY A

PAR = PLYMSTOCK NGR = SX48525332
PRN = SX45SE-682 MAP 3 No. 112

In 1668, on a plan by de Gomme of the Citadel and its defences, an earthwork battery with embrasures for nine guns is shown on the shore to the W of the tower. In 1716 Col. Lilly notes a battery as being thrown up under Old Tower. This may be the 1668 battery or a new battery established by Lilly. Later, in 1768, the French spy de Beville proposed siting two batteries on the spit leading towards Mount Batten from Fort Stamford in the event of the French landing and investing the Citadel and dockyard. These were of course never constructed.

The battery shown in 1668 was probably located on the shore immediately W of the later WWII searchlight engine-house. No identifiable surface remains are visible, and the site appears to have been quarried.

Present condition

Demolished.

Sources

General

M, O, Q.

Specific

1668	Plan of Citadel and defences by de Gomme. BL: Add Mss 16731 D
1716	Map by Col. Lilly of defences of Plymouth. BL: Kings Mss 45 f.34
1768	Plan of Plymouth and its Defences by M. de Beville. PRO: MR 1111

MOUNT BATTEN REDOUBT (PROPOSED)

MOUNT BATTEN REDOUBT (PROPOSED)

PAR = PLYMSTOCK, NGR = SX48605332, MAP 3 No. 112a

In January 1780 a redoubt and blockhouse for 300 men was proposed by Col. Dixon, but no reference appears in other contemporary sources and there is no evidence that it was ever built or started.

Sources
General
5

MOUNT BATTEN BATTERY B

MOUNT BATTEN BATTERY B

PAR = PLYMSTOCK, NGR = SX48555332, PRN = SX45SE-683, MAP 3 No. 113

In August 1942, according to the Drake's Island Fort Record Book, two 12-pdr QF guns were transferred from Drake's Island to Mount Batten, presumably to form another battery for anti-motor torpedo boat defence. They were accompanied by three WWII illuminated area searchlights and their engine-house, although these may have been established earlier to light the minefield between Mount Batten & Drake's Island, and replaced two searchlight emplacements shown on the S coast of Mount Batten in 1911. According to Saunders the guns were manned by 160 Coast Battery Royal Artillery and were put in care and maintenance in April 1943.

The guns were sited behind the searchlights on the S.W shore, on the crown of the existing outcrop at the top of the concrete steps.

An alternative site for the guns, overlooking Jennycliff Bay (NGR = SX49205230), has previously been suggested by Cobb. However there is no evidence of gun positions on the ground, except for the 6-inch BL Lord Howard's Battery.

Also belonging to this period is a probable LAA gun position just W of the tower. It consists of a concrete slab containing a ring of sawn-off mounting bolts, surrounded by covered concrete ?ammunition shelters.

On the S.W shore of Mount Batten two of the three WWII searchlight emplacements survive complete (at NGRs = SX48515330 & 48565326); the easternmost emplacement (SX48585325) has been demolished. The eastern two emplacements may have been built on the sites of those shown in 1911.

The two emplacements are of brick & shuttered concrete construction, and retain their original double steel entrance doors, protective armour plating on the inside of the light slits, and cable ducts and conduits. At the rear is a small closet. The N emplacement has a single light slit & faces W.S.W towards Drakes Island, the other has two slits and faces S.W. The concrete base only of the E emplacement remains.

The engine house accompanying the searchlights was sited (SX48515332) at the bottom of the slope to the N. It was a rectangular shuttered concrete structure with a flat bitumen roof, which had been heavily altered & used as a bar. No original fittings such as steel window shutters or doors survived. It was probably associated with a telephone fusebox immediately to the south. This holds three fuseboxes, perhaps belonging to each of the three searchlights.

Present condition
The site of the gun positions is heavily overgrown; no remains which could be identified with QF gun positions are currently visible. The condition of the two remaining searchlight emplacements is very good, and they retain nearly all internal fittings bar the searchlights. The eastern emplacement and the engine house have been demolished, although the fusebox still remains.

Sources
General
22; K, O, Q.
Specific
1943 Reference. PRO: WO192/135
n.d. Drake's Island Fort Record Book. PRO: WO 192/294

MOUNT BATTEN WWII OBSERVATION POST

MOUNT BATTEN WWII OBSERVATION POST

PAR = PLYMSTOCK, NGR = SX48725336, MAP 3 No. 114

This is located at the head of a slipway on the N. coast, and was probably a minewatcher's post. It faces N, and had two viewing slits cut through its N.W & N.E corners, protected by steel shuttering, and an armoured door in its S wall. The interior was not viewed.

Present condition
Probably demolished.

Source
General
R

DRAKE'S ISLAND (ST. NICHOLAS ISLAND)

PAR = ST. ANDREW, NGR = SX46905280, PRN = VARIOUS, MAP 3 Nos 115-123

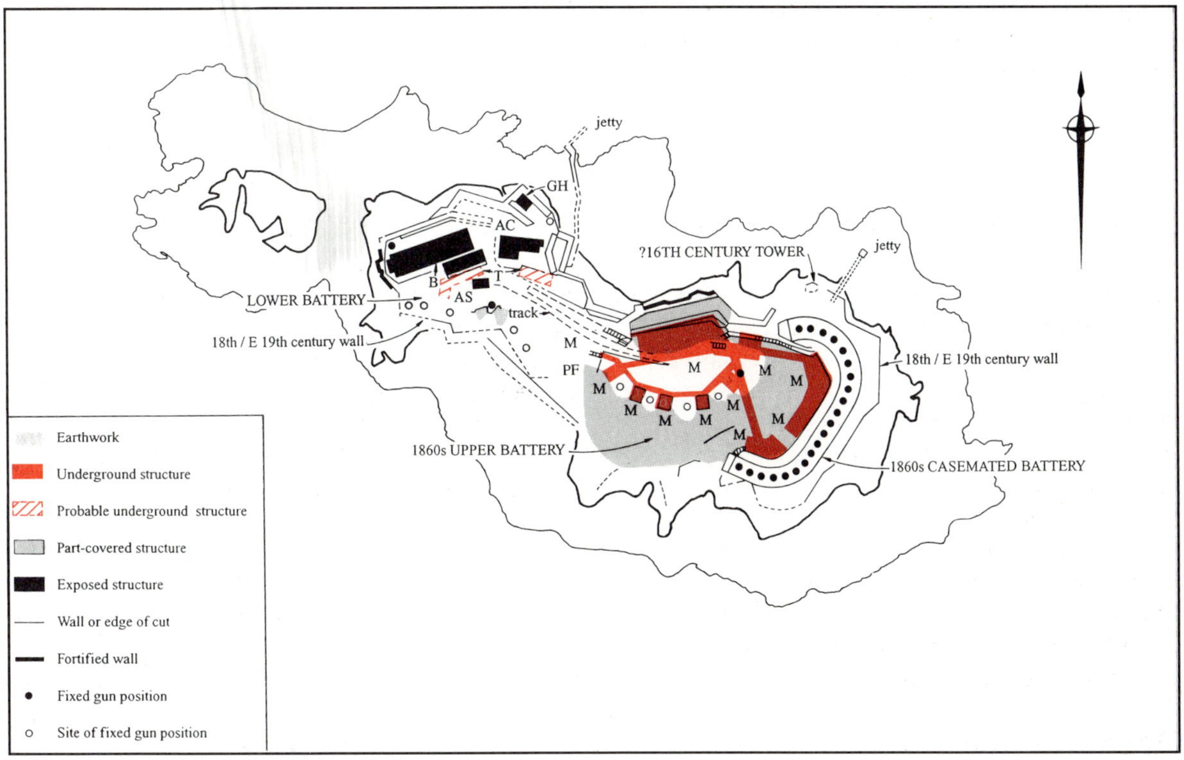

Fig. 68 Drake's Island, 16th century to the 1860s

This is located in the middle of the Sound and commands the immediate approaches to the Cattewater and Sutton Harbour anchorages and the approach channel to the late 17th-century dockyard. As such it held a position of considerable strategic importance and was fortified from 1548 until *c.*1945. During the medieval period there was a chapel (initially dedicated to St. Michael and later to St. Nicholas) on the highest point of the island which was owned by Plympton Priory. However, from the 1540s its history is purely one of fortification, which has been described in detail by Woodward (1991).

Drake's Island was first fortified in 1548-9 when a 'fort' or castle replaced the chapel, followed by a perimeter wall in the 1570s (Brayshay). On Grenville's map of 1586-8 eight heavy guns are shown at various points around the coast of the island, together with a castle and enclosure housing two smaller guns. Fourteen guns are shown on Robert Adams' plan of 1592, together with a perimeter wall and a gateway close to the present one and a probable guardhouse adjoining. There is a low wall all around the island together with a substantial wall at the W end facing N. The present gatehouse is generally thought to be 18th-century, but Brayshay has suggested that it may contain 16th-century work. By the early 17th century barracks had been built on the island and a parapet around its perimeter. It was held by Parliament during the Civil War but after the Restoration was used as a prison for a short time.

In the early 1700s two batteries (of 19 & 14 guns) were built on the island to assist in the protection of the dockyard and the Hamoaze. These were presumably located on the N & E sides, probably down near the waterline where the later 18th- and early 19th-century batteries were placed.

In 1716 Col. Lilly recommended various improvements to the defences, including raising the number of guns to 57. The plan of 1725 shows one battery and a number of platforms on the island, together with the old castle, a powder magazine, barracks and a guardroom. Batteries with gun embrasures are shown at the W end to the N of the present Commanding Officer's House, at the western extremity where the present barracks and a loop-holed wall are situated, and at various locations around the S & E shores.

In the 1750s and in 1779-80 the defences were further improved by General Ligonier and Col. Dixon. Dixon built an upper battery on the site of the demolished castle on top of the island facing S, barracks on the site of thc present one and a magazine on the site of the earlier 1725 one, together with a smaller battery to the W of the upper battery facing S. Most of the earlier embrasures in the perimeter wall facing E & N were blocked up and a rampart with *banquette* built around the E, N & W coasts. Two embrasures overlooking the landing beach were retained or remodelled however, and there was a guardroom on the site of the present CO's house. Further small improvements were made during the Napoleonic Wars, including the

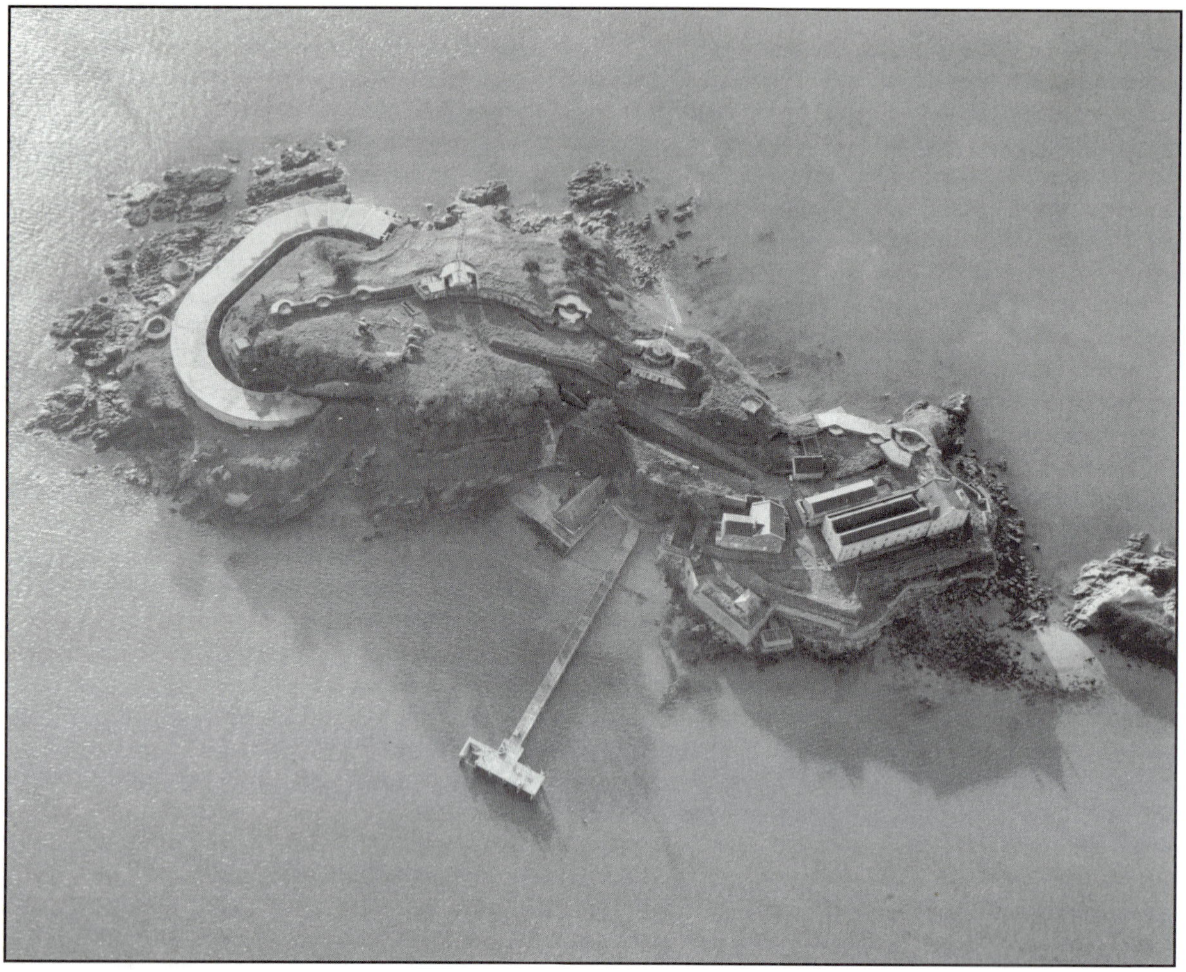

Plate 98 Drake's Island (Photograph: F.M. Griffith, Devon County Council. Frame DAP/UT14. Copyright Devon County Council)

construction of the Master Gunner's House adjoining the early guardroom. In the 1830s this guardroom was largely demolished and the present CO's house and barrack and ablution blocks were built.

The Royal Commission of 1860 (and Jervois in 1858) felt that the existing battery of 22 guns was insufficient, and recommended the construction of a 30 gun battery with casemated accommodation for 180 men behind. A casemated battery designed (by Major

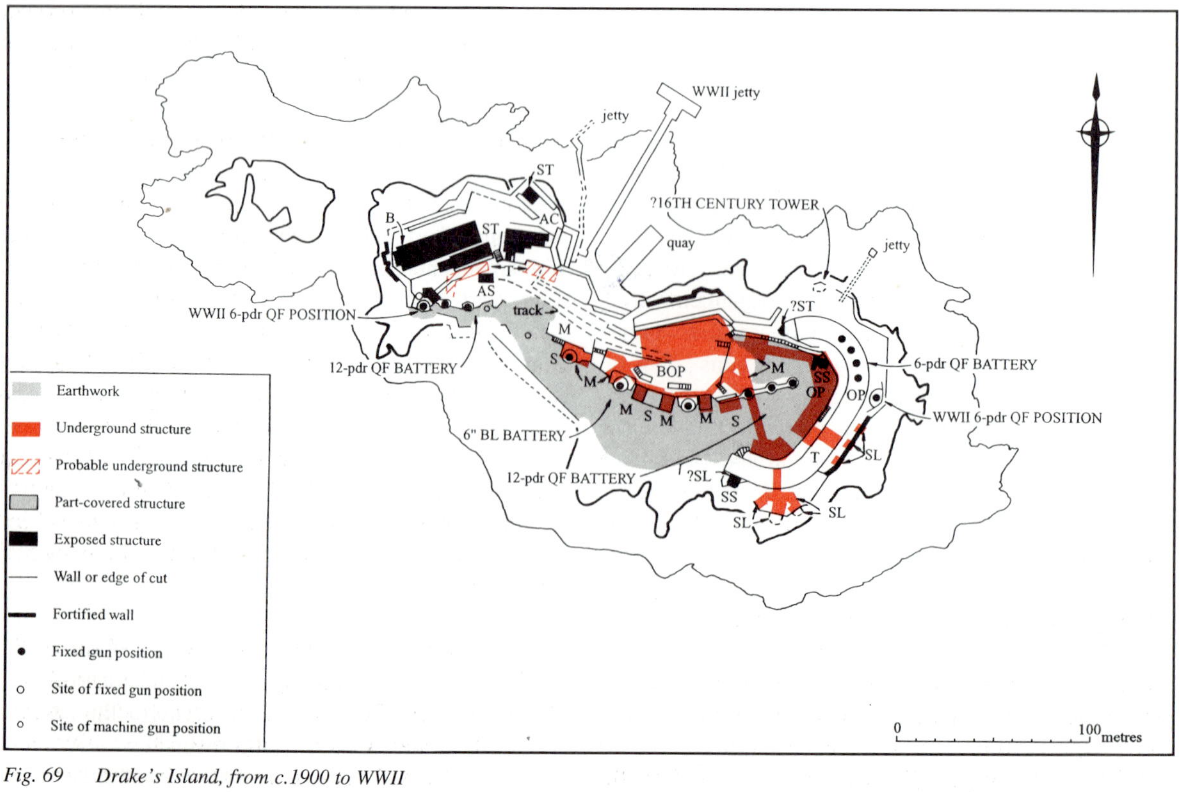

Fig. 69 Drake's Island, from c.1900 to WWII

Porter) for twenty-one 9-inch 12-ton guns was complete (except for shields & full armament) by 1867, and in 1868-69 a further five *en barbette* emplacements (the 'main (or upper) battery') were built on top of the island. These were intended for the heaviest RMLs then available (12-inch 23-ton guns), and were to be adapted to accommodate the Moncrieff mounting should it be adopted. They were served by separate expense magazines, supplied from the main magazine underneath. In the W half of the island the small earlier battery facing S.W was remodelled & extended around to the W to form the lower battery. On the completion of the batteries the total armament was formidable (although the casemated battery was never fully armed) and consisted in 1885 of thirteen 9-inch RMLs in the casemated battery, five 11 & 12-inch RMLs in the main battery, six 80-pdr and two 64-pdr RMLs on the W & S faces of the lower battery, two 8-inch SB howitzers on its E face and one 18-pdr SB gun in an open emplacement. The location of the E face is not clear; it may be represented by the embrasure(s) facing E over the landing bay adjoining the main gate. The open emplacement may be the single embrasure at the W extremity of the island, although later this gun is listed under the main battery to the E.

In the mid to late 1890s the heavy guns were gradually replaced by QF guns; four 6-pdr QF guns were proposed for the northern casemates in 1893 & 1895, and the western 12-pdr QF battery was proposed in 1895 & built in 1898. In 1901 the 6-pdrs were replaced in their role (which was probably to cover a minefield - first proposed in 1877 - between the island and Mount Batten) by the eastern 12-pdr QF battery, and a 6-inch BL gun battery replaced the heavy guns. This is sited on the old 'main battery', and utilised some of the earlier gun positions and expense magazines. In the late 1890s three searchlights (fighting lights) were emplaced on the S coast to light the area for the 6-inch battery. Also, a Brennan torpedo station has previously been thought to have been constructed in the late 1880s on the site of these searchlights. However, there is no known documentary reference to it and there is no physical evidence remaining of a torpedo slipway or of the other large, extensive structures which accompanied it such as engine and boiler rooms, torpedo store, and shelters for those manning the establishment. There is not enough room for the scale of establishment which was built at Pier Cellars.

By 1903 the batteries were fully armed with three 6-inch BL guns and six 12-pdr QF guns, and three searchlights were present; all the RMLs had been dismounted. After WWI the armament was reduced to two 6-inch BLs and four QFs (two of which were held in reserve).

During WWII the present jetty was built and the island was the HQ of Drake Fire Command, responsible for the close defence of the Sound within the Breakwater. The 6-inch battery remained in use, and two minefield control posts were built at the E end of the island. In 1942 two twin 6-pdr QF guns were mounted on the island, one on the site of the earlier western QF battery, and the other immediately in front of the casemated battery looking E. Of the remaining 12-pdrs two were removed to Mount Batten. The 6-inch BL battery was disbanded in 1947; after the abolition of Coast Artillery in 1956 the island was used for training until 1963 when it was leased to the National Trust and others who ran it as an adventure centre. The lease was then taken over by Plymouth CC and it remained an adventure centre until 1989. Since then the island has been unoccupied except for a temporary lease to the Plymouth Groundwork Trust, and it has recently been sold.

The following description relates to the various lengths of coastal and fortified walling, related features, individual military buildings and other miscellaneous features of various dates visible around the island. Individual batteries and other discrete fortifications are dealt with separately below. The walling around the perimeter of the island is described in sequence from the main gateway westwards, regardless of period.

Gateway

The main gate faces S.E across the landing beach on the N shore of the island, and in the 19th century a small masonry jetty extended N from it down to the low water mark. It consists of an outer gateway with granite ashlar surrounds. Beyond a brick-vaulted passage steps up into an inner courtyard, with an inner gateway of similar design giving access to the interior of the island. The courtyard is protected by a parapet wall with a walkway or firing-step behind, and has a later iron winch or crane-base on its E wall. The gate is thought to be 18th-century although Brayshay suggests that parts may be 16th-century in origin; a gateway is shown here on Adams' 1592 map. The earliest known representation of the inner gateway (which however lacks the courtyard), is on a 1725 plan, and the current arrangement is only first depicted clearly in 1780.

Coastal & perimeter walls and related features

The stretch of wall to the N of the gate is built of rubble limestone and has similar granite quoins to the gateway, and may therefore be contemporary. It appears to be depicted in 1780 & possibly in 1725 and therefore is probably 18th-century or earlier in date. Its parapet contains an embrasure depicted in 1780, the S side of which has been rebuilt relatively recently and forms part of the decorative archway located immediately to the S (which has replaced the other embrasure shown in 1780). Sloping granite paving similar to that used in gun platforms survives behind the embrasure, which may have formed the E face of the 'Lower Battery' in 1885.

The coastal wall continues around to the W end of the island, on the alignment depicted in 1780 & possibly in 1725, although of it is of different construction. Above it is a thick wall with a firing-step behind. This is of similar date, and is sited to the N of the barracks.

Plate 99 Drake's Island, 18th century wall & firing step (Exeter Archaeology)

Originally it turned eastwards at its E end and continued towards the CO's House. At its W end is an embrasure, with racer rails for a traversing carriage behind. The granite setts for the rear racer are still visible and appear to postdate the paving belonging to the 1830s barrack building. One of the 80-pdr RMLs listed in 1885 may have been mounted here, or the 18-pdr signal gun. Although the embrasure itself may be earlier in date, it is not depicted in 1811 (*Fig. 70*) or 1780.

Plate 100 Drake's Island, loopholed wall at W end (Exeter Archaeology)

At the W end of the island the coastal wall incorporates a projecting rectangular tower. This contains two brick-vaulted chambers which appear to be 18th/19th-century in date. The tower is topped by a loop-holed wall which has been thought to be of possible 17th-century date. However, the main build of the tower predates the loop-holed wall and therefore is either earlier than the brick-built chambers it contains, or the loop-holed wall is of 18th-century or later date. The tower is not depicted in 1780 or 1811, implying it, and the loopholed wall, are of later date, perhaps contemporary with the construction of the adjoining barracks in 1830. The loop-holed wall is of rubble limestone with musketry loops along the faces and at the corners. Gun embrasures are depicted in this position in 1725, and a rampart with *banquette* behind is shown here in 1780 and 1811.

The coastal wall to the S of the tower is of several different builds, and is faced in places with fine limestone ashlar. Its alignment closely reflects the wall depicted in 1780 although there is an earlier wall depicted in this position on the 1725 plan. In places it has been eroded away, but it probably continued around to join a substantial length of wall to the east. This is of battered profile and consists of limestone ashlar with rougher work above. It follows the line of the wall illustrated on Dixon's 1780 plan, although its southern section continues beyond where Dixon's wall turns E. It may therefore date to the 19th century, and currently retains the earthwork of the 6-inch BL battery. Above its N end is a short length of wall which probably represents the parapet depicted in 1780 & 1811.

To the S.E, on and above two small headlands, are at least three lengths of rubble walling. These may be the walling depicted on the 1725 plan immediately to the E of Crown Platform or may be of earlier origin, perhaps belonging to the wall circuit built in the 1570s. Some walling is also shown here in 1811, though not in 1780. Most was covered over when the 'main battery' above was built in the 1860s.

The coastal wall around the E end of the island extends from the S end of the casemated 1860s battery around to an earlier masonry tower to the N, and represents the wall depicted in 1780, with some sections reflecting that depicted in 1725. It may continue beyond the tower (as shown in 1811), but if so is obscured by vegetation. At the S it has been partly demolished and overlain by the later casemates, and has also been partly removed by the construction of searchlights in the late 1890s and further to the N in the 1940s, where it is also topped by a late loop-holed wall. It is a high rubble wall of slightly battered profile with dressed limestone quoins.

The landing bay on the N side of the island was protected by two lengths of fortified walling, one loopholed and the other with a *banquette* to the rear. The loop-holed wall lies immediately N of the main magazine built to serve the 1860s batteries and follows a zig-zag course. It is sited to cover the area around the landing-place and the angle of depression of the musketry loops reflects this. It is probably 1860s in date, replacing an earlier rampart with *banquette* behind shown in 1780 & 1811. The wall behind it retains the earthen traverse protecting the N flank of the main magazine. To the W is a length of wall with a *banquette* to the rear (visible near the entrance of the covered way to the main magazines & casemated battery), which is depicted in 1780 & 1811, and may date to 1779-80 or the 1750s. Between it and the loopholed wall to the E is a rectangular masonry tower which is shown in 1780 and also possibly in 1725. It overlooks a later landing-stage and contains granite string-courses and a granite coping course. It may originally have been a loading platform. It has later been heightened and is now topped by a concrete crane base. A contemporary wall containing a masonry relieving arch adjoins it to the W as does a stub of wall to the E.

Other features

These include a jetty and ramp sited on the foreshore at the N.E of the island, which was probably built in the 1860s for the unloading of guns to be mounted in the batteries. The S end of the ramp is visible where it cuts through the shoreline and the granite foundation of the N end remains. The present quay and landing-stage on the N shore are WWII in date.

Buildings

'Commanding Officer's House'
This is sited adjoining the gateway and from the 1830s was occupied by the commanding officer of the garrison. By 1896 however it had become the canteen. A guardhouse is depicted on this site on Dixon's 1780 plan, which by 1811 had had a master gunner's house added to its S. In the 1830s it was partly rebuilt.

Three different periods of building are visible. The earliest lies on the site of the master gunner's house and is represented by the S end of the W wing. It has quoins of local stone and no limestone ashlar. A later ?early 19th-century extension to the N contains granite quoins and other details of high quality. This itself was later extended to the E, probably in the 1830s, and this extension contains limestone ashlar quoins and thresholds and a contemporary outshot & walled garden.

'Guardhouse'
This is sited on the platform to the N of the C.O's House and is thought to have been the guardhouse. It was built between 1780 & 1811 and may have become the guardhouse after the conversion of the earlier guardroom into the C.O's House in the 1830s. By 1896 it had become a coal store. It is a small rectangular structure with a slate roof, which has been extended & heightened.

Barracks
These were built in *c.*1830 on the site of earlier barracks built by Dixon in 1781. There is also an earlier structure, unlabelled, shown on this site in 1725. Soldiers & NCOs were accommodated in the E part, and the officers in the W part, a dichotomy which is clearly reflected in the quality of internal fittings such as stairways and fireplace surrounds. Much of the original timberwork, joinery and fireplaces survive *in situ.*

'Ablution block'
This is sited to the rear of the barracks, with which it was associated and probably contemporary. It is a two-storey building, with the ground floor terraced into the slope and an access passage around the rear. Fireplaces at first-floor indicate that it was used as living accommodation with perhaps wash-rooms below. The water supply for this block, the barracks and presumably the whole island was stored in two sets of underground tanks sited to the S & E. These are extensive, and the W set are brick vaulted.

Artillery Store
This is sited to the S of the ablution block and probably dates to the 1860s. It is a single-storey structure with a sloping, rebuilt roof.

Present condition
The condition of most of the walls and buildings described is reasonable, although very overgrown in parts, and suffering ongoing coastal erosion in others. The early walls in the S are generally heavily overgrown and largely covered by the earthworks of the later 1860s and *c.*1900 batteries, and in places are under pressure from this material mounded up behind them. Most of the buildings were being cleared in 1993, and were in reasonable condition, except for the barracks. These were empty, and in many rooms the upper floor was unsafe and rotten because of a leaky roof.

Sources
General
2 - 9, 11 - 15, 17, 19 - 24; B, F - H, M - Q.
Specific
These are listed under the entries below

16TH CENTURY FORT & DEFENCES

PAR = ST. ANDREW, NGR = SX46935279, PRN = SX45SE-611, MAP 3 No. 115

In 1548-9 a fort or castle was built on the highest point on the island, replacing a medieval chapel. It is illustrated on Grenville's 1586-8 plan, on another plan of 1588, and on the siege map of 1644. It was still present in 1725 but was demolished by 1780 when a battery was built by Dixon on its site. This was subsequently replaced by the 'main' or upper battery built in the late 1860s, which was in turn replaced by the 6-inch BL battery in 1901. There are no visible remains; the site lies approximately under the E 6-inch gun position.

Another feature thought to have dated to this period is a rubble stone tower located (NGR = SX46985286, PRN = SX45SE-26) on the N shore at the E end of the island. However, it is not depicted on Grenville's or Adams' maps. It is polygonal in shape, lit by one rough window; no other openings are evident, except a later access hatch. It contains a brick barrel-vaulted chamber of 18th/19th-century date and was probably used as a tank or cistern, or possibly for incarceration. The E & W walls appear to be later than the front wall, indicating that part of the structure may be earlier in date.

There are also remains of early perimeter walling (described above) on the S slopes of the island to the W of the casemates; these may in part date to the 1570s.

Present condition
The fort or castle has been demolished, although below-ground remains may survive outside the areas of the later 1860s magazines.

Sources
Specific
1592 Plan by Robert Adams. Hatfield: CPM II 31
1725 Plan of the island. BL: Kings Top. XI.91
1992 Brayshay, M. Lecture, Oct. 14th
1995 Brayshay, M 'The Sixteenth Century Protection of Sutton Harbour and Plymouth Sound: the documentary evidence' in Ray, K (ed) *Archaeological Investigations and Research in Plymouth, Vol. 1, 1992-93* pp 83-90. Plymouth Archaeology Occasional Publication No. **2**

18TH CENTURY BATTERIES

PAR = ST. ANDREW, NGR = Various, PRN = SX45SE-609, MAP 3 Nos 116 & 117

The development of the fortifications during this period is summarised above and described in detail by Woodward and illustrated by Lilly's report of 1716 & plans of 1725 & 1780 in particular. There are few surface remains which belong specifically to this period, except for the lengths of coastal and fortified walls described above and probably the embrasure looking out over the landing beach to the N of the gate.

In 1780 the main upper battery (completed in March 1779 & mounting twenty-one 32-pdr guns) was sited on that of the later 'Main Battery', with a smaller battery (completed in July 1779 with two 18-pdrs in embrasures) sited to the W, immediately S of the main magazine. Two 13-inch mortars were installed to the N of the main battery, and other guns probably retained on the lower lines around the shore, which was defended along the E, N & W by a fraised rampart with *banquette* behind. Between 1780-1811 a new main magazine (NGR = SX46865284, PRN = SX45SE-724) was built on or near the site of an earlier powder magazine marked on the 1725 map and on the site of a store house and gunner's quarters proposed by Dixon in 1780. It was still standing in 1898 when it was used as the magazine for the western QF battery, but was demolished when the 6-inch BL battery was built in 1900-01. According to the 1898 plan it consisted of a vaulted and earth-covered cartridge and shell-store surrounded by a buttressed wall. The site now remains as a terrace.

Elsewhere much of the coastal wall probably dates to this period, and a stretch of rampart with *banquette* survives facing N adjoining the entrance to the later covered way.

Present condition
Most of the gun batteries & other structures belonging to this period have been demolished or covered over by later fortifications. However, below-ground remains

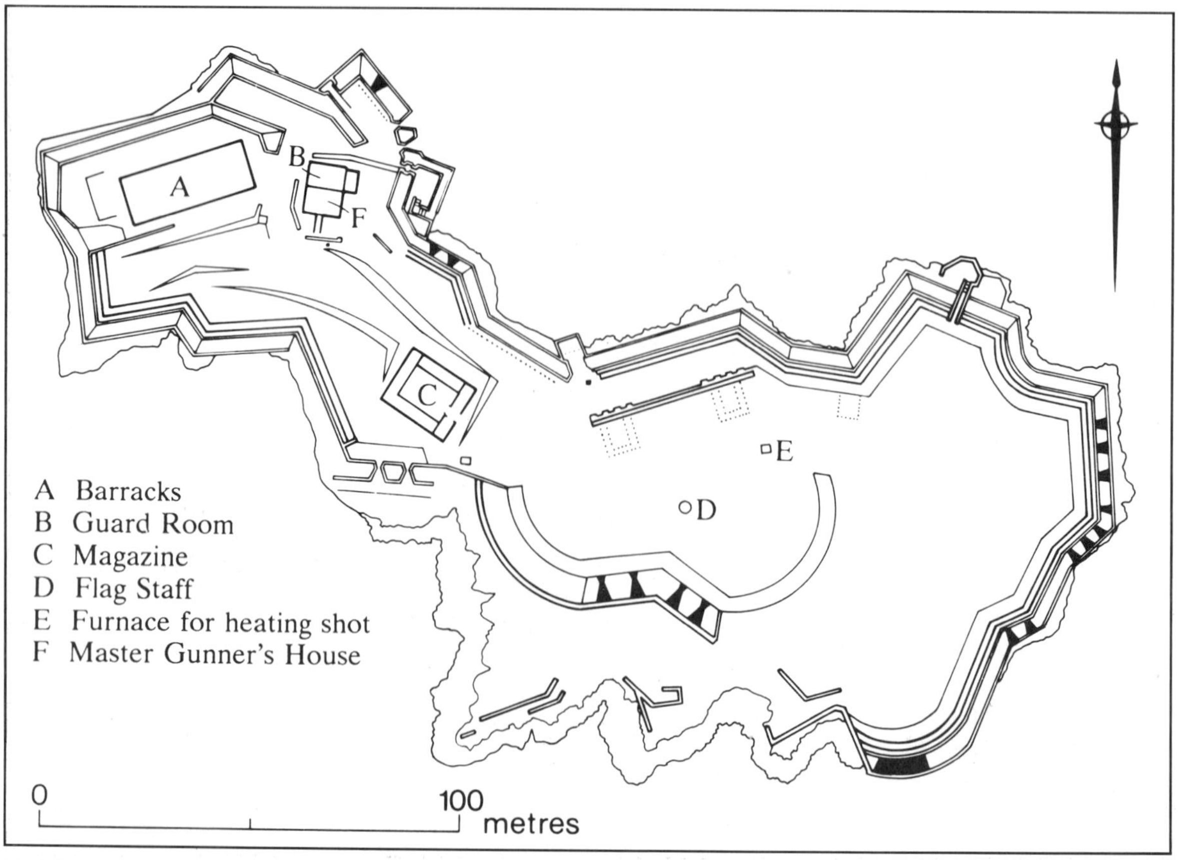

Fig. 70 Drake's Island in 1811 from PRO: MPH 233; reproduced from Devon Archaeology No. 5

may well survive, as well as fabric incorporated into later structures.

Sources

Specific

1700	Estimates for constructing batteries. BL: Add Mss 5439 f.193
1716	Report by Col. Lilly. BL: Kings Mss 45
1725	Plan of the island. BL: Kings Top. XI.91
1780	Plan of magazine & new battery. PRO: MPH 379
1780	Plan of magazine & new battery. PRO: MPH 727
1811	Plan of the island. PRO: MPH 233

CASEMATED BATTERY

PAR = ST. ANDREWS, NGR = SX47005280, PRN = SX45SE-22, MAP 3 No. 118

This consists of a casemated 21-gun battery with brick vaults and granite embrasures located at the E end of the island. Access to it from the rest of the island was via a covered way. It was connected to the main magazine located underneath the N side of the island at SX46945283 by two subterranean passages. Construction began in 1860-61 to a design by Major Porter and was largely complete (except for the shields) by 1864 when it was armed with 68-pdr SB guns on traversing garrison carriages. Three expense magazines at the rear of the passage running behind the casemates served seven guns each. In 1868-69 these were supplemented by a fourth magazine and racers for heavier guns were being installed. The installation of the iron shields were approved in 1864 and probably ordered in 1866, but by 1870 none had yet been provided, and in 1880 some were still missing and were ordered to be installed at once. However most were probably in place by 1873 when trials were carried out at Fort Picklecombe. The northern two casemates however remained unarmed, as they covered the Hoe, and were not provided with shields at all. In 1885 thirteen out of the twenty-one casemates were armed with 9-inch RML guns. The remaining casemates were never fully armed, and in 1895 the armament was reduced to eight 9-inch RMLs facing S.E & four 6-pdr QF guns were to be mounted facing N.E in casemate Nos 14-17. These were replaced by a 12-pdr QF battery built on the site of the upper RML battery in 1901.

Plate 101 Drake's Island, casemated battery (Exeter Archaeology)

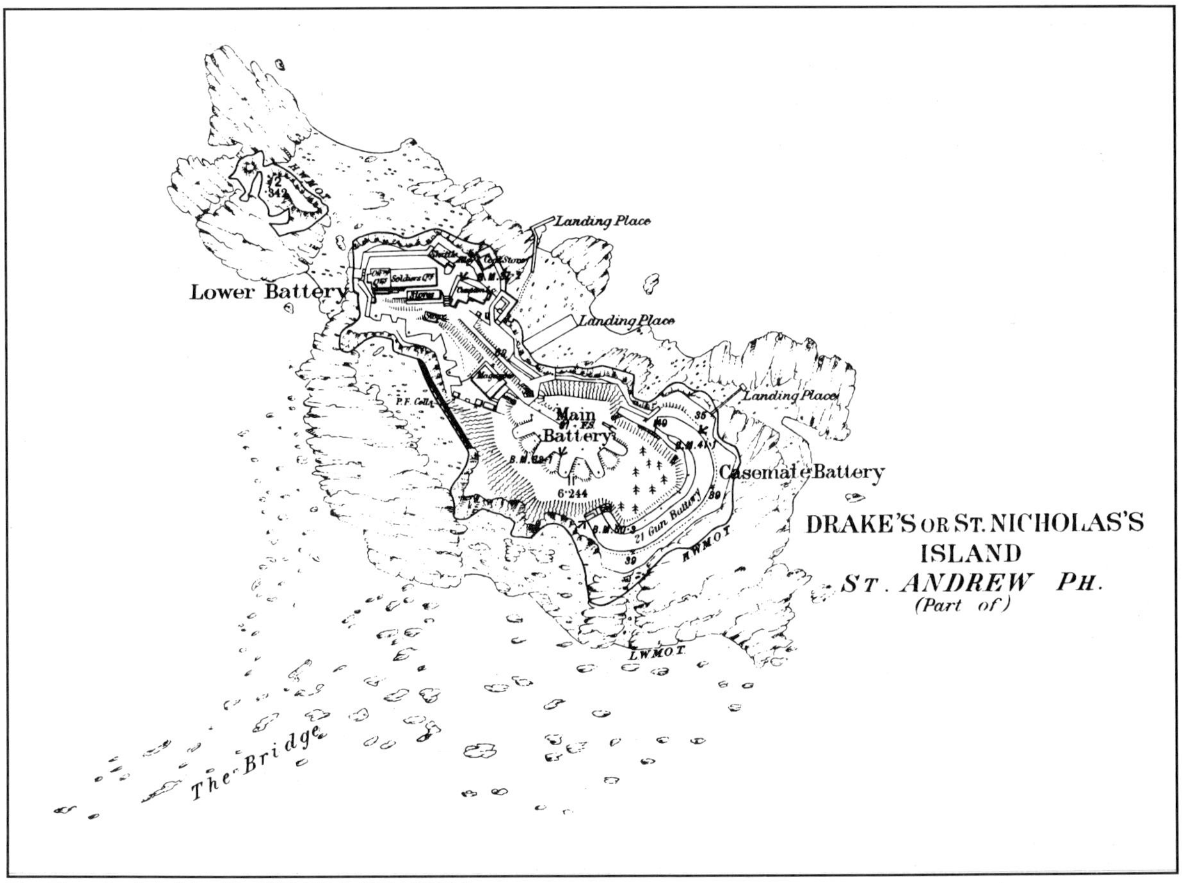

Fig. 71 Drake's Island in 1896 (PRO: WO 78/2314)

The battery remains largely intact although casemate No. 4 has been modified by the construction of searchlight emplacements on the shore below shortly after 1895. Tanks were also later installed beneath casemate No. 9. Casemate Nos 1-9 were fitted with a different design of iron shields to Casemates 10-18; perhaps one set dated to 1870-80 & the other to after 1880. Nos 19-21 remained shieldless. According to a 1895 plan casemates 20-21 were used as an artillery store and the rooms to the N as a straw and coal store. Later in WWII another ?store building was added to the W.

Plate 102 Drake's Island, rear of casemated battery (Exeter Archaeology)

The casemates are brick-vaulted and in many cases the original stone steps and the ramps for the ammunition trolleys leading up to the rear still survive, together with the dwarf walls and some of the wooden window framing. Most remain empty and some retain original features such as racer rails, mantlet bars & shields. No. 4 has been modified to accommodate the ramp down to the searchlight emplacements below, & No. 15 still retains a label above the embrasure reading '[6]-pdr QF No. 2', referring to the 6-pdr QF guns installed here after 1895. Casemate Nos 11-14 have had their shields removed and replaced in brick, presumably during WWII, and the embrasures of Nos 18-21 have been infilled with shuttered concrete. No. 21 has sliding iron shutters behind the window embrasure, perhaps indicating use during WWII as a searchlight emplacement or observation post related to the minefield (the control post for which is sited on the slope immediately behind this casemate).

The four expense magazines to the rear survive complete and usually consist of one cartridge store and one shell store separated by lamp-rooms. They are lit via a lamp-passage running within the top part of the access passage to their rear. Some retain their original suspended wooden flooring.

Plate 103 Drake's Island, hoist in main magazine (Exeter Archaeology)

The main magazine is located on the site of earlier magazines depicted in *c*.1780 and consists of three central broad vaulted chambers flanked by two long narrower chambers. In 1895 three were used as shell stores and two as cartridge stores. There is a separate lamp passage around the front and down the sides. The main access passage, sited at the rear, contains two hoists serving the expense magazines for the Main Battery above.

Present condition

The battery is largely empty though part of the main magazine, for example, has been used in the past as a discotheque. Some sections of the lamp passage have been blocked off and doorways have been knocked through into the central shell and cartridge stores. Ventilation shafts have been cut through the roofs of some of the chambers. The expense magazines are empty and largely derelict. Several of the windows and issuing hatches are blocked up; others remain open. Most of the casemates remain empty although several have recently been or are used for storage for example. Casemate Nos 1-10 and 15-17 still retain their iron shields.

Sources

Specific

1881 Plans of buildings. PRO: WO 78/2997

1895 Site plan. PRO: WO 78/4200

MAIN (UPPER) & LOWER BATTERIES

PAR = ST. ANDREW, NGR = SX46945281 & 46805285, PRN = SX45SE-544/2, MAP 3 No. 119

The main battery occupies the site of Dixon's 1780 upper battery at the E end of the island, sited above and firing over the casemated battery. It was approved in February 1867 and was built in 1868-*c*.1870. In 1885 it mounted two 12-inch and three 11-inch 23-ton RML guns, the former being removed shortly after 1895; the remaining guns were probably removed when the succeeding 6-inch BL battery was built in 1901.

The lower battery was sited at the W end of the island, and probably included Dixon's small 18-pdr battery which was extended to the N.W. It represents a remodelling of the earlier rampart in this area to accommodate several individual gun positions, in which six 80-pdr & two 64-pdr RMLs were mounted in 1885. The 64-pdrs were mounted on the S face, which probably represents the 1780 battery; these were removed by 1893 & two PF cells built in their place by 1896 (*Fig. 71*). The lower battery also included two 8-inch SB howitzers mounted on its E face, which by elimination is probably the two 1780 embrasures overlooking the landing beach N of the gate; these had been removed by 1893. The 80-pdrs remained in place until shortly after 1895, when three 12-pdr QFs were proposed (the Western QF Battery, No. 120).

The main battery had five *en barbette* emplacements facing S & E, separated by vaulted earth-covered expense magazines. These are underlain by a series of alternating cartridge and shell stores with an access passage to their rear. Access to this was via tunnels from the W & N, and branch passages lead at each end to hoist shafts down to the main magazine below. From W to E the gun emplacements were subsequently utilised as follows: No. 1 is occupied by the central emplacement of the later BL battery, No. 2 by a shelter for this battery, No. 3 for the E emplacement, No. 4 is now occupied by a stairway down from the Eastern 12-pdr QF battery to the magazines below, & No. 5 has been demolished, although its foundations have been recently re-excavated and one of four RMLs found in 1963 has been remounted in it (*Plate 9*). The underlying expense magazines survive complete, & were re-used in the 1900s as magazines for the 6-inch BL and 12-pdr QF batteries.

The western part of the lower battery has been partly removed and overlain by the later western 12-pdr QF battery, whilst the southern section has been overlain by the earthwork and spoil resulting from the construction of the W emplacement of the 6-inch BL battery in 1901. However one 80-pdr embrasured emplacement survives immediately E of a later Maxim machine-gun position. This is labelled as an 80-pdr emplacement on a plan of 1898. Within the emplacement the rear granite racer rail remains visible together with tackle loops and an ammunition recess to the W. Another recess to the W probably belonged to another emplacement on the site of the easternmost QF position. Above the gate, the platform and one embrasure belonging to the E face remains visible.

Present condition

Main battery

The underground structures remain in good condition; the remaining expense magazines at the upper level are also in good condition although those flanking emplacement No. 5 have been demolished.

Lower battery

Largely demolished or covered over when later batteries built. The remaining 80-pdr emplacement on its S.W face is in good condition although partly overgrown. The E face of the battery has been half removed by the construction of an ornamental archway to the S.

Sources

Specific

1898	Royal Engineers' plan of western QF battery. Copy held by F.W.Woodward, original by Plymouth City Council Planning Dept.
1901	Royal Engineers' plan of the 6-inch BL and eastern QF batteries. Copy held by F.W.Woodward, original by Plymouth City Council Planning Dept.
1901	Plan. PRO: WO 78/5046

WESTERN QF BATTERY

PAR = ST. ANDREW, NGR = SX46805285, PRN = SX45SE-608, MAP 3 No. 120

This is sited on the earlier lower battery and was proposed in 1895, and covered the shallow water (the Bridge) between the island and Mount Edgcumbe. It was commissioned in 1897 and completed in 1898 for three 12-pdr QF guns. According to the 1898 plan the battery initially used the magazine built to the E in 1780-1811. The armament was reduced to two guns shortly after WWI, which were held in reserve in 1930 & in August 1942 were removed to Mount Batten and replaced by a twin 6-pdr QF gun built on the westernmost 12-pdr emplacement.

Only the two eastern emplacements now survive. Both retain their steel mounting-plates and ammunition lockers; the area to the rear has been infilled. Immediately to the E a Maxim machine-gun emplacement covered the shallow Bridge channel and perhaps a minefield or other obstacle. This was largely extant in 1961, and utilised the parapet wall of the earlier 80-pdr emplacement to its rear. Its front wall is no longer visible although there is a slight square platform towards the W end which may have been the gun position.

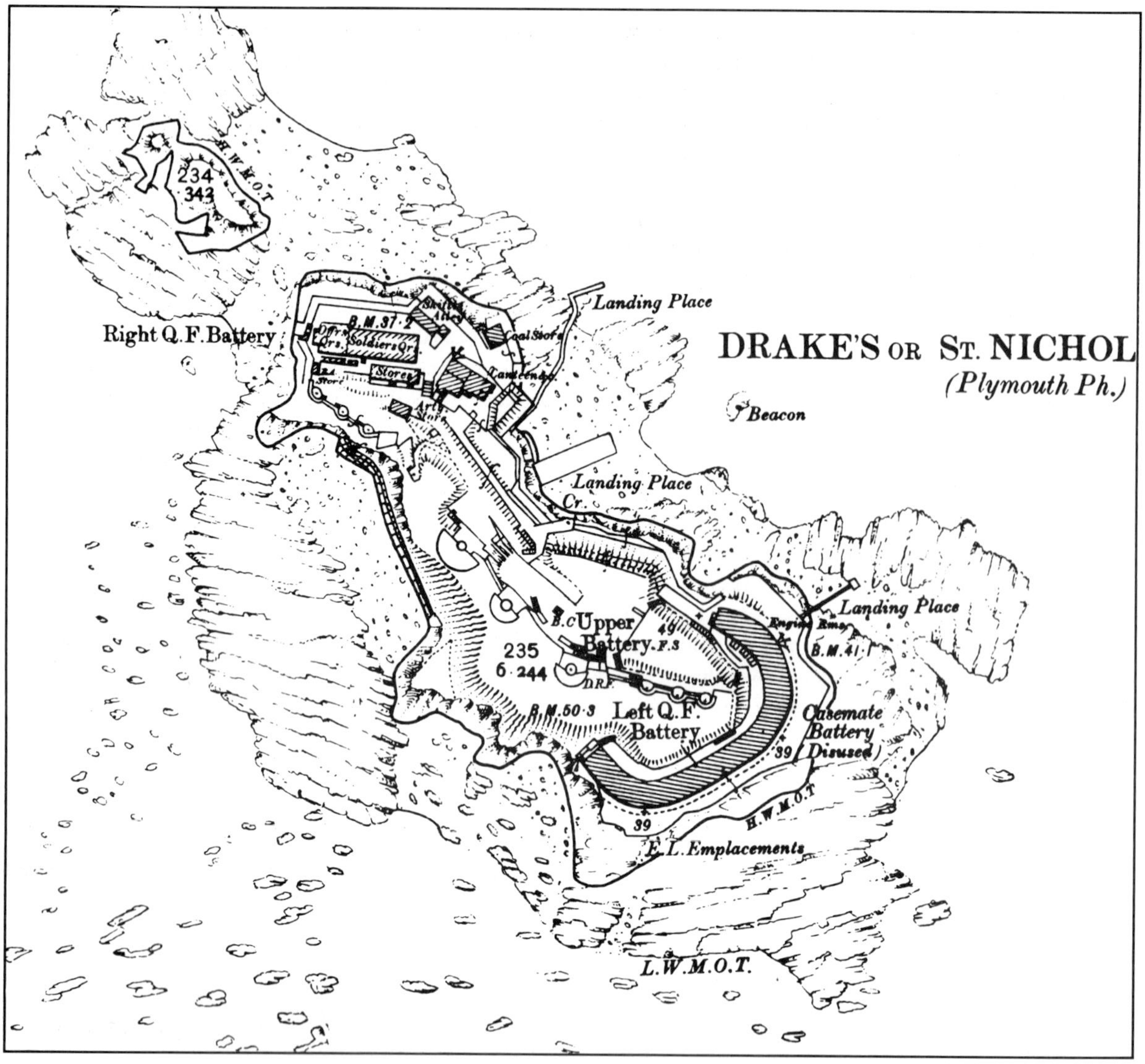

Fig. 72 Drake's Island in 1911 (PRO: WO 78/2314)

Present condition

Two emplacements survive in reasonable condition, although one mounting plate has been covered over. The main magazine has been demolished, and the LMG position infilled - its S wall is no longer visible and it is vulnerable to coastal erosion.

Sources

Specific

1898 Royal Engineers' plan of western QF battery. Copy held by F.W.Woodward, original by Plymouth City Council Planning Dept.

1911 Plymouth Defences index plan, with additions c.1930. PRO: WO 78/5066

1961 1:500 survey

n.d. Drake's Island Fort Record Book. Original lost, another version composed in c.1946. PRO: WO 192/294

6-INCH BL BATTERY

PAR = ST. ANDREW, NGR = SX46895282, PRN = SX45SE-544, MAP 3 No. 122

This is located in the centre of the island facing S, on the site of the earlier main battery built in 1868-70. It was commissioned in 1900 and completed in April 1901. The gun from the W emplacement was removed between 1920 & 1930 & the emplacement was probably occupied during WWII by an AA gun. In 1911 a DRF was sited at the E end of the battery & a Battery Command Post (probably accommodating the O.C.E.L (Officer Commanding Electric Lights) for the inner defences) to the rear. In WWII a new Fire Command Post and Observation Post were built.

Associated with this battery (& perhaps also with the eastern QF battery) were three searchlights (NGR = SX46975275, PRN = SX45SE-729) built on the shore below casemate Nos 4 - 6. They first appear on a sketch dated 1895, although may not necessarily have been built for some time after. They were operational from at least 1903 to after WWI, when the W one became redundant on the removal of the W 6-inch BL gun. By 1936 however the number increased to three again, & in WWII three others were built to the N to accompany the twin 6-pdr QF installed in 1942. In 1911 a Director Post is shown to the N.

All three 6-inch emplacements survive intact together with cartridge and shell lifts to the magazines below. However, mast bases occupy all three gun pits. The eastern two emplacements made use of earlier RML positions and the earlier expense magazines below, to which new lifts were constructed. New stairwells were constructed at the rear of each emplacement down to the rear access passage serving the magazines underneath. The W emplacement was freshly built, involving the demolition of the late 18th- or early 19th-century magazine sited immediately to the N. It is underlain by a cartridge and shell store and shelter. Several fittings, such as the wooden and metal mechanism for some of the hoists, brackets for fighting lights and the steel shutters of the ammunition lockers still survive.

The searchlight emplacements consist of three shuttered concrete cells (with brick cavity walling) built within the cliff face immediately to the S of casemate No. 4. They are linked by a passage and the searchlights were apparently transported down a ramp constructed within casemate No. 4. This had been thought to have formed part of an earlier Brennan torpedo station. Later, perhaps in WWII, two new searchlight emplacements were built on the rock foreshore immediately in front of the central and eastern cells. Three further buildings similar to searchlight emplacements or observation/direction posts are depicted in 1961 on the ground above these searchlights, directly in front of the casemates. The E one of these may have been a searchlight director post, the others may have been searchlight emplacements at some time, or observation posts, perhaps related to the minefield which has probably been present between the island and Mount Batten from the beginning of WWI (and probably earlier) up to the end of WWII. All three have been demolished; the W one has been replaced by a WWII minefield control post, and the other two are visible as platforms.

Present condition

The battery is empty, and in generally good structural condition, although the magazine & shelter under the W position have been recently damaged by unfinished structural alterations. The late 19th century searchlight emplacements are empty, and the brick walling is collapsing; the later emplacements built in front have been demolished, as have those other three structures sited above. Foundations are still visible however, and probably survive below-ground.

Sources

Specific

1895	Sketch plan of searchlight emplacements. PRO: WO 78/4900(4)
1899?	Plan of electric light emplacements. PRO: WO 78/4066
1901	Royal Engineers' plan of the 6-inch BL and eastern QF batteries. Copy held by F.W.Woodward, original by Plymouth City Council Planning Dept.
1911	Plymouth Defences index plan, with additions c.1930. PRO: WO 78/5066
1943	Letter/plan? PRO: WO 199/154 B/1
1961	1:500 survey
1978	Report of the Joint Working Party from the FSG and the UK Forts Club, led by C. Foss.
n.d.	Drake's Island Fort Record Book. Original lost, another version composed in *c*.1946. PRO: WO 192/294

EASTERN QF BATTERY

PAR = ST. ANDREWS, NGR = SX46975281, PRN = SX45SE-23, MAP 3 No. 121

This is located at the E end of the island directly above the 1860s casemated battery & faces S. It was approved in 1900 and completed in November 1901. It was fully armed with three 12-pdr QF guns by 1903, with the armament reduced to two between 1920 & 1930. These were in place at the beginning of WWII, and were replaced by the twin 6-pdr QF gun on the coast to the E in 1942.

It consists of three gun emplacements with ammunition lockers to their rear and an underground shelter at the W end. A contemporary stairwell leads down to the two N 1860s expense magazines, which were utilised as magazines for the QF battery. Fittings such as the steel mounting-plates and steel doors of the ammunition lockers remain.

Present condition

Good, although the shelter is semi-derelict and difficult of access, and the metalwork is deteriorating.

Sources

Specific

1901	Royal Engineers' plan of the 6-inch BL and eastern QF batteries. Copy held by F.W.Woodward, original by Plymouth City Council Planning Dept.
1911	Plymouth Defences index plan, with additions c.1930. PRO: WO 78/5066
1931	Letter/plan. PRO: CAB 16/105
1961	1:500 survey
n.d.	Drake's Island Fort Record Book. Original lost, another version composed in *c*.1946. PRO: WO 192/294

WWII QF BATTERY & MINEFIELD CONTROL TOWERS

PAR = ST. ANDREW, NGR = SX46795285 & 47025281, PRNs = SX45SE-29, 607, MAP 3 No. 123

Two twin 6-pdr QF guns were emplaced at the W & E ends of the island in 1942, replacing the earlier 12-pdr QF batteries. The W one was sited on the W emplacement of the earlier battery, and covered the 'Bridge'; the E one was sited outside casemate Nos 13 & 14. Three searchlights were provided to the S, with local defence being provided by a loopholed wall above. The area was also lit by three searchlights emplaced at Mount Batten. The guns were probably removed shortly after the end of the war.

Plate 104 Drake's Island, western twin 6-pdr QF emplacement (Exeter Archaeology)

Also belonging to this period are two minefield control towers sited at each end of the 1860s casemated battery to view the minefield to the E.

The central gun mounting of the W emplacement survives intact together with the parapet, concrete apron and magazine & shelter at the rear, to which access was via a ramp from the N.E. The observation tower which would have been sited to the rear has been demolished.

The E emplacement retains its concrete parapet, iron ring gun-mounting, gun platform, apron and ammunition trolley rails. The magazines were probably sited within casemates Nos 13 & 14 to the rear and there was an observation tower (now demolished) on the roof of No. 14.

The three illuminated area searchlights are sited within the earlier sea wall in front of casemate Nos 9 - 11. They are of shuttered concrete construction, face E, and each contain a pair of light slits. Access down to them appears to have been via a stairwell to the rear, in front of casemate No. 9. The central emplacement retains its internal armour plating. Above the searchlights is a zigzag length of brick wall containing concrete loop-holes. This fronts a lower area to the rear, containing the stairwell to the searchlights below. Access into this area was originally via casemate No. 11, whose iron shield has been replaced by a brick wall and door. This wall and lower area has previously been thought to date to 1902-3 and to represent an emplacement for a Maxim machine-gun. However, the wall clearly overlies the WWII searchlights and is therefore contemporary.

Plate 105 Drake's Island, minefield control tower, casemates & blocked up searchlight emplacement (bottom) (Exeter Archaeology)

The northern of the two minefield control towers is sited to the rear of, and looks over, casemate Nos 18/19, presumably to observe the minefield laid down between the island and Mount Batten. It is a two-storey rectangular shuttered concrete structure. The sides facing N, N.E & S.E contain horizontal viewing slits. The southern tower is of the same design and is sited immediately outside casemate No. 1, to which it is attached. It overlies an earlier length of coastal wall & a possible earlier searchlight emplacement or observation post. Neither post appears to retain their armoured shutters, although the interiors were not viewed.

Present condition

The gun emplacements survive in reasonable condition, as do the searchlight emplacements, loop-holed wall & control towers. All are empty, except the S tower which is a studio.

Sources

Specific

1961	1:500 survey
n.d.	Drake's Island Fort Record Book. Original lost, another version composed in *c*.1946. PRO: WO 192/294
n.d.	?WWII Plan? PRO: WO 199/954 B/1

3.3.2 Devonport & Stonehouse

STONEHOUSE TOWN WALL

PAR = E. STONEHOUSE, NGR = SX46125420 - 46425416, PRN = SX45SE-11/1, MAP 3 No. 124

This is located on a limestone ridge overlooking Stonehouse Pool to the S, defending the medieval and 16th-century town and port of Stonehouse to the N. It is illustrated on the 1540 panorama (*Fig. 2*) and on a map of 1725. It was previously erroneously identified by Worth as the fortified wall of Stonehouse Manor. It extended from a blockhouse (No. 125) on Stonehouse Pool in the W and in the E joined an earlier park boundary just to the N.W of Millbay, at or near the junction of Barrack Place and Emma Place Ope. It seems to have part of a programme of fortification by Sir Piers Edgcumbe (who held Stonehouse) in the late 15th/early 16th century which also included perhaps the blockhouses at Devil's Point and Firestone Bay. The wall was crenellated, and included a bastion and main gate as well as the blockhouse on Stonehouse Pool.

A 110m length of the wall now survives although the W blockhouse has been demolished, as has the gatehouse which probably lies under Renwicks Garage at the junction of Emma Place and Durnford Street. There are however the remnants of the bastion depicted to the W of the gate and a small late-medieval gun-port just to the W. The wall consists of roughly coursed, rubble limestone, and survives to near its original height in the central section where it retains a parapet and sentry walk. Its alignment to E & W survives in the form of property boundaries shown on later 19th-century and early 20th-century O.S. maps.

Present condition

The surviving length is in reasonable condition but has been undermined by quarrying to the N and is also affected by vegetation roots; this has been remedied by a recent programme of repair. At present it forms the boundary wall to Stonehall Flats to the S and also to the forecourt of the garage to the E. Below-ground remains may survive elsewhere, although the area of the gateway has been heavily disturbed by later cellaring.

Sources

General

1, 8; O, Q.

Specific

1725 Board of Ordnance plan of Plymouth and surrounds. PRO: MR 902

1864 1st ed. OS 1:2500 map sheet CXXIII.11. WDRO

1886 Worth, R.N 'Notes on the early history of Stonehouse' *Jnl. Plymouth Institution* 9, 338-374.

1894 2nd ed. OS 1:500 map sheets CXXIII.11.9 & 10. PCM/WDRO

1955-58 Copeland, G.W & Masson Phillips, E.N *The Ancient Buildings of Plymouth*

1975 Gaskell Brown, C *Stonehouse: an archaeological survey and policy*

1992 Pye, A.R & Stead, P.M *Archaeological evaluation of Renwicks Garage Forecourt, Durnford Street, Stonehouse* Exeter Archaeology Report No. **92.42**

Forthcoming Ray, K *Stonehouse Artillery Wall* City of Plymouth Archaeology Report GD. **12/94**

Forthcoming Ray, K 'Stonehouse : archaeological studies and the early port' in Ray, K (ed) *Archaeological Investigations and research in Plymouth. Vol 2: 1994-95*' Plymouth Archaeology Occasional Publication No. **4**.

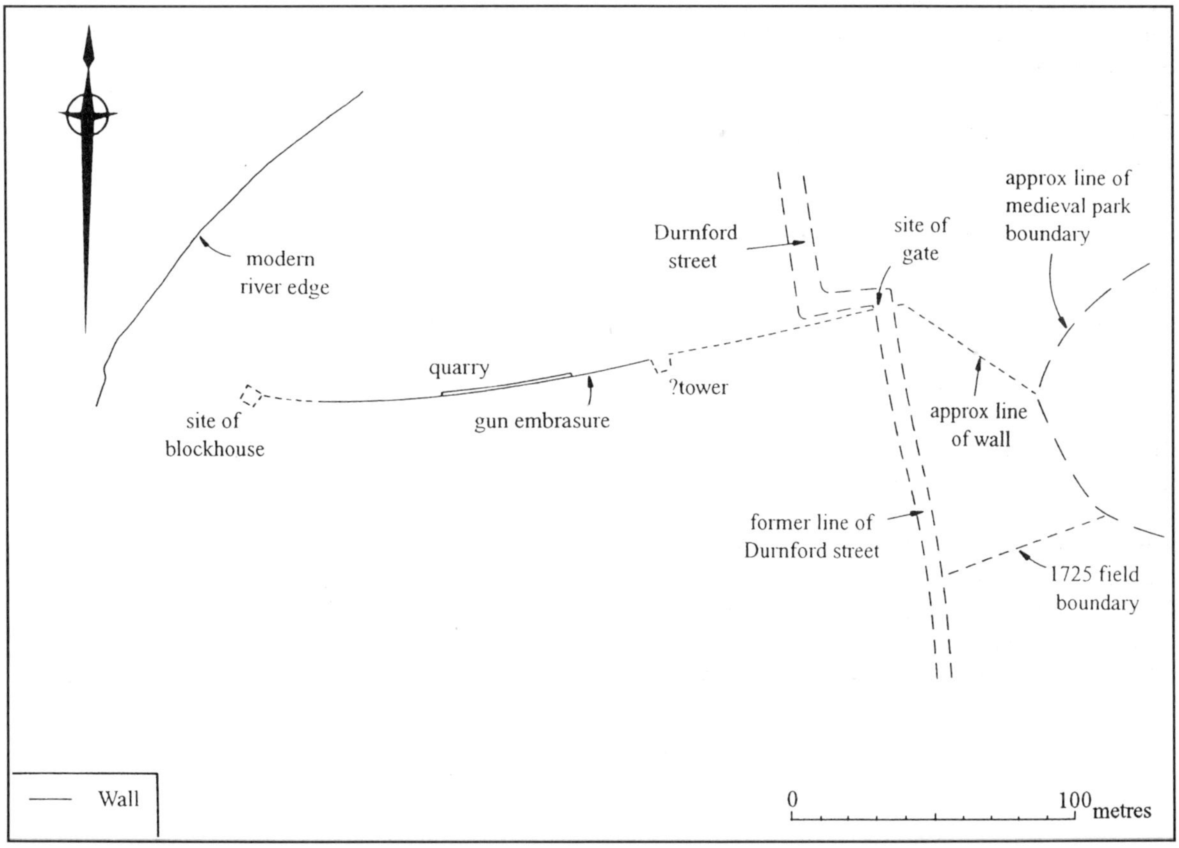

Fig. 73 Stonehouse Town Wall

STONEHOUSE BLOCKHOUSE

STONEHOUSE BLOCKHOUSE

PAR = E. STONEHOUSE NGR = SX46125420
MAP 3 No. 125

This is a two-storey polygonal crenellated blockhouse depicted in *c*.1540 at the W end of Stonehouse Town Wall on the E shore of Stonehouse Pool. A building is shown on the site as late as 1894, but has since been demolished.

Present condition
Demolished, although below-ground remains may survive.

Sources
General
1
Specific
1725 Board of Ordnance plan of Plymouth and surrounds. PRO: MR 902
1864 1st ed. OS 1:2500 map sheet CXXIII.11. WDRO
1894 2nd ed. OS 1:500 map sheets CXXIII.11.9 & 10. PCM/WDRO
Forthcoming Ray, K 'Stonehouse : archaeological studies and the early port' in Ray, K (ed) *Archaeological Investigations and research in Plymouth. Vol 2: 1994-95'* Plymouth Archaeology Occasional Publication No. **4**

STONEHOUSE POOL BLOCKHOUSE (NORTH)

STONEHOUSE POOL BLOCKHOUSE (NORTH)

PAR = STOKE DAMEREL, NGR = SX46015424, MAP 3 No. 126

This has been identified (Ray) from the depiction on 19th century illustrations of a structure very similar in character, and probably therefore contemporary, to the late medieval blockhouses elsewhere. It is sited on the W shore of Stonehouse Pool, almost exactly opposite the end of the Town Wall on the E shore, between Richmond Walk and the waterfront. It would have been built to cooperate with another blockhouse to the S and with the blockhouse and wall opposite in the defence of the approach to the medieval port of Stonehouse. There are no visible remains.

Present condition
Demolished, although below-ground remains may survive.

Source
Specific
Forthcoming Ray, K 'Stonehouse : archaeological studies and the early port' in Ray, K (ed) *Archaeological Investigations and research in Plymouth. Vol 2: 1994-95'* Plymouth Archaeology Occasional Publication No. **4**.

STONEHOUSE POOL BLOCKHOUSE (SOUTH)

STONEHOUSE POOL BLOCKHOUSE (SOUTH)

PAR = STOKE DAMEREL, NGR = SX45995417, MAP 3 No. 127

This has been recently identified (Ray) from 19th century illustrations and was sited on the W shore of Stonehouse Pool between Richmond Walk and the waterfront. It was probably contemporary with another blockhouse to the N and co-operated with this and the town wall opposite in the defence of the approach to the medieval port of Stonehouse. There are no visible remains.

Present condition
Demolished, although below-ground remains may survive.

Source
Specific
Forthcoming Ray, K 'Stonehouse : archaeological studies and the early port' in Ray, K (ed) *Archaeological Investigations and research in Plymouth. Vol 2: 1994-95'* Plymouth Archaeology Occasional Publication No. **4**.

DEVONPORT (DOCK) LINES

DEVONPORT (DOCK) LINES

PAR = STOKE DAMEREL, NGR = Various, PRNs = SX45NE-356 & 712, MAP 3 No. 128

This is a bastioned *enceinte* surrounding the landward side of the late 17th century Dockyard and the six barrack squares built in the 1750s. From 1780 it formed an integrated defensive system with various redoubts and batteries sited both outside and within the Lines. Outside the Lines Mount Pleasant and Stonehouse Hill Redoubts (Nos 146 & 147) were sited on hills commanding the land approach, Bluff Battery (a *tête de pont*, No. 143) overlooked the passage (and later the bridge) across Stonehouse Pool, and Obelisk Redoubt and musketry lines in Cornwall (Nos 9 & 10) covered the rear. Other proposed redoubts (not in the event built) at Torpoint (No. 11), Keyham, Stoke and on the W end of Stonehouse Hill (Nos 132, 133 & 148) would have completed the ring. Batteries were also sited on the Lines itself to fire out over the *glacis* (now Devonport Park and the Brickfields) above the New Gun Wharf (Cavalier Battery, No. 129), at the apex of George's Bastion (No. 144) and at the S end of the Lines (Lower Mount Wise Battery, No. 137); there may also have been another at the southernmost bastion above the Old Gun Wharf (No. 135). Close defence was provided by guns firing through embrasures in the faces and flanks of the bastions over the *glacis* and along the ditch and other guns sited on platforms midway along the curtains between bastions; in the mid-19th century this was supplemented by gun casemates in the S flank of a remodelled George's

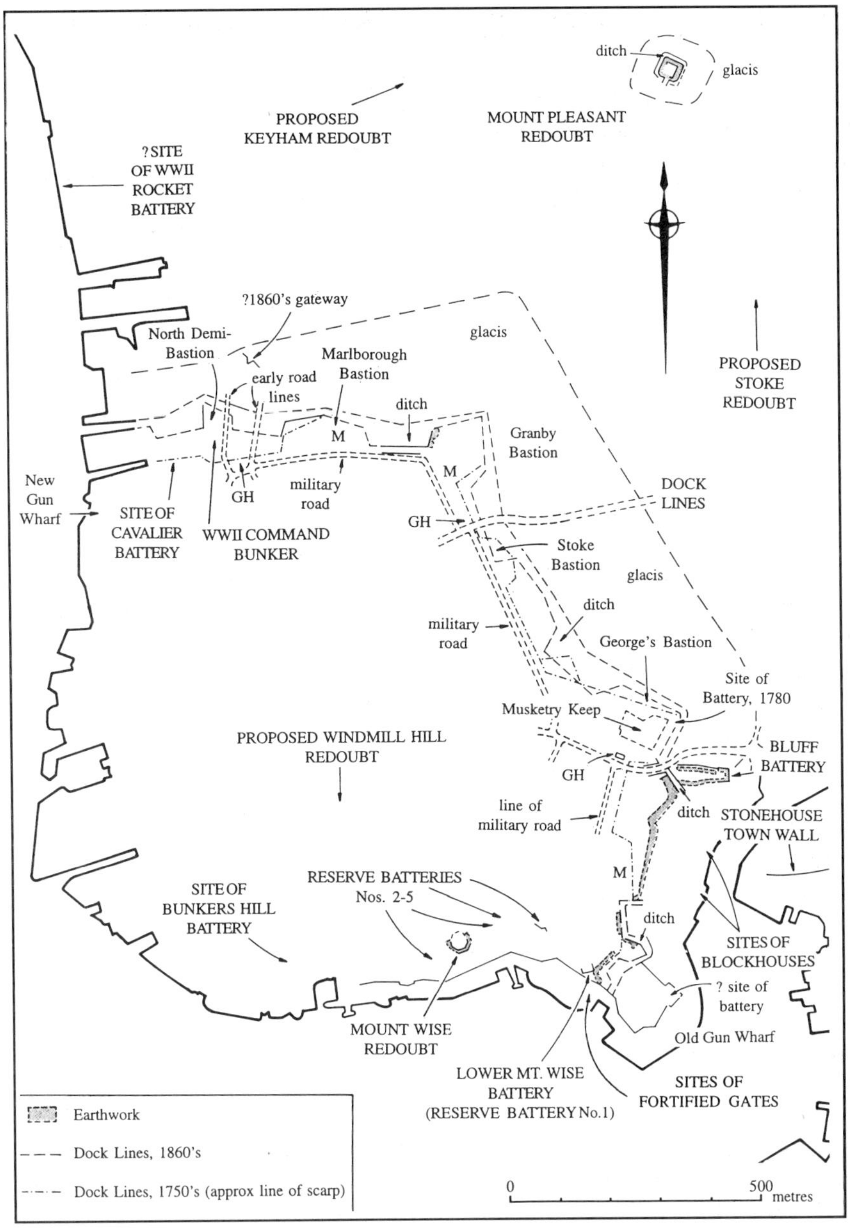

Fig. 74 Devonport (Dock) Lines & related defences

Bastion, a musketry keep (No. 145) with gun platforms on the same bastion, and fortified gates fronted by ditches sited across Richmond Walk at the S extremity of the Lines (No. 142). Strongpoints within the Lines were represented by Mount Wise Redoubt and by the proposed Windmill Hill Redoubt (Nos 136 & 130), and seaward fire was provided by Mount Wise Redoubt, Lower Mount Wise Battery, the slightly later Mount Wise Naval Reserve Batteries (Nos 138-141), and Bunkers Hill Battery (No. 131).

The Devonport (initially named Dock) Lines were begun in 1756 during the Seven Years' War. At first it consisted of an earthwork rampart fronted by a shallow unrevetted ditch. It extended from the New Gun Wharf at Morice Town eastwards to Granby Bastion, then southwards to Devonport (formerly Passage and/or Ferry House) Hill and Mount Wise. The circuit was complete by 1765, with gateways through the Lines to the S of George's Bastion, and through one face of Stoke Bastion at the E end of Fore St; there may have been a further entrance at the N end of Queen St. Three major phases of improvement works were subsequently carried out: in the emergency of 1779-80, between 1809-16, and between 1853-68.

Improvement works carried out during 1779-80 included the deepening of the rock-cut ditch to 10 feet and the 'fraising and sodding' of the earthen rampart. A new length of ditch and rampart running across the promontory at the S end of the Lines to meet the Hamoaze adjoining Lower Mount Wise Battery may also have been built at this time; it was present by 1788. In 1788-89 a new road and gateway were built through the curtain of the earlier Lines to the W of Marlborough Bastion to the new ferry across to Torpoint and a military road had also been built around the rear of the bastions by this time. Further large-scale improvements began in 1809 and were abandoned in 1816. These included the re-alignment further to the N of the section of Lines to the W of Marlborough Bastion (including the construction of the N. Demi-Bastion and a new N gate to the E of it), the construction of a new rampart faced with stone, including sally ports adjoining some of the major bastions (to the W of Marlborough Bastion for example), the deepening of the ditch and its facing in ashlar, and the provision of guardhouses at all three gates and magazines for each of the bastions (although some were already present). Before they were halted these works reached a point midway between George's Bastion and Stoke Bastion to the N, and included the replacement of the gate through the latter with another to the N. Between 1853 and *c.*1868 some further re-alignment occurred to the S of Granby Bastion and the Lines were considerably strengthened. A new, larger bastion sited further to the S replaced Stoke Bastion, and George's Bastion was re-modelled to include a musketry keep and gun casemates facing along the ditches fronting the gate and flanking the bastion. The keep, built in 1855-56, was raised above the Lines (on a 'cavalier') and included gun platforms. By 1861 the realignment was complete down to Devonport Hill. Between 1861-68 the section to the S was completed, including a new rampart along the top of the quarry face to the E and a new bastion at the S end. The Devonport Hill gate was protected by loopholed walls to each side, and was originally fronted by a drawbridge; other measures included the construction of fortified gates across Richmond Walk and the re-building and re-arming of the reserve batteries at Mount Wise. Other minor alterations included the construction of a fortified gate protecting the N entrance to the Morice Yard, and the second realignment (to form New Passage Hill) of the road leading out to the Torpoint ferry. The Lines as completed are clearly illustrated on the 1872 panorama (*Fig. 8*). However they were soon to become redundant, with the musketry keep for example being demolished in 1866 to make way for a military hospital. In 1882 a proposal to demolish the Lines from Devonport Road (Fore St.) to Passage Hill (Devonport Hill) was approved, with demolition and infilling presumably occurring shortly after.

The initial armament totalled 30 guns (mainly 12-pdrs), increasing to 61 during the 1779 invasion scare. By 1805 there were forty-nine 24-pdrs and thirty-eight 18-pdrs in place. In 1850 all the armament, totalling 28 SB guns and three mortars, was concentrated at the S end of the Lines around Government House and Mount Wise, except for three 8-inch guns on the North Cavalier (probably the N. Demi-Bastion). No proposed armament is given in the 1860 Royal Commission Report, where the Lines receive little attention as they were considered to lie too close to the Dockyard to be of use. After the approval of the partial demolition of the Lines in 1882 the remaining armament was concentrated on the Mount Wise Batteries (described separately) and largely consisted of 64-pdr RML guns and mortars.

All the surviving elements of the Lines system are described below, from the N at Morice Town around to the S adjoining Mount Wise; the numbered batteries and redoubts form separate entries.

Much of the walls of the North Demi-Bastion, the ditch in front of it, and Marlborough and Granby Bastions

Plate 106 Granby Bastion, blocked embrasures (Exeter Archaeology)

(and the curtain in between and the revetment wall at the rear of the rampart) are still visible, complete with blocked up embrasures in the face and flanks of the latter. The bastion walls survive to their full height and are faced with limestone ashlar. The W face of the N Demi-Bastion is complete, and the N face revets a railway cutting; the remainder of the N & E faces lie under a car park. The interior of the bastion was occupied by a reservoir during the later 19th century which has since been filled in. A 300m length of the counterscarp wall of the ditch is visible to the E, and continues eastwards as the boundary between the park and the industrial units; a short length of scarp wall appears to adjoin New Passage Hill to the S and may continue to the W as a break of slope. All other sections of the ditch around to Devonport Hill and W to the Hamoaze have been completely infilled.

Plate 107 1860s rampart & banquette to S of Bluff Battery (Exeter Archaeology)

To the S of Devonport Hill a section of earthen rampart built in 1861-68 remains along the E edge of the Cricket Ground, fronted by a deep rock-cut ditch to the rear of Bluff Battery and by the Richmond Walk Quarries. It has a *banquette* on its rear face, and a flat sloping top; both become less clear to the S where the rampart has been graded and partly removed. The earlier Lines crossed Devonport Hill further to the W and ran S through the centre of the Cricket Ground. To the S the 1850s bastion in the grounds of Admiralty House survives largely complete, together with most of the ditch surrounding it, a short length of rampart to the N, and the rampart and ditch (now occupied by a building) extending W to the Hamoaze. This section of ditch was probably widened in the 1850s and the cordon of its scarp wall is clearly visible where it adjoins Richmond Walk. The bastion is faced with ashlar masonry, wheras the ditch has a rubble stone counterscarp. On its N flank are two embrasures served by a bomb-proof expense magazine, and a series of musketry loops in its S.E face enfilade the earlier curtain wall leading S towards the bastion above the old gun wharf on Stonehouse Pool. This bastion is located adjoining the site of the old gun wharf and represents the original S end of the Lines. On later 19th century maps a broad gun platform is depicted on its N.E & S.E faces, on which may have been mounted the six 24-pdrs mentioned in 1779-80 at the old gun wharf (although this may refer to Lower Mount Wise Battery which had the same armament). The bastion wall is built of roughly-coursed rubble stone, as is probably the curtain. No ditch is visible.

To the W the defensive circuit continues in effect as the N wall of Richmond Walk. This is first shown in 1789, and appears to have been built as a defensible line, presumably covering Mount Wise from landings along the shore. It is built of rubble stone, *c.*3m high and of battered profile throughout, and consists of a series of straight lengths of wall, each of which could be covered by neighbouring lengths or from the bastion at its E end or from an apparent bastion near its W end below Mt Wise Redoubt; in the W it ends just short of Mutton Cove. Adjoining the bastion in the E is a possible sally port, and in places the S sections are topped by a decorative course of 18th or early 19th century bricks, similar to those on the parapets of contemporary batteries at Staddon and Lower Mount Wise. Currently the higher ground to the rear of the wall slopes down level with its top, although it is possible that there was originally a sentry walk at a lower level. Below Lower Mt Wise Battery it has been remodelled and realigned in the 1850s, presumably when the ditch was widened and the fortified gates built across Richmond Walk at this point, and the wall displays several different builds. It also contains later intrusions, including a gateway dated 1847 (replacing an earlier one) providing access from Admiralty House to Mount Wise Hard, and a more recent blocked gateway and the wall of a ?WWII transformer house to the S.

Within the N section of the Lines the line of the military road survives as St Aubyn Rd and Granby St, to the E it turned S and runs under modern housing. To the S of Fore St its line is represented by Raglan and Madden Rd and joined Cumberland Rd slightly E of the present junction. To the S it ran under the Garrison Cricket Ground to Mount Wise. Of the three guardhouses built by 1811, the N one was located to the W of the junction of New Passage Hill and St Aubyn Rd and its site is now a car park, the E one, a rectangular structure fronted by a verandah, was located under the verge to the W of the junction of Fore St with St Nazaire Approach, and the S one still survives complete at the top of Devonport Hill. This is a single-storey limestone ashlar building fronted by a stepped verandah, with a later extension at the rear. In

Plate 108 Napoleonic guardhouse at the top of Devonport Hill (Exeter Archaeology)

1811 each access road was carried across the ditch by a drawbridge, all of which were replaced and re-sited in the 1850s. Prior to 1811 the E access road ran to the S of Fore St. and out through the face of Stoke Bastion; a remnant remains as York St. On Devonport Hill the ends of two masonry piers belonging to the bridge built in the 1850s are visible in the rock cut ditch to the S of the present carriageway, and one is visible in the stairwell to the N; both are aligned slightly askew to the present carriageway. Later brick vaulted tunnels run under the road. The approach to the bridge is protected by a loop-holed wall along the N flank of Bluff Battery and by fire from two guns stationed at the S.E corner of the contemporary musketry keep on George's Bastion. Loop-holed walls continue up the hill from the bridge on both sides, providing defence against any infantry who penetrated that far. The bridge itself and the underlying ditch were protected by gun casemates and musketry galleries in the flank of George's Bastion and by loop-holes in the scarp immediately S of the bridge; all of these survive although the ditch to the N has been infilled.

Plate 109 1860s loopholed wall on Devonport Hill (Exeter Archaeology)

Present condition

The best preserved lengths of the Lines lie between Devonport Hill and Mount Wise and elsewhere substantial sections of the scarp walls of Marlborough, Granby, and the N Demi-Bastions survive to their full height and generally in good condition although they are overgrown in parts and the rampart has been removed from the rear and the interiors developed for housing. Elsewhere the rampart has been levelled (in the late 1880s) and the ditch infilled (apart from sections at Mount Wise, Bluff Battery and the N Demi-Bastion), although the ditch has been shown to survive to its full depth in front of Marlborough Bastion and around George's Bastion. Substantial below-ground remains of the ditch and of the bastions (including those of the original 1750s Lines) are therefore very likely to survive elsewhere, such as around Granby Bastion and within the Brickfields, and under the Garrison Cricket Ground in Mount Wise; much of the course of the ditch is open ground, although some sections are occupied by industrial units and housing. On Devonport Hill the guardhouse and the later 1850s bridge and defensive arrangements survive virtually complete, although partly buried and covered by the later road carriageway, and below-ground remains of the other two guardhouses, bridges and magazines may also survive. Outside the Lines most of the *glacis* survives as Devonport Park and the Brickfields, and the 1850s fortified gateway at the N entrance to the Morice Yard survives complete.

Sources
General
5 - 9, 11 - 13, 15, 17, 19; J, M, O, Q.
Specific
1756 Plan. BL: Kings Top. XI 77
1756 (1859) Copy of map of lands taken under Defence Act for building Dock Lines. Held by Cdr Clegg, Dockyard Museum.
1757 An exact plan of the ground humbly proposed to be purchased at the Dock of Plymouth. PLSL
1757 Act for securing of land to build the Dock Lines. WDRO: Acc 227/1/11
1765 Map by Benjamin Donn.
1782 Plan of Gun Wharf. PRO: MR 572
1788 Map of Plymouth & environs (Sturt). PRO: MR 1176
1789 Plan of Dock Lines & Town. PRO: MR 1427
1789 Plan and sections of Dock Lines. PRO: MPH 757
1790 Gun Wharf - loop-holed gallery at. PRO: MPH 406
1805 Sections through the Lines. PRO: MPHH 146
1809-16 Plans of improvements to Lines. PRO: WO 55/798, WO 78/1145, MPHH 20/3-7, MPHH 61, MPHH 288, MPHH 584, MPHH 788
1811 Mercer's plan of the Lines. PRO: MPH 233/1
1838 Plan of the Town of Devonport. WDRO: Acc 1469
1840 Tithe map of Stoke Damerel parish. DRO
1850 Armament table and plan. Officers' Mess, Royal Citadel
1854 Proposed reform of Lines. PRO: MR 1425
1856 Military edition of O.S. 1:2500 map sheet CXXIII.11. WDRO
1857 1st ed. OS 1:500 sheet Nos 65, 41, 53, 40. PCM
1857 Military edition of O.S. 1:500 maps. PRO: MPHH 629
1858 Defence works for Devonport PRO MR 1261 (WO78/497)
1859 Plan of Lines. PRO: WO 78/2569(2)
1861 (revised 1880, 1887 & 1893) Map & Chart of Plymouth Sound & Hamoaze. PCM
1862 Plan of Royal Albert Hospital. WDRO: Acc 1073/1
1864 1st ed. OS 1:2500 map. Devon sheet CXXIII.11 WDRO
1872 Illustrated London News panorama
1880 Gun Wharf at Devonport. PRO: WO 78/3101
1893 Gun Wharf at Devonport. PRO: WO 78/2924
1894 2nd ed. OS 1:500 map sheet CXXIII.7.17. PCM
1933 OS revised 1:2500 edition. Devon sheet CXXIII.7 WDRO/DRO
1992 Stead, P.M *Archaeological evaluation of the former MoD car park off New Passage Hill, Devonport* Exeter Archaeology Report No. **92.57**
Forthcoming Pye, A 'The Inner Defences of the Dockyard' in Ray, K (ed) *Archaeological Investigations and Research in Plymouth, Volume II: 1994-95* Plymouth Archaeology Occasional Publication No. **2**.
n.d. Plan, including Cavalier & N. Demi Bastion. PRO: WO 78/4481

CAVALIER BATTERY

PAR = STOKE DAMEREL, NGR = SX44975498,
PRN = SX45NW-501, MAP 3 No. 129

This was located on the westernmost bastion of the N section of the Lines above the New Gun Wharf. It was built between August 1779 and January 1780 on the orders of Col Dixon (and is marked 'V' on his plan). It mounted seven 12-pdrs and was intended to cover the Ordnance Arsenal (the new gun wharf) and to strengthen the weaker part of the Lines. Although described in Dixon's 1780 report as a permanent battery and as being armed, it is not mentioned in contemporary remarks on the new defences erected at Plymouth nor is it illustrated on Cowl's 1780 plan. After the shift northwards of this section of the Lines in 1811-12 the original battery would probably have become redundant, with its role perhaps being fulfilled by guns sited on the N Cavalier Bastion sited next to the river (at NGR = SX 44875506) and on the N Demi-Bastion (NGR = SX 45055509) to the E; this may have overlooked and therefore commanded the former. Both bastions contain a series of emplacements in 1857 and in 1850 three 8-inch SB guns were mounted on the 'North Cavalier'.

The site of the 1780 battery is an area of higher ground, sited to the N of Queen St and overlooking the gun wharf to the W and lower ground to the N; it is currently a car park. The N Demi-Bastion lies to the N.E and much of it still remains, although its interior was converted into a reservoir and has subsequently been infilled; there is no surface trace of gun emplacements. The site of the N Cavalier Bastion lies within the Morice Town Yard to the N.W, immediately to the S of a slipway or canal which formed the ditch in this area.

Present condition

Both the 1780 battery site and the interior of the N Demi-Bastion are currently car parks. Below-ground remains may survive, but the degree of survival may have been affected by the construction of a nearby railway cutting and also of the tunnels which run under both sites. The N Cavalier Bastion has been demolished and from the map its site is occupied by a quay and associated buildings; the site was not visited however.

Sources
General
5 - 7; O, Q.
Specific
1811 Mercer's plan of the Lines. PRO: MPH 233/1
1850 Armament table and plan. Officers' Mess, Royal Citadel
1857 Military edition of O.S. 1:500 PRO: MPHH 629
n.d. 19th-century plan PRO: WO 78/4481

WINDMILL HILL REDOUBT (PROPOSED)

WINDMILL HILL REDOUBT (PROPOSED)

PAR = STOKE DAMEREL, NGR = SX45325438,
PRN = SX45SE-711, MAP 3 No. 130

A redoubt on Windmill Hill was recommended by Dixon in January 1780 as an interior defence to the Lines. The site is marked as 'W' on his 1780 plan but there is no evidence that it was completed; it does not appear on other contemporary or later sources.

The site is a prominent knoll within the Dock Town, which slopes away steeply to the north and west; it is occupied by Devonport Town Hall which was erected in 1822. This probably involved some considerable truncation of the hilltop, as the area surrounding the column immediately to the N is some 2-3m higher.

Present condition
Site occupied by buildings; any remains of an unfinished redoubt may have been truncated during their construction although the survival of some below-ground remains cannot be discounted.

Sources
General
5 - 7.

BUNKERS HILL BATTERY

BUNKERS HILL BATTERY

PAR = STOKE DAMEREL, NGR = SX45175404,
PRN = SX45SE-705, MAP 3 No. 131

A battery of this name is referred to in 1808; there are no other known references. The site is probably Kings Hill in South Yard, where subsequently a gazebo was built on the occasion of a visit by George III in 1822. There are no obvious surface remains although the surrounds were not examined in detail.

Present condition
Demolished, although below-ground remains may survive.

Sources
Specific
1808 Plan or letter? PRO: WO 55/798
1931 Bracken, C.W *History of Plymouth & Her Neighbours* p. 171

KEYHAM REDOUBT (PROPOSED)

KEYHAM REDOUBT (PROPOSED)

PAR = STOKE DAMEREL, NGR = SX45405577,
PRN = SX45NE-347, MAP 3 No. 132

A redoubt was proposed by Dixon in January 1780 to cover the N side of the Lines and the Powder Magazines at Keyham Point. There is no evidence that it was ever built; it does not appear on any other sources and there are no visible remains. The proposed site occupies the crest of a slope, underneath the Herbert public-house, and has been truncated to the E by the railway.

Source
General
5

STOKE REDOUBT (PROPOSED)

STOKE REDOUBT (PROPOSED)

PAR = STOKE DAMEREL, NGR = SX46105530,
PRN = SX45NE-346, MAP 3 No. 133

A redoubt was proposed by Dixon in January 1780 to the S of Stoke village to command the approach to the Lines around the S of Mt Pleasant Redoubt. There is no evidence that it was ever built; it does not appear on any other sources. The proposed site lies at the E end of a small spur, within very overgrown former gardens.

Source
General
5

DEVONPORT DOCKYARD ROCKET BATTERY

DEVONPORT DOCKYARD

PAR = STOKE DAMEREL NGR = SX?44705550
PRN = SX45NW-548 MAP 3 No. 134

This was apparently established in the Dockyard in 1941 when it was manned by 142 Z Battery; it was capable of firing 64 rockets. It is thought to have been located in the area of quays to the N of Morice Town and the Torpoint Ferry; no trace has been identified by FSGSW. The site was not viewed.

Present condition
Not available; probably demolished.

Source
General
25

OLD GUN WHARF BATTERY

PAR = STOKE DAMEREL, NGR = SX45935397,
PRN = SX45SE-712/15, MAP 3 No. 135

The Old Gun Wharf was located on the W shore of Stonehouse Pool, below Mount Wise. In *c.*1780 six 24-pdr guns are mentioned as being mounted there, although this probably refers to Lower Mount Wise Battery which had the same armament at this time and was built by January 1780. There is no other known reference to a battery at this location.

Guns were however probably sited on the southernmost bastion of the Dock Lines; this overlooks the site of the gun wharf and was built by 1765. Maps show a broad gun platform along its two faces. The bastion is built of rubble stone, and was probably topped by a decorative course of brick which has since been removed or obscured by the construction of a fence along the top. The interior was not viewed.

Present condition

Appears good, although the construction of the fence has caused some damage to the parapet.

Sources

General

5, 7

Specific

1765	Map by Benjamin Donn.
1789	Plan of Dock Lines & Town. PRO: MR 1427
1811	Mercer's plan of the Lines. PRO: MPH 233/1
1838	Plan of the Town of Devonport. WDRO: Acc 1469

MOUNT WISE REDOUBT

PAR = STOKE DAMEREL, NGR = SX45515408,
PRN = SX45SE-170, MAP 3 No. 136

This is an octagonal redoubt built on the highest point of Mount Wise to cover the approach channel to the dockyard and the rear of Obelisk Redoubt and musketry lines at Cremyll on the opposite shore, and to fortify the position against attack. Previously thought to have been constructed by 1770, it is described in *c.*1780 as having been begun in 1778 and completed in May 1779. Stuart (M) does not note its presence on any maps until its appearance on a chart of 1777-79 with an armament of eight 32-pdrs and two 10-inch mortars. This is the armament given in most contemporary sources except one which mentions eight 24-pdrs instead. In 1850 it had an armament of three 10-inch guns, and is referred to in 1860 but is not included in plans for improving the defences. Some remodelling however may have occurred, and in 1885 three 64-pdr RMLs were mounted, and were retained until shortly after 1895.

From 1806, and possibly from 1785 or earlier, a telegraph and/or signal station was present, and remained until early this century, utilising the guardroom/magazine building of the earlier redoubt. This was demolished in the 1960s when Onslow Court was built.

On a 1780 plan a building used as a guardhouse and magazine/store is marked in the centre of the redoubt

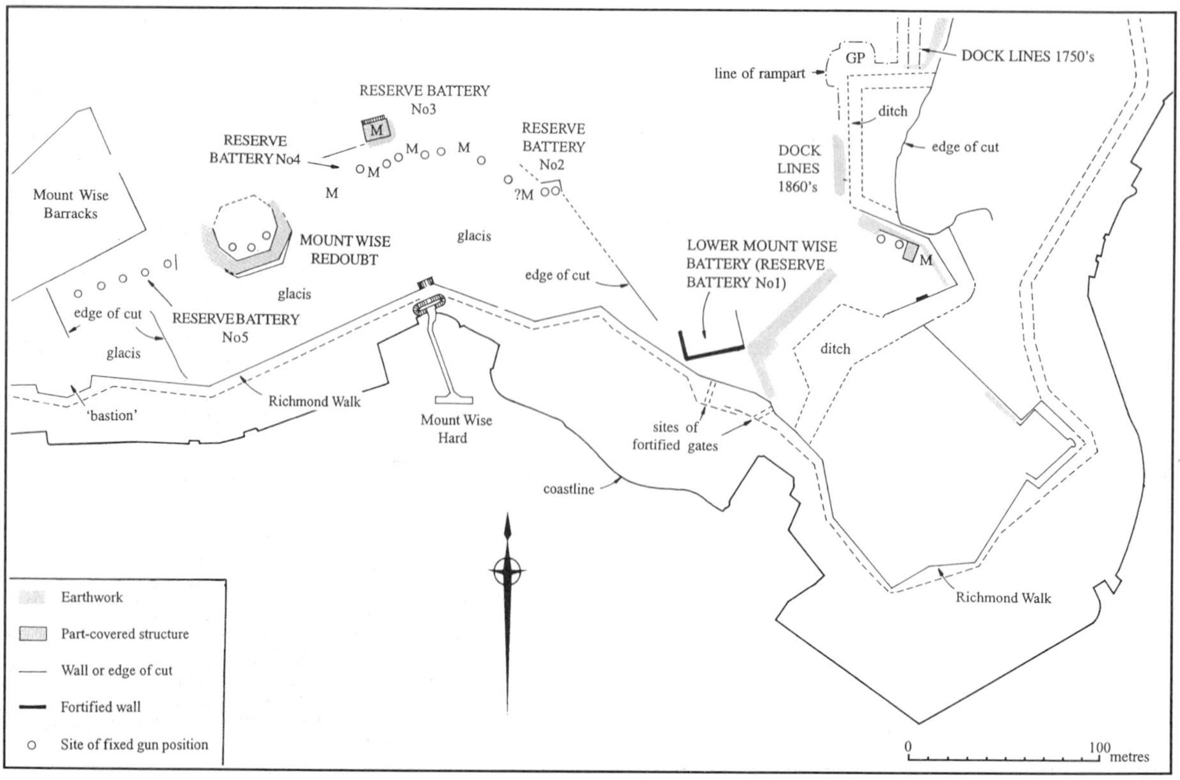

Fig. 75 Mount Wise

with a reservoir sited immediately to the E. A *terreplein* or gun platform is shown to the rear of the three sea facing sides and a *banquette* to the rear of the others. The rampart was surrounded on the outside by a ditch which was fraised; this continued around the S flank but the ditch did not. The redoubt was entered over a drawbridge from the N. In 1896 three sets of racer rails are depicted, belonging to the three 64-pdr RMLs.

Plate 110 Mount Wise Redoubt & glacis from Richmond Walk (Exeter Archaeology)

The ramparts on the seaward side of the redoubt survive complete with external and internal stone revetment walls and small ammunition recesses in three sides. The N walls of the redoubt have been mostly demolished, although substantial below-ground remains of these, the internal buildings and racer rails for the 64-pdr RMLs were observed when Onslow Court was recently demolished; the ditch, although infilled, also survives. The *glacis* is evident on the seaward side, with the junctions between its different planes clearly visible.

Present condition

Although partly demolished in the 1960s, substantial above and below ground remains survive in reasonable condition, although truncated and partly overgrown. The *glacis* is very clear, and lies within a public park.

Sources

General

4 - 8, 12, 13, 17, 19; M, O, Q.

Specific

1780	Plan of Mt Wise Battery. PRO: MPH 372
1780	Plan? PRO: WO 78/372
1785	Print of Mt Wise showing battery and signal station. PRO: MPHH 544
1811	Mercer's plan of the Lines. PRO: MPH 233/1
1812	Plan. PRO: WO 44/239
1838	Plan of the Town of Devonport. WDRO: Acc 1469
1850	Armament table and plan. Officers' Mess, Royal Citadel
1856-7	Military edition of O.S. 1:2500 map, Devon sheet CXXIII.11. WDRO
1880	Print showing Admiralty House and Government House, with redoubt and telegraph/signal station in the background. Copy in Dockyard Museum (Cdr Clegg)
1890	Photo on postcard showing redoubt. Copy held by F.W. Woodward
1907	2nd edition O.S. 1:2500 map sheet Devon CXXIII.11. WDRO

LOWER MOUNT WISE BATTERY

PAR = STOKE DAMEREL, NGR = SX45765403, PRN = SX45SE-706, MAP 3 No.137

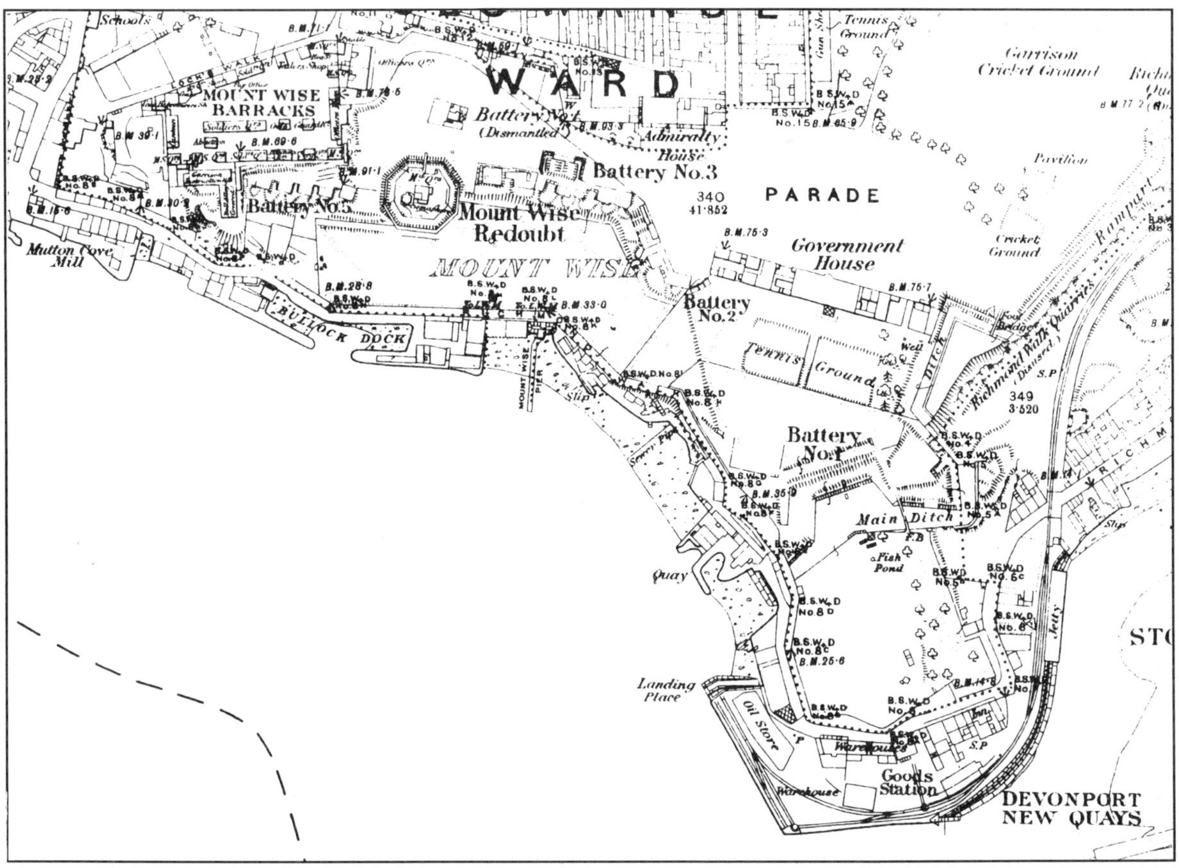

Fig. 76 Mount Wise in 1896 (PRO: WO 78/2314)

A coast battery located in the grounds of Government (now Admiralty) House facing S out over the Hamoaze, defending the inner approaches to the dockyard. It was built in January 1780 on the orders of Lt Col. Dixon, and mounted six 24-pdrs *en barbette*. Another map of 1780 gives its armament as six 32-pdrs. Later in the late 18th or early 19th century it became one (No. 1) of five Naval Reserve batteries, which in an emergency were manned by sailors from nearby naval barracks. In 1850 it was probably known as 'Govt House 1' battery and mounted eight 32-pdr guns. It is not mentioned by the 1860 Royal Commission report, and was not subsequently re-modelled; no armament was present in 1885.

Plate 111 Lower Mount Wise Battery (Exeter Archaeology)

It consists of a rectangular terrace with early brick parapets on the S & W sides with sloping granite gun platforms to their rear. These form a continuous platform and remain largely intact. The E side is retained by a higher, contemporary brick wall with a more recent stone wall sited immediately to the E. Six 6-pdr saluting guns on wheeled naval carriages are currently present. The site of the magazine which served this battery is not evident. Access to the battery was probably via a track down from the N.W.

Present condition

Very good; it is maintained as part of the Admiral's private garden. Some granite slabs at the S.W corner of the platform are missing however.

Sources

General

4 - 8, 12, 13, 17, 19; J, M, O, Q

Specific

1780? Plan. PRO: WO 78/372
c.1789 Plan of Town of Plymouth Dock (Durnford). PRO: MPH 406(3)
1811 Mercer's plan of the Lines. PRO: MPH 233/1
1838 Plan of the Town of Devonport. WDRO: Acc 1469
1850 Armament table and plan. Officers' Mess, Royal Citadel
1861 Map and Chart of Plymouth Sound and Hamoaze. PCM
1907 2nd ed. OS 1:2500 map. Devon sheet CXXIII.11. WDRO
Forthcoming Pye, A 'The Inner Defences of the Dockyard' in Ray, K (ed) *Archaeological Investigations and Research in Plymouth, Volume II: 1994-95* Plymouth Archaeology Occasional Publication No. **2**.

MOUNT WISE BATTERY No. 2

PAR = STOKE DAMEREL, NGR = SX45655411, PRN = SX45SE-707, MAP 3 No. 140

One of five reserve batteries (to be manned by sailors from the naval barracks) at Mount Wise which (except No. 1 - Lower Mt Wise Battery) are first depicted in 1784. They commanded the inner approach channel and formed the last line of defence against sea-borne attack; the channel turns sharply at this point, exposing the ships' decks and sides to concentrated fire from above. No. 2 was sited immediately W of Government (now Admiralty) House and faced S & S.W. In 1850 it was split into 'Govt House No. 2' and 'No. 2 Battery', and mounted two 32-pdr and two 8-inch SB guns *en barbette* along a single open gun platform. In 1860-65 it was remodelled and included at least one bomb-proof expense magazine and four individual gun positions, presumably accommodating four of the 64-pdr RML guns mounted in 1885; some of these were removed in 1891-93 and the remainder shortly after 1895. Its N.W section was demolished between 1904-7, and the remainder probably during WWII.

Part of the wall at the rear of the gun platform at the E end of the battery is still visible, together with vestiges of the earthwork rampart to the front.

Present condition

Small fragments of the rear wall survive, the remainder is earthwork and under grass. It is not clear whether the earthwork has been levelled and pushed down the slope, or whether the rear has been infilled. Some of the material downslope contains concrete and may represent later rubble/spoil from WWII activity. The area to the rear is used for parking and storage; the earthworks lie in public parkland. Although demolished some below-ground remains of the gun positions and magazine(s) are likely to survive.

Sources

General

5, 8, 13, 17, 19; M, O, Q.

Specific

c.1789 Plan of the Town of Plymouth Dock (Durnford). PRO: MPH 406(3)
1838 Plan of the Town of Devonport. WDRO: Acc 1469
1850 Armament table and plan. Officers' Mess, Royal Citadel
1856-7 Military edition of O.S. 1:2500 map, Devon sheet CXXIII.11. WDRO
1861 Plan and Chart of Plymouth Sound and Hamoaze. PCM
1904 Plan of Mount Wise Admiralty House and its environs prior to construction of new road. Copy held in Dockyard Museum (Cdr Clegg)
1907 2nd ed. O.S. 1:2500 map sheet Devon CXXIII.11. WDRO
Forthcoming Pye, A 'The Inner Defences of the Dockyard' in Ray, K (ed) *Archaeological Investigations and Research in Plymouth, Volume II: 1994-95* Plymouth Archaeology Occasional Publication No. **2**.

MOUNT WISE BATTERY No. 3

PAR = STOKE DAMEREL, NGR = SX45595412, PRN = SX45SE-708, MAP 3 No. 139

This was located at the crest of the coastal slope between Nos 2 & 4 and faced S. It was built between 1780 & 1784 and in 1850 was armed with three 32-pdr and two 8-inch SB guns. It originally consisted of an open gun platform, with the addition between 1838 & 1857 of a furnace for heating shot. In 1861 it was remodelled to accommodate five guns in separate positions firing through earthwork embrasures and separated by two bomb-proof expense magazines. To the rear was a bomb-proof main magazine and guardroom. In 1885 it was armed with five 64-pdr RMLs, most of which remained until shortly after 1895, and the gun positions were demolished between 1904 & 1907 when the present access road was built. During WWII Canadian troops apparently cut a number of tunnels in this area.

The battery was built (with No. 4) within a terrace at the crown of the slope, and is sited within the gardens of Seymour House. The main magazine survives intact and consists of two rooms; one is lit by windows and is presumably the guardroom, the other has lamp windows and a shifting lobby and is the magazine. Substantial below-ground remains of the expense magazines and gun platforms were observed under the lawn to the front in 1994. The road runs along the rampart.

Present condition
The 1861 magazine survives intact and in reasonable structural condition apart from the timberwork, which is original. In 1994 it was empty and unused. Substantial below-ground remains of the gun platforms and expense magazines survive within the garden to the S, although the rampart to the S was levelled when the road was constructed. The *glacis* slope is public parkland.

Sources
As for Battery No. 2

MOUNT WISE BATTERY No. 4

PAR = STOKE DAMEREL, NGR = SX45555412, PRN = SX45SE-709, MAP 3 No. 138

This was located at the crest of the coastal slope between No. 3 & the Redoubt and faced S. It was built between 1780 & 1784 and in 1850 was armed with one 13-inch and two 10-inch mortars; three mortar positions are depicted in 1857. In 1860-65 it was remodelled and its site shifted to the W; in 1885 it was armed with three land-service mortars, which were subsequently retained for drill until their removal in 1891-93. Three square mortar positions separated by a bomb-proof expense magazine are depicted in 1896.

The battery was sited in a terrace at the crest of the slope, and in the 1860s was extended to the W into the side of the hill on which the redoubt stands. Part is sited within the garden of Seymour House, where the stone wall retaining the rear of the terrace is visible, and part under and to the W of the present road.

Present condition
Most of it was demolished in 1904-7 when the road was driven through, although the W section was infilled and still survives below-ground. The remaining section of retaining wall is in reasonable condition.

Sources
As for Battery No. 2.

MOUNT WISE BATTERY No. 5

PAR = STOKE DAMEREL, NGR = SX45455405, PRN = SX45SE-710, MAP 3 No. 141

This was located along a ridge at the crest of the coastal slope to the W of and below the redoubt, and above Mount Wise Barracks to the N. It faced S. It was built between 1780 & 1784. In 1784 and 1789 another possible battery platform is depicted (at approx. NGR = SX45345404) immediately W of the barracks (built 1789-1811), but does not appear subsequently. In 1850 No. 5 was a Saluting Battery armed with 6-pdr and three 32-pdr and two 8-inch SB guns. Between 1838 & 1857 a furnace for heating shot was provided and the slope in front scarped to form a *glacis*. In 1860-65 it was remodelled to form five separate gun positions separated by traverses, presumably containing ammunition recesses. No main magazine is evident. In 1885 it was armed with five 64-pdr RMLs, most of which remained until shortly after 1895. It was demolished on the construction of Hamoaze Court in the 1960s.

Visible remains consist of part of the easternmost 1860s gun platform and an adjoining arched ammunition recess. To the W, remains of the 18th century battery and of the later 1860s gun positions were observed during the recent demolition of Hamoaze Court, and the *glacis* slope, defined by a rock scarp to the E, can be seen to the S.

Present condition
Mostly demolished when Hamoaze Court was built and the E section heavily terraced; however below-ground remains of both batteries (*c*.1784 & 1860s) survive, particularly towards the W end of the site, and the extant ammunition recess is in good condition. The earthen rampart fronting the 1860s battery has been levelled and pushed down the *glacis* slope to the S, which otherwise survives intact.

Sources
As for Battery No. 2.

RICHMOND WALK FORTIFIED GATES

PAR = STOKE DAMEREL, NGR = SX45765400, MAP 3 No. 142

These were built across Richmond Walk at the S end of the Lines below Lower Mount Wise Battery and adjoining the former Royal Clarence Baths; they were constructed between 1838 and 1856-7 and probably date to improvements earlier in the 1850s. They pre-date the subsequent widening of the Lines ditch at this point; one is aligned on the counterscarp of the late 18th century Lines ditch and the other is sited immediately below Lower Mt. Wise Battery. Both consist of a wall containing a central gate and fronted by a narrow ditch. By 1896 they had been removed.

The walk has been widened at this point and the retaining wall on the N.E re-aligned when the gates were constructed. Both have been demolished, although closer inspection may reveal evidence of their former presence in the build of the boundary walls.

Present condition

Both have been demolished, although below-ground remains are likely to remain.

Source

Specific

1856-7 Military edition of O.S. 1:2500 map, Devon sheet CXXIII.11. WDRO

BLUFF BATTERY

PAR = STOKE DAMEREL, NGR = SX46005439, PRN = SX45SE-704, MAP 3 No. 143

This was built by Dixon between August 1779 and January 1780, and was also referred to as 'Rocks Battery' and 'Bridge Battery'. It was intended as a *tête de pont* to command Stonehouse Bridge and the road from Plymouth and the armament at this time is variously given as six 9-pdr or 12-pdr guns. In 1804 it

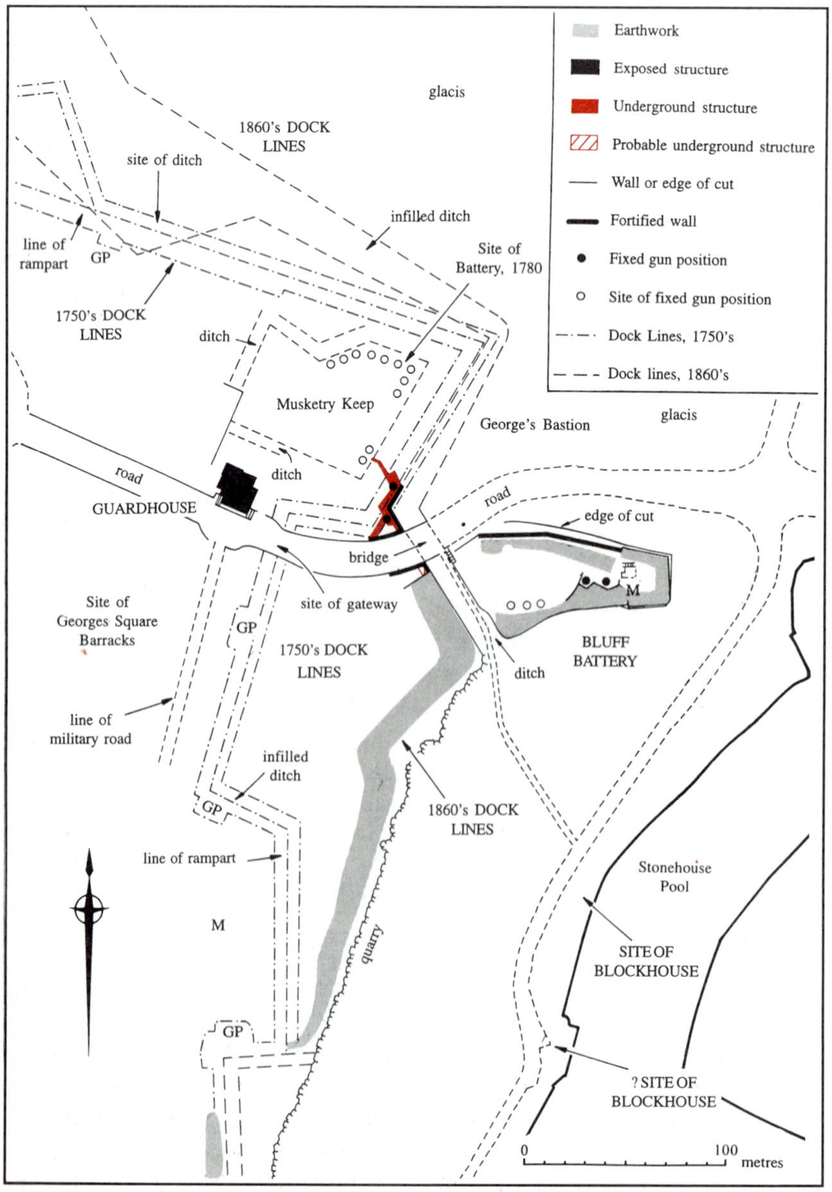

Fig. 77 George's Bastion, Bluff Battery & Stonehouse Pool blockhouses

was apparently rebuilt as a separate limestone battery for six 9-pdrs. In 1850 it contained a magazine but no armament, and was probably remodelled in 1860-68 to include gun positions along the S face to enfilade the front of the Lines along the top of the quarry to the S, and loopholes protecting the approach to the new gate. It was not armed in 1885, and was released by the MoD in 1975.

It is located on a limestone bluff overlooking Stonehouse Bridge. At the E end there is a battered limestone ashlar wall (of similar style to the early 19th century facing of the N section of the Lines) retaining an earthen rampart behind. On the N flank is a loop-holed wall covering the approach to the bridge and gateway built in 1860-68 at the top of the hill. An earthen embankment (traverse) along the rear protected those manning the loopholes from incoming fire from the S, and the gun crews to S from fire from the N. At the E there are two *en barbette* gun positions facing S.W, both retain small ammunition recesses and a sloping granite platform is visible in one. To the W is one certain and two possible further splayed embrasures cut through the earthen rampart, covering the front of the Lines to the S; these may have been added in 1860-65. At the E end foundations of a guardhouse/store room are exposed; the magazine depicted to the S in 1856-7 is not visible. No gun platforms or *terreplein* is visible at the E end overlooking the bridge, although presumably these would have been provided.

Present condition

The W part of the interior is occupied by a modern house; the remainder is a garden. Parts of the E emplacements and the foundations of the guardhouse have been recently exposed. Parts of the garden are heavily vegetated, and the fringes - the ramparts, traverse and loopholed wall - are overgrown. Overall the battery remains largely complete, and probably contains further below-ground remains of gun emplacements and the magazine.

Sources

General

5 - 7; O, Q.

Specific

1850	Armament table and plan. Officers' Mess, Royal Citadel
c.1850-3	Plan/section. PRO: WO 55/807
1855-6	Military edition of 1:500 O.S. map sheet No. 53. PRO: MPHH 629
1856-7	Military edition of O.S. 1:2500 map, Devon sheet CXXIII.11. WDRO
1864	Ist ed. OS 1:2500 sheet CXXIII.11

GEORGE'S BASTION BATTERY

PAR = STOKE DAMEREL, NGR = SX45875453, PRN = SX45SE-712/4, MAP 3 No. 144

A battery of six 9-pdr guns mounted *en barbette*, described as 'cavalier battery in Windmill Field', was erected in February 1780 and is depicted on the N face of George's Bastion. An earlier gun platform is shown at the apex of the bastion in 1765. The battery was subsequently incorporated into, or replaced by, gun platforms forming part of the musketry keep built in 1855-56 (No. 145).

Present condition

This area appears to have been levelled when the Lines were demolished after 1882; no remains of this battery have been identified during recent redevelopment.

Sources

General

6, 7.

Specific

1765	Map by Benjamin Donn.
1811	Mercer's plan of the Lines. PRO: MPH 233/1
1838	Plan of the Town of Devonport. WDRO: Acc 1469

GEORGE'S BASTION MUSKETRY KEEP

PAR = STOKE DAMEREL, NGR = SX45855445, PRN = SX45SE-712, MAP 3 No. 145

This formed one of the improvements to the Dock Lines carried out between 1853 & 1868. It was proposed in 1854 and completed by 1855-56, and was located within George's Bastion, on the site of an earlier battery (No. 144). It was sited to cover the area in front of the Lines to the N and the approach to the gate at the top of Devonport Hill. Nine guns were to be mounted on platforms at its N.E corner, and three on a platform at the S.E corner to cover the approach. All were sited at a higher level (i.e on a cavalier) and fired over the parapet of the surrounding Dock Lines. An earthen *banquette*, revetted in stone and fronted by a shallow ditch, provided local defence on the S & W sides should an enemy break through the Lines elsewhere; the main gate was sited in the centre of the S side. There is no evidence of any internal structures such as magazines; these would have had to be present, and were probably constructed under the higher N gun platforms. It is not clear whether the keep was actually armed; it was demolished in 1866-68 when a military hospital was built on the site, although the Lines themselves remained.

Recent investigations in advance of and during redevelopment have revealed the foundations of the keep wall surviving to varying heights on all sides, together with those of the main gateway. Most had been levelled to bedrock when the hospital was built, and several of these remnants have been removed as a result of redevelopment. However, substantial remains of the wall survive at the S.E corner, together with those of two gun platforms and an arched doorway down to the rampart of the Lines below; remnants of the N.W gun platform also survive, together with the whole of the (infilled) 1860s ditch belonging to the Lines; this contained *machicolations* in its scarp wall.

Present condition

The keep was levelled down to bedrock when the hospital was built in 1866-68. However substantial sections of wall and gun platform survive at the S.E corner where the ground slopes away; most of this has been retained during the recent redevelopment. More below-ground remains of the N.W gun platform probably survive immediately to the N.W of Damerel House, and the surrounding ditch of the Dock Lines is virtually complete, though infilled.

Sources

Specific

1854	Plan showing proposed reform of the Dock Lines. PRO: MR 1425
1856	Military edition of O.S. 1:2500 map, Devon sheet CXXIII.11. WDRO
1856-57	O.S. 1:500 map sheet CXXIII.12.3. PCM
1857	Military edition of O.S. 1:500 PRO: MPHH 629
1859	Plan of completed keep. PRO: WO 78/2569(2)
1861	Map and chart of Plymouth Sound & Hamoaze. PCM
1868	Plans of Devonport Female Hospital. PRO: MPH 628
1994	Pye, A et al. *Archaeological Assessment and Phase I Field Evaluation of Cumberland House, Devonport, Plymouth* Exeter Archaeology Report No. **94.75**
1995	Pye, A & Sage, A *Phase II Field Evaluation: Damerel House, and Excavation and Recording: Cumberland House, Devonport* Exeter Archaeology Report No. **95.19**
Forthcoming	Pye, A 'The Inner Defences of the Dockyard' in Ray, K (ed) *Archaeological Investigations and Research in Plymouth, Volume II: 1994-95* Plymouth Archaeology Occasional Publication No. **2**

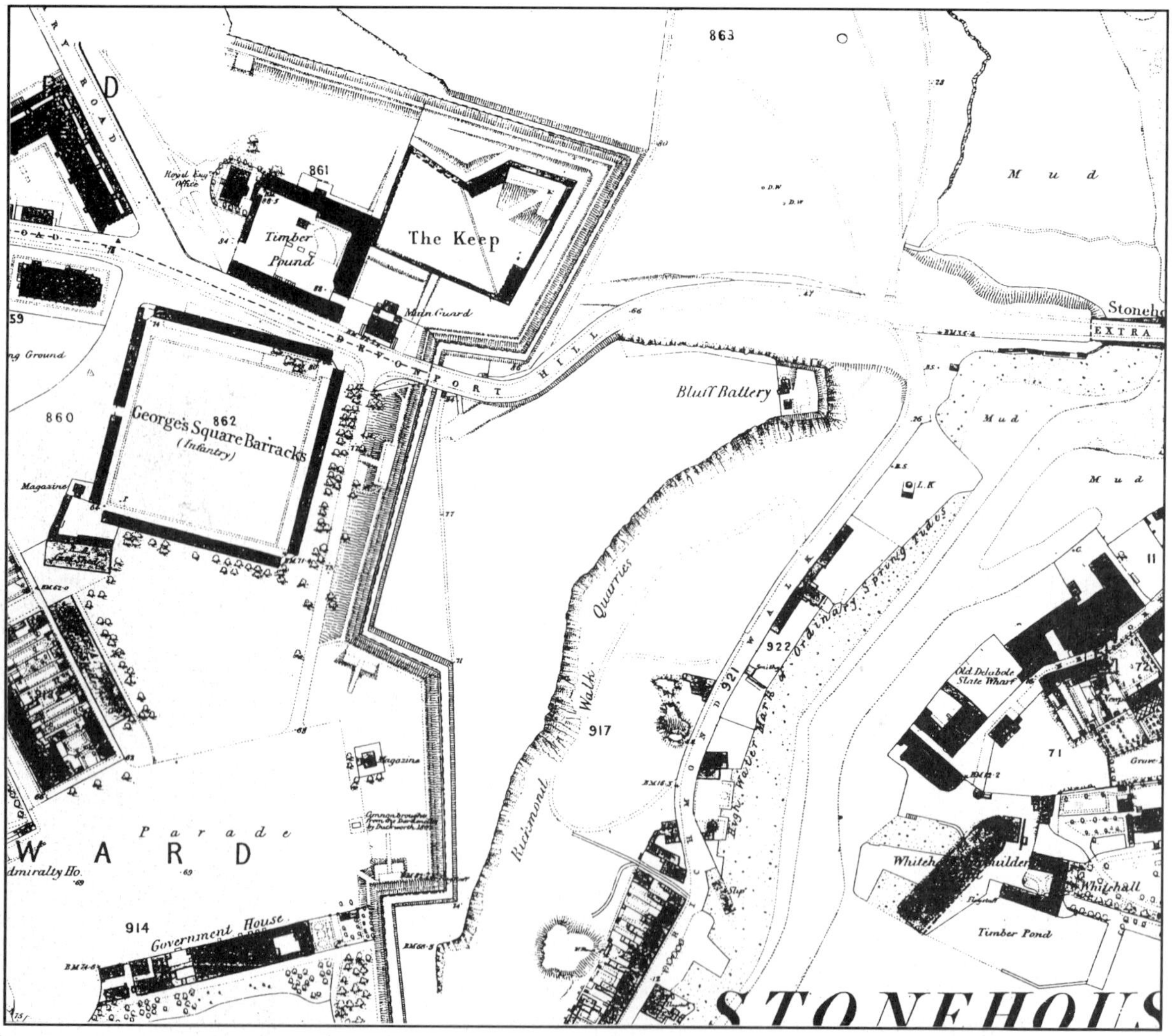

Fig. 78 George's Bastion & Keep in 1857 (WDRO: military edition of O.S. 1:2500 map)

MOUNT PLEASANT REDOUBT

PAR = STOKE DAMEREL, NGR = SX45925575, PRN = SX45NE-91, MAP 3 No. 146

This is a square earthwork redoubt located on a knoll sited on the watershed between two valleys going down to the Tamar and Stonehouse Creek, and commanding the easiest route of approach to the Dockyard. It was proposed in January 1780 by Dixon, and does not appear to have been completed or armed until after March that year. Earlier maps do not show a blockhouse on this hill; the structure which appears in some may be the 'Stoke Summerhouse'. A survey dated by Stuart to 1777-79 (but containing later additions) gives its armament as eight 3-pdrs, eight 12-pdrs in the blockhouse (somewhat unlikely, given the limited space), thirteen 18-pdrs on the two N faces, and swivel-stocked blunderbusses and musketry. In 1787 it was armed with eleven 18-pdrs mounted *en barbette* on its N & E faces, and in 1811-16 the *terreplein* appears to have been remodelled to contain eleven individual gun positions and was re-surfaced in stone. In 1855 the

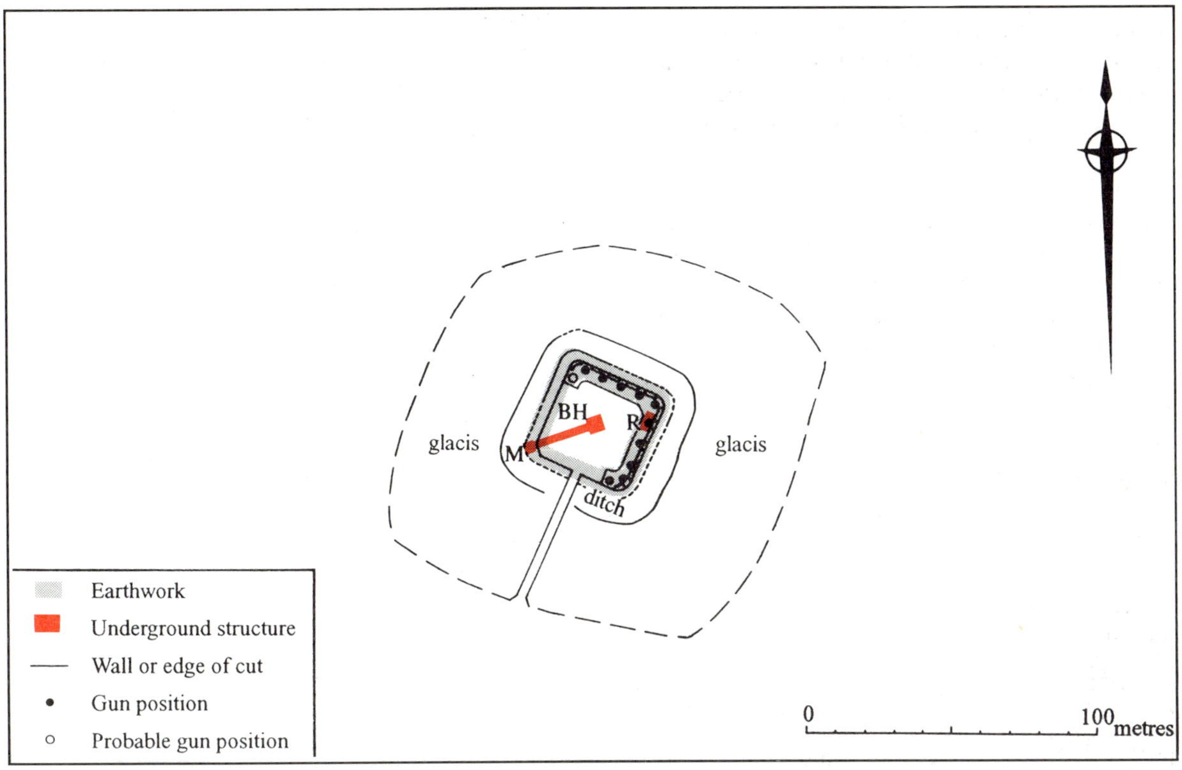

Fig. 79 Mount Pleasant Redoubt

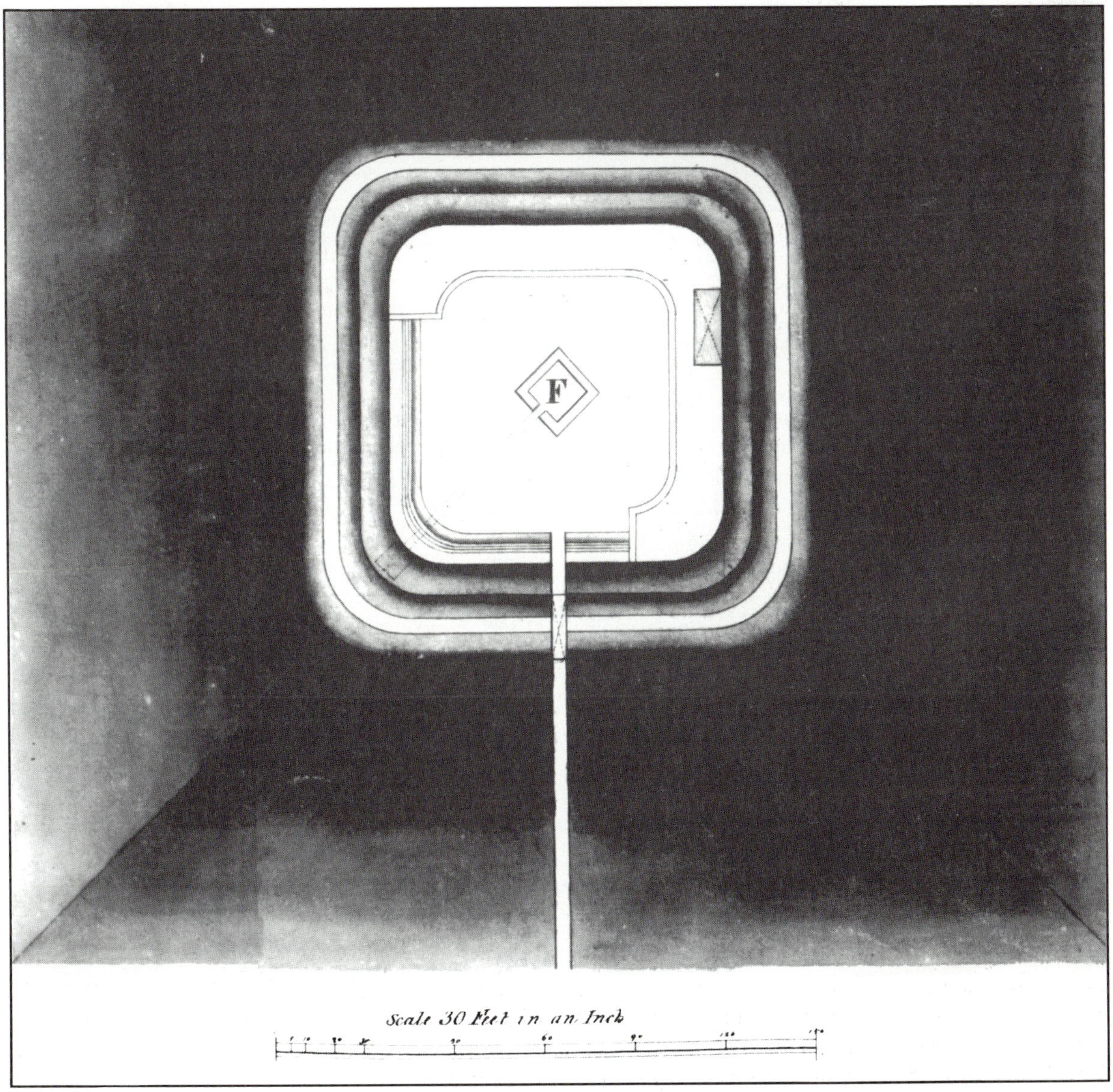

Fig. 80 Mount Pleasant Redoubt in 1794 (PRO: MR 725)

central blockhouse was burnt down and in 1860 the Royal Commission recommended that the redoubt be used as a supporting post for an outer line of works extending from St. Budeaux and Cattedown, and that it be armed with ten guns and be provided with barracks for 100 men. However, after the line was moved further out from the Dockyard the redoubt became redundant, although by 1885 two 64-pdr RMLs had been approved (but not mounted). At the beginning of WWII at least one AA gun was present, and a barrage balloon was anchored on the remains of the blockhouse.

A plan of 1784 shows a gun platform along the N & E faces of the redoubt and a *banquette* along the others. It is surrounded on all sides by a levelled *glacis*, on which there were further barriers such as thorn entanglements and ditches containing sharpened stakes at the bottom. In the centre is a two-storey fortified blockhouse with magazine under, connected via an underground passage to a magazine in the S.W corner. There was a reservoir under the E platform.

Plate 112 Mount Pleasant Redoubt, gun platform (Exeter Archaeology)

The redoubt contains a sloping granite and limestone gun platform, with originally eleven separate gun positions defined by a brick parapet, embrasures and guttering at the front; on the rear sides a 1950s platform has replaced the original *banquette*. The surrounding ditch as a brick scarp and a stone counterscarp, and in 1784 was fraised; it has been partly infilled and the original drawbridge replaced. The planes and full extent of the surrounding *glacis* is clearly visible.

Present condition

The structure has been recently conserved and is in good condition. The ditch remains partly infilled. There are no visible remains of the blockhouse, passage or magazine, although the latter has been reportedly entered in the recent past, and probably survives complete. The *glacis* still survives largely complete and is a public park.

Sources
General
4 - 8, 12, 17; M, O, Q.
Specific
1784 Plans and sections. PRO: MR 725
1787 Report on armament. PRO: Supp. 5/46
1793-1816 Series of letters. PRO: WO 55/133, 798; WDRO: Acc 112, 152
1811 Plan. PRO: MPH 233/4
1855-6 Military edition of O.S. 1:500 maps. PRO: MPHH 629
1856 1st ed. O.S. 1:500 town map sheet No. 16. PCM
1992 Pye, A *An Archaeological Survey of Mount Pleasant Redoubt, Plymouth* Exeter Archaeology Report No. **92.12**
1992 Pye, A 'An archaeological survey of Mount Pleasant Redoubt, Plymouth' *Proc. Devon Arch. Soc.* **50**, 137-161

STONEHOUSE REDOUBT A

PAR = E. STONEHOUSE, NGR = SX46755430, PRN = SX45SE-466, MAP 3 No. 147

This is one of two redoubts recommended by Dixon in January 1780 sited to cover the approach to the Dock Lines from Plymouth and any possible landings in Millbay. It was sited at the E end of the hill, whilst the other was sited towards the W., and was probably completed by the end of 1784, when it was depicted on one of Gardner's maps of that date. A 1808 plan (*Fig. 7*) shows the redoubt as square with projecting bastions at each corner and surrounded by a ditch. It is shown on most 19th-century maps up until the 1850s and is mentioned in the 1860 Royal Commission report as being of little military use and obstructed by housing. The site is illustrated as quarries in 1861, and now survives as the street name Battery Road.

Present condition

Demolished, although it is not currently clear whether the whole site has been quarried away. The area is now built up.

Sources
General
5, 6, 8, 12; O, Q.
Specific
1808 Plan. PRO: MR 1201 & 1202
1809 Plan of Stonehouse Hill. PRO: MR 1180
1811 ?Plan. PRO: MPH 233
1857 Military edition of 1:500 O.S. map. PRO: MPHH 629
1861 Chart of Plymouth Sound and Hamoaze. PCM
1864 1st ed O.S. 1:2500 map sheet Devon CXXIII.11. WDRO

STONEHOUSE REDOUBT B (PROPOSED)

PAR = E. STONEHOUSE, NGR = SX46455425, MAP 3 No. 148

This is the western of two redoubts recommended by Dixon in January 1780 to defend the approach to the Lines. The proposed site lies just N.E of the junction of Market St. & Emma Place; there is no evidence that it was ever built; it does not appear on any other sources.

Source
General
5

3.3.3 The North-East Defences

These were built on the recommendation of the Royal Commission of 1860 to protect the dockyard and other military establishments around the city from bombardment and attack. Initially the proposed line was sited closer in to the city, extending from St Budeaux to the Cattewater, but in July 1861 a different line sited further away from the city was adopted, largely to reduce the cost of land purchase. It was designed by Capt. du Cane, and consists of a line of mutually defensible batteries and forts extending from Ernesettle above the Tamar in the W to Efford above Marsh Mills in the E. Each work (except three open batteries - Deer Park, Efford and Laira Emplacements) was defended by a ditch and *caponiers* and musketry galleries, and each covered the front of its neighbour as well as the ground and *glacis* to the front. They are sited along ridges to the S of tributary valleys of the Tamar and Plym, commanding the valleys in front and the slopes opposite, and in places are linked with dry ditches covered by galleries and *caponiers*. As with the Staddon Heights Defences, clearance rights in the event of war extended over a much wider area to the N. All the works are linked by a military road to their rear, protected along much of its length from incoming fire by an earthen 'parapet' or embankment; this usually had a sloping top and *banquette*, allowing infantry to fire over it at an advancing enemy. The key to the system was a large detached fort (Crownhill) set slightly forward of the main line, which commanded the watershed between the two valleys and the main route N to Tavistock. The line was also supported by a fortified keep at Eggbuckland; three other proposed keeps (at St Budeaux, Widey, and Efford) were not in the event built. Most of the works were only armed to any extent between 1885 and 1893, and were disarmed shortly after; in 1911 and during WWI & WWII they formed the general line of defence to the N.E of Plymouth, and foxholes and light machine-gun emplacements from this period remain on the ramparts. Each of the forts and batteries are described separately below. Most of the military road survives as modern roads and streets (as Crownhill Road from St. Budeaux to Crownhill, Fort Austin Avenue from Crownhill to Fort Austin, and as 'Military Road' from Fort Austin to Laira Battery), and substantial sections of embankment survive (to a maximum height of *c.*10m and width of at least 10m) adjoining Ernesettle Battery, near St. Budeaux Church, to the W of Woodland Fort, to the S of Fort Austin, and around Deer Park Emplacement and the Efford Position.

Present condition

Although there has been much development in this area which has obscured the layout of the defences, cluttered many of the *glacis* slopes and removed sections of road and embankment, the structure of the defence system remains largely intact. The *glacis* slopes of Ernesettle Battery, Woodland Fort, Bowden Battery and Efford Fort survive intact, although overgrown in some cases, as do large sections of military road and embankment, especially adjoining Ernesettle Battery and between Fort Austin and Laira Battery. The Efford Position (Efford Fort & Emplacement, Laira Battery & Emplacement) survives particularly well as it has remained relatively undeveloped; it retains the original network of military roads and embankments, as well as the structure and gun positions of the fortifications themselves, although much of the interiors have suffered damage and relative neglect.

Sources

General

12 - 15, 19, 22.

Specific

1861	Plymouth defences plans, incl. some of N.E defences. PRO: MR629
1862	Plymouth defences plans, incl. some of N.E defences. PRO: MR1849
*c.*1870?	Coloured military 6-inch map, showing forts and clearance area. WDRO
1878	O.S. survey of N.E Defences. PRO: WO 78/566
1933	O.S 1:2500 & 6-inch maps, various sheets. PLSL

ERNESETTLE BATTERY

PAR = ST BUDEAUX, NGR = SX44805930, PRN = SX45NW-512, MAP 1 No. 149

This is sited on a spur between two small tributary valleys and forms the westernmost position of the defences. It was designed by Capt. du Cane, and after the approval of the plans in January 1862 construction began in 1863 and was completed shortly after 1868. It was intended for 15 guns in open battery and six mortars under bombproof arches (i.e. casemates) on the W flank. There were three expense magazines under traverses, a casemated barrack for 60 men, and an ample but not very well protected magazine whose alteration was recommended in 1869; the battery was protected by a 30-foot deep rock-cut ditch flanked by musketry galleries, and had a 30-foot high gorge wall. An armament of eight 7-inch RBL guns and two 8-inch RML howitzers was recommended in 1875, and by 1885 two of the RBLs had been mounted (on naval slides) on the E flank. In 1885 an armament of two 5-inch BL and three 64-pdr RML guns (blocked up) was recommended for the W salient and W face; these were mounted by 1893 and the 7-inch RBLs withdrawn. It was disarmed shortly after, and in 1911 (and presumably in WWI & WWII) formed part of the 'General Line of Defence' around Plymouth. During WWII it was possibly used as an anti-aircraft observation post/fire-watching post; subsequently it was used as Royal Navy Stores.

It is an irregular five-sided polygonal work, with deep ditches on the W., N., N.E., & S.E flanks protected by musketry galleries; an open gallery in the south salient protects the W part of the gorge, which is in two sections. The main entrance (*Plate 114*) is of

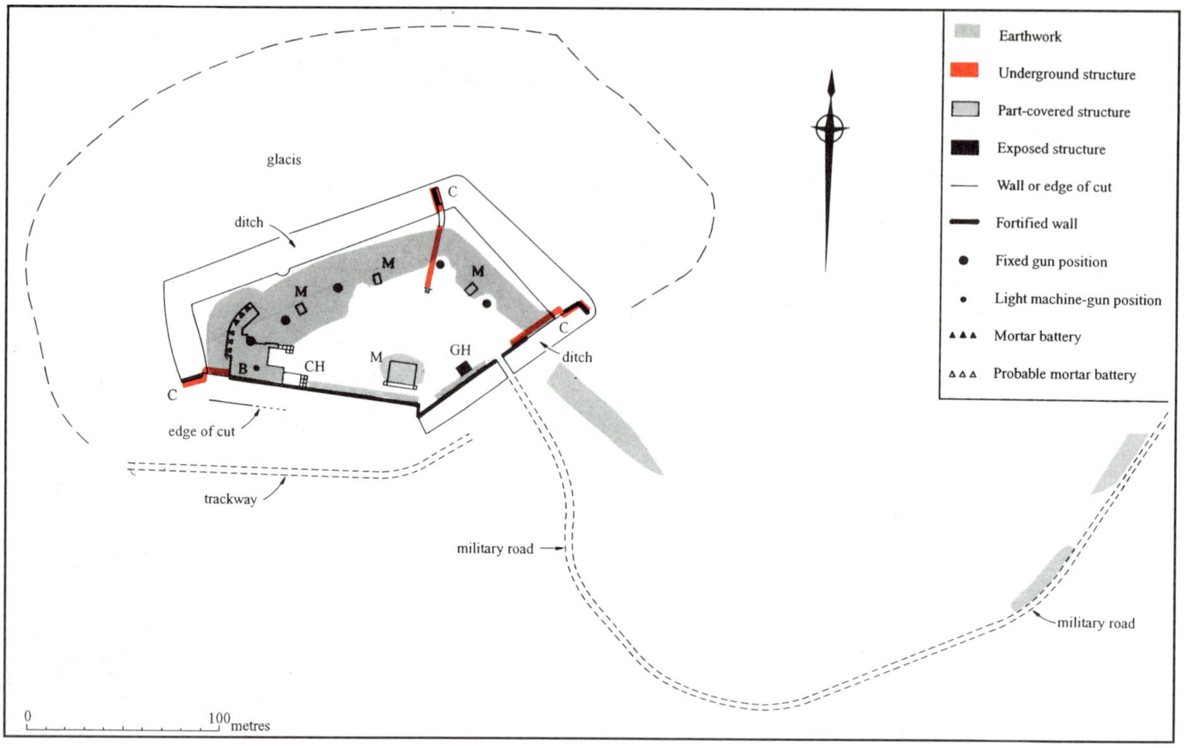

Fig. 81 Ernesettle Battery

monumental ashlar work with a 1866 datestone above the arch and is sited in the centre of the E part of the gorge; all the gorge is protected by a loop-holed wall. An extensive *glacis* survives to the N, and a section of military road and embankment lie to the rear. Concrete positions for the five guns mounted 1885-93 are visible on the N & N.W ramparts, separated by three bombproof expense magazines; the main magazine, unusually for this period, is sited under a separate earthen traverse towards the rear of the parade, suggesting that the modernisation recommended in 1869 was not carried out. The casemated barrack block lies under the S.E corner of the *terreplein*, with a casemated mortar battery of three bays in front of it facing N.W; another three bays were partially constructed immediately to the S but have been subsequently infilled. Later 19th-century buildings include an artillery store sited just inside the main gate, and a cookhouse & armoury attached to the E end of the barracks. Remains dating to WWII consist of a Lewis/Bren gun-pit on top of the barracks and two steel ?fire-watching posts. Latterly the parade was occupied by Nissen huts, which have been demolished.

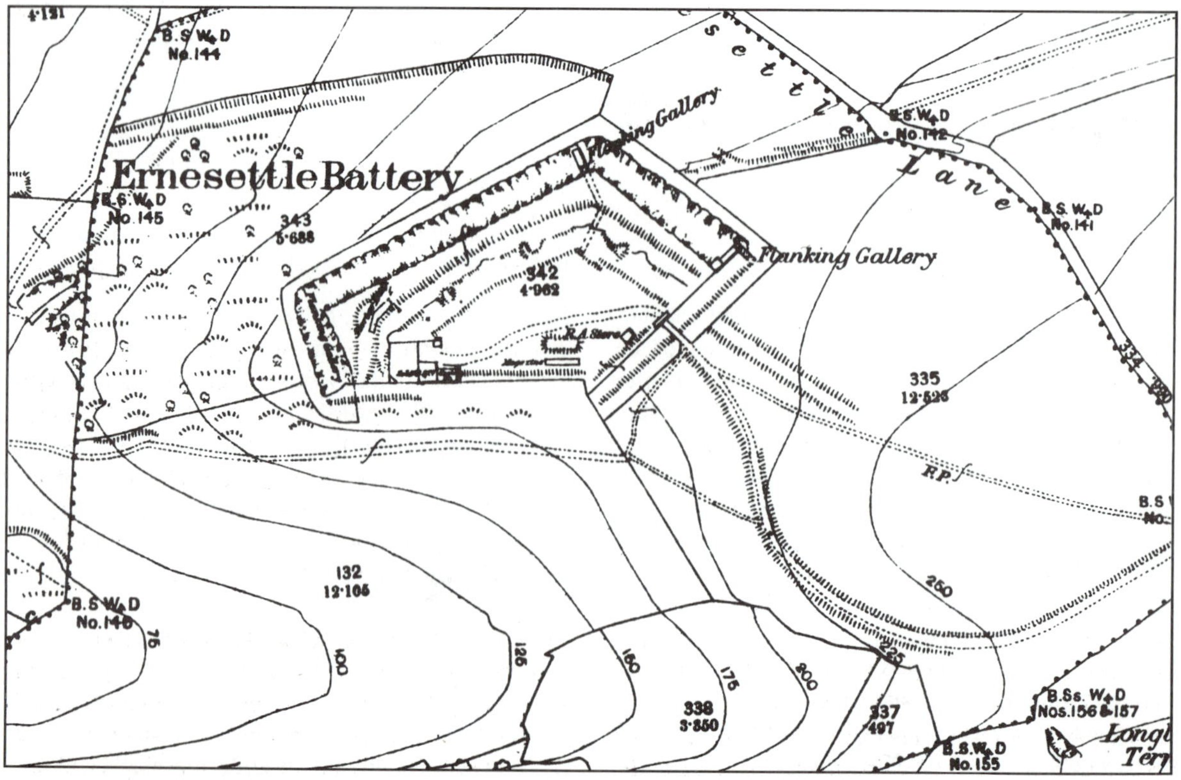

Fig. 82 Ernesettle Battery in 1896 (PRO: WO 78/2314)

Plate 113 Ernesettle Battery & glacis (Photograph: F.M. Griffith, Devon County Council. Frame DAP/UU15. Copyright Devon County Council)

Plate 114 Ernesettle Battery, main gate (Exeter Archaeology)

Present condition

The battery is currently empty and unused; all the structures are either blocked up or locked. The external structural condition is very good, with the exception of the cookhouse, which is roofless and in a ruinous state; no interiors were accessible. The ditch and the front of the ramparts are overgrown, as are the musketry galleries. Some of the gun positions have been partially removed by terracing for the Nissen huts.

Sources
General
12 - 15, 17, 19, 22; O, Q.
Specific
1972 Plan. PSA

AGATON FORT

PAR = ST BUDEAUX, NGR = SX 45505950, PRN = SX45SE-71, MAP 1 No. 150

This is a small fort located on a knoll slightly forward of and commanding the *glacis* slopes of Ernesettle and Knowle Batteries; it is connected to both by a military road defended by an embankment. It was designed by Capt. du Cane, with the plans being approved in January 1862. Construction began in 1863 and was completed shortly after 1869. It was intended for 20 guns in open battery and one in a Haxo casemate with six mortars in two nests on the exterior of the rampart, and was to be defended by a deep ditch flanked by guns and musketry. It was unarmed in 1875, when fifteen 7-inch RBLs, five 8-inch rifled howitzers and ten SB flank guns were recommended; by 1885 three 7-inch RBLs had been mounted (two on naval slides and the other in the Haxo casemate) and five 64-pdr RMLs and four 32-pdr SBBL guns were recommended. The five RMLs were mounted by 1893 but the 32-pdrs still remained to be added. It was disarmed shortly afterwards, although it formed part of the 'General Line of Defence' in 1911 and presumably during WWI & WWII. During WWII it was the main Royal Army Service Corps Depot supplying the S. W and was released by the MoD in 1958.

It is a five-sided polygonal work, with a deep rock-cut ditch on all sides except the gorge; this was protected by musketry loops in its parapet and casemates, and enfiladed by gunfire from the S.E *caponier*. The remaining flanks were protected by one single and one double *caponier*, and a counterscarp gallery, all

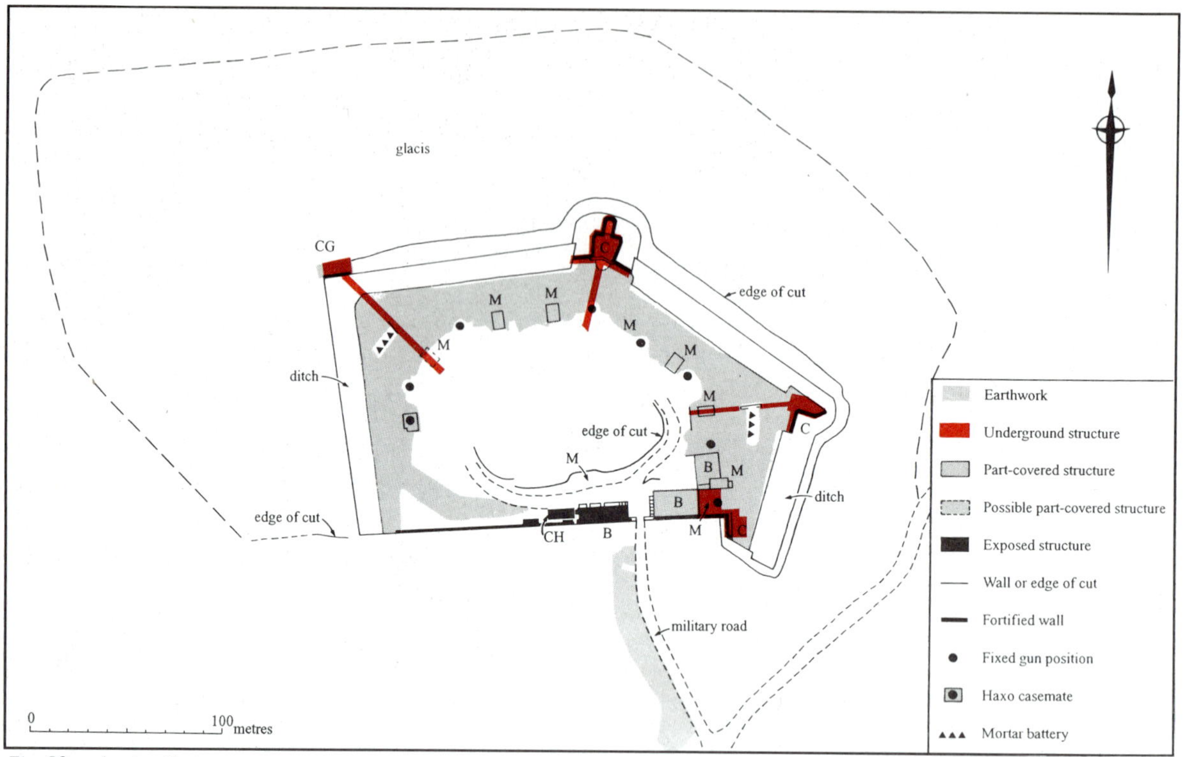

Fig. 83 Agaton Fort

bombproof and designed to contain guns and musketry. The *caponiers* are protected by drop ditches. On the inside, the recently-widened gateway is flanked by an officers' quarters building (displaying fine architectural detail), cookhouse and store to the W and by bombproof casemated barrack accommodation to the E. The main magazine is located under the S.E corner of the rampart, with another separate one (now demolished) located opposite the officers' quarters. On the rampart are seven concrete gun emplacements dating to 1885-93 and one earlier stone Haxo casemate on the W flank; there were seven expense magazines dating to the 1860s, of which five now survive. There are well-preserved remains of later foxholes at the E, N.E and N.W salients. The two 1860s mortar nests remain intact at the E and N.W salients; access to these, the N.W and E *caponiers* and the counterscarp gallery was via (blocked) tunnels from the parade ground. This is at the same level as the gun platforms, with the rear of the Haxo being protected by a traverse (now demolished), and the barracks and officers' quarters by a scarp. The interior was formerly occupied by Nissen huts and buildings (now demolished) and from the 1970s by the present HGV Testing Station; all the parade has been tarmaced except for a ?1930s or 1950s detached house in the S.W corner and contemporary garages/stores on the S side.

The fort is approached from the S by a military road, defended by loop-holes sited to each side of the gate and by embankments. The embankment to the E of the road has been levelled and its site is occupied by the

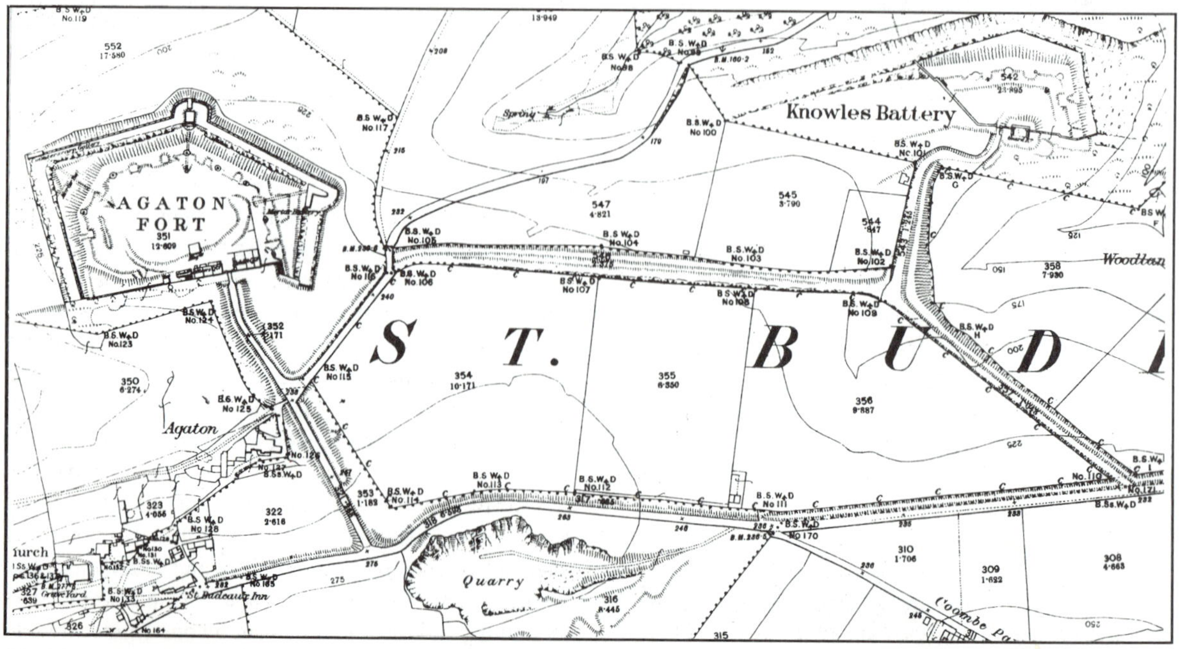

Fig. 84 Agaton Fort, Knowle Battery, military roads & embankments in 1896 (PRO: WO 78/2314)

Plate 115 Agaton Fort (Photograph: F.M. Griffith, Devon County Council. Frame DAP/UY9. Copyright Devon County Council)

recently extended Agaton Social Club and car park; the area to the W is occupied by a new housing estate, although the embankment still survives. A large area of *glacis* remains as a public open space to the N.W, together with fragments in the grounds of Ernesettle Primary School to the N.E; the remainder is occupied by housing estates.

Plate 116 Agaton Fort, musketry gallery (Exeter Archaeology)

Plate 117 Agaton Fort, stairwell (Exeter Archaeology)

Present condition

The parade ground and *terreplein* is used by the Dept. of Transport as a HGV Testing Station. The stairwells to the tunnels leading to the mortar batteries and *caponier* have been infilled, and the rear of the N.E rampart and two expense magazines have been removed. The rest of the magazines are blocked up; the gun positions however are open and in reasonable condition. The officers' quarters, cookhouse, store, and counterscarp gallery and double and E *caponiers* are all blocked up and presumably empty, as is the S.E *caponier* and main magazine. Most of the barrack casemates are used for storage, and the house and compound are occupied. The ramparts, mortar batteries and ditch are overgrown; the ditch remains open though some intermittent small-scale dumping is occurring. Most of the structures appear sound, although the store is ruinous and in need of repair and re-roofing; the cookhouse, officers' quarters, E and double *caponiers* and counterscarp gallery were not accessible and therefore their internal condition was not assessed, though the double *caponier* has largely lost its floor. The floors and other internal detail of the S.E *caponier* survive intact, together with the flanking musketry gallery and the main magazine.

Sources
General
12 - 15, 17, 19, 22; O, Q

KNOWLE BATTERY

PAR = ST BUDEAUX, NGR = SX46305960, PRN = SX45NE-72, MAP 1 No. 151

This is sited between Agaton and Woodland Forts on a spur overlooking a valley to the N. Its right flank enfilades the front of Woodland Fort, whilst it is protected to the north by a ditch and its *glacis* is swept by fire from Agaton and Woodland; there are no *caponiers* or musketry galleries.

The design (by Capt. du Cane) was approved in January 1862 & construction began in 1863 and was completed soon after 1869. It was designed for 13 guns in open battery and one in a Haxo casemate on the right flank, with 3 expense magazines in traverses and a reserve magazine in the guardhouse. In 1869 the 30-foot high gorge wall was flanked by a cannon and five loop-holes in each side of the two-storey guardhouse, which was protected by parapets on its roof. In 1875 an armament of nine 7-inch RBLs & three SB flank guns was proposed. In 1885 it was armed with one 7-inch RBL gun in the Haxo casemate and contained three others unmounted; by 1893 it mounted two 7-inch RBLs and three 64-pdr RMLs, and was disarmed soon after. The 1896 map shows one Haxo and one probable 7-inch RBL position on the E face and three probable 64-pdr RML positions and two expense magazines on the N face & N.E salient. It was used in WWII by the RAF as a base for the barrage balloon system in Plymouth. The date it was released by the MoD is not known.

The battery was protected by a rock-cut ditch to the N; part of the scarp survives at the front of the battery and to the rear of garages *c.* 80m to the W. The land to the E & N was extensively landscaped to form a *glacis*; there was no ditch along the gorge.

The interior of the battery has been much altered due to the construction of Knowle Primary School. All the gun positions and magazines on the ramparts have been demolished or covered over, except for one 64-pdr RML position at the N.E salient which has been retained as a decorative feature and embellished with a new stone parapet and concrete surround. The two-storey guardhouse survives intact, although its ground floor (not accessible) has been converted to changing-rooms and its roof to an (empty) swimming-pool. Its architectural character suggests it may have been originally intended as the gateway, but this was in the event sited to the W. On each side it has a single gun embrasure on the middle floor enfilading the gorge; they may originally have been supplemented by musketry loops or embrasures below, which have since been replaced by mullioned windows. In the centre is a

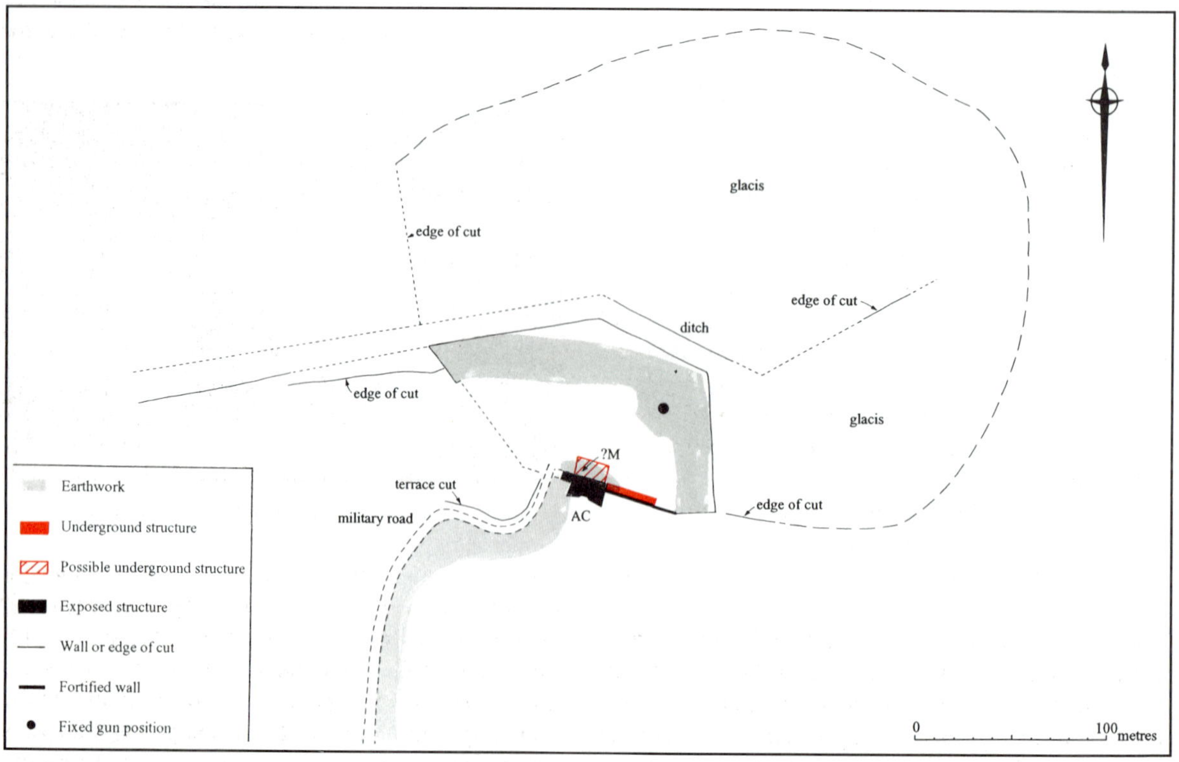

Fig. 85 Knowle Battery

Plate 118 Knowle Battery, guardhouse (Exeter Archaeology)

small magazine; this and the gun casemates are served by an access corridor to the rear, with (blocked) stairways (with rails intact) to the ground floor and roof. To the rear there is an ammunition lift, probably serving an underground magazine under the earthen mound to the rear, as at Bowden Battery. Both levels are well-lit by windows to the S and there are two ?later doorways at ground level. The roof was fortified with a parapet with a firing-step behind. The loop-holed gorge wall contains a musketry gallery and survives to its full height to the E; to the W it and the gateway have both been demolished. Part of the *glacis* to the N & E has been built up and truncated by Ringmore Way and Budshead Road; however, a large area remains as woodland although it has been cut off from the battery by Ringmore Way.

Present condition

The interior is occupied by the Knowle Primary School buildings, and the area to the S.W by landscaped playing fields. The rear of the rampart has been truncated, except for the N.E corner and at the W; the front of the rampart is wooded, and the ditch to the N infilled and its counterscarp removed or lowered by the construction of Ringmore Way and associated development. The military road embankment, guardhouse and gorge wall are all intact and structurally complete, though the guardhouse is now (1993) empty and is suffering from damp. Much of the floor is rotten and unsafe; the middle level is empty or is used for the storage of unwanted school furniture; the lower level is disused and is blocked up against vandals.

Sources
General
13 - 15, 17, 19; O, Q.

WOODLAND FORT

PAR = ST BUDEAUX, NGR = SX47105930, PRN = SX45NE-73, MAP 1 No. 152

This is sited on the S side of the valley between Knowle Battery and Crownhill Fort; it was intended to cover the front of the former and the S.W flank of the latter. The design (by Capt. du Cane) was approved in April 1863 & construction began shortly after; it was completed soon after 1869.

It was designed for 18 guns (two in Haxo casemates on the flanks), with a defensible guardhouse and casemated barracks for 100 men and additional accommodation in the *caponier* and 'double' or 'two-way' counterscarp gallery protecting the ditch, and with ample room for powder and shell in three expense magazines in traverses and in the main magazine. In 1875 the proposed armament was twelve 7-inch RBLs & six SB flank guns. By 1885 a single 7-inch RBL gun had been mounted on the N.W face, although a further seven of these lay dismounted within the fort. By 1893 two 7-inch RBLs were mounted in the Haxo casemates on the E & N.W faces and three 64-pdr RMLs elsewhere, with a further two 7-inch RBLs and four 32-pdr SBBL guns for the *caponier* and counterscarp gallery to come. It was disarmed shortly after, and, after accommodating various units during WWI, was sold by the MoD in 1920. It was occupied by various units again during WWII.

The fort was protected by rock-cut ditches on all sides, which were in turn intended to be enfiladed by 32-pdr guns and musketry in each side of the guardhouse and in a *caponier* and counterscarp gallery at the N.W & N.E salients. The counterscarp gallery has two faces, and commands the N & E sections of ditch. All these structures are bomb-proof and survive structurally intact although they have been blocked up and are inaccessible; the ditch is open except at the S.W & S.E corners and along the gorge, where it is infilled and partly overlain by Crownhill Road. Loop-holes and musketry galleries in the gorge wall enfilade the guardhouse and protect the rear; further protection may have been provided by an embankment along the military road.

Plate 119 Woodland Fort, guardhouse (Exeter Archaeology)

The two-storey guardhouse has fine Norman-style archways to front and rear, with 16th-century style drip courses over the rear windows, and retains the drawbridge pulley and chain. The two-storey barrack block consists of four pairs of vaulted casemates with a matching limestone ashlar frontage, a first-floor balcony similar to that at Crownhill Fort, and a parapet at roof level. Blocked tunnels at each end (ground

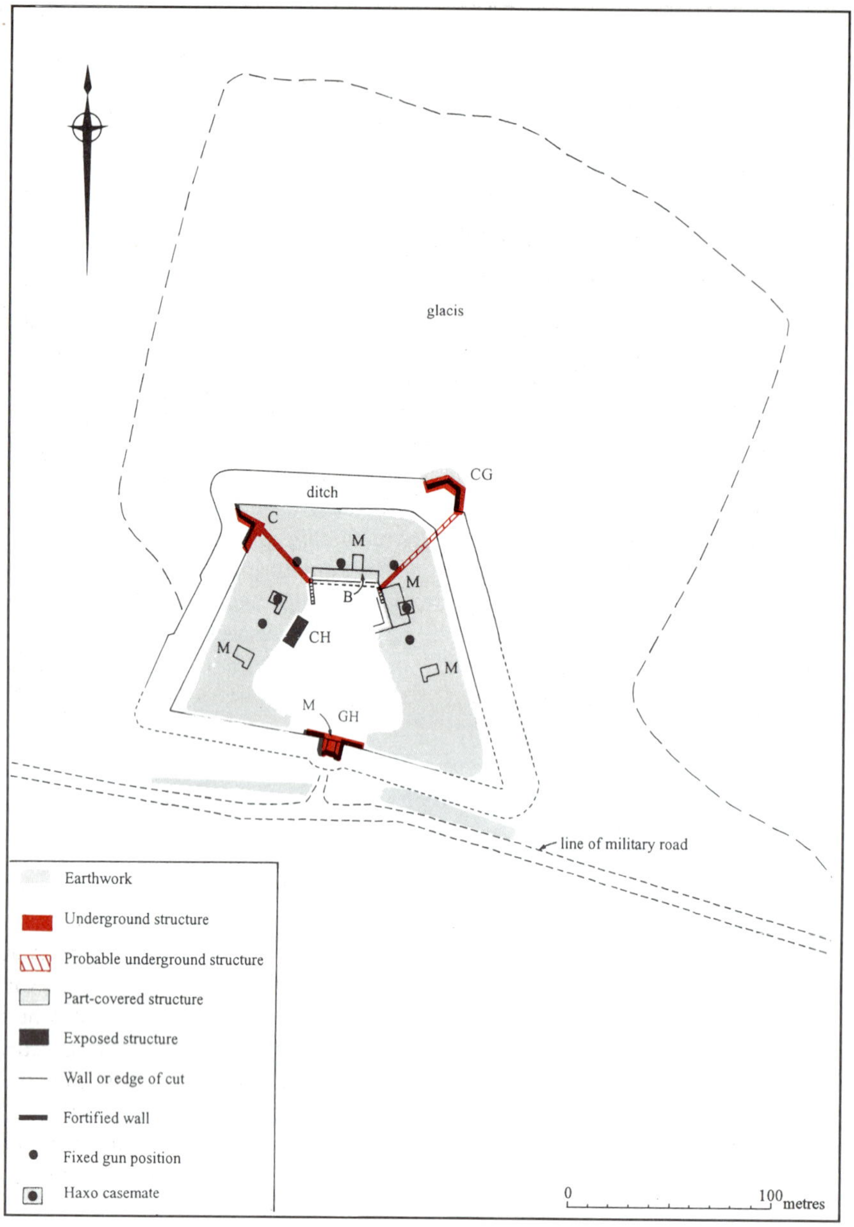

Fig. 86 Woodland Fort

floor) gave access to the *caponier* and counterscarp gallery. The main magazine adjoins the barracks to the E, and consists of three vaults (?stores) opening onto the parade with a larger magazine vault and lamp-passage behind; no original internal features such as lamp window shutters are visible. The cookhouse, complete with its original verandah, ornate iron stove-vent shutters and slated roof, lies within the builder's yard on the W of the parade.

Plate 120 Woodland Fort, barracks (Exeter Archaeology)

Remains on the rampart consist of two complete 1860s Haxos, three 1860s expense magazines, two concrete 1880s 64-pdr RML positions at the N.E & N.W salients and three concrete 1880s ?7-inch RBL positions in the centre of each flank. Few internal features are visible, except for an ornate vent grille in the east barrack casemate and the stove-vent shutters in the cookhouse, light brackets in the Haxos, and some of the door and window frames in the barracks, magazine, guardhouse and *caponier*; the first two have been converted and adapted whilst the expense magazines have been vandalised; further features may survive in the counterscarp gallery. Later remains include several well-preserved foxholes (with corrugated-iron revetments) on the N & W faces and a concrete hut base adjoining the entrance.

On the outside the extensive landscaped *glacis* survives complete, except to the E where it has been affected by the construction of Whitleigh Way and a cricket field. The military road lies on the line of the modern Crownhill Road, although segments of its protective embankment survive in the central reservation.

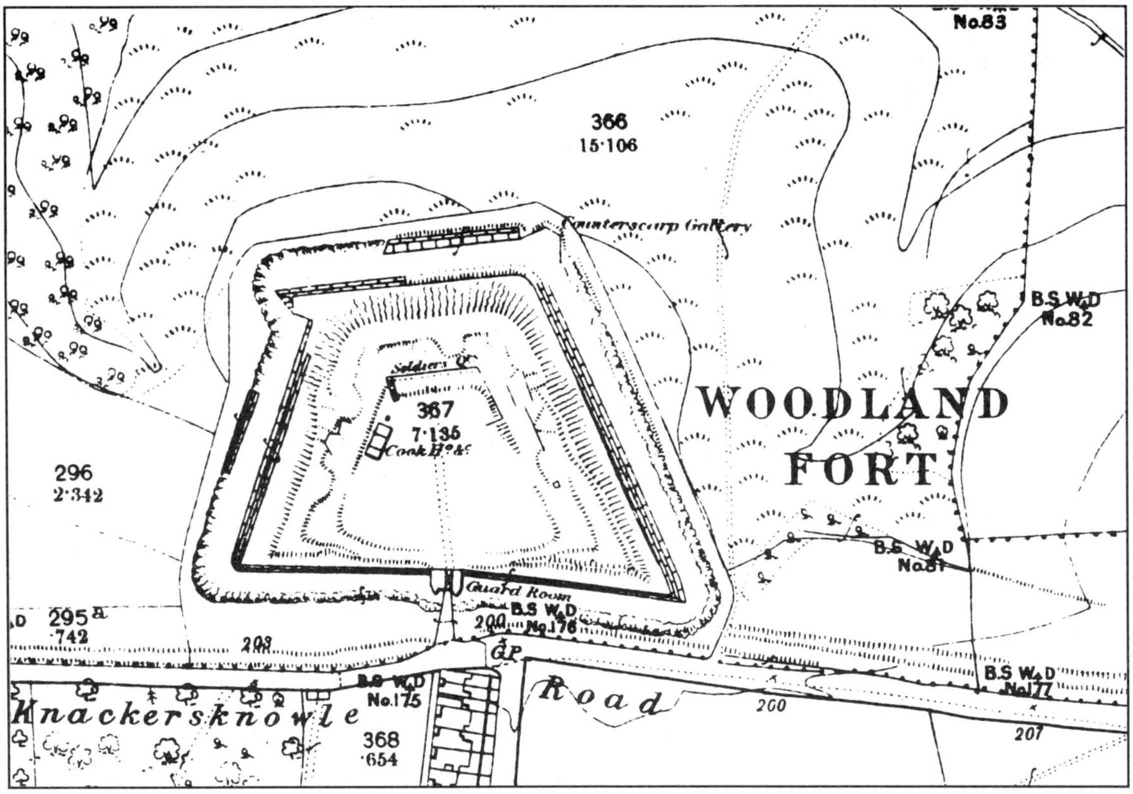

Fig. 87 Woodland Fort in 1896 (PRO: WO 78/2314)

Present condition

The fort is currently owned by Devon C.C and used as a sub-library and community centre; the *caponier* was formerly a youth club and the W part of the parade is occupied by a derelict builder's yard & the empty cookhouse. The ramparts are heavily overgrown, with the undergrowth obscuring some of the gun positions and probably further WWII foxholes; the expense magazines are derelict and have been vandalised. The guardhouse, *caponier* and gallery are blocked up and empty. Most structures remain sound although the cookhouse is in need of repair and re-roofing; the floor of the *caponier* survives, although those of the guardhouse have largely gone. The ground floor of the *caponier* is waterlogged whilst the lower floor of the guardhouse is also very damp and partly filled with rubble. The frontage of the barrack block is obscured by various modern concrete-block accretions and many of the original fittings have either been covered over or removed. The gorge wall has been buried at the E end and a modern access has been cut through it to the W of the guardhouse; the embankment in the central reservation is still visible although it has probably been altered and truncated by the widening of Crownhill Road. The ditch has been infilled along the gorge, and along the E face.

Sources

General

13 - 15, 17, 19; O, Q.

CROWNHILL FORT

PAR = EGGBUCKLAND & TAMERTON FOLIOT,
NGR = SX48705920, PRN = SX45NE-56, MAP 1 No. 153

Designed by Capt. du Cane, this formed the principal fort of the N.E defences. It was located on the watershed between tributary valleys flowing E & W to the Rivers Plym and Tamar, commanding the main route into Plymouth from the north. It also lies on the probable site of an earlier defensive enclosure, reflected in the occurrence of 'castle' in the field names in 1840. The fort was connected to Woodland Fort and Bowden Battery by a military road protected by embankments.

After approval of the design in April 1863, construction began shortly after and was completed in 1872. It was originally designed for 32 guns (4 in Haxo casemates) and 6 mortars, with casemated barracks for 300 men and provision for magazines and artillery and side-arms stores. In 1875 the proposed armament was twenty-three 7-inch RBLs, six 8-inch RML howitzers & fifteen SB flank guns. By 1885 it had been armed with thirteen 7-inch RBLs, at least two of which were in Haxos and a further two on counterweight (Moncrieff) mountings, and, unusually for the land defences, fourteen 32-pdr SBBL guns had actually been mounted in the *caponiers*, reflecting the strategic importance of this fort. A further twelve guns lay unmounted within the fort. In 1893 the fort mounted eleven 7-inch RBLs, five 64-pdr RMLs, six 25-pdr RMLs & the fourteen 32-pdr SBBL guns; it also housed two moveable 64-pdr RML guns (for drill) and probably the moveable armament of eighteen 5-inch BL & 8-inch RML howitzers assigned to the Ernesettle - Crownhill section of the defences.

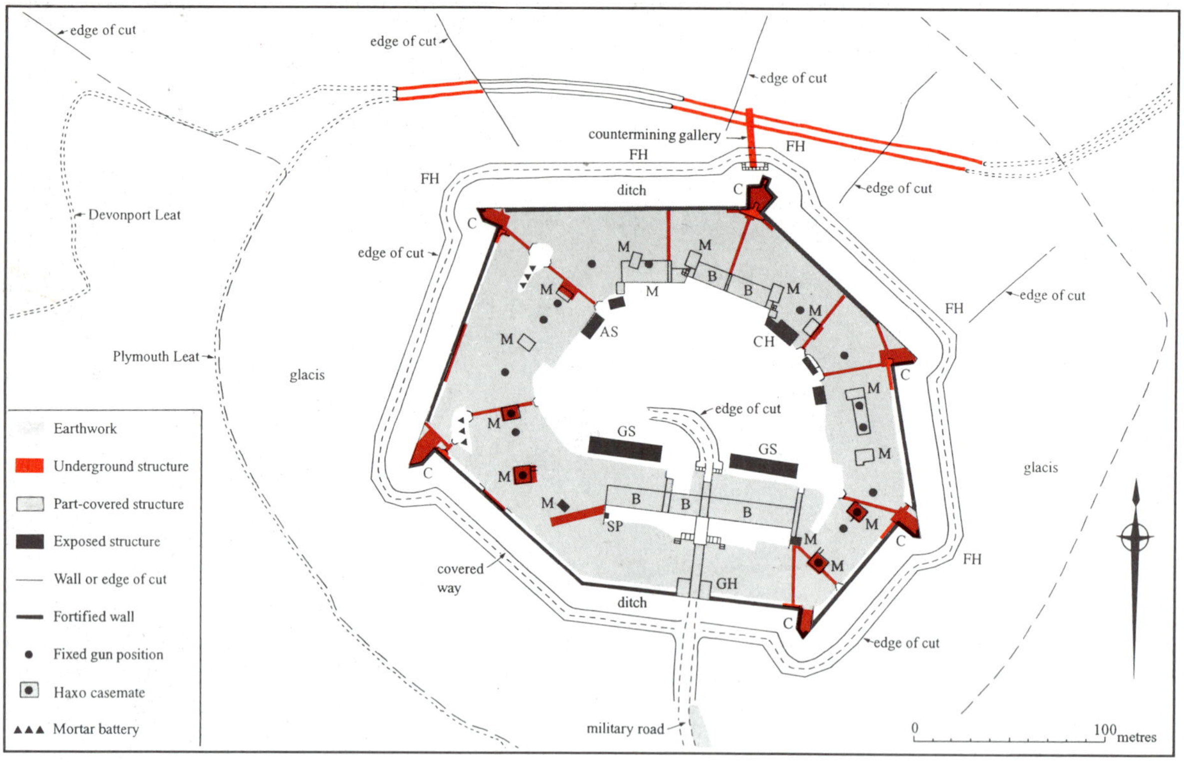

Fig. 88 *Crownhill Fort*

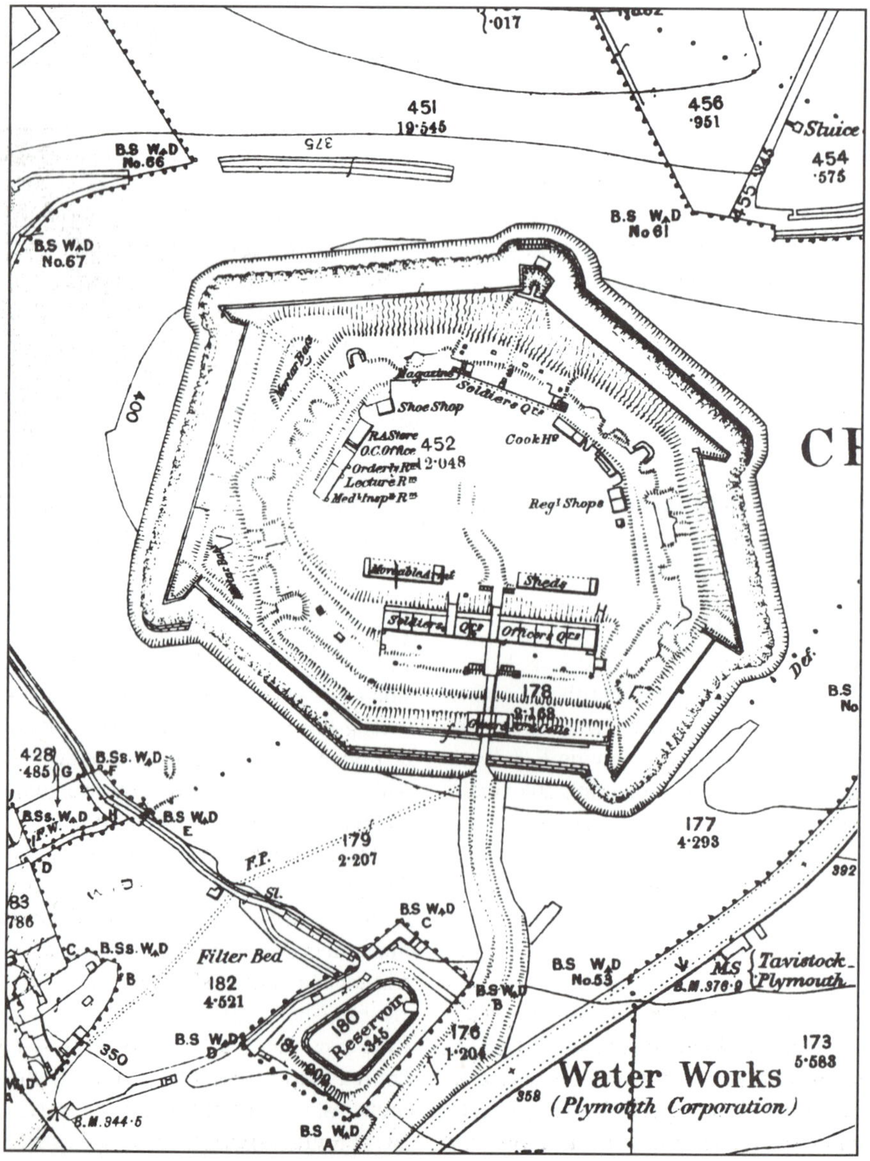

Fig. 89 *Crownhill Fort in 1896 (PRO: WO 78/2314)*

Plate 121 Crownhill Fort (Photograph: F.M. Griffith, Devon County Council. Frame DAP/UV9. Copyright Devon County Council)

Plate 122 Crownhill Fort, double Haxo casemate (Exeter Archaeology)

From *c*. 1900 it was the depot and store for the Royal Garrison Artillery manning the Plymouth defences, and in 1911 and during WWI & WWII was a strongpoint in local defence. After WWII it was used as barracks for the Garrison HQ and various units, and in the 1950s housed an AA gun operations room. It was used in 1944 and 1982 as an assembly point for D Day and the Falklands War. Military occupation ceased in 1983 and the fort was subsequently bought by the Landmark Trust in 1986.

The fort is a 7-sided polygonal work, with fixed armament on 6 sides and provision for stationing moveable armament along the gorge in front of the officers' quarters. It is surrounded by a 30ft deep rock-cut ditch protected by 5 single and 1 double *caponier* mounting 32-pdr SBBL guns, and by a covered way and extensive *glacis* beyond, large parts of which are still extant to the N & N.E. The ditch & covered way are covered by a *chemin des rondes*, a loopholed and partly earth-covered sentry walk around the top of the ditch scarp. Of particular interest is the countermining gallery opposite the double *caponier*. This utilises the earlier Plymouth and Devonport Leats and is the only known example extant in Britain.

The ramparts contain a double Haxo casemate and four single Haxo casemates built in the 1860s, together with ten concrete open gun positions built in the 1870s & 1880s. These include two emplacements at the N.W & E salients for 7-inch RBL guns on Moncrieff (disappearing) mountings. At intervals there are six bomb-proof 1860s expense magazines, and a further three (one not bomb proofed) serve the fortified roof level of the soldiers' barracks and the gun platform for mobile armament along the gorge. A further four underground expense magazines served, via hoists, the four individual Haxo casemates on the S.E & S.W faces, and each *caponier* also contained a magazine. There are mortar batteries in the S.W & N.W salients, but there is no record of them ever having been armed. The *caponiers* were designed to accommodate up to 15 32-pdr SBBL guns, and mounted fourteen. In *c*.1878-82 the S.E & E *caponiers* were used to test the firing drill for the 32-pdr SBBL guns.

Earth-covered bomb-proof buildings present within the fort include the guardroom and cells flanking the main entrance, casemated officers' quarters under the traverse, and casemated soldiers' quarters and the main magazine under the north rampart. Much of the

Plate 123 Crownhill Fort, Moncrieff emplacement for a 7-in RBL gun (Exeter Archaeology)

Plate 124 Crownhill Fort, 1880s emplacement for a 64-pdr RML gun (Exeter Archaeology)

Plate 125 Crownhill Fort, 1880s emplacement for a 7-in RBL gun (Exeter Archaeology)

masonry throughout is high quality, with limestone ashlar being used on the officers' quarters for example, and the main gate being framed by a high-quality reproduction Norman arch. Seven other buildings surround the parade ground, including two 'gun sheds', which may have housed stabling as well as the mobile armament, and also an artillery store, latrines and cookhouse.

Several well-preserved WWI/WWII foxholes survive along the covered way and on the main ramparts; the covered section of the leats was apparently used as a Water Board air raid shelter in World War II, and the leats themselves may have formed an advanced line of defence.

Plate 126 Crownhill Fort, Officers' Quarters (Exeter Archaeology)

Plate 127 Crownhill Fort, main gate (Exeter Archaeology)

Present condition

The recent clearance & conservation work undertaken by the Landmark Trust, together with its relatively recent release from MoD stewardship, means that the fort is in generally excellent condition. However few of the original *caponier* floors survive and the fort as a whole contains few of the internal fittings still present at Staddon Fort. The barrack blocks, gun sheds and other buildings have recently been restored, and are mostly in use. Later post-1896 buildings have been removed from the parade, as well as WWI and 1930s rifle ranges and a gas chamber from the ditch, which is now open. The ramparts and gun positions have now been cleared, and the trees are managed. Outside the fort the countermining gallery & covered way survives intact, and includes a series of well preserved foxholes and infantry emplacements. The *glacis* however has been largely built up, except to the N & N.E where it is covered by scrub and grassland. A short section of military road, embankment and *glacis* also survives outside the main gate.

Sources

General

13 - 15, 17, 19; O, Q.

Specific

1904 Plan of fort. PRO: WO 78/3196

1908 Plan & section of fort. PRO: WO 78/3757

1933 1:500 Royal Engineers plan. Copy held by K. Rawlings (FSGSW)

1943 Record plan of ground floor. PSA: 023312X

c.1949 Plan of double *caponier*. PSA: 023313B

1955 Plan of E *caponier*. PSA: 023338B

1971 Plan of main magazine. PSA: 009876E

1990 Cobb, P & Moore, D *Crownhill Fort, Plymouth* Palmerston Forts Society

BOWDEN BATTERY

PAR = EGGBUCKLAND, NGR = SX49675834, PRN = SX45NE-74, MAP 1 No. 154

This is located on the S side of Forder Valley and was connected to Forder Battery, Eggbuckland Keep and Crownhill Fort by a military road protected by an embankment. It was designed by Capt. du Cane, and was intended to cover the valley in front, the N face of Forder Battery and the rear of Crownhill Fort. It was designed for 12 guns in open battery and a battery of three mortars, with a bombproof defensible guardroom containing a magazine and accommodation for 16 men, and musketry galleries in the ditches. The design was formally approved in April 1863 and construction began shortly after and was completed some time after 1868. In 1875 the proposed armament was eight 7-inch RBLs, four 8-inch howitzers and two SB flank guns, but in 1885 it had still not yet been armed, although seven 7-inch RBLs were lying in the battery unmounted. By 1893 however two 7-inch RBL and four 64-pdr RML guns had been mounted on the ramparts. The guardroom and the mortar batteries remained unarmed throughout. The battery was released by the MoD in 1963 and is now a garden centre.

The rampart remains intact on the E and N.E faces but has been levelled elsewhere; all four of the original bomb-proof 1860s expense magazines survive, although the two western ones have lost their earth covering. Three concrete 64-pdr RML emplacements dating to the 1880s survive on the N.E face complete with pivots and racer rails, and one infilled 7-inch RBL emplacement is visible on the E face; of the other two emplacements depicted in 1896 one has been demolished and the other may lie under a greenhouse. The earthwork mortar battery in the N.E salient remains complete, whilst the other has been infilled.

The rock-cut ditches on the N.W, N.E, & E flanks are open, together with the continuation eastwards towards Forder, but the gorge ditch has been infilled; the two musketry galleries covering the ditches appear intact although part of the E gallery may have been demolished by a new stable block. Both are buried to roof level and flooded; the access tunnels from the interior are blocked.

The guardroom has two levels, with four embrasures covering the gorge and a roof level protected by a parapet. The lower level now lies below ground and contains two embrasures, two small projecting musketry *caponiers*, and an ammunition lift and magazine to the rear; all now are empty and suffer from damp. The upper level is of the same plan, excluding the magazine. The main gate was sited through the gorge wall immediately to the W and retains its drawbridge pulleys and chains; the bridge itself may still lie under the tarmac. A new entry has been cut through the gorge wall immediately to the W. The gorge wall is loop-holed throughout.

To the N the levelled *glacis* extends down to the valley bottom, and a further section extended down to the road to the E; it is clear of vegetation and is a rare example of where its inter-relationship with the battery can be clearly appreciated.

Present condition.
The interior is occupied by the buildings and stock of the garden centre, and the N, N.E & E ramparts and ditches are an overgrown wildlife area; the gorge ditch has been infilled and is now a car park. The N.W section of the rampart has been levelled and the mortar

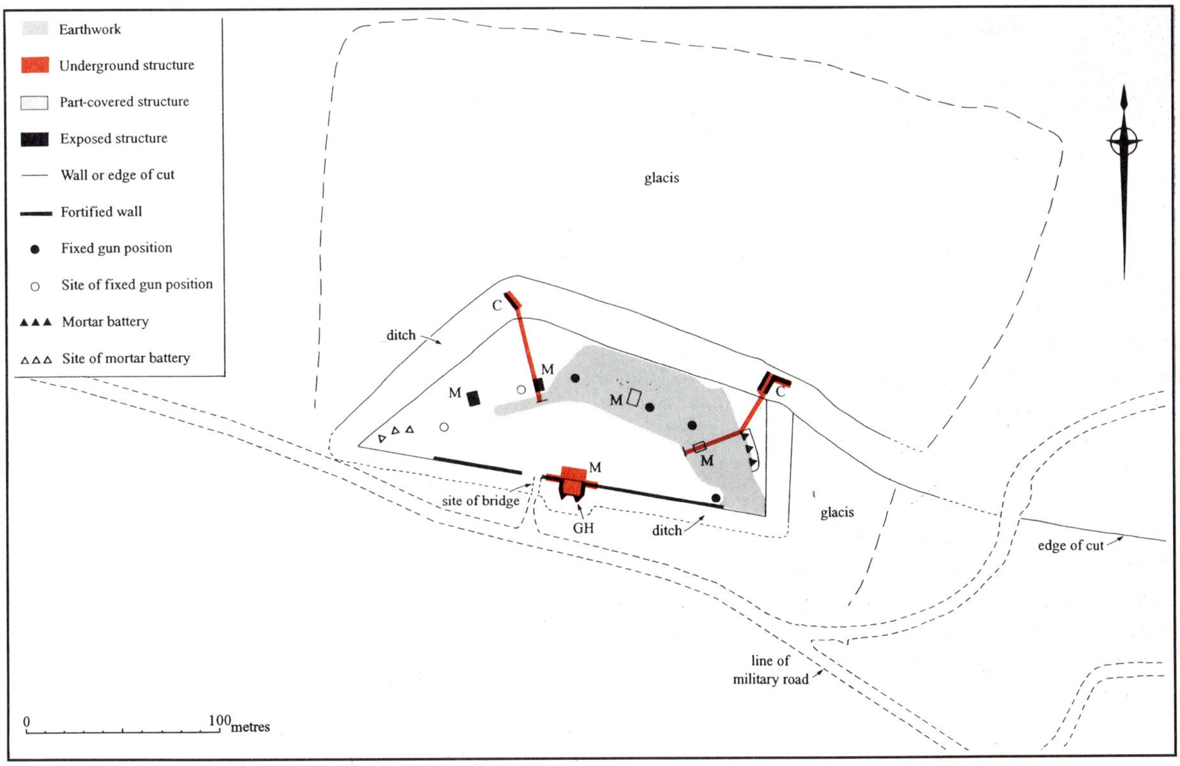

Fig. 90 Bowden Battery

battery infilled; the area is occupied by greenhouses and storage areas. The expense magazines and the remaining rampart, gun emplacements and mortar battery remain in good condition, though the ditch has silted up in places and the *caponiers* have been flooded, and it contains a recently-built stable block. The guardroom remains in reasonable structural condition although is very damp.

Sources
General
13 - 15, 17, 19; O, Q.

EGGBUCKLAND KEEP

PAR = EGGBUCKLAND, NGR = SX50025811, PRN = SX55NW-14, MAP 1 No. 155

This forms the only one of four fortified keeps or barracks proposed for the N.E Defences in 1861 to be built, and can be said to be the last 'keep' to be built in Britain. It occupies the highest point of the N.E section and lies above and to the rear of Bowden and Forder Batteries and Austin Fort. It is connected to Forder Battery via a tunnel and to all three via a military road protected by an embankment. It was designed (by Capt. du Cane) to cover the rear of Forder (which had no gorge wall or gatehouse) and to be the main barrack and magazine for the three batteries. It was intended as a defensible keep or barracks housing 230 men and ample store room for powder and shell, surrounded by a *glacis* and a ditch defended by four musketry *caponiers*. The military road leading to the main gate in the gorge was sited in a cutting to protect it from incoming fire.

The design was approved in April 1863 and construction began shortly after, and was completed in 1872. In 1875 an armament of five 7-inch RBL guns was recommended, but in 1885 it remained unarmed. By 1893 three 0.45-in machine-guns had been installed, presumably on the rampart. The keep was released by the MoD in 1947, and is now a DIY Store and there is a house & garden on the roof.

The keep consists of a five-sided two-storey bomb-proof (earth-covered) structure built within a rock-cut depression, surrounded by a ditch. This is rock-cut, except for its masonry scarp wall and the counterscarp wall of the gorge. Single-storey musketry *caponiers* with pitched roofs project from each corner and enfilade the ditch. A loop-holed parapet wall along the gorge protected the approach to the main entrance, which is now fronted by a corrugated iron *porte cochère*. Further loops flank the doorway and drawbridge at the rear leading to the tunnel to Forder Battery.

Internally, the general arrangement of both floors is of rooms arranged along either side of a central corridor, with the barrack accommodation being sited on the outer side and lit by windows in the ditch scarp, and

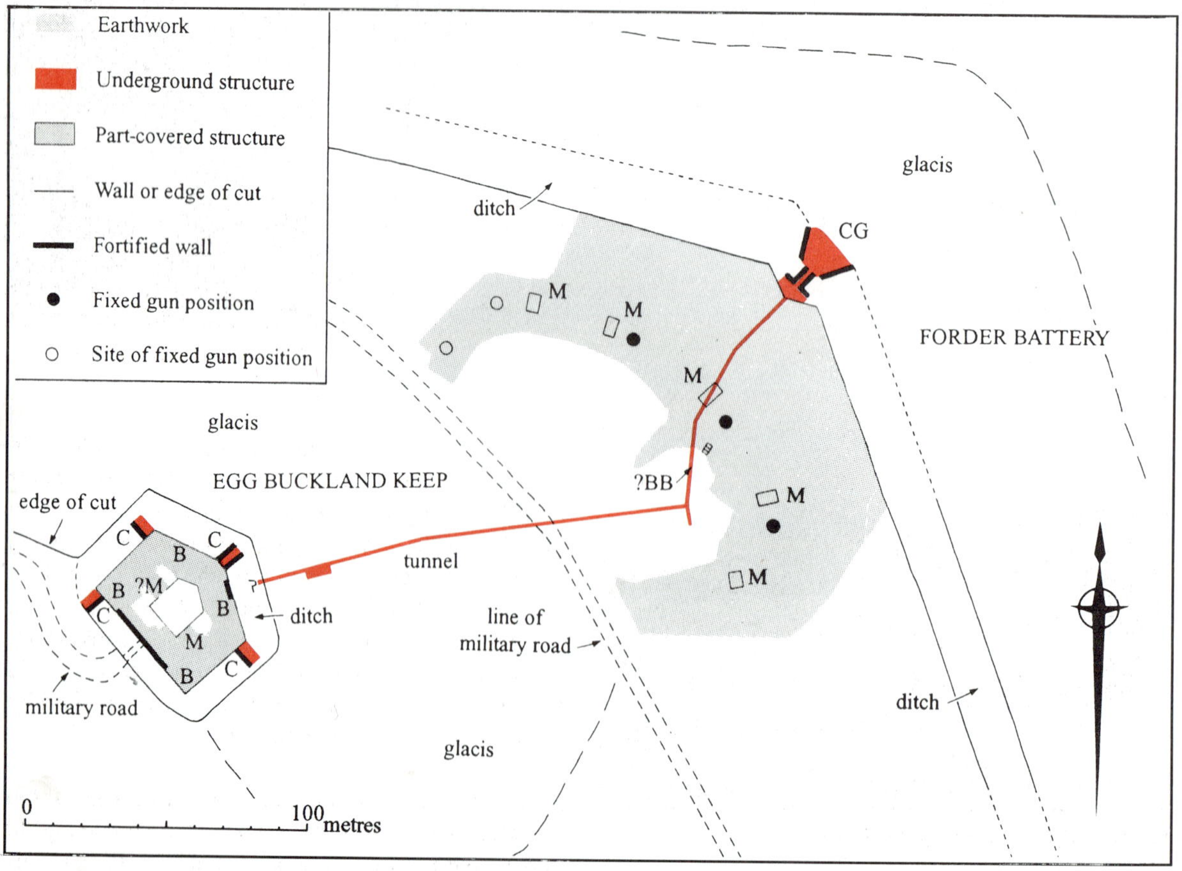

Fig. 91 Eggbuckland Keep & Forder Battery

Plate 128 *Eggbuckland Keep, with Forder Battery (background) (Photograph: F.M. Griffith, Devon County Council. Frame DAP/UV13. Copyright Devon County Council)*

Plate 129 *Eggbuckland Keep (Exeter Archaeology)*

store-rooms being sited on the inner side. The magazines were sited under earthwork traverses at each end of the gorge. Within the limited number of these rooms viewed, any original fittings were largely obscured by modern decoration, shelving and rolls of carpets. Visible original features include much of the flooring and doorframes, iron stair rails flanking the main entrance tunnel on the interior, the 1872 datestone over the main entrance, and drawbridge chains flanking the rear entrance.

Two spiral stairs provide access to the roof level; this is surrounded by an earthen rampart except along the gorge where there is a loop-holed wall. No gun emplacements were identified.

To the N a *c.* 350m long tunnel leads to Forder Battery; this was ventilated by shafts at intervals, and includes three vaults which later contained urinals. At the E end it forks, one fork leading up stairs into Forder Battery and one down a flight of stairs to the counterscarp gallery (or 'reverse *caponier*').

Present condition

The keep is mostly occupied by a DIY and building supplies store, except for the N.W corner which is a health club. Any original fittings which may survive are obscured by shelving and stock; most rooms, including the S magazine and the *caponiers*, were not accessible. Little major structural alteration is apparent except in the area of the health club. The *caponiers* are used for storage and suffer from damp due to the partial infilling of the ditch. The roof level is a private residence & garden. The gorge ditch is used for storage; the remainder has been infilled to half its width, partly burying the *caponiers*. The counterscarp wall at the S end of the gorge has been demolished. The tunnel to Forder Battery is intact; the first 30m is used for storage. The *glacis* is completely built up; the original access road is still used.

Sources

General

13 - 15, 17, 19; O, Q.

Specific

1940 Plan. Copy held by K. Rawlings (FSGSW)

1944 Plan. Copy held by K. Rawlings (FSGSW)

FORDER BATTERY

PAR = EGGBUCKLAND, NGR = SX50175817, PRN = SX55NW-35, MAP 1 No. 156

This is located on a spur between Bowden Battery and Fort Austin, and was connected to them by a military road and to Eggbuckland Keep to the rear via a tunnel. It was intended to cover Forder Valley and Estover and was designed (by Capt. du Cane) for 16 guns in open battery, separated by five traverses containing expense magazines. A gatehouse, main magazine and gorge wall were not provided as Eggbuckland Keep accommodated the garrison and munitions and covered its rear. The design was approved in April 1863 & the battery was largely complete by 1869. In 1875 an armament of twelve 7-inch RBL & six SB flank guns was recommended, but by 1885 it remained unarmed, although six 7-inch RBLs were lying in the battery unmounted. By 1893 four 64-pdr RMLs & one 7-inch RBL had been mounted on the ramparts, and two 32-pdr SBBL guns were installed in the counterscarp gallery. It was released by the MoD in 1900.

The W half of the parade is occupied by modern buildings, the E half is overgrown and empty except for foundations of demolished Nissen huts, and an ?anchor point for a WWII barrage balloon (the steel anchor rope for which is lying on the adjacent *terreplein*). The rampart remains intact except for some terracing and partial removal of the *terreplein* and access ramps; all five 1860s bomb-proof expense magazines survive, together with three concrete 64-pdr RML emplacements dating to the 1880s. Two further emplacements probably lie under undergrowth on the W face. The scarp of the ditch protecting the front of the battery survives but the counterscarp has mostly been removed and the ditch itself filled in, except for a *c.*100m length to the S. The ditch contained a double counterscarp gallery (or 'reverse *caponier*') with embrasures for four flank guns, which covered the long ditches extending either side to Austin Fort & Bowden Battery. Although this has been partly demolished and a new house sited over it, its lower level and the access tunnel from Forder and Eggbuckland Keep remain. Access to the gallery was via a loop-holed passage across the bottom of the ditch, which contained two sally ports.

Present condition

All of the rampart and the E part of the interior is overgrown; the W part has been developed. At both ends the rear of the rampart has been removed by road

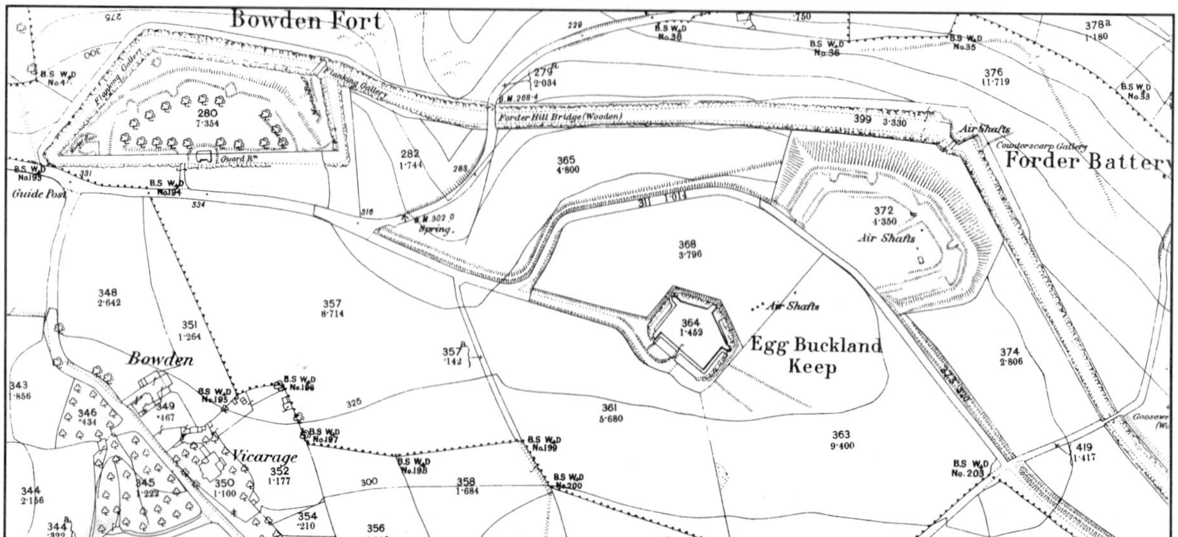

Fig. 92 Bowden Battery, Eggbuckland Keep & Forder Battery in 1896 (PRO: WO 78/2314)

widening; a small electricity sub-station has been terraced into the W end. The N.W corner of the rampart face has recently been heavily terraced in preparation for development; trackways have also been cut into the slope on the N & N.E flanks. The counterscarp gallery and *glacis* have been demolished/occupied by new housing, although the gallery remains under the house above. The remaining open section of ditch is overgrown and a wildlife area; the section running S to Fort Austin has been filled in, and the embankment protecting the road to either side has mostly been removed by road re-alignment.

Sources
General
13 - 15, 17, 19; O, Q

AUSTIN FORT

PAR = EGGBUCKLAND, NGR = SX50615764, PRN = SX55NW-34, MAP 1 No. 157

This is located on a spur overlooking the junction of the Forder Valley and a tributary valley to the S, and forms part of an arrow-shaped position comprising Bowden and Forder Batteries and Eggbuckland Keep; it is connected to them and to the Efford-Laira Position to the S via a military road protected by embankments. After approval of the design (by Capt. du Cane) in April 1863 construction began and was completed soon after 1868. It was designed for 15 guns and five mortars, wth five traverses containing expense magazines. The ditches were flanked by gun casemates and musketry galleries, connected by a loop-holed gallery; the 30ft high gorge was flanked by a large central guardhouse containing two tiers of guns and musketry galleries with accommodation for *c*. 60 men and a reserve magazine.

In 1875 an armament of ten 7-inch RBL guns, ten 8-inch rifled howitzers and four SB flank guns were proposed, but by 1885 none had been mounted, although five of the RBLs & three howitzers were lying unmounted within the fort. An armament of four

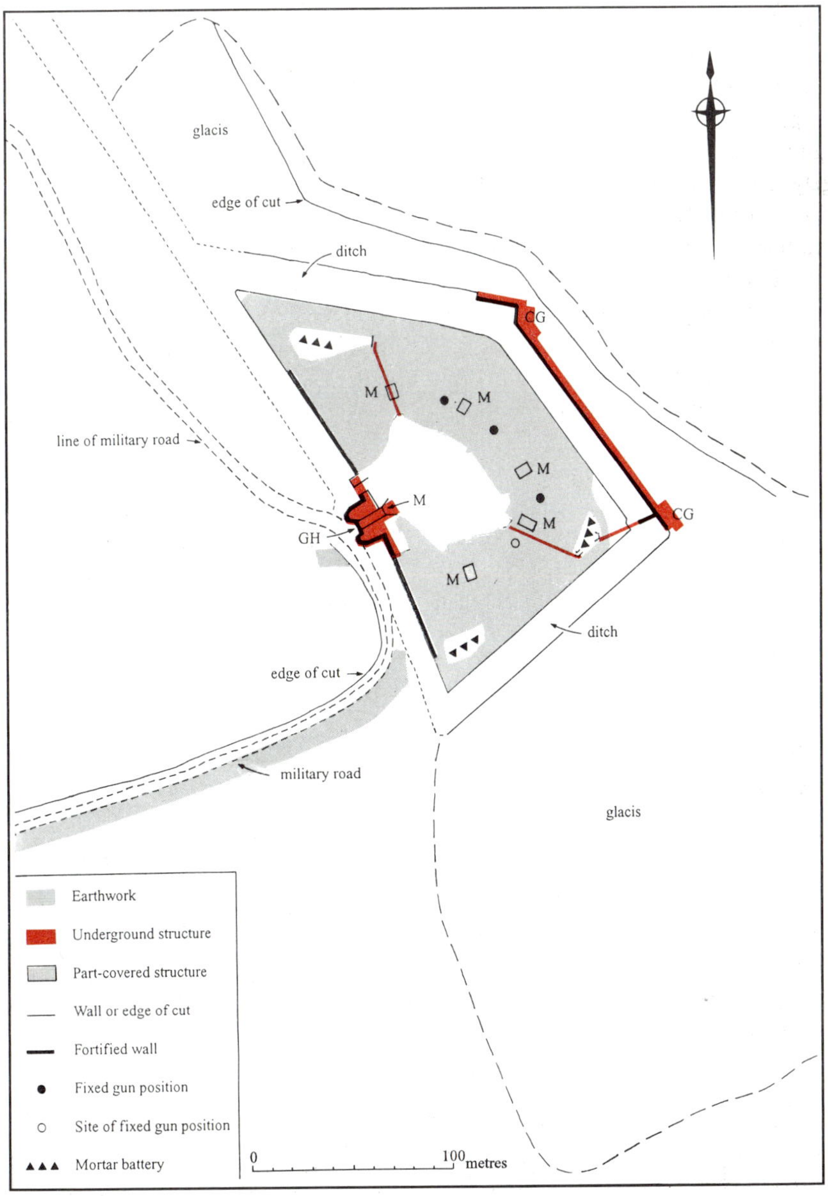

Fig. 93 Austin Fort

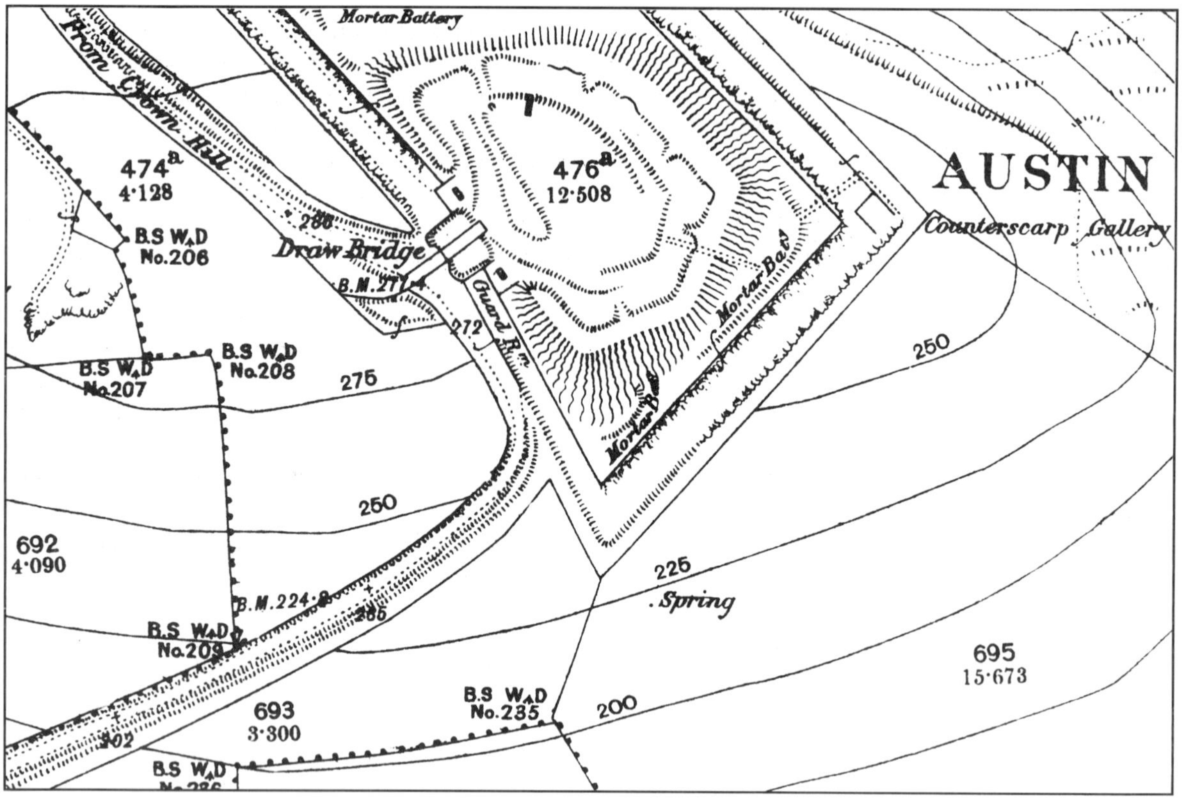

Fig. 94 Austin Fort in 1896 (PRO: WO 78/2314)

64-pdr RMLs & six 32-pdr SBBLs were proposed, and by 1893 the former were mounted (but not the 32-pdrs). It was probably disarmed shortly after, and was released by the MoD in 1958 after occupation during WWII by the 'Devon & Cornwall Auxiliary Unit'. In 1984 the guardhouse was converted into the Plymouth City Emergency Centre for Civil Defence, and the rest of the fort has been used for some time as the City Engineer's Dept and workshops.

Austin Fort is a four-sided work, protected by ditches (largely infilled) to the N, N.E & S.E, which are in turn enfiladed by two pairs of gun casemates (each with expense magazine) located in the counterscarp at the N.E & E salients. Access to these was via a tunnel (now blocked) from the parade and through another under the ditch at the E salient, with a loop-holed gallery (containing a sally port) connecting the two. The gorge ditch (now infilled) was enfiladed by two pairs of gun embrasures in each flank of the guardhouse; these in turn were enfiladed by fire from musketry galleries in the gorge wall and over a parapet above.

The fort was originally entered via a drawbridge (now removed) and through an arched gateway in the centre of the guardhouse. This gateway is flanked on either side by musketry loops in two small projecting *caponiers*. The present entrance has been cut through the gorge wall to the N, removing most of the musketry galleries.

The guardhouse is two-storey, each of which contains four gun casemates, a central passage and flanking musketry galleries; the reserve magazine lies on the lower level to the rear. Spiral stairs give access to the rampart to either side; the roof was originally completely earth-covered and the rear was protected by a traverse (see *Fig. 94*). On the ramparts five 1860s expense magazines in traverses separate four 1880s concrete gun emplacements; two of these have the curved parapets typical of 64-pdr RML emplacements

Plate 130 Austin Fort, counterscarp gallery (Exeter Archaeology)

Plate 131 Austin Fort, guardhouse (Exeter Archaeology)

and two have the straight parapets typical of 7-inch RBL emplacements (although only 64-pdrs were mounted in 1885-93). In the N.W, E, & S salients are three overgrown mortar batteries. No WWII foxholes are visible on the ramparts, which have been heavily landscaped or are overgrown. There was an extensive *glacis* to the N.W & S; to the N.E the ground drops away sharply and was probably covered by Forder Battery.

Present condition

The parade and ramparts are now occupied by prefab and concrete buildings and storage areas belonging to the City Engineer's Dept; the central traverse has been removed and the top of the rampart on the N.E & S.E faces levelled; a new entrance has been cut through the gorge wall. The earth cover has been removed from the rear of the guardhouse, which has recently been converted into an 'emergency centre' containing map/operations rooms, briefing rooms, toilets, and communications facilities, generators and a new floor. All the expense magazines survive complete, although four have lost all or part of their earth covering; three are used for storage, one is blocked and another (on the S face) lies open and empty. Three gun positions are occupied by buildings and one has been demolished or infilled. The sections of rampart along the gorge and S face have been little altered and are heavily overgrown, as are the three mortar batteries. The counterscarp galleries remain open and derelict, and are currently accessible, although much of them has been buried by the relatively recent infilling of the S.E & E ditches. The gorge ditch has been infilled and is used as a car park, and is occupied by the back gardens of houses fronting Fort Austin Avenue (the former military road). The S part of the *glacis* is a housing estate (Thetford Gardens etc) whilst the N & E sections remain open ground; the scarp along the E side is clearly visible. Overall, despite the levelling of some rampart and the occupation of the site by functional buildings of variable attractiveness, the structure of the fort remains largely intact.

Sources

General

13 - 15, 17, 19; O, Q.

DEER PARK EMPLACEMENT

PAR = EGGBUCKLAND, NGR = SX51005680, PRN = SX55NW-107, MAP 1 No. 158

This is an earthwork battery platform sited on a spur overlooking the Forder Valley; it faced E to cover the N flank of Efford Fort. It is connected to Efford and Austin Forts by a military road protected by an embankment. It was built by 1869 for five guns and in 1875 the proposed armament consisted of four 64-pdr RML guns on travelling carriages which were to be kept at Efford Fort. In 1885 no guns were listed, and no armament was proposed. The date of release by the War Dept. or MoD is not known.

It is located on a bend of the military road which runs along its rear; in effect it is a continuation of the embankment protecting the road but has a *terreplein* or gun platform. No individual gun positions or embrasures are visible, and no expense magazines present.

Present condition

The earthwork and the military road are largely complete, although the rampart has been truncated and remodelled in places. It is heavily overgrown.

Sources

General

13 - 15, 17, 19; O, Q.

EFFORD FORT

PAR = EGGBUCKLAND, NGR = SX51365661, PRN = SX55NW-30, MAP 1 No. 159

This represents the key to the eastern end of the N.E Defences, and forms (with Laira Battery & Laira & Efford Emplacements) part of an integrated fortified position commanding the junction of the Forder and Plym valleys and the lowest crossing of the Plym (at Long Bridge; SX51905673). The fort is sited on a steep hill, overlooking Laira Battery to the S. It was connected to the rest of the position and the N.E Defences by a military road protected by an embankment. The design (by Capt. du Cane) was approved in April 1863, with construction beginning in 1865 and being completed shortly after 1868.

It was designed to mount 21 guns on the *terreplein*, with three in Haxo casemates with ammunition lifts to magazines underneath. In 1868 there were two expense magazines, one with a magazine under, five gun casemates on the flank and a further two lower down flanking the ditch fronting Efford Emplacement. Its rear was protected by a 20ft high gorge wall and a defensible guardroom, and it contained casemated barracks for five officers and 108 men. No *caponiers* however were provided for the ditch around its N & E faces, either perhaps because the steepness of the slope was considered enough on this side or because they were cut out due to financial constraints.

In 1875 an armament of nineteen 7-inch RBLs, five 64-pdr RMLs & three SB flank guns was proposed, and by 1885 a single 7-inch RBL had been mounted in the Haxo casemate on the S.E face, and five others in the casemates within the slope below. A further five 7-inch RBLs lay unmounted within the fort. In 1885 it was proposed to mount a further three 7-inch RMLs and three 64-pdr RMLs on the rampart faces, together with two 5-inch BL guns on disappearing mountings at the E & N.E salients & two 32-pdr SBBL guns in the S *caponier* below the casemated battery. All these guns, except the 32-pdrs, had been mounted by 1893, when a moveable armament of RML howitzers & 40-pdr RBLs is listed as being present to cover the section from Crownhill to Laira, and also the 'Catdown Position' - the undefended gap between Laira and the Staddon Heights Defences. At least some of these were probably stored in the gun shed at Efford Fort. The fort was probably disarmed shortly after, and in WWII the barrack casemates were used for ammunition storage and a light-gauge railway built within the fort; fuel tanks were built on the upper parade. It was released by the MoD in 1961 and now provides accommodation for the Showmen's Guild.

The fort is an irregular polygonal work, defended by rock-cut ditches on the E & N.E faces & gorge, a steep scarp to the N and an earlier ?quarry face to the S. The parapet of the rampart lies at a considerable height above the ditch on all sides except the gorge, which is defended by a fortified guardhouse including gun casemates and by another gun embrasure placed at the N end of the gorge wall. The ditch and *glacis* to the N would have been covered by Deer Park Emplacement, and to the E by Laira Battery; the junction of the N.E & E ditches appears unfinished and may have been the intended site of a musketry gallery or *caponier*. On the S flank a battery of five gun casemates separated by expense magazines (and with a stair to a spotter position) covers the front of Efford Emplacement and Laira Battery; the S *caponier* (with four cannon) covers the ditch fronting the former and a musketry gallery protects the S section of the gorge ditch. Another single embrasure covers the rear of Efford Emplacement. All these are reached from the parade ground via a long staircase flanked by ramps, which formed an incline plane down which the guns and ammunition were brought.

On the ramparts there are six open concrete 1880s gun positions (and one which has been demolished), and three 1860s Haxo casemates on the S, S.E & E faces; one of these has subsequently been buried and overlain

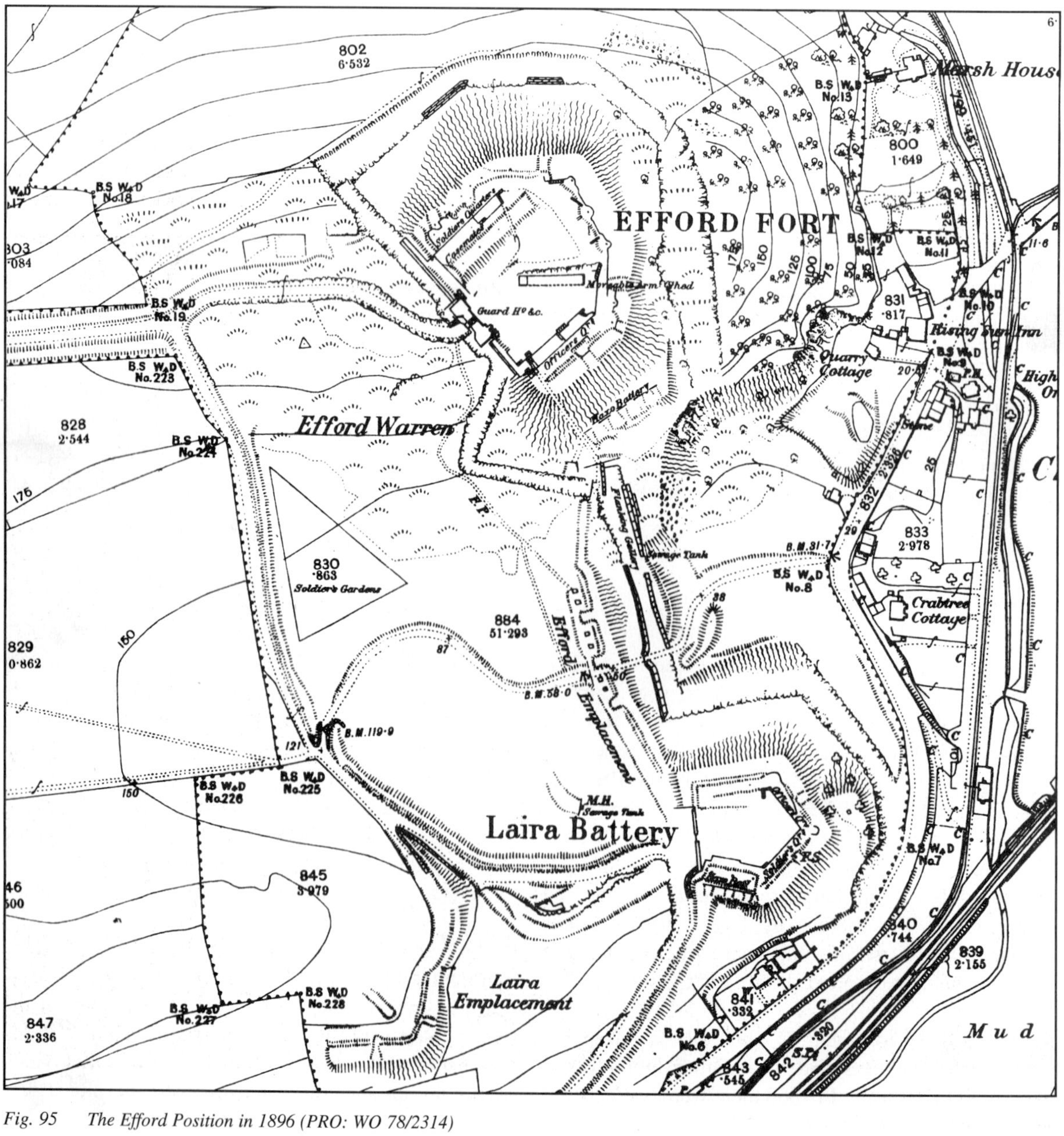

Fig. 95 The Efford Position in 1896 (PRO: WO 78/2314)

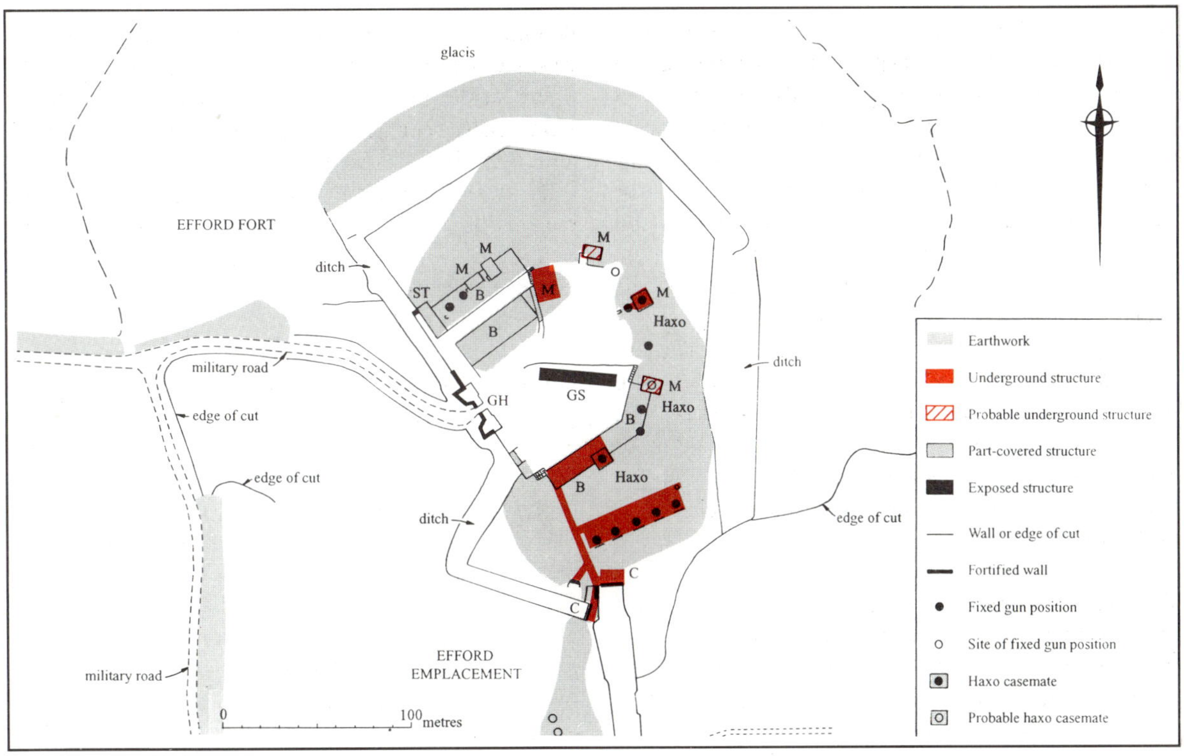

Fig. 96 Efford Fort

by an 1880s gun position, and another has been blocked in. The third remains open, and each had an underlying magazine (now inaccessible). There are three 1860s expense magazines on the other faces. One of the 1880s positions, sited at the E salient, has a high parapet and was presumably the site of one of the two 5-inch BL guns on disappearing mountings proposed in 1885.

The main magazine lies under the N.E end of the central traverse, which also houses five barrack casemates. A further two-storey block of ten barrack

Plate 132 Efford Fort (foreground) & Laira Battery (background) (Photograph: F.M. Griffith, Devon County Council. Frame DAP/UX5. Copyright Devon County Council)

casemates (with stores to the N.W), and a three-storey block of 19 officers' casemates underlie the N.W & S ramparts respectively. The large amount of accommodation may have housed the officers and men manning the mobile artillery stored in the gun shed on the parade as well as the garrison of the fort itself, and perhaps an infantry reserve to man Deer Park, Efford and Laira Emplacements.

Plate 133 Efford Fort, officers' quarters (2nd floor), with infilled stairwell in front (Exeter Archaeology)

The officers' quarters, which included an orderlies' room and store-room, were strengthened and adapted during WWII, when the basement was used as a laundry. A light-gauge railway was built linking the soldiers' casemates (used for ammunition storage?) and two other buildings (since demolished) to the S of the central traverse. No foxholes are visible on the ramparts, which are heavily overgrown. The *glacis* displays little evidence of landscaping, except for a scarp adjoining the gorge.

Plate 134 Efford Fort, main gate in 1910 (FWW)

Present condition

Overall the condition of the fort is poor and semi-derelict, although most of basic structure remains intact; much of the stores, barrack casemates, main magazine and gun shed are used for storage and as workshops, together with the buried Haxo on the N.E

Plate 135 Efford Fort, main gate in 1993 (Exeter Archaeology)

face. The lower and upper parades are occupied by the prefabs and semi-permanent caravans of the Showmen's Guild. The gate arch was apparently demolished when the Guild leased the fort from the City Council, and the gatehouse has been blocked up and much of the gorge infilled to form a lorry park; the remainder of the ditches are generally heavily overgrown. Two of the expense magazines are blocked up; the third is open and derelict; most of the ramparts are overgrown and one of the open gun positions has recently been removed. The gun casemates on the S face are mostly blocked up and derelict but still retain iron tackle fittings and mantlet bars. The S *caponier* has lost its floors but is otherwise complete, as is the adjoining musketry gallery.

The lower two storeys of the officers' quarters were fronted by a large open stairwell which has been infilled; the basement floor frontage (which survives complete, together with its original brass window catches) is encased by a WWII concrete wall but the first-floor frontage is bowing in under the pressure; most of the floor boards have also been removed, although some of the woodwork around the doors and stair survives, together with the occasional wrought-iron fireplace. However, although the interior is dangerous due to the pressure of the infill and the lack of floors, the 19th century structure appears sound, although one of the concrete supporting pillars installed in WWII is collapsing.

Apart from the gorge the ditches remain open. The *glacis* is largely wooded, except to the N where it is used for pasture; the military road survives complete outside the gate, although to the W the embankment has been lowered to accommodate a former gipsy camp.

Sources
General
13 - 15, 17, 19; O, Q.

EFFORD EMPLACEMENT

PAR = EGGBUCKLAND, NGR = SX51385640,
PRN = SX55NW-106, MAP 1 No. 160

This is an open earthwork battery sited across a small valley between Efford Fort and Laira Battery, facing due E and commanding the chicane approach to the sally port it bestrides. It had been built by 1869, when it was described as a curtain with emplacements for four guns. In 1875 the proposed armament was four 64-pdr RML guns. By 1885 none of these had been mounted, and six 8-inch RML howitzers (three emplaced & three on travelling carriages) were proposed. These were present in 1893 although dismounted; six separate gun positions are depicted in 1896. It was probably released by the MoD at the same time as Efford Fort.

It consists of a rampart with *banquette* (still visible in places) and *terreplein* behind; the six overgrown gun positions are protected by three earthen traverses and served by an expense magazine sited off the tunnel underlying it. This tunnel and the road connecting it to the main military road to the rear is of military origin and was probably intended as a 'sally port' for troops issuing to defend the Long Bridge crossing. The road to the E was protected by embankments and was in the form of a chicane, to force an enemy to expose himself to fire from the emplacement above.

Access to the *terreplein* was via a ramp down from Laira Battery to the S. It was defended by a deep rock-cut ditch to the front which was in turn enfiladed by the S *Caponier* of Efford Fort; another gun placed on the flank of Efford Fort enfiladed its rear.

Present condition

Most of the *terreplein* is pasture covered with patches of scrub and undergrowth; the rampart and the N part of the ditch are woodland, whilst the S part has been infilled and forms the back gardens of houses built along Willow Close. The (blocked-up) expense magazine is derelict and inaccessible to all but children. The S end of the rampart and *terreplein*/ramp has been covered by dumped material from the demolished N rampart of Laira Battery. The road to the W survives but the section outside to the E has been removed (together with the embankment) by a new housing estate.

Sources
General
13 - 15, 17, 19; O, Q.

LAIRA BATTERY

PAR = EGGBUCKLAND, NGR = SX51505630,
PRN = SX55NW-31, MAP 1 No. 161

This forms the S.E end of the N.E Defences and is sited on a hill overlooking the Plym valley and the main road into Plymouth from the E. It also covers to some extent the gap in the defences between Laira and the Staddon Defences to the S. It forms part of a coherent defensive position with Efford Fort and Efford, Laira and Deer Park Emplacements, to which it is connected by a military road protected by embankments.

After approval of the design (by Capt. du Cane) in April 1863, construction began in *c.* 1865 and was completed *c.* 1871. It was designed to mount 10 guns

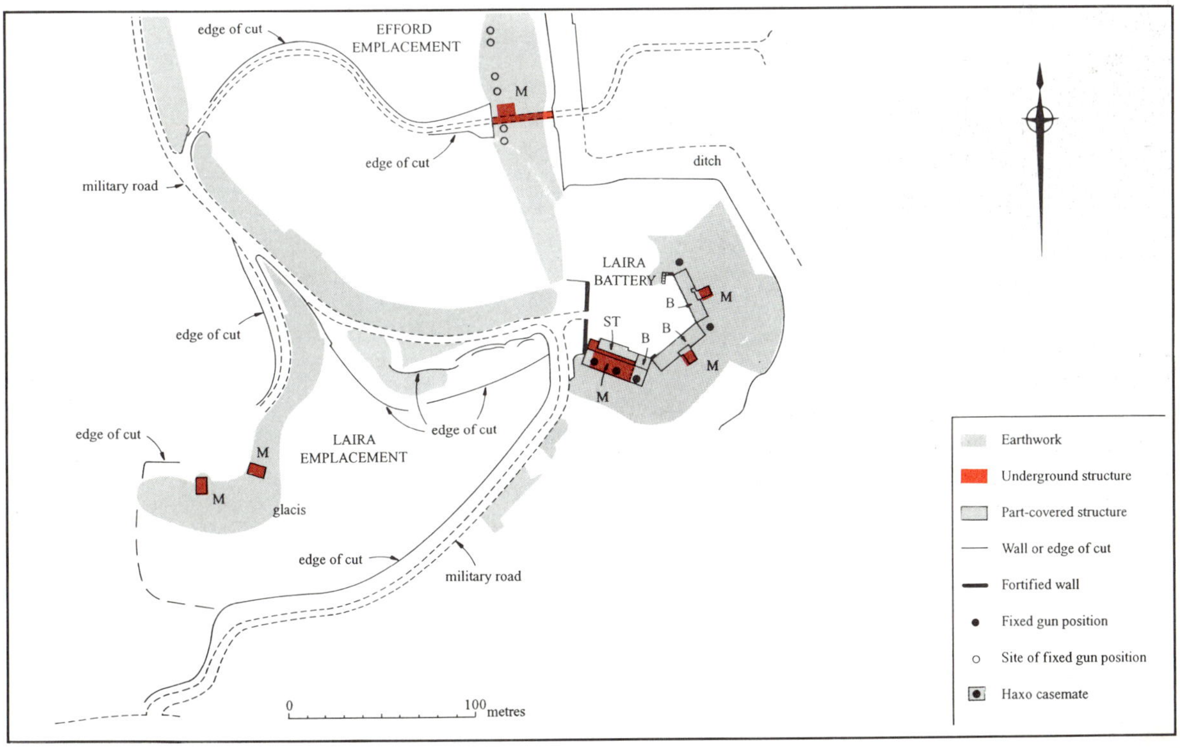

Fig. 97 Laira Battery & Emplacement

in embrasures and three in Haxo casemates to cover the valley southwards towards Staddon Heights, with ample magazine capacity and accommodation for two officers and 30 men. The gorge was closed with a simple wall and could be covered from Efford. In 1875 the proposed armament consisted of eleven 7-inch RBLs & two SB flank guns. In 1885 three of the 7-inch RBLs were mounted in the triple Haxo casemate, and a further five of these guns lay unmounted within the battery. A further two 64-pdr RMLs were proposed and were mounted in 1893. Shortly after it was disarmed, and was released by the MoD in 1961. It is currently occupied by a plant hire firm.

It is a five-sided work, protected by a ditch (now infilled) to the N & N.E and by a rock scarp to the E & S.E; the S flank was enfiladed from Laira Emplacement and the military road embankment, and the gorge from Efford Fort. The gorge is protected by a loop-holed wall and a parapet above; outside there are the remains of (unfinished) scarping to provide a clear field of fire. The gate-arch has been demolished and there was no gatehouse or guardroom. The N rampart has been levelled and pushed northwards towards the ditch scarp; it was originally topped with an earthen parapet with *terreplein* and ramp behind. There are two infilled concrete 64-pdr RML emplacements at the N.E & S.E salients, separated by two bomb-proof 1860s expense magazines with lifts and chambers under. On the S.W face there is a triple Haxo casemate. This includes two expense magazines & survives complete, although two of the casemates are occupied by later concrete partitions and floors. Powder and shot was brought up from the main magazine below via a lift shaft.

The main magazine survives complete, and consists of three vaults with a lamp passage to the rear, and an issuing hatch and shifting room to the W; casemated stores front the parade to the S. Eight barrack casemates lie under the N.E & S.E ramparts, and a ninth to the E of the magazine. Surviving fixtures and fittings include: the wooden sliding doors of the ammunition lockers and the racer rails for the gun

Plate 136 Laira Battery, interior of Haxo casemate (Exeter Archaeology)

carriages in the Haxos; wooden doors, frames (with labels), lamp-window shutters and clothes pegs in the main magazine; and shelf brackets in the expense magazines on the rampart. There may be further features in the disused barrack casemates.

Present condition

Modern buildings on the parade and some of the barrack casemates are used by the plant hire firm as workshops; the remainder are stores or are empty and derelict, as are the expense magazines and Haxo casemates. The rest of the parade and the area of the levelled N rampart is used for parking vehicles, and abandoned machines litter areas of levelled rampart between the expense magazines and gun positions. These have been mostly infilled although the parapets remain visible. Much of the (empty) main magazine is difficult of access. The stores are also empty or contain later oil tanks; the gorge wall and ramparts are heavily overgrown, and the N & N.E ditches have been largely infilled and occupied by the gardens of new houses built along the counterscarp. The gorge is occupied by the military road and by a (partly covered over) ramp down onto the *terreplein* of Efford Emplacement; there does not appear to have been a gorge ditch (see *Fig. 95*).

Sources
General
13 - 15, 17, 19; O, Q.

LAIRA EMPLACEMENT

PAR = EGGBUCKLAND, NGR = SX51245620,
PRN = SX55NW-56, MAP 1 No. 162

Previously described as 'Laira Fort', this earthwork battery is sited on a spur overlooking the Plym valley and the gorge of Laira Battery, to which it is connected by a military road. It was designed in 1869 to mount six guns, two to bear on the right of Laira Battery and four on the Laira river and Saltram opposite, and was probably completed shortly afterwards. In 1875 an armament of six 64-pdr RMLs was proposed. None had been mounted by 1885, when four 8-inch RML howitzers were proposed; these were mounted by 1893. It was probably disarmed shortly after, and released by the MoD at the same time as Laira Battery (1961).

An earthwork battery, with access from the N via a spur of the military road protected by an embankment to the S.E. It has two (E & S) faces, with an expense magazine and chamber under in the centre of each and a *terreplein* behind. No individual gun positions or embrasures are now visible, except possibly in the S.E salient. The rear is protected by an earthen traverse, and the area in front landscaped to form a *glacis*; the military road runs below the battery in a cutting fronted by a protective embankment (now largely removed).

Present condition

The rampart is largely complete, although partly removed or slighted to the N of the E expense magazine and elsewhere overgrown with brambles. The trackway to the rear has been infilled to the level of the *terreplein*. The expense magazines are derelict and vandalised and one has lost its floor. Below-ground remains of the gun positions are likely to survive. The *glacis* is grassland.

Sources

General

13 - 15, 17, 19; O, Q

3.3.4. Staddon Heights to Wembury

The bulk of the sites in this area belong to the Staddon Heights Defences of the 1860s; an integrated and well preserved system of defences which face both landward and seaward. It also includes Breakwater Fort, earlier and later sea-facing batteries and other related works. Anti-aircraft batteries and other installations of the last war are mostly described in section 3.3.5 below.

THE STADDON HEIGHTS DEFENCES

PAR = WEMBURY/PLYMSTOCK, NGR = Various, PRNs = SX45SE-443; 444/1, 3 - 8

These were first proposed by Jervois in a memo of 1858, with a modified version being recommended by the Royal Commission in February 1860. This was further amended by the addition of Fort Turnchapel (later re-named Stamford) in October 1860, and by 1869 the defences were largely complete, although unarmed. The bulk of the defences faced landward, and were intended to deny Staddon Heights (which overlooks the old part of the city, the approach channel and the harbours of Sutton Pool and the Cattewater) to an enemy. Defence of the sea approaches was provided by Fort Bovisand and by guns on the S.W face of Fort Stamford. Large areas of land (shown as white on *Fig. 99*) were purchased, with clearance rights extending over a wide area (shaded on *Fig. 99*) beyond.

The land defences comprise two forts and three batteries, linked by a military road and protected by extensive *glacis* slopes, ditches, scarps and embankments, and form a completely integrated, interdependent defensive system. This was designed to operate as follows. Heavy guns on the ramparts of Staddon and Stamford Forts and Brownhill Battery were intended to keep the enemy far enough away to

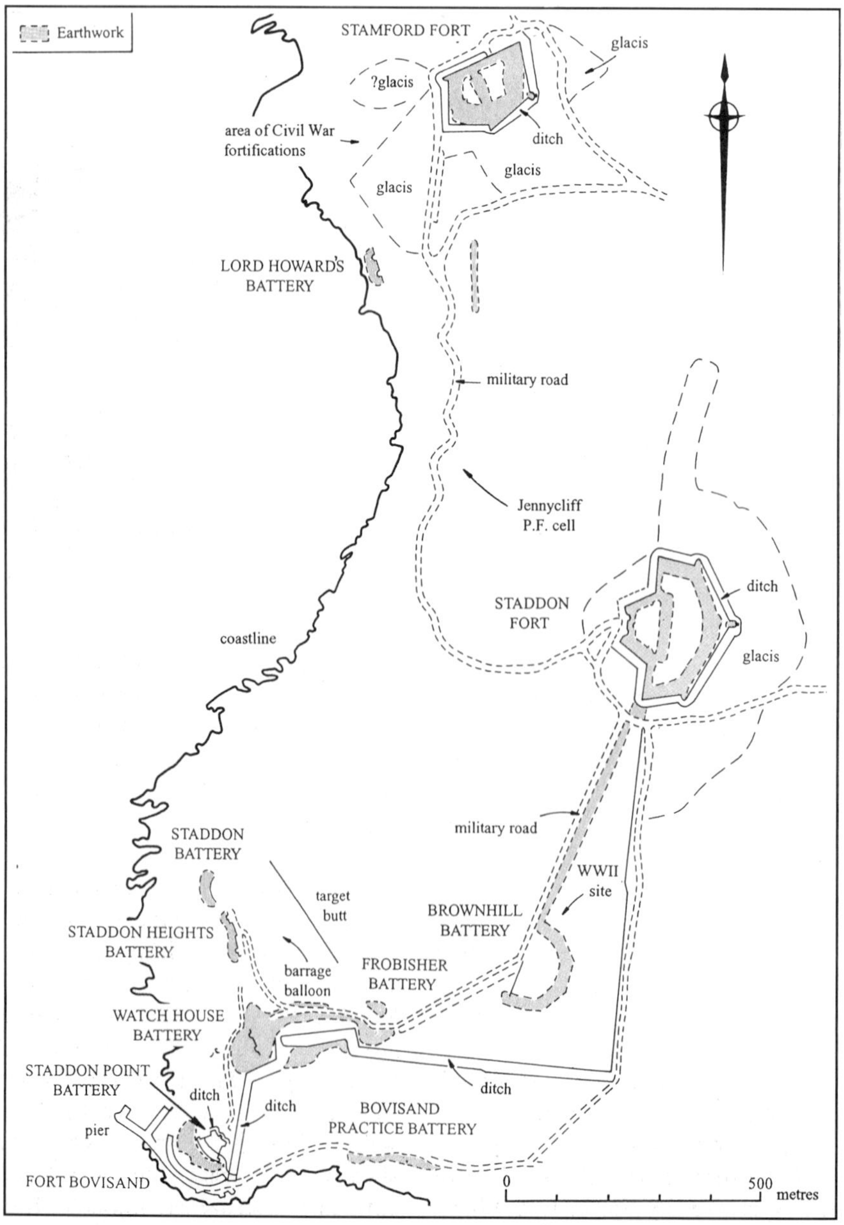

Fig. 98 Staddon Heights

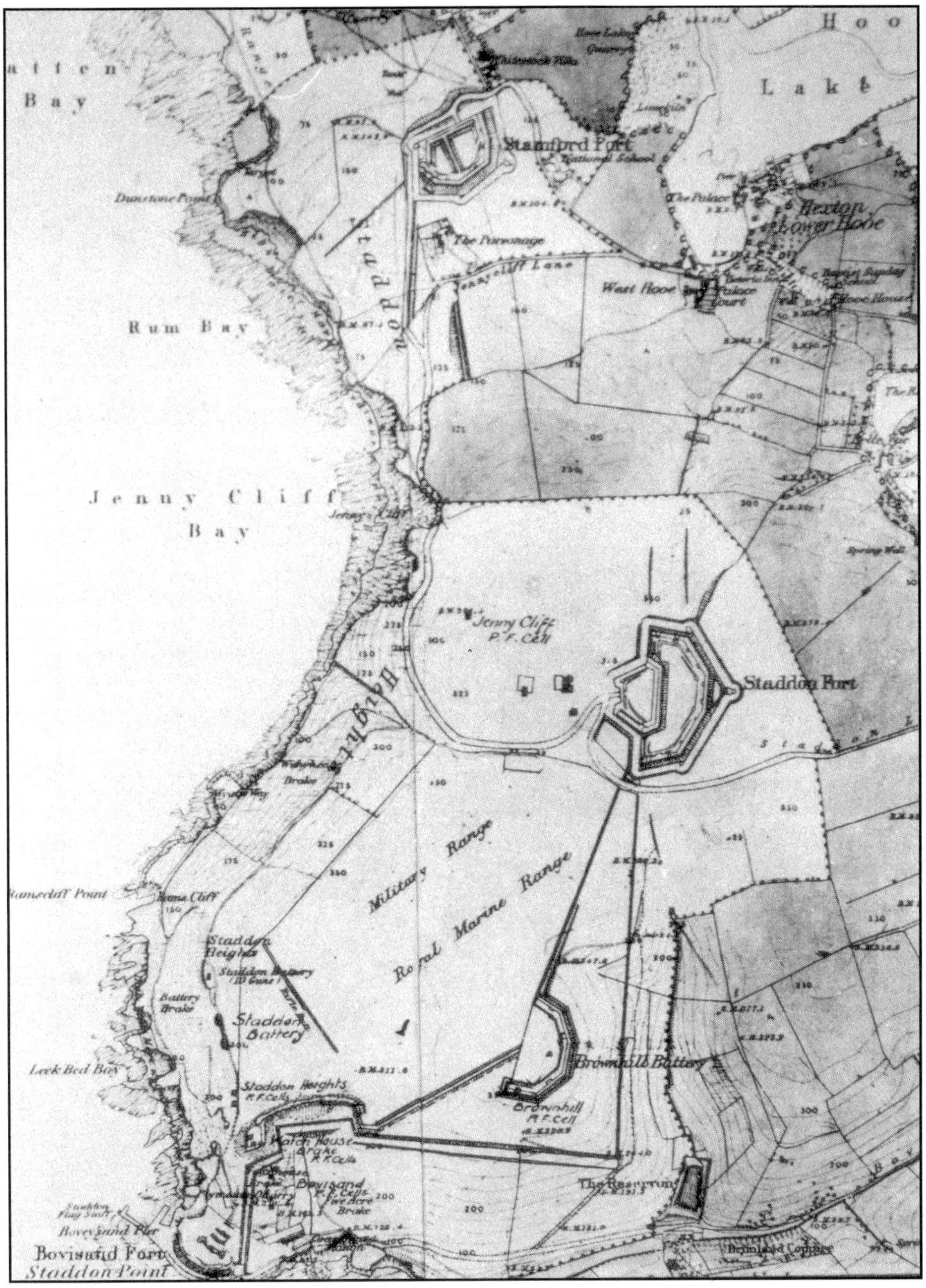

Fig. 99 *The Staddon Heights defences in c.1870, with later fortifications added (by hand) in 1894 (Plymouth Proprietary Library)*

prevent bombardment of the city, anchorages and the forts themselves, and to cover the areas in front and the valley to the S in the event of attack. Closer defence was provided by a levelled *glacis* slope in front of the forts, which was swept by the fire of the guns on the ramparts above and by musketry fire from infantry stationed on a covered way along the outside edge of the ditch of Fort Staddon.

The line to the S of Staddon Fort was protected by a scarp and a deep dry ditch around and down to Fort Bovisand, and to the N the floor of a coombe down to Hooe Lake was levelled to form a *glacis*. This was raked by the fire of heavy guns stationed on the N flank of Staddon Fort, whilst equivalent guns on the S flank fired along the scarp in front of Brownhill Battery. The section of dry ditch between Brownhill and Twelve Acre Brake Batteries was raked by gunfire from Watch House Brake Battery, whilst the section between the latter two was raked from Twelve Acre Brake Battery. The section running down the hill to Fort Bovisand was covered by gun fire from Watch House Brake Battery above, supplemented by musketry galleries in the bottom of the ditch below this battery and adjoining Fort Bovisand.

If the enemy gained access around the N of Fort Staddon he was exposed to fire from Fort Stamford, and from infantry firing over embankments sited alongside the military road to the S. To the S of Staddon Fort a similar last line of defence was provided by infantry firing over an embankment along the military road to each side of Brownhill Battery, the front of which was covered by the loopholed gorge wall of Brownhill Battery and presumably by guns sited on its N face. The ditches of both forts were covered by cannon and musketry fire from *caponiers* and galleries.

Plate 137 The Staddon Heights Defences, target butts & sea-facing batteries (Photograph: F.M. Griffith, Devon County Council. Frame DAP/UT5. Copyright Devon County Council)

Plate 138 Glacis from rampart of Staddon Fort (Exeter Archaeology)

Plate 139 Military road & embankment (with banquette) near Stamford Fort (Exeter Archaeology)

The forts and batteries are described as separate items below. The *glacis* slopes to the N, E and S of Staddon Fort are very extensive and clearly visible, as are those of Stamford Fort (although cluttered and obscured to a large extent by modern development). The ditch and scarp to the S of Staddon Fort is rock-cut, revetted in places with masonry, except between Watch House Brake and Twelve Acre Brake where it has been built as a free-standing ditch across a small combe. The N side of this section is formed by a battered and buttressed rubble stone wall and its S side by a dump of spoil forming a bank.

The embankments to the W of Brownhill Battery and S of Stamford Fort all have a level top sloping gently down from the rear face to the front, and some retain vestiges of an infantry *banquette* on the rear face (*Plate 139*). The embankment to the N of Brownhill has a pointed top, probably because it was only to protect the road behind from incoming fire, the protection afforded by the guns on the S face of Staddon Fort and the N face of Brownhill Battery presumably being thought sufficient.

The military road comprises the lane running S from Staddon Fort to Watch House Battery, and the road which follows the contours around to Stamford Fort. Most of this is not protected by embankments as it is sheltered from incoming fire by the hill to the E. To the N of Stamford Fort and between Watch House and Twelve Acre Brake Batteries it is built on an embankment.

Present condition

The *glacis* slopes around Staddon Fort are complete, clear and uncluttered, and, whilst some of those surviving around Stamford Fort have been built over, large sections still remain as allotments or as open field. The ditch and scarp is largely overgrown with scrub, but survives complete. However the drystone masonry of the scarp wall adjoining Watch House Brake Battery and between Watch House and Twelve Acre Brake Batteries is in poor condition and deteriorating rapidly. Most of the embankments survive complete and in good condition, although in places overgrown. Small parts have been modified to accommodate golf tees and a small section has been completely removed to the rear of Lord Howard's Battery. Therefore, although there has been some modification due to the construction of later coastal batteries and also some more recent damage, in total the Staddon Heights Defences survive virtually complete, and represent a very clear, easily understandable and nationally important example of the theory and practice of Victorian military fortification.

Sources
General
11 - 16, 19.

STAMFORD FORT

PAR = PLYMSTOCK, NGR SX49355275, PRN = SX45SE-16, MAP 3 No. 165

This forms the N element of the Staddon Heights Defences, defending the high ground overlooking the Sound and the S.E land approach to Plymouth; it also covers both the Laira and the merchant ship anchorage of Jennycliff Bay, and the N flank of Staddon Fort. It is connected to Staddon Fort by a military road protected by embankments. It was not proposed in the 1860 Royal Commission report, but was added to the scheme in October 1860, when it was known as Fort Turnchapel. Construction probably commenced late in 1861 or early in 1862, and was completed shortly after 1869. The fort was built on or near the site of a Civil War work.

In 1869 it was described as containing casemated barracks for 200 men, officers and NCOs in the gorge, a good and sufficient magazine, and a central traverse protecting the interior from view from the high ground to the E. It was intended to mount seven (9-inch) 12-ton (RML) guns on the two sea-facing sides, 13 guns on the land fronts and six mortars in the salients; the ditch (50 feet wide and 30 feet deep) and gorge were protected by one double and two single two tiered *caponiers* and two gun casemates in the counterscarp. In 1875 the proposed armament was five 7-inch RBLs, four 64-pdr RMLs, three 8-inch RML howitzers and sixteen SB flank guns. In 1877 two 10-inch RML guns were recommended for the S.W sea-facing side, and were mounted by 1880. In 1885 these had been joined by a 7-inch RBL gun on a Moncrieff carriage at the S.E salient, and five 64-pdr RMLs and eight 32-pdr SBBL guns (for the *caponiers*) were proposed. Eight other guns were lying in the fort. By 1893 the 64-pdr RMLs had been mounted, but the SBBLs were not. In 1903 four 40-pdr RBLs and four 8-inch howitzers were present. The fort was probably disarmed shortly after and was released by the MoD in 1963.

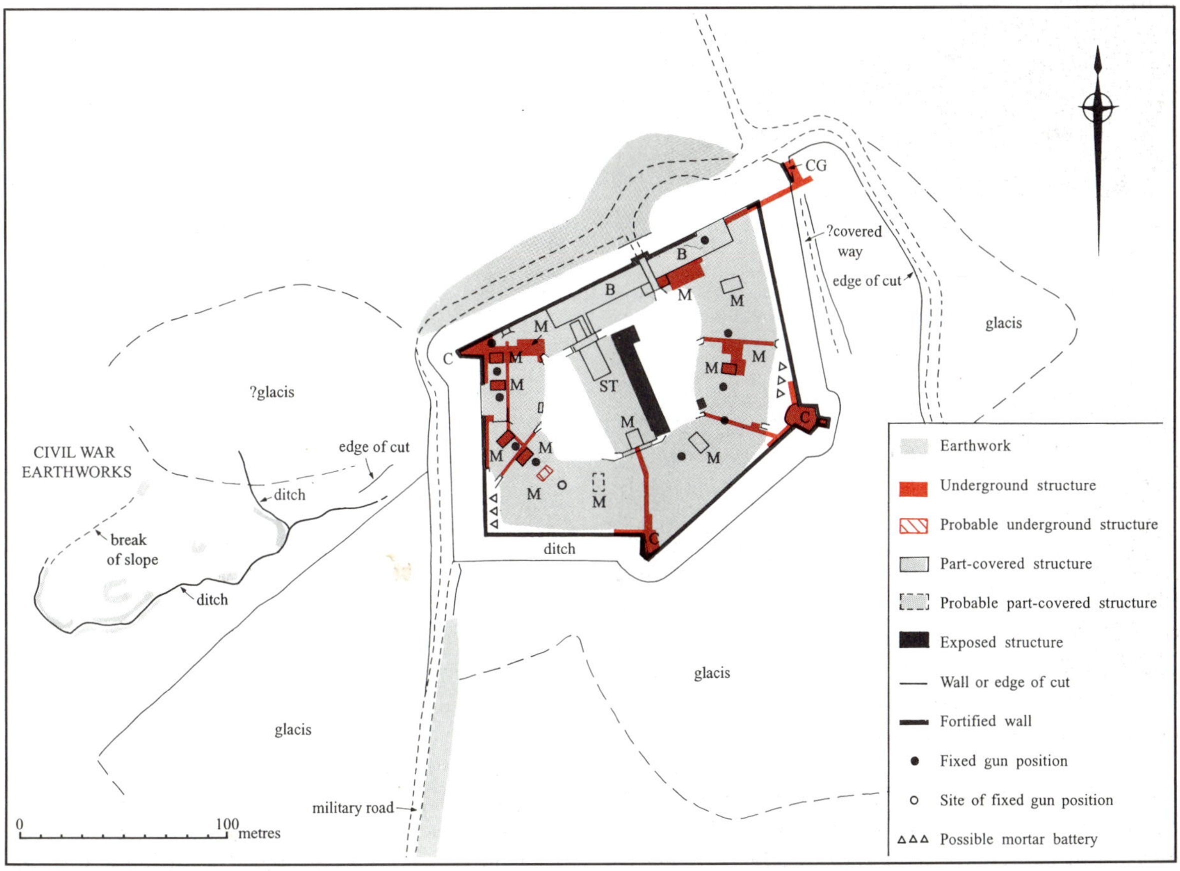

Fig. 100 Stamford Fort & earthworks

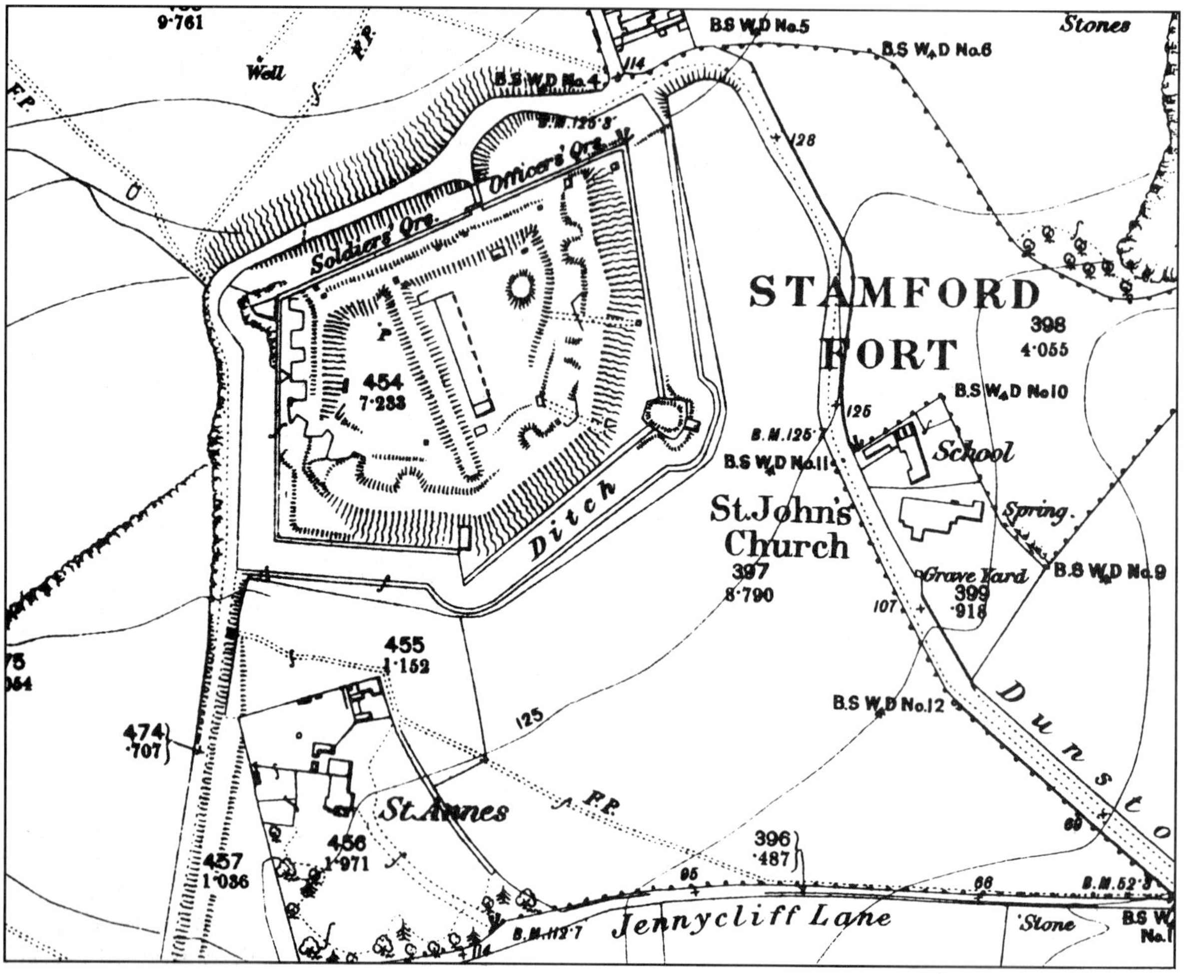

Fig. 101 Stamford Fort in 1896 (PRO: WO 78/2314)

Plate 140 Stamford Fort (Photograph: F.M. Griffith, Devon County Council. Frame DAP/US15. Copyright Devon County Council)

It is a five-sided polygonal work; three sides face landwards and one seaward, with a gorge overlooking the Cattewater. This is 50 feet high and contains bomb-proof casemated barracks and large magazines at its W end and adjoining the gate. The fort is divided in two by a central traverse; this contains stores, and to the E is a much-altered building which may have been intended as a gun shed. The W magazine retains most of its original wooden flooring (a rare survival) and iron lamp-housing; it served the RML guns mounted on the W and S.W sea faces in 1877-1880 via a series of four expense magazines on a level above the magazine, which in turn underlie others sited on the rampart between the gun positions. The other magazine served the guns to the E of the traverse. In total ten open gun positions are currently visible on the ramparts, five on the W & S.W sea faces, four (including one Moncrieff emplacement) on the S.E & E land faces, and one at the E end of the gorge, covering the access road from the N.E; they are separated by seven expense magazines. There are mortar batteries at the S.W & S.E salients.

Plate 141 Stamford Fort, main gate (Exeter Archaeology)

The gorge scarp contains an imposing gateway (with 'VR' over) flanked by 13 sets of barrack casemates on two floors, each lit by a double window with ashlar surrounds. The gorge was protected by a loop-holed wall along the scarp and by two gun casemates in a counterscarp gallery at the N.E end of the ditch. The other ditches were protected by one double (eight-gun) and two single (two and four-gun) *caponiers*, all enfiladed by musketry galleries. A *chemin des rondes* runs along all the scarps except part of the W one, and there are the remains of an ?unfinished covered way along the east face. Most of the *glacis* slope to the E & S.E has been built over, although some to the N.E remains open as allotments; St Anne's Parsonage to the south was not included in the *glacis* although presumably would have been cleared in time of war. To the S.W the land was heavily scarped to provide a clear field of fire for the heavy guns covering Jennycliff Bay, and there is a possible unfinished area of levelling to the N.

Plate 142 Stamford Fort, sally port door with loopholes (Exeter Archaeology)

Original fittings which remain include the main gate doors and drawbridge pulley wheels, flooring and lighting arrangements in the W magazine, tackle loops, stair rails and doorframes in the N.W *caponier*, together with the sally port door, stair rails, tackle-loops, flooring and door-frames, racer rails (not *in situ*), and the remnants of glazing, hammock-hooks and wooden musket-racks in the double *caponier*. The barrack casemates, counterscarp gallery or the S *caponier* were not accessible.

Present condition

The interior of the fort is used as a country club and caravan park; in the process the barrack casemates have been converted into flats and the ramparts have been levelled in places and at least one structure (?expense magazine at the S.W corner) demolished. The Moncrieff pit is occupied by a caravan. However the W magazine and the N.W and S *caponiers* are empty and unused; the double *caponier* is used as a private gym and most of the expense magazines on the ramparts and the stores within the central traverse are used for storage. The long building to the E of the traverse has been converted and partly extended and is the service and reception block. The ditch remains open except for a car park in the gorge (partly infilled at its west end) and a squash club in the eastern section. The counterscarp gallery has been modified and is used for storage. The W & S.W sections of the *glacis* remains open land; the remainder has been built on or is used as allotments.

Sources

General

13 - 17, 19, 23; O, Q.

Specific

c.1860 Plan (design). PRO: MR 1849

1928 Plan. EH: WD 574

STAMFORD HILL CIVIL WAR FORTIFICATIONS

PAR = PLYMSTOCK, NGR = SX49105265, PRN = SX45SE-212, MAP 3 No. 166

These are located on a spur extending westwards from Fort Stamford, overlooking Mount Batten to the N & a coombe containing Lord Howard's Battery to the S. This area was fortified by the Parliamentarian defenders of Plymouth in October and November 1643, when it and Mount Batten were taken by the besieging Royalists, and it was subsequently re-fortified by the Royalists in February 1645. A recently discovered map and account of the siege of October-November 1643 depicts the Parliamentary fortifications and the Royalist siege works, and there are other contemporary written accounts.

In October 1643 the Royalists attempted to surround the Parliamentary Fort Stamford (under the 1860s fort) by building a square work to the N. E of the fort and a line with half moons around the Parliamentary fort. This was slighted by the Parliamentarians who then built a line of communication with half moons at each end to either side of the fort. The fort, which was triangular, and the lines to each side are depicted on a plan of the action drawn up by a Royalist officer, John Pasman, together with another square Parliamentarian work to the N.E & a Royalist breastwork, batteries & half-moon in the valley below to the S.E. These Parliamentarian fortifications were taken by the Royalists on the 6th November 1643 and held by them until June 1644 when they withdrew. They then re-occupied and re-fortified Fort Stamford in February 1645 when they constructed a breastwork to each side of it in the manner of a line.

The Parliamentarian Fort Stamford was almost certainly sited under the later Victorian fort of the same name, with the line of communication and square work lying to the N.W overlooking Hooe Lake. To the S of the fort is a ridge, which contains a trench extending along the crown of the slope from N.E to S.W. This area was generally left unaffected by the scarping of the *glacis* of Stamford Fort in the 1860s. To the S. is a coombe, where the Royalist breastwork depicted in 1643 was sited.

The trench along the ridge is clearly depicted on an aerial photograph of 1946 and is visible on the ground, although the section to the N has been ploughed over and partly infilled. The trench follows a sinuous course, with some sections projecting forward of the general line, presumably to provide covering fire along the line to either side and over the slope in front. A slight bank remains in places along the southern side, and also in places along the northern side. In the centre is a communicating ditch leading northwards which has a slight bank on its western side for part of its length. At its western end the ditch and bank curves around the crown of the slope to the north and is heavily overgrown, although the ditch survives to a depth of at least 1m. Its line appears to continue as a break of slope around to the N.E around the crown of the hill overlooking Mount Batten. Just behind the line, on the summit of the slope, are two horseshoe-shaped earthworks, one substantial one towards the W and another in the centre. There are also other slight linear features and terraces/platforms which may belong to later use of the site, and a possible area of *glacis* to the N, which has been cut by later hut terraces.

The linear trench may represent the Parliamentary line of communication shown on Pasman's map, especially as both loop round at the S.W end, although Pasman does not show all the indentations elsewhere. Another context may be the Royalist breastwork constructed in 1644. An alternative explanation is that the trench, because it appears so fresh and sharp on the 1946 photograph, may have been dug in WWI or WWII, either as a defensive line or for practice purposes. However, it is sited further up the slope from the *glacis* scarp to the S.E, thus creating 'dead ground' very near the line where an attacker could shelter with impunity. For this reason a more practicable alignment for a defensive line post-dating the scarp would seem to be along the top of it. The possibility remains however that it was dug solely for practice.

Present condition

The site is open rough grassland with scrub encroaching from the west.

Sources

General

3

Specific

1860 'Account of the siege of Plymouth by the Royal Army in 1643', accompanied with notes by Capt. E. F du Cane. *Professional Papers of the Royal Engineers* Paper **XVI**

1875-6 Worth, R.N 'The siege of Plymouth' *Reports & Transactions of Plymouth Institution* **5**

1946 Aerial photograph. PCM

1988 Gaskell-Brown, C 'The later history of Mount Batten' in Cunliffe, B *Mount Batten, Plymouth. A Prehistoric and Roman Port* Oxford University Monograph No. **26**

1993 Stoyle, M *A List of Civil War fortifications at Plymouth* Exeter Archaeology Report No. **93.82** (City of Plymouth Archaeology Report GD. **1293**)

1994 Gray, T & Stoyle, M 'A Cavalier Cartographer' *History Today* **44(3)**

LORD HOWARD'S BATTERY

PAR = PLYMSTOCK, NGR = SX49105240, PRN = SX45SE-465, MAP 2 No. 167

This was armed with two 6-inch BL guns and was built to cover the merchant ship anchorage in Jennycliff Bay and the approach channel through the Sound to the Dockyard. It is sited on the top of the coastal cliffs, just S.W of Stamford Fort; it took over the function of the guns on the S.W face of the latter. It was probably recommended in 1905 and completed in 1909, and armed by 1910 when it first appears on the Defence Scheme maps (it does not appear in 1908). The guns were dismounted in 1916 although they appear to have been present in 1920 & 1927; they had been removed by 1936. Two 6-inch guns were mounted again in 1941, and were to be manned by 71 Coast Training Regiment from Fort Staddon on the order to 'Stand to'. The guns were finally dismounted in 1946.

Plate 143 Lord Howard's Battery, blockhouse (Exeter Archaeology)

The emplacements have been filled in, although the concrete aprons and parapet walls are still extant. Access was via a road down from the main road above; this is still in use but the lower area of magazines, stairwells and sunken roadway sited behind the emplacements has been infilled. The magazine was sited below-ground between the two emplacements as at Lentney. Small terraces in the slope behind represent two possible sites of the battery observation post, and immediately to the N of the cafe there is a concrete blockhouse. This probably dates to WWI or earlier, is rectangular and has a six-sided rear wall. There are loops in both side walls and in the rear wall. Other buildings, probably shelters and an artillery store, were sited to each side of the emplacements, and there was also a DRF; this would either have been sited immediately to the S or to the N of the guns; the sites and functions of this and other buildings are probably depicted on the two battery plans. The cafe building is relatively modern.

Present condition

Consists of coastal 'parkland', largely grass with some scrub along the coastal cliffs. The site of the battery is clear, although the surface buildings (except the blockhouse) have been demolished and the remainder infilled. Substantial below-ground remains of the gun pits, mountings and magazines below probably

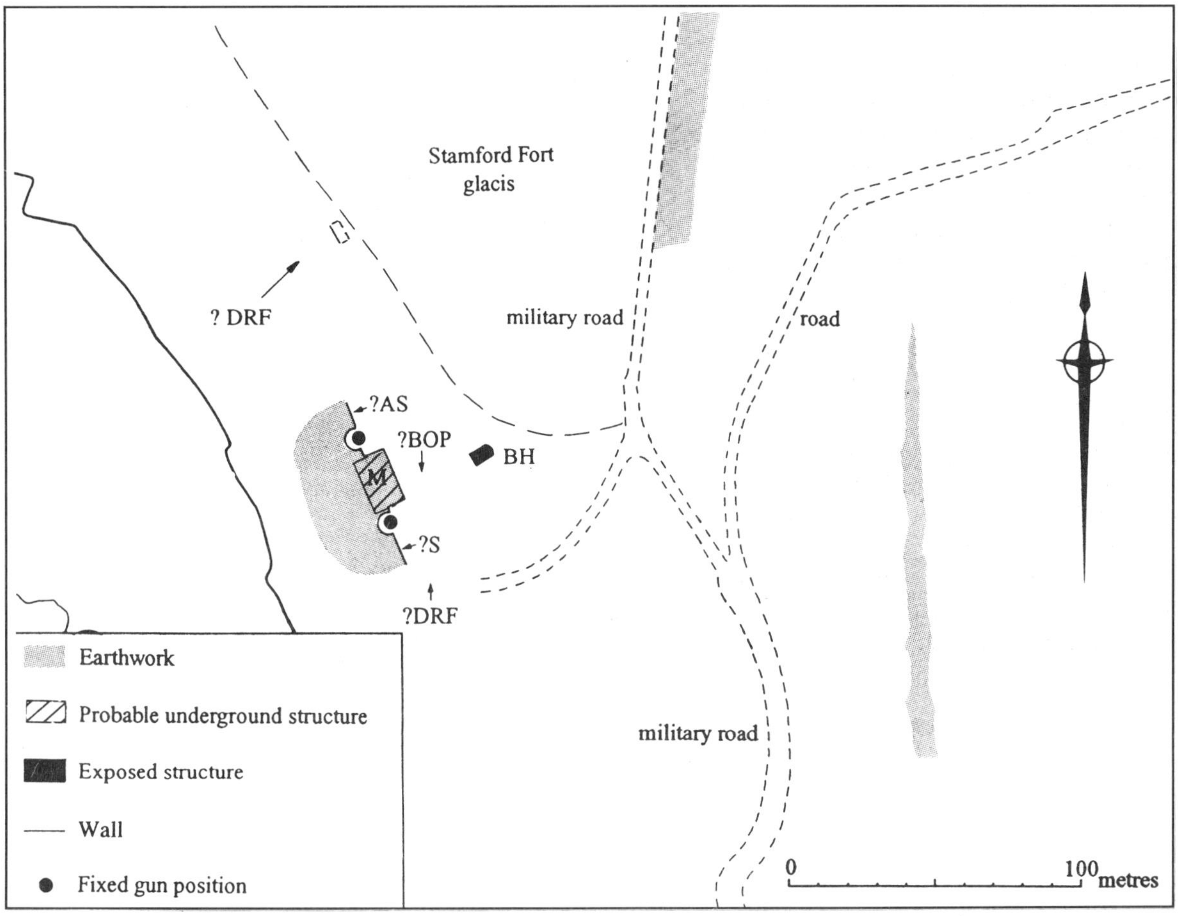

Fig. 102 Lord Howard's Battery

survive. The blockhouse is in good condition and is used for storage.

Sources
General
21, 22, 24; K, O, Q.

Specific

1907	Plan of battery. PRO: WO 78/5061
1927	?Armament table. PRO: CAB 36/16
n.d.	PRO: CAB 13/1
n.d.	Fort Record Book, including plan. PRO: WO 192/291

JENNYCLIFF PF CELL

PAR = PLYMSTOCK, NGR = approx SX 49305200, PRN = SX45SE-178, MAP 2 No. 168

This is marked (as a later annotation of 1894 and probably in an incorrect location) on the 1870 map and on a map of 1896. It was still in use in 1903, but had become redundant by 1915. Presumably it was intended for use with the guns of Staddon Heights Battery.

The site of the PF cell is on the brow of the coastal slope with a good view W over the Sound. No remains were found at its site as depicted in 1894; the site as marked on the 1896 map has not been visited.

Present condition
Not known.

Sources
General
16, 19, 23, 24.

STADDON FORT

PAR = PLYMSTOCK, NGR = SX49705171, PRN = SX45SE-42, MAP 2 No. 169

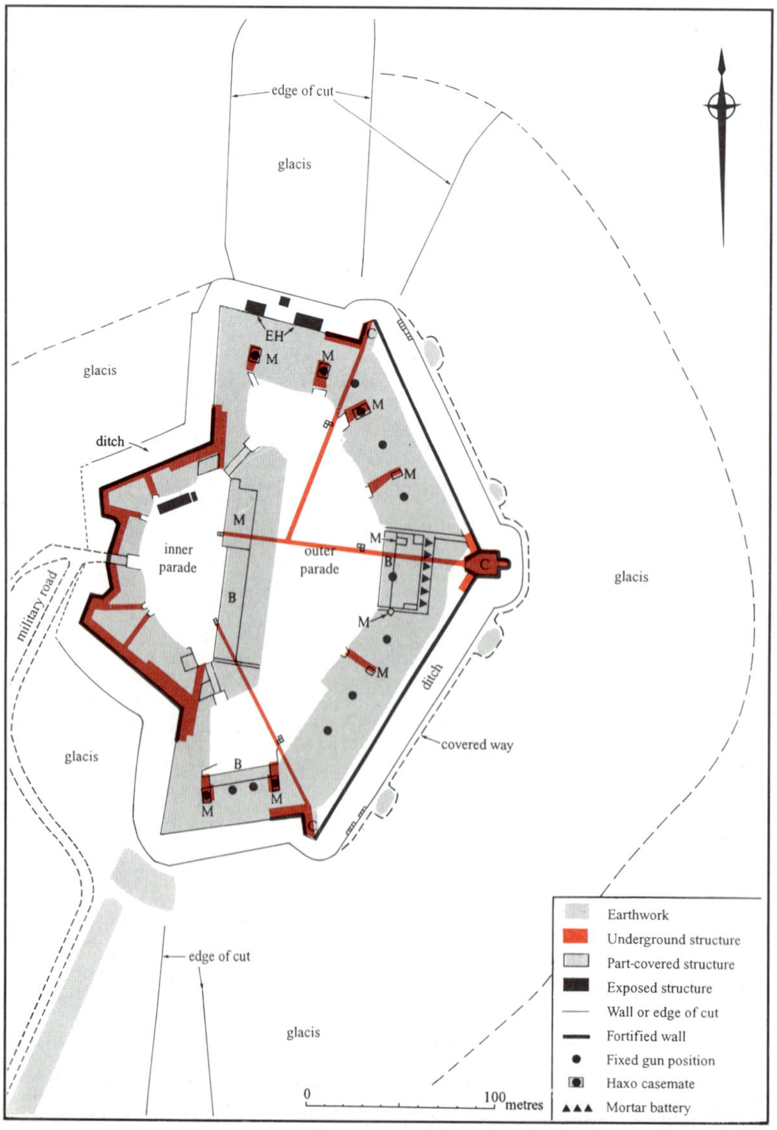

Fig. 103 Staddon Fort

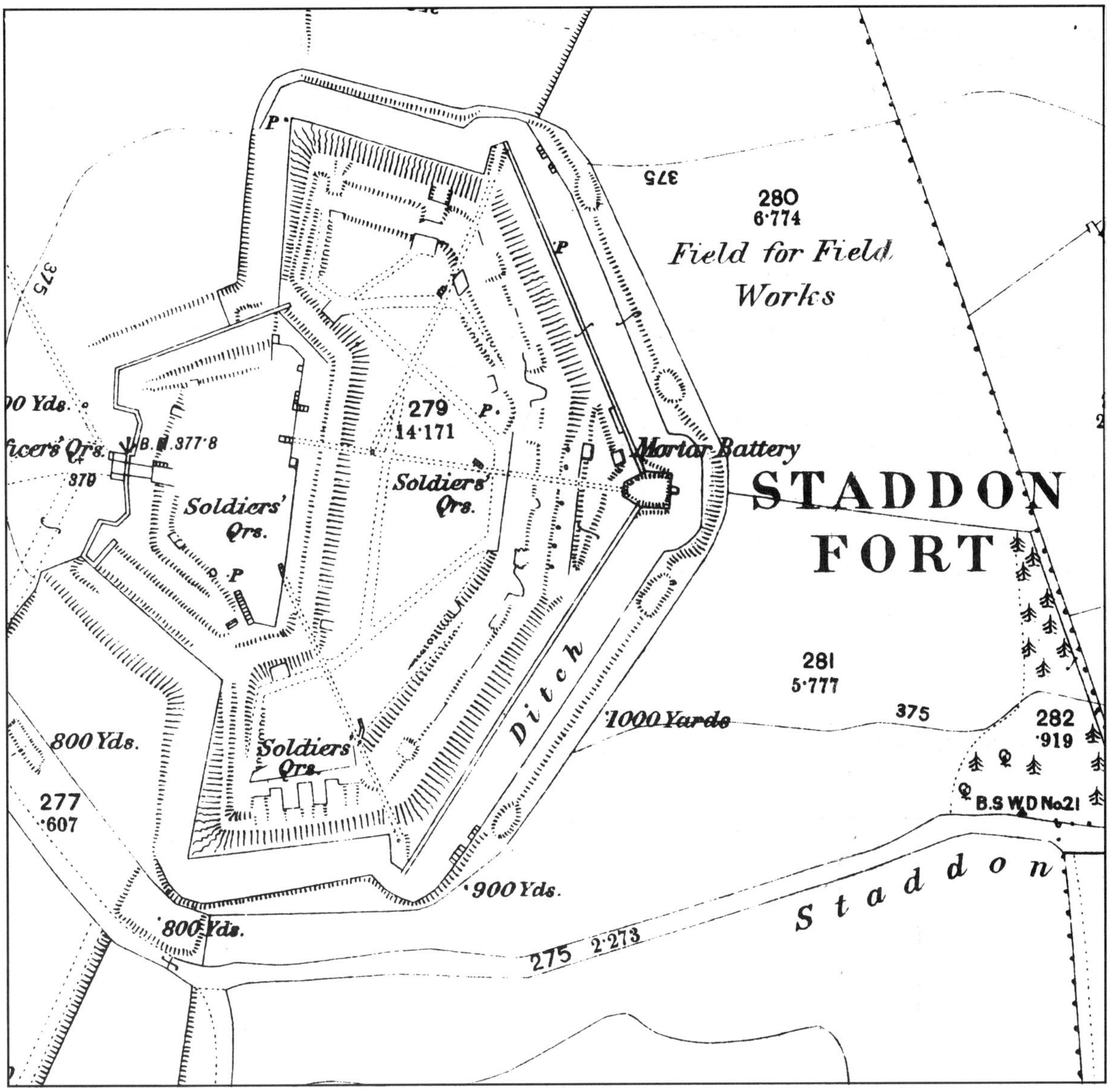

Fig. 104 Staddon Fort in 1896 (PRO: WO 78/2314)

This is the principal land fort of the Staddon Heights Defences; it occupies the highest point astride the watershed between valleys leading down to Hooe Lake and Bovisand, commands the approach to the Heights and overlooks Fort Stamford and the road from Queens Bridge as it approaches Laira Bridge. A work on this site was initially proposed in 1858 by Jervois as the central work of three, and was to have 35 guns and casemated barracks for 200 men and a 'tower' at the gorge. It was the principal work of the two proposed in 1860 by the Royal Commission, and was to have 30 guns and barracks for 400 men. It is connected to Stamford Fort and Brownhill, Twelve Acre Brake and Watch House Brake Batteries by a military road protected by an embankment/parapet.

The initial design included a keep at the rear, but this was modified in January 1862 when ordinary permanent barracks were substituted for casemated barracks in a keep. Designed by Capt. du Cane, construction began on 30 April 1861 and was completed on 15 March 1869, when it is described as intended for 16 guns on the *terreplein*, 12 on the keep (i.e. the ramparts of the 'inner parade'), 6 in Haxo casemates and for 6 mortars in casemates, with ample magazines and barracks for about 250 men. Its front faces were protected by a 50 foot wide and 30 foot deep ditch, flanked by two tiers of guns in *caponiers* and galleries. In 1875 the proposed armament was for twenty-five 7-inch RBLs, two 64-pdr RMLs, four 8-inch RML howitzers and thirty SB flank guns. However, by 1885 only two 7-inch RBLs were mounted, although there were two 8-inch RML howitzers and ten 7-inch RBLs lying in the fort. At this time an armament of thirteen guns was proposed for the ramparts, including two 7-inch RBLs on Moncrieff mountings, together with eight 32-pdr SB guns for the *caponiers* and two machine-guns to flank the main gate. By 1893 there were four 7-inch RBLs, five 64-pdr RMLs, and two 5-inch BL guns mounted on the ramparts, and eight 32-pdr SB guns in the *caponiers* and two machine-guns in the casemates flanking the gate. In 1903 the armament had declined to two 40-pdr and one 16-pdr RML and two unidentified guns, and the fort was probably disarmed shortly after.

It is a polygonal work, with four faces and a gorge from the centre of which the W half of the original (uncompleted) keep projects and forms an inner parade ground with a large traverse which covers it to the E.

Plate 144 Staddon Fort (Photograph: F.M. Griffith, Devon County Council. Frame DAP/US7. Copyright Devon County Council)

Plate 145 Staddon Fort, ditch (Exeter Archaeology)

Plate 147 Staddon Fort, mortar battery (Exeter Archaeology)

Plate 146 Staddon Fort, rampart, with Moncrieff emplacement in foreground (Exeter Archaeology)

The gate is protected by flanking gun casemates, but not, it appears, by a ditch, and gives on to the inner parade. The ditch extends around the other sides of the fort, and is flanked by two single and one double *caponier* and by gun casemates in the scarp wall of the 'keep'. A covered way, protected at intervals by traverses and by a *chemin des rondes*, lies on the front two flanks, with access via sally ports in the scarp wall and stairways in the masonry counterscarp. These are discontinuous, having a gap at the half-landing which could be bridged by troops issuing from the sally port; this bridge would then be removed in the event of retreat. Extensive landscaped *glacis* slopes extend to the N down to Hooe Lake and to the E and S, where its constant plane is clearly evident. On the ramparts of the outer parade are nine open gun emplacements (including two Moncrieff pits at the salients), six Haxo casemates and three expense magazines. Other magazines underlie these and the Haxo casemates, and serve the casemated mortar battery, *caponiers*, and gun casemates flanking the gorge. The *caponiers* and casemates were built to accommodate a total of 30 flank guns. The central traverse contains the main magazine and casemated barracks; there are further barracks within the S & E flanks of the outer parade and in the gorge wall flanking the gate. Further accommodation was available in the *caponiers* and gun casemates. The rampart of the inner parade has no gun emplacements but does have loop-holed parapet walls along the gorge and a rampart on the central traverse separating it from the outer parade. The parapet adjoining the gate also has *machicolations* and squinch loops, these are features of medieval origin which provided a means of firing at any attackers who had managed to get close up to the wall.

Plate 148 Staddon Fort, 32-pdr SBBL position in double caponier, with shelving & musket rack (right) (Exeter Archaeology)

Throughout the fort much internal detail and fittings survive, including gun tackle loops, racer rails, glazing, fireplaces, stoves, musket racks, coat and hammock hooks, and labels above doors, as well as later 19th-century and early 20th century light fittings, bathrooms and furnishings, and remnants of its subsequent use. Later remains include a brick building in the inner parade, terracing for huts on the ramparts and in the outer parade, and two 1930s/WWII engine-houses and a ?guardhouse in the ditch on the N side. These are similar in form to those powering searchlights elsewhere.

Present condition

Much of the fort, except the main magazine and two of the Haxos, is now empty. Apart from later adaptation of the barracks and main magazine the fort is in excellent condition; of particular importance is the survival of the *caponiers* complete with floors, gun tackle, stoves, musketry racks, coat-hooks and original glazing and also embrasure shutters in some cases. The ditch is mostly clear although sections have been infilled near the adjoining golf club and a new stable block, together with a substantial length along the S side of the 'keep'. The *glacis* remains open and unaltered.

Sources

General

11 - 17, 19, 23; O, Q.

Specific

c.1860	Plan (design). PRO: MR 1849
WWI	Postcard photo of gate and gorge. F.W. Woodward, FSGSW
1926	Plan, 1:500 (Royal Engineers). 2 copies, 1 held by K. Rawlings, FSGSW; 1 by the caretaker of Staddon Fort

BROWNHILL BATTERY

PAR = WEMBURY, NGR = SX49435105, PRN = SX45SE-43, MAP 2 No. 170

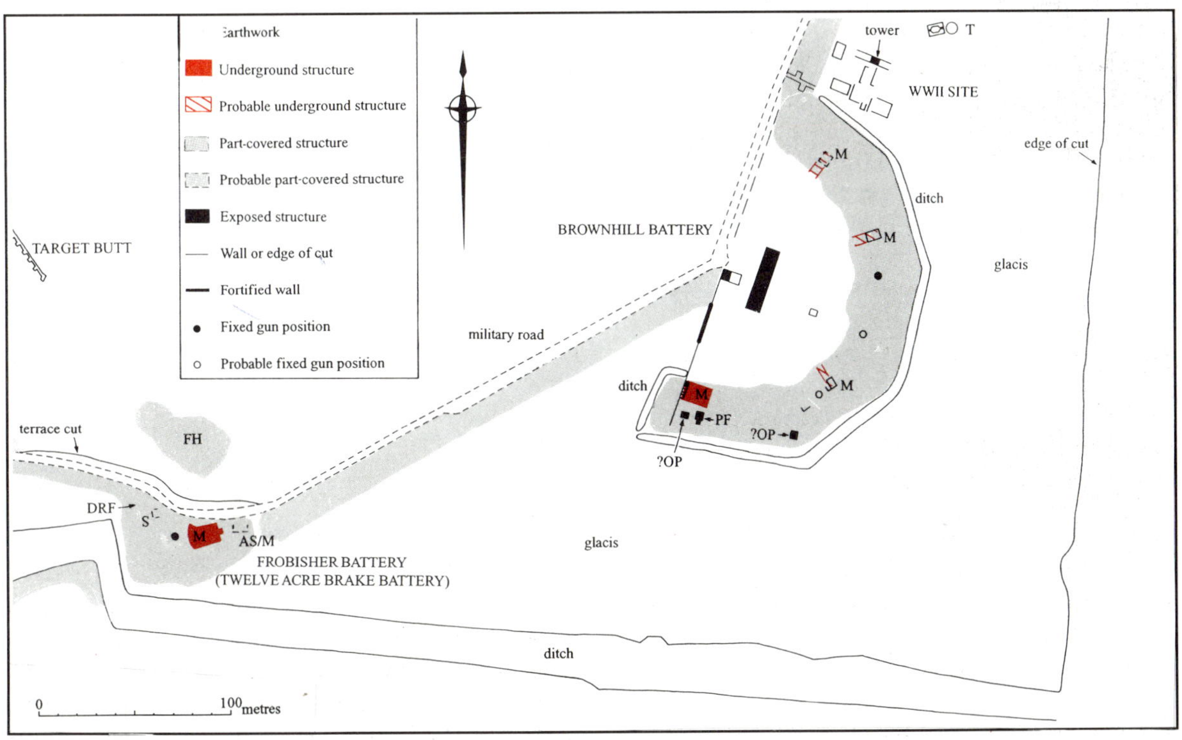

Fig. 105 Brownhill & Frobisher Batteries

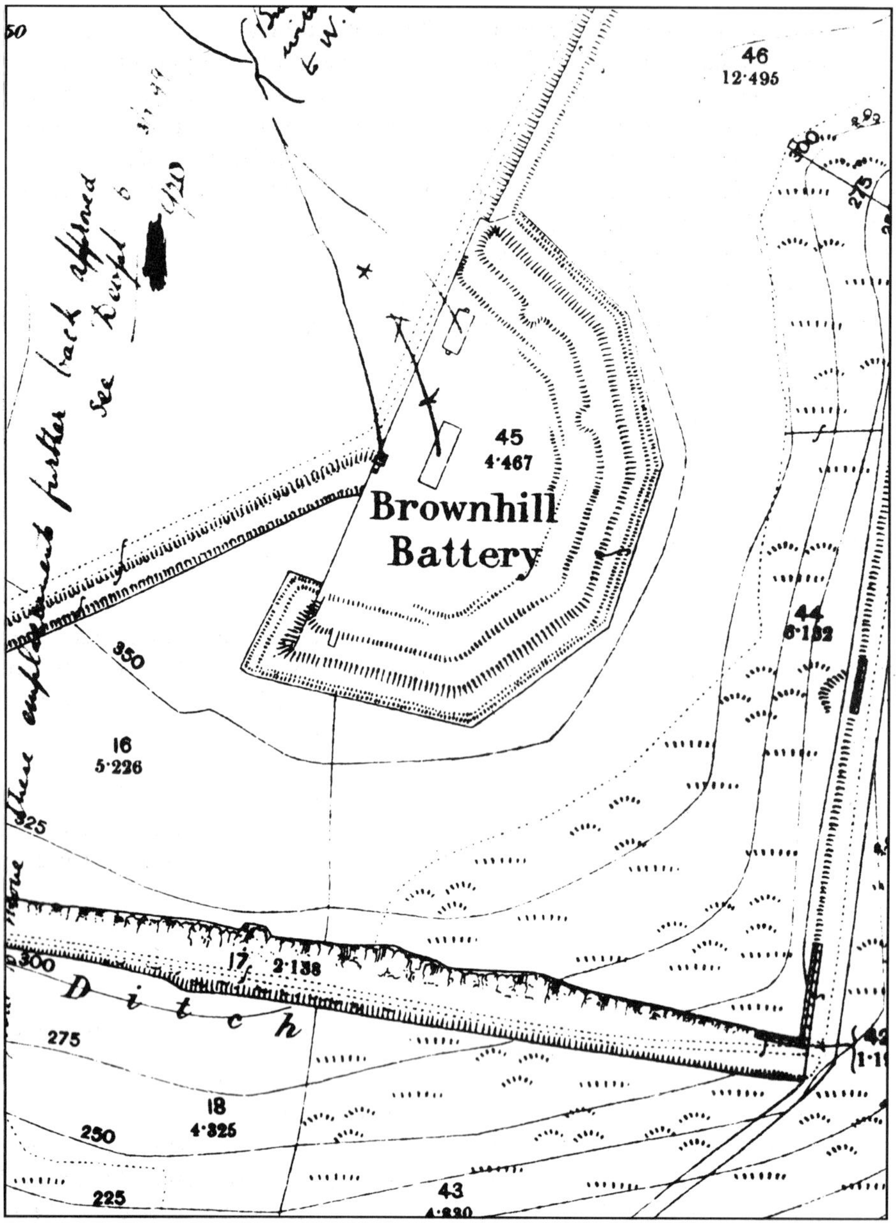

Fig. 106 Brownhill Battery in 1896 (PRO: WO 78/2314)

A redoubt (to be armed with 15 guns) in this approximate position was first recommended by Jervois in 1858, and Brownhill formed one of the two works (Staddon Fort being the other) recommended by the Royal Commission to deny Staddon Heights to an enemy. They were to be connected by a ditch and rampart, with lines closing the gaps at each end down to Hooe Lake and Bovisand Bay. Brownhill was to have 20 guns and accommodation for 200 men. Its function was to cover the ground in front of the lines and the scarp which surrounds it on the E and S, i.e. the valley below and the clearance area extending as far as Down Thomas. It was probably complete by 1867, and in 1869 was described as having space for 14 guns, with four bomb-proof chambers and an open gorge. In 1875 an armament of eight 64-pdr RMLs on travelling carriages was recommended (to be stored at Staddon Fort), and in 1885 six 8-inch RML howitzers were proposed, and were mounted by 1893. These were still in place in 1903, together with two 40-pdr RMLs, but were presumably removed shortly afterwards. In 1879 gun-cotton for use in submarine mines was stored in the battery, and a PF cell is depicted on its S rampart in 1894 and 1903. The battery was probably disused by WWI.

The battery has five faces, with an earthwork rampart fronted by a small ditch. On the S flank there is a loopholed wall covering the face of the rampart protecting the military road running S.W to Twelve Acre and Watch House Brake Batteries. The remainder

Plate 149 Brownhill Battery, expense magazine (Exeter Archaeology)

of the gorge (rear) of the battery is open. One probable and two possible gun positions are visible on the ramparts, although obscured by scrub. Two expense magazines remain on the E & S.E faces, and probably another on the N.E face. A larger magazine, consisting of a cartridge-store and a shell-store with a davit above is sited at the S.W corner. On the S rampart are the remains of the PF cell and two later (?WWII) observation posts. A stone building (possibly a small guard house) adjoins the entrance and in the centre is a long shed of recent build. Several concrete hut bases, presumably WWII in date and possibly associated with the site to the N, are visible in the interior.

Present condition

The ramparts are overgrown and unused, although the large magazine is used to shelter animals. The guard house is a pig sty and the shed a stable; the rest of the interior is occupied by a riding paddock (with the rear of the rampart being scarped in places to accommodate it) and dung-heaps.

Sources
General
11, 12, 14 -17, 19, 23; F, O, Q

BROWNHILL WWII RADAR INSTALLATION

PAR = WEMBURY, NGR = SX49505125, PRN = SX45SE-691, MAP 2 No. 171

This is sited immediately N of Brownhill Battery; access to it from the military road is through the 1860s embankment via a tunnel which has a guardroom to each side. The interior contains a concrete tower sited at the N end of a hut-base and underlain by a passage, and four other concrete hut-bases, some retaining remnants of breeze-block walls and entrance steps. There is also a water-tank and demolished pumping-house within a pasture field to the N.E. It is probably the site of the control room and radar for the Hooe Hill Rocket Battery to the N (No. 198) and was built by February 1944. It is the only known example of its type in or around Plymouth.

Present condition

The main site is fenced off and largely overgrown. All the buildings have been demolished apart from the tower.

TWELVE ACRE BRAKE BATTERY

PAR = WEMBURY, NGR = SX49155090, PRN = SX45SE-44, MAP 2 No. 172

Although not specified by the Royal Commission, this earthwork battery was added later when the Staddon Heights Defences scheme was finalised and was completed by 1867 for three guns, and included an expense magazine. The emplacements covered the section of ditch W towards Watchhouse Brake Battery. In 1872 it is labelled as two-gun battery, and in 1875 an armament of one SB flank gun was recommended; this was lying in the battery in 1885 but was removed shortly after. In 1888-92 it was rebuilt as Frobisher Battery (No. 173).

Present condition

The site is infilled and overgrown; most of the earthwork survives and probably originally dates to the 1860s; the expense magazine may have been re-used as the artillery store of Frobisher Battery.

Sources
General
12, 14 - 17; Q.
Specific
1871 General plan of Bovisand area. PRO: WO 78/3847
1872 War Dept. plan. PRO: WO 78/623

FROBISHER BATTERY

PAR = WEMBURY, NGR = SX49155090, PRN = SX45SE-044, MAP 2 No. 173

Frobisher Battery was built over and within the earlier Twelve Acre Brake Battery (No. 172). It was proposed in 1885, construction began in 1888 and was completed in 1892; it was armed with one 12.5-inch RML gun and was intended to bombard ships entering the Sound. It was still apparently armed in 1903 but was disarmed shortly after as its role was taken over by Watch House Battery. The magazine and artillery store was sited to the E of the gun, and a shelter and DRF to the N. In 1902 sites for two 5-inch BL guns (part of Bovisand Practice Battery) were approved immediately to the E of the battery, but it is not clear whether they were emplaced.

The emplacement, magazine and other structures were apparently filled in 10-15 years ago, but probably still survive below ground; the concrete apron is visible. To the N of the road there is a largely complete network of WWI or WWII trenches/foxholes (PRN = SX45SE-44/1; NGR = SX49115100). Some retain corrugated-iron revetment, and include at least one sunken bunker. They are dug into an earlier earthen mound and may have either been constructed to block off access around the S end of the target butts or for practice. The mound, as it is not depicted in 1870 but is in 1896, may have originated from the excavation of the Frobisher Battery magazine.

Present condition

The battery has been infilled but substantial remains probably survive below-ground. Much of the area is overgrown. The foxholes are largely complete and relatively well preserved for such features.

Sources

General

16, 17, 19, 23; O, Q.

Specific

1895 Frobisher Battery record plan. PRO: WO 78/4169

WATCH HOUSE BRAKE BATTERY

PAR = WEMBURY, NGR = SX48855090, PRN = SX45SE-019, MAP 2 No. 174

Although not originally proposed by the 1860 Commission this earthwork battery was completed in 1869, when it was described as a redoubt containing an expense magazine and positions for five guns. Its purpose was to cover the sections of the dry ditch running E towards Twelve Acre Brake Battery and Brownhill Battery and S down to Fort Bovisand. An armament of three 64-pdr RMLs was recommended in 1875, and was further proposed in 1885; two were finally mounted by 1893, and were removed in 1900. Plans of 1872 and 1896 show three apparent gun positions, two facing E along the ditch and one S.E towards the beach. The ditch down to Bovisand was covered by a musketry gallery below the battery. From *c*.1894 (*Fig. 99*) three PF cells were located in the battery together with another probable cell immediately to the W of the ditch; all were redundant by 1903. These, together with other cells in the area (Nos 182, 183 & 170), presumably located the targets for the RML guns at Staddon Heights and Frobisher Batteries.

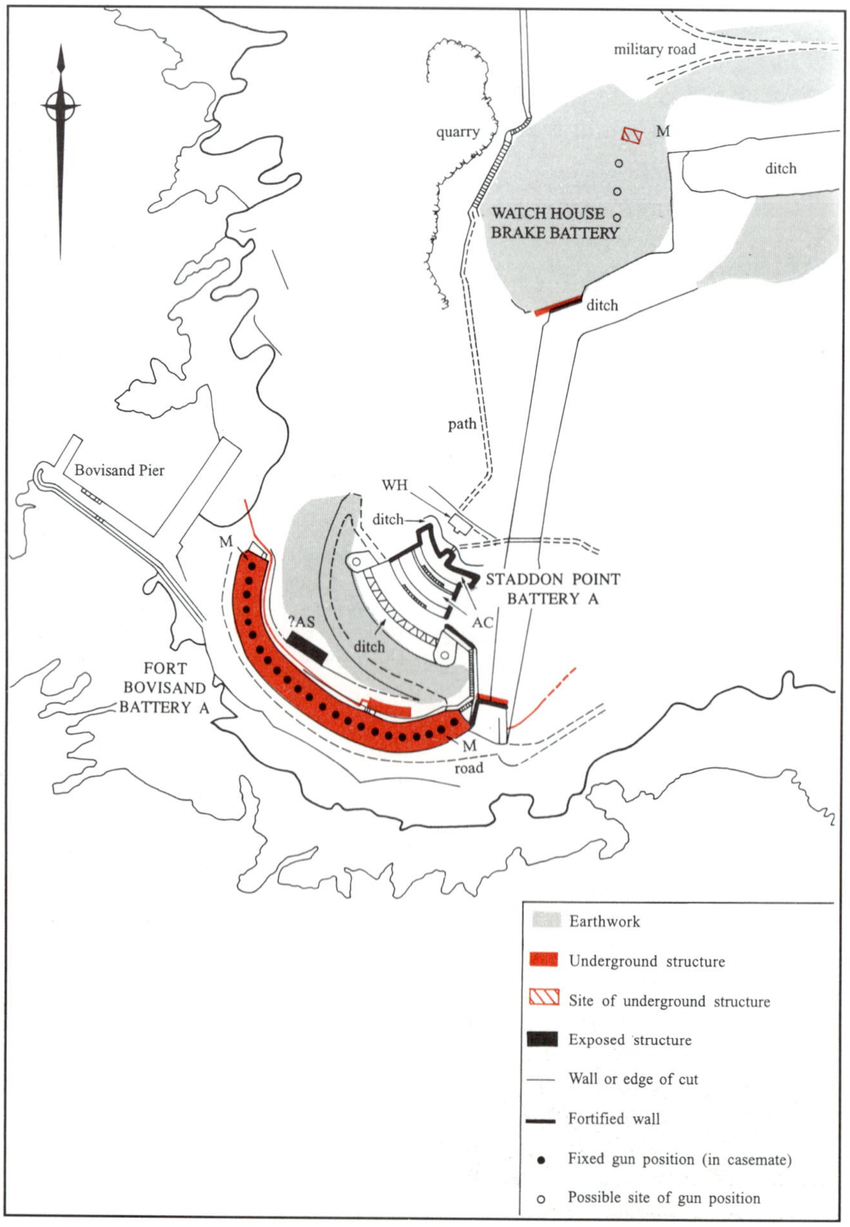

Fig. 107 The Staddon Point fortifications in the mid 19th century

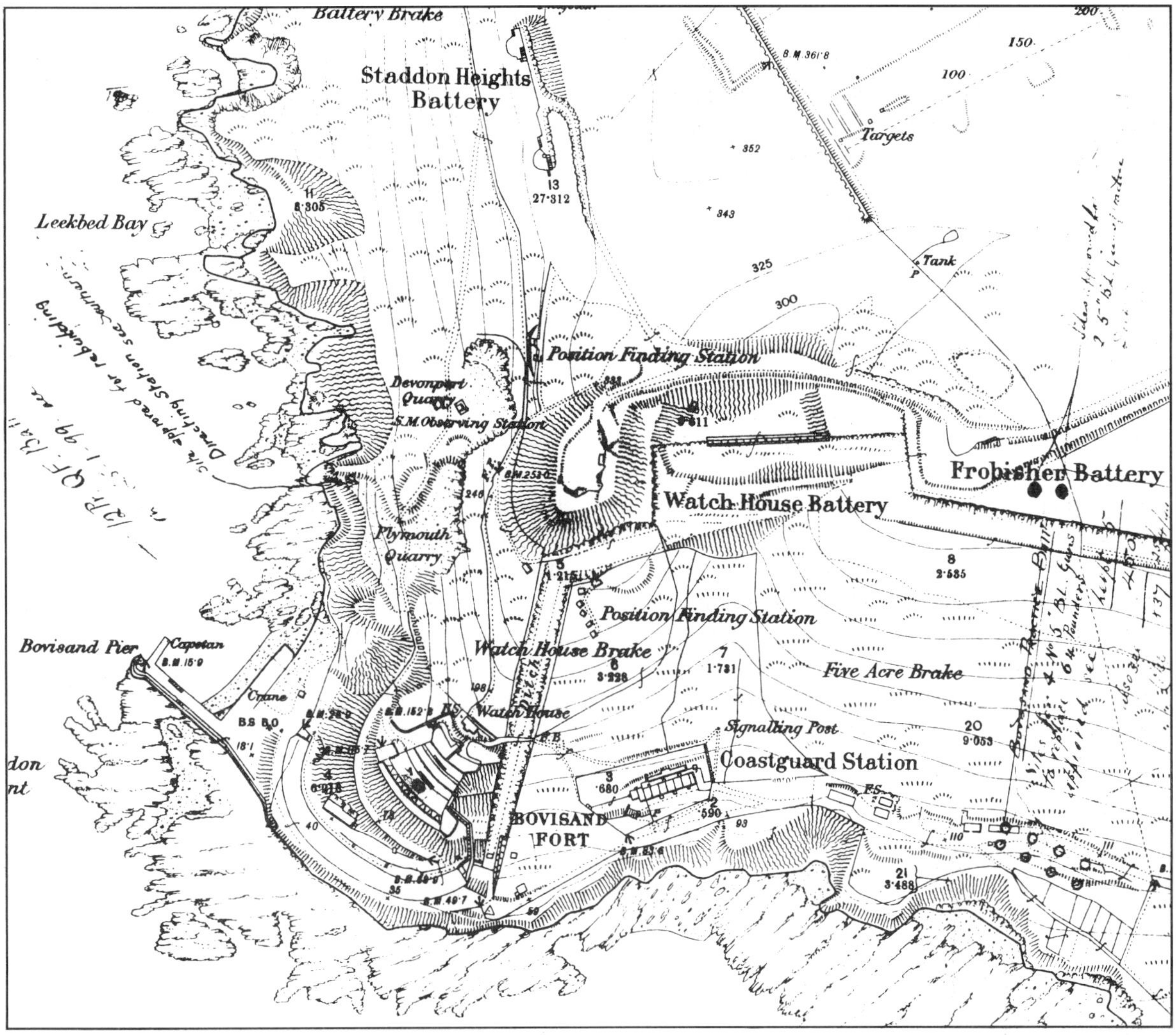

Fig. 108 The Staddon Point fortifications in 1896 (PRO: WO 78/2314)

Within the battery, the emplacements, magazine and PF cells were either covered over or removed when Watch House Battery was completed in 1904. Little therefore remains visible except for the ditch and musketry gallery. The ditch is rock-cut, *c*. 10-15m deep and 20-30m wide, and to the E has been artificially created where it crosses a valley, using buttressed dry stone walling to form its N side. Access to the musketry gallery is via a tunnel from the W; subsequently another entrance has been cut through into the ditch to provide access to the Watch House Brake PF Station S of the ditch. The gallery has a brick vaulted roof, stepped interior and 11 loop-holes. The nearby PF cell is of shuttered concrete with a flat roof; its viewing window at the front continues around part of the sides. It is adjoined by a later directing post (see Watch House Battery, No. 175).

Plate 150 Dry ditch looking east from Watch House Battery (Exeter Archaeology)

Present condition

Internal features of the battery have probably been largely removed but remains may survive below ground. The musketry gallery is in very good condition, but some of the walled sections of the ditch to the E of the battery are collapsing and are in urgent need of consolidation. The PF cell is in reasonable condition.

Sources

General

12, 13, 15, 16, 17, 19, 23; Q

Specific

1871	Plan of Bovisand area. With later amendments. PRO: WO 78/3847
1872	1:2500 plan. PRO: WO 78/623
n.d.	Watch House Fort Record Book. PRO: WO 192/292

WATCH HOUSE BATTERY

PAR = WEMBURY, NGR = SX48855090, PRN = SX45SE-019, MAP 2 No. 175

This battery was completed by November 1901, when it was armed with two 6-inch BL guns; its purpose was to cover the seaward approaches to the Sound. At 352 feet above sea level, it is the highest battery of this type in the country. It was armed during WWI, and the guns remained mounted through the inter-war period and WWII; they were dismounted in 1952. Initially the battery probably made use of the earlier searchlights built on Bovisand Pier to serve the 12-pdr QF battery at Staddon Point; in 1912 these were augmented by two 'fighting lights' sited immediately to the E of Fort Bovisand (PRNs = SX45SE-18/7 & 8; NGR = SX 48845065 & 48875065), which remained in use during WWII. A DRF was sited to the north, and by 1911 an EL (Electric Light) Director Post had been built behind the guns on the roof of the guardhouse. The earlier PF cell on the W edge of the ditch below the battery was extended and is labelled as a 'Night Director' and O.C.E.L. (Officer Commanding Electric Lights) Post in 1911 (PRN = SX45SE-19/2). Local defence measures in WWI included the erection of fences around this post and the battery and of a small block-house (see under Watch House Brake PF Station, No. 182) in the bottom of the ditch below - to protect both the battery and the Watch House PF Station. At this period a Battery Observation Post (BOP) was built below the guns.

In 1940 it was proposed to emplace another 6-inch BL gun to the N., but this was not done and the battery continued in operation with the same armament until it was stood down in 1946. The DRF position to the N may at this time have been converted into a machine-gun or LAA gun emplacement to protect against strafing, and a new BOP (now demolished) was built immediately to the S of it, together with a brick sentry post at the N.E entrance to the battery. It was probably at this time that a 'Battle' observation post was added between the two earlier Staddon Heights PF cells (see under No. 183).

The gun emplacements, magazines, and associated buildings such as shelters, guard-house, artillery store, lamp-room and the DRF position remain largely complete. In common with other BL batteries of this period the magazine is of standard type, with two pairs of shell and cartridge stores to each side of a central passage (where personnel changed into safety clothing). The cartridge stores are placed to the rear, behind the shell stores, and are enclosed with a brick wall and lit by lamp windows; a serving hatch gives onto an area at each end where the shells and cartridges were transferred up to the gun above via separate manually-operated lifts. Most internal fittings such as shelf supports, light fittings, cartridge lifts, and the lower parts of the shell lifts have been removed although the labels mostly survive. Above the magazines the two gun emplacements survive complete with the degrees of traverse incised in the cement surround and retain many of the iron doors to the ammunition lockers and also the cartridge and shell lifts. The original guard-rails, and the davits which provided an alternative method for lifting up shells and cartridges from the magazines, remain.

Plate 151. Watch House Battery, 6-inch BL emplacement (Exeter Archaeology)

The two searchlight emplacements on the coast E of Fort Bovisand have been demolished. The W one was sited on an area retained by a curved rubble stone wall; this is clearly marked on all plans from 1872 onwards, when it formed the retaining wall for a road down to the fort, and probably either dates to the 1860s or to 1816-24 when the harbour, pier and sea wall were built by Rennie.

The WWI BOP below the battery is a rectangular concrete and brick structure, containing an instrument pillar. The searchlight directing post (SDP; OCEL Post - see above) adjoining the earlier PF cell is built of brick and concrete, and contains two rooms, both of which have large seaward facing windows. The entrances are from the rear, where there is a insulated cupboard which was used as an ammunition locker or fusebox.

Present condition

The battery

The buildings are presently used as accommodation and are relatively well maintained although they suffer from vandalism when not occupied. Some of the concrete structure however is suffering from damp, as are the steel girders; the wooden shell lifts have lost their steel covers and until recently were exposed to the elements and deteriorating as a consequence.

Searchlight emplacements

Both of these are demolished, though foundations may survive below ground. The early retaining wall is being eroded and has partly collapsed at its E end.

PF Cell; SDP/OCEL Post; WWI BOP

All these are unused, open to the weather and consequently deteriorating. Most, however, are still largely structurally complete, although the PF Cell has a collapsing roof, and the BOP is partly infilled.

Sources
General
21 - 24; F, O, Q.
Specific

1896	War Office O.S 1:2500 map with c.1910 amendments. PRO: WO 78/5041(1)
1904	Plan and sections etc. PRO: WO 78/5058
1911	Plymouth Defences. Index plan. With later amendments. PRO: WO 78/5066
1920s	Lease plan for Staddon Battery property. Mr Forster, Staddon Cottage
1938	Plan of Bovisand Fort. PSA: 023210X
1940	Plan, sections and elevations. PRO: WO 78/5058
1942	War Dept. plan. Copy held by J. Symons (FSGSW)
n.d.	Watch House Fort Record Book. PRO: WO 192/292
n.d.	Block plan. EH: P/229

STADDON POINT BULWARK

PAR = WEMBURY, NGR = SX48785067, PRN = SX45SE-018, MAP 2 No. 176

Three cannon pointing out over the Sound, together with a barricade on the landward side, are depicted at Staddon Point on Grenvyle's map of proposed defences dating to 1586-88, and are labelled 'new bulworke'. It is not clear whether such a bulwark was in the event constructed; if it was its site lies under the later batteries. There are no identifiable surface remains.

Sources
General
2; M (No. 4)

STADDON POINT BATTERY A

PAR = WEMBURY, NGR = SX48805072, PRN = SX45SE-447, MAP 2 No. 176

This, with Picklecombe and Eastern King, was one of three batteries recommended by the Inter Service Committee on Harbour Defences in 1844; it covered the E entrance to the Sound around the end of the recently completed breakwater whilst Picklecombe covered the W entrance. It also served to protect the harbour and pier (PRNs = SX45SE-454, 692 & 693) built by Rennie between 1816 and 1824 for the watering (via barrels and piping from a reservoir sited above Bovisand Bay) of ships moored in the Sound. Construction began in October 1845 and was completed in 1847, as a datestone above its entrance records. It was originally designed to accommodate three officers and 90 men, and to be armed with six 32-pdr and four 8-inch guns on dwarf traversing platforms. In 1850 it mounted seven 68-pdr guns and three 10-inch shell-guns, and nine guns of unspecified type in 1858. In 1862 an Anderson's cupola for heating iron to fill Martin's liquid-iron shells was apparently installed on trial. On a map of 1871 eight embrasures with racer rails and pivots behind are depicted, together with a racer rail and pivot on each of the flanking towers.

On the completion and arming of Bovisand Fort in 1870-2 Staddon Point was disarmed and used as accommodation for the officers and garrison. A covered way protected by a loop-holed wall was provided between the two batteries and they were also connected by a road. An earlier 'Watch House' (in 1864 a Coastguard lookout station) is sited just outside the N gate of the battery, and after 1872 the whole of the battery was enclosed by a boundary wall to the N. A pathway (PRN = SX45SE-19/5), protected in places by a wall on its seaward side, linked it with Staddon (No. 184) and Watch House Brake Batteries (No. 174) to the N, and later with Staddon Heights Battery (No. 185) and PF cells (No. 183). In 1898-99 a 12-pdr QF battery (Staddon Point Battery B) was built within the ditch.

Plate 152 Staddon Point Battery A (1847) (Exeter Archaeology)

Apart from the construction of a new gateway in the 1860s and the partial demolition of the towers and the remodelling of the *terreplein* in 1898-9, the battery remains largely complete. It is built on three levels, with the lowest being occupied by the *terreplein* with, according to a plan of 1901, a range of stores at its rear. The middle level accommodated (in 1901) the Officers' Mess, kitchens and servants' quarters, and a later WWII concrete observation post is sited on the terrace; the upper level was the Officers' Quarters. The higher status of the upper two levels is reflected in the superior quality of the stone facework. The whole structure is built of limestone and was defended on all sides by a dry ditch, which remains visible around the N. This was enfiladed by musketry fire from loop-holes in the side walls of the projecting gatehouse, whilst the approaches were protected by a loop-holed parapet on the roof of the Officers' Quarters. The approaches to the flanks were similarly protected by loop-holed walls and the flanks themselves were enfiladed by fire from the parapet wall on the Officers'

Quarters and by others at the rear of the towers (shown on *Plate 7*). The E flank was later also enfiladed by a loop-holed wall protecting the 1860s covered way down to Fort Bovisand. Few original fittings survive except for three iron water-pumps, one complete with its handle, and the drawbridge mechanism in the gatehouse. Access to the battery was originally via the gatehouse and drawbridge, and probably also through a wider gateway (subsequently blocked) in the E wall of the *terreplein*. The present monumental gateway through the W wall is clearly a secondary insertion and probably dates to the construction of Bovisand in the 1860s and the provision of the road linking the two.

Present condition

The structure of the battery survives largely intact, except for the alterations made in 1898-99. Few fittings appear to survive, except for the pumps and drawbridge mechanism. The three levels of barrack and store accommodation is well-maintained; some forms a private flat, while the remainder has been recently refurbished as additional accommodation for the diving centre. The earlier watch-house building is roofless and used at present as a garden.

Sources

General

10, 11, 12, 16; F, G, I, O, Q.

Specific

1850	Maps and armament tables. Royal Citadel: Officers Mess
1862	Map, with later additions. PSA: 023213B
1864	Plan of Bovisand. Royal Citadel: Officers Mess
1869	Plan of Bovisand and area. RCHME: PLM/535
1871	Plan of Bovisand area. With later amendments. PRO: WO 78/3847
1872	1:2500 plan. PRO: WO 78/623
1896	War Office 1:2500 map, with amendments c.1910. PRO: WO 78/5041(1)
1890s	Photograph (Plate 7). R.C.F. Serpell.
1901	Plan of Officers' Quarters and QF magazine. Reproduced in McDonald, 1981 (I)
1950s	Plan and section of roof level. PSA: 023228X
n.d.	Photographs in PLSL.

FORT BOVISAND BATTERY A

PAR = WEMBURY, NGR = SX48785067, PRN = SX45SE-018, MAP 2 No. 177

Bovisand was one of two powerful casemated coastal batteries proposed in the Royal Commission Report of 1860 to cover the entrances at each end of the Breakwater. It covered the E entrance whilst Picklecombe Fort in Cornwall covered the W. Both superseded batteries (Staddon Point Battery A and Picklecombe Battery, Nos 176 & 13) built in the 1840s for the same purpose; Bovisand is also located at the southern end of contemporary fortifications guarding against land attack from the E (The Staddon Heights Defences).

Jervois, in his memo of February 1858, recommended the construction of a battery of about 60 guns in three tiers at Staddon Point, with another at Picklecombe and also a casemated battery at each end of the Breakwater. However, the latter were not recommended in 1860 (a sea fort, Breakwater Fort, being preferred instead), although Picklecombe and Bovisand were. The final design (by Major Porter) for Bovisand which was accepted in November 1861 was for a 'granite casemated battery of two tiers, to mount fifty 68-pdr and 110-pdr guns, protected by iron shields, with a large detached magazine at the rear'. In 1864, when the foundations and basement had been largely completed to this plan, the specification was changed to one casemated tier of 23 guns of 12 and 18 tons, with the magazines now being housed underneath them in the basement. Bovisand was completed on 25th November 1869 and in 1872 was apparently armed with 22 9-inch RML guns and one 10-inch RML gun. By 1880 this had changed to its final armament (nine 9-inch and 14 10-inch RML guns) and at least one Watkins Depression Range-finder was installed. This may have been sited on the flank, beyond the gun casemates, or on the roof, where there are two observation stations (present by 1886). The RML guns were removed between 1895 and 1903. Later gun emplacements on the roof, and searchlights along the shore, belong to other batteries (Fort Bovisand Batteries B & C, Staddon Point Battery B, and Watch House Battery). All the searchlights were probably powered by diesel engines sited in casemate Nos 1 and 2. In World War II casemate nos 11 & 16 were used as magazines for the twin 6-pdr QF guns sited on the roof, and in the early 1950s the fort was converted and used as the Plymouth Fortress Seaward Defence HQ, until the disbandment of Coast Artillery in 1956.

The main structure of the battery survives complete, although most of the casemates and magazines have since been adapted for other uses. It consists of 23 stepped granite casemates set in a curving frontage, sloping down from E to N.W. A typical casemate has an iron shield (up to 3 feet thick, and consisting of a sandwich of wrought iron plates with teak and/or iron concrete in between) within the granite embrasure,

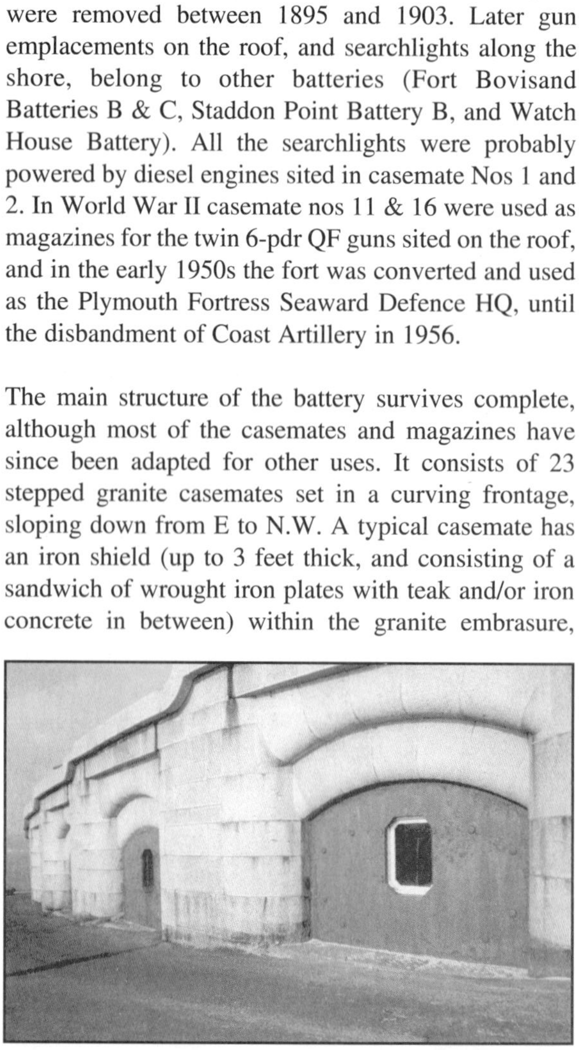

Plate 153 Fort Bovisand, casemates & shields (Exeter Archaeology)

Plate 154 Fort Bovisand, interior of casemate (Exeter Archaeology)

behind which was a rope mantlet for the protection of the gun crews. The RML gun was placed on a traversing carriage at the front of the casemate, with the rear being reserved for barrack accommodation. In the front wall there is a cartridge lift between each embrasure, and fireplaces alternate with shell-lifts in the dividing walls to the rear. Most of the lifts are blocked, although some of the pulley loops and davits for the cartridge lifts still remain visible (e.g. between casemate Nos 13 & 14). Mantlet bars survive in casemate Nos 12 - 14 at least, together with labels (in Nos 12 & 13) above each embrasure detailing the specification of the gun emplaced there (e.g. '10-inch 18-ton RML gun XIII' in No. 13). An arched verandah runs around the rear of the casemates, originally divided off from the latter by glazed timber partitions; two spiral staircases provide access from it to the magazines below.

The magazine level consists of alternating barrel-vaulted shell-stores and cartridge-stores, with each being placed directly under a casemate and each serving two adjoining guns. Access is via a passage running under the verandah around the rear of the stores. The shell-stores and lifts open directly onto it, whilst the cartridge-stores open into branch passages. These each have a hatch giving into a narrow unlit passage running round inside the front wall of the casemates; cartridge lifts are placed in its roof. The main access passage was lit by lamps opposite each branch passage, which were serviced from a narrow lamp passage running under the road to the rear. Further light may also have been provided by lamps placed within shafts in the ceiling adjoining each branch passage and shell lift. These do not appear in the floor of the verandah above, which has been re-paved.

Most of the internal fittings of the magazines have been removed. Two of the shell lifts retain their labels, and one its wooden lining; several of the cartridge lifts in the front passage still possess their wooden lining and the occasional metal voice-pipe. Labels survive above some of the doors of the shell stores, whilst at least one of the cartridge hatches retains its original door.

The E flank of the battery is protected by a deep dry ditch which continues around the Staddon Heights position to the N. The section adjoining Bovisand is enfiladed by a musketry gallery below Watch House Brake Battery, and its seaward end is defended by two musketry galleries, access to which was gained from inside Bovisand and which include a sally port. A covered way protected in part by a loopholed wall provided a safe route between Bovisand and Staddon Point Battery A, which was used as accommodation. Other surface buildings subsequently added to the rear of the main battery during the later 19th century and early 1900s include various store buildings and a possible concrete observation post for the later 6-pdr Hotchkiss battery (Fort Bovisand Battery B). An original iron water tank to the rear of casemate No. 23 also survives.

On the roof of the casemates the two observation stations survive largely complete, at the rear of the casemates and of later gun emplacements.

Present condition

All the casemates and magazines are presently used by the diving centre and are generally maintained in good condition, although some of the few remaining cartridge-lift and shell-lift linings and labels above doorways may be vulnerable to removal in order to accommodate pipes and services. Damp is a general problem throughout the battery.

Sources

General

11 - 17, 19, 23; F - I, K, O, Q.

Specific

1861	Proposed works on Staddon Position. PRO: MR 1849
1862	General plan of area, with reservoir etc, and 1869 additions. PSA: 023213B
1864	Plan. Royal Citadel: Officers' Mess
1869	General plan of area. PSA: 023211X
1869	General plan of area, with reservoir and pier. RCHME: PLM/535
1871	Overall plan and basement and first floor plans and sections. PRO: WO 78/3847
1872	Plan. PRO: WO 78/623
1876	Basement and general plan, with ?1886 and later amendments. PRO: WO 78/3847
1880	Map of Bovisand Bay. PRO: WO 78/2735
1893	General plan of area. PSA: 023216X
1896	O.S. 1:2500 map with 1910 amendments. PRO: WO 78/5041(1)
1890s	Photographs. PLSL
1890s	Photograph. R.C.F Serpell (Plate 7)
1910	General plan of area. PSA: 023215X
1910	War Office 1:500 survey. PRO: WO 78/5041(2)
1920s	Lease plan for Staddon Battery property. Mr Forster, Staddon Cottage
1938	Ground floor plan of battery. PSA: 023210X
1940s	Plan & section of casemates 6 - 8. PSA: 023226B
1951	Plan of casemates 6 & 7. PSA: 023227X
n.d.	Bovisand Fort Record Book. PRO: WO 192/265

FORT BOVISAND BATTERY B

PAR = WEMBURY, NGR = SX48785067, PRN = SX45SE-018, MAP 2 No. 178

In 1885 three pairs of Hotchkiss 6-pdr QF guns were proposed for the defence of the minefield between Bovisand and the Breakwater; emplacements for these are sited on the roof of the casemates in front of the earlier observation stations. In 1893 they were dismounted and in 1903 were apparently used for practice purposes; there is no record of them thereafter and they were probably removed by WWI. They were replaced in their original role by the six 12-pdr QF guns installed in 1899 (Staddon Point Battery B).

The E pair of emplacements survive complete. Three other emplacements are partly visible under the World War II twin 6-pdr QF gun positions to the W.

Plate 155 Fort Bovisand, pair of 6-pdr QF positions & observation station (left) & later twin 6-pdr QF emplacement (right) (Exeter Archaeology)

Present condition
See above.

Sources
General
17, 19, 23; I, Q.
Specific
1950s Plan of casemate roof level. PSA: 023229X
n.d. Fort Bovisand Fort Record Book. PRO: WO 192/295

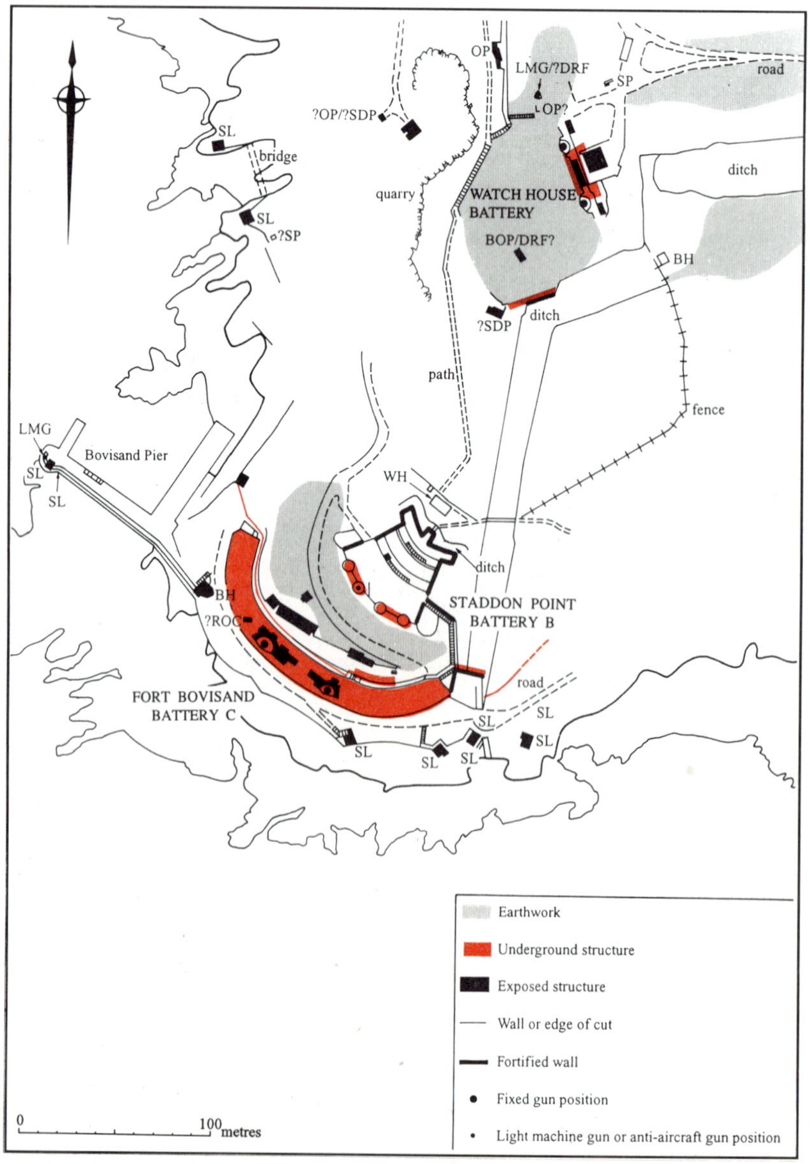

Fig. 109 The Staddon Point fortifications in c.1900

FORT BOVISAND BATTERY C

PAR = WEMBURY, NGR = SX48785067,
PRN = SX45SE-018, 18/3-6, MAP 2 No. 179

In 1942 two twin 6-pdr QF guns were mounted on the roofs of casemate Nos 11 and 16, which housed their magazines. The guns were positioned to defend against motor torpedo boats using the E entrance to the Sound, and replaced the obsolescent 12-pdr QF guns on Staddon Point Battery (B) above, which were removed. Four new illuminated area searchlights (CASLs) were built on the shoreline below the casemates, powered by a new engine-room in casemate No. 3. Local defence measures during WWII included a machine-gun position at the pier head (PRN = SX45SE-454/3), a blockhouse (probably doubling as an earlier searchlight position; PRN = SX45SE-468) at the landward end of the pier, and spigot mortar positions guarding the access from the E & N.E. All guns and searchlights were removed in 1957.

Plate 156 Fort Bovisand, twin 6-pdr QF emplacement with observing tower (Exeter Archaeology)

The gun emplacements survive complete with their observation towers and adjoining shelters, and are the only ones to do so in the Plymouth area. They overlie earlier 6-pdr QF emplacements. They are of brick and shuttered concrete construction, reinforced with iron girders. Immediately to the W is a glass-roofed building which may perhaps have been a (?Royal Observer Corps) post for observing aircraft.

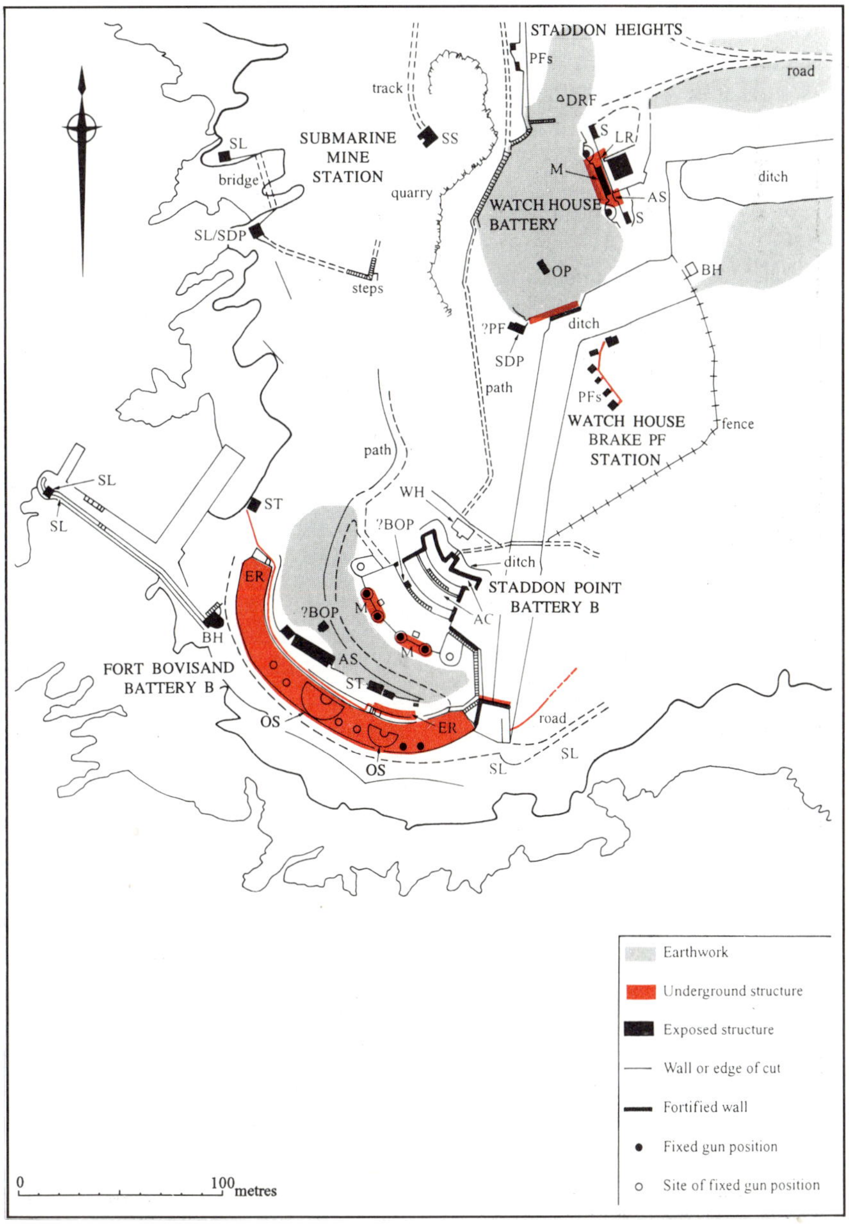

Fig. 110 The Staddon Point fortifications in WWII

Plate 157 Fort Bovisand, WWII searchlight emplacements (Exeter Archaeology)

The four searchlight emplacements (PRNs = SX45SE-18/3-6; NGRs = SX48765063, SX48825063, SX48845064, SX48865064) are all sited at the high water mark, and face S. Three are cut into an early 19th century sea wall. The western two each have a pair of light slits in the front face, the eastern two have three. Access is from the rear through armoured doors; each is of shuttered concrete and brick construction, with a flat bitumen roof containing a central vent directly above the searchlight. Only the E emplacement was accessible; this retained its armoured door, iron shutters covering the light slits, and wiring conduits.

The machine-gun position at the pier head retains its pivot; the gun was fired through an embrasure within a heightened section of parapet wall, presumably at boats attempting to round the pier into the harbour. The blockhouse is described under Staddon Point Battery B.

Present condition

The gun emplacements were not built as permanent domestic structures, and are consequently suffering from damp penetration and decay, especially the W observation tower. Both emplacements survive complete, and have been converted into domestic use, the E one into accommodation and the W one into a cafe/bar; both gun pits have been enclosed and roofed over - it is possible that the gun mountings still remain beneath the floors. The searchlight emplacements again remain complete, and three are used for storage or accommodate tanks; the fourth lies open and derelict, and retains several rusting internal fittings. The machine gun position survives intact.

Sources
General
F, I, Q, R.
Specific

1950s	Plan of casemate roof. PSA: 023229X
n.d.	Bovisand Fort Record Book. PRO: WO 192/295

STADDON POINT BATTERY B

PAR = WEMBURY, NGR = SX48805072, PRN = SX45SE-447, MAP 2 No. 180

In 1898-9 emplacements for four 12-pdr QF guns and their accompanying magazines were built within the ditch of the earlier 1840s battery, just forward of its parapet wall, to cover the E. entrance to the Sound against motor-torpedo boats and other fast moving craft. At the same time two searchlights (PRNs = SX45SE-454/2; NGR = SX 48625077 & 48635065) were emplaced on the pier below, facing S.W. and lighting up the sea area; in 1915 these were re-sited together in a building (PRN = SX45SE-468; NGR = SX 48695071) which appears from its design to have doubled as a blockhouse protecting the landward end of the pier.

Between 1903 and 1908 two further 12-pdr guns were emplaced, probably on the two flanking towers, which may have been levelled at this time or during WWI (Fort Record Book); the extra guns were removed by 1910. The remaining four (*Plate 16*) were retained in service until their replacement in 1942 by the twin 6-pdr QF guns emplaced on the roof of Fort Bovisand below. Emplacement No. 2 was subsequently adapted to accommodate first a projector (rocket launcher) and then a Bofors 40mm LAA gun in 1943. Early in the Second World War two brick loop-holed walls were built on the remains of the flanking towers for local defence and an Observation Post was constructed on the terrace above. The three levels of the original battery continued to be used as offices and accommodation until the release of the site in 1956-7.

Plate 158 Staddon Point 12-pdr QF battery (Exeter Archaeology)

The battery survives intact although the gun positions on the levelled towers are not now visible. The later adaptation of emplacement No. 2 is also evident and one of the brick loop-holed walls still survives. The original mounting plates for all four QF guns remain, and their magazines (a cartridge-store and shell-store to each gun) still retain several of their fittings such as hatch doors, doorjambs, serving tables and some labelling. The davits by which the ammunition was lifted up to the guns have however been removed.

The W searchlight emplacement is sited at the pier head and is a small flat-roofed rectangular concrete structure with a blocked slit opening on its S.W side. It may have been re-built in WWII, when it was apparently operational. The other emplacement, sited immediately to the E, has been demolished; its position is indicated by two blocked splay openings cut through the parapet wall of the pier; again, it may still have been operational in WW II.

The double searchlight emplacement/blockhouse at the landward end of the pier is a hexagonal concrete flat-roofed structure with loops protected by armour-plating in all sides, except the seaward. It has a rectangular extension to the north-west which appears to be contemporary and also contains firing-slits. There are two windows facing seawards.

Present condition

QF Battery

The gun emplacements and mounting plates survive virtually intact and in good structural condition. The magazines however are damp and little used, except as a cluttered, temporary store; consequently the surviving fittings are vulnerable to neglect and accidental damage, and the concrete work, wooden fittings and iron girders are deteriorating due to the damp.

Searchlight emplacements

The W one is used as a Diving Control Room, and is in reasonable structural condition. The interior was not viewed. The E one has been demolished.

Blockhouse

This is presently used as a small generator-house; condition good. The interior was not viewed.

Sources

General

19 - 24; F, G, I, O, Q.

Specific

1871	Plan of Bovisand area. With later amendments. PRO: WO 78/3847
1896	War Office 1:2500 map, with amendments c.1910. PRO: WO 78/5041(1)
1898	War Office drawings of proposed electric light emplacements. PRO: WO 78/4058 (1-3)
1901	Plan of Officers' Quarters and QF magazine. Reproduced in McDonald, 1981 (I)
1908	Plan of pier. PSA: 023217X
1910	General plan. PSA: 023215X
1911	Plymouth Defences. Index plan. With later amendments. PRO: WO 78/5066
1920s	Lease plan for Staddon Battery property. Mr Forster, Staddon Cottage
1938	General plan of Fort Bovisand. PSA: 023210X
n.d.	Bovisand Fort Record Book. PRO: WO 192/295

BOVISAND SUBMARINE MINE OBSERVATION STATION

PAR = WEMBURY, NGR = SX48805094, PRN = SX45SE-451/1, MAP 2 No. 181

This is located in a quarry above and to the N of Fort Bovisand and was built in 1896 to observe and control the minefield lying between the end of the breakwater and Bovisand pier. A matching establishment was built behind and above Fort Picklecombe at the same time to control an equivalent minefield at the W entrance to the Sound. Minefields in both these areas were in place by 1880, and in 1885 they were to be protected by 6-pdr QF guns installed at Fort Bovisand (Battery B, No. 178) and Fort Picklecombe. At Bovisand the structures built in 1896 consisted of the mine observation station, and the construction/adaptation of three vaulted chambers sited at the fort, under the road to the rear of the casemates. Later, in *c.* 1900 two searchlight emplacements were built facing W on the coast below (PRNs = SX45SE/450 & 450/1; NGR = SX 48705093 & 48725090) to light the minefield. The observation station presumably became redundant in 1905, when submarine mining of harbour entrances ceased on the orders of the First Sea Lord, Admiral Fisher, although the S searchlight at least remained in use in 1915. An Observation Post (PRN = SX45SE/451; NGR = SX 48785095) sited immediately N of the station was present by 1910, although whether it was associated with the latter during its operation prior to 1905 is not clear; it is labelled as a Directing Post on a plan of 1911.

The observation station and post were approached via trackways from Staddon and Staddon Heights Batteries (Nos 184 & 185) and Fort Bovisand, and were linked by a path and flight of steps to the searchlights below.

The station is a semi-sunken concrete structure built around an earlier stone building associated with the quarry. It consists of a pair of observation cells, each approached by steps from the rear and with a slab/'table' containing an instrument socket or recess. The roofs of the cells are protected by armour plating, and the viewing slits by sliding iron shutters (still extant). A levelled area in front provided a clear field of view of the minefield. Therefore it was masked from vessels below, and was protected to some extent from incoming fire.

The two searchlight emplacements are square flat-roofed concrete and brick structures; both have a broad rectangular opening on the seaward side and a door at the rear. A bridge connected the two. Access to them was originally via a pathway along the coast from the S and down the steps from the observation station above. At the foot of the steps was a small building which may have been a sentry post.

The observation post is a small rectangular concrete structure with a door at the rear and a broad opening at the front. This was shuttered, faces seawards and is open to the sides as well as to the front. It may perhaps have operated as a subsidiary directing post for the searchlights below.

Present condition

Observation station

This is the only one of the two built at Plymouth to survive (that above Picklecombe having been demolished), and survival in such completeness of equivalent installations elsewhere is likely to be rare. It is currently abandoned and unsecured. Structurally in apparently good condition, although the steel shutters are heavily rusted.

Searchlight emplacements
Both appear to be in good condition, though their foundations are highly vulnerable to coastal erosion. The steps are intact but heavily overgrown; the bridge and the ?sentry post have been demolished.

Observation post
This is complete, although the front section of roof has collapsed.

Sources
General
13, 17, 19, 21, 22 - 24.
Specific
1896 War Office plan submarine mining station. PRO: WO 78/2735(14)
1896 War Office 1:2500 map, with amendments c.1910. PRO: WO 78/5041(1)
1910 General plan. PSA: 023215X
1911 Plymouth Defences. Index plan. With later amendments. PRO: WO 78/5066

WATCH HOUSE BRAKE PF STATION

PAR = WEMBURY, NGR = SX48885084, PRN = SX45SE-19/3, MAP 2 No. 182

This is sited on the slope below Watch House Battery and was completed by 1894. It was used to supply target data to Staddon Heights and Frobisher Batteries (Nos 185 & 173); in 1903 and in 1911 it was in use but in WWI appears to have been redundant as it is not included in the telephone network (*Fig. 14*).

Plate 159 Watch House Brake, PF cells (Exeter Archaeology)

Plate 160 Watch House Brake, instrument pillars inside PF cell (Exeter Archaeology)

It consists of six brick and concrete PF cells connected by an underground passage at the rear. In common with other PF cells they are semi-sunken rectangular structures, retaining a clear view seawards whilst being masked from the view of ships below. They were surrounded by a fence to the S and E and by the 1860s ditch on the other sides. Access to the complex was through an entrance in the fence protected by a blockhouse (PRN = SX45SE-19/4) and a doorway cut into the 1860s musketry gallery. A flight of steps leads up from the ditch into the N cell. This looks W and is of different character to the others - it has masonry walls and an older concrete roof with a viewing window protected by a grille and iron plating. The other cells are brick-built with concrete roofs and look S.W. Some still contain three pillars for the PF instruments; in one these retain script on the rear face, giving distances to known points such as the Breakwater and the height above water table of the instrument.

The blockhouse is a small rectangular single-storey masonry building containing loops in its E, N and S walls.

Present condition
All are in fair to good condition although the roofs of two cells are collapsing due to the steel girders supporting the concrete roof rotting away. All are derelict and are difficult of access. They form a complete group, with detail such as the script on the pillars being a particularly important survival. The blockhouse is roofless and empty, although most walls survive to their full height.

Sources
General
16, 19, 23, 24.
Specific
1896 War Office O.S 1:2500 map with amendments c.1910. PRO: WO 78/5041(1)
1911 Plymouth Defences. Index plan. With later amendments. PRO: WO 78/5066
1920s Lease plan for Staddon Battery property. Mr Forster, Staddon Cottage

STADDON HEIGHTS PF CELLS

PAR = WEMBURY, NGR = SX48845097, PRN = SX45SE-19/1, MAP 2 No. 183

These two PF cells were constructed by 1894 within an earlier masonry covered way (PRN = SX45SE-19/5), presumably to supply Staddon Heights and Frobisher Batteries (Nos 185 & 173) with target data. A WWII 'Battle' observation post belonging to Watch House Battery has subsequently been built in between them.

The cells have brick walls and concrete roofs supported on steel girders; the viewing windows extend around the whole of the front and part of the side walls. The WWII OP is of similar construction; it faces W and its front wall contains two large horizontal windows.

Present condition

All three are derelict and unused; no internal features survive. Overall their condition is fair except for the roof of the S cell which is collapsing.

Sources

General

16, 19, 23, 24.

Specific

1920s Lease plan for Staddon Battery property. Mr Forster, Staddon Cottage

1942 War Dept. plan. Copy held by J. Symons (FSGSW)

STADDON BATTERY

PAR = WEMBURY, NGR = SX48755125, PRN = SX45SE-467, MAP 2 No. 184

This is sited overlooking the Sound on the brow of the coastal slope N of Bovisand. In the late 18th and 19th centuries it is named 'the battery above Withy Hedge'. Construction began in July 1782 and the battery was probably completed shortly afterwards for ten guns mounted *en barbette*, although it is not shown on Gardner's map of 1784. In 1805 it was armed with ten small 12- & 18-pdr SB guns, and probably retained this armament until the completion of Staddon Point Battery A in 1847. In 1860 the Royal Commission recommended the retention of the battery, to prevent enemy ships anchoring in the Sound, and in 1870 it is marked as accommodating 10 guns; in 1885 it was armed with two 64-pdr RMLs; these were removed by 1893.

The battery survives largely intact, consisting of a semi-circular terrace cut back into the hillside. This was fronted by a masonry parapet behind which the guns were stationed on garrison carriages. The guard/store-room is sited at the rear of the terrace together with a pair of magazines (originally earth-covered). These are brick barrel-vaulted and have lamp passages and retain door fittings. A George IV Board of Ordnance plaque is visible on the S wall of the guard-house. The two guns at present on the battery *terreplein* were apparently brought from Saltram House in the 1920s and their carriages were built by thc present owner, Mr Forster. Granite slabs which originally formed the gun platforms have mostly been moved and are now used as paving around the front of

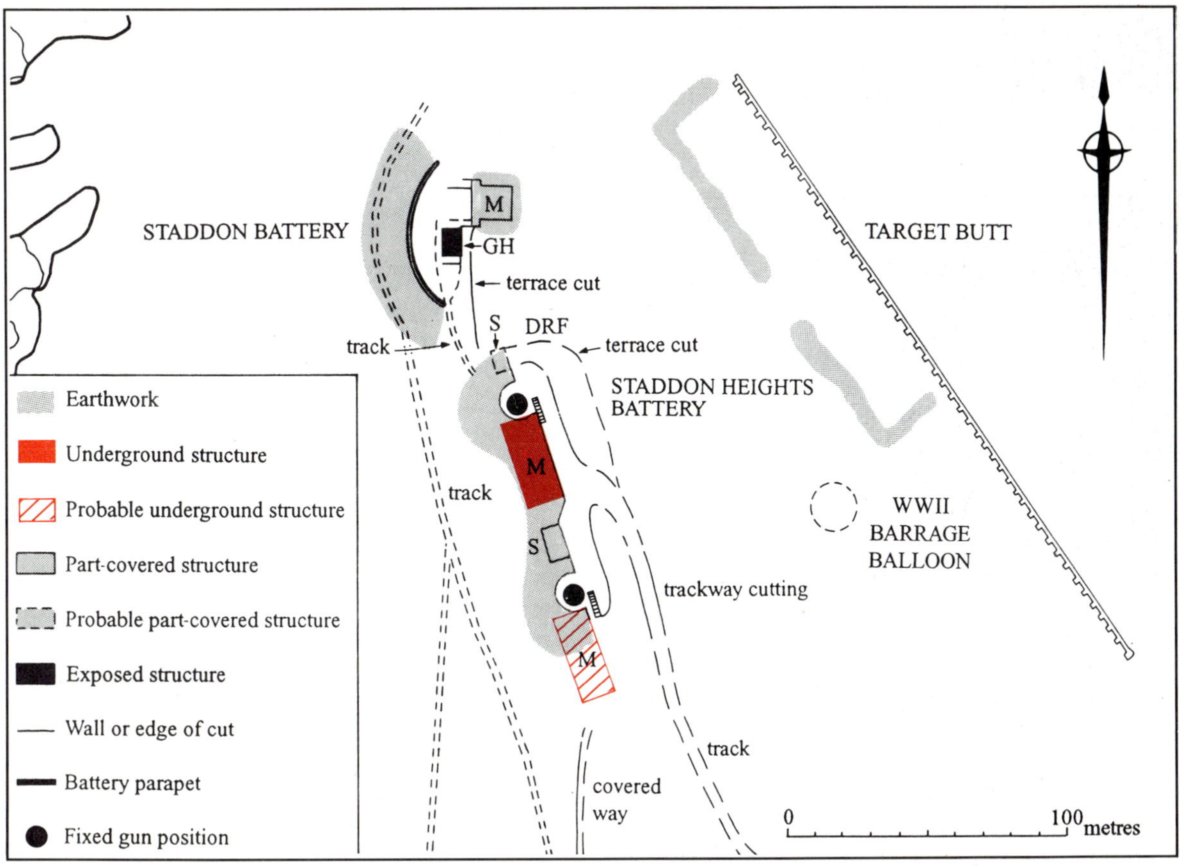

Fig. 111 Staddon & Staddon Heights Batteries

Plate 161 Staddon Battery (Exeter Archaeology)

the guard-house; others may survive *in situ* beneath the turf. The slope of the lawn down to the parapet reflects the original slope of the battery *terreplein*.

Present condition

The magazines are used as a store-room and workshop; the earth covering the roof has been removed and the protective earthen bank (traverse) at the front has been replaced by a new building. The guard/store-room is domestic accommodation (Staddon Cottage) and all the buildings are well maintained.

Sources

General

8, 9, 12, 16, 17, 19; E, O, Q.

Specific

1780	Staddon Hill Battery. PRO: MPH 424
1811	Staddon Hill Battery. PRO: MPH 233
1846	Staddon Heights Battery-guard & store room. PRO: MPH 424
*c*1850	Watercolour PCM

STADDON HEIGHTS BATTERY

PAR = WEMBURY, NGR = SX48805115, PRN = SX45SE-445, MAP 2 No. 185

This was proposed in 1885 and built in 1893 when it was armed with two 12.5-inch RML guns. The guns apparently remained in 1903 but were superseded in their role by Watch House Battery (completed 1901) and removed shortly after. Its purpose was to bombard ships entering the Sound and in this complemented Maker Battery on the W shore. Target information was provided by several PF cells nearby (Staddon PF & Watch House Brake PF Station - Nos 183 & 182).

Although heavily overgrown and partially infilled the structure of the battery survives largely intact. The S emplacement has been infilled although the concrete apron is still visible. The entrance to its magazine is visible as a precipitous gorse-covered hole; access was not possible. The magazine lay to the S of the gun underneath the present trackway, and probably still survives underground. The N emplacement is partially visible under encroaching garden waste. The concrete apron is clear, as is the gun pivot (a re-used upturned cannon). The magazine lies underneath the *terreplein* to the S of this gun position and includes an almost complete ammunition hoist and a cartridge-store, shell-store and lamp-room. Electric light fittings, doorframes and labels still remain. To the S at *terreplein* level is the shelter for the S gun. The shelter for the N gun has been filled in, and the DRF sited behind the N gun is not visible. Access to the battery was via a sunken trackway from the S; part has been infilled, part is visible. In the 1920s there was also a small building on the apron of the S emplacement, presumably built after the battery was disarmed; it was a Battery Office and Store in 1942 and was demolished in the 1970s.

Present condition

Overall most of the battery survives, although it is heavily overgrown and the S emplacement and stairwell to its magazine has been infilled; however the mounting and magazine are very likely to survive below-ground. Garden waste is gradually infilling the N emplacement. The magazine is very damp and half-full of rubbish, and the hoist is heavily rusted although almost wholly intact.

Sources

General

13, 16, 17, 18 (misnamed Frobisher), 19, 23; O, Q.

Specific

1896	Staddon Heights Battery record plan. PRO: WO 78/4163
1920s	Lease plan for Staddon Battery property. Mr Forster, Staddon Cottage
1942	War Dept. plan. Copy held by J. Symons (FSGSW)

TARGET BUTTS

PAR = WEMBURY, NGR = SX49005120, PRN = SX45SE-619/1

This dates to after 1860, and is a very prominent local landmark. The N half was built for the army (when it was converting to high-velocity rifles) between 1860 & 1870 and the S half for the Royal Marines between 1872 and 1894; the junction is clearly visible. It is a high buttressed masonry wall about 300m long and aligned N.W - S.E. At the rear are two (?contemporary) earthwork enclosures, the function of which is unclear. Some mounded firing positions are extant to the N.E.

Present condition

In good structural condition; the ranges are now a golf course and scrubland lies to the S.W.

Sources

General

16, 19.

Specific

1860	Defences Act 1860: lands to be taken. DRO: DP266, 267

WWII BARRAGE BALLOON SITE

PAR = WEMBURY, NGR = SX48905115, PRN = SX45SE-177, MAP 2 No. 187

This is sited on sloping ground in between the target butts and Staddon Heights Battery. It consists of a circle of 24 concrete anchor points with a central square block, and is clearly visible on a 1940s aerial photograph and on the ground today.

Present condition

Land use: scrub and grassland. It survives complete, and currently is the only known such site in Plymouth to do so.

Source

Specific

1940s? Oblique aerial photograph. Held by Mr Forster, Staddon Cottage.

BOVISAND PRACTICE BATTERY

PAR = WEMBURY, NGR = SX49145071, PRN = SX45SE-448, MAP 2 No. 188

This is located in a car park on the present road c.350m E of Fort Bovisand overlooking the bay. It was built *c.*1870, and used for training Royal Artillery militia and volunteer gunners until Whitsand Bay Practice Battery was built, both on current artillery pieces and to test-fire new pieces such as the 7-inch Mark I Moncrieff gun recorded here in 1872/3. A gun pit (labelled in 1893 as a Moncrieff pit) is depicted at the E end of the battery on all plans from 1871/72 to 1910. A plan of 1871 (amended in 1876) shows an upper battery containing two sets of four platforms for guns on garrison carriages, two emplacements for guns on traversing carriages, an emplacement for a gun on a Moncrieff mounting, together with a field expense magazine, artillery store, expense magazine, shell-filling room and gun shed. A lower battery, below the car park at its W end, is also shown, and contains four gun platforms and two mortar positions. This arrangement is reflected in the armament of the battery in 1885, when there were nine 64-pdr RMLs and two 7-inch RMLs (one presumably the Moncrieff) mounted on the upper battery and four 32-pdr SB guns and two 8-inch mortars on the lower battery. The guns for the battery (and for the other batteries on Staddon Heights) were probably brought to the battery by boat from Devonport, and offloaded at a gun wharf in Bovisand Bay (at NGR = SX49245060; PRN = SX45SE-695) or on the ramp within the harbour at Fort Bovisand.

By 1893 the lower battery had become disused, and only the nine 64-pdr RMLs and one 7-inch RML were present; the Moncrieff had been removed. In *c.*1899 four 5-inch BL guns were emplaced slightly to the N of and replacing the 64-pdr RMLs. These were still present in 1903 and probably in 1911, when DRFs are marked to the rear of the battery and within the former Moncrieff pit. It is not clear when the battery ceased to be used.

The field expense magazine, artillery store and gunshed have all been demolished but the remainder of the magazines survive together with two other structures built by 1896. Two concrete 5-inch BL gun emplacements are visible in the surface of the car park

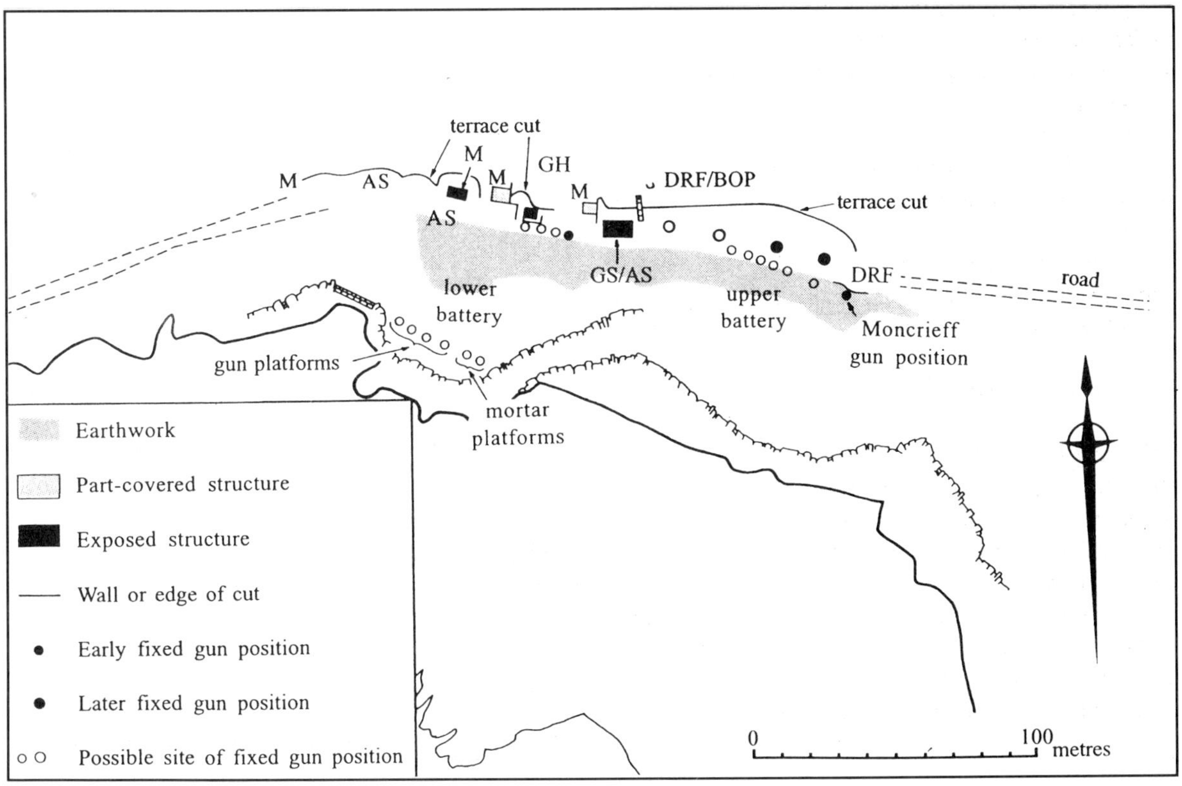

Fig. 112 Bovisand Practice Battery

just N of the road. An earlier granite platform for a gun on a garrison carriage lies outside the shell-filling room. The Moncrieff gun pit remains, although adapted and perhaps partially infilled to accommodate the later DRF. The other DRF retains its instrument pillar and is sited on the hillside behind the battery, up a flight of steps. There is also a square brick building, probably a guard-house built during World War II.

Present condition

All the remains, including the gun-pit and the DRF on the hill are in good condition except for the timber building (built *c*.1896). The upper battery is used as a car park, and further gun positions may lie just under the surface. The buildings are empty except for the two built in *c*.1896 - one is used as an ice-cream parlour and the other as a store. All are in reasonable condition, except for the store, which is timber. The lower battery site was not examined, and is overgrown and probably threatened by coastal erosion.

Sources

General

17, 19, 23; F, Q.

Specific

1871	Plan of Bovisand area, with amendments c.1876. PRO: WO 78/3847
1872	War Dept. plan. PRO: WO 78/623
1893	General plan of area. PSA: 023216X
1910	General plan of area. PSA: 023215X
n.d.	Late 19th century photograph apparently showing gun firing. PLSL

BREAKWATER FORT

PAR = N/A, NGR = SX47165048, PRN = SX45SE-20, MAP 2 No. 163

This is a powerful seafort located 100 yards behind the centre of the Breakwater (which was completed in 1844 to provide a sheltered anchorage for the fleet). In 1860 a casemated work mounting 100 guns and accommodating 600 men was recommended by the Royal Commission to close the gap between Picklecombe and Bovisand Batteries and protect any ships lying at anchor behind the Breakwater. The fort was originally designed in October 1860 as a masonry work of four levels encased in granite, with two tiers of granite gun casemates protected by iron shields mounting 33 guns, and a further 7 guns on the roof. Work began in 1861 and the foundations were completed in 1865. Experiments between 1860 and 1869 showed that only an iron structure would resist heavy shell-fire from rifled guns and in April 1866 a revised design was approved for seventeen (subsequently increased to eighteen) RML guns in iron casemates (with accommodation for 60-180 men) with magazines and stores below, and pair of two-gun turrets (mounting four of the heaviest guns) on the roof. In 1873 the turrets were omitted from the design, and in 1875 the approved armament consisted of fourteen 38-ton RML guns (the heaviest available) to cover the sea in front and the channels to each side, and four lighter 18-ton RML guns to cover the anchorage behind.

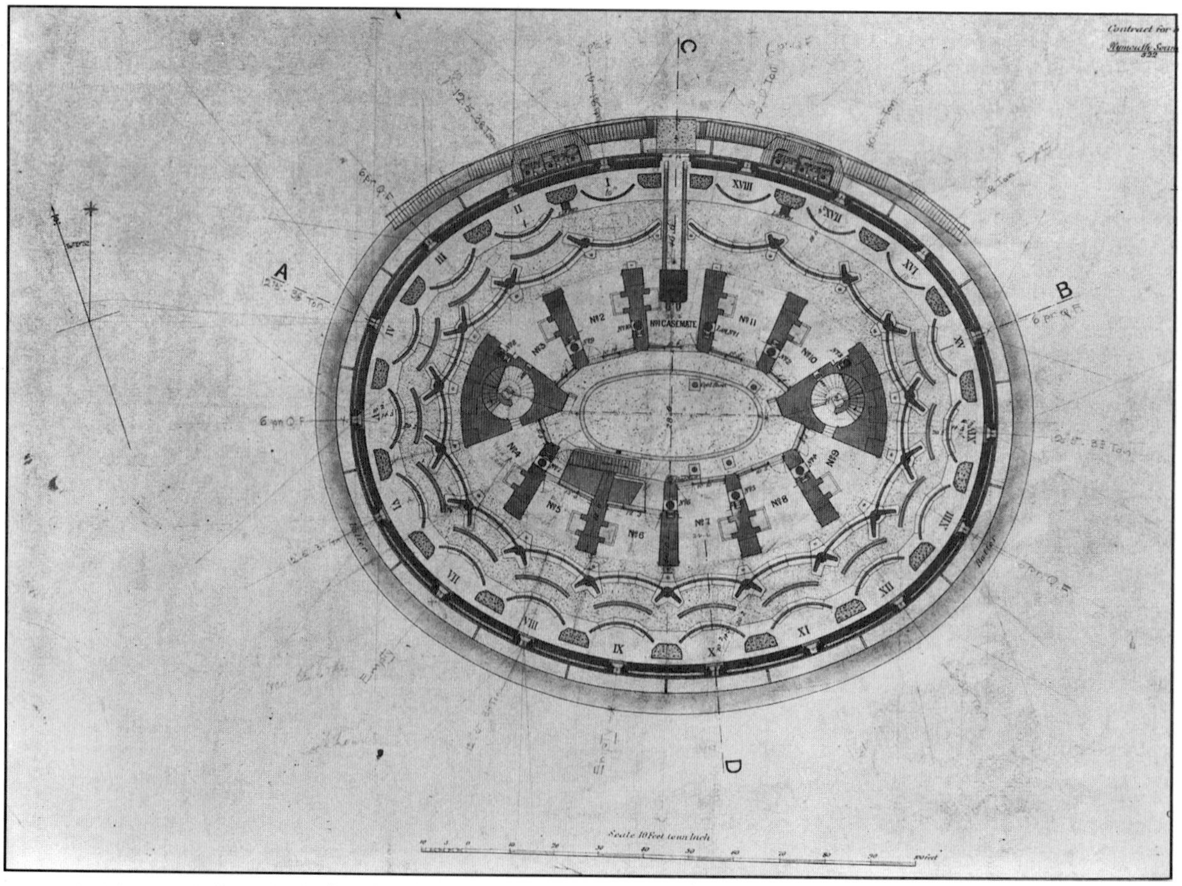

Fig. 113 Breakwater Fort, gun casemates in 1884 (RCHME: PLM/494)

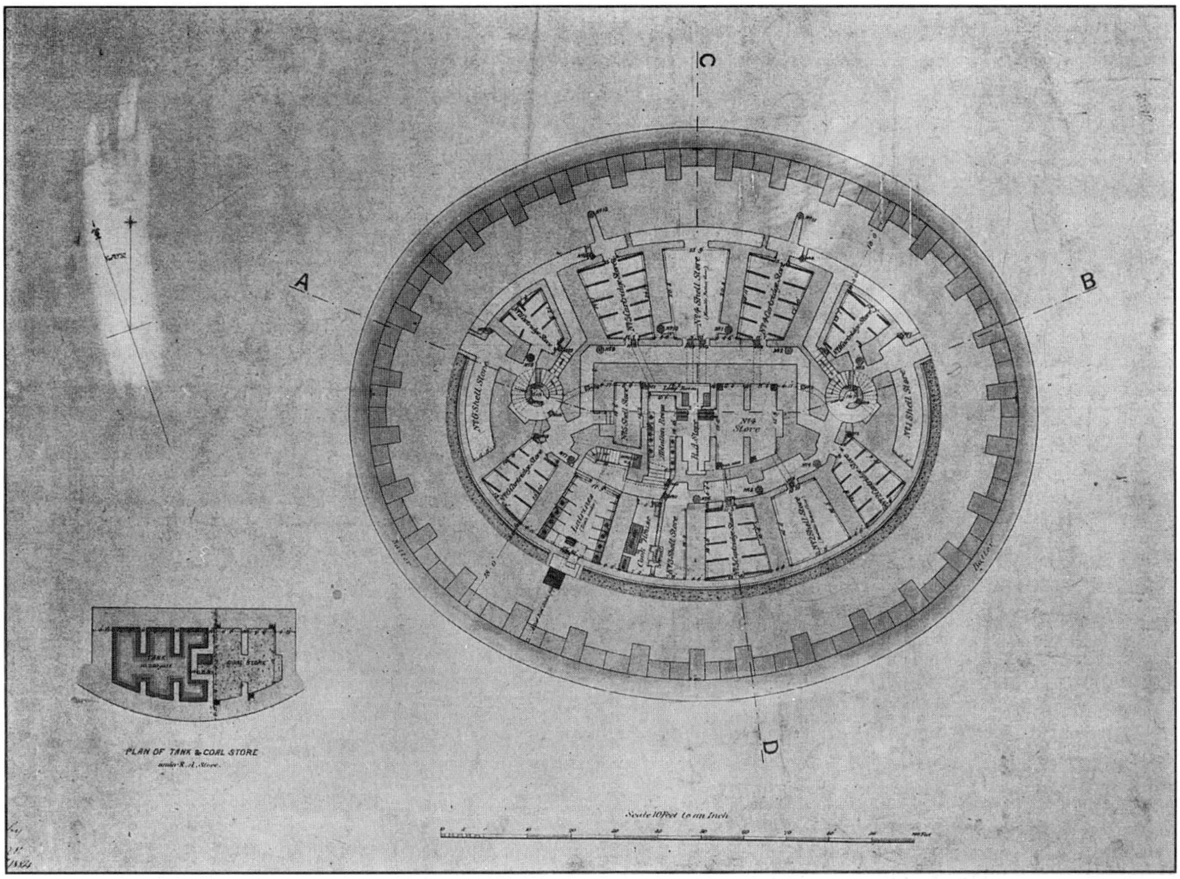

Fig. 114 Breakwater Fort, magazine level in 1884 (RCHME: PLM/495)

'Small port' (muzzle-pivoting) carriages were developed for the casemates. The iron framing at the front of the casemates is filled with concrete and is about 2 feet thick; the iron shields of the gun-ports are between 1 ½ and 2 feet thick. The first 12.5-inch 38-ton RML gun was installed in 1879 and by 1880 the fort was being fully armed with fourteen 12.5-inch and four 10-inch RML guns. In 1885 it was proposed to remove seven of the 12.5-inch guns to new batteries (on Staddon and Maker Heights) and place four 6-pdr QF guns in the vacant ports; these proposals had been implemented by 1893. In the late 19th century the exterior was painted in a black and yellow chequer pattern (much of which still remains) to obscure the positions of the gun-ports and thereby confuse an attacker. By 1903 a further 12.5-inch RML gun had been removed, and shortly after a searchlight was installed on the roof, supplemented by 1911 by another

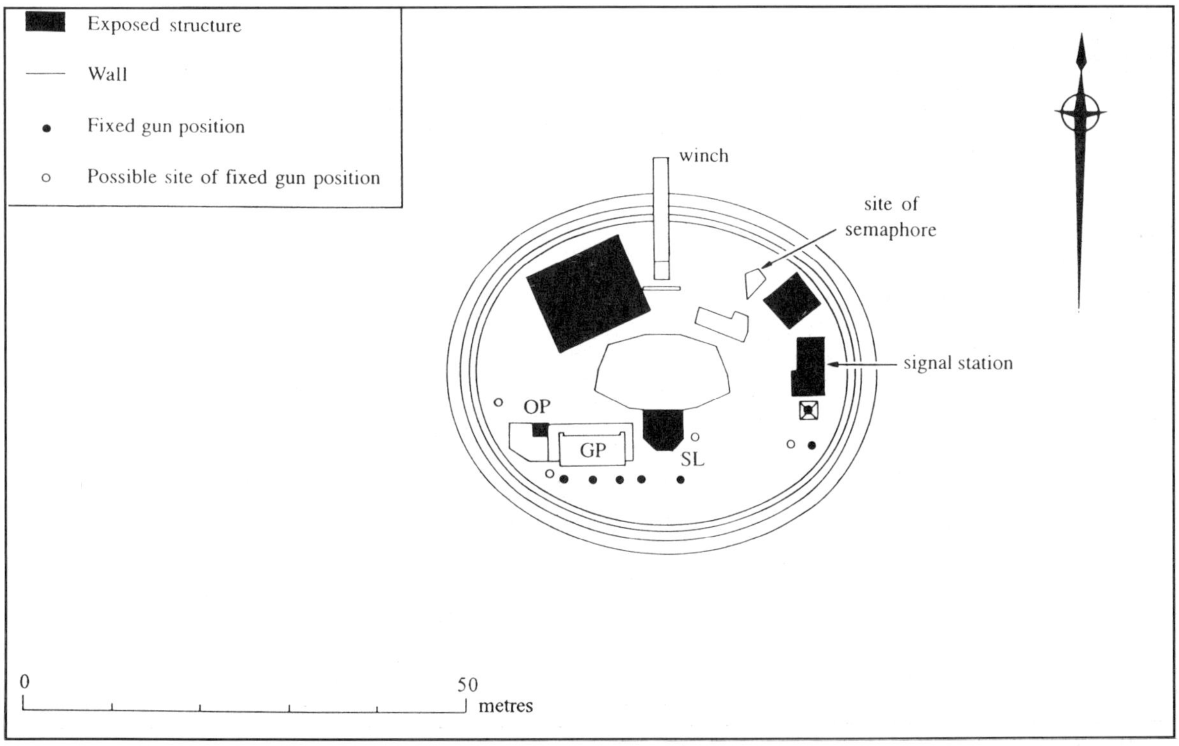

Fig. 115 Breakwater Fort, roof level

Plate 162 Breakwater Fort (Exeter Archaeology)

Plate 164 Breakwater Fort, gun casemate (Exeter Archaeology)

in one of the W gun-ports. By 1905 two more 6-pdrs had been emplaced to either side of the entrance, but were removed shortly afterwards. By WWI the fort had apparently been disarmed, although the searchlights were still operational, and it became the Port War Signal Station, a role it retained during WWII. In 1936 it became an anti-aircraft (AA) training school, with additional AA gun positions and other buildings being constructed on the roof at this time and during WWII. The fort went out of military use in 1976.

Plate 163 Breakwater Fort, roof level, later gun mountings (Exeter Archaeology)

The structure of the fort remains largely intact, although there have been some alterations related to its subsequent use. The original iron travelling crane used to lift the guns up into the fort from lighters below remains intact, together with a series of later structures, gun platforms and AA gun mountings belonging to the later AA training school. The WWI Port War Signal Station is no longer present, although later WWII buildings still remain. Other structures include a 'signal homster' or 'magnetic hut', a WWII observation post, and the searchlight emplacement built in *c.* 1903 (converted in 1936). At casemate level there are positions for 18 guns, with 11 casemates behind them providing accommodation; these contain fireplaces and shell/cartridge lifts in their brick party walls. Internal fittings such as the lifts (and labels), iron hose brackets, gun pivots, tackle loops and racer rails remain, together with later features such as wooden partitions. Two spiral stairs, only one of which is now open, gave access to the magazine level below. This is arranged as an inner core containing stores and a lamp-room, surrounded by a passage and an outer ring of alternating shell and cartridge stores. Each of these has a hydraulic lift, and several contain WWII Davy Paxman diesel engines; in one room there is the remains of a WWII operations room. In the centre, below the stores, are a water tank and coal store (both flooded).

Present condition

The fort is currently used as a diving centre. The structures on the roof are mostly empty although some are used for storage; the burnt out remains of the WWI signal station have recently been removed and the roof surface sealed. Some of the casemates are used by the Diving Centre, together with the gun positions flanking the entrance; the remainder are largely empty; loose material has recently been cleared out from these and from the magazine level below, which remains empty except for the engines and the WWII operations room. Most attached fittings remain *in situ*, but remain vulnerable to decay and inadvertent damage.

Sources

General

12 - 15, 17, 22 - 24; H, I, O, Q.

Specific

1884	Plans, sections and elevations. RCHME: PLM/498
1902/3	Plan. PRO: WO 78/4066
1936	Plan of Anti-aircraft training school, with later additions *c.*1945. BPFM: 031380
1937	Plan of part of roof and basement levels. BPFM: 031363
1994	Pye, A.R *Archaeological Survey of the Roof Level of Breakwater Fort, Plymouth* Exeter Archaeology Report No. **94.94**

OBSERVATION POSTS ON THE BREAKWATER

PAR = N/A, NGR = SX46765043 & 47685034, PRN = SX45SE/459 & 460, MAP 2 No. 164

These are two concrete WWII observation posts located towards each end of the Breakwater where it changes angle. They each have a viewing window at the front with railings around a viewing platform on the roof. They presumably operated in conjunction with the port war signal station on Breakwater Fort.

Present condition
Generally good.

LENTNEY BATTERY

PAR = WEMBURY, NGR = SX49304950, PRN = SX44NE-004, MAP 1 No. 189

This is located on the coast just N of Renney Battery, and, with Watch House and Lord Howard's Batteries, was one of three 6-inch BL batteries built to cover the E side of the Sound; it shared accommodation and storage with Renney Battery (Renney/Lentney Camp). It is the last complete example of this type of battery in the Plymouth area, as both its surface features and internal fittings such as shell and cartridge lifts survive virtually untouched.

The battery was completed in 1905; although originally designed for three 6-inch BL guns only two were installed. By 1910 the battery had been put into reserve as its role was better fulfilled by Watch House Battery; the guns were still present in 1920 but were removed by 1930. By 1912 one searchlight emplacement (fighting light) had been built below the battery on the coast, and another was proposed to the N in 1915. In 1914 a blockhouse and unclimbable fence were built for local defence. In 1941 the battery was re-armed with guns of the same calibre, when a new Battery Observation Post was built on the site of the earlier one, above and to the rear of the guns. Other armament installed during WWII for training purposes included one twin 6-pdr QF gun, two 6-inch BL naval guns, and two 12-pdr QF guns (site not identified).

Plate 165 6-in BL gun at Lentney Battery in WWII (Ian V. Hogg)

During WWII Lentney was the practice battery for the coast artillery training regiment housed in Staddon Fort. The men from this regiment manned the 6-inch

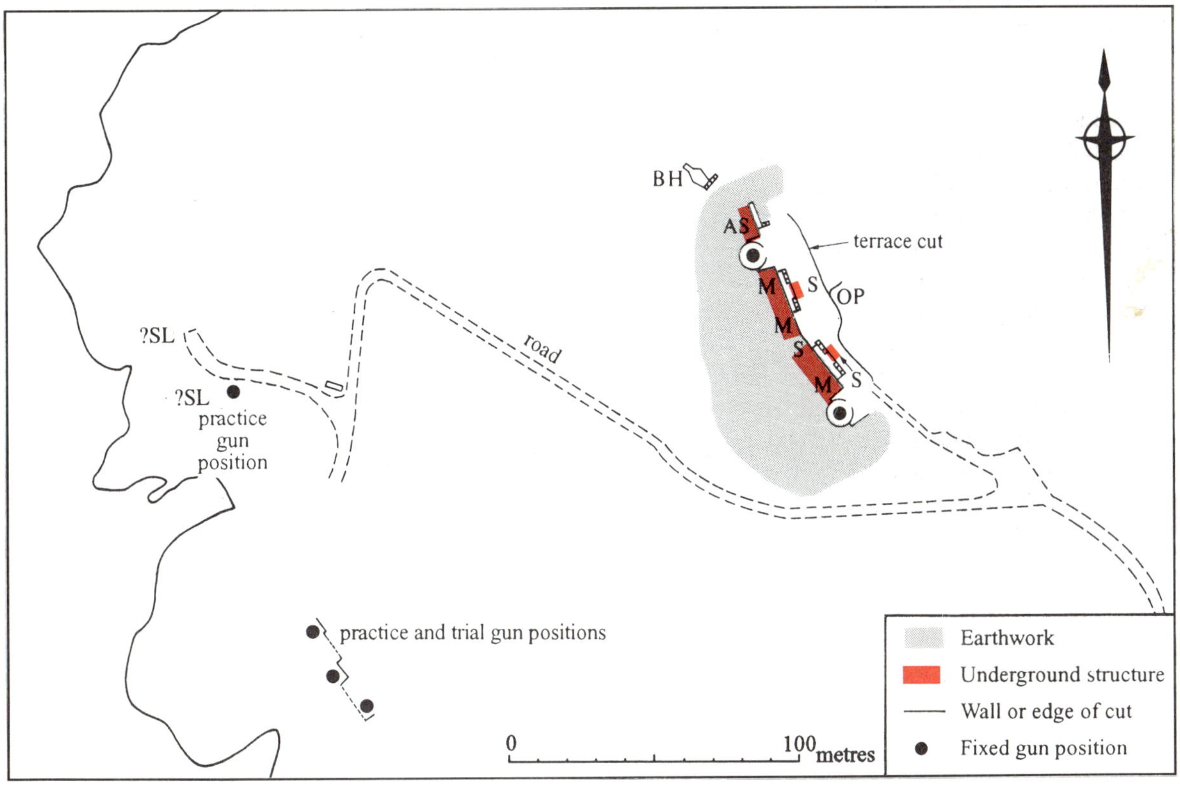

Fig. 116 Lentney Battery

Plate 166 6-in BL emplacement at Lentney Battery in 1993 (Exeter Archaeology)

Plate 168 Lentney Battery, base of shell lift (Exeter Archaeology)

Plate 169 Lentney Battery, top of shell lift (Exeter Archaeology)

BL battery on the call to 'Stand to'. After the war the 6-inch and twin 6-pdr guns formed the main practice battery for the coast artillery school in the Royal Citadel. The school also carried out trials at Lentney of British equipment (the 3.7-inch HAA gun in a coast role) and of captured German equipment. The guns were removed in 1956, and the site released in 1991.

Most of the two 6-inch BL gun emplacements survive complete, including the shell and cartridge lifts, most of their gearing, their steel lids and doors (and those of the ammunition lockers), and the davits at the corners of the stairwells down to the magazines. Three underground magazines (including one for the gun which was not installed), shelters and store-rooms are located between and behind the emplacements. The magazines contain original wooden fittings and light fittings, and cartridge and shell stores and lifts for each of the two guns which were installed, and a cartridge and shell store and empty lift shafts for the central gun which was not. The concrete apron of its emplacement lies buried; the Battery Observation Post has been demolished. Some 25m N of the battery is the bottle-shaped concrete blockhouse built in 1914, partly surrounded by unclimbable fence. It contains a machine-gun port at its N.W end and rifle loops high up in the side walls. On the coastal path the concrete apron of the filled in twin 6-pdr QF emplacement is visible, together with three other mountings to the S; these are probably for the two 6-inch BL naval guns and for the trial firing of captured guns.

Plate 167 Lentney Battery, shell store (Exeter Archaeology)

Present condition

The battery is complete and very well preserved and has not been modified; it retains complete examples of shell and cartridge lifts and other equipment and fittings, and is the only battery to do so in the Plymouth area. As such it is of considerable regional and national significance. The blockhouse is overgrown but complete, as are the practice gun mountings.

Sources

General

20 - 22, 24; F, O, Q.

Specific

1903	Lentney Battery. Plan. PRO: WO 78/5064
1911	Plymouth Defences. Index Plan. PRO: WO 78/5066
1950s	Various photos of 6-inch BL gun and emplacement. (I. Hogg; Plate 12)
n.d.	Lentney Fort Record Book, incl. a plan. PRO: WO 192/296

RENNEY BATTERY

PAR = WEMBURY, NGR = SX49404890, PRN = SX44NE-003, MAP 1 No. 190

One of two powerful coastal batteries (the other being Penlee) sited each side of the Sound and designed to keep the largest battleships out of range of the Dockyard. Renney was armed with three heavy 9.2-inch BL guns and covered the eastern approaches whilst Penlee (with two, and then three similar guns) covered the western. Penlee has been infilled so Renney is the only remaining example in the Plymouth area. It shared accommodation and stores (Renney/Lentney camp) with the contemporary 6-inch BL Lentney Battery, sited some 400m to the N.

The battery was built in 1905-6, with test rounds being fired from the guns in 1907. The armament was progressively modernised, including the installation of 35-degree mountings in WWII which increased their range to 35000 yards, until the guns were removed in 1957. The final improvement occurred in 1947 when the gun in the southern emplacement was remounted on a Mark VII mounting; this was power-operated throughout, except for the breech, and was the most efficient in service. Other armament at various times during WWII included two 60-pdr guns (Mark I; field service) in various unidentified positions, one mobile 6-pdr gun in an anti-tank role, and two 40mm Bofors LAA guns and two spigot mortars for air and local defence.

Earlier, local defence measures undertaken in 1914 involved the construction of three concrete infantry blockhouses linked by an unclimbable fence, forming a circuit around the front of the battery. In 1933 two searchlight emplacements and a probable directing post were built on the coast in front of the guns, and in WWII a new Battery Command Post, Observation Post and Plotting Room were built to the S of the gun emplacements. After the disarming of the battery in 1957 it was used as a training establishment until its release in 1991.

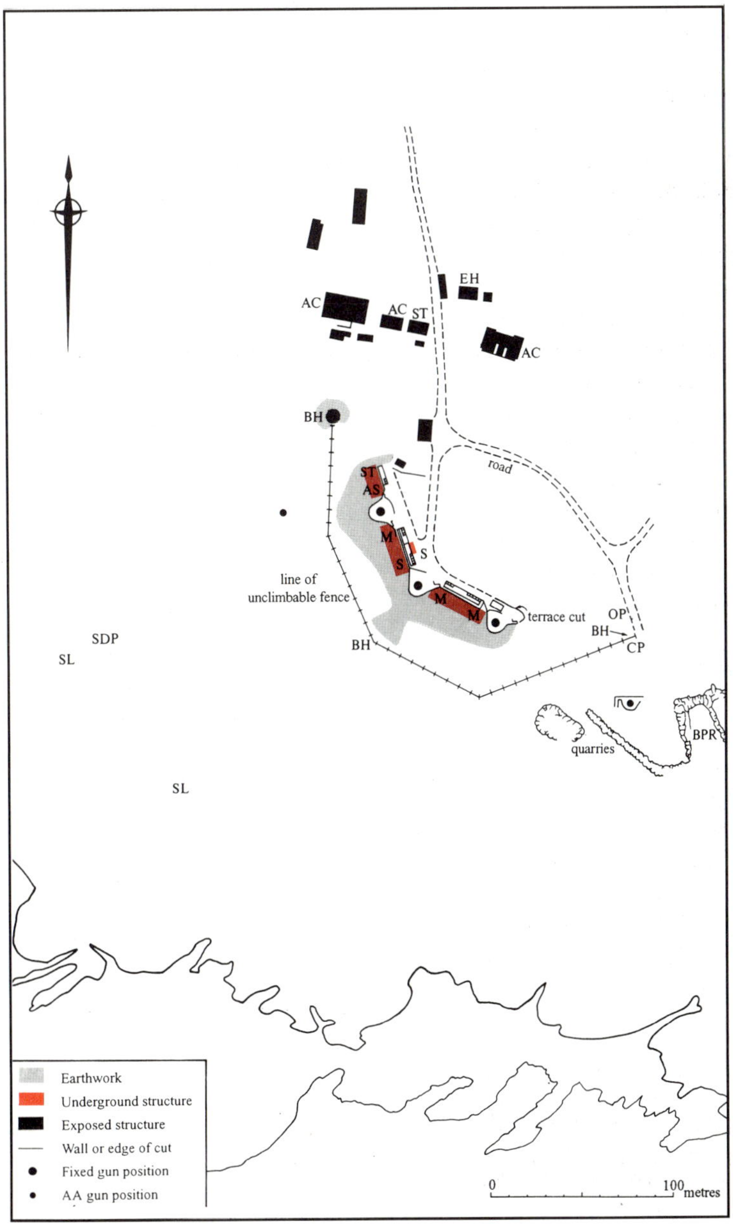

Fig. 117 Renney Battery

Plate 170 9.2-in BL emplacement at Renney Battery (Exeter Archaeology)

All three 9.2-inch emplacements survive complete, together with three underground magazines sited in between them and underground stores, shelters and lamp room adjoining. They mostly retain their original steel doors and the ammunition hoists. The S emplacement contains modifications for the powered mounting installed in 1947 and all three have brick blast-protection walls, built in 1941, across the rear; all contain rifle loops. There are the foundations of a small WWII building behind the S emplacement.

Of the local defence measures, all three blockhouses and the unclimbable fence were extant in 1963, but only the N blockhouse now survives. This is 12-sided and built of concrete; it retains its original steel door at the rear (E), flanked by a pair of horizontal loops to each side; the remaining nine sides each have a single loop, some of which retain their steel shutters. Two of the sides contain square ports low-down for machine guns and/or 'motor headlamps' to cover and light up the unclimbable fence. The other two blockhouses have been demolished, although part of one wall of the S one survives. To the S of the battery is a small sunken concrete gun-pit; this contains ammunition lockers and may have accommodated one of the Bofors LAA guns; foxholes adjoin it and may have been present elsewhere around the perimeter. Some 50m to the W of the N emplacement is a small circular terrace; this may have been the site of the other Bofors although it does lie in front of the 9.2-inch emplacement.

The WWII Battery Command Post (earlier the Officers' Watch Shelter) has been demolished except for part of its N.E wall; an earlier blockhouse adjoined it to the N. The WWI/WWII Battery Observation Post to the N and the WWII Battery Plotting Room (sited in a quarry to the S) have both been demolished, as have the two searchlight emplacements and directing post. The concrete searchlight engine house and accompanying transformer building still survived in 1991 and are sited within the camp to the N. The engine house retains its original steel doors and window shutters and concrete ventilation grilles; it was built in 1941 to replace another (site unknown) built in 1933 with the searchlights.

Within the camp are a row of high-quality limestone buildings constructed in 1905/6 to accompany the two batteries. The three single-storey buildings lying to the W of the road were a double shelter, artificer's shop and artillery store in 1911, and were latterly used as officers' and NCO's mess, and stores, with stone outbuildings to the rear. To the N of the road is a pair of semi-detached single-storey buildings which were originally a double caretakers' quarters, and were latterly the Master Gunners' Quarters.

Present condition

The battery, together with most of its fittings, survives largely complete and is currently lying empty; as Penlee has been infilled it is the only example to survive in this area. The N blockhouse is also largely complete and in relatively good condition for its type and age; substantial below-ground remains probably survive of the central blockhouse, the site of which is a now a mound. The other blockhouse, searchlight emplacements and WWII structures have all been demolished, although below-ground remains may survive. The S Bofors emplacement is complete and represents the only known survival in the Plymouth area. The camp buildings and engine house were (in 1991) lying empty and in good condition; the site has since been re-developed and some of the buildings refurbished/converted and probably others demolished.

Sources

General

20 - 22, 24; F, O, Q, R.

Specific

1907	Renney Point Battery. Plan etc. PRO: WO 78/5063
1911	Plymouth Defences. Index Plan. PRO: WO 78/5066
1915	Renney Point Battery. Plan. PRO: WO 78/5063
1932	Renney Point Electric Lights (searchlightss). PRO: WO 78/5065
1955	Renney Point Battery. Plan. PRO: WO 78/5063
n.d.	Renney Fort Record Book, incl. 1940s cable plan. PRO: WO 192/293

WEMBURY PF STATION

PAR = WEMBURY, NGR = SX50104850, PRN = SX54NW-96, MAP 1 No. 191

This was built by 1911 to provide the guns at Renney with target information, and consisted of two PF cells and one fire-commander/night-director cell surrounded by an unclimbable fence; these were present in 1915, and in 1922 an experimental 100 foot Barr & Stroud range-finder was installed. This was returned to Woolwich in 1934 and the emplacement destroyed in December 1941 by grenades. During WWII early warning radar was installed, and it was one of the two main Fortress Observation Posts (Rame Head being the other).

The site lies at the brow of the coastal slope, within the perimeter of H.M.S Cambridge; no visit has been made.

Present condition

N/A.

Sources

General

22, 24.

Specific

1911 Plymouth Defences. Index Plan. PRO: WO 78/5066

n.d. Renney Fort Record Book. PRO: WO 192/293

WORSEWELL BATTERY

PAR = REVELSTOKE, NGR = SX53304762, PRN = SX54NW-102, MAP 1 No. 215

This is located on the S shore of the Yealm estuary near its mouth, and probably faced W. A square enclosure is marked on a 1863 map; this is named 'Worsewell Fort' and has an entrance in the N side. By 1912 a cottage had been built within it and it is named 'Battery Cottage'. It may have been one of the fortifications built by General Simcoe in the Napoleonic Wars, and may be the Yealm Redoubt and barracks referred to by Breihan (although he places it at St. Werburgh's Church, Wembury, on the opposite side of the river). This was built in 1803 and decommissioned in 1817. The site has not been visited.

Present condition

N/A

Sources

Specific

1863 Ist edition O.S. 6-inch map. Devon sheet 130 PLSL

1912 Revised edition of O.S. 1:2500 map. Devon sheet 130.10 PLSL

1990 Breihan, J.R 'Army barracks in Devon during the French Revolutionary and Napoleonic Wars' *Trans. Devonshire Assoc.* **122**, 133-158

3.3.5. Other World War II sites

BERE ALSTON HEAVY ANTI-AIRCRAFT BATTERY

PAR = BERE ALSTON, NGR = SX45306604, PRN = SX46NE-556, MAP 1 No. 192

This is located on a spur between the valleys of the Tamar and Tavy *c.* 0.5km to the S of Bere Alston and *c.* 12km to the N of Plymouth. It faces N., and defended against aircraft using the landmarks of the rivers Tavy and Tamar to approach Plymouth from the N. It was probably built in 1942, and was apparently abandoned and then reoccupied in 1944; it presumably became redundant shortly after the end of the war in 1945-6. It was probably armed with four 3.7 or 4.5-inch HAA guns. An aerial photograph of 1946 shows four gun emplacements in an arc facing N, with a command post to the rear and a group of accommodation buildings in an adjoining field some 200m to the N. A magazine is not visible, nor is a gun laying radar platform; this was most likely located in the field between the guns and the accommodation. The magazine may have been a Nissen magazine, perhaps represented by one or both of the demolished buildings sited alongside the road to the E.

The battery consists of four gun emplacements in an arc facing W., N.W., N.E., & E, with a semi-sunken command post on the S side; no remains of a magazine is visible. The site is bisected by an earlier field bank and ditch, which have been partly removed to accommodate two of the emplacements. These all survive complete with gun mountings, ammunition lockers and side shelters; they are of a type associated with 3.7 or 4.5-inch HAA guns, and the gun mountings are very similar to those at Down Thomas. The command post is also complete and faces N. Access was from the W, where a sentry post survives; other buildings sited to the E have been demolished, together with the accommodation buildings to the N.

Present condition

All the emplacements, the command post and the sentry post survive complete and in very good condition; the emplacements each have substantial well-maintained roofs and are used as stock shelters and farm stores. The command post however is empty and overgrown, although it still retains its roof and is complete apart from its internal fittings.

Sources

General

25; R

Specific

1946 Vertical aerial photograph. SMR: RAF/CPE/UK 1890. Frame 4308

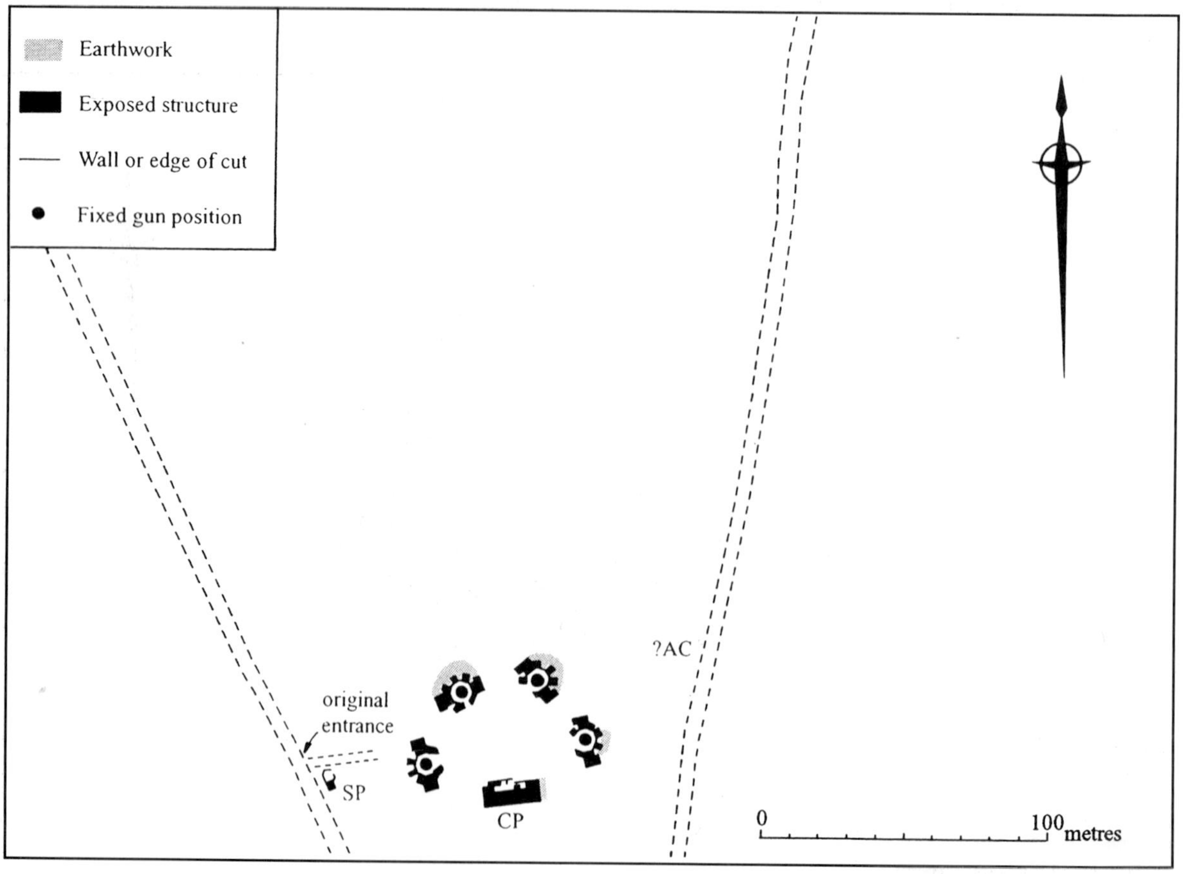

Fig. 118 Bere Alston HAA Battery

CENTRAL PARK HEAVY ANTI-AIRCRAFT BATTERY

PAR = STOKE DAMEREL, NGR = SX47305560, PRN = SX45NE-343, MAP 3 No. 193

This is a heavy AA battery which was possibly established in *c.* 1942, and apparently mounted four 4.5-inch guns. It was located on the spur overlooking the main station and the town and Sound to the S. It now lies within a landscaped public park; no remains are visible.

Present condition

Demolished, although below-ground remains may survive.

Source

General

25

SEATON BARRACKS HEAVY ANTI-AIRCRAFT BATTERY A

PAR = EGGBUCKLAND, NGR = SX49455900, PRN = SX45NE-6, MAP 1 No. 194

This is located on a spur between Forder Valley to the N and a tributary valley to the S, *c.* 0.5km E of Crownhill Fort. It lies within the grounds of Seaton Barracks which after the war was the HQ of the AA Brigade (F.W Woodward pers. comm.). This battery was built in 1940 for four 3.7-inch guns, and probably manned by 165 HAA Battery. It was supplemented in 1943 when four 5.25-inch guns were emplaced (Battery B). An aerial photograph of 1946 shows four gun emplacements in an arc facing E, with a command post in the centre, two magazines at each end of the arc and a surface ?gun store to the rear (W). In an arc to the S of the southern magazine lie two to three slightly smaller emplacements. A group of accommodation buildings lie to the N.W. The position of the gun-laying radar platform is not clear, but may be represented by a probable ramp sited just to the N of the 5.25-inch battery to the E.

The visible remains consist of an arc of four filled-in gun emplacements facing N.E., E, & S.E. They are of the same plan as those at Down Thomas, octagonal in shape with an entrance at the rear and the remains on the inside of partly demolished ammunition lockers and shelters. They do not have external shelters, and are surrounded by embankments for additional protection. The access road to the rear of the emplacements continues in a loop to the N.W and forms the main access to the site. There are two semi-sunken ?5-bay magazines on each flank to the rear of the emplacements and a surface concrete building (the probable WWII gun store). An earthen mound is present to the S of this and of the S magazine, and represents the site of the infilled emplacements visible in 1946; the central command post has also been infilled.

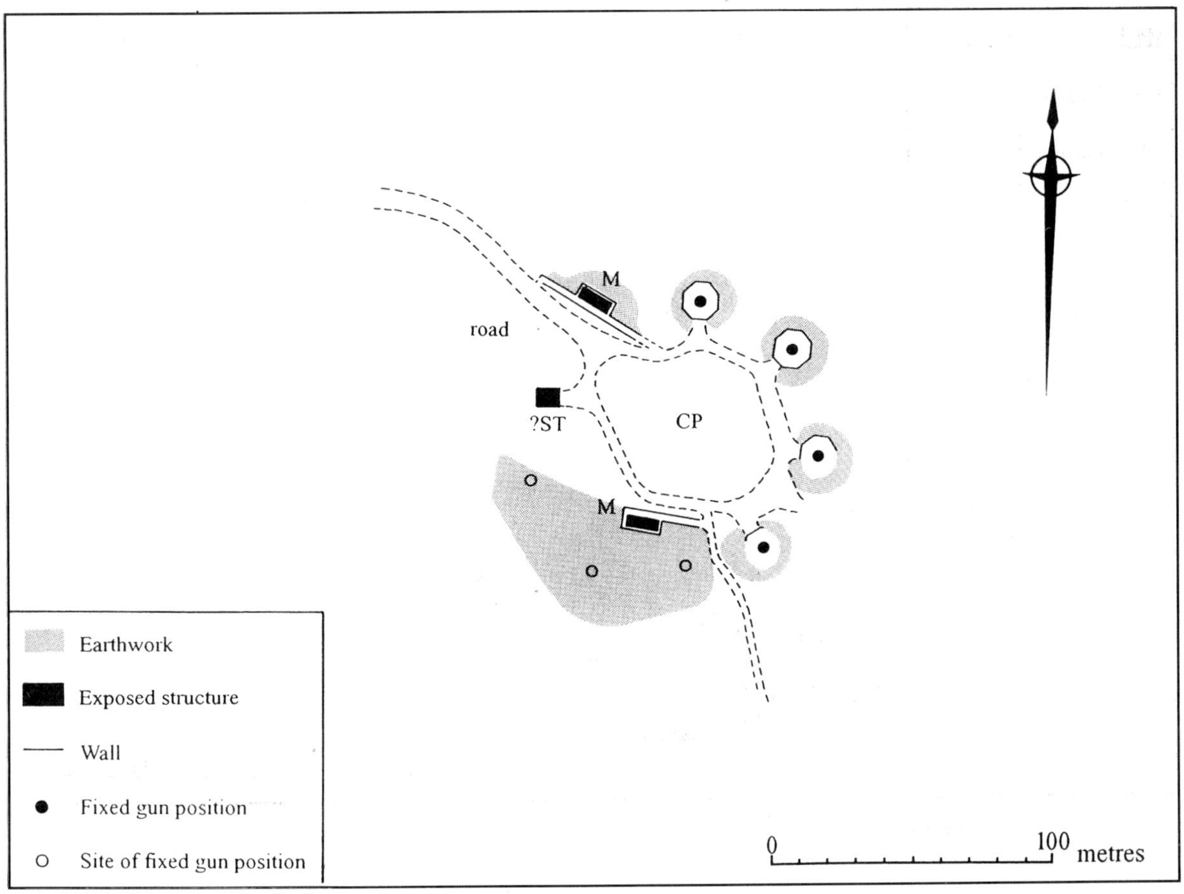

Fig. 119 Seaton Barracks HAA Battery A

Present condition

The area of the battery is grassed over; the magazines and gun store are in use. Although the emplacements and control post have been filled in substantial remains of these and of the magazine are present on the surface or as probable below-ground archaeological remains.

n.b 1996 - all the buildings have now been completely demolished and removed.

Sources

General

25; R

Specific

1946 Vertical aerial photograph. SMR: RAF/CPE/UK1890. Frame 1117

SEATON BARRACKS HEAVY ANTI-AIRCRAFT BATTERY B

PAR = EGGBUCKLAND, NGR = SX49655895, PRN = SX45NE-6/1, MAP 1 No. 195

This is the site of the four 5.25-inch HAA guns emplaced late in WWII. Four gun pits and ancillary structures are visible on an aerial photograph of 1946, arranged in an arc around an access loop at the end of a road leading out of the earlier HAA battery (A) some 200m to the W; the access road to the emplacements of the earlier battery is not visible, suggesting that it and the emplacements had become redundant by this time. Along the road to the later battery are a series of buildings, including a rectangular one of the same plan as that at St Winolls Battery B in Cornwall which presumably housed the engine room.

No surface remains of the battery or associated buildings are visible; the site lies under a sports field.

Present condition

Demolished and infilled, although substantial below-ground remains may still survive.

Sources

General

25; R

Specific

1946 Vertical aerial photograph. SMR: RAF/CPE/UK1890. Frame 1117

WOODFORD HEAVY ANTI-AIRCRAFT BATTERY

PAR = PLYMPTON ST MARY, NGR = SX52305740, PRN = SX55NW-105, MAP 1 No. 196

This is thought to have been built in the later stages of WWII and to have had an armament of four 5.25-inch HAA guns. It was sited on a spur on the W side of the River Plym to the N.W of Plympton, and has extensive views to the S and W. It was probably intended to defend Plymouth from aircraft approaching from the E and from the N, using the River Plym and the darker edge of the moor.

The hilltop, the most likely site for the gun emplacements, is fairly level but there are no surface remains of any emplacements. A building which was probably associated with the battery was sited (at SX52335729) to the S.E but has been demolished. Access to the field is currently from lower down the slope off Woodford Avenue via a concrete track; this does not appear to approach the hilltop and therefore may either represent an access to accommodation buildings or perhaps to a more recent unfinished housing development.

Present condition

The field is presently under grass, with the demolished building and the S.W part of the site occupied by a relatively new housing estate. Below-ground remains of the gun pits, which were substantial, may still however survive.

Sources

General

25; R

COLESDOWN HILL HEAVY ANTI-AIRCRAFT BATTERY

PAR = PLYMPTON ST MARY, NGR = SX52655427, PRN = SX55SW-147, MAP 1 No. 197

This was probably established in 1940 and was manned in August 1941 by 210 Heavy Aircraft Battery (who also manned the Down Thomas battery at this time), when it was armed with four 3.7-inch HAA guns. The site is located just off Colesdown Hill, within Moorcroft Quarry. An arc of six emplacements (four hexagonal and two rectangular) facing S.E are visible on an aerial photograph of 1946 and represents a similar arrangement to Down Thomas and elsewhere. A command post or magazine is visible in the centre, with groups of accommodation buildings to the N and to the W.

Present condition

The gun emplacements have been quarried away, although remains of the accommodation buildings adjoining Colesdown Hill to the N may remain within woodland.

Sources

General

25; R.

Specific

1946 Vertical aerial photograph. SMR: RAF/CPE/UK 1890. Frame 2173

HOOE HILL ROCKET BATTERY

PAR = PLYMSTOCK, NGR = SX504051780, PRN = SX55SW-148, MAP 2 No. 198

This is located on the top and N flank of a spur *c.* 500m E of Staddon Fort. It was probably built in *c.* 1941 and manned by 144Z Battery (rocket). It consisted of 64 rocket projectors arranged about 8-10 yards apart in a large square. Each fired a single U2P (unrotating two-inch projectile), and all the rockets were fired simultaneously at a target, with the target information initially being provided from a control room on site, which received the information from a central control centre in Plymouth. Later in the war target information was provided from the battery's own radar set and control room, sited in a field some 0.75 of a mile to the south. This included accommodation buildings for the ATS personnel who manned the equipment, and was probably the WWII site located immediately N of Brownhill Battery (No. 171). There is one recorded hit of an aeroplane from this battery in late 1944.

An aerial photograph of 1946 shows strings of buildings along Hooe Hill and the N edge of the site, and another group to the S.W. In the field in between are 2 to 3 lines of regularly spaced light rectangles, which may represent the positions of the projectors. The battery was presumably abandoned shortly after 1945, if not before.

Several ruined concrete block buildings are present alongside Hooe Hill and in the woods along the N boundary there are an extensive range of concrete hut platforms, representing barrack buildings, guardroom and urinals (which survive intact). Most prominent is the magazine, sited near the top of Hooe Hill, and to the N is the probable remains of a control or command post, with instrument pillar adjoining. The main entrance to the site was at the N.W corner from Hooe Hill; a sentry-post survives together with the base of the probable guardroom adjoining.

Plate 171 Hooe Hill Rocket Battery, magazine (Exeter Archaeology)

Present condition

In 1993 most of the site was a hayfield, with woodland along the N edge; recently a rugby pitch has been laid out and the magazine is being converted into a club house, presumably destroying most of the internal features in the process. The other buildings generally survive as hut-bases within clumps of woodland or scrub within the field or the adjoining woodland.

Sources

General

25; R.

Specific

1946 Vertical RAF aerial photograph SMR: RAF/CPE/UK/1890/4122

1996 Letter from P.J.Calnan to FWW

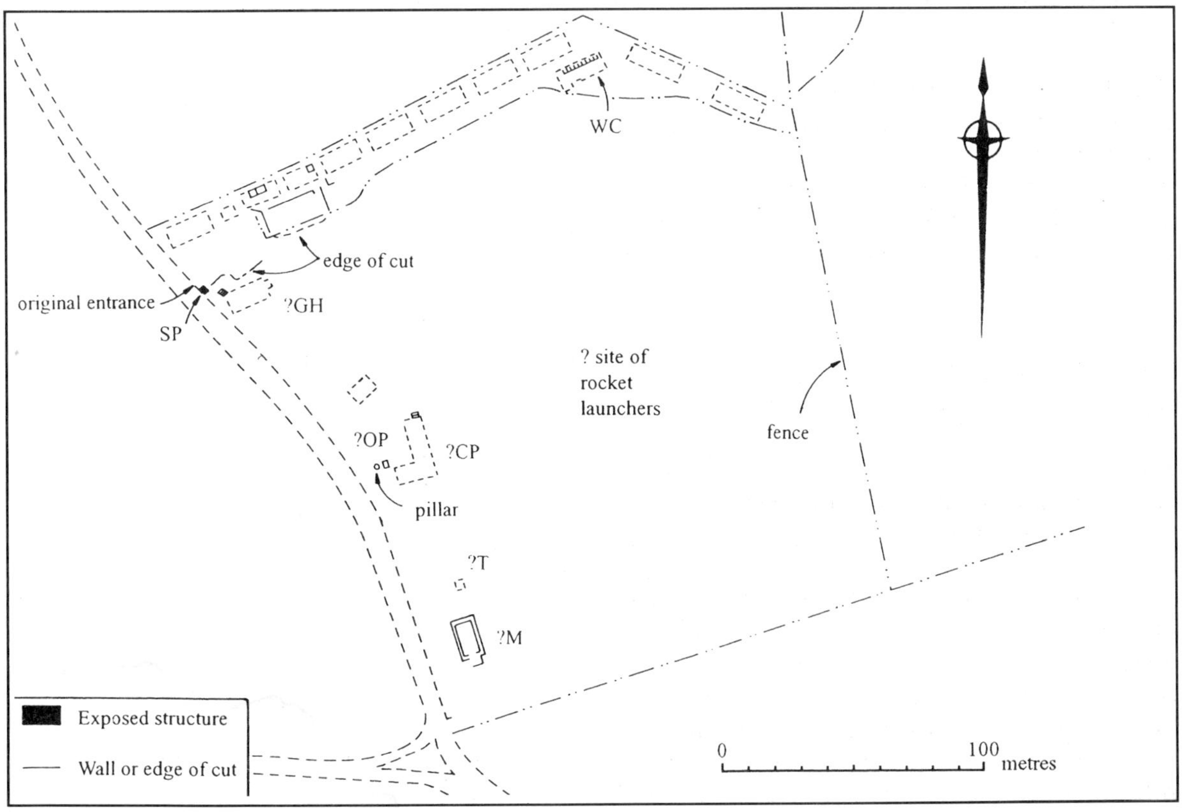

Fig. 120 Hooe Hill Rocket Battery

DOWN THOMAS HEAVY ANTI-AIRCRAFT BATTERY

PAR = WEMBURY, NGR = SX50774912, PRN = SX54NW-13, MAP 1 No. 199

This (*Plate 21*) is sited in an arable field about 600m N of the coast off the road to HMS Cambridge. The battery was built in 1940 for four 3.7-inch guns and manned by 210 HAA Battery in August 1941. Subsequently two other rectangular emplacements were added for 3.7-inch and/or 4.5-inch guns.

An aerial photograph of 1946 shows six emplacements arranged in an arc facing S & W, with a magazine and command post within the arc and a ?MT (Motor Transport) workshop or gun store on the N edge of it. Groups of accommodation buildings are sited to each side of the entrance and also some 150-200m to the W of the battery, and there are other faint indications of other structures (possibly gun-laying radar) *c.* 50m S.W and 100m N.W of the battery.

A concrete road provides access to the site and to each of the four original octagonal concrete gun emplacements, to the gun store and via ramps to the magazine. The four octagonal and two rectangular emplacements are all built of shuttered concrete and concrete blocks, and are embanked with earth for extra protection. Each has a series of ammunition lockers and holdfast mountings for the gun. In the centre there is a semi-sunken command post protected by earth banks, with observation platforms and a pillar for a

Plate 172 Down Thomas HAA Battery, command post (Exeter Archaeology)

Plate 173 Down Thomas HAA Battery, magazine (Exeter Archaeology)

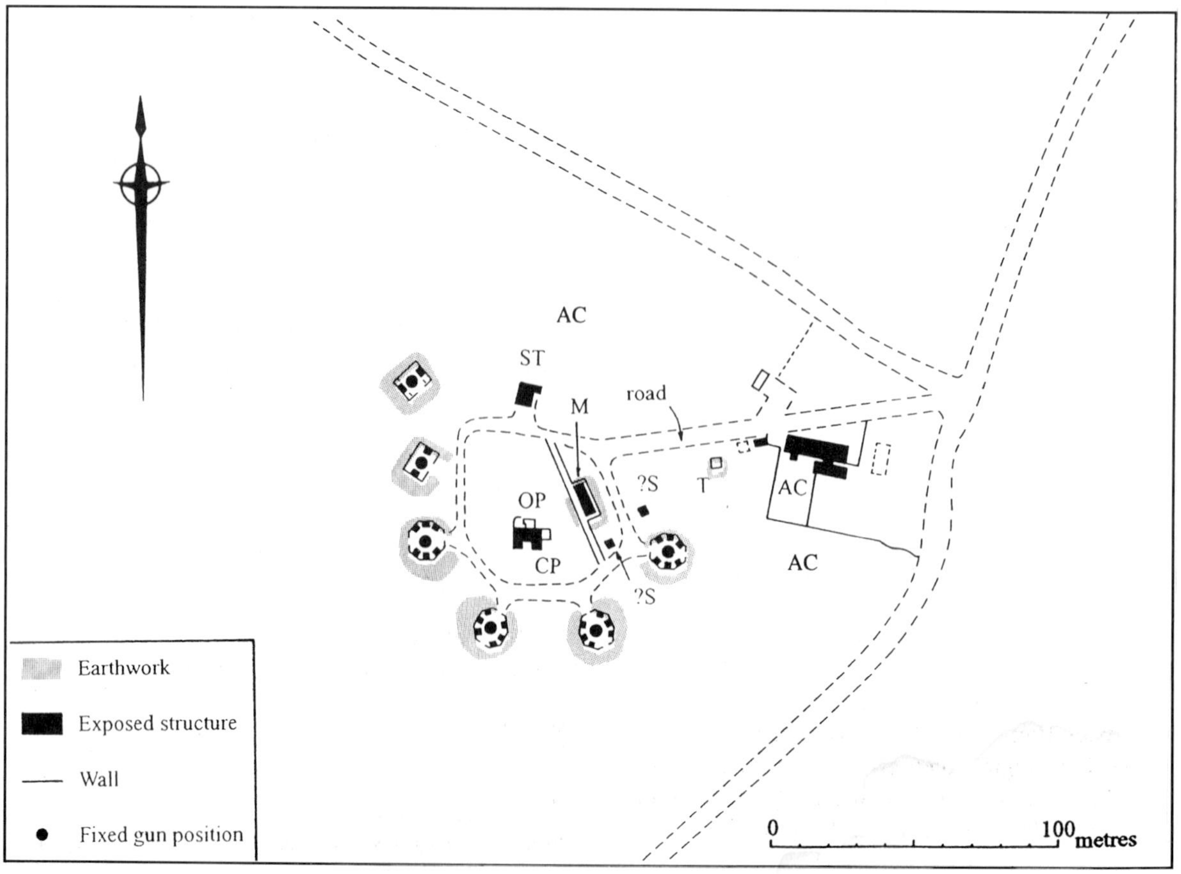

Fig. 121 Down Thomas HAA Battery

height (range) finder on the outside, together with a semi-sunken 5-bay magazine protected by concrete blast walls. Each bay still retains its labelling. The guardhouse (Princes Cottages) is sited adjoining the entrance. No other buildings survive, except for at least two small semi-sunken small ?shelters within the arc of the gun emplacements.

Present condition

Most emplacements are used for the storage of timber and some farm equipment and rubbish; until recently it was used as a camp by travellers who have left several old vehicles behind; several are partly overgrown. The two rectangular emplacements are open although one has been partly filled in. The command post and magazine are open and empty and are not used, nor are the small shelters. The guardhouse is inhabited and another building adjoining it and the MT workshop are used for storage. The surrounding field is arable; no remains of the two groups of accommodation buildings or of the other structures are visible and are unlikely to survive.

Sources

General

25; R.

Specific

1946	Vertical RAF aerial photograph SMR: RAF/CPE/UK/1890/3109

NETTON HEAVY ANTI-AIRCRAFT BATTERY

PAR = NEWTON FERRERS, NGR = SX55604630, PRN = SX54NE-54, MAP 1 No. 200

This was apparently established in 1942, and was probably armed with 3.7- and/or 4.5-inch HAA guns. An aerial photograph of 1946 clearly shows its location and layout. An arc of six gun emplacements (apparently four hexagonal and two square, mirroring the arrangements at Down Thomas and Maker) faces seaward, astride the lane leading S from the present car park. In the field to the W there is another loose group of structures some 250m to the S.W, which appear to include at least three other smaller emplacements arranged around a turning loop at the end of an access road; these may represent emplacements for LAA guns. Between this group and the main battery to the N.E is the outline of a hexagonal enclosure with a building in the centre, which is probably a gun laying radar platform surrounded by a false datum. Accommodation buildings are sited alongside the lane to the N. The battery was demolished just after the war.

Present condition

The battery has been demolished although scatters of rubble are visible across the arable fields and in hedgerows; some of the gun positions are visible as slight depressions and there may be below-ground remains.

Sources

General

25; R

Specific

1946	Vertical RAF aerial photograph. SMR: RAF/CPE/UK1890. Frame 1082.

NETTON OBSERVATION POST

PAR = NEWTON FERRERS, NGR = SX54474595?, PRN = SX45NW-29/1, MAP 1 No. 201

The only reference to this is in the Renney Fort Record Book which records that the Netton FOP (presumably a 'Forward' or 'Fortress' Observation Post) was installed with a J.PF Mk 4 (presumably a 'J' position finder Mk 4) in 1940. A possible site is at the brow of the coastal slope some 1.5km W of Netton HAA Battery, where a rectangular flat-roofed building is shown on an aerial photograph of 1946. Site not visited.

Present condition

N/A

Sources

Specific

1946	Vertical aerial photograph. SMR: RAF/CPE/UK 1890 Frame 1082
n.d.	Renney Fort Record Book. PRO: WO 192/293

WEMBURY BOMBING DECOY

PAR = WEMBURY, NGR = SX52954875, PRN = SX54NW-97, MAP 1 No. 202

This is the control shelter for a bombing decoy built in 1941; the decoy was located in a field *c.* 300m to the S.W, and on a S-facing spur about 1km N of the coast and about 1km to the S.E of Wembury. The control shelter is a single storey concrete building set into a hedgebank; it contains two windowless rooms off a central corridor with a tank? on the roof above.

Present condition

The shelter is in relatively good condition.

Sources

General

R.

Specific

1941	PRO: Air 20/4352
1946	Vertical aerial photograph. SMR: RAF/CPE/UK 1890 Frame 3104

WWII BUILDING NEAR WEMBURY

WWII BUILDING NEAR WEMBURY

PAR = WEMBURY, NGR = SX52964890, PRN = SX54NW-98, MAP 1 No. 203

This is a two-storey concrete building located at the end of a green lane some 250m W of Old Barton Farm and about 250m N of the control shelter of Wembury bombing decoy. Its function is not known; it may be similar to another two-storey tower adjoining Brownhill Battery (No. 171) on Staddon Heights. It may have been an observation post sited at a safe distance from the bombing decoy.

STADDISCOMBE PILLBOX A

STADDISCOMBE PILLBOX A

PAR = WEMBURY NGR = SX51155135 PRN = SX55SW-151 MAP 2 No. 204

This is located in a pasture field at the junction of Bovisand Lane and Hooe Lane at the end of a spur overlooking Staddiscombe village; it commands the main access road to Staddon Heights and the military installations there and probably operated in conjunction with another pillbox (B) located *c.* 300m to the S.E. It is a hexagonal Type 22 or 24 WWII pillbox of shuttered concrete construction with a flat roof; five-sides have a single loop for a light machine-gun, the sixth (N.E) side has a door.

Present condition
Structurally sound; interior was not accessible.

STADDISCOMBE PILLBOX B

STADDISCOMBE PILLBOX B

PAR = PLYMSTOCK, NGR = SX51305125, PRN = SX55SW-153, MAP 1 No. 205

This is located at the S corner of a field on the N side of the junction of Hooe Lane with Staddiscombe Road. Hedgebanks obscure its S & E sides. It may have defended a checkpoint at the entrance to Hooe Lane which led to the military installations on Staddon Heights, and probably operated in conjunction with another pillbox (A) sited *c.* 300m to the N.W. It is a hexagonal Type 22 or 24 pillbox of shuttered concrete construction; a later 'porch' adjoins its E side. Interior not viewed.

Present condition
Good.

LOOSELEIGH LANE PILLBOX, CROWNHILL

LOOSELEIGH LANE PILLBOX, CROWNHILL

PAR = TAMERTON FOLIOT, NGR = SX481602, PRN = SX46SE-65, MAP 1 No. 206

This is located at the bottom of a garden at the junction of Looseleigh Lane and Tamerton Road. It is a polygonal ?six-sided concrete structure, probably a Type 22 or 24 pillbox, and lies half buried and largely infilled; part of its N.W wall forms the garden boundary and faces onto the road.

Present condition
Most of the structure survives complete, although half buried and largely infilled. Sited in a domestic garden.

Source
General
R

YENNADON DOWN WWII SITE

YENNADON DOWN WWII SITE

PAR = MEAVY, NGR = SX54256830, PRN = SX56NW-200, No. 207

This is sited on the S.W flank of Yennadon Down at 250-260m O.D, to the east of Yelverton airfield and with extensive views to the W & S. Visible remains consist of four concrete Nissen hut bases, access to which is via a track (originally tarmaced) from Dousland. From its location it may have represented a radar installation of some kind, although no remains of receiver blocks and masts have been identified to date. It may also have been a AA battery, although again no gun positions were identified.

Present condition
Demolished.

WOTTER RADAR INSTALLATION

PAR = SHAUGH PRIOR, NGR = SX55106220,
PRN = SX56SE-133, MAP 1 No. 208

This is located on a S-facing slope on the S.W edge of Dartmoor; it overlooks the Plym valley and Plymouth and the Sound are visible in the distance. It represents one of the 'West Coast Type' Chain Home Stations.

The remains consist of a number of concrete hut-bases and other buildings which were originally surrounded or covered by earthworks. Access to the site is via a hardcore track which may once have been tarmaced and which leads directly up the slope from the main road. There is also another unmetalled track leading off at an angle which may be earlier. Sandwiched between the two tracks is an area of accommodation and service blocks and a possible guardhouse adjoins the main entrance. The remainder of the buildings are arranged around a track branching off at right angles to the main access track and consist of two earth-covered brick buildings, which may represent buried reserve transmitter or receiver blocks, a terraced area which may have been the guard dog compound, and embanked buildings at the junction of the two tracks and at the end of the branch. These probably represent receiver and/or transmitter blocks; the western one may have been a Type C (completely earth-covered), whilst from its shape the eastern one may have been a Type B.

There are also various toilet blocks and two mast-bases & balance weights for transmitter masts on the up-slope side of the main complex. In between these is the base of a generator. The wooden receiver towers would have been sited elsewhere, perhaps nearer the road to the S. There would also normally have been two transmitter blocks and perhaps a standby set house, sited away from the receiver blocks.

Plate 174 Wotter Radar Station, mast base (Exeter Archaeology)

Present condition

Most huts have been demolished and at least one of the buried reserves has been partly demolished, although the roof of one survives. The receiver or transmitter blocks have been partly demolished although the outline of the side walls are visible together with the surrounding earthworks. Overall the site is in reasonable condition in archaeological terms and at present is an open area of moorland with public access for leisure purposes and probably light grazing by sheep.

Sources
General
R
Specific

1983 Collis, J 'Field systems on Shaugh Moor and at Wotter, Dartmoor' *Proc. Devon Archaeol. Soc.* **41** 47-62.

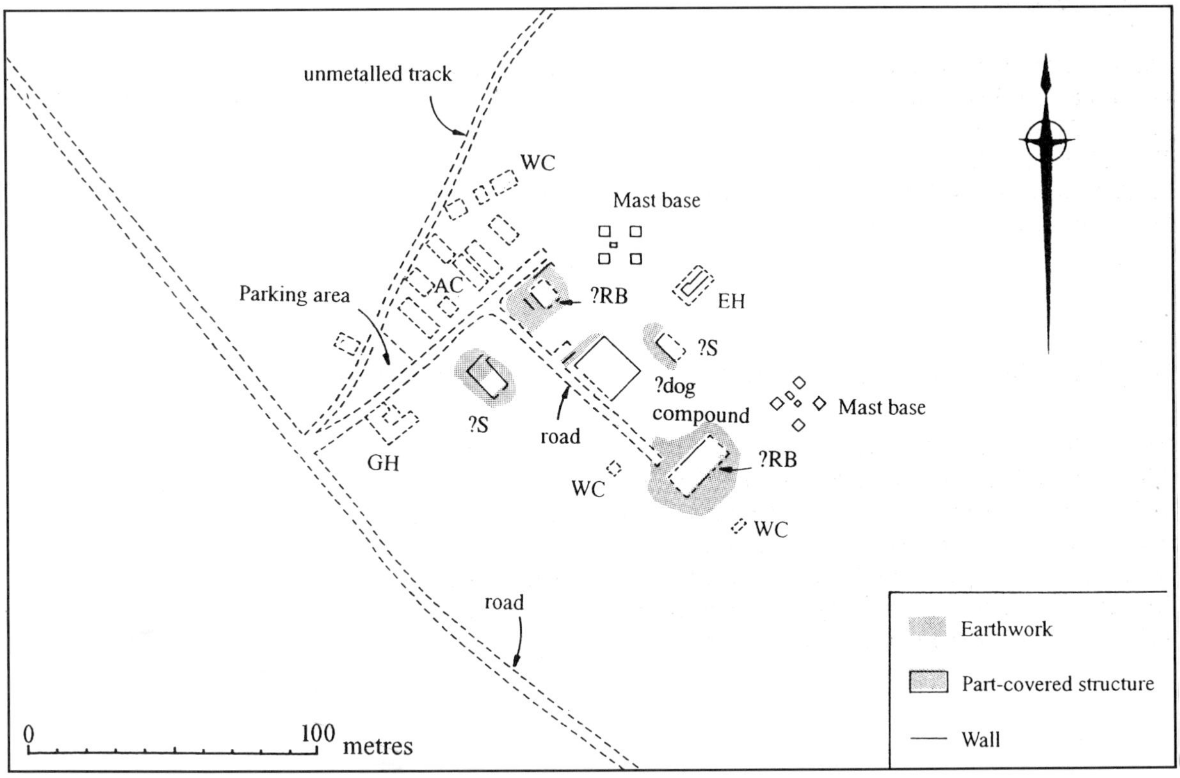

Fig. 122 Wotter Radar Station

STADDISCOMBE RADAR INSTALLATION

STADDISCOMBE RADAR INSTALLATION

PAR = WEMBURY, NGR = SX 50505070, PRN = SX55SW-159, MAP 2 No. 209

This consists of two apparent masts set within square enclosures on a hill near Staddiscombe, visible on a RAF aerial photograph of 1946. The southern of the two enclosures is larger. They may represent the twin gantries of a Chain Home Low radar station.

Present condition
N/A

Sources
General
R
Specific
1946 RAF Vertical aerial photograph. SMR: CPE/UK/1890 Frame 2125

LONG BRIDGE PILLBOX

LONG BRIDGE PILLBOX

PAR = EGGBUCKLAND, NGR = SX51905673, PRN = SX55NW-239, MAP 1 No. 210

This was sited on the N side of the old A38 road at the W end of Long Bridge, near Marsh Mills. It is no longer extant.

Present condition
Demolished.

HIGHER SPRIDDLESTONE PILLBOX

HIGHER SPRIDDLESTONE PILLBOX

PAR = BRIXTON, NGR = SX53065163, PRN = SX55SW-90, MAP 1 No. 211

This faces N.E & covers a cross-roads. It is a hexagonal concrete pillbox, possibly a Type 22 or 24.

Present condition
Appears largely complete & in reasonable condition.

WEMBURY BEACH PILLBOX (EAST)

WEMBURY BEACH PILLBOX (EAST)

PAR = WEMBURY, NGR = SX51764844, PRN = SX54NW-33, MAP 1 No. 212

One of a pair of concrete pillboxes built to defend Wembury beach. Only the base now remains.

Present condition
Largely removed by erosion.

WEMBURY BEACH PILLBOX (WEST)

WEMBURY BEACH PILLBOX (WEST)

PAR = WEMBURY, NGR = SX51614850, PRN = SX54NW-101, MAP 1 No. 213

One of a pair of concrete pillboxes built to defend Wembury beach. Only the base now remains.

Present condition
Largely removed by erosion.

WEMBURY PILLBOX

WEMBURY PILLBOX

PAR = WEMBURY, NGR = SX51934872 PRN = SX54NW-103, MAP 1 No. 214

This is a polygonal concrete pillbox sited on rising ground at the head of the coombe extending inland from Wembury beach. Now sited within a private garden.

Present condition
Good.

Appendix 1 Abbreviations

AC	accommodation (mess & barracks)
AM	Ammunition Shelter
AS	Artillery Store
ATS	Auxiliary Territorial Service
B	barracks
BB	barrage balloon
BCP	Battery Command Post
BH	blockhouse
BL	Breech-loading
BOP	Battery Observation Post
BPR	Battery Plotting Room
BR	bunker
BS	boundary stone
BT	Brennan Torpedo Station
C	caponier
CG	counterscarp gallery
CH	cook house
CP	command post
CS	cart shed
DRF	depression range finder
EH	engine-house
ER	engine room
ES	engine shaft
FH	foxhole
FS	firing-step
GH	guardhouse/gatehouse
GP	gun platform
GR	guardroom
GS	gun shed
H	Hospital
HAA	Heavy anti-aircraft
HDA	Harbour Defence Asdic (sonar)
HQ	Headquarters
LAA	Light anti-aircraft
LMG	light machine-gun position
LR	lamp room
M	magazine
MT	motor transport
OP	Observation Post
OS	Observation Station
O.S.	Ordnance Survey
PB	pillbox
pdr	pounder
PF	position finder
QF	quick fire breech-loading
R	reservoir
RA	Royal Artillery
RB	Receiver Block
RBL	rifled breech-loading
RE	Royal Engineers
RML	rifled muzzle-loading
ROC	Royal Observer Corps Post
ROCMP	Royal Observer Corps Monitoring Post (1950s)
S	Shelter
SB	smooth bore
SBBL	smooth bore breech-loading
SDP	searchlight directing post
SE	stable
SL	searchlight
SP	sentry post
SPT	Sally Port
SS	Submarine Mine Observation and/or Control Station
ST	store
T	tank/cistern
WC	toilet
WH	Watch House
WS	workshops

Appendix 2 Glossary

ADVANCED WORKS	Additional works beyond the GLACIS but still commanded from the main defences.
BANQUETTE	An infantry firing step.
BARBETTE	BREASTWORK of a BATTERY sufficiently low that guns may fire over it without the need for EMBRASURES.
BARBICAN	OUTWORK for the protection of a gateway or approaches to a bridge.
BASTION	Projection from the general line of a FORTRESS from which the garrison can defend by flanking fire the ground between the RAMPARTS. From the mid-sixteenth century generally a four-sided projection.
BATTER	Inward slope of the face of a wall or revetment.
BATTERY	Any place where guns or mortars are mounted.
BERM	Level space between the edge of a ditch or moat and the foot of a RAMPART.
BLOCKHOUSE	Small detached FORT at a strategic point, late often a wooden structure.
BULWARK	Early term for a BASTION or BLOCKHOUSE.
CAPONIER	Covered communications way across a dry ditch leading to OUTWORKS, usually loopholed. Also a powerful CASEMATED WORK projecting into or across a ditch to provide flanking fire.
CASEMATE	Bombproof vaulted chamber within the ramparts providing an emplacement for a gun and/or a barracks room.
CAVALIER	Raised BATTERY usually built on a BASTION to provide an additional tier of fire.
CHEMIN DES RONDES	Passage or sentry path at top of the SCARP WALL with a PARAPET for cover.
CHICANE	A zig-zag approach to a gate, exposing an attackers' flank to fire from the ramparts.
CITADEL	Self-contained FORTRESS usually within a town's fortifications intended as a place of last resort.
COMMAND	Elevation of one work above another or above the surrounding country.
CORDON	Continuous rounded projection at the junction of the sloping SCARP REVETMENT with the vertical PARAPET.
COUNTERFORTS	Buttreses behind SCARP walls, and often arched over, to provide additional strength within a RAMPART.
COUNTERSCARP	Exterior slope or revetment of a ditch.
COUNTERSCARP GALLERY	Loopholed passage behind the COUNTERSCARP WALL to defend a ditch.
COVERED WAY	Continuous communication on the outer edge of the ditch protected by an earthwork PARAPET from enemy fire.

CRÉMAILLÈRE	Indented or saw-toothed TRACE to allow greater flanking cover, usually applied to fieldworks.
CRENEL	Gaps in a PARAPET between MERLONS enabling the fire of archers or gunners, hence Crenellations or Battlements.
CROCHETS	Passages round the head of TRAVERSES to allow continuous access on the covered way.
CURTAIN	Length of RAMPART between two BASTIONS on the main line of a defensive work.
DROP DITCH	A deeper section of ditch along the faces of casemates or musketry galleries, preventing easy access to them by an attacker.
EMBRASURE	Opening in a PARAPET or wall through which a gun can be fired.
ENCEINTE	Also known as 'the body of the place'. The main defensive enclosure of a FORTRESS, excluding the OUTWORKS.
ENFILADE	Fire coming from a flank which sweeps the length of a fortification.
ESCALADE	The climbing of walls by the means of ladders.
ESCARP	Outer slope or revetment of a rampart. Also SCARP.
EXPENSE MAGAZINE	Small MAGAZINE close to a BATTERY in which a small supply of ammunition is kept for immediate use.
FACE	(of a BASTION). Outer sides of a work which meet at a salient angle projecting towards the field.
FLANK	Side of a work, usually a BASTION, between the FACE and the CURTAIN. The principal defensive element of a BASTIONED fortification.
FLANKER	BATTERY mounted in the flank of a BASTION from which flanking fire is directed across a CURTAIN.
FORT	Position or building designed primarily for defence.
FORTRESS	Major fortified place, often a town, capable of containing a large force.
FRONT	(Of fortification). The distance between the SALIENTS of two adjacent BASTIONS.
FRAISES	Stakes or palisades set horizontally on the outward slope of a RAMPART to counter an infantry rush.
GABION	Cylindrical wicker basket filled with earth and used to protect BATTERIES and to supplement PARAPETS.
GARDE-FOU	A free-standing wall, running along the top of a revetment, protecting sentries behind it (as with a chemin des rondes) or the guns and the gunners (as with that along the rear of the Citadel terreplein).
GLACIS	PARAPET of the COVERED WAY extended in a long slope towards the FIELD.
GORGE	Rear, whether open or closed, of any work. Usually the NECK of a BASTION or a DETACHED WORK.
GUÉRITE	Sentry box projecting from the angle of a BASTION at PARAPET level.

HAXO CASEMATE	Vaulted CASEMATE for a gun built on the TERRE-PLAIN of a RAMPART, invented by General Haxo.
KEEP	Principal and strongest tower of a castle and the final point of defence.
LINE OF DEFENCE	Theoretical line drawn from the junction of a FLANK and a CURTAIN to the SALIENT of an adjacent BASTION.
MACHICOLATION	Projecting gallery corbelled out from a wall-top with openings for vertical defence of the foot of a wall.
MANTLET	Moveable rope screen for a gun, often in a casemate
MERLON	Solid part between two CRENELS of a battlemented PARAPET.
MOTTE	Generally artificial steep-sided mound in or on which is set the principal tower of a castle.
MOUNT	Artificial mound of earth on which guns can be mounted.
ORILLON	Projection of the FACE of a BASTION beyond the line of a RETIRED FLANK, serving to protect a FLANKER.
PALISADE	Obstacle of close-set pointed wooden stakes.
PARADE	Ground on which regular musters and exercises are held.
PLACE OF ARMS	Assembly point at the RE-ENTERING or SALIENT ANGLES of the COVERED WAY to enable the formation of troops for a sortie or for the defence of the OUTWORKS.
PLATFORM	Hard surface of timber, stone, etc. on which guns in BATTERY can be placed.
PORTE-COCHÈRE	Roofed structure extending out from an entrance.
POSTERN	(or SALLYPORT). A small entrance and tunnel leading out of the fortifications.
RAMP	Inclined track on the rear slope of a RAMPART to allow the movement of troops and guns on the TERRE-PLEIN.
RAMPART	Mass of excavated earth on which the troops and guns of the garrison are raised and forming the main defence of the FORTRESS.
RAVELIN	Traingular, detached WORK with or without FLANKS in the ditch in front of the CURTAIN and between two BASTIONS.
REDAN	OUTWORK consisting of two FACES forming a SALIENT ANGLE.
REDOUBT	Small enclosed WORK without BASTIONS, sometimes in the form of a REDAN, either used as an OUTWORK or placed inside a BASTION or RAVELIN.
REDUIT	Small CITADEL of last resort, sometimes used to protect parts of a town independant from its CITADEL.
RE-ENTRANT	Angle facing inwards from the FIELD as opposed to the SALIENT.
RETIRED FLANK	Recessed plaform or CASEMATE within a BASTION FLANK.
RETRENCHMENT	Interior works behind the ENCEINTE to provide defence in depth and to make good a breach.

REVETMENT	Retaining wall of a RAMPART or for the sides of ditches.
RICOCHET FIRE	Method of firing by which the projectile is made to glance or bounce along the length of a WORK.
SALIENT	An ANGLE projecting outwards toward the FIELD.
SALLYPORT	See POSTERN.
SCARP	Outer slope or REVETMENT of a RAMPART or inner side of a ditch. Also ESCARP.
SHOULDER	(of a BASTION). Angle at the meeting of the FACE and the FLANK..
SPUR	Arrow-shaped projection from the face of a CURTAIN WALL.
STORM POLES	As FRAISES.
TENAILLE	Low-lying WORK in the ditch between BASTIONS for the protection of the CURTAIN.
TERREPLEIN	Level surface on top of a RAMPART and below the PARAPET where guns are mounted.
TÊTE-DE-PONT	Fortification on the vulnerable side of a bridge.
TRACE	Plan of a fortified place and its angles of fire.
TRAVERSE	Earthwork thrown up to bar enfilade fire along any line of a WORK which is liable to it.
WORK	General term for any work of defence

Appendix 3 General sources

Abbreviations

BL	British Library
BODL	Bodleian Library, Oxford
BPFM	Building Property Facilities Management Ltd
CRO	Cornwall Record Office
DCO	Duchy of Cornwall Record Office
DRO	Devon Record Office
EH	English Heritage
FSGSW	Fortress Study Group South West
FWW	F.W. Woodward
MECP	Mount Edgcumbe Country Park
MODHD	Ministry of Defence Hydrographic Dept., Taunton.
MODWL	Ministry of Defence Whitehall Library
NMM	National Maritime Museum
PCM	Plymouth City Museum
PLSL	Plymouth Local Studies or History Library
PPL	Plymouth Proprietary Library
PRO	Public Record Office
PSA	Former Property Services Agency
RCHME	Royal Commission on Historic Monuments, England
SMR	Devon County Sites & Monuments Register
WCSL	Westcountry Studies Library
WDRO	West Devon Record Office

Primary

1. c.1540	Panoramic map showing existing and proposed defences. BL: Cotton Ms Augustus I; 35-6, 38-9
2. c.1586-88	Map showing defence scheme for Plymouth proposed by Sir Richard Grenvyle. PRO: MPF 6
3. 1644	'A true mapp and description of the towne of Plymouth and the Fortifications thereof, with the workes and approaches of the Enemy, at the last Seige anno 1643' Engraved by Wenceslas Hollar. PPL
4. 1779	Chart of Plymouth Sound, compiled by Mackenzie in 1777-79, with additions in 1780 & 1797. MODHD: D881 Press 15b. (Stuart No. 159)
5. 1780	Report and accompanying map on the existing and proposed defences of Plymouth, January 1780. By Col. Matthew Dixon. BL: Kings Top. XI. 79
6. 1780	Chart of Sound and map of Plymouth by Richard Cowl. WCSL: B/PLY/1780 COWL
7. c.1780	Remarks on new defences erected at Plymouth. PRO: WO 30/54
8. 1784-86	Maps of Plymouth and the surrounding country produced by William Gardner. PRO: MR 1199, MR 1385, OS 5/4; BL: Kings Top. XI. 80.
9. 1805	Board of Ordnance List (reproduced in Woodward, F. W *Citadel* p. 69)
10. 1844	Report of the Committee of Harbour Defences. Plymouth 23 Oct 1844. PRO: ADM1/5543
11. 1858	Memo on defences proposed for the protection of the Naval Arsenal at Devonport, by Maj. Jervois. PRO: ZHC1/2577

12. 1860 Report of the Commissioners appointed to consider the defences of the U.K. PRO: ZHC1/2577

13. 1860-93 Précis of correspondence relating to the defences of Plymouth (including an armament table of 1875). PRO: WO33/2772

14. 1867 Report on the progress made in the construction of the fortifications ..... PRO: ZHL1/1747

15. 1869 Report of the Committee appointed to enquire into the construction of the fortifications.... PRO: ZHL1/1884

16. c.1870 Plan of the Staddon Heights Position (with later amendments dated 1894). PPL

17. 1885, 1893 Armament tables, Plymouth. RA/RE Works Committee. MODWL 1895

18. 1894 Naval and Military Record, 11th January. BL (Colindale) & PLSL

19. 1896, 1911 Military editions of O.S. 1:2500 maps. PRO: WO 78/2314

20. 1908 Coastal Defence Scheme. PRO: WO 33/451

21. 1908-36 Maps, including armament tables. PRO: WO 78/5060

22. 1911 Plymouth Fortress Defence Scheme. PRO: WO 33/525

23. c.WWI Hawkins Fort Record Book (including map of 1903 showing batteries and armament, and PF stations). PRO: WO 192/120

24. c.WWI Grenville Fort Record Book (including map of 1915 showing searchlights and minefields, and diagram of 1915 depicting the Plymouth Fortress Telephone Network). PRO: WO 192/122

25. WWII List of Plymouth Anti-aircraft and rocket battery sites during the Plymouth Blitz, 1941, and some later batteries. FSGSW (1993).

Secondary

A. Barber, J. 1973-79 'New Light on Old Plymouth' *Trans Plymouth Athenaeum*, **IV**, 55-66

B. Brayshay, M. 1987 'Plymouth's Coastal Defences in the year of the Spanish Armada' *Trans Devonshire Assoc.* **19**, 169-196

C. Evans, D. 1986 *History of the defences of Maker Heights.* Mss held by CAU.

D. Evans, D. 1988 'The Duke of Richmond, James Glenie, Maker and the Fortifications Bill' *FORT* **16**, 73-82.

E. Evans, D. 1990 'The Duke of Richmond as designer'. *FORT* **18**, 83-93

F. Hogg, I.V 1974 *The Coast Defences of England and Wales, 1856-1956.*

G. Hunt, I. 1980 'Plymouth Sound? The defence of the naval station' *FORT* **11**, 78-108

H. Linzey, R. *Plymouth's Victorian Defences.* Unpublished undergraduate thesis, Univ. of Plymouth.

I. Mc Donald, K. 1981 *Bovisand. The Book.*

J. Maurice-Jones, Col. K.W. 1959 *The History of Coast Artillery in the British Army.*

K. Saunders, A. n.d. Mss notes (Cornwall, with some Devon)

L. Sheppard, P. 1975 'Maker Fortifications'. *Old Cornwall* **8**, No. 5. 236-247

M. Stuart, E. 1991 *Lost Landscapes of Plymouth. Maps, Charts and Plans to 1800*

N. Woodward, F.W. 1987 *Citadel*

O. Woodward, F.W. 1990 *Plymouth's Defences. A short history.*

P. Woodward, F.W. 1991 *Drakes Island.* Devon Archaeology **5**.

Q. Woodward, F.W. & FSGSW 1993-94 Historical notes on Plymouth's Defences. Mss

R. Brown, I. et al. 1995 *20th Century Defences in Britain.* Council for British Archaeology

Alphabetical Index of Sites